OPERATIONS MANAGEMENT

DECISION MAKING IN THE OPERATIONS FUNCTION

McGRAW-HILL SERIES IN MANAGEMENT

Keith Davis and Fred Luthans, *Consulting Editors*

Allen Management and Organization

Allen The Management Profession

Argyris Management and Organizational Development: The Path from XA to YB

Beckett Management Dynamics: The New Synthesis

Benton Supervision and Management

Brown Judgment in Administration

Buchele The Management of Business and Public Organizations

Campbell, Dunnette, Lawler, and Weick Managerial Behavior, Performance, and Effectiveness

Cleland and King Management: A Systems Approach

Cleland and King Systems Analysis and Project Management

Cleland and King Systems, Organizations, Analysis, Management: A Book of Readings

Dale Management: Theory and Practice

Dale Readings in Management: Landmarks and New Frontiers

Davis Human Behavior at Work: Organizational Behavior

Davis and Newstrom Organizational Behavior: Readings and Exercises

Davis, Frederick, and Blomstrom Business and Society: Concepts and Policy Issues

DeGreene Systems Psychology

Dunn and Rachel Wage and Salary Administration: Total Compensation Systems

Edmunds and Letey Environmental Administration

Fiedler A Theory of Leadership Effectiveness

Finch, Jones, and Litterer Managing for Organizational Effectiveness: An Experiential Approach

Flippo Personnel Management

Glueck Business Policy and Strategic Management

Glueck Readings in Business Policy from *Business Week*

Glueck Strategic Management and Business Policy

Hampton Contemporary Management

Hicks and Gullett Management

Hicks and Gullett Modern Business Management: A Systems and Environmental Approach

Hicks and Gullett Organizations: Theory and Behavior

Johnson, Kast, and Rosenzweig The Theory and Management of Systems

Karlins The Human Use of Human Resources

Kast and Rosenzweig Experiential Exercises and Cases in Management

Kast and Rosenzweig Organization and Management: A Systems and Contingency Approach

Knudson, Woodworth, and Bell Management: An Experiential Approach

Koontz Toward a Unified Theory of Management

OPERATIONS MANAGEMENT

DECISION MAKING IN THE OPERATIONS FUNCTION

ROGER G. SCHROEDER
University of Minnesota

McGRAW-HILL BOOK COMPANY

New York   St. Louis   San Francisco   Auckland   Bogotá   Hamburg
Johannesburg   London   Madrid   Mexico   Montreal   New Delhi
Panama   Paris   São Paulo   Singapore   Sydney   Tokyo   Toronto

This book was set in Bembo by Progressive Typographers.
The editors were John F. Carleo, Kathi A. Benson, and James B. Armstrong;
the designer was Anne Canevari Green;
the production supervisor was John Mancia.
The drawings were done by Fine Line Illustrations, Inc.
Von Hoffmann Press, Inc., was printer and binder.

OPERATIONS MANAGEMENT
Decision Making in the Operations Function

234567890 VHVH 8987654321

Library of Congress Cataloging in Publication Data

Schroeder, Roger G
    Operations management.

    (McGraw-Hill series in management)
    Includes bibliographies and index.
    1. Production management. 2. Decision-making.
I. Title.
TS155.S335   658.5'036   80-21008
ISBN 0-07-055612-1

ABOUT THE AUTHOR

Roger G. Schroeder is Professor, Graduate School of Business Administration, University of Minnesota, specializing in operations management and management science. He received his B.S. degree in industrial engineering with high distinction from the University of Minnesota, MSIE University of Minnesota, and his Ph.D. in operations research from Northwestern University. Prior to joining the faculty at the University of Minnesota, he was a member of the faculty of the U.S. Naval Postgraduate School, Monterey, California, and an analyst for the office of the Assistant Secretary of Defense. Professor Schroeder has conducted research for the Ford Foundation, the Exxon Education Foundation, and the American Production and Inventory Control Society, and he has published numerous research articles. His current research interests include decision making in operations management, materials requirements planning systems, and management of service operations. Professor Schroeder has been awarded the Morse-Amoco award for outstanding teaching at the University of Minnesota. He is on the faculty of the Minnesota Executive program and has been a consultant for many public and private organizations. Professor Schroeder is currently Director of the Ph.D. program in Business Administration.

TO
MARLENE,
KRISTEN,
AND
BETHANY

CONTENTS

ix

PREFACE

This book is intended for the introductory course in production and operations management offered by most schools of business administration and some schools of engineering. It may be used at either the undergraduate or introductory graduate level, and it addresses the "production" accreditation requirement of the AACSB for both manufacturing and service industries.

This book has several features which set it apart from others in the field.

1. *Functional emphasis.* In this text, operations is treated as a major functional area of business along with the marketing and finance functions. While other books recognize operations as a functional area of business, they do not always stress the management of the operations function—rather, they tend to emphasize quantitative analysis or a systems approach to the design of operations systems. As a result, students can become confused about the organizational importance of operations and the role of the operations function in a business enterprise.

2. *Decisions in operations.* In this text, the important decision responsibilities in operations are organized into five major decision categories—process, capacity, inventory, work force, and quality—each of which is the theme of a major part of the text. Each chapter within a part is devoted to one or more critical decisions topics, while the systems approach and quantitative analysis are treated as underlying disciplines supporting decision making. This is the first text to use this decision-making framework.

3. *The general business student.* This text is written for the general business student as well as those students who may go on in operations. For this audience, it is important to stress management decision making, responsibilities, and the relationship of operations to other business functions. The main chapters do not require prior preparation in quantitative analysis, the behavioral sciences, economics, or other underlying disciplines. For courses in which quantitative disciplines are taught, chapter supplements are provided. The chapter supplements generally treat more advanced quantitative methods, while the basic methods are included in the chapters themselves.

4. *Manufacturing and service industries.* The manufacturing and service industries are presented together in a common conceptual framework. For each decision topic, the book provides a framework which is independent of any particular industry. The examples are then balanced between manufacturing and service industries.

xiii

In other texts, material on service industries has often been "tacked on" and not properly integrated with manufacturing topics.

5. *Case studies.* Cases are included in the text to improve the student's skill in the identification and formulation of problems. These are substantive cases derived from real companies and not just "enlarged problems." Seventeen case studies are included in the last part of the book under major section headings. This permits the use of cases which are somewhat more integrative than the short case sketches typically included at the end of each chapter.

6. *New material.* Since it is based on a great deal of research, this book provides an up-to-date treatment of the field. About one-third of the material in it is new or revised over that found in other operations management textbooks. Important chapters with new material are those on process selection, choice of technology, productivity, materials requirements planning, planning quality, and operations policy and strategy.

The book's educational objectives can be summarized as follows:

- To provide an understanding of operations as a major functional area of business, including its five management decision areas in operations.
- To show how operations decision making can be improved by utilizing all the underlying disciplines: behavioral, quantitative, economic, and systems.
- To present manufacturing and service industries within a common conceptual framework.

Before writing this book, a survey was conducted of professors of operations management throughout the United States. This book's design—both in its approach and in its specific content areas—represents much of their input. During the survey, it became apparent that a wide diversity of courses are taught in the operations management field. A modular approach was therefore chosen, so that different courses can stress different parts of the subject matter.

In writing this text, I have continually attempted to integrate the different parts. This aim is facilitated by use of the decision-making framework and by reference in each chapter to the ways in which decisions are interrelated. Since operations decisions may not occur in any particular sequence, particularly in ongoing operations, this text stresses the interrelationship of decisions rather than the sequence of decision making.

To emphasize the decision-making approach, a typical decision problem is included near the beginning of each chapter. These problems, written in a case format, help to show how decisions are made in an organizational context. They also help to integrate the text and make it more relevant to students.

Many people have helped to prepare this book. The reviewers were Joseph D. Blackburn of Vanderbilt University, William T. Boore of Portland State University, James S. Dyer of the University of Texas, Edward F. Stafford, Jr., of the University of Oklahoma, and Steven C. Wheelwright of Stanford University. I want to express my appreciation to those reviewers and to Fred Luthans of the University of

Nebraska, one of the McGraw-Hill Management Series editors. All these individuals read the manuscript thoroughly and helped to refine and improve the material presented.

I also want to acknowledge the contributions of my colleagues on the faculty at the University of Minnesota. Those who provided me with advice and counsel were John Anderson, Norman Chervany, Gordon Davis, Arthur Hill, and Thomas Hoffmann. There were also many students at the University of Minnesota who commented on the text, particularly the operations management classes from spring 1979 to winter 1980. Several students who assisted in preparation of the manuscript and the Instructor's Manual were Nancy Browning, Douglas Chard, Lori Larson, Nancy Melone, Linda Novotny, T. J. Wharton, and Edna White.

Finally, I wish to thank my family for their patience and perseverance during the three years of text development and editing. I would also like to thank the secretaries who typed various portions of the manuscript: Cyndy Krey, Mary Lamm, and Joan Peterson. To all these individuals I express my appreciation for their contributions and assistance.

Roger G. Schroeder

OPERATIONS MANAGEMENT

DECISION MAKING IN THE OPERATIONS FUNCTION

PART I
INTRODUCTION

PROCESS

CAPACITY

QUALITY

INVENTORY

OPERATIONS
MANAGEMENT
DECISIONS

WORK FORCE

The introductory part of this book will provide an overview of the operations management field and a survey of some of the underlying disciplines required for further study. In Chapter 1, a decision-making framework is developed which is the basis for organizing the remainder of the text. This framework identifies five major decision responsibilities of the operations function in all organizations: process, capacity, inventory, work force, and quality. Each subsequent section of the book is devoted to one of these decision types.

In Chapter 2, the fundamentals of decision making in operations are developed. These fundamentals include formulation of decision problems, decision criteria in operations, important tradeoffs required, and mathematical modeling for decisions. This chapter provides a basis for the development of decision-making ideas in the remainder of the text.

An important input for all operations is the design of the product or service, as discussed in Chapter 3. Product design, however, should not precede the design of the productive process; rather, product and process should be designed together. Product design is viewed as interfunctional in nature, requiring close cooperation between the product designers and the operations function.

Forecasting, discussed in Chapter 4, is the second major input to operations decision making. Chapter 4 describes the types of forecasting methods available and the interaction between forecasting and operations decisions. Some of the important organizational considerations for the use of forecasting in operations are also discussed, along with the requirements for a successful forecasting system.

After studying this section, the reader should be able to define the operations management field, describe important elements of decision making in operations, and discuss the relationship of product design and forecasting to operations. The reader should also have gained some basic skills of model building and have learned how to apply these skills to forecasting and product decisions. The skills and knowledge gained will provide background for studying the five major decision responsibilities of operations in the remainder of the text.

CHAPTER 1
THE OPERATIONS FUNCTION

In the broadest sense, operations management is concerned with the production of goods and services. Every day we come in contact with an abundant array of goods or services, all of which are produced under the supervision of operations managers.

One example of an operations manager is the plant manager who is in charge of a factory. All other managers who work in the factory—including production and inventory control managers, quality managers, and line supervisors—are also operations managers. Collectively, this group of factory managers is responsible for producing the supply of products in a manufacturing business. Carrying this example one step further, we should also include in the group of operations managers all manufacturing managers at the corporate or divisional level. These managers might include a corporate vice president of operations (or manufacturing) and a group of corporate staff operations managers concerned with quality, production and inventory control, facilities, and equipment.

But operations managers are not employed only in manufacturing companies; they work in service industries as well. In the government, for example, there are operations managers in the post office, welfare department, and housing department, to name only a few. In private service industries, operations managers are employed in hotels, restaurants, airlines, and retail stores. In each of these organizations, operations managers—much like their counterparts in manufacturing who produce the supply of goods—are responsible for providing the supply of services.

On the surface, it may appear that service operations have very little in common with manufacturing operations. However, a unifying feature of these operations is that both can be viewed as transformation processes. In manufacturing, inputs of raw materials, energy, labor, and capital are transformed into finished goods. In service operations, these same types of inputs are transformed into service outputs. Managing the transformation process in an efficient and effective manner is the task of the operations manager in any type of organization.

There has been a tremendous shift in our economy from the production of goods to the production of services. It comes as a surprise to many people that, today, more than 70 percent of the American work force is employed in service industries.[1] We have already shifted from a manufacturing-based economy to a service-based economy. Because of the importance of both service and manufacturing operations, they will be treated on an equal basis in this text.

For many years, when the field was related primarily to manufacturing operations, operations management was called "production management." Later, the name was expanded to "production and operations management," or, more simply, "operations management" to include the service industries as well. The term "operations management" as used in this text refers to both manufacturing and service industries.

1.1 DEFINITION OF OPERATIONS MANAGEMENT

The above ideas can be summarized by the following definition:

Operations managers are responsible for producing the supply of goods or services in organizations. Operations managers make decisions regarding operations functions and the transformation systems used. Operations management is the study of decision making in the operations function.

There are three points in this definition which deserve emphasis:

1. FUNCTION. As we have indicated, operations managers are responsible for managing those departments or functions in organizations that produce goods and services. These departments, however, often have different names in different industries. In manufacturing companies, the operations function may be called the manufacturing, production, or operations department. In service organizations, the operations function might be called the operations department, or it may be given some other name peculiar to the particular industry. In general, the generic term "operations" is used to refer to the function which produces goods or services in any organization. Treating operations management in this manner, as an organizational function, puts it on a similar footing with other business functions such as marketing and finance.

---

[1] U.S. Bureau of the Census, *Statistical Abstract of the United States,* Washington, D.C., 1977, pp. 402–404.

2. SYSTEM. The above definition refers to transformation systems which produce goods and services. The systems view provides not only a common ground for defining service and manufacturing operations as transformation systems but also a powerful basis for design and analysis of operations. Using the systems view, we consider operations managers as managers of the conversion process in the firm.

The systems view of operations also provides insights for the design and management of productive systems in functional areas outside the operations function. For example, a sales office within a marketing function may be viewed as a productive system with inputs, transformation, and outputs. The same is true for an accounts payable office and for keypunch operations within a data processing center. In terms of the systems view, operations management concepts have applicability beyond the functional area of operations.

3. DECISIONS. Finally, the above definition refers to decision making as an important element of operations management. Since all managers make decisions, it is natural to focus on decision making as a central theme in operations. This decision focus provides a basis for dividing operations into parts based on major decision types. In

BOX 1.1 **TYPICAL DECISION PROBLEM**

In reviewing earnings reports for the fourth quarter of 1980, Linda Farwell, president of American Car Rental Company, noticed that profits were down once again. This was the third successive quarter in which profits had dropped, and Linda decided that she must act. She picked up her phone and called the vice president of operations, Tom Storch. After briefly explaining the situation, she asked Storch to meet with her later in the day to go over the recent figures. During the meeting, Linda observed that the primary cause of poor profits could be found in the operations department. Car inventories were up, and the unit cost of rental operations had increased over the past year. About the only bright spot in operations was that the quality of service had not deteriorated over time. She also noted that union relations had been getting progressively worse over the past few months.

Storch replied that costs could be cut and car inventories reduced, but not without adverse effects on customer service, quality, and union relations. Storch argued that reduced inventories would offer less model variety for the customer, and some customers would not get the car they wanted at the time and place of their choice. Rental costs could be reduced by layoffs of personnel, but this might aggravate the already deteriorating union situation. Storch suggested, with tongue in cheek, that the problem could be solved by more aggressive marketing, since sales had dropped along with profits. Storch added, "I am sorry, but there is no such thing as a free lunch. If costs are to be reduced, something else must give. We simply have too much capacity for the present level of sales."

At this point, Storch suddenly realized that the problem went deeper than simply cutting back present operations to improve profits. To prevent this situation from occurring again in the future, he must do a better job of planning, decision making, and managing within the operations function. This could be done by identifying the critical decisions in operations and assuring that these decisions were made in a timely manner with the best information available by professional operations managers. Storch, therefore, set out to develop a system of decision making in operations to ensure that the operations department would consistently meet its cost, quality, and customer-service objectives. He also agreed with the president that drastic actions would have to be taken now to cut costs, despite possible adverse effects. Storch vowed that this situation would not arise again in the future.

this text, we identify the five major decision responsibilities of operations management as: process, capacity, inventory, work force, and quality. These decisions provide the framework for organizing the text and describing what operations managers do. See Box 1.1 for a typical decision problem faced by an operations manager.

Since the operations management field can be defined by function, systems, and decisions, we will expand on these three elements in detail in this chapter. Before doing so, however, we shall make a brief historical survey of operations management.

1.2 HISTORY OF OPERATIONS MANAGEMENT

Operations management has existed for as long as people have produced goods and services. Although the origins of operations can be traced to early civilizations, most of our attention in this section will be focused on the last two hundred years.

In the following discussion, the recent history of operations management is organized according to major schools of thought rather than in strict chronological terms. On this basis, there are seven major areas of contribution to the operations management field.

DIVISION OF LABOR. The division of labor is based on a very simple concept. Specialization of labor to a single task can result in greater productivity and efficiency than the assignment of many tasks to a single worker. This concept was recognized in 400 B.C. by Plato in *The Republic* when he said, "A man whose work is confined to such a limited task [e.g., shoe stitching] must necessarily excel at it." [See George (1968).] The ancient Greeks also recognized the concept of the division of labor when they assigned some workers to do nothing but sharpen stone chisels.

The first economist to discuss the division of labor was Adam Smith, author of the classic *Wealth of Nations* (1776). Smith noted that specialization of labor increases output because of three factors: (1) increased dexterity on the part of workers, (2) avoidance of lost time due to changing jobs, and (3) the addition of tools and machines. Later, in 1832, Charles Babbage expanded on these ideas with his study of pin manufacturing. [See Babbage (1832).] He noted that specialization of labor not only increases productivity but also makes it possible to pay wages for only the specific skills required. Although division of labor has been widely applied, it is now being reevaluated because of its effect on worker morale, turnover, job boredom, and job performance. We shall discuss this issue at length later.

STANDARDIZATION OF PARTS. Parts are standardized so that they can be interchanged. According to Chase and Aquilano, standardization was practiced in early Venice, where rudders on warships were made to be interchangeable. [See Chase and Aquilano (1977), p. 5.] This provided a great advantage when rudders were damaged in battle. Eli Whitney used interchangeable parts in musket production. Prior to his time, musket parts and even ammunition were tailored to each individual musket. When Henry Ford introduced the moving automobile assembly line in 1913, his concept required standardized parts as well as specialization of labor. The idea of standardized parts is by now so ingrained in our society that we rarely stop to think of it. For example, it is difficult to imagine light bulbs which are not interchangeable.

INDUSTRIAL REVOLUTION. The industrial revolution was in essence the substitution of machine power for human power. Great impetus was given to this revolution in 1764 by James Watts's steam engine, which was a major source of mobile machine power for agriculture and factories. The industrial revolution was further accelerated in the late 1800s with the development of the gasoline engine and electricity. Early in this century, mass-production concepts were developed but they did not gain widespread use until World War I, when heavy demands for production were placed on American industry. The age of mass marketing has continued this pressure for automation and high-volume production. However, our society has now entered a postindustrial period, characterized by a shift to a service economy and greater concern for the natural and social environment.

SCIENTIFIC STUDY OF WORK. The scientific study of work is based on the notion that the scientific method can be used to study work as well as physical and natural systems. This school of thought aims to discover the best method of work by using the following scientific approach: (1) observation of the present work methods, (2) development of an improved method through scientific measurement and analysis, (3) training the workers in the new method, and (4) continuing feedback and management of the work process. These ideas were first advanced by Frederick Taylor in 1911 and later refined by Frank and Lillian Gilbreth throughout the early 1900s. [See Taylor (1911).] The scientific study of work has come under attack by labor unions, workers, and academics. In some cases, these attacks have been justified because the approach was misapplied or used as a "speedup" campaign by management. Nevertheless, the principles of scientific management can still be applied in today's world by recognizing the interaction between the social and technical work environments.

HUMAN RELATIONS. The human relations movement recognized the central importance of motivation and the human element in work design. Elton Mayo and others developed this line of thought in the 1930s at Western Electric, where the now famous Hawthorne studies were conducted. [See Wren (1972).] These studies indicated that worker motivation—along with the physical and technical work environment—is a crucial element in improving productivity. This led to a moderation of the scientific management school, which had emphasized the more technical aspects of work design. The human relations school of thinking has also led to job enrichment, now recognized as a method with a great deal of potential for "humanizing the work place" as well as improving productivity.

DECISION MODELS. Decision models can be used to represent a productive system in mathematical terms. A decision model is expressed in terms of performance measures, constraints, and decision variables. The purpose of such a model is to find optimal or satisfactory values of decision variables which improve systems performance within the applicable constraints. These models can then help guide management decision making. One of the first uses of this approach occurred in 1915 when F. W. Harris developed an economic order-quantity formula for inventory management. In 1931, Shewhart developed quantitative decision models for use in statistical quality control work. In 1947, George Dantzig developed the simplex method of linear programming, which made possible the solution of a whole class of mathematical models. In the 1950s, the development of computer simulation models contributed much to the study and analysis of operations. Since the 1950s, the use of various decision models in operations has been greatly expanded.

COMPUTERS. The use of computers has dramatically changed the field of operations management since computers were introduced into business in the 1950s. Most manufacturing operations except very small ones now employ computers for inventory management, production scheduling, quality control, and costing systems. In addition, computers are rapidly making inroads on the automation of office work, and they are used in virtually all types of service operations. Today, the effective use of computers is an essential part of the operations management field.

Each of these seven areas of contribution has advanced the operations management field in a major way. Furthermore, the contributions are still applicable to the management of modern operations, although sometimes in modified form. At later points in the text, these basic developments will be amplified and discussed in more detail.

1.3 THE OPERATIONS FUNCTION

In this section, we will expand the idea that operations management is a functional area of business. Figure 1.1 helps describe this idea by showing four types of business administration fields: functional areas, methodology areas, industry areas, and integrating areas.

Functional areas are concerned with a particular focus of responsibility or decision making in an organization. The marketing function is typically responsible for creating demand and generating sales revenue, the operations function is responsible for the production of goods or services (generating supply), and finance is responsible for the acquisition and allocation of capital. Functional areas tend to be closely associated with organizational departments because businesses typically are organized on a functional basis.

Figure 1.1 also shows methodology areas, which are characterized by a particular methodology or discipline base. For example, the quantitative methods area deals with the use of mathematical models for decision support; the systems area deals with the study of organizations as systems; and organizational behavior deals with the study of human behavior in organizations. Methodology areas develop methods or tools which can be applied to problems in any of the functional areas.

Industry areas involve the study of a particular industry such as banking, insurance, transportation, and manufacturing. Industry areas may draw on ideas from both methodology and functional fields.

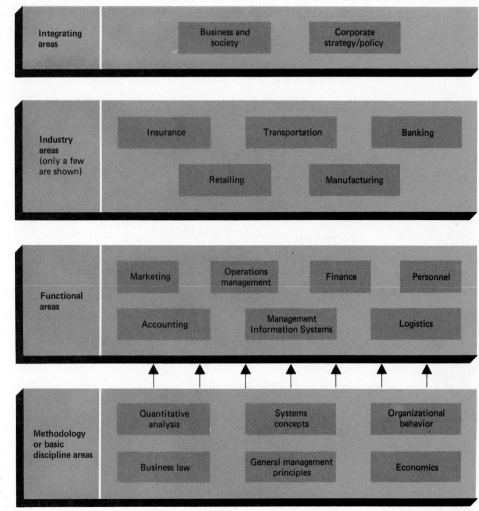

**Figure 1.1
Fields of study
in business
administration.**

Finally, there are two integrating areas. The business and society area is concerned with the relationship of business to its societal, governmental, and economic environment. Corporate strategy is concerned with top management, the integration of the functional areas within business, and the formulation and implementation of strategy.

This view of business administration clearly illustrates the relationship between methodology areas and functional areas. In general, each of the functional areas utilizes a blend of the appropriate methodology areas to address its specific problems and decisions. This textbook follows the blend approach throughout; certain chapters draw heavily on quantitative analysis, while others draw on systems concepts, organizational behavior, economics, general management principles, or a combination of these areas.

Managers in operations functions practice operations management. They do not practice behavioral science, quantitative methods, or systems analysis, although they utilize these underlying disciplines. Likewise, doctors do not practice biology, although they know how to use biological methods. While methodologies are certainly important, they are not the essence of operations management.

Figure 1.1 also indicates the distinction between operations management and the manufacturing industry. Operations functions occur in every industry, such as manufacturing, banking, and retailing. As we discussed earlier, operations management is not industry-specific.

1.4 OPERATIONS AS A PRODUCTIVE SYSTEM

We have also defined operations management as the management of transformation systems which convert inputs into goods and services. As discussed in the first section, this approach views the field as a productive system. [For an excellent treatment of this view, see Buffa (1976).]

In general, a productive system can be defined as a process for converting resource inputs into goods and services, as illustrated in Figure 1.2. The inputs to this system are energy, materials, labor, capital, and information. These inputs are converted into goods and/or services by the process technology, which is the particular method used to transform the various inputs into outputs. Changing the technology alters the way one input is used in relation to another, and it may also change the outputs produced.

Figure 1.2 also shows feedback information used to control the process technology or inputs. It is essential in operations that feedback be used for control purposes

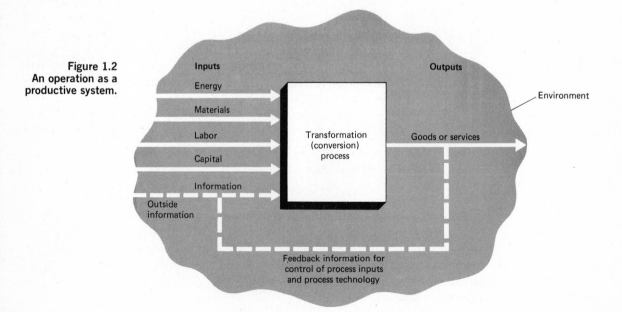

**Figure 1.2
An operation as a
productive system.**

TABLE 1.1 **EXAMPLES OF PRODUCTIVE SYSTEMS**

Operation	Input	Output
Bank	Tellers, staff, computer equipment, facilities, and energy	Financial services (loans, deposits, safekeeping, etc.)
Restaurant	Cooks, waitresses, food, equipment, facilities, and energy	Meals, entertainment, satisfied customers
Hospital	Doctors, nurses, staff, equipment, facilities, and energy	Health services, healthy patients
University	Faculty, staff, equipment, facilities, energy, and knowledge	Educated students, research, public service
Manufacturing plant	Equipment, facilities, labor, energy, raw materials	Finished goods
Airline	Planes, facilities, pilots, flight attendants, maintenance people, labor, energy	Transportation from one location to another

to produce the desired outputs. It is the operations manager's responsibility to use feedback information to continually adjust the mix of inputs and technology needed to achieve desired outputs. These mix decisions are complex and require constant attention to the tradeoffs available.

The types of inputs used will vary from one industry to another. If the operation is automobile manufacturing, inputs of capital and energy for machines, facilities, and tools will be necessary. Labor will be required to operate and maintain the equipment, and materials inputs will form the basis for the conversion process from raw materials to finished goods.

Operations in the service industries use a somewhat different mix of inputs from those used in manufacturing. For example, an airline operation requires inputs of capital for aircraft and facilities, highly skilled labor (pilots, maintenance), low-skilled labor, and a great deal of energy. Very little raw material input is used in comparison with the requirements of a manufacturing company. The primary service provided by the airline is transportation, although other services such as hotel reservations and air freight are also provided.

Table 1.1 provides some additional examples of productive systems in society. By studying operations as transformation systems, a great deal can be learned about how to improve operations design and decision making.

1.5 OPERATIONS DECISIONS—A FRAMEWORK

Since operations management is concerned with decision making in the operations function, a framework which categorizes and defines decisions in operations is needed. Although many different frameworks are possible, the primary one used here is a functional scheme for grouping decisions. In this framework, similar decision responsibilities concerning facilities or inventories, for example, are grouped together.

A functional grouping of decisions may conform quite closely to the assignment of management responsibilities within an operations organization. However, management assignments will vary from one operation to another on the basis of local organizational preferences. What is proposed here is a theoretical framework of decision responsibility for operations which groups decisions according to their function or purpose.

In the proposed framework, operations has five major decision responsibilities: process, capacity, inventory, work force, and quality. These decision responsibilities are found in most, if not all, operations.

1. *Process*. Decisions in this category are related to design of the physical productive process including selection of process type, choice of technology, process-flow analysis, and facility layout. Process decisions define how the product or service is made. Process design is highly interactive with product design and thus requires close coordination between marketing and operations.
2. *Capacity*. Capacity decisions are aimed at providing sufficient output capacity for the organization—not too much and not too little. Capacity decisions include developing capacity plans over long-, medium-, and short-term ranges. Forecasting, facilities planning, aggregate planning, and scheduling decisions are all part of capacity planning and control.
3. *Inventory*. Inventory is an important asset which must be managed by operations. Inventory managers make decisions concerning when to order and how much to order. They manage the logistics system from the purchasing stage through the inventorying of raw materials, work in process, and finished goods.
4. *Work force*. This area of decision responsibility is concerned with managing the work force in operations. Responsibilities include line management, productivity improvement, job design, and work measurement. Close attention to the management of people and productivity is one of the most important responsibilities of the operations function.
5. *Quality:* The operations function is typically responsible for the quality of goods and services produced. In this text emphasis will be placed on both the planning and control of quality. The management of quality will be considered for all types of operations including manufacturing and services.

Careful attention to the five decision areas is the key to management of successful operations. Indeed, the well-managed operations function can be defined in terms of the decision framework. If each of the five decision areas is functioning properly and well integrated with the other areas, the operations function can be considered well managed.

In some cases, students feel that operations management is a hodge-podge of techniques and methods—that there is no central theme. The decision framework was specifically designed to overcome this problem. Each major section of this text is devoted to one of the five decision categories. The framework thus provides an integrating mechanism for the text.

1.6 DECISION FRAMEWORK—EXAMPLE

To illustrate the use of the decision framework, a company will be described in terms of the five decision categories. The example is a simplified description of Pizza U.S.A., Inc., a company which produces and markets pizza pies on a national basis. It consists of 100 company-owned and franchised outlets (each called a store) in the United States. The operations management function in this company exists at two levels: the corporate level and the level of the individual store.

The major operations decisions made by Pizza U.S.A. can be described as follows:

PROCESS. Since uniformity across different stores is desired, most of the process decisions are made by the corporate staff. They have developed a standard facility which is simply sized to fit a particular location. The standard facility incorporates a limited menu with high-volume equipment. As pizzas are made, customers can watch the process through a glass window; this provides entertainment for both children and adults as they wait for their order to be filled. Because this is a service facility, special care is taken to make the layout attractive and convenient for the customers. The location of facilities is based on a mathematical model which is used to project revenues and costs for particular sites. Each potential site must have an adequate projected return on investment before construction can begin.

CAPACITY. Pizza U.S.A. faces a series of decisions related to the maximum level of output. First, when the initial location and process decisions are made, the corporate staff fixes the physical capacity of each facility. Individual store managers then plan for annual, monthly, and daily fluctuations in service capacity within the available physical facility. During peak periods, they employ part-time help, and advertising is used in an attempt to raise demand during slack periods. In the short run, individual personnel must be scheduled to shifts to meet demand around the clock.

INVENTORY. The individual store managers buy the ingredients required to prepare the recipes provided by corporate staff. They select their own suppliers and decide how much flour, tomato paste, sausage, etc., to order and when to place orders. Store operators must carefully integrate purchasing and inventory decisions to control the flow of materials in relation to capacity.

WORK FORCE. Store managers are responsible for hiring, training, supervising, and, if necessary, firing workers. They must decide on exact job responsibilities and on the number of people needed to operate the store. They also advertise job openings, screen applications, interview candidates, and make the hiring decisions. They must measure the amount of work required in relation to production and also evaluate the performance of each individual. Management of the work force is one of the most important daily responsibilities of the store manager.

QUALITY. Finally, the corporate staff has set certain standards for quality which all stores must follow. These standards include procedures to maintain service quality and to ensure the quality of the pizzas served. While service quality is difficult to measure, the quality of the pizzas can be more easily specified by using criteria such as temperature at serving time, the amount of raw materials used in relation to standards, and so on. In Pizza U.S.A., each store manager must carefully monitor quality to make sure that it meets company standards.

The five decision categories provide a framework to describe the important operations decisions made by Pizza U.S.A. It should be recognized, however, that these five types of decisions cannot be made separately; they must be carefully integrated with one another and with decisions made in other parts of the business.

BOX 1.2   **MANAGEMENT POSITIONS IN OPERATIONS**

Operations Manager. In manufacturing organizations, titles include plant manager and vice president of manufacturing operations. In service industries, titles include store manager, office manager, and vice president of operations. These positions are concerned with overall coordination and direction of the operations function. Specific responsibilities include strategic planning, policy setting, budgeting, management of other managers, and control of operations.

Materials Manager. This position is concerned with managing and integrating the flow of materials from raw materials to finished products. The materials manager will typically have subordinate managers in purchasing, inventory control, and production control.

Purchasing. The purchasing manager is concerned with assuring an adequate flow of raw materials. Purchasing managers work closely with vendors. They negotiate prices, perform vendor selection, and evaluate vendor performance.

Inventory Manager. The inventory manager is concerned with ordering the proper amount of material at the right time. Inventory managers often utilize computerized systems to help them provide the best customer service at the lowest possible inventory cost.

Production Control and Scheduling Manager. The production control manager is responsible for developing a production plan and ensuring the best use of resources in meeting that plan. Production control responsibilities include planning schedules, balancing workloads, and making sure that the product is delivered on time. In the service industry, this function is often called scheduling.

Quality Manager. The quality manager is concerned with planning and controlling product quality. Responsibilities include setting quality standards, developing quality control standards, developing quality control systems, and assisting workers in producing quality. The quality manager monitors the quality of the product or service at every stage.

Facility Manager. The facility manager is concerned with the design and control of operations facilities and processes. Responsibilities include work-flow analysis, technology management, facilities choice, facilities location, and equipment planning.

Line Manager. The line manager is concerned with the management of the work force and of operations units. Job titles include first-line supervisor and unit manager. The line manager is concerned with proper performance of work, personnel development, work organization, and reward systems.

Operations Planning Analyst. An operations planning analyst deals with the overall planning, budgeting, and control of an operation. A planning analyst serves as staff to the operations manager and may develop models and information systems to support planning and decision making.

Toward this end, a section is provided at the end of the text which specifically addresses the integration of decisions within operations and the firm.

While Pizza U.S.A. is one example of an operation, students often ask, "What do operations managers do in more general terms?" Box 1.2 provides examples of nine typical operations management positions and describes the associated decision-making responsibilities. The descriptions have been greatly simplified, perhaps oversimplified, for illustration purposes.

As Box 1.2 indicates, there are a great variety of management positions in operations. These range from first-level supervisory positions to middle- and top-management positions of considerable responsibility. These positions also cut across all the functions of operations and apply to both manufacturing and service operations.

Operations managers must have both behavioral and quantitative skills. While the line supervisory positions require more behavioral skill, the supporting staff positions often require a greater degree of quantitative skill.

Furthermore, some positions are more concerned with day-to-day operations, while others are more concerned with policy and planning. Typically, the staff and higher-level management positions are more concerned with policy and planning than with day-to-day operations. Lower- and middle-line managers are more concerned with daily operations.

1.7 DECISIONS IN OPERATIONS—ANOTHER VIEW

Another way of classifying operations decisions is: (1) decisions affecting the design of the operations function and (2) decisions related to utilization of an existing operation. While the design decisions tend to be strategic, long-range, and irreversible for long periods of time, the utilization decisions are tactical, short range, and implementation-oriented. In Pizza U.S.A., there was a tendency for corporate staff to handle design decisions and for store managers to be responsible for utilization decisions.

Table 1.2 is a matrix which shows how the five decision categories are related to design and utilization decisions. Each decision category contains some decisions of both types. For example, some decisions in the inventory area involve long-range design considerations, while others are concerned with utilizing an existing inventory system. The functional decision categories, therefore, do not correspond to either long- or short-range decisions; rather, both types of decisions are included in each category.

In making decisions in operations, no particular sequence is followed in practice. There is, however, a tendency for many of the process and physical capacity decisions to precede other decisions in the inventory, work force, and quality areas. Because of this tendency, process and capacity decisions are treated first in the text. The reader should be cautioned, however, that decisions are often intertwined; therefore no strict, logical sequence can be constructed, particularly for ongoing operations. This phenomenon makes it difficult to organize the operations management field using a sequential decision approach. This book, therefore, groups decisions into functional categories and discusses interrelationships rather than sequence.

TABLE 1.2   **DESIGN AND UTILIZATION DECISIONS IN OPERATIONS**

Decision category	Design decisions (strategic)	Utilization decisions (tactical)
Process	Select process type Choose equipment	Analyze process flows Provide for maintenance of equipment
Capacity	Determine facilities size Determine facilities location Set work force levels	Decide overtime Arrange for subcontracting Determine scheduling
Inventory	Set overall inventory size Design inventory control system	Decide when to order and how much to order
Work force	Design jobs Select compensation system	Provide supervision Set work standards
Quality	Set quality standards Decide on quality organization	Decide on amount of inspection Control quality to meet standards

1.8 PRODUCERS OF SERVICES AND GOODS

Throughout the text we will be describing decisions in both service and manufacturing operations. It is therefore important to compare these two types of operations as a prelude to further discussion. Before going further into the distinction between goods and services, however, some definitions will be helpful. A good is a tangible entity. Since goods are physical in nature, they can be stored, transformed, and transported. A service is intangible in nature. A service can be defined as something which is produced and consumed more or less simultaneously. Because it is intangible, a service cannot be stored or transported. A product may be either a good or a service or both. A product is the output of an operation.

Because services are intangible, service producers differ from goods producers in important aspects of their operation. Several of the more interesting differences are described below. [For an excellent treatment of services, see Sasser, Olsen, and Wyckoff (1978).]

CAPACITY AND INVENTORY. A service can be viewed as an extremely perishable product; it cannot be stored as inventory for future use. Thus, the delivery of services presents a special problem for inventory and capacity planning. The service producer needs to build capacity in advance of demand as workers are hired, facilities are built, and equipment is installed. If the demand does not materialize, the capacity is wasted and high costs result. On the other hand, a goods producer can use current capacity to produce an inventory of goods for consumption in future periods.

QUALITY. Since a service is intangible, quality cannot be readily assessed by potential customers. In service organizations, reputation is crucial because much of the quality image for services is passed on by word of mouth. The future customer often cannot look at the product and form an impression of quality. Reputation and quality are special problems for service producers.

DISPERSION. Service organizations are often dispersed geographically. Since a service cannot be stored and shipped, it must be produced at the point of consumption or the customer must be brought to the service. This leads to a dispersion of service outlets. Examples are retail stores, barbershops, car-rental agencies, banks, and hospitals. On the other hand, goods producers can centralize their operations because their goods can be shipped to the final destination. The degree of centralization is an extremely important operations decision which will be discussed later.

MARKETING AND OPERATIONS. In service organizations, the operations and marketing functions tend to be closely related. This is because services are consumed at the same time and place that they are produced. Service organizations are both marketing and operations entities. In goods-producing organizations, the opposite is true. Marketing and operations are organized as separate functions because goods are produced and sold separately. The integration of marketing and operations then becomes a difficult problem for goods producers.

The distinction between goods producers and service producers can be made even more precise by referring to Box 1.3, which is a detailed classification of industries in terms of firms that primarily produce goods and those that mainly provide services.

BOX 1.3   **PRODUCERS OF GOODS AND SERVICES**

Primarily goods producers	Primarily service producers
Agriculture, forestry, fishing	*Transportation and public utilities*
Agricultural production—crops	Railroad transportation
Agricultural production—livestock	Local and interurban passenger transit
Agricultural services	Trucking and warehousing
Forestry	U.S. Postal Service
Fishing, hunting, and trapping	Water transportation
	Transportation by air
Mining	Pipelines except natural gas
Metal mining	Transportation services
Anthracite mining	Communication
Bituminous coal and lignite mining	Electric, gas, and sanitary services
Oil and gas extraction	
Nonmetallic minerals except fuels	*Wholesale trade*
	Wholesale trade—durable goods
Construction	Wholesale trade—nondurable goods
General building contractors	
Heavy-construction contractors	*Retail trade*
Special trade contractors	Building materials and garden supplies
	General merchandise stores
Manufacturing	Food stores
Food and kindred products	Automotive dealers and service stations
Tobacco manufactures	Apparel and accessory stores
Textile-mill products	Furniture and home furnishings stores
Apparel and other textile products	Eating and drinking places
Lumber and wood products	Miscellaneous retail
Furniture and fixtures	
(Continued)	*(Continued)*

BOX 1.3   **PRODUCERS OF GOODS AND SERVICES** (*Continued*)

Primarily goods producers	Primarily service producers
Manufacturing (continued) Paper and allied products Printing and publishing Chemicals and allied products Petroleum and coal products Rubber and miscellaneous plastic products Leather and leather products Stone, clay, and glass products Primary metal industries Fabricated metal products Machinery except electrical Electric and electronic equipment Transportation equipment Instruments and related products Miscellaneous manufacturing industries	*Finance, insurance, and real estate* Banking Credit agencies other than banks Security, commodity brokers and services Insurance carriers Insurance agents, brokers, and service Real estate Combined real estate, insurance, etc. Holding and other investment offices *Services* Hotels and other lodging places Personal services Business services Auto repair, services, and garages Miscellaneous repair services Motion pictures Amusement and recreation services Health services Legal services Educational services Social services Museums, botanical and zoological gardens Membership organizations Private households Miscellaneous services *Public administration* Executive, legal, and general Justice, public order, and safety Finance, taxation, and monetary policy Administration of human resources Environmental quality and housing Administration of economic programs National security and international affairs

Industries listed are based on the U.S. Department of Commerce Standard Industrial Classification System.

Many organizations produce a mixture of goods and services. Thus a classification of industries on a continuous scale between pure goods and pure services is appropriate. In Figure 1.3, point *a* represents the pure goods producers. These producers might include factories, farms, mines, and other organizations that typically produce goods only. Pure goods operations have little or no customer contact and they do not offer services as part of their marketing package.

Point *b* in Figure 1.3 represents an organization which produces both goods and services. Many companies manufacturing consumer goods are in this category. For

**Figure 1.3
Continuum of
goods and
services.**

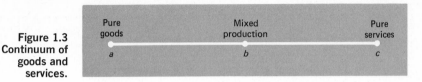

example, automobile manufacturers provide many services in addition to the automobiles they sell. These services include financing, insurance, warranty, repair, and so on. Another example of a producer of both goods and services is the fast-food outlet.

Point c represents the pure service producer. Any tangible good delivered in connection with the service is incidental. For example, dentists provide fillings for teeth, but these materials are incidental to the main service provided. Other examples of pure service producers are consulting firms, government agencies, hospitals, banks, education, and personal services.

Richard Chase (1978) has suggested that service organizations be classified by the percentage of time during which the producer is in direct contact with the customer while the product is being produced. Pure goods producers would have zero percent contact and pure service producers would have 100 percent contact. This proposal provides a precise method of classification for all types of operations.

Chase goes on to point out that operations with low customer contact can be made more efficient, since the customer is not involved as much in the process of production. On the other hand, systems with a high degree of customer contact must respond to customers' time and quality demands, and they suffer a corresponding loss in efficiency of operations.

As will be noted at many points in the text, the service industries present a substantial challenge to operations management. They are often not professionally managed to the same degree as are goods producers. Most operations management concepts can be applied in service organizations, but they have not been widely used in these areas.

1.9 KEY POINTS

The purpose of this book is to provide a broad overview and survey of the field of operations management for a first course. Decision making, responsibilities, and the relationship of operations to other business functions are stressed. The functional orientation and the five decision categories are used as major organizing principles.

The following key points are stressed in the chapter:

- Operations management is defined as decision making for operations functions and systems which produce goods or services.
- The history of operations management includes seven major contributions: division of labor, standardization of parts, industrial revolution, scientific study of work, human relations, decision models, and computers.

- Operations management, like marketing and finance, is a functional area of business. As a functional area, the focus is primarily on decision-making responsibility and secondarily on methodology.
- Managers in operations manage the transformation process which supplies goods and services. The transformation process converts inputs (materials, energy, labor, capital, and information) into outputs (goods or services).
- Operations management is defined by five key types of decision responsibilities: process, capacity, inventory, work force, and quality. These five decision categories are useful for describing an existing operation or identifying the decisions required to establish a new operation.
- A service is produced and consumed more or less simultaneously. Service-producing and goods-producing organizations differ on the following characteristics: capacity, quality, dispersion of operations, and the relationship of marketing and operations. Service and goods producers may be described on a continuous scale from pure goods producers to pure service producers.

QUESTIONS

1. Some definitions of operations management from other textbooks are given below. Contrast and compare these definitions with the one given in this chapter.
   a. "Conceptually POM [production and operations management] includes all types of productive work which are geared to the criteria of efficiency and effectiveness." [Levin et al. (1972).]
   b. "Thus, productive systems are man's unique invention: They are the means by which we create the endless list of goods and services that are needed to sustain modern society . . . and the management of these productive systems is called operations management." [Buffa (1976).]
   c. "Operations Management may be defined as the performance of managerial activities entailed in selecting, designing, operating, controlling, and updating productive systems." [Chase and Aquilano (1977).]
2. What is the difference between the terms "production management" and "operations management"? *Goods vs Goods + Svcs*
3. How does the function of an operations manager differ from the function of a marketing manager or a finance manager? How are these functions similar?
4. How is the operations management field related to the fields of quantitative analysis, computer systems analysis, economics, and organizational behavior?
5. Describe how the concept of division of labor applies to the following situations:
   a. College teaching *Bus, Mgmt, Hist* c. The construction trades *welder, mason*
   b. Accounting *tax, specialties* d. A fast-food restaurant *cashier, cook*
6. Using the history of operations management, what approaches have been used to improve productivity over the last century? Can these same approaches be used to improve productivity in today's world and in the future?
7. What did the scientific study of work contribute to the operations management field? How can these principles be used today?
8. Discuss the impact of mathematical models and computers on the field of operations management.
9. Describe the nature of operations management in the following organizations. In doing this, first identify the purpose and products of the organization, then use the five decision types to identify important operations decisions and responsibilities.
   a. A college library
   b. A hotel

10. For the organizations listed in question 9, describe the inputs, transformation process, and outputs of the productive system.
11. Describe the functional view and the productive system view of operations management. Why are both these views useful in studying the field of operations management?
12. Contrast and compare a service organization to a goods-producing organization. Use the decision framework to identify important points of similarity and difference.

SELECTED BIBLIOGRAPHY

BABBAGE, CHARLES: *On the Economy of Machinery and Manufactures,* London: Charles Knight, 1832.

BUFFA, ELWOOD S.: *Operations Management: The Management of Productive Systems,* New York: Wiley, 1976.

CHASE, RICHARD B.: "Where Does the Customer Fit in a Service Operation?" *Harvard Business Review,* November–December 1978.

———, and NICHOLAS J. AQUILANO: *Production and Operations Management: A Life Cycle Approach,* rev. ed., Homewood, Ill.: Irwin, 1977.

COLLEY, JOHN L., JR., ROBERT D. LANDEL, and ROBERT R. FAIR: *Production Operations Planning and Control,* San Francisco: Holden-Day, 1977.

CONSTABLE, C. J., and C. C. NEW: *Operations Management: A Systems Approach through Text and Cases,* London: Wiley-Interscience, 1976.

GEORGE, CLAUDE S., JR.: *The History of Management Thought,* Englewood Cliffs, N.J.: Prentice-Hall, 1968.

LEVIN, RICHARD, et al.: *Production/Operations Management: Contemporary Policy for Managing Operations Systems,* New York: McGraw-Hill, 1972.

MARSHALL, PAUL W., et al.: *Operations Management: Text and Cases,* Homewood, Ill.: Irwin, 1975.

SASSER, W. EARL, R. PAUL OLSEN, and DARYL WYCKOFF: *Management of Service Operations: Text, Cases and Readings,* Boston: Allyn and Bacon, 1978.

SHORE, BARRY: *Operations Management,* New York: McGraw-Hill, 1973.

SMITH, ADAM: *An Inquiry into the Nature and Causes of the Wealth of Nations,* London: A. Strahn & T. Cadell, 1776.

STARR, MARTIN K.: *Operations Management,* Englewood Cliffs, N.J.: Prentice-Hall, 1978.

TAYLOR, FREDERICK W.: *The Principles of Scientific Management,* New York: Harper, 1911.

VOLLMANN, THOMAS E.: *Operations Management: A Systems Model-Building Approach,* Reading, Mass.: Addison-Wesley, 1973.

WREN, DANIEL A.: *The Evolution of Management Thought,* New York: Ronald Press, 1972.

CHAPTER 2
DECISION MAKING IN OPERATIONS

In the last chapter, we stressed the importance of decision making in the operations function. But precisely what is decision making, how should decisions be formulated by operations managers, and how do operations decisions interact with each other? These questions will be addressed in depth in this chapter.

Decision making can be viewed from many different perspectives. From a narrow point of view, decision making is the act of choosing from among different alternatives. In this case one can view the decision maker as agonizing over the choice at the moment of decision. From a broader perspective, decision making is the whole process of arriving at a decision, from initial identification of the problem through generation and evaluation of alternatives and finally to the choice itself. This definition of decision making as a process can be broadened even further to include implementation of the decision and control of the decision process to determine when additional decisions are required. In this case decision making becomes practically synonymous with managing.

A broad view of decision making, which includes the entire process of deciding and implementing, has been proposed by Simon (1960). This text follows his lead in taking the broad view of decision making. Box 2.1 illustrates how the decision-making process is used for a typical operations decision problem.

22

BOX 2.1   **TYPICAL DECISION PROBLEM**

The Midwest Bedding Company makes a wide line of mattresses and beds which are sold throughout the United States. Among the critical components of the company's mattresses are the spring coils used inside the mattress. The supplier from whom Midwest has always purchased these coils just announced a 20 percent price increase, from 50 cents per coil to 60 cents. The result of this action is to increase the cost of the entire mattress by about 10 percent, since half its cost is in the springs.

According to the purchasing agent, Shelly Rodgers, "Midwest cannot accept this large price increase and continue in business. Something must be done soon to alleviate the situation." Her boss, Harold Anderson, the vice president of operations, agreed that action should be taken, but what action? Together they outlined several alternatives: (1) talk to the supplier and see if something can be done to reduce the price increase to a more manageable level, (2) seek out alternate sources of supply, (3) start making the springs in house, and (4) acquire a spring manufacturing company.

According to Anderson, "Cost is not the only issue here. We must carefully consider the quality of the springs, the ability to deliver the springs when we need them, and the flexibility of operations to meet changes in spring design. Each of the alternatives will have different strengths and weaknesses in meeting these objectives, and we must, therefore, carefully evaluate the tradeoffs involved."

Anderson continued by stating that he would like to see a cost model used in evaluating the alternatives. The cost model should include both fixed and variable costs, since the different alternatives require different levels of investment. Once complete, the cost model could be used to sharpen the comparison among alternatives and the assumptions required, even though some of the noncost factors are excluded.

Anderson and Rodgers set out to collect the information they would need to make the decision. This required contacting the present supplier, finding alternate suppliers, costing out manufacturing facilities, and asking the finance department to investigate the feasibility of acquisitions. Even though the process they followed pertained to this particular decision, Rodgers observed that the decision-making process used could be applied to decisions of all types.

2.1 THE DECISION-MAKING PROCESS

Decision making can be described as a sequence of steps: problem definition, generation of alternatives, evaluation of alternatives, choice, and implementation. Although these steps are ordered in a logical sequence, they are not necessarily completed one after another. A great deal of looping or iteration may be required between steps before a decision is reached, as shown in Figure 2.1.

PROBLEM DEFINITION. At the outset of the decision-making process, a need must be recognized by one or more decision makers. This need is often seen as either a problem or an opportunity of some sort. As a result, the decision-making process is set in motion. Decision makers will then seek to identify the nature of the problem or opportunity more clearly. How broad is the problem? Does it extend beyond operations, or is it limited to some part of operations? What other parts of the organization are affected by the decision, and what constraints, assumptions, and criteria must be considered? As a result of exploring these questions, the decision problem will not only be recognized but also well defined.

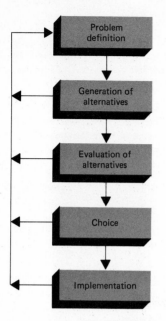

**Figure 2.1
The decision-
making process.**

GENERATION OF ALTERNATIVES. One or more alternatives to the existing situation must be generated before a decision can be made. In some cases, the generation of a single alternative from the status quo may be quite difficult. This is especially true in decisions which require consensus of a political nature, where the decision makers do not agree on constraints, criteria, or assumptions about the problem. In other cases, a great many alternatives may be considered. Sometimes, so many alternatives are possible that sophisticated mathematical models are needed to evaluate all the possibilities systematically. Regardless of the circumstances, however, the generation of alternatives is often difficult and requires a great deal of creative effort.

EVALUATION OF ALTERNATIVES. The evaluation of alternatives depends on the selection of proper decision criteria. Since criteria are so important, an entire section of this chapter will be devoted to decision criteria in operations. The evaluation of alternatives also frequently requires the decision maker to deal with conflicting criteria. For example, the decision to introduce a new machine in operations may reduce costs, but it may also decrease the flexibility of operations. Thus tradeoffs must be made between the various criteria and conflicting objectives.

In many cases, the evaluation of alternatives is facilitated by use of a formal mathematical model. This allows the decision maker(s) to quantify the criteria and constraints and to evaluate a variety of alternatives based on the model framework. How this can be done will also be treated later in the chapter.

CHOICE OF AN ALTERNATIVE. Despite the quality of the analysis done to evaluate alternatives, the choice will seldom be clear or easy. This is so because decision problems are difficult to represent completely in quantitative terms and because conflicting criteria are present. As a result, the decision maker often seeks to clarify assumptions, constraints, or problem conditions before selecting a preferred alternative.

Decision makers must also operate in an environment of imperfect or incomplete information. Often, all the information which is pertinent to the problem cannot be obtained in the time available for the decisions. All the possible alternatives cannot be explored for similar reasons. Herbert Simon calls this "bounded rationality." A decision is rarely perfectly rational; it is more often bounded by real-world conditions. As a result, the decision may not be optimal with respect to the conditions and criteria specified in the problem. Instead, the decision maker may accept a satisfactory solution, one which is an improvement over the present situation but which is not the best (or optimal) solution. Simon calls this process of reaching an acceptable or satisfactory decision "satisficing."

IMPLEMENTATION. A decision is not complete until it is carried out and put into practice. The implementation step is thus as crucial as the whole process of deciding. Implementation requires changing the way people behave. It has been found that it is often easiest to change people's behavior if they have been involved in the decision process itself. Thus implementation may begin well before the last step of the decision process is taken.

Since implementation requires change, the decision maker can be viewed as a change agent. It is important to consider the behavioral side of decision making as well as the quantitative side; this will help the decision maker to implement the decision and to change the organization. Understanding organizational change is the key to implementation.

The decision process applies to all areas of business, not just operations management. In the remainder of this chapter, however, we will be expanding on the general ideas described above to show their application to the operations function.

2.2 SYSTEMS IN OPERATIONS

When operations is viewed as a transformation system the decision-making process is greatly facilitated. The systems view is particularly useful in problem identification and formulation. By using the systems view, the decision can be put in the proper context and all the relevant decision variables and criteria can be identified.

When the systems approach is used for decision making, the first step is to define the relevant operations system. This step, in turn, rests on the following definition of a system: A system is a collection of interrelated elements whose whole is greater than the sum of the parts.

The human body is a system. It consists of interrelated organs including the lungs, heart, muscles, etc. But the human body as a whole is certainly more than the sum of the individual parts. By itself, the heart is merely a pump. The brain cannot function without the heart and lungs. Each part of the body contributes to the functioning of the whole.

A business organization is a system. Its parts are the functions of marketing, operations, finance, and so on. But the business as a system accomplishes more as a whole than the individual functions could accomplish. A single function accomplishes nothing by itself. A business cannot sell a product which it cannot produce. It does no good to produce a product which cannot be sold. When the different parts of a system work together, a synergistic effect is achieved where the output of the system is greater than the sum of the individual contributions.

Every operation can be viewed as a system by identifying a transformation or conversion process, as described in Chapter 1. The transformation process must be isolated from its environment and defined in terms of inputs, outputs, and the transformation method used. The most difficult part of using the systems approach for decision making, however, is defining the system boundary which separates the operations system from its environment. The boundary tells us, for purposes of analysis, how large or small the system is. The selection of a boundary is arbitrary; the system can be as large or as small as desired, depending on the particular decision problem being studied. The boundary should encompass all important interactions within the system, but it is always difficult to define exactly what should be included or excluded.

In making operations decisions, the largest system ordinarily considered is the entire operations function. Whenever a larger system needs to be considered, the decision will usually concern general management as well as operations management. In making operations decisions, managers also consider subsystems which are only a a part of operations. Examples include the production and inventory control subsystem, the quality subsystem, and so on.

To illustrate these ideas regarding systems and problem definition, consider a typical small bank which we shall call the First City Bank. This bank is located in a community of 100,000 people, and there are five other banks in the town. First City Bank employs twenty people; seven of these are cashiers, including a drive-up window cashier; six employees record transactions from checking, savings, and loan accounts; two employees work with new-customer accounts; and five work in the loan department. The bank utilizes the services of a computer through a correspondent bank, which processes transactions and keeps the bank's books.

The bank is considering the installation of a new automatic teller. What would the relevant system for this decision be? Applying the principles that we have just discussed, all parts of the business affected by this decision should be included in the systems definition. The new teller machine will affect the cashiering function, since cash will be distributed directly to customers and deposits will be taken by the new machine. We can safely assume that the loan department is outside the system boundary, since loans are not affected. New accounts are affected, since new customers will probably be offered the services of the automatic teller when they come to the bank. Accounting is not affected, assuming the transactions coming from the machine teller will be exactly the same as those that come from human tellers.

The systems approach to problem formulation thus helps us define the system boundary and identify those parts of operations and the business which are affected by the proposed decision. In a similar way, we would proceed to identify the effect of the decision on the inputs, outputs, and transformation process of operations. These effects in First City Bank include effects on labor skills and on the services offered to the customer. Maintenance skills will be required to keep the automatic teller in operating condition. Services from the automatic teller can be offered outside normal business hours. All these effects and others must be identified as part of the problem definition.

2.3 CRITERIA FOR OPERATIONS DECISIONS

After defining the system of interest in a decision problem, the decision criteria or objectives should be identified. This process is simplified by recognizing that there are generally four objectives in operations: cost, quality, dependability, and flexibility. [See Wheelwright (1978).]

COST. The cost objective is of extreme importance in operations; and it can be roughly equated to efficiency. When costs for decisions are evaluated, all relevant costs should be included. The concept of relevant cost requires that costs which vary with the decision should be identified and considered in the decisions. Those costs which are not affected by the decision should be ignored. Examples of how to isolate relevant costs will be given later.

QUALITY. The quality objective is concerned with the quality of the product or service produced by operations. This objective is influenced by both the design of the product and the way the product is made in operations. Quality is, in turn, affected by a host of decisions in operations, including decisions about the product, the process, the work force, and the approach taken to quality control.

DEPENDABILITY. Dependability as an objective involves the dependability of the supply of the good or service. In operations, dependability may be measured by the percentage of stockout, the percentage of delivery promises met, and other criteria. Depend-

**Figure 2.2
Operations
objectives.**

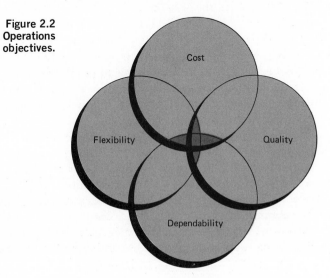

ability is also affected by many of the decisions made in operations, ranging from scheduling to inventory to process-design decisions.

FLEXIBILITY. Flexibility involves the ability of operations to make changes in product design or in the volume of product delivery. Flexibility may be measured by the amount of time it takes to change from one product to another or from one output level to another. The flexibility objective is sometimes overlooked in operations, but it is very important in decision making of all types.

The decision facing First City Bank regarding the automatic teller involves tradeoffs among all these objectives. Cost is, of course, an important consideration in any capital investment decision. If we expect more revenue from the automatic teller than from a human teller, we may need to consider profits rather than costs as the objective. Otherwise, we can simply compare the relevant costs of the automatic and human tellers.

If First City Bank installs the automatic teller, the quality of services offered will also be affected. In this case the quality can be measured by response time to provide service, the range of services offered, the hours of service available, and the degree to which customers needs are met by the service.

The dependability of service for the automatic teller can be measured by the downtime of the machine. This will be a function of both machine design and the level of maintenance provided. Dependability of operations will be high if the machine is operating whenever the customer comes to the bank to use it.

The flexibility of the new automatic teller in adapting to changes in the services offered will probably be less than that of a human teller. On the other hand, the automatic teller will have more flexibility than the human teller with respect to hours worked. The operations manager will need to consider flexibility carefully, because the risk of obsolescence involved in adopting the automatic teller is offset by the advantages of operating during extended hours.

2.4 TRADEOFFS IN OPERATIONS DECISIONS

Evaluating decisions in operations requires numerous tradeoffs among the decision criteria defined in the last section. Thus it is important to understand the nature of these tradeoffs and the way in which one should go about making tradeoff decisions. Many failures in operations can be attributed to a lack of awareness of important tradeoffs or a faulty analysis of the tradeoffs available.

Tradeoff decisions in operations can be classified in many different ways. One classification has been presented by Wickham Skinner (1969) in his classic article on manufacturing strategy (see Box 2.2). It is apparent that Skinner's tradeoff decisions can also be generalized to service operations without much difficulty.

It can be seen from the table that tradeoff decisions occur in every operations decision area: process, capacity, inventory, work force, and quality. Tradeoffs are made among the decision criteria of cost, quality, dependability, and flexibility. These criteria should be the basis for evaluating tradeoff decisions and for choosing a particular alternative.

BOX 2.2

**SOME IMPORTANT TRADEOFF DECISIONS IN MANUFACTURING—
OR "YOU CAN'T HAVE IT BOTH WAYS"**

Decision area	Decision	Alternatives
Plant and equipment	Span of process	Make or buy
	Plant size	One big plant or several smaller ones
	Plant location	Locate near markets or near materials
	Investment decisions	Invest mainly in buildings, equipment, inventories, or research
	Choice of equipment	General-purpose or special-purpose equipment
	Kind of tooling	Temporary, minimum tooling or "production tooling"
Production planning and control	Frequency of inventory taking	Few or many breaks in production for buffer stocks
	Inventory size	High inventory or lower inventory
	Degree of inventory control	Control in great detail or in lesser detail
	What to control	Controls designed to minimize machine downtime, labor cost, or time in process or to maximize output of particular products or usage of certain materials
	Quality control	High reliability and quality or low costs
	Use of standards	Formal, informal, or none at all
Labor and staffing	Job specialization	Highly specialized or not highly specialized
	Supervision	Technically trained first-line supervisors or supervisors who are not technically trained
	Wage system	Many job grades or few job grades; incentive wages or hourly wages
	Supervision	Close supervision or loose supervision
	Industrial engineers	Many or few such engineers
Product design engineering	Size of product line	Many customer specials, few specials, or none at all
	Design stability	Frozen design or many engineering change orders
	Technological risk	Use of new processes unproved by competitors or follow-the-leader policy
	Engineering	Complete packaged design or design-as-you-go approach
	Use of manufacturing engineering	Few or many manufacturing engineers
Organization and management	Kind of organization	Functional or product focus; geographical or other
	Executive use of time	High involvement in investment, production planning, cost control, quality control, or other activities
	Degree of risk assumed	Decisions based on much or little information
	Use of staff	Large or small staff group
	Executive style	Much or little involvement in detail; authoritarian or nondirective style; much or little contact with organization

Some managers have difficulty in seeing tradeoffs in operations decisions. The view sometimes prevails that an operation with modern equipment, new facilities, up-to-date methods, a cooperative work force, a computerized management information system (MIS), and an enlightened management will be a "good" operation. But what is good operation? Does it minimize lead time or inventories? Both cannot be minimized. Does it minimize purchased materials or investment in equipment? Both cannot be minimized. Does it emphasize process flexibility or low unit costs? The operation cannot have both.

One of the classic tradeoff decisions in operations is the tradeoff between inventory and capacity. In the face of fluctuating demand, it is possible to maintain a low level of inventory by varying capacity with demand. If capacity is high in periods of high demand and low in periods of low demand, then little inventory is carried. However, it is usually undesirable—as well as costly—to vary capacity from one period to the next. Therefore, a tradeoff decision between capacity and inventory is required.

There is a need to focus operations. There is no such thing as a universally "good" operation. Important tradeoff decisions are constantly required to link operations with corporate strategy and to focus the attention of operations on the important tasks and objectives. What is "good" for one company is not good for another company with a different strategy and different objectives, even in the same industry.

An analysis of the cost tradeoffs involved in First City Bank's decision on an automatic teller is given below. The cost tradeoff decision can be made by first identifying all fixed and variables costs, as shown:

Machine teller alternative

Investment cost   = $10,000
Variable cost of operations = $100 per month (including maintenance and electricity)

Assume an estimated volume of 8000 transactions per year.

Human teller alternative

Initial training cost   = $700
Variable cost of operations = $700 per month (including salary and fringe benefits)

Assume an estimated volume of 6000 transactions per year.

Suppose for the moment that volume is treated as the number of transactions processed. It follows that the fixed cost and the variable cost of the alternatives can be compared, as shown in Figure 2.3. The figure shows that the machine teller has a high fixed cost initially but a low cost of operations per transaction. The human teller has a lower fixed cost initially but a much higher operations cost per transaction. Thus, a tradeoff exists between fixed and variable costs.

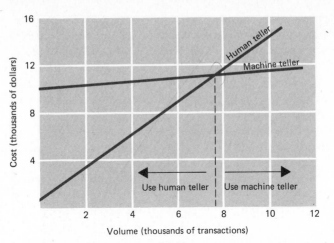

**Figure 2.3
Cost comparison
for First City
Bank.**

The costs of these alternatives can be expressed mathematically as follows:

$$C = F + VX$$

where C = the total cost (shown on the y axis)
     F = fixed cost (does not vary with the volume of transactions)
     V = variable cost (expressed as a cost per transaction)
     X = number of transactions processed by the teller (shown on the x axis)

The information given for each alternative is converted into equations, as follows:

    Machine teller $C = 10{,}000 + [100(12)/8000]X$

    Human teller $C = 700 + [700(12)/6000]X$

In each case the monthly operation costs were converted to unit transaction costs by multiplying the monthly cost by 12 and dividing by transactions per year. The two costs equations plotted in Figure 2.3 intersect at a value of $X = 7440$. This value of X can be computed by setting the cost equations equal and solving for X, as follows:

$$10{,}000 + [100(12)/8000]X = 700 + [700(12)/6000]X$$

$$X(1.4 - .15) = 10{,}000 - 700$$

$$X = \frac{9300}{1.25} = 7440$$

This value of X represents the indifference point between the two alternatives. If less than this volume of transactions is expected, the human alternative is less costly. If more than 7440 transactions are expected, the machine alternative is less costly. At exactly 7440 transactions, we are indifferent between the machine and human teller.

    In this case the indifference point will be achieved by the automatic teller in slightly less than a year. Since the expected lifetime of the machine would probably be several years, the machine alternative might be preferred if all other operations criteria are also judged to be satisfactory.

There are other forms of financial analysis which could be used in this example, including present-value analysis and internal rate of return. These methods, which allow consideration of the time value of money, will be treated later in the text.

2.5 MATHEMATICAL MODELS IN OPERATIONS

A mathematical model is a representation of a system or decision problem in mathematical terms. A model of the entire operations system or of some subsystem can be constructed. The model will usually incorporate a set of decision tradeoffs which allows the decision maker to evaluate different decision alternatives in terms of the model.

In the last section, a simple mathematical model was developed in which the relevant subsystem was the bank teller. The teller's output was represented by customer transactions. Inputs were expressed in terms of costs. The model of the teller subsystem was the equation

$$C = F + VX$$

This equation (or model) represented the relationship between costs and transaction volume. It incorporated the tradeoff between fixed and variable costs.

In general, a mathematical model can be defined as follows: A mathematical model is a representation of a system in terms of equations, inequalities, or other mathematical expressions. A mathematical model is used to assist managers in evaluating decision alternatives.

A mathematical model can be expressed as:

$$P = f(U_i, C_k)$$

where P = a vector of performance or criteria variables
U_i = the ith uncontrollable external variable
C_k = the kth controllable decision variable
f = a vector of functions relating variables to performance criteria

Thus a model represents the relationship between decision variables, external variables, and decision criteria in formal mathematical terms. A mathematical model allows one to study the effects of decision alternatives before a particular alternative is selected.

In general, there are two types of models: normative and descriptive. A normative model describes things as they should be. It therefore requires an objective function which is maximized or minimized. Another term for normative models is "optimization models." These models result in an optimal or best set of decision variables which optimize the chosen decision criteria.

Descriptive models simply describe the relationship between the variables and the decision criteria. Descriptive models do not include an objective function or an optimization criterion. The cost model used in the last section was a descriptive model, since it described the relationship between costs and volume. Descriptive models are very helpful because they serve to clarify important relationships in the decision problem.

At first it would appear that one would always prefer optimization models because the decision criterion is incorporated directly into the model. But the situation is not quite so simple. First, optimization models do not match reality exactly, so the optimal decision from the model cannot be simply implemented. Sensitivity analysis must be performed to determine how the optimal decision will change as input assumptions vary. Furthermore, optimization models must frequently be highly simplified to make them computationally tractable. As a result, one must often modify the "optimal" decision to make it conform more closely to reality. Since descriptive models are usually more complex, they are more realistic and accurate. However, descriptive models simply predict or describe, they do not identify the "best" alternative.

Many different techniques—such as simulation, linear programming, and calculus—can be used to solve mathematical models. Some of these techniques will be described at appropriate points in the text. It is not our purpose here to discuss techniques; we simply wish to illustrate the role of models in decision making in operations. A detailed description of simulation is given in the chapter supplement, along with more details on the process of modeling.

There are many uses of mathematical models in operations. Some of the important uses can be described by the five decision categories, as follows:

1. PROCESS. Mathematical models are used in process design for two types of decisions: first, the choice of technology or equipment and, second, the layout of facilities. The choice of equipment is often facilitated by the use of cost models and cash-flow modeling. Specific types of decisions include equipment replacement or substitution of equipment for labor. These decisions often involve tradeoffs between fixed and variable costs. They also have differing cash-flow streams which require present-value or discounted cash-flow treatment.

Facility layout decisions are also very amenable to mathematical modeling. Many types of layout models have been used, including simulation and optimization models. Since these decisions have long-range implications and may require great amounts of capital, a careful mathematical analysis is often required.

2. CAPACITY. Much use has been made of modeling in this area of operations. The applications include forecasting, facilities planning, aggregate planning, and scheduling.

Forecasting models are used to develop short- and medium-range forecasts for use in planning capacity or inventories. These forecasts are often made by individual product type and may reflect trend and seasonal data patterns. The model types include time-series analysis, exponential smoothing, and regression. Forecasting models are of the descriptive type, and they have been highly refined to produce useful forecasts under a wide variety of conditions.

Capacity models are concerned with the acquisition of facilities and efficient use of available facilities, people, and equipment. These models assist in planning and scheduling of capacity and in making tradeoff decisions between capacity and inventory. The modeling techniques include facility location models, linear programming for aggregate planning of operations, and simulation of various detailed capacity decisions.

3. INVENTORY. Modeling is highly developed in the inventory area. Decisions include what to carry in inventory, when to reorder material, and how much to order. Optimization models are often used to deal with these issues. Although some inventory models are highly simplified, they can be adapted to a wide variety of inventory problems. Inventory modeling also includes material requirements planning, which can be viewed as a way of relating output plans to input requirements. The resulting materials model is often simulated in order to answer "what if" questions. This allows one to examine the effects of proposed changes in the material plan before the changes are implemented.

4. WORK FORCE. Work-force management makes little use of mathematical models. Instead, this area relies heavily on the behavioral sciences and on general management principles. Even though models are not used, work-force management is just as important to overall management of the operations function. Work-force management has, however, sometimes been slighted because it does not rely on an underlying quantitative discipline. Within the philosophy of this book all the five functions of operations are considered important to the well-managed operation.

5. QUALITY. Models can be used in quality control to determine how to inspect the product. Should all the items produced be inspected? If only some items are inspected, how many should be sampled, and how should the sample be selected? How many defectives can be tolerated in the sample before the entire production run is rejected? All these questions can be analyzed by the use of statistical models. The models assist the manager in assessing risks and in defining a coherent quality control process.

2.6 KEY POINTS

Decision making in operations occupies a central role. Operations managers are judged by their effectiveness in the decision-making process. Therefore, this chapter is devoted to describing important aspects of decision making in the operations function.

The key points from the chapter are as follows:

- In a narrow sense, decision making is the act of choosing among alternatives. In the broad sense, decision making is a process which includes problem definition, generation of alternatives, evaluation of alternatives, choice, and implementation.
- Decisions are often made in the face of imperfect information; this results in

bounded rationality. Therefore the decision maker seeks a satisfactory solution rather than an optimal (or best) solution.

- The systems approach is useful in defining the appropriate decision problem. A system boundary must be identified which includes all the important effects of the decision and excludes those effects which are of lesser importance.
- Four criteria used in evaluating operations decisions are cost, quality, dependability, and flexibility. Most decisions require tradeoffs among one or more of these criteria. A particular decision must therefore consider all the relevant criteria and tradeoffs.
- Mathematical models are very helpful in quantifying tradeoffs faced in operations decisions. A model is defined in relation to a system of interest by representing the productive system through equations, inequalities, or other mathematical expressions. By using the model, the decision maker can evaluate various decision alternatives.

QUESTIONS

1. Describe a decision that you have made recently in terms of the entire decision-making process used.
2. Discuss the role of the systems approach in the decision-making process.
3. A manufacturing company is trying to decide whether it should make a particular part or buy it from outside. If it makes the part, it will have to buy a machine, hire new employees, and find the space for production. If it buys the part from outside, it will have to obtain one or more suppliers.
    a. Describe the important characteristics of this decision in terms of cost, quality, dependability, and flexibility.
    b. Can you think of other important criteria which are not included in part (a)?
4. A service station does car washing by hand, but it is considering the installation of an automatic car-washing machine. What effect would this change have on the flexibility of operations?
5. Using Skinner's tradeoff framework from Box 2.2, identify some of the important tradeoff decisions in the following operations:
    a. Airline
    b. Sawmill
6. A car wash is considering installing a new car-washing machine. The machine will cost more to buy but less to operate than the present manual method. The cost information is as follows:

    Manual method: 76 cents per wash variable cost; no fixed costs

    Machine: Investment cost = $5000

    Variable cost = 50 cents per wash

    a. Conduct a tradeoff analysis similar to that shown in Figure 2.3 between the machine and manual labor.
    b. What factors other than cost should be considered?
7. Comment on the issues raised by the following types of tradeoffs:
    a. Higher inventory costs versus better customer service
    b. High quality control costs versus defects sent to customers
    c. High wages versus lower personnel turnover
    d. High inventory versus capacity changes to meet seasonal demand

8. A factory has a department with 10 identical machines producing a product. These machines are subject to failure and require skilled repairers to fix them. The management is trying to decide whether one, two, three, or four repairers should be hired. When there are more repairers available, there will be less machine downtime, as shown below. However, each repairer is paid $15,000 per year in salary and benefits. Thus, management must make a tradeoff decision between the cost of time lost due to machine breakdowns and the cost of the repairers. Assume that each hour of machine downtime costs $50 in lost contribution to profit and overhead. Also assume there are 250 working days per year. How many repairers should management hire?

Number of repairers	Total hours of downtime per day
1	8
2	5
3	3
4	2

9. What are the differences between normative and descriptive models?
10. Decribe several ways in which models might be useful in improving operations decisions.

SELECTED BIBLIOGRAPHY

ACKOFF, R. L.: "Towards a System of System Concepts," *Management Science,* vol. 17, July 1971, pp. 661–667.

BOULDING, K. E.: "General Systems Theory—The Skeleton of Science," in P. P. Schroderbek (ed.), *Management Systems,* 2d ed., New York: Wiley, 1971.

BUFFA, ELWOOD S.: *Modern Production Management,* 5th ed., New York: Wiley, 1977, chap. 3.

CHURCHMAN, C. W.: *The System Approach,* New York: Delacorte, 1968.

DRAKE, A. W., R. L. KEENEY, and P. M. MORSE: *Analysis of Public Systems,* Cambridge, Mass.: M.I.T. Press, 1972.

JOHNSON, RICHARD A., FREMONT E. KAST, and JAMES E. ROSENZWEIG: *The Theory and Management of Systems,* 2d ed., New York: McGraw-Hill, 1967.

SIMON, HERBERT A.: *The New Science of Executive Decision Making,* New York: Harper & Row, 1960.

SKINNER, WICKHAM: "Manufacturing—Missing Link in Corporate Strategy," *Harvard Business Review,* May–June 1969.

VOLLMANN, THOMAS E.: *Operations Management: A Systems Model-Building Approach,* Reading, Mass.: Addison-Wesley, 1973, chap. 3.

WHEELWRIGHT, STEVEN: "Reflecting Corporate Strategy in Manufacturing Decisions," *Business Horizons,* February 1978, pp. 57–66.

SUPPLEMENT: SIMULATION

In the last part of Chapter 2 we discussed mathematical modeling and simulation as an aid to decision making. Simulation is a technique which can be used to formulate and solve a wide class of models. The class is so broad that it has been said, "If all else fails, try simulation." Simulation models include business games, analogue simulators, and flight simulators, which all represent a real situation in terms of a model. In this supplement, however, our discussion of simulation will be limited to computer simulation of business decision problems.

In describing simulation, we will present the simulation modeling process, which is applicable to other types of models as well. Simulation methodology is therefore a good place to start, because the simulation modeling process can be generalized.

As discussed in the foregoing chapter, simulation provides a descriptive model of a decision problem. Specific optimization criteria cannot be incorporated directly into simulation models. Simulation can only be used to predict or describe what will happen under a given set of circumstances, not what *should* be done relative to specific decision criteria.

Simulation is typically used for dynamic models which include multiple time periods. Dynamic simulation models are incremented from one time period or one event to the next as the situation unfolds over time. In this way the effect of successive decisions can be evaluated.

Simulation should be used in situations where it is too expensive or too difficult to experiment in the real situation. In these cases, the effects of a decision can be tested on a simulation model before the decision is implemented. A large number of situations have been simulated in this way, including the flow of patients in clinics, the operation of physical distribution networks, the organization of curricula in colleges, factory operations, and arrivals and departures of all types (ships, aircraft, students, blood shipments, etc.), to name only a few.

We will begin this supplement with a simple example of simulation. This will be followed by a discussion of the general simulation method, and some comments on the uses of simulation in operations.

A SIMULATION EXAMPLE: BETTY'S BAKERY

Betty's Bakery orders a number of bakery products each day; these are carried in stock. One product Betty carries is a special type of whole wheat bread. Betty wanted to determine how much of this bread she should order each day to maximize her profits. If she ordered too little, she would lose sales and profit. If she ordered too much, the excess would be wasted. For simplicity, we assume that all bread not sold during the day would be given away the next day at a total loss. (In real life, the leftover bread could, perhaps, be sold as day-old bread at only a partial loss.)

Betty collected data on the daily demand for her bread for 100 days, obtaining the following demand frequencies:

Demand (loaves)	Midpoint	Frequency
20–24	22	.05
25–29	27	.10
30–34	32	.20
35–39	37	.30
40–44	42	.20
45–49	47	.10
50–54	52	.05

Betty had been managing her bread inventory by ordering an amount equal to demand on the day before. Sometimes this decision rule left her with too much bread and sometimes she did not have enough. Therefore, Betty wondered whether there was a better decision rule that she might use. For example, how would profits be affected if she ordered an amount of bread equal to the average past usage? For this case, average past usage is equal to 37 loaves per day.

$$\overline{X} = .05(22) + .10(27) + .20(32) + .30(37)$$
$$+ .20(42) + .10(47) + .05(52) = 37$$

To resolve this issue, we will construct a simulation model incorporating the following two decision rules:

Rule 1: Order a number of loaves equal to demand on the previous day.
Rule 2: Order 37 loaves each day regardless of past demand.

The best rule will be selected on the basis of maximum profit over the total number of days simulated. We will use 15 days of simulation, just for purposes of illustration. In a real application, many more days would be used to obtain reliable results.

To simulate this problem, we will generate a series of random daily demands with frequencies equal to those given above. To visualize the demand-generation procedure, imagine a large

wheel of fortune with 100 positions on it. Five of those positions are labeled with a 22, corresponding to the .05 frequency above. Ten of the positions are labeled with a 27, corresponding to the .10 frequency, and so on. The wheel is spun once for each day, and where it stops determines the daily demand. As a result, provided that the wheel is truly random, random demands with the proper frequencies are generated.

Although this process of generating random demands is helpful conceptually, it can be made more efficient by using a random number table. The random number table shown in Appendix B consists of a series of random numbers arranged in rows and columns. The numbers are randomized across rows, down columns, and by digits within numbers. The table can be used by selecting an arbitrary starting point and proceeding either across rows or down columns. Some of the digits can be thrown away if they are not needed, because the numbers in the table are completely randomized.

For example, suppose we wish to generate 15 two-digit random numbers for Betty's Bakery. Suppose we start in the upper left-hand corner of the table (arbitrarily) and proceed across the first row. Taking the first two digits of each number and throwing the rest of the digits away, we obtain:

27, 43, 85, 88, 29, 69, 94, 64,
32, 48, 13, 14, 54, 15, 47

In this case, we could also have used all the digits in each number, or proceeded down the columns instead of across rows, or used any other pattern we liked as long as the pattern was consistent.

Now that we have generated 15 random numbers, we can convert them to loaves of bread demanded. This is done by associating the entire range of 100 random numbers with the demand distribution, as follows:[1]

---

[1] In the table, 00–04—a total of 5 numbers out of 100—is assigned to the first category. Similarly, 05–14 contains 10 numbers, or a frequency of .10.

Demand midpoint	Frequency	Random numbers
22	.05	00–04
27	.10	05–14
32	.20	15–34
37	.30	35–64
42	.20	65–84
47	.10	85–94
52	.05	95–99

The random numbers that we have generated above are converted to loaves of bread demanded, as shown in Table S2.1. For example, the first random number, 27, corresponds to a demand of 32 loaves; the second random number, 43, corresponds to a demand of 37 loaves; and so on. In this way we can simulate the demand for bread on each of the 15 days of the problem by what is commonly called the Monte Carlo method.

The next step will be to calculate the corresponding sales and amount ordered on each day. These calculations depend on the rule chosen;

therefore, two sets of calculations are shown in Table S2.1. With rule 1, the amount ordered can be filled in the table, since demand is known. Sales is then just the minimum of the amount ordered and the amount demanded on each day. Betty cannot sell more than she ordered, and she cannot sell more than the demand. Similar daily calculations are made for rule 2.

The total amount ordered and the total amount sold over the 15 days is obtained in Table S2.1. These figures can be multiplied by the unit cost and selling price to derive profits. Assume that bread sells for 50 cents a loaf, and it costs 25 cents to purchase a loaf wholesale. The total profit over 15 days for each rule then is:

$$\text{Rule 1: Profit} = .50(500) - .25(550)$$
$$= \$112.50$$
$$\text{Rule 2: Profit} = .50(515) - .25(555)$$
$$= \$118.75$$

Rule 2, therefore, offers some improvement in profit contribution over rule 1.

TABLE S2.1
BETTY'S BAKERY

Day	Random number	Demand	Rule 1 Amount ordered	Rule 1 Sales	Rule 2 Amount ordered	Rule 2 Sales
0		37				
1	27	32	37	32	37	32
2	43	37	32	32	37	37
3	85	47	37	37	37	37
4	88	47	47	47	37	37
5	29	32	47	32	37	32
6	69	42	32	32	37	37
7	94	47	42	42	37	37
8	64	37	47	37	37	37
9	32	32	37	32	37	32
10	48	37	32	32	37	37
11	13	27	37	27	37	27
12	14	27	27	27	37	27
13	54	37	27	27	37	37
14	15	32	37	32	37	32
15	47	37	32	32	37	37
		587	550	500	555	515

GENERAL METHODOLOGY

The example we have just discussed represents an application of the generalized simulation method. The steps used in every simulation study are shown in Figure S2.1 and described below; it is assumed that a computer is being used in the simulation process.

Define the problem

A relevant decision problem must be isolated and defined for study. Considerable experience and insight are required if a problem for simulation is to be properly isolated from its environment. Problem definition also includes deciding on the objectives, constraints, and assumptions which will be used. After the problem is defined in general terms, a specific quantitative model can be developed.

In Betty's Bakery, a problem regarding a specific type of bread was isolated. It was assumed that if the whole wheat bread was not available, the sale would be lost. Customers' substitution of other types of bread or other bakery products was not considered possible. It was also assumed that Betty's objective was to maximize profits, and a variety of other explicit or implicit assumptions were made. These assumptions collectively define the problem.

Develop the model

In the development of simulation models, the controllable variables, the uncontrollable variables, measures of performance, decision rules, and model functions must be defined. In this way a specific mathematical representation of the problem will be developed. As we indicated in the foregoing chapter, every model can be expressed in the form

$$P = f(U_i, C_k)$$

In developing the simulation model, we are simply specifying the P, f, U_i, and C_k values in the model.

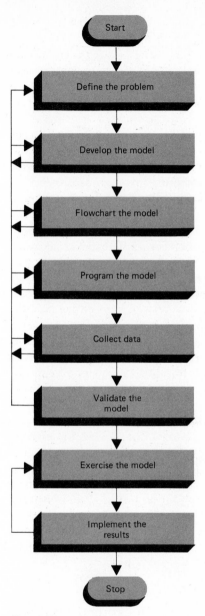

**Figure S2.1
Simulation method.**

In the model, the uncontrollable variables U_i, or parameters, are fixed constants which are outside the control of the decision maker. For example, in Betty's Bakery, the initial demand level, the frequency distribution of demand, the cost of purchasing bread, and the price of bread were all considered fixed values and therefore uncontrollable variables.

The controllable variables (or decision variables) in a simulation model can be controlled by the decision maker. These variables will change in value from one run to the next as different decisions are simulated. In Betty's Bakery, the amount ordered each day was the controllable decision variable. The values of this variable were specified by a decision rule which determined the amount ordered each day.

Finally, a decision model has one or more measures of performance P and function(s) which relate the variables to performance. In Betty's Bakery, the measure of performance was profit. A specific formula was used to calculate profit as a function of the controllable and uncontrollable variables in the model.

After all the model elements have been defined, the model is ready for computer flowcharting and programming. Before a flowchart can be constructed, however, the analyst must decide whether the model will be incremented by fixed or variable time increments. Every simulation model has a "clock" which keeps track of the time increments in the model. In a fixed-time-increment model, the clock is advanced in fixed time periods (e.g., Betty's Bakery). In a variable-time-increment model, the clock is advanced to the next event. For example, if patient flows in a hospital are simulated, each arrival and departure can be treated as an event. The clock is then advanced to the next arrival or departure time, which results in variable time increments.

Flowchart the model

A simulation model should always be flowcharted prior to computer programming. Flowcharting helps clarify the precise computational logic of the model. This facilitates computer programming and helps the model builder discover logical errors in the model.

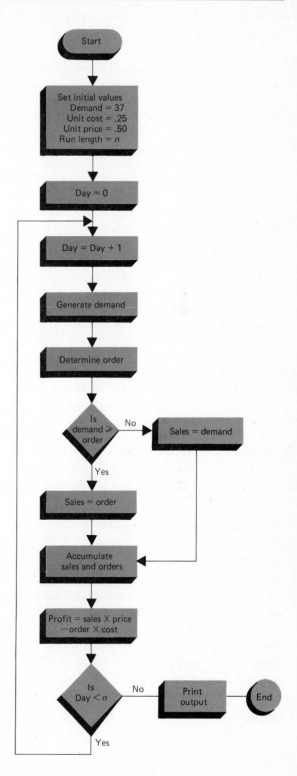

**Figure S2.2
Flowchart for Betty's Bakery.**

A flowchart for Betty's Bakery is shown in Figure S2.2. The flowchart simply represents the logic used to construct the data recorded in Table S2.1. Each day of the simulation, a demand value is generated. The order quantity is then determined by using the appropriate decision rule and comparing the order quantity to the demand. If the demand is greater than or equal to the order quantity, sales are set equal to the order quantity, since Betty will sell all she has on hand. If demand is less than the order quantity, sales are set equal to demand and the rest of the available bread will be given away. Using the quantities for sales and order size, profit is then computed, and the simulation is recycled until it reaches the desired number of periods. When the simulation is finished, a report showing the various value of sales, order quantities, demand, and profit is printed.

The flowchart is a representation of the mathematical model being simulated. On each step of the simulation, we compute values for the equation $P = f(U_i, C_k)$. In the case of Betty's Bakery, we use the mathematical model already described above to compute sales and profit on each step of the flowchart.

In constructing simple flowcharts, two types of symbols are used:

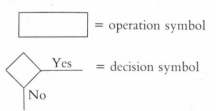

An operation may consist of generating a demand, setting a value of a variable, or other tasks in the simulation. A decision results in a branch in the simulation model depending on a comparison or test of variables. Flowcharts are normally drawn from top to bottom. (See Figure S2.2.)

Program the model

A good flowchart will make it easy to program the simulation model for computer operation.

For example, a simple FORTRAN program for Betty's Bakery is shown in Figure S2.3. The program uses the following fixed inputs: demand for day zero, the decision rule being used for order quantity, the demand distribution, unit cost, unit price, and run length. The output of the program when rule 1 is used is shown in Table S2.2. This table provides the same information as the data recorder we constructed earlier by hand. The advantage of the program, of course, is that we can easily change the run length and other input parameters when we are using the simulation model for decision making.

Simulation programming can be done in a variety of computer languages—general languages such as FORTRAN, PASCAL, and BASIC as well as special simulation languages such as GASP and GPSS. The advantage of the special languages is that they simplify the programming through the use of special simulation statements. For example, GASP has statements which can be used to generate arrivals, build queues, and maintain statistics commonly used in simulation.

Collect data

After the model is programmed, data must be collected to specify the input parameters. In the case of Betty's Bakery, data are required for unit cost, price, and the demand distribution. The unit cost might be available from the accounting department or it might be derived from past purchase orders. The price is easily obtained from current practice. The demand data might be derived from available records or collected by a special study. A minimum of about 20 days would be needed to obtain even rough estimates of demand frequencies. It would be better to have as many as 100 days of past demand data for stable estimates of demand frequency.

The collection of data is often one of the most costly and time-consuming parts of the simulation study. Because of the time required, data collection is often done at the same time as

```
          DIMENSION D(100),Q(100),PROFIT(100),SALES(100)
C   INITIALIZE VARIABLES
          TPROF=0
          TDEMAN=0
          TSALES=0
          TQTY=0
          D1=37
          C=.25
          P=.5
          N=100
          DO 100 I=1,N
C   GENERATE DEMAND
          NX=RANF(0)*100.
          IF(NX.GE.0..AND.NX.LE.4.)    D(I)=22
          IF(NX.GE.5..AND.NX.LE.14.)   D(I)=27
          IF(NX.GE.15..AND.NX.LE.34.)  D(I)=32
          IF(NX.GE.35..AND.NX.LE.64.)  D(I)=37
          IF(NX.GE.65..AND.NX.LE.84.)  D(I)=42
          IF(NX.GE.85..AND.NX.LE.94.)  D(I)=47
          IF(NX.GE.95..AND.NX.LE.99.)  D(I)=52
C   DECISION RULE
          IF (I.EQ.1) THEN
             Q(I)=D1
          ELSE
             Q(I)=D(I-1)
          ENDIF
C   SALES
          IF(D(I).GE.Q(I)) SALES(I)=Q(I)
          IF(D(I).LT.Q(I)) SALES(I)=D(I)
C   PROFIT CALC
          PROFIT(I)=SALES(I)*P-Q(I)*C
  100 CONTINUE
C   HEADINGS
          PRINT 110
  110 FORMAT(///,1X,28X,6HAMOUNT,/,3X,3HDAY,8X,6HDEMAND,8X,7HORDERED,
     *    8X,5HSALES,10X,6HPROFIT,//)
C   SUMMATION
          DO 200 I=1,N
          TPROF=PROFIT(I)+TPROF
          TDEMAN=TDEMAN+D(I)
          TSALES=TSALES+SALES(I)
          TQTY=TQTY+Q(I)
          PRINT 180,I,D(I),Q(I),SALES(I),PROFIT(I)
  180 FORMAT(3X,I3,10X,F3.0,12X,F3.0,11X,F3.0,9X,F7.2,/)
  200 CONTINUE
          PRINT 210,TDEMAN,TQTY,TSALES,TPROF
  210 FORMAT(1X,5HTOTAL,6X,F7.0,8X,F7.0,7X,F7.0,7X,F9.2)
          STOP
          END
```

Figure S2.3
FORTRAN program.

DAY	DEMAND	AMOUNT ORDERED	SALES	PROFIT
1	37.	37.	37.	9.25
2	52.	37.	37.	9.25
3	42.	52.	42.	8.00
4	32.	42.	32.	5.50
5	37.	32.	32.	8.00
6	22.	37.	22.	1.75
7	32.	22.	22.	5.50
8	32.	32.	32.	8.00
9	42.	32.	32.	8.00
10	37.	42.	37.	8.00
11	27.	37.	27.	4.25
12	42.	27.	27.	6.75
13	37.	42.	37.	8.00
14	27.	37.	27.	4.25
15	32.	27.	27.	6.75
TOTAL	530.	535.	470.	101.25

Table S2.2
Betty's Bakery output.

the programming. In this case, when the programming is done, the data is also available to begin validation of the model.

Validate the model

Validation determines whether the simulation model is a sufficiently accurate portrayal of the real world. To be useful, the model does not have to reflect every real-world condition and as-

sumption. As a matter of fact, a simplified description of the real world is often necessary to make the model controllable and affordable. Therefore, simplifying assumptions incorporated into the model must be checked by the process of validation.

There are several types of validation: of input parameters, of outputs, and of run length. Validation of input parameters is aimed at determining whether the inputs used by the model match the correct values. For example, in the case of Betty's Bakery, we should test whether the demand distribution for bread generated by the model is a good match for the assumed distribution. Figure S2.4 shows a plot of 100 values of the demand distribution used in a simulation run versus the true values of the demand distribution. In each case, there are errors between the true demand and the observed values used in the simulation. Standard statistical tests can be used (e.g., the chi-squared test) to determine whether or not the observed distribution is a sufficiently close fit to the true distribution. If not, perhaps more runs may be needed or there may be an error in the coding itself.

Similar tests can be made on output values to determine whether the simulator is predicting properly or not. In the case of Betty's Bakery, an output test would be a comparison of actual sales and profit data with the outputs from the model under similar conditions. These output comparisons can be tested statistically in the same way as the inputs.

Finally, validity can be related to run length.

Figure S2.4
Betty's Bakery: true versus simulated demand.

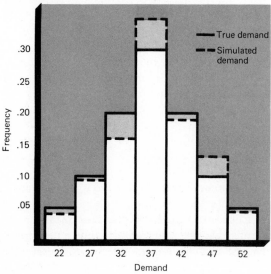

In simulation, run length is set to obtain stable or realistic results. One way to determine run length is to plot the output results of the model versus run length and determine when output stability occurs. In Figure S2.5, both sales and profit are plotted as a function of run length. As may be noted, there are wide fluctuations for small run lengths, but the output stabilizes as run length increases. Often, simulators have initial starting conditions which are arbitrarily selected. Therefore, the simulator must be run long enough to arrive at steady-state results. Standard statistical tests can be run on the output to determine when stability occurs.

In order to determine model validity, it may be necessary to revise the model. Therefore, Figure S2.1 shows a feedback loop from validation to all earlier steps in the modeling process. In addition to guiding model revision, validation should help determine an appropriate run length. When validation is completed, the model is ready to be used.

Exercise the model

To aid decision making, the simulation model is exercised or *run* through several cases of interest. In the case of Betty's Bakery, a run is made for each of the two decision rules and the effects on sales and profits are compared. For 100 periods, the following results are obtained:

	Rule 1	Rule 2
Profit	$ 749	$ 810
Sales	$1687	$1735

In this comparison, exactly the same daily demand is used for both rules, so demand variability is the same in both cases.

In simulation studies, sensitivity analysis is required to test the sensitivity of the results to input assumptions. In the case of Betty's Bakery, for example, there may be some uncertainty with regard to the unit cost figure. In the example, a cost of 25 cents per loaf was used, but the cost might really be 30 or 20 cents a loaf, depending

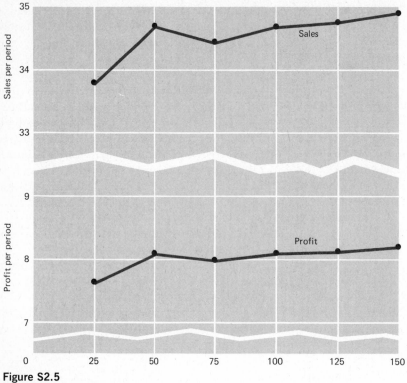

Figure S2.5
Outputs versus run length.

on the assumptions made. Would these changes in cost affect our preference for the rule used? In order to answer this question, we make two additional calculations: one with $C = .30$ and the other with $C = .20$. The results of these calculations are:

	C = .20		C = .30	
	Rule 1	Rule 2	Rule 1	Rule 2
Profit	$936	$995	$561	$625

As indicated above, rule 2 is still preferred to rule 1 on the basis of profit.

As part of the decision-making process, similar sensitivity runs could be made for price and demand. In many cases, sensitivity runs are the most valuable part of the analysis because they give the decision maker a "feel" for the situation.

For Betty's Bakery, additional decision rules

should also be investigated. For example, why should we order at the average of past demand? Should we not also consider other values of constant ordering levels? Figure S2.6 shows profit as a function of various constant ordering levels, indicating that it is most profitable to order 40 loaves a day (slightly more than the past average of demand). As part of the analysis, other rules should also be investigated.

Implement the results

In the pursuit of model building, we sometimes forget that the simulation study is not useful until it has some impact on decision making. This means that the result of the study must cause a change in behavior or—at a very minimum— provide confirmation that the present actions are

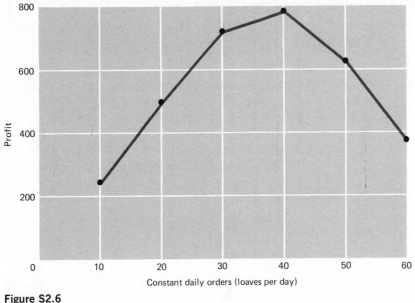

Figure S2.6
Sensitivity analysis.

correct. In the latter case, the study may have prevented undesirable change.

Implementation therefore requires us to consider the behavioral reactions of decision makers and the people they manage. In the case of Betty's Bakery, rule 2 is preferred; fortunately, it has the least behavioral impact on the supplier, since a constant number of loaves are ordered each day.

VARIABLE-TIME-INCREMENT SIMULATION

As we have already indicated, variable-time-increment simulation is not based on discrete time periods; instead, the "clock" is advanced from one event to the next. As a result, the clock could read time 1, 3, 9, 12, and 17, for example, in a simulation run consisting of five events and 17 time units. The principles of designing a variable-time-increment simulation model are exactly the same as those of designing the fixed-

time-increment model. Therefore, following the same steps in model design, we will provide a variable-time-increment example below.

Suppose we are trying to design dock facilities for ships. Since docks are very expensive, we want to decide whether to use one or two docks in a particular harbor. To solve this problem, we need an arrival-time distribution for the ships. In particular, suppose the ships arrive at random with a specified mean time between arrivals, according to the exponential arrival distribution described below. We also assume, for the sake of convenience, that the time to service a ship is a constant number of days, such as 5. Service in this case involves unloading a ship and refueling it at a dock. Under these conditions, we are interested in how long the ships will have to wait in the harbor before they are unloaded. After finding the waiting time, we might convert waiting time to waiting cost in order to trade off the cost of the waiting ships with the cost of the additional dock.

In developing this model, we need to generate exponential ship arrivals. When we assume an average time of 6 days between ship arrivals, the exponential distribution of arrival times is as shown in Figure S2.7. These times are derived from the following formula:[2]

$$P(x \leq t) = 1 - e^{-\lambda t}$$

where

λ = mean rate of arrivals, $\lambda = \frac{1}{6}$
$1/\lambda$ = mean time between arrivals = 6 days
t = time
x = interarrival time

Random times for ship arrivals can be gen-

[2] This formula is the exponential distribution which specifies the time between arrivals for a Poisson arrival distribution.

erated by using the discrete probability distribution shown in Figure S2.7a or the continuous distribution shown in Figure S2.7b. The discrete distribution is used in the same way as in the previous example, by assigning random numbers to the distribution. The continuous distribution is used by generating a random number for the y axis between 0 and 1 and computing the corresponding t coordinate from the following equation. For example, if $y = .7$ is generated, this corresponds to a ship arrival time of 7.22 days between arrivals.

$$t = -\frac{1}{\lambda} \ln(1 - y) = -6 \ln(1 - .7) = 7.22$$

Figure S2.7
Distribution of arrival times.

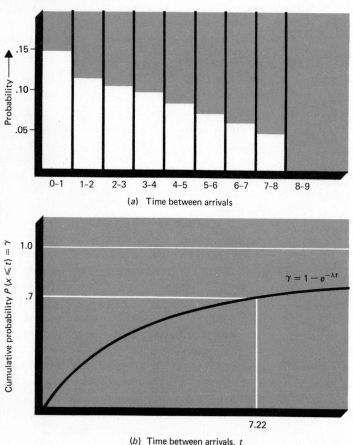

(a) Time between arrivals

(b) Time between arrivals, t

This computation is shown in Figure S2.7*b*, where the $y = .7$ value is projected onto the t axis.

The arrival times generated with the continuous exponential distribution are shown in Table S2.3, which also shows the corresponding times the ship enters and leaves service. For the single dock, if another ship is in the dock when an arrival occurs, the ship joins the waiting line and waits until the preceding ship is finished. As a result, the waiting time for each ship can be calculated from the table.

The remaining steps in using an event-oriented model, flowcharting, programming, data collection, validation, experimentation, and implementation are exactly the same as with the time-oriented model described above. These steps will therefore not be repeated here.

APPLICATIONS OF SIMULATION IN OPERATIONS

Applications of simulation in operations are numerous. Well-known applications include the following:

1. Facilities design. These applications are related to the size of facilities or the number of servers required. Examples include the number of check-out counters in a supermarket, the number of runways in an airport, and the number of toll booths on a freeway. Simulation models are useful in cases like these where a physical flow of customers, materials, or other objects can be identified.

2. Aggregate planning. Where an operation's aggregate capacity must be determined, simulation models are used to find the cost of alternative plans. Specific aggregate-planning decisions that may involve simulation are described in Chapter 10.

3. Scheduling. Simulation has been used in the evaluation of alternative scheduling rules. In scheduling patients for surgery, for example, should the longest operation be scheduled first or last? In Chapter 11, the scheduling of jobs in a machine shop is discussed and alternative dispatching rules are evaluated by simulation.

4. Inventory. Many inventory models are evaluated by simulating the effects of ordering rules. In complex inventory situations, it is often necessary to simulate proposed rules before they are put into effect to determine the impact on customer service and cost.

TABLE S2.3
SHIP EXAMPLE

Arrival number	Arrival time	Enter service	Service time	Depart service	Ship waiting time	Server idle time
1	3.5	3.5	5	8.5	0	0
2	4.7	8.5	5	13.5	3.8	0
3	8.3	13.5	5	18.5	5.2	0
4	12.8	18.5	5	23.5	5.7	0
5	13.7	23.5	5	28.5	9.8	0
6	28.7	28.7	5	33.7	0	0.2
7	34.7	34.7	5	39.7	0	1.0
8	52.1	52.1	5	57.1	0	12.4
9	59.9	59.9	5	64.9	0	2.8
10	65.0	65.0	5	70.0	0	0.1

5. Materials-requirements planning. When MRP is used to plan and control manufacturing, simulation is used to evaluate proposed changes in the manufacturing plan before the changes are put into effect. As a result, "what if" questions can be asked by management before decisions are made. These applications are described in greater detail in Chapter 14.

Simulation is a broad methodology which has wide applicability to operations decisions. As the book develops, many other applications of simulation will be cited.

QUESTIONS

1. Discuss the differences between fixed- and variable-time-increment simulation models. When would one model or the other be preferred?
2. Suppose you are simulating the arrival of customers at a barber shop so as to determine the number of chairs needed. Develop an approach to model validation in this case.
3. How should you decide how long to run a simulation model?
4. Show how random times can be developed from a normal distribution using the cumulative normal distribution function.
5. Discuss the advantages and disadvantages of making a simulation model completely realistic.
6. Sketch out a flowchart for the ship-arrival simulation problem described in the supplement.
7. What is the purpose of using sensitivity analysis in simulation studies?
8. How does simulation differ from linear programming?

PROBLEMS

1. The owner of the ABC grocery store is trying to decide whether to install one or two checkout counters. The time between customer arrivals is exponentially distributed with an average of 15 minutes between arrivals. The time to service a customer is also exponentially distributed with an average of 10 minutes per customer. Customers are served on a first-come first-served basis.
   a. Simulate this problem either by computer or manually. If the simulation is done manually, use 15 arrivals.
   b. Calculate the average waiting time of the customer and the percent idle time of the server(s).
   c. How would you decide between the alternatives?
2. An inventory of a certain repair part is maintained in a garage. At present, when the supply of the part drops to 30 units, an additional 20 units are ordered. It takes 2 days to get the parts after they are ordered. The daily demand is exponentially distributed with a mean of 13 units. Assume a starting inventory of 40 units.
   a. Simulate this problem by computer or by hand. For hand computations, use 20 days of simulated demand.
   b. How many orders are placed, how much inventory is carried on average, and how many stockouts occur?
   c. How would you validate your model in this case?
3. An assembly operation requires processing through two stations in sequential order. The amount of time required for processing at each station is a random variable, as shown on the next page. Assume that station 2 must wait whenever there is no work available from station 1. Also assume that there is no buffer between the stations.
   a. How long will it take to process 10 jobs through both stations, assuming the stations are empty when starting?
   b. How much time do stations 1 and 2 spend waiting?
   c. What is the effect on waiting time of placing a buffer between the two stations?

Station 1		Station 2	
Minutes	Probability	Minutes	Probability
1.0	.1	1.5	.2
1.1	.2	1.6	.2
1.2	.4	1.7	.2
1.3	.2	1.8	.2
1.4	.1	1.9	.2

4. A florist is trying to decide how many bouquets of fresh flowers to cut for each day. Any flowers cut and not sold during the day can be sold at half price the following day. The variable cost of growing and cutting flowers is $2 per bouquet, and the price is $3 per bouquet. The following demand distribution has been observed in the past:

Number of bouquets	Probability	Random # Range
25	.1	0 - 9
30	.2	10 - 29
35	.4	30 - 69
40	.2	70 - 89
45	.1	90 - 99

The florist would like to evaluate policies of cutting 40 and 45 bouquets each day.
   a. Simulate each policy for 20 days.
   b. Which policy maximizes profit?   45/DAY

5. A laundromat is considering installation of 10 washers and 5 dryers. On average, a customer arrives at the laundromat every 10 minutes with one or more baskets of clothes. The time between arrivals is distributed according to the exponential distribution. The number of washer loads per customer is distributed as follows:

Loads	Probability
1	.2
2	.3
3	.3
4	.2

Each dryer will handle two loads from the washer. It takes 20 minutes to wash a load of clothes and 40 minutes to dry a load.
   a. Simulate the operation of this laundromat for 4 hours. Build a table to describe the status of the washers, the dryers, and the waiting loads.
   b. How much idle time is there for the washers and dryers? How much waiting time for customers?
   c. What actions might be suggested by your simulation?

6. A repairer tends three different machines. Each machine has an exponential distribution of time between failures, with a mean of 120 minutes. When the machine fails, it takes an average of 30 minutes to repair it with an exponential service time. Assume all machines are in operation at the beginning of the simulation.
   a. Simulate the problem for a total of 8 hours.
   b. How much idle time is there for the machines and for the repairer?
   c. If the repairer is paid $10 per hour and lost machine time costs $30 per hour, evaluate the suggestion to add another repairer.

SELECTED BIBLIOGRAPHY

GORDON, GEOFFREY: *The Application of GPSS V to Discrete System Simulation,* Englewood Cliffs, N.J.: Prentice-Hall, 1975.

HERSHAUER, JAMES C., and RONALD G. EGERT: "Search and Simulation Selection of a Job-Shop Sequencing Rule," *Management Science,* vol. 21, no. 7, March 1975, pp. 833–843.

KWAK, N. K., P. J. KUZDRALL, and HOMER H. SCHMITZ: "The GPSS Simulation of Scheduling Policies for Surgical Patients," *Management Science,* vol. 22, no. 9, May 1976, pp. 982–989.

NANDA, R.: "Simulating Passenger Arrivals at Airports," *Industrial Engineering,* vol. 4, no. 3, March 1972, pp. 12–19.

NAYLOR, THOMAS H., et al.: *Computer Simulation Techniques,* New York: Wiley, 1966.

NEW, C. C.: "Matching Batch Sizes to Machine Shop Capabilities: An Example in Production Scheduling," *Operations Research Quarterly,* vol. 23, no. 4, December 1972, pp. 561–572.

PACKER, ARNOLD H.: "Simulation and Adaptive Forecasting as Applied to Inventory Control," *Operations Research,* vol. 15, no. 4, July–August 1967, pp. 660–679.

PETERSEN, CLIFFORD C.: "Simulation of an Inventory System," *Industrial Engineering,* vol. 5, no. 6, June 1973, pp. 35–44.

ROCHETTE, RENE, and RANDALL P. SADOWSKI: "A Statistical Comparison of the Performance of Simple Dispatching Rules for a Particular Set of Job Shops," *International Journal of Production Research,* vol. 14, no. 1, 1976, pp. 63–75.

SCHRIBER, THOMAS J.: *Simulation Using GPSS,* New York: Wiley, 1974.

SHANNON, ROBERT E.: *Systems Simulation: The Art and Science,* Englewood Cliffs, N.J.: Prentice-Hall, 1975.

WYMAN, F. PAUL, and GERALD CREAVEN: "Experimental Analysis of a GPSS Simulation of a Student Health Center," *Socio-Economic Planning Science,* vol. 6, no. 5, October 1972, pp. 489–499.

CHAPTER 3
PRODUCT DESIGN FOR GOODS AND SERVICES

3.1 STRATEGIES FOR NEW-PRODUCT INTRODUCTION
3.2 NEW-PRODUCT DEVELOPMENT PROCESS
3.3 DISCUSSION OF THE NEW-PRODUCT DEVELOPMENT PROCESS
3.4 INTERACTION BETWEEN PRODUCT AND PROCESS DESIGN
3.5 PRODUCT VARIETY
3.6 MODULAR DESIGN
3.7 KEY POINTS
    QUESTIONS
    SELECTED BIBLIOGRAPHY

New-product design is crucial to the survival of most firms. While a few firms experience little product change, most firms must continually revise their products. In fast-changing industries, new-product introduction is a way of life and highly sophisticated approaches have been developed to introduce new products.

Product design is seldom the responsibility of the operations function, but operations is greatly affected by new-product introduction and vice versa. Operations is on the "receiving end" of new-product introduction. At the same time, new products are constrained by existing operations and technology. Therefore, it is extremely important to understand the new-product design process and its interactions with operations.

This chapter is divided into three major parts. First, there is a discussion of a new-product design process. The view presented is that product design is interfunctional in nature and requires a great deal of cooperation between organizational functions. The second part of the chapter presents a model of product-process interaction which stresses the important relationship of product and process design. In the third part, product variety and the effect of multiple products on operations are discussed.

A product can be defined as the output of the operations function. As stated in Chapter 1, the word "product" is used in this book to refer to both goods and services. The material in this chapter, therefore, refers to the design of outputs for all types of productive systems.

Product decisions affect each of the five decision-making areas of operations. Therefore product decisions should be closely coordinated with operations—to ensure that operations is integrated with product design. Through close cooperation between operations and marketing, the market and product strategy can be integrated with decisions regarding process, capacity, inventory, work force, and quality.

Product design is a prerequisite for production, along with a forecast of production volume. The result of the product-design decision is transmitted to operations as product specifications. These specifications state the desired characteristics of the product and allow production to proceed. Box 3.1 illustrates a typical decision problem resulting from conflict over product specifications between different departments.

BOX 3.1   **TYPICAL DECISION PROBLEM**

Mary Bennett, the director of the Welfare Department in the state of Wisconsin, leaned back in her chair and pondered the events of the past few days. On her desk lay two memos; one, from her direct subordinate Ann Jones, stated that a new welfare service which was being offered in her department was coming along fine. The other letter, from the Federal Welfare Administration, stated that unless the services from the program improved and certain irregularities were corrected, federal funds would be canceled. What had gone wrong? How could a program which had gotten off to such a good start and that offered a badly needed service now be in such trouble?

The program was intended to provide stamps for winter heating oil to the needy people of the state. After the enabling legislation was passed, representatives from all the state and federal departments met and agreed on objectives for the new program as well as a timetable to introduce the new service. In some cases, the directors of the departments concerned could not attend the initial meeting, so their assistants or junior assistants attended in their place.

The first thousand applications for assistance were processed without a hitch. Then one day the governor's office called and asked for certain changes in the procedures being used. The result was that some applications were delayed while the changes were put into effect and some individuals who had expected to receive assistance proved to be no longer qualified. Later, the State Finance Office, during its regular annual audit, noticed that some state procedures were not being properly followed. As a result, new forms had to be printed and additional information requested from the applicants. This change added about 50 percent to the length of the application form.

Some of these changes had an adverse effect on the personnel in welfare operations. In the beginning, they had taken pride in rendering this badly needed service and in designing the procedures and forms that would be used. More recently, they had become disgruntled as changes were introduced; consequently, productivity dropped and more errors were made in administering the program.

From her past experience in industry and in the state, Mary concluded that the problems being encountered here were not unique. These were problems of organizational coordination and cooperation between departments and individuals. New-product introductions that start smoothly, with great enthusiasm, often become embroiled in conflict, finally ending up with operations problems. Mary decided to investigate this problem more deeply to find out how the present situation could be corrected and how similar difficulties could be avoided in the future.

3.1 STRATEGIES FOR NEW-PRODUCT INTRODUCTION

There are three fundamental ways to view the new-product introduction process: it may be seen as market-driven, technology-driven, or interfunctional in nature.

1. **MARKET-DRIVEN.** According to this view, "You should make what you can sell." In this case, new products are determined by the market with little regard to existing technology and operations processes. Customer needs are the primary (or only) basis for new-product introduction. According to this view, one can determine the types of new products which are needed through market research. These products are then produced.

2. **TECHNOLOGY-DRIVEN.** This approach would suggest that "You should sell what you can make." Accordingly, new products should be derived from production technology, with little regard for the market. It is marketing's job to create a market and to "sell" the products that are made. This view is dominated by vigorous use of technology and simplicity of operations changes. Through aggressive R&D and operations, superior products are created which have a "natural" advantage in the marketplace.

3. **INTERFUNCTIONAL VIEW.** In this view, new-product introduction is interfunctional in nature and requires cooperation among marketing, operations, engineering, and other functions. The new-product development process is neither market-driven nor technology-driven but determined by a coordinated effort between functions. The result should be new products which meet market needs and at the same time are compatible with existing operations. Using this approach, the new-product design will fall somewhere between "making what you can sell" and "selling what you can make." New-product introduction, therefore, is viewed as a continuum of possibilities, as shown in Figure 3.1.

    The interfunctional view usually produces the best results. [See Souder (1977).] It is also the most difficult approach to implement because of interfunctional rivalry and friction. In many cases, special organizational mechanisms, such as matrix designs or task forces, are used to integrate diverse organizational elements. The specific details of these organizational mechanisms are beyond the scope of the present discussion. [See Galbraith (1971) or George (1977) for more information.] The result of a lack of cooperation, however, is shown in Figure 3.2.

Figure 3.1 Interfunctional view of new-product introduction.

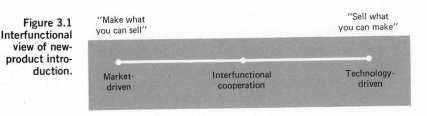

The factory designs a swing for the children.

As proposed by the marketing department.

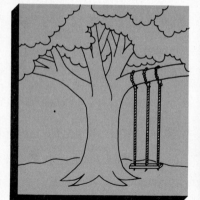

As specified in the product request.

As designed by the senior designer.

As produced by manufacturing.

As used by the customer.

What the customer wanted.

Figure 3.2
Lack of cooperation in designing a swing.

3.2 NEW-PRODUCT DEVELOPMENT PROCESS

Regardless of the organizational approach used for new-product development, the steps followed in developing new products are usually the same. Figure 3.3 is an idealized model of the new-product development process, which consists of the six steps described below.

1. IDEA GENERATION. Ideas can be generated either from the market or from the existing technology. Market ideas are derived from customer needs. For example, there might be a need for a new breakfast food which is nutritional and still good to eat or for a new type of house paint which does not peel. Identification of market needs can then lead to the development of new technologies and products to meet those needs. Market needs can also be identified by observing the performance of other products. Many of the most successful products began as imitations or slight modifications of earlier products that had done well.

On the other hand, ideas can spring from available technology. When nylon was invented by Du Pont, a whole range of new products was made possible. Examples of other technologies which have spawned new products are those involving plastics, semiconductors, integrated circuits, computers, and microwaves. Thus, exploitation of technology can also be a rich source of ideas for new products.

2. PRODUCT SELECTION. Not all new ideas should be developed into new products. New-product ideas need to meet at least three tests: (1) market potential, (2) financial feasibility, and (3) operations compatibility. Before a new-product idea is put into preliminary design, it should be subjected to analysis organized around these three tests.

The purpose of product selection analysis is to screen out the worst ideas, not to reach a conclusive decision to market and produce the product. After initial develop-

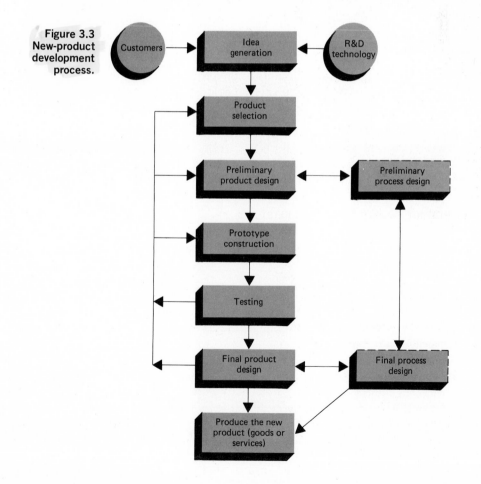

Figure 3.3 New-product development process.

ment, more extensive analysis may be conducted through test markets and pilot operations before a final decision is made to introduce the product. Thus product selection analysis may be quite subjective in nature and based on somewhat limited information.

To assist in product selection analysis, several methods have been developed. One is a checklist scoring method that involves developing a list of factors along with a weight for each. To evaluate a given product idea, each factor is rated on a scale and a total weighted score is computed. If the total score is above a certain minimum level, the new-product idea may be selected for further development. Alternatively, the method may be used to rank products in priority order for selection. An example of this type of scoring is given in Table 3.1.

A new-product idea may also be subjected to more rigorous financial analysis by computing an approximate return on investment. The calculation is as follows:

$$RI = \frac{P_T \times P_c \times AV \times p \times L}{TDC}$$

where RI = return on investment
P_T = probability of technical success $(0 \le P_T \le 1)$
P_c = probability of commercial success in the market, given technical success $(0 \le P_c \le 1)$
AV = annual volume in units of the product
p = profit contribution per unit sold
L = lifetime of the product in years
TDC = total development cost of the product

The RI is simply the projected profit margin divided by the total investment required for product development. The RI is thus a return-on-investment figure; it is not, however, discounted for the time value of money.

TABLE 3.1	PRODUCT SELECTION BY CHECKLIST						
Product characteristics		Poor	Fair	Good	Very good	Excellent	Weight
Selling price			✔				15%
Product quality					✔		10%
Sales volume				✔			20%
Operations compatibility		✔					10%
Competitive advantage					✔		10%
Technical risk			✔				15%
Fit with corporate strategy					✔		20%
							100%

Each rating in the table is valued as follows: poor = 1, fair = 2, good = 3, very good = 4, and excellent = 5. The total weighted product score is computed as follows: Total score = .15 (2) + .10 (4) + .20 (3) + .10 (1) + .10 (4) + .15 (2) + .20 (4) = 2.9. In this formula the weights have been multiplied by the product characteristic scores and added.

Both the above methods should be used with care because the estimates are likely to be very subjective. As the methods become known throughout the organization, most new products will routinely pass these screening tests. In other words, the methods will have a tendency to become self-fulfilling prophecies. Thus, management needs to continue to ask probing questions about new-product screening decisions. [See Gluck and Foster (1975).]

3. PRELIMINARY PRODUCT DESIGN. This stage of the product-design process is concerned with developing the best design for the new-product idea. If the preliminary design is approved, a prototype or prototypes may be built for further testing and analysis. In preliminary design, a great number of tradeoffs between cost, quality, and product performance are considered. The result should be a product design which is competitive in the marketplace and producible by operations. These design goals are, of course, exceedingly difficult to meet.

As a result of product selection, only the bare bones of a product will be defined. Preliminary product design must then specify the product completely. For example, suppose that a new CB radio is to be designed because the product selection phase has identified a weakness in the existing products on the market. It is thought that a radio with top-of-the-line performance can be designed for a middle-of-the-line price by incorporating new advances in miniature electronics. If such a radio can be built it will lend considerable strength to marketing efforts. This is the extent of the information available at the end of the product selection phase.

During preliminary design of the radio, a great number of tradeoff decisions will be made. The radio will contain many components, and each of them has cost-performance tradeoff features. Furthermore, size may be a problem assuming the radio must eventually fit into a small housing. During preliminary design, all tradeoff decisions should be based on the design objective: a medium-priced radio with top-of-the-line performance. As part of preliminary design, the radio will probably be built in a laboratory to test the integration and performance of the circuits. If these tests are successful, drawings of the preliminary design will be made.

4. PROTOTYPE CONSTRUCTION. Prototype construction can take many different forms. First of all, several prototypes which closely resemble the final product may be made by hand. For example, the auto industry regularly makes clay models of new automobiles.

In the service industry, a prototype may be a single site where the service concept can be tested in actual use. Service can be modified, if necessary, to better meet customer needs. When the prototype has been tested successfully, the final design can be finished and the service franchised or developed on a large-scale basis.

Ray Kroc, the owner of McDonald's restaurants, started with a prototype restaurant in San Bernardino, California. [See Boas and Chain (1976).] It was characterized by a very clean appearance, the original red and white colors, the limited menu, low prices, and so on. Kroc closely duplicated this facility as the McDonald's franchise began to expand. The original restaurant was, in effect, a prototype service installation. In the future, as more services are standardized, greater use may be made of service prototypes.

5. TESTING. Testing of prototypes is aimed at verifying marketing and technical performance. One way to assess market performance is to build enough prototypes to support a test market for the new product. Test markets typically last from six months to two years and are limited to a small geographical region. The purpose of a test market is to gather quantitative data on customer acceptance of the product.

Prototypes are also tested for technical product performance. For example, all new military aircraft are tested by use of prototypes. Up to six prototype planes may be built and tested extensively before management approves the final production design. Engineering changes initiated as a result of prototype testing are then incorporated as part of the final design package.

6. FINAL DESIGN. During the final design phase, drawings and specifications for the product are developed. As a result of prototype testing, certain changes may be incorporated into the final design. If changes are made, the product may be tested further to ensure final product performance. Attention will then focus on completing the design specifications so that production can proceed.

For services, the final design phase corresponds to fine tuning of standards and procedures which are prescribed for delivery of the service. For example, in the case of a bank, waiting-time standards for certain types of bank services may be specified.

3.3 DISCUSSION OF THE NEW-PRODUCT DEVELOPMENT PROCESS

The process of new-product development described thus far can be thought of as a funnel or filter. A great many ideas originate at the beginning, but only a few are successfully introduced to the market as products; see Figure 3.4.

**Figure 3.4
The new-product
filtering process.**

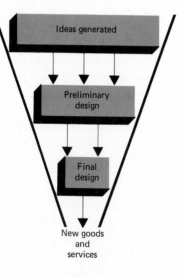

Ideas generated

Preliminary
design

Final
design

New goods
and
services

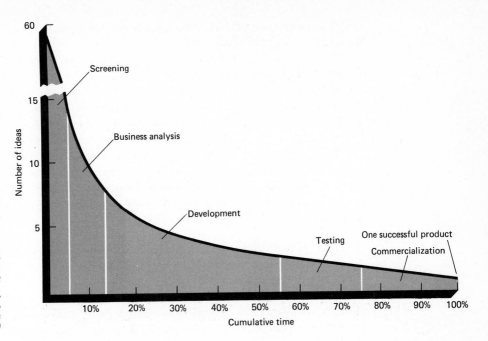

**Figure 3.5
Mortality of new-
product ideas.**

*(Source: David B. Uman,
New-Product Programs:
Their Planning and
Control, New York:
American Management
Association, 1969,
p. 67. Reprinted by
permission of the
publisher. All rights
reserved.)*

David Uman has depicted this process of elimination graphically in Figure 3.5. His study of the mortality of new-product ideas in 51 companies indicates that only one out of 60 new-product ideas results in a successful product. The greatest reduction, however, takes place before preliminary product design begins. Thus, one must place great weight on the initial product selection phase and the associated analysis.

It should be noted that new-product design can result in a good deal of iteration between stages. For example, prototype testing may require a return to the preliminary design phase or to prototype construction. In actual practice, the new-product design process does not proceed sequentially from beginning to end; some steps may be skipped and others may be repeated several times.

The production process should be designed in parallel with the new product. Figure 3.3 shows a preliminary process design and a final process design which are developed simultaneously with the corresponding stages of product design. This implies that process design should not wait until product design is completed but that process design should be developed as part of the product design process.

Sometimes in practice, process design follows product design. When this happens, a product which is costly or impossible to produce may result. This is one reason why operations personnel should be involved in product design from the start. In this way, process design and product design can proceed together.

If communications between functions has been effective, a productive process will be designed which is effective, efficient, and sufficiently flexible for future operations. Also, good communications should allow the product to be put into production faster than a design approach where process design follows product design.

A new technology, computer-assisted design (CAD), is being developed to reduce costs and speed up the new-product development process. Using CAD, an engineer can design a product at a cathode ray tube connected to a computer. As the product is traced out on the screen with a light pen, the computer records the product design in its memory. The design engineer can easily make design changes and look at the product from different angles by means of the computer. In some cases, the performance characteristics of the product can also be simulated by the computer. When the design is completed, the engineer can request drawings from the computer memory, or the product design can be transmitted directly to numerically controlled machine tools. CAD is already being used successfully in the automobile industry, electronics, aircraft, shipbuilding, and other heavy-design industries. This new technology promises to greatly simplify the engineering tasks required for new-product development. [For more information on this subject, see Decker (1978).]

To this point, goods and services have been treated as distinct categories of product design. In actual practice, most productive systems produce neither pure goods nor pure services.

A ride in a taxicab—transportation from one point to another—is a service. However, the taxi service is delivered by means of a facilitating good, the taxicab. Likewise, telephone companies use facilitating goods—telephones, wires, and equipment—and so do most other service operations.

Therefore, when either a good or service is purchased, the consumer actually buys a bundle of goods and services. In designing products, it is important to specify the nature of this bundle. For services, the entire bundle is designed as a unit. For goods, the physical product may be designed separately from the services. But both are delivered to the consumer as a bundle.

Sasser et al. (1978) have defined a service bundle as consisting of three components:

1. The physical items or facilitating goods
2. The sensual benefits or explicit services
3. The psychological benefits or implicit services

In the case of a restaurant, the physical items consist of food, drinks, napkins, etc. The sensual benefits are taste, waiter service, the facility and its appearance, and the sounds and sights of people. The psychological benefits include comfort, status, and a sense of well-being.

The key to the design of service products is to properly define the items in the service bundle. An appropriate mix of each of the three components should be delivered. But it is not enough to define the attributes of good service in general terms; one must also specify standards. These standards should cover each of the attributes in the goods-services bundle; they should be specifically defined and measurable. The standards can thus be used as a basis for training, quality control, and measurement of management performance.

3.4 INTERACTION BETWEEN PRODUCT AND PROCESS DESIGN

We have been discussing the process of new-product development prior to initial production. But products are also developed or changed during their product life cycle; this might be called product redesign. This section focuses on the product innovation process after initial product introduction, with special emphasis on the nature of product and process interaction.

Products in use are continually being subjected to redesign and innovation. Good examples are automobiles, telephones, and appliances. Abernathy has studied this phenomenon of product and process innovation. As a result of these studies, Abernathy and Townsend (1975) have suggested that product-process innovation typically follows three stages.

STAGE I. The early life of products is characterized by constant change brought about by uncertain market conditions and technological advances. The production process is typically suited to low volume and it is "uncoordinated" in nature. Typically, the product is made on general-purpose equipment which can be changed as the product changes. The situation for both product and process can best be described as fluid. The rates of product and process innovation are high, and there is great product diversity among competitors. The production process itself is largely uncoordinated between various operations. Bottlenecks and excess capacity result from the lack of a stable product flow. Decisions in operations are oriented toward the flexibility objective in this stage.

While we often think in terms of physical products, the situation is similar for services. For example, consider the high rate of initial innovation in health maintenance organizations, no-fault auto insurance, and fast-food chains. In these cases both the product and the process were initially in a highly fluid state.

STAGE II. As development takes place, price competition becomes more intense. Operations managers respond by becoming more cost-conscious. The result is better integration of product flow, more specialized tasks, greater automation, and better production planning and control. The process is best characterized at this stage by the term "islands of mechanization." Some subprocesses may become highly automated with specific process equipment while others continue to rely on general-purpose equipment. Such automation cannot occur, however, until the product line is mature enough to have high volume and at least a few stable product designs. This stage might best be described by the phrase "product and process standardization with increasing automation."

STAGE III. As the product reaches maturity, competition becomes even more intense. Further standardization is required and even more emphasis is placed on cost reduction, while acceptable dependability and quality standards are maintained. At this point the process becomes highly integrated and automated. A change in any part of it is likely to make an impact on the entire process as product and process become interdependent and hard to separate. Further changes in the product are exceedingly

TABLE 3.2   RELATIONSHIPS OF PRODUCT-PROCESS INNOVATIONS

	Innovation	Product line	Production process	Organizational control	Kind of capacity
			Fluid boundary		
	Frequent and novel product innovation—market stimulated.	High product-line diversity produced to customer order.	Flexible, but inefficient. Uses general-purpose equipment and skilled labor.	Loosely organized. Entrepreneurially based.	Small-scale, located near technology source or user. Low level of backward vertical integration.
	Cumulative product innovations usually incorporated in periodic changes to model line. —and—	At least one model sold as produced in substantial volumes. Dominant design achieved.	Increasingly rationalized process configuration with line-flow orientation, relying on short-duration tasks and operative skills of the work force.	Control achieved through creation of vertical information systems, lateral relations, liaison, and project groups.	Centralized general-purpose capacity where scale increases are achieved by breaking bottlenecks.
Normal direction of transition (→)	Increase in process innovation—internally generated. —and— Technology-stimulated innovation.	Highly standardized product with a few major options. Commoditylike product specified by technical parameters.	"Islands" of specialized and automated equipment introduced in some parts of process. Integrated production process designed as a "system."	Control achieved by means of goal setting, hierarchy, and rules as the frequency of change decreases.	Facilities located to achieve low factor input costs, minimize disruption, and facilitate distribution.
	Cost-stimulated incremental innovation predominates. Novel changes involve simultaneous product and process adaptations and are infrequently introduced.		Labor tasks predominantly ones of systems monitoring.	Bureaucratic, vertically integrated, and hierarchically organized with functional emphasis.	Large-scale facilities specialized to particular technologies; capacity increases achieved only by designing new facilities.
			Specific boundary		

Source: W. J. Abernathy and James Utterback, "Innovation and the Evolving Structure of the Firm," Harvard Business School Working Paper 75-18, June 1975, p. 18.

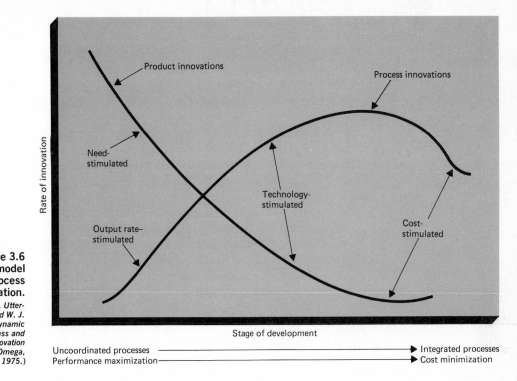

**Figure 3.6
A dynamic model
of product-process
innovation.**
*(Source: J. M. Utter-
back and W. J.
Abernathy, "A Dynamic
Model of Process and
Product Innovation
by Firms," Omega,
1975.)*

difficult and costly to make. Change comes more slowly but may be caused by sudden alterations in the inputs, in government regulations, or in the marketplace. Examples of processes in this stage of development are automobile assembly lines, chemical plants, food processors, and high-volume services such as social security, medicare, and the telephone company.

The preceding discussion has been summarized by Abernathy and Utterback (1975) in Table 3.2. This table illustrates how innovation, product line, production process, organizational control, and kind of capacity all develop together throughout the product-process life cycle.

Figure 3.6 illustrates the nature of process-product interaction and development While product innovation declines as the product matures, process innovations increase once the product becomes standardized. In the mature stage, both types of innovations drop off as the product and process become intertwined and difficult to change.

3.5 PRODUCT VARIETY

We have been dealing with the problems of designing and redesigning an individual product. This section will address product-design decisions dealing with multiple products. The key question addressed is: How much product variety is enough?

The issue of product variety must be considered from both a marketing and an ityWe

operations point of view. In each case, there are advantages and disadvantages in having a large number of products.

From a marketing point of view, the advantage of a large number of products is the ability to offer customers more choices. Marketing often argues that sales will drop if the firm does not offer as many products as its competitors. Marketing managers may also argue for a complete product line to meet nearly all conceivable customer needs.

But high product variety also makes the marketing function difficult. Too many products can confuse the customer, who may not differentiate between similar products. It is more difficult to train salespeople, and advertising is more costly and less focused with high product variety. Thus, it is possible that too much product variety may lead to lower sales, just as too little product variety does. Nevertheless, marketing managers tend to prefer more product variety.

From an operations viewpoint, high product variety is seen as leading to shorter production runs, higher costs, greater complexity, and more difficulty in specializing equipment and people. The ideal operations situation is often seen as a few high-volume production runs with stabilized product configurations. Operations managers often prefer less product variety.

On the basis of the foregoing discussion, it is possible to formulate an economic theory of product variety. We have argued that high product variety may lead to lower sales—through confusion of the customers—and to difficulties in advertising. On the other hand, too little product variety may also lead to low sales. This is illustrated in Figure 3.7. At the same time, we have argued that higher product variety leads to higher unit production costs due to shorter runs and increasing complexity. This effect is also shown in Figure 3.7, along with the resultant effect on profits. We therefore theorize that there is an optimum amount of product variety which results in maximum profits. Both too little and too much product variety will lead to low profits.

In using this theory, one of the key problems is the analysis of a given product line to determine whether or not there are too many products. This analysis immediately raises the question of how to allocate fixed costs to product lines.

**Figure 3.7
An economic
theory of product
variety.**

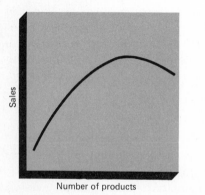
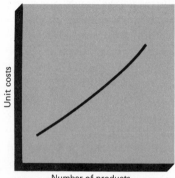
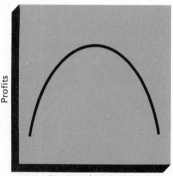

In the short run, the argument is made that as long as a product contributes to overhead and profits, it should be retained. Thus, in the short run, a product need only cover its variable expenses and none of the fixed expense. Although this reasoning is correct, it leads to the dangerous practice of retaining the products in the long run also, where the short-run reasoning does not apply. Therefore, except in special circumstances, it is best to retain only products which carry their full cost, including allocated overhead. This is difficult for managers to accept, because the immediate effect of trimming out a product which has a positive contribution margin is to reduce profits. However, as inventory is worked off, accounts receivable are collected, and overhead labor is reduced, long-run profits will be improved. It is the desire on the part of managers for short-run profits which often leads to inflated product lines and, eventually, lower profits.

Herbert Woodward (1976) illustrates the problem with a story about product proliferation:

> A few years ago, one of our operating companies disposed of a line of portable positive-displacement pneumatic machines that had an annual sales volume of about $500,000. Although the line was a natural companion to a much larger and long-established line of fan-operated equipment and a prodigious effort had been devoted to get it going, it had not made money and the prospects of success were poor. We finally made the painful decision to sell the line for a nominal amount. The buyer was one of our employees, who set it up as a separate business that later proved modestly successful.
>
> The beneficial effects of that sale on the company's operation were substantial and almost instantaneous. Our balance sheet improved dramatically as we collected the remaining accounts receivable, worked off the inventory, and—by buying no more material—cut our accounts payable. Our earnings improved more than the elimination of this relatively minor line seemed to justify. Only then did top management realize how much this one activity had demanded in attention and effort from almost everyone in the parent company. The product line had had a disproportionately high overhead, but the figures didn't show it.
>
> The advantages of simplification are hard to quantify, but they are real. Despite all that the computer can do to make possible a wide span of control, there is no better road to efficiency than to eliminate complexity entirely, usually by shrinking the business to a smaller and more manageable size.

In the short run, the problem of product variety can be analyzed as a product-mix problem, utilizing the linear programming technique. This approach determines the optimum number of products to produce based on the production and marketing constraints in place and the profit margins of various products. The details of both the product-mix problem and the linear programming technique are given in the chapter supplement.

3.6 MODULAR DESIGN

The problem of product variety requires not only an analysis of product lines but also a way to limit and control the number of products. The concept of modular design is one approach to this problem. [See Starr (1965).]

Modular design makes it possible to have relatively high product variety and low component variety at the same time. The basic idea is to develop a series of basic product components (or modules) which can be assembled into a large number of different products. To the customer, it appears there are a great number of different products. To operations, there is only a limited number of basic components.

Controlling the number of different components which go into products is of great importance to operations, since this makes it possible to produce more efficiently in longer runs while also allowing standardization of processes and equipment. A large number of product variations greatly increases the complexity and cost of operations.

Modular design offers a fundamental way to change product-design thinking. Instead of designing each product separately, the company designs products around standard component modules. If this is to be done, the product line must be carefully analyzed and divided into basic modules. Common modules should be developed that can serve more than one product line, and unnecessary product frills should be eliminated. This approach will still allow for a great deal of product variety but the number of unnecessary product variations will be reduced.

The usual way to develop products is to design each one separately without much attention to the other products in the line. Each product is optimized, but the product line as a whole is not. Modular design requires a broader view of product lines, and it may call for changes in individual products to optimize the product line in its entirety.

The modular-design approach can best be illustrated by an example. Recently, a group of M.B.A. students at the University of Minnesota studied the operations of a large manufacturer of beds—a company that produces over 2000 different combinations of mattresses. The team discovered that 50 percent of these combinations accounted for only 3 percent of sales. Market surveys showed that this much product variety was not advantageous to marketing. At the same time, the amount of variety had increased costs. Therefore, modular production was suggested as a way to trim the product line.

On the basis of modular-design ideas, a mattress product line would be produced in four basic sizes: regular, twin, queen, and king. The inside construction of the mattress would be limited to only a few different spring arrangements and thicknesses of foam padding. A moderate variety of mattress covers would be used to meet consumer preferences for color and type of design. The result would be a greatly reduced number of mattress components but still a substantial amount of variety for the customer. For example, if there were four bed sizes, three types of spring construction, three types of foam, and eight different covers, a total of 288 different mattresses would be possible.

$$4 \times 3 \times 3 \times 8 = 288 \text{ combinations}$$

Not all the mattresses would be produced because some might be unacceptable to the customer, e.g., the expensive springs with the thin foam pad. Although there are still many product combinations in the example, the number of components has been limited.

The team suggested that marketing, operations, and engineering get together to define the basic components that would be made and the product combinations desired. They also suggested that the company rigorously adhere to those components once the decision had been made, with a periodic revision perhaps once a year. Thus the team not only dealt with the problem of product proliferation but, by using the concept of modular production, retained the advantages of product variety.

3.7 KEY POINTS

New-product development has a great impact on the operations function, because any new product which is designed must be produced by operations. Furthermore, existing operations may constrain the development of new products.

Product decisions are a prerequisite to production. Product specifications must be provided to operations before production can begin and before some major decisions in operations can be made. Other operations decisions such as process design, however, should not wait until the product specifications are completed. Rather, process-design decisions should be made at the same time as the product is being designed.

This chapter deals with the nature of product design and its relationship to the operations function. Major points are:

- A product is the output of a productive system. The product may be either a good or a service or both.
- There are three ways to view the new-product introduction process: as market-driven, technology-driven, or interfunctional. The market-driven view corresponds to "making what you can sell," while the technology-driven view is "selling what you can make." The interfunctional view is a combination of these two, which requires cooperation between the functions in designing products. The interfunctional approach usually produces the best results. However, it requires an organizational structure which cuts across functional lines.
- The new-product development process consists of six steps: idea generation, product selection, preliminary design, prototype construction, testing, and final design. In practice, this process does not proceed sequentially from the beginning to end. Many iterations may be required.
- In defining products, it is important to specify the bundle of goods and services desired. The bundle includes facilitating goods, explicit services, and implicit services. Design of service is completely specified by the standards of service desired. Design of goods is specified by engineering drawings and specifications of the physical product.
- During the life cycle of a product, there are three stages of product-process interaction: the fluid stage, the semiautomated stage, and the fully automated stage. During these stages of product development, there is a great deal of interaction between product and process.
- The product greatly affects the objectives of operations: cost, dependability,

quality, and flexibility. When the product is first introduced, flexibility may be the most important objective. Later, when price competition develops, cost may be the most important objective.

- An economic theory of product variety was proposed where both too little variety and too much variety result in low profit. According to this theory, there is an optimum amount of product variety.
- Modular production is an approach used to produce a wide variety of products from a limited number of product components. This approach can be used to control product proliferation by limiting the number of components or modules available.

QUESTIONS

1. Why is interfunctional cooperation important for new-product design? What are the symptoms of a possible lack of interfunctional cooperation?
2. Under what circumstances might a market-driven approach or a technology-driven approach to new-product design be the best approach?
3. Describe the steps which might be required in writing and producing a play. Compare these steps to the six steps for new-product development described in Section 3.2. Is there a correspondence?
4. Consider the development and production of a new course in a college setting. Describe how this course might proceed through the three stages of product-process interaction. How would the course be taught at each stage? How would the "product" develop?
5. Why has there been an increase in product variety in our economy?
6. Three new-product ideas have been suggested. These ideas have been rated as follows:
   a. Using an equal point spread for all five ratings (i.e., P = 1, F = 2, G = 3, VG = 4, E = 5), determine a weighted score for each product idea. What is the ranking of the three products?

	Product			
	A	B	C	Weight
Development cost	P	F	VG	10%
Sales prospects	VG	E	G	15%
Producibility	P	F	G	10%
Competitive advantage	E	VG	F	15%
Technical risk	P	F	VG	20%
Patent protection	F	F	VG	10%
Compatibility with strategy	VG	F	F	20%
				100%

P = poor, F = fair, G = good, VG = very good, E = excellent.

   b. What are some of the advantages and disadvantages of this method of product selection?
7. Suppose the products from question 6 have been further rated as shown in the table on the next page.
   a. Compute the undiscounted return on investment for each product idea.

	Product		
	A	**B**	**C**
Probability of technical success	.9	.8	.7
Probability of commercial success	.6	.8	.9
Annual volume (units)	10,000	8000	6000
Profit contribution per unit	$6	$5	$10
Lifetime of product in years	10	6	12
Total development cost	$50,000	$70,000	$100,000

     b. Does this computation change your ranking of the products over that obtained in question 6?

8. How can the modular-design concept control production variety and at the same time allow product variety?

9. How can the bundle of goods and services be specified for the following products? Describe the attributes of the facilitating goods, the explicit service, and the implicit service.

    a. A hospital stay   c. Travel by commercial aircraft

    b. A checking account   d. A theater performance

10. What is the proper role of the operations function in product design?

11. What form does the product specification take for the following firms: a travel agency, a beer company, and a consulting firm?

SELECTED BIBLIOGRAPHY

ABERNATHY, W. J.: "Production Process Structure and Technological Change," *Decision Sciences,* vol. 7, no. 4, October 1976, pp. 607–619.

———, and P. L. TOWNSEND: "Technology, Productivity and Process Change," *Technological Forecasting and Social Change,* vol. 7, August 1975, pp. 377–396.

———, and JAMES UTTERBACK: "Innovation and the Evolving Structure of the Firm," Harvard Business School Working Paper 75-18, June 1975.

BOAS, MAX, AND STEVE CHAIN: *Big Mac: The Unauthorized Story of McDonald's,* New York: Mentor, 1976.

BUFFA, ELWOOD S.: *Modern Production Management: Managing the Operations Function,* 5th ed., New York: Wiley, 1977.

CHASE, RICHARD B., and N. J. AQUILANO: *Production and Operations Management: A Life Cycle Approach,* rev. ed., Homewood, Ill.: Irwin, 1977.

DECKER, ROBERT: "Computer Aided Design and Manufacturing at GM," *Datamation,* May 1978, pp. 159–165.

GALBRAITH, JAY R.: "Matrix Organization Design," *Business Horizons,* February 1971, pp. 29–40.

GEORGE, WILLIAM W.: "Task Teams for Rapid Growth," *Harvard Business Review,* March–April 1977, pp. 71–121.

GLUCK, FREDERICK, AND R. N. FOSTER: "Managing Technological Change: A Box of Cigars for Brad," *Harvard Business Review,* September–October 1975, pp. 139–150.

HISE, RICHARD, AND M. A. McGINNIS: "Product Elimination: Practices, Policies and Ethics," *Business Horizons,* June 1975, pp. 25–32.

LEVITT, THEODORE: "Production-Line Approach to Service," *Harvard Business Review,* vol. 50, no. 5, September–October 1972, pp. 41–52.

MOORE, FRANKLIN G., AND T. E. HENDRICK: *Production/Operations Management,* 7th ed., Homewood, Ill.: Irwin, 1977.

SASSER, W. EARL, R. PAUL OLSEN, AND D. DARYLE WYCKOFF: *Management of Service Operations: Text, Cases, and Readings,* Boston: Allyn and Bacon, 1978.

SOUDER, WILLIAM: "An Exploratory Study of the Coordinating Mechanisms Between R&D and Marketing as an Influence on the Innovation Process," Working Paper, Technology Management Studies Group, Department of Industrial Engineering, University of Pittsburgh, Pittsburgh, Pa., August 1977.

STARR, MARTIN K.: "Modular Production: A New Concept," *Harvard Business Review,* November–December 1965, pp. 131–142.

UTTERBACK, J., AND W. J. ABERNATHY: "A Dynamic Model of Process and Product Innovation," *Omega,* vol. 3, no. 6, 1975, pp. 639–656.

WOODWARD, HERBERT H.: "Management Strategies for Small Companies," *Harvard Business Review,* January–February 1976, pp. 113–121.

SUPPLEMENT: LINEAR PROGRAMMING

In Chapter 3, one of the important decisions discussed was the breadth of the product line. In certain cases this decision can be made with the assistance of linear programming (LP). We will therefore begin this supplement with an LP formulation of the product-mix decision problem.

PRODUCT-MIX PROBLEM

For the sake of simplicity, suppose a furniture company can make only two types of products: tables and chairs. The company has limited resources of lumber, labor, and finishing capacity with which to produce these items. The management of the company would like to determine the best mix of products to make: all chairs, all tables, or some mix of chairs and tables. Management defines the best mix of products as the one which maximizes the total contribution to profit and overhead subject to the limited availability of resources already mentioned.

The product-mix problem can be formulated in mathematical terms as follows.

Let: X_1 = the number of tables produced
X_2 = the number of chairs produced

Both X_1 and X_2 are unknown variables to be determined by the solution of the LP problem. Also assume that the following unit production technology matrix is given. This matrix describes the transformation process used to convert the scarce resources (lumber, labor, and finishing capacity) into tables or chairs. For example, it takes 30

board feet to make one table and 20 board feet to make one chair.

Resources used per unit produced

	Tables	Chairs
Lumber, board feet	30	20
Labor, hours	2	2
Finishing capacity, hours	4	6

We also assume that the amount of scarce resources available is given: 120 board feet of lumber, 9 hours of labor, and 24 hours of finishing capacity.

If we multiply the values in the unit production technology matrix by the number of units produced and add over both products, we will obtain the total resources of each type required. These requirements must be less than the amount of resources available. Thus we have:

$$30X_1 + 20X_2 \leq 120$$

$$2X_1 + 2X_2 \leq 9$$

$$4X_1 + 6X_2 \leq 24$$

Since 30 board feet are required for each table, $30X_1$ board feet will be required for X_1 tables, as shown in the first constraint above. Likewise, $20X_2$ board feet are required to produce X_2 chairs. The total amount of lumber required for both tables and chairs $(30X_1 + 20X_2)$ must be less than or equal to the amount available (120). A similar logic can be used to derive the second two constraints.

Management wishes to find the values of X_1 and X_2 which will maximize the contribution to profit and overhead. To formulate this objective function, we assume that each table contributes $10 and each chair $8 to profit and overhead. Then the total contribution for X_1 tables and X_2 chairs is:

$$10X_1 + 8X_2$$

Finally, we require that X_1 and X_2 be nonnegative values, since we cannot produce a negative number of tables or chairs. Gathering together the constraints and objective function that we have specified, the product-mix problem can be summarized as follows:

> Objective: max $10X_1 + 8X_2$
>
> Subject to: $30X_1 + 20X_2 \leq 120$
>
> $2X_1 + 2X_2 \leq 9$
>
> $4X_1 + 6X_2 \leq 24$
>
> $X_1 \geq 0, X_2 \geq 0$

When this problem is solved by the methods described below, optimal values of X_1 and X_2 will be found. These optimal values, however, are a solution to the mathematical problem as stated and not necessarily a solution to the manager's original decision problem. The mathematical problem is always an abstraction of the manager's real problem; therefore the optimal solution must be carefully evaluated before a decision can be made.

In practice, a series of product-mix problems may be formulated and solved before the manager is satisfied. For example, suppose the optimal solution to our problem is to produce all tables and no chairs. Also assume that this solution conflicts with the marketing strategy in the company. Therefore, either the marketing strategy must be modified or the production constraints altered or other changes made in the formulation to make the mathematical solution consistent with the real decision problem. Even though the optimal solution to the product-mix problem is not implemented, it may provide important insights into possible coordination problems between market-

ing and production, possibly leading to further analysis and ultimate solution of the decision problem.

GENERAL LP PROBLEM

The problem that we have just formulated is a member of a class of general problems—called linear programming or LP problems—the notation for which follows:

> Objective:
>
>   max $C_1X_1 + C_2X_2 + \cdots + C_nX_n$
>
> Subject to:
>
> $a_{11}X_1 + a_{12}X_2 + \cdots + a_{1n}X_n \leq b_1$
>
> $a_{21}X_1 + a_{22}X_2 + \cdots + a_{2n}X_n \leq b_2$
>
> $a_{m1}X_1 + a_{m2}X_2 + \cdots + a_{mn}X_n \leq b_m$
>
> $X_1 \geq 0, X_2 \geq 0, \ldots, X_n \geq 0$

In this formulation the C_j, a_{ij}, and b_i values are given constants and the X_j are called decision variables. The problem is to find the values of the n decision variables ($X_1, X_2, \ldots, X_n$) which maximize the objective function subject to the m constraints and the nonnegativity conditions on the X_j variables. The resulting set of decision variables which maximizes the objective function is called an optimal solution. In this problem, "max" may be replaced by "min" and $\leq$ may be replaced by $\geq$ or $=$ signs to obtain the general set of LP problems.

The general LP problem as formulated above is based on the following four assumptions:

1. *Linearity*. Both the objective function and the constraints must be linear functions of the X_j. This implies that no cross products, powers of X_j, or other nonlinearities are permitted in the problem. It also implies that resource utilization is proportional and additive, e.g., if it takes 2 hours to produce one

table, it will take 4 hours to produce two tables.

2. *Divisibility*. The X_j variables are permitted to take on continuous values. Thus we can obtain a solution to the product-mix problem, for example, of 20.5 chairs and 30.2 tables. Sometimes the continuous solution can be rounded off or interpreted as the average production per day. In other cases, special integer programming problems must be formulated to provide integer solutions.

3. *Nonnegativity*. The decision variables must have nonnegative values. In many problems this assumption is natural and presents no difficulties. If negative values are needed, however, the LP formulation can be modified to handle these cases.

4. *Certainty*. All constants, C_j, a_{ij}, and b_i, are assumed to have certain values. If these values are probabilistic, other special chance-constrained or stochastic programming problems can be formulated.

Although LP problems have some rather restrictive assumptions, a large class of real decision problems can still be solved by LP methods. In addition, LP methods sometimes form the nucleus for more advanced nonlinear, stochastic, or integer programming methods.

Linear programming can be used to solve a general class of resource-allocation problems including product-mix, blending, and scheduling problems. All these decision problems are concerned with finding the best allocation of scarce resources. In the product-mix problem, the scarce resources are allocated to the products; in the blending problem, the best mix of resource inputs to meet a prescribed product blend is determined; and in scheduling problems, available machine times may be allocated to the required products. In each of these cases, scarce resource inputs are allocated among several economic activities. This is a general characteristic of most, if not all, LP problems.

Graphical solution method

The graphical solution method may be used to solve LP problems with two variables. Although two variables are not enough to describe real problems, the graphical method provides important insights into LP solution procedures. For illustration purposes, we will solve the product-mix problem formulated above.

The first step in the graphical procedure is to plot the constraint equations. The three constraints from the product-mix example are shown in Figure S3.1. Each constraint is plotted on the figure by first considering the $\leq$ sign as an $=$ sign. The first constraint is thus plotted as the equation $30X_1 + 20X_2 = 120$. By setting $X_1 = 0$ in this equation, we have $X_2 = 6$; and setting $X_2 = 0$, we have $X_1 = 4$. These two coordinates are placed on the graph and connected with a straight line. The original constraint equation, however, includes all points smaller than or equal to the right-hand side. Thus all points to the left of the lines in Figure S3.1 are permitted by the constraints.

The intersection of points from all three constraint equations plus the nonnegativity conditions forms the feasible region shown in white in Figure S3.1. All points within this feasible region *simultaneously* satisfy all the LP constraints. The problem then is to find the one or more points (or solutions) in the feasible region which maximize the original objective function. This point(s) will be the optimal solution(s).

The optimal solution is found by graphing the objective function on the same graph as the feasible region. For illustration purposes, we have drawn the feasible region again in Figure S3.2 and plotted a series of objective functions or isoprofit lines on the graph. Each isoprofit line is obtained by setting the objective function equal to an arbitrary value. For example, suppose we arbitrarily set the objective function equal to 60. Then the line $10X_1 + 8X_2 = 60$ is plotted just as we plotted the constraints. Since the value of the objective function is unknown, a series of arbi-

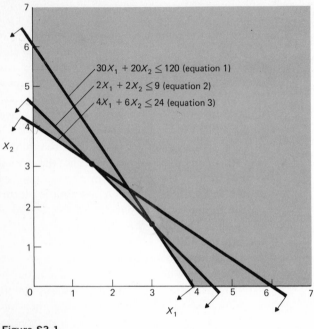

Figure S3.1
Product-mix problem.

Inside the figure:
$30X_1 + 20X_2 \leq 120$ (equation 1)
$2X_1 + 2X_2 \leq 9$ (equation 2)
$4X_1 + 6X_2 \leq 24$ (equation 3)

trary values is selected to generate a series of parallel isoprofit lines, as shown in Figure S3.2.

The problem now is to find the isoprofit line which has the largest profit and is still in the feasible region. This can be done by starting at the origin or any other point inside the feasible region and moving the isoprofit line out away from the origin parallel to itself until the last point in the feasible region is reached. In this example the last feasible point is the corner labeled c ($X_1 = 3$, $X_2 = 1.5$), which maximizes the value of the isoprofit line and is therefore the optimal solution to the LP problem.

The exact coordinates of the optimal solution may be found by solving for the intersection of equations 1 and 2, which define the optimal corner c. These two equations in two unknowns are solved simultaneously for the values of X_1 and X_2. As a result, we find $X_1 = 3$ and $X_2 = 1.5$. Although X_2 is a fractional number of chairs, this solution might still be perfectly realistic. For example, suppose we produce 3 tables

and 1.5 chairs a day over a period of several weeks. The 1.5 chairs can then be interpreted as an average production rate per day.

The optimal solution will always occur on at least one corner point (or extreme point) of the feasible region. In the example, there was only one optimal solution because a single corner point was reached. If the isoprofit line had been parallel to a side of the feasible region, then two corner points and all the points in between would have been optimal solutions. In this case, we would have had alternate optimal solutions, different values of X_1 and X_2 which yield the same value of the objective function.

The fact that the optimal solution occurs at one or more extreme points is exploited in LP methods. The simplex method, described next, is an adjacent-extreme-point method. It moves from one corner point to the next until an optimal solution is found. Since there are only a finite number of corner points but an infinite number of feasible solutions inside the feasible region,

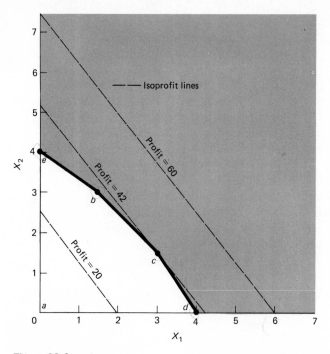

Figure S3.2
Product-mix problem solution.

the general solution to linear programming problems is greatly simplified when only adjacent extreme points are examined.

SIMPLEX METHOD

The simplex method is a general algebraic method which can be used to solve LP problems with a very large number of variables and constraints. When more than a few variables and constraints are involved, the computerized simplex method is required. Nevertheless, for purposes of instruction, we shall illustrate the simplex method by hand computations. An understanding of the simplex method's mechanics facilitates interpretation of LP results.

With the simplex method, the problem must be put in a special format and specific computational rules must be followed. To illustrate, we will use the product-mix problem which has al-

ready been solved graphically. The first step in the simplex method is to convert the LP problem to the proper format by changing all the inequality constraints into equalities. This is done by adding a slack variable to each constraint inequality, as shown below.

Objective:

$$\max 10X_1 + 8X_2 + 0X_3 + 0X_4 + 0X_5$$

Subject to:

$$30X_1 + 20X_2 + 1X_3 + 0X_4 + 0X_5 = 120$$
$$2X_1 + 2X_2 + 0X_3 + 1X_4 + 0X_5 = 9$$
$$4X_1 + 6X_2 + 0X_3 + 0X_4 + 1X_5 = 24$$
$$X_1 \geq 0, X_2 \geq 0, X_3 \geq 0, X_4 \geq 0, X_5 \geq 0$$

In the first constraint, variable X_3 is added to the left-hand side to take up the slack between the value of the original left-hand side and the right-hand side of the inequality. Then X_3 must also be restricted to be nonnegative, so that it properly represents the slack on the left-hand side of the first constraint. Similarly, X_4 and X_5 are added as slack variables to the second and third constraints respectively. Since we do not want these slack variables to affect the profit, they are entered with zero coefficients in the objective function. The revised problem will have exactly the same optimal solution for X_1 and X_2 as the original problem.

Now that the problem is in the required form for the simplex method, we can construct the first tableau. The term "tableau" refers to the special simplex tables which are constructed to keep track of the computations. The first tableau is shown in Figure S3.3.

The tableau is constructed by detaching the coefficients from the variables and displaying the resulting coefficients by themselves in the appropriate rows and columns of the tableau. For example, the first row in the body of the tableau is the first constraint equation, the second row is the second equation, and so on. In the right-hand column of the tableau, the right-hand side of the constraints is placed under the heading "Solution quantity." In every tableau, this column will represent the values of the X_j variables for the current solution. The particular X_j variables in the solution are shown in the box labeled "Solution

variables" on the left-hand side of the tableau. For example, the initial solution is $X_3 = 120$, $X_4 = 9$, $X_5 = 24$. All variables not in the solution are always assumed to have zero values. Thus, $X_1 = 0$, $X_2 = 0$ in the first tableau.

On the very top row of the tableau, the objective function coefficients are displayed corresponding to the columns represented by each X_j variable. For example, the profit coefficient of X_1 is 10, which is written directly above the symbol X_1. The values of the C_j which correspond to the solution variables are listed to the left of the solution variables in the tableau. In the first tableau, these C_j values are all zero, since only slack variables are in the initial solution.

Finally, the tableau has two rows on the bottom labeled Z_j and $C_j - Z_j$. The Z_j row is computed by multiplying the C_j values on the left by the coefficients in each column and adding. For example, Z_1 is computed as follows:

$$Z_1 = 0(30) + 0(2) + 0(4) = 0$$

In the first tableau, the resulting values of Z_j are always zero, since all the C_j values are zero.

The last row in the tableau, $C_j - Z_j$ is the result of subtracting the Z_j value we have just computed from C_j at the top of the tableau.

The Z_j values can be interpreted economically as the gross profit due to introducing *one*

Figure S3.3
First tableau—product-mix problem.

C_j			10	8	0	0	0	
↓	Solution variables		X_1	X_2	X_3	X_4	X_5	Solution quantity X_j
0	X_3		30	20	1	0	0	120
0	X_4		2	2	0	1	0	9
0	X_5		4	6	0	0	1	24
	Z_j		0	0	0	0	0	0
	$C_j - Z_j$		10	8	0	0	0	

unit of the corresponding X_j variable. For example, in column 1, if one unit of X_1 is introduced to the solution, the value of X_3 must be reduced by 30 to maintain the equality in the first row, X_4 must be reduced by 2 to maintain the equality in the second row, and X_5 must be reduced by 4 to maintain equality in the third row. Therefore, the coefficients in the X_1 column represent the physical rates of substitution between X_1 and each of the variables in the solution. When these substitution rates are multiplied by their respective profit coefficients, the result is Z_1, the gross profit lost when one unit of X_1 is introduced. The profit gained by introducing one unit of X_1, however, is the value $C_1 = 10$. Therefore, the value $C_1 - Z_1$ represents the *net* profit gained by introducing one unit of X_1. It stands to reason, then, that introducing either X_1 or X_2 into the solution of the first tableau will improve the net profit because the $C_1 - Z_1$ and $C_2 - Z_2$ values are positive.

All the facts required to solve the LP problem are represented in the tableau: the current solution values on the right, the substitution ratios of each variable for the others in the tableau body, and the net profit contribution for increasing the value of each variable on the bottom.

As we mentioned earlier, the simplex method works by moving from one corner of the feasible region to an adjacent corner. The first tableau represents corner a at the origin in Figure S3.2, because we have $X_1 = 0$, $X_2 = 0$, in the tableau. All three constraints have slack in them ($X_3 = 120$, $X_4 = 9$, and $X_5 = 24$) at the origin. There are only two possible ways to move from the origin to an adjacent extreme point without "cutting across" the feasible region. One way to move is to increase X_1 until we reach corner d, at a value of $X_1 = 4$. At this point, we will also have $X_3 = 0$, since there will no longer be slack in constraint number 1. The other adjacent extreme point can be reached by increasing X_2 until $X_2 = 4$ at corner e. In this case $X_5 = 0$, since constraint 3 no longer has slack.

The simplex method selects between these two options on the basis of the largest net profit

contribution per unit ($C_j - Z_j$). Since $C_j - Z_j$ is largest for X_1, the simplex method will move to corner d by increasing X_1 and simultaneously decreasing X_3 to zero. In the language of the simplex method, X_1 is introduced into the solution and X_3 is removed from the solution, since its new value is zero.

Without reference to the graphical picture, we can determine which variable will enter the solution and which one will leave by using the following rules:

Entering rule. To enter the solution, select the variable with the largest value of $C_j - Z_j$. Call this the key column.

Leaving rule. Take the ratio of the solution quantities to the key-column coefficients for those coefficients which are positive. Select the row variable with the minimum ratio to leave. Call this the key row.

In the first tableau, the application of the entering rule is: X_1 is chosen to enter. The application of the leaving rule produces the following ratios, one for each row: 120/30, 9/2, and 24/4. Since 120/30 is the smallest ratio for the first row, the variable represented in the first row, X_3, will be leaving the solution. Intuitively, as the value of X_1 is increased in column 1, X_3 will be the first variable in the current solution to reach zero. This fact is determined by calculating the above ratios for positive coefficients. The key column and key row are denoted in the first tableau by small arrows. The intersection of these arrows is called the "pivot element," which is circled in the tableau.

After applying the entering and leaving rules, the next step in the simplex method is to transform the tableau to the new solution by using the pivot element. This is done by the process of gaussian elimination which transforms the tableau but maintains the same solution to the constraint equations. In gaussian elimination, any row in the tableau may be multiplied or divided by a nonzero constant and placed in the new tableau. Also, any row may be multiplied by a nonzero constant and added to any other row, with the sum placed in the new tableau. What we are doing with the gaussian elimination method is solving simultaneous equations.

According to the gaussian rules, all coefficients in the key row are divided by the pivot element and the result is placed in the new tableau; see Figure S3.4. Then the key row is multiplied by a constant and added to a row other than the key row, so the result is a zero in the key column. The appropriate constant is selected for each nonkey row. For example, the constant $-2/30$ is multiplied by the key-row coefficients and added to each coefficient in the second row, with the sum placed in the second row of the new tableau. The constant value of $-2/30$ was selected so that the key column for row 2 will be zero in the new tableau. Similarly, the key row is multiplied by $-4/30$ and added to the third row to get the new third row in tableau 2. This completes the gaussian procedure which puts the second tableau in the proper format and ensures that the solution set is not changed.

After this step is completed, the values of Z_j and $C_j - Z_j$ are computed by updating the computations with the new coefficient values in tableau 2. The new tableau is exactly like the old one except that we have replaced column 3 by column 1 in the solution. Notice that column 1 in the new tableau has a 1 in the first position; the

rest are zeros. At every step of the simplex, the variables in the solution have a 1 in some position and the rest zeros, yielding an identity matrix in the tableau. This makes it possible to read the solution directly from the tableau. In the second tableau, we have $X_1 = 4$, $X_2 = 0$, $X_3 = 0$, $X_4 = 1$, and $X_5 = 8$. By following the gaussian elimination rules, we are computing a solution of three equations and three unknowns for each tableau until the optimal tableau is reached.

The second tableau is not yet optimal, since a positive increase in net profit is shown in the $C_j - Z_j$ row. Since $C_2 - Z_2$ is the largest positive value, column 2 is the key column. Taking the ratios, we find that row 2 has the minimum ratio, so row 2 is the key row and X_4 leaves the solution. Pivoting on column 2 and row 2, we obtain the third tableau (Figure S3.5) by gaussian elimination. Since no values of $C_j - Z_j$ are positive, we have arrived at the optimal solution; no further improvement in net profit is possible. The optimal solution in the third tableau is $X_1 = 3$, $X_2 = 3/2$, $X_3 = 0$, $X_4 = 0$, $X_5 = 3$.

Since the simplex method is rather long, a brief recap of the main steps might be helpful.

1. Put the constraints in equality form by adding slack variables. Set up the first tableau.
2. Pick the key column to enter the solution, on the basis of largest positive, $C_j - Z_j$

Figure S3.4
Second tableau.

C_j		10	8	0	0	0	
	Solution variables	X_1	X_2	X_3	X_4	X_5	Solution quantity
10	X_1	1	2/3	1/30	0	0	4
0	X_4	0	2/3	−2/30	1	0	1
0	X_5	0	10/3	−4/30	0	1	8
	Z_j	10	20/3	10/30	0	0	40
	$C_j - Z_j$	0	4/3	−10/30	0	0	

C_j		10	8	0	0	0	
	Solution variables	X_1	X_2	X_3	X_4	X_5	Solution quantity
10	X_1	1	0	1/10	−1	0	3
8	X_2	0	1	−1/10	3/2	0	3/2
0	X_5	0	0	6/30	−5	1	3
	Z_j	10	8	2/10	2	0	42
	$C_j - Z_j$	0	0	−2/10	−2	0	

Figure S3.5
Third tableau.

value. If no $C_j - Z_j$ values are positive, an optimal solution has been reached.

3. Calculate the ratio of the right-hand side to all positive coefficients in the key column. Select the key row on the basis of the minimum ratio.
4. Transform the tableau by pivoting on the key row and key column using the gaussian elimination procedure. Recalculate the values of Z_j and $C_j - Z_j$ and then return to step 2.

The simplex solution of the product-mix problem may be interpreted in direct economic terms. The simplex method started with zero production of both products—an initial feasible solution but not a very profitable one. Product 1 was then introduced to the solution because it had the largest profit contribution ($10 per unit versus $8 per unit). The simplex method is a method of "steepest ascent." It moves in the direction of the greatest unit profit improvement at each tableau. Then as much of product 1 as possible was introduced, until a constraint was reached. In this case the constraint on lumber was the most binding constraint and limited the amount of X_1 to four units. When four units of X_1 were produced, the profit was increased from zero to $40.

Next, a calculation was made to determine whether the profit could be improved even more by introducing some of the second product. This

calculation required a substitution between product 1 and product 2. As product 2 was increased, less of product 1 was produced because the constraints limited the total amount of resources available.

The net effect on profit of increasing product 2 and decreasing product 1 is represented by the $C_2 - Z_2$ calculation, which indicated that profit could be improved by $4/3 per unit of X_2 produced. Next, it was found that a maximum of $1^1/2$ units of X_2 could be introduced to the solution due to the combination of the lumber and labor constraints. Increasing the value of X_2 to $1^1/2$ units also reduced X_1 to three units. The net effect of these changes in X_1 and X_2 was an improvement in profit to $42. At this point the simplex method determined that no further improvement in profit was possible.

In economic terms, the simplex method starts with a feasible solution and introduces one product at a time provided that profit is improved. When no further incremental improvement in profit is possible, the optimal solution is reached.

SHADOW PRICES

After the optimal solution has been computed, much information can be obtained from the final tableau. One type of data comprises "shadow prices," which are used to evaluate the scarce resources available. The precise interpretation of a shadow price is the amount of improvement in the objective function per unit change in a right-hand-side value. For example, in the product-mix problem, there are shadow prices for lumber, labor, and finishing capacity. The shadow price for each of these resources is the amount of improvement in profit possible if an additional unit of the resource is made available. One can thus use the shadow prices to evaluate proposed changes in resources as they might affect the objective function. For example, the shadow price for lumber is 20 cents per board foot; therefore any proposal to make additional lumber available at less than this price would improve profits up to the point where the constraints of labor and finishing capacity become binding. Shadow prices are used to evaluate potential right-hand-side changes. This evaluation procedure is called sensitivity analysis, since the optimal solution's sensitivity to changes in the problem formulation is being evaluated.

The shadow prices for the product-mix problem can be obtained directly from the final tableau (Figure S3.5). The negative of the shadow price appears in the $C_j - Z_j$ row under the slack variables. Since X_3 was the slack variable in the first constraint, $-(C_3 - Z_3)$ is the shadow price $2/10$ (or 20 cents per board foot) for lumber. Similarly, $-(C_4 - Z_4)$ is the shadow price, $2 per hour for labor, in the second constraint. The third constraint, represented by the X_5 slack variable, has a shadow price of $-(C_5 - Z_5) = 0$. This value of zero is logical, since there is excess finishing capacity at the optimal solution. The economic value (or shadow price) of this resource is therefore zero.

As another illustration, suppose someone offers to work for you at $4 per hour. Since the shadow price of labor is only $2 per hour, it would not pay to use the additional labor. In this case profit is improved by only $2 per hour while the additional resource costs $4 an hour—a net loss of $2 per hour for each additional hour of labor used.

MINIMIZATION PROBLEM

Linear programming can also be used to solve minimization problems. The procedures require some modifications, however, which will be described later. As an example of a minimization problem, suppose that a machine shop has two different types of machines, machine 1 and machine 2, which can be used to make a single product. These machines vary in the amount of product produced per hour, in the amount of labor used, and in the cost of operation. Also assume that at least a certain amount of the product must be produced and that we would like to utilize at least the regular labor force. Under these conditions, how much should we utilize each machine in order to minimize total costs and still meet the requirements?

This problem can be formulated as a linear programming problem by letting:

X_1 = hours of machine 1 time

X_2 = hours of machine 2 time

We also assume that machine 1 can produce 20 pounds of product per hour, machine 2 can produce 15 pounds of product per hour, and at least 100 pounds of product are required from both machines. This constraint is expressed mathematically as:

$$20X_1 + 15X_2 \geq 100$$

Suppose also that 2 hours of labor are required for each hour of machine 1 operation, 3 hours of labor are required for each hour of machine 2 operation, and we must use at least the 15 hours of regular-time labor available. This constraint is expressed mathematically as:

$$2X_1 + 3X_2 \geq 15$$

Finally, we assume that it costs $25 per hour (labor and materials) to operate machine 1 and $30 per hour to operate machine 2. Our desire to minimize total costs of operation is expressed as follows:

$$\text{Min } 25X_1 + 30X_2$$

The problem as stated above, along with the $X_1 \geq 0$, $X_2 \geq 0$ constraints, is graphed in Figure S3.6. The constraints are plotted as equations just as before, but the feasible region for $\geq$ signs is to the *right* of the line, since the feasible points must exceed the line. The isoprofit lines are also shown in Figure S3.6. Since we are minimizing, the isoprofit line closest to the origin is chosen as the minimum in this case. This results in an optimal solution at the intersection of the two constraints. The solution of those constraints as simultaneous equations yields $X_1 = 2.5$, $X_2 = 3.33$ for the optimal solution. The corresponding minimum cost is \$162.50.

This problem can also be solved by the simplex method with some minor modifications. Just as before, the first step is to convert the inequalities to equations. Since the inequalities are $\geq$, a variable must be *subtracted* from the left-hand side to make the two sides equal. This variable is called a surplus variable, but it serves the same function as the slack variable for $\leq$ signs. The resulting LP problem is:

Objective:

$$\min 25X_1 + 30X_2 + 0X_3 + 0X_4$$

Subject to:

$$20X_1 + 15X_2 - X_3 \qquad = 100$$
$$2X_1 + 3X_2 \qquad - X_4 = 15$$
$$X_1 \geq 0, \ X_2 \geq 0, \ X_3 \geq 0, \ X_4 \geq 0$$

The simplex method requires a nonnegative feasible solution as a starting point. If we were to set $X_1 = 0$, $X_2 = 0$ as we did before, we would have $X_3 = -100$ and $X_4 = -15$. Since this solution violates the nonnegativity conditions, a feasible starting point is not available in this problem. To correct this situation, we add an artificial variable to each equation with a very large positive coefficient (called large M) in the objective function. Since we are minimizing costs, artificial variables will be driven out of the solution by the simplex method due to their large cost coefficients. This is, of course, just what we want, since artificial variables cannot remain in the optimal solution.

Figure S3.6
Minimization problem.

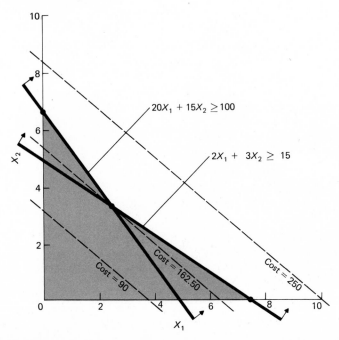

C_j		25	30	0	0	M	M	
	Solution variables	X_1	X_2	X_3	X_4	X_5	X_6	Solution quantity
M	X_5	20	15	−1	0	1	0	100
M	X_6	2	3	0	−1	0	1	15
	Z_j	$22M$	$18M$	$-M$	$-M$	M	M	$115M$
	$C_j - Z_j$	25 $-22M$	30 $-18M$	0 $+M$	0 $+M$	0	0	

Figure S3.7
First tableau—minimization problem.

The purpose of artificial variables is to provide a feasible starting point for the simplex method.

With the use of artificial variables, the LP formulation becomes:

Objective:
min $25X_1 + 30X_2 + 0X_3 + 0X_4 + MX_5 + MX_6$

Subject to:
$$20X_1 + 15X_2 - X_3 + X_5 = 100$$
$$2X_1 + 3X_2 - X_4 + X_6 = 15$$
$$X_1 \geq 0, X_2 \geq 0, X_3 \geq 0, X_4 \geq 0, X_5 \geq 0, X_6 \geq 0$$

Now we have achieved an LP formulation with an initial starting solution of $X_1 = 0$, $X_2 = 0$, $X_3 = 0$, $X_4 = 0$, $X_5 = 100$, and $X_6 = 15$. The initial cost is then $100M + 15M$, which is very large, since M is an arbitrarily large positive number. This problem is now ready to go into the first simplex tableau, shown in Figure S3.7.

With minimization, the entering variable is based on the largest *negative* $C_j - Z_j$, since we want to reduce the objective function as much as possible on each iteration. In the first tableau, the entering column is therefore X_1, which has the largest negative M coefficient in the $C_j - Z_j$ row. The rest of the simplex method is now applied in exactly the same way as in the maximization problem. On the basis of the minimum

Figure S3.8
Second tableau.

C_j		25	30	0	0	M	M	
	Solution variables	X_1	X_2	X_3	X_4	X_5	X_6	Solution quantity
25	X_1	1	15/20	−1/20	0	1/20	0	5
M	X_6	0	3/2	2/20	−1	−2/20	1	5
	Z_j	25	$75/4$ $+3/2M$	$-5/4$ $+1/10M$	$-M$	$5/4$ $-1/10M$	M	$125 + 5M$
	$C_j - Z_j$	0	$45/4$ $-3/2M$	$5/4$ $-1/10M$	$+M$	$5/4$ $+11/10M$	0	

C_j		25	30	0	0	M	M	
	Solution variables	X_1	X_2	X_3	X_4	X_5	X_6	Solution quantity
25	X_1	1	0	−1/10	1/2	1/10	−1/2	5/2
30	X_2	0	1	1/15	−2/3	−1/15	2/3	10/3
	Z_j	25	30	−1/2	−15/2	1/2	15/2	162.5
	$C_j − Z_j$	0	0	1/2	15/2	−1/2 +M	−15/2 +M	

Figure S3.9
Third tableau.

ratio, X_5 is the leaving variable. The pivot element is then used to perform a gaussian transformation to the second tableau, shown in Figure S3.8.

In the second tableau, X_2 is selected as the incoming variable, since it has the largest negative value of $C_j − Z_j$. Taking the minimum ratio over positive coefficients of column 2 yields X_6 as the leaving variable. Performing a gaussian transformation then yields the third tableau, shown in Figure S3.9.

The third tableau is optimal, since all $C_j − Z_j$ are positive; no further reduction in the objective function is possible. From the tableau, the optimal solution is $X_1 = 5/2$, $X_2 = 10/3$, and cost = $162.50. The shadow prices are 50 cents for each additional pound of product produced and $7.50 for each additional hour of labor required. The marginal cost of 50 cents per pound can be used to help decide whether additional orders should be taken. The marginal labor cost of $7.50 per hour can be used to help decide whether all the labor should be utilized. For example, it will pay for some people to be idle if their wage rates are less than $7.50 per hour.

In summary, there are two main effects on the simplex method for a minimization problem. First, the entering-column criterion is the largest negative $C_j − Z_j$ instead of the largest positive $C_j − Z_j$ value. Second, the simplex method stops at the optimal solution when all $C_j − Z_j \geq 0$.

Otherwise, all features of the simplex method are the same as in the maximization case.

APPLICATIONS OF LP IN OPERATIONS

LP has been applied to a wide range of decisions both inside and outside operations. Within operations, well-known applications include the following:

1. **Product mix.** A simplified version of the product-mix decision was formulated in the first part of this supplement, where scarce resources were allocated to products. In real situations, additional constraints—such as minimum or maximum production levels of each product and multiple time periods—may be introduced to provide more realism. As we have indicated, one benefit of the optimal-product-mix solution is to identify coordination problems between production and marketing, since the best mix of products from a production point of view is provided by the LP solution. If this optimal mix of products is not being marketed, either marketing strategy or production resources should be adjusted.

2. **Blending.** The blending decision determines the best resource inputs to make a blended prod-

uct such as gasoline or sausage. In the sausage-blending decision, certain specifications such as fat content, water content, pork percentage, and beef content are given for the final product. These specifications are frequently stated as maximums or minimums. Several types of raw-meat stocks are available which vary in their cost and product-specification characteristics. The problem is to find the best blend of raw-meat stocks which meets the final product specifications and minimizes the cost of the product.

3. Scheduling. A wide range of scheduling decisions have been supported by LP, including the operation of blast furnaces, project scheduling, and scheduling of nurses in hospitals. Scheduling decisions typically include the assignment of available resources to jobs or tasks which must be completed. One example is a situation in which a number of blast furnaces can be used to produce several types of steel and each furnace varies in both its cost and steel output characteristics. Under these circumstances, LP is used to determine which furnaces should be scheduled for the production of each steel product in order to minimize the cost of production.

4. Distribution. LP has been applied to a wide range of distribution decisions such as optimal shipping patterns and optimal location of plants and warehouses. In these decisions, goods may be shipped from one location to another through a variety of alternate paths and locations. The best shipping paths and patterns can then be identified by an LP formulation. One simple version of this problem, the transportation problem, will be described in the supplement to Chapter 9.

5. Aggregate planning. The aggregate-planning decision, described in Chapter 10, determines the best mix of inventory, employment, subcontracting, and other resources to meet a given demand. Demand is typically specified for several months into the future on an aggregate or total basis. This decision can be formulated as an LP problem or in several other ways. LP helps select the best aggregate plan when the conditions of the problem are linear in nature.

Although only a few examples are given above, LP has been used to solve many hundreds of real problems in operations. Remember, LP did not solve these problems, it merely assisted the manager in reaching a better decision. LP did, however, solve the mathematical formulation of the manager's problem.

QUESTIONS

1. Define the following terms:
   a. Slack variable
   b. Constraint
   c. Objective function
   d. Artificial variable
   e. Extreme point
   f. Optimal solution
   g. Feasible solution
2. What information is provided by shadow prices?
3. Explain the concept of a shadow price by using the LP graph in Figure S3.2.
4. The simplex method is an adjacent-extreme-point method. Explain.
5. How do we know when an optimal solution for a minimization problem has been reached by the simplex method?
6. What is the purpose of using gaussian elimination in going from one tableau to the next?
7. How are corner points represented by the simplex tableau?
8. Why is a large M value assigned to artificial variables?
9. Why does the optimal solution to an LP problem always occur at a corner point? How is this fact exploited in finding the optimal solution?
10. In the simplex method, what are the differences between minimization and maximization problems?

PROBLEMS

1. Solve the following LP problem by the graphical method:

   Objective:
   $$\max 3X_1 + 4X_2$$

   Subject to:
   $$5X_1 + 2X_2 \leq 10$$
   $$2X_1 + 6X_2 \leq 12$$
   $$X_1 \geq 0, X_2 \geq 0$$

2. Solve the following problem by the graphical method:

   Objective:
   $$\min 6X_1 + X_2$$

   Subject to:
   $$X_1 + X_2 \geq 5$$
   $$4X_1 - X_2 \geq 6$$
   $$X_1 \geq X_2 \geq 0$$

3. A company manufactures two types of plastic toys: trucks and cars. Each truck requires 1 minute of molding time, 2 minutes of painting time, and 1 minute of packing time. Each car requires 2 minutes of molding time, 1 minute of painting time, and 2 minutes of packing time. There are a total of 400 minutes of molding time, 600 minutes of painting time, and 500 minutes of packing time available each day. Both cars and trucks contribute $1 per unit to profit.
   a. Formulate this problem.
   b. Solve it graphically.
   c. Solve it by the simplex method.
   d. If only one of the three resources can be increased in capacity, which one would you choose?

4. The x-ray department of a hospital has two machines, A and B, which can be used to develop x-ray film. The maximum daily processing capacity of these machines is A = 80 films, and B = 100 films. The department must plan to process at least 150 films per day. The operating costs per film are $2 for machine A and $3 for machine B. To minimize costs, how many films per day should each machine process?
   a. Solve this problem graphically.
   b. Solve it by the simplex method.
   c. How much would you be willing to pay for additional capacity on machine A?

5. Gasoline is blended from several stocks to obtain minimum required octane ratings. Suppose an order for 2000 gallons of 80-octane gasoline has been received. There are three blending stocks available. Stock A has 90 octane and costs $1.20 per gallon. Stock B has 70 octane and costs $1 per gallon. Stock C has 85 octane and costs $1.10 per gallon. There are only 1000 gallons of stock A, 1500 gallons of stock B, and 1000 gallons of stock C available. Assume that octane numbers combine in proportion to the volume of the stocks which are blended together. How much stock of each type should be used to minimize the total cost of filling the order?
   a. Solve this problem by the simplex method.
   b. How much would you be willing to pay per additional gallon of stock A?

6. Brand X animal feed is made from a combination of wheat and corn. Wheat contains 10 percent protein, 40 percent starch, and 50 percent fiber by weight. Corn contains 15 percent protein, 50 percent starch, and 35 percent fiber by weight. The recipe for brand X feed calls

for a minimum of 45 percent starch and 40 percent fiber; there is no restriction on protein. If a batch of at least 1000 pounds of brand X is produced, how many pounds of corn and how many pounds of wheat should be used to minimize costs? Corn costs 5 cents per pound and wheat costs 3 cents per pound.

SELECTED BIBLIOGRAPHY

CHARNES, ABRAHAM, and W. W. COOPER: *Management Models and Industrial Applications of Linear Programming,* New York: Wiley, 1961.

DAELLENBACH, HANS G., and EARL J. BELL: *User's Guide to Linear Programming,* Englewood Cliffs, N.J.: Prentice-Hall, 1970.

DANTZIG, GEORGE B.: *Linear Programming and Extensions,* Princeton, N.J.: Princeton University Press, 1963.

GASS, SAUL I.: *Illustrated Guide to Linear Programming,* New York: McGraw-Hill, 1970.

GRINOLD, RICHARD C.: "Input Policies for a Longitudinal Manpower Flow Model," *Management Science,* vol. 22, 1976, pp. 570–575.

LEE, SANG M.: *Linear Optimization for Management,* New York: Petrocelli/Charter, 1976.

LYONS, D. F., and V. A. DODD: "The Mis-Feed Problem," *Operational Research,* Amsterdam: North-Holland Publishing, 1975.

NAYLOR, THOMAS H., EUGENE T. BYRNE, and JOHN M. VERNON: *Introduction to Linear Programming: Methods and Cases.* Belmont, Calif.: Wadsworth, 1971.

ZIERER, T. K., W. A. MITCHELL, and T. R. WHITE: "Practical Applications of Linear Programming to Shell's Distribution Problems," *Interfaces,* vol. 6, no. 4, August 1976, pp. 13–26.

CHAPTER 4
FORECASTING

Forecasting is the art and science of predicting future events. Until the last decade, forecasting was largely an art, but it has now become a science as well. While managerial judgment is still required for forecasting, the manager is aided today by sophisticated mathematical tools and methods. Forecasting has indeed come a long way from the black art of viewing chicken entrails, tea leaves, or crystal balls.

Many different methods of forecasting and their uses are described in this chapter. One of its main points is that a forecasting method must be carefully selected for the particular use it is intended to serve. There is no universal forecasting method for all situations and circumstances.

In the first part of the chapter, a descriptive framework of forecasting is presented. Several methods and their potential applications are then discussed at length. Following this, the uses of forecasting in organizations are described.

4.1 A FORECASTING FRAMEWORK

Although there are many types of forecasting, this chapter will focus on the forecasting of demand for output from the operations functions. Whenever this demand is not constrained by capacity or other management policies, the forecasting of demand will be the same as the forecasting of sales. Otherwise, sales may be somewhat below real customer demand.

We should also clarify at the outset the difference between forecasting and planning. Forecasting deals with what we think *will* happen in the future. Planning deals with what we think *should* happen in the future. Thus, through planning, we consciously attempt to alter future events, while we use forecasting only to predict them. Good planning utilitizes a forecast as an input. If the forecast is not acceptable, a plan can frequently be devised to change the course of events.

Forecasting is one input to all types of business planning and control, both inside and outside the operations function. Marketing uses forecasts to plan products, promotion, and pricing. Finance uses forecasting as an input to financial planning. The main focus in this chapter, however, will be on forecasting for the operations function, where it serves as an input for decisions on process design, capacity planning, and inventory. A typical forecasting problem is described in Box 4.1.

For process-design purposes, forecasting is needed to decide on the type of process and the degree of automation to be used. If a low demand is forecasted, the process design might have an intermittent product flow with little automation. For higher-demand forecasts, a line process with more automation might be justified. Since the process and product are often selected together, a forecast might be made by marketing for purposes of product selection, and it might then also be used by operations for process selection and design. Such a market forecast should normally extend several years into the future with a reasonable degree of accuracy.

Capacity decisions utilize forecasts at several different levels of aggregation and precision. For planning the total capacity of facilities, a long-range forecast several years into the future is needed. For medium-range-capacity decisions extending through the next year or so, a more detailed forecast by product line will be needed to determine hiring plans, subcontracting, and equipment decisions. Besides being more detailed, the medium-range forecast should be more accurate, if possible, than the long-range forecast. Short-range-capacity decisions include assignment of available people and machines to jobs or activities in the near future. The associated short-range forecasts should be detailed in terms of individual products, and they should be highly accurate.

Inventory decisions resulting in purchasing actions tend to be short-range in nature and deal with specific products. The forecasts that lead to these decisions must meet the same requirements as short-range scheduling forecasts: they must have a high degree of accuracy and individual product specificity. For inventory and scheduling decisions, because of the many items usually involved, it will also be necessary to produce a large number of forecasts. Thus a computerized forecasting system may be needed for these decisions.

BOX 4.1 **TYPICAL DECISION PROBLEM**

Ted Hickford, vice president of operations for Pizza U.S.A., was meeting with Harold Foster, the corporation president, to discuss the upcoming budgeting cycle. Ted began, "Harry, I'm tired of operations being whiplashed by changing forecasts every month. Every fall just before budgeting time, the marketing people make their annual sales forecast, which, as you know, is updated monthly. As far as I can tell, this forecast is merely a composite of all the 'wish lists' submitted by the marketing people in the field. After the marketing vice president receives these forecasts, he simply adds them together and sometimes adjusts the results if he thinks they're too high or too low. Harry, I think these 'seat of the pants' methods of forecasting are too crude, and something must be done about them."

Harry replied, "Well, Ted, I appreciate your concern, but we are doing the best we can. As you know, the market is very dynamic in our business and Tom tries to stay in close touch with the market. But if you have a better approach to forecasting our monthly demand, we'll be happy to give it a try."

Ted indicated that he had recently taken a short course in operations management and had learned about some new quantitative methods that were available for forecasting. These methods relied on computer analysis of past data patterns and trends and could be used to forecast future demand. Ted continued, "I'm not sure how well these methods will work for us, but perhaps we should investigate them."

At this point, Tom Peters, the marketing vice president, walked into the office, and Ted and Harold explained the entire situation to him. Tom said, "I'm very skeptical that a computer can be used to replace the marketing judgment that we've spent years developing. How can computer methods project upturns and downturns when so many factors are involved?"

At this point Tom proposed that a test be instituted. Ted would develop a computer forecasting model using all available historical data except those for the past year. This model would then be used to forecast demand for the past year, and the results would be compared to actual demand and to the market forecasts. All three managers agreed to meet again when the model was complete to review the results of the test and decide how to proceed from there.

In summary, there are different types of decisions in operations and different associated forecasting requirements, as shown in Table 4.1. The table also indicates the three types of forecasting methods to be described next: qualitative, time series, and causal.

In general terms, qualitative forecasting methods rely on managerial judgment; they do not use specific models. Thus different individuals can use the same qualitative method and arrive at widely different forecasts. Qualitative methods are useful, however, when there is a lack of data or when past data are not reliable predictors of the future. In this case, the human decision maker can utilize the best available data and a qualitative approach to arrive at a forecast. Some of the well-known qualitative methods to be described later in this chapter are the Delphi technique, market surveys, the life-cycle analogy, and informed judgment.

There are two types of quantitative forecasting methods: time-series and causal forecasting. In general, quantitative methods utilize an underlying model to arrive at a forecast. The basic assumption for all quantitative forecasting methods is that

TABLE 4.1   FORECASTING USES AND METHODS

Uses of forecasting for operations decisions	Time horizon	Accuracy required	Number of products	Management level	Forecasting methods
Process design	Long	Medium	Single or few	Top	Qualitative and causal
Capacity planning Facilities	Long	Medium	Single or few	Top	Qualitative and causal
Aggregate planning	Medium	High	Few	Middle	Causal and time series
Scheduling	Short	Highest	Many	Lower	Time series
Inventory management	Short	Highest	Many	Lower	Time series

past data and data patterns are reliable predictors of the future. Past data are then processed by a time-series or causal model to arrive at a forecast.

Time-series forecasts are based on the past history of demand for a product. This history is analyzed for data patterns such as trends, seasonality, or cycles, and the resulting demand patterns are projected ahead into the future. Since demand patterns often do not hold over the long range, time-series methods are primarily useful for short- to medium-range forecasts. Common time-series methods to be described later in this chapter are the moving average, exponential smoothing, mathematical models, and the Box-Jenkins method.

Causal forecasting methods relate demand to one or more intrinsic or extrinsic variables. For example, a publisher might relate the demand for newspapers to population, economic activity, and per capita income. Since causal methods relate demand to independent variables other than time, turning points and fundamental changes in demand patterns can be predicted. Causal forecasting methods are therefore generally more accurate than time-series methods for medium- to long-range forecasts. The causal methods described later in the chapter are regression, econometric models, input-output models, and simulation models.

The relationship between the methods and uses of forecasting is summarized in Table 4.1. As may be noted, each method has certain uses for which it is particularly well suited.

In the remainder of this chapter we will be referring to long, medium, and short time ranges. "Long range" will mean 2 years or more into the future, which is a common horizon for the planning of facilities and processes. "Medium range" is defined as from 6 months to 2 years, which is the normal time frame for aggregate planning decisions, budgeting, and other resource acquisition and allocation decisions. "Short range" will refer to less than 6 months, where the decisions involve procurement of materials and scheduling of particular jobs and activities. For short-range decisions, forecasts that extend through procurement or production lead times are sufficient.

4.2 QUALITATIVE FORECASTING METHODS

As we have indicated, qualitative forecasting methods utilize managerial judgment, experience, relevant data, and an *implicit* mathematical model. Because the model is implicit, two different managers both using qualitative methods often arrive at widely different forecasts.

Some people think that qualitative forecasts should be used only as a last resort. This is not strictly true. Qualitative forecasts should be used when past data are not reliable indicators of future conditions. When this happens, past data must be tempered by judgment before a forecast can be developed. Qualitative forecasting must also be used for new-product introductions, where a historical data base is not available. In this case, qualitative methods can be used to develop a forecast by analogy or by the selective use of market research data. As we shall see, a systematic approach is possible even though an explicit mathematical model is not formulated.

Table 4.2 describes four of the best-known qualitative methods and some of the characteristics of each. As can be seen, qualitative methods are typically used for medium- and long-range forecasting involving process design or capacity of facilities. For these decisions, past data are not usually available or, if they are, may show an unstable pattern.

One of the qualitative forecasting methods, the so-called Delphi method, is used to obtain a forecast from a panel of experts or managers. A feature of this method is that all estimates from the panel are treated anonymously. This tends to eliminate the influence of the supposed greatest authority as well as the bandwagon effect which is so common when face-to-face panels are used.

The Delphi method, named after the famous Greek oracle of Delphi, proceeds through a series of rounds. On the first round, each person on the panel provides a written response to the questions asked. After these responses are tabulated, they are fed back to the panel along with statistics on the mean, median, interquartile range, and standard deviation. Each member of the panel is then asked to reconsider his or her previous answers and to respond once again to the questions. The responses from the second round are again summarized and fed back to the panel for a third round, and so on. This procedure is often repeated for four to six rounds (a minimum of three) until sufficient convergence is achieved. The estimates from the last round are then used as the forecasts.

The Delphi method has sometimes been referred to as "pooled ignorance." This criticism is derived from the tendency of the feedback process to force convergence toward the group center. Nevertheless, the method can be used to obtain reasonable forecasts in the face of a great deal of uncertainty and a lack of data.

An example of the use of the Delphi method to obtain a 5-year forecast of sales for facility-planning purposes was reported by Basu and Schroeder (1977). In this case, sales at American Hoist and Derrick had been constrained by insufficient capacity and were therefore not a reliable predictor of future demand. Furthermore, economic conditions were changing rapidly, making past data unreliable. Therefore, the Delphi method was used to bring managerial judgment to bear on the available past data and to reflect expected future conditions.

TABLE 4.2
QUALITATIVE FORECASTING METHODS

Qualitative methods	Description of method	Uses	Accuracy				Relative cost	References
			Short-term	Medium-term	Long-term	Identification of turning point		
1. Delphi	Forecast developed by a panel of experts answering a series of questions on successive rounds. Anonymous responses of the panel are fed back on each round to all participants. Three to six rounds may be used to obtain convergence of the forecast.	Long-range sales forecasts for capacity or facility planning. Technological forecasting to assess when technological changes might occur.	Fair to very good	Fair to very good	Fair to very good	Fair to good	Medium to high	North and Pyke; Basu and Schroeder
2. Market surveys	Panels, questionnaires, test markets, or surveys used to gather data on market conditions.	Forecasts of total company sales, major product groups, or individual products.	Very good	Good	Fair	Fair to good	High	Bass, King, and Pessemeier
3. Life-cycles analogy	Prediction based on the introduction, growth, and saturation phases of similar products. Uses the S-shaped sales growth curve.	Forecasts of long-range sales for capacity or facility planning.	Poor	Fair to good	Fair to good	Poor to fair	Medium	Spencer, Clark, and Hoguet
4. Informed judgment	Forecast may be made by a group or by an individual on the basis of experience, hunches, or facts about the situation. No rigorous method is used.	Forecasts for total sales and individual products.	Poor to fair	Poor to fair	Poor to fair	Poor to fair	Low	

Source: Reprinted by permission of the *Harvard Business Review.* Exhibit adapted from John C. Chambers, Satinder K. Mullick, and Donald D. Smith, "How to Choose the Right Forecasting Technique," July–August 1971, p. 55. Copyright © 1971 by the President and Fellows of Harvard College; all rights reserved.

In this case, a panel of 23 managers who had knowledge of the overall market and sales picture was selected from different functional parts of the corporation. This panel was given a questionnaire which requested three estimates—the GNP, industry sales, and company sales—for each of the next 5 years. These three estimates were requested in order to encourage panel members to think about the interrelationships between the economy, industry, and the company and to allow validity and correlation checks on the results. The managers were given the past 5 years of data on these three scales and asked simply to fill in their best estimate of the curve for the next 5 years.

Both the anonymous estimates of all the managers and summary statistics were fed back on the second round. The data indicated a fairly wide spread of estimates. For example, the industry sales estimates in one year ranged from a low of 0 percent increase to a high of 35 percent increase with a mean of 9.5 percent and a standard deviation of 8 percent.

In addition to a revised estimate, the panel members were asked to give their reasons for their estimates on the second round; this resulted in an outpouring of views on future conditions. These reasons were then fed back, along with the revised estimates and statistics for the third round.

The result of the three successive rounds was a striking convergence of the managers' forecasts. For GNP in one year, the first-round forecast ranged from 0 to 12 percent increase, while the third-round estimate had converged to a 5 to 8.5 percent increase. In addition to providing a forecast, the convergence produced a common outlook among the managers, which had been lacking before the use of the Delphi procedure.

Top management at American Hoist and Derrick was presented with three forecasts: the Delphi forecast, another developed using regression, and a third using exponential smoothing. The Delphi forecast was considered most credible by top management because it incorporated the judgment of 23 knowledgeable corporate managers. This confidence was subsequently justified when corporate sales for the first year were within one-third of 1 percent of the forecast and the second-year sales were within 4 percent of the forecast. In the past, forecasting errors of ± 20 percent had been common.

Three additional qualitative forecasting methods are described in Table 4.2. Notice that all these qualitative methods are best suited to long-range forecasting problems, where judgment is required to deal with inherent variability. Also notice that the Delphi and market-survey methods are fairly expensive and therefore must be used sparingly for only the most important decisions.

4.3 TIME-SERIES FORECASTING

Time-series methods are used to make detailed analyses of past demand patterns over time and to project these patterns forward into the future. One of the basic assumptions of all time-series methods is that demand can be divided into components such as average level, trend, seasonality, cycle, and error. A sample of these components for a representative time series is shown in Figure 4.1. When the components are added together (or in some cases multiplied), they will equal the original time series.

The basic strategy used in time-series forecasting is to identify the magnitude and form of each component based on available past data. These components (except the random component) are then projected forward into the future. If only a small random component is left over and the pattern persists into the future, a reliable forecast will be obtained.

One example of the decomposition of a time series is as follows:

$$y(t) = (a + bt)[f(t)] + e \tag{4.1}$$

**Figure 4.1
Decomposition of
time-series data.**

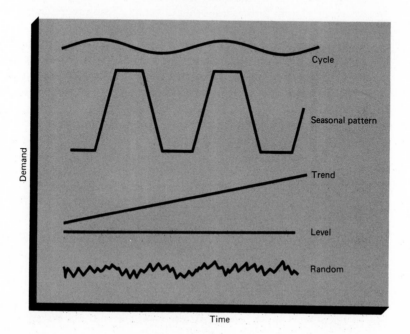

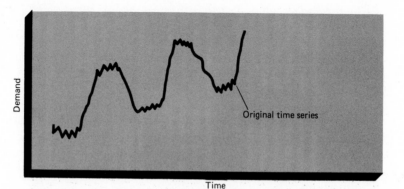

where $y(t)$ = demand during period t
$\quad a$ = level
$\quad b$ = trend
$\quad f(t)$ = seasonal factor (multiplicative)
$\quad e$ = random error

As can be seen, this time-series model has a level, trend, seasonal factor, and a random-error term. Each of these terms would be estimated from past data to develop an equation which is then used to forecast future demand.

In discussing time-series forecasting, the following symbols and terminology are used:

	Observed demands							Forecasts at time t			
Data	D_1	D_2			D_{t-2}	D_{t-1}	D_t	F_{t+1}	F_{t+2}	F_{t+3}	
Period	1	2	$\cdots$		$t-2$	$t-1$	t	$t+1$	$t+2$	$t+3$	$\cdots$

$\quad D_t$ = demand during period t
F_{t+1} = forecast demand for period $t+1$
$\quad e_t = D_t - F_t$ = forecast error in period t
$\quad A_t$ = average computed through period t

The general picture is that we are at the end of period t, just having observed the value of D_t, and are making a forecast for periods $t+1$, $t+2$, $t+3$, etc.

Moving average

The simplest method of time-series forecasting is the moving-average method. For this method, it is assumed that the time series has only a level component plus a random component. No seasonal pattern, trend, or cycle components are assumed to be present in the demand data. More advanced versions of the moving average can, however, include all the various components; see, for example, Wheelwright and Makridakis (1977).

When the moving average is used, a given number of periods N is selected for the computations. Then the average demand A_t for the past N periods at time t is computed as follows:

$$A_t = \frac{D_t + D_{t-1} + \cdots + D_{t-N+1}}{N} \tag{4.2}$$

Since we are assuming that the time series is flat, the best forecast for period $t+1$ is simply a continuation of the average demand observed through period t. Thus we have

$$F_{t+1} = A_t$$

Each time F_{t+1} is computed, the most recent demand is included in the average and the oldest demand observation is dropped. This procedure maintains N periods of demand in the forecast and lets the average *move* along as new demand data are observed.

In Box 4.2, a three-period moving average is used for forecasting purposes. Notice how the moving *average* is offset by one period to obtain the moving *forecast*. The forecast error is also shown in the box as the difference between actual and forecast demand. Always use the forecast for period t, F_t, in computing forecast errors, not the average for period t, A_t.

The graph in Figure 4.2 shows the demand data from the example, the three-period moving average, and a six-period moving average. Notice how the six-period moving average responds more slowly to demand changes than the three-period moving average. As a general rule, the longer the averaging period, the slower the response to demand changes. A longer period thus has the advantage of providing stability in the forecast but the disadvantage of responding more slowly to real changes in the demand level. The forecasting analyst must select the appropriate tradeoff between stability and response by selecting the averaging length N.

One way to make the moving average respond more rapidly to changes in demand is to place relatively more weight on recent demands than on earlier ones. This is called a weighted moving average, which is computed as follows:

$$F_{t+1} = A_t = W_1 D_t + W_2 D_{t-1} + \cdots + W_N D_{t-N+1} \tag{4.3}$$

with the condition

$$\sum_{i=1}^{N} W_i = 1$$

BOX 4.2 **MOVING AVERAGE FORECASTS**

Period	D_t (demand)	A_t (three-period moving average)	F_t (three-period forecast)	$D_t - F_t$ (error)
1	10			
2	18			
3	29	19.0		
4	15	20.7	19.0	−4.0
5	30	24.7	20.7	+9.3
6	12	19.0	24.7	−12.7
7	16	19.3	19.0	−3.0
8	8	12.0	19.3	−11.3
9	22	15.3	12.0	10.0
10	14	14.7	15.3	−1.3
11	15	17.0	14.7	0.3
12	27	18.7	17.0	10.0
13	30	24.0	18.7	11.3
14	23	26.7	24.0	−1.0
15	15	22.7	26.7	−11.7

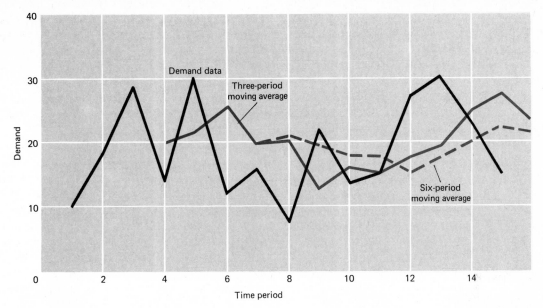

**Figure 4.2
Time-series data.**

With the weighted moving average, any desired weights can be specified so long as they add up to 1. For example, if we have the three demands $D_1 = 10$, $D_2 = 18$, and $D_3 = 29$, the ordinary three-period moving average is 19.0. With weights of .5, .3, and .2, the three-period weighted moving average is 21.9. In this case the weight of .5 was applied to the third period, .3 to the second period, and .2 to the first period. Notice how the weighted moving average has responded more rapidly to the increased demand. Notice also that the simple moving average is just a special case of the weighted moving average with all weights equal ($W_i = 1/N$).

One of the disadvantages of a weighted moving average is that the entire demand history for N periods must be carried along with the computation. Furthermore, the response of a weighted moving average cannot be easily changed without changing each of the weights. To overcome these difficulties, the method of exponential smoothing has been developed.

Exponential smoothing

Exponential smoothing is based on the very simple idea that a new average can be computed from an old average and the most recent observed demand. Suppose, for example, we have an old average of 20 and we have just observed a demand of 24. It stands to reason that the new average will lie between 20 and 24, depending on how much weight we want to put on the demand just observed versus the weight on the old average.

To formalize the above logic, we can write:

$$A_t = \alpha D_t + (1 - \alpha)A_{t-1} \tag{4.4}$$

In this case A_{t-1} is the old average (20), D_t the demand just observed (24), and α the proportion of weight placed on the new demand versus the old average ($0 \leq \alpha \leq 1$).

To illustrate, suppose we use the values $\alpha = .1$, $D_t = 24$ and $A_{t-1} = 20$. Then, from Equation (4.4), we have $A_t = 20.4$. If $\alpha = .5$, we have $A_t = 22$, and if $\alpha = .9$, we have $A_t = 23.6$. Thus A_t can vary between the old average of 20 and the demand of 24, depending on the value of α used.

If we want A_t to be very responsive to recent demand, we should choose a large value of α. If we want A_t to respond more slowly, then α should be smaller. In most forecasting work, α is given a value between .1 and .3 to maintain reasonable stability.

In simple exponential smoothing, just as in the case of moving averages, we assume that the time series is flat with no cycles and that there are no seasonal or trend components. Then the exponentially smoothed forecast for the next period is simply the average obtained through the current period. That is,

$$F_{t+1} = A_t$$

In this case the forecast is also offset one period from the smoothed average.

We can substitute the preceding relationship into Equation (4.4) to obtain the following equation:

$$F_{t+1} = \alpha D_t + (1 - \alpha)F_t \tag{4.5}$$

Sometimes this alternate form of simple (or first-order) exponential smoothing is more convenient to use than Equation (4.4) because it uses forecasts instead of averages.

Another way to view exponential smoothing is to rearrange the terms on the right-hand side of Equation (4.5) to yield:

$$F_{t+1} = F_t + \alpha(D_t - F_t)$$

This form indicates that the new forecast is the old forecast plus a proportion of the error between the observed demand and the old forecast. The proportion of error used can be controlled by the choice of α.

Students often wonder why the name "exponential smoothing" has been given to this method. This can be explained by writing Equation (4.5) in terms of all the previous demands. By substitution for F_t into Equation (4.5), we have

$$F_{t+1} = \alpha D_t + (1 - \alpha)[\alpha D_{t-1} + (1 - \alpha)F_{t-1}]$$

Then, substituting for F_{t-1} in the above equation, we have

$$F_{t+1} = \alpha D_t + (1 - \alpha)\alpha D_{t-1} + (1 - \alpha)(1 - \alpha)[\alpha D_{t-2} + (1 - \alpha)F_{t-2}]$$

If this substitution is continued, we will arrive at the expression

$$F_{t+1} = \alpha D_t + (1 - \alpha)\alpha D_{t-1} + (1 - \alpha)^2 \alpha D_{t-2}$$
$$+ \cdots + (1 - \alpha)^{t-1}\alpha D_1 + (1 - \alpha)^t F_1$$

This expression indicates that the weights on each preceding demand decrease exponentially until the demand from the first period and the initial forecast F_1 is reached.

If $\alpha = .3$ and $t = 3$, for example, we will have

$$F_4 = .3D_3 + .21\ D_2 + .147\ D_1 + .343\ F_1$$

Notice that the weights on the demands decrease exponentially over time and all the weights add up to one. Therefore, exponential smoothing is just a special form of the weighted average, with the weights decreasing exponentially over time.

In Box 4.3, two exponentially smoothed forecasts are computed for $\alpha = .1$ and $\alpha = .3$ using the same demand data as in Box 4.2. As can be seen, the $\alpha = .3$ forecast responds more rapidly to demand changes but is less stable than $\alpha = .1$. Which of these forecasts is then the best?

To answer this question, two measures of forecast errors are computed in Box 4.3. One measure is simply the arithmetic sum of all errors, which reflects the bias in the forecasting method. Ideally this sum should be 0. In Box 4.3, both methods have a positive bias, with $\alpha = .1$ producing more bias than $\alpha = .3$.

The second measure of forecast error is the absolute deviation. In this case the absolute value of the errors is added, so that negative errors do not cancel positive errors. The result is a measure of variance in the forecasting method. The total absolute deviation for $\alpha = .1$ is less than for $\alpha = .3$.

Thus, we have the interesting result that the $\alpha = .1$ forecast has more bias but less absolute deviation than the $\alpha = .3$ forecast. In this case there is no clear choice

BOX 4.3   **EXPONENTIAL SMOOTHING***

Period	D_t (demand)	F_t $\alpha = .1$ (forecast)	$D_t - F_t$ (error)	F_t $\alpha = .3$ (forecast)	$D_t - F_t$ (error)	MAD_t $(\alpha = .3)$	T (tracking signal)
1	10	15	−5.0	15	−5.0	6.4	−.8
2	18	14.5	3.5	13.5	4.5	5.8	−.1
3	29	14.85	14.15	14.85	14.15	8.3	1.6
4	15	16.26	−1.26	19.09	−4.09	7.1	1.3
5	30	16.14	13.86	17.86	12.14	8.6	2.5
6	12	17.52	−5.52	21.50	−9.50	8.8	1.4
7	16	16.97	−.97	18.65	−2.65	7.0	1.4
8	8	16.87	−8.87	17.85	−9.85	7.9	−.1
9	22	15.98	6.02	14.90	7.10	7.6	.9
10	14	16.58	−2.58	17.03	−3.03	6.2	.6
11	15	16.33	−1.33	16.12	−1.12	4.7	.6
12	27	16.19	10.81	15.78	11.22	6.7	2.1
13	30	17.27	12.73	19.15	10.85	7.9	3.1
14	23	18.54	4.46	22.40	0.60	5.7	4.4
15	15	18.99	−3.99	22.58	−7.58	6.4	2.8
$\Sigma(D_t - F_t)$			36.01		17.74		
$\Sigma\lvert D_t - F_t\rvert$			95.05		103.38		

* Assume $F_1 = 15$, as an arbitrary starting point. Also assume $MAD_0 = 7$. See pages 102–103 for definitions of MAD and tracking signal.

BIAS ERROR —

ABSOLUTE ERROR —

between the two methods; it just depends on one's preference between bias and deviation. However, if a forecast has both lower deviation and lower bias, then it is clearly preferred.

The procedure for choosing a value of α is now clear. A forecast should be computed for several values of α. If one value of α produces a forecast with less bias and less deviation than the others, then this value of α is preferred. If no clear choice exists, then a tradeoff between bias and deviation must be made in choosing the preferred value of α.

Unfortunately, simple exponential smoothing cannot always be used in practice because of trends or seasonal effects in the data. When these effects are present, second-order smoothing, third-order smoothing, trend-corrected smoothing, or seasonal smoothing might be used. Some of these more advanced methods are presented in the chapter supplement. [See Brown (1963) and Wheelwright and Makridakis (1977).]

Forecast errors

When exponential smoothing is used, whether it is simple smoothing or more advanced smoothing, an estimate of forecast error should be computed along with the smoothed average. This error estimate might be used for several purposes:

1. To set safety stocks or safety capacity and thereby ensure a desired level of protection against stockout
2. To monitor erratic demand observations or outliers which should be carefully evaluated and perhaps rejected from the data
3. To determine when the forecasting method is no longer tracking actual demand and needs to be reset

The first use will be covered later in the text, but the last two uses are described more completely below.

When exponential smoothing is used, it is common to calculate the smoothed mean absolute deviation or MAD, which is defined as follows:

$$\text{MAD}_t = \alpha|D_t - F_t| + (1 - \alpha)\text{MAD}_{t-1}$$

In this case the new MAD, or MAD_t, is simply a fraction α of the current absolute deviation plus $(1 - \alpha)$ times the old MAD. This is analogous to Equation (4.4), since the MAD is being smoothed in the same way as the average.

The current MAD_t should be computed each period along with the forecast average. The MAD can then be used to detect an outlier in demand by comparing the observed deviation with the MAD. If the observed deviation is greater than 3.75 MAD, we have reason to suspect that the demand may be an extreme value. This is comparable to determining whether an observed demand value lies outside three standard deviations for the normal distribution. In Box 4.3 MAD was computed for $\alpha = .3$. As can be seen, none of the demand errors fall outside 3.75 MAD, so no outliers are suspected in the data.

The second use of MAD is to determine whether the forecast is tracking with the actual time-series values. To determine this, a tracking signal is computed, as follows:

$$\text{Tracking signal} = T = \frac{\text{cumulative sum of forecast deviation}}{\text{MAD}}$$

The tracking signal is thus a computation of bias in the numerator divided by the most recent estimate of MAD. If demand variations are assumed to be random, then control limits of ±6 on the tracking signal should ensure only a 3 percent probability that the limits will be exceeded by chance.[1] Thus, when the tracking signal exceeds ±6, the forecasting method should be stopped and reset to more nearly equal observed demand. In Box 4.3, the tracking signal does not exceed ±6 in any period. Therefore the forecast is considered to be tracking sufficiently close to actual demand.

In computerized forecasting systems it is extremely important to incorporate error controls of the type discussed above. This will ensure that the system does not run out of control. Instead, the user is notified when outliers in demand are detected or when the tracking signal becomes too large.

Advanced time-series forecasting

A variation of exponential smoothing which has received considerable recent attention is *adaptive* exponential smoothing. In one form of this approach, Chow (1965) used first-order smoothing but varied the smoothing coefficient at each forecast by ±.05 to determine which of the three forecasts had the lowest forecast error. The resulting value of α was used for the next period forecast. The smoothing coefficient was allowed to increase to a maximum of .95 and to decrease to a minimum of .05.

Another type of adaptive smoothing called variable-response smoothing is used by IBM in its INFOREM inventory software package. For this method, α is set equal to the value of the tracking signal normalized to be between 0 and 1. If there is a large forecasting error, the tracking signal and α will be large until the forecast comes back on track. When the tracking signal is smaller, α will also be small and a stable forecast will result. This method appears to work quite well for retail and wholesale inventory forecasting situations. [See IBM (1978).] For other references on adaptive smoothing, see Whybark (1972), Trigg and Leach (1967), and Raine (1971).

Table 4.3 summarizes four time-series-forecasting methods. We have already discussed two of them, moving average and exponential smoothing, at some length. The remaining two are described briefly below.

Any desired mathematical model can be fitted to a time series such as the one

---

[1] These numerical limits and probabilities are based on the normal probability distribution and a value of $\alpha = .1$. [See Thomopoulos (1980), p. 306.]

TABLE 4.3
TIME-SERIES-FORECASTING METHODS

Time-series methods	Description of method	Uses	Accuracy			Identification of turning point	Relative cost	References
			Short-term	Medium-term	Long-term			
1. Moving averages	Forecast is based on arithmetic average or weighted average of a given number of past data points.	Short- to medium-range planning for inventories, production levels, and scheduling. Good for many products.	Poor to good	Poor	Very poor	Poor	Low	Neter and Wasserman
2. Exponential smoothing	Similar to moving average, with exponentially more weight placed on recent data. Well adapted to computer use and large number of items to be forecast.	Same as moving average.	Fair to very good	Poor to good	Very poor	Poor	Low	Brown, Adams, Wheelwright, and Makridakis
3. Mathematical models	A linear or nonlinear model fitted to time-series data, usually by regression methods. Includes trend lines, polynomials, log-linear, Fourier series, etc.	Same as moving average but limited, due to expense, to a few products.	Very good	Fair to good	Very poor	Poor	Low to medium	
4. Box-Jenkins	Autocorrelation methods are used to identify underlying time series and to fit the "best" model. Requires about 60 past data points.	Limited, due to expense, to products requiring very accurate short-range forecasts.	Very good to excellent	Fair to good	Very poor	Poor	Medium to high	Box-Jenkins and Nelson

Source: Reprinted by permission of the *Harvard Business Review.* Exhibit adapted from John C. Chambers, Satinder K. Mullick, and Donald D. Smith, "How to Choose the Right Forecasting Technique," July–August 1971, pp. 55–56. Copyright © 1971 by the President and Fellows of Harvard College; all rights reserved.

shown in Equation (4.1), with level, trend, and seasonal components. For example, a model can be fitted by the methods of linear regression or Fourier series analysis. In some cases the resulting model may provide a more accurate forecast than exponential smoothing. However, a custom-fitted model is more expensive, so the tradeoff between accuracy and model cost must be made.

Within the past few years, the sophisticated Box-Jenkins method has been developed for time-series forecasting. This technique has a special phase for model identification, and it permits more precise analysis of proposed models than is possible with the other methods. The Box-Jenkins method, however, requires about sixty periods of past data and is too expensive to use for routine forecasting of many items. For a special forecast of sales involving a costly decision, however, the use of Box-Jenkins may be warranted.

In summary, time-series methods are useful for short- or medium-range forecasts when the demand pattern is expected to remain stable. Time-series forecasts are often inputs to decisions concerning aggregate output planning, budgeting, resource allocation, inventory, and scheduling. Time-series forecasts are not typically useful for decisions on facility planning or process selection because of the long time spans involved.

4.4 CAUSAL FORECASTING METHODS

In general, causal forecasting methods develop a cause-and-effect model between demand and other variables. For example, the demand for ice cream may be related to population, the average summer temperature, and time. Data can be collected on these variables and an analysis conducted to determine the validity of the proposed model. One of the best-known causal methods is regression, which will be described next, followed by very brief descriptions of additional causal methods.

For regression methods, a model must be specified before the data are collected and the analysis is conducted. The simplest case is the following single-variable linear model:

$$\hat{y} = a + bx$$

where $\hat{y}$ = estimated demand
  x = independent variable (hypothesized to cause $\hat{y}$)
  a = y intercept
  b = slope

For this model, we assume that n pairs of x and y values have been observed. We denote these pairs $(x_1, y_1), (x_2, y_2), \ldots, (x_n, y_n)$. Notice that the symbol y denotes observed values of y and that the symbol $\hat{y}$ denotes points on the line expressed by the equation $\hat{y} = a + bx$.

The situation is shown in Figure 4.3. The y values which have been observed do not fall exactly on the line because of random errors in the data. For each observed point, the error can be expressed as $\hat{y}_i - y_i$, and the total variance or squared error

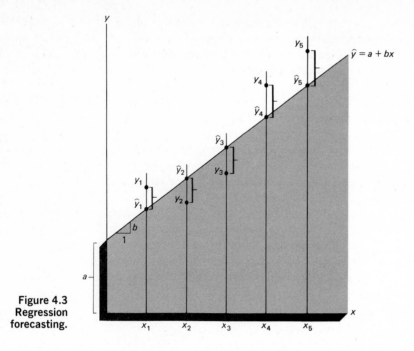

Figure 4.3
Regression
forecasting.

due to all the points is then

$$\Sigma(\hat{y}_i - y_i)^2 = \Sigma(a + b\,x_i - y_i)^2$$

In regression analysis, the objective is to minimize the error equation shown above by choosing values of a and b. The minimum error can be found by using calculus, which results in the following set of equations:

$$a = \frac{\Sigma y_i}{n} - b\,\frac{\Sigma x_i}{n} \tag{4.6}$$

$$b = \frac{n\Sigma x_i y_i - [(\Sigma x_i)(\Sigma y_i)]}{n\Sigma x_1^2 - (\Sigma x_i)^2} \tag{4.7}$$

For a given set of n data pairs (x_1, y_1), (x_2, y_2), . . . , (x_n, y_n), the values of a and b can be found from Equations (4.6) and (4.7). These values describe the straight line which is the best (least squares) predictor of demand y based on the independent variable x.

We can also calculate the strength of the relationship between y and x by means of r^2, the coefficient of determination.[2] The value of r^2 represents the proportion of variation in y which is explained by the relationship with x; the remainder of the variation $1 - r^2$ being due to chance or factors other than x. It is therefore desirable to have the value of r^2 as close to 1 as possible.

---

[2] The correlation coefficient r is the square root of the coefficient of determination. However, r^2 has a direct physical meaning, which r does not have.

A value of $r^2 = .8$ indicates that 80 percent of the variation in y is predicted or explained by the regression line with x; only 20 percent is due to chance. In this case, a quite reliable forecast for y can be obtained when the value of x is known.

The quantity r^2 can be computed as follows:

$$r^2 = \frac{[n\Sigma x_i y_i - (\Sigma x_i)(\Sigma y_i)]^2}{[n\Sigma x_i^2 - (\Sigma x_i)^2][n\Sigma y_i^2 - (\Sigma y_i)^2]}$$

We will illustrate linear regression forecasting with a simple example. Suppose we are interested in estimating the demand for newspapers on the basis of the local population. The demand for newspapers over the past 8 years and the corresponding population in a small town are shown in Table 4.4. Using the available data, the first step is to compute the values of a and b for the line. This is done by computing the cross product of xy and the values of x^2 as shown in the table. If the totals of all columns are obtained, the data are then available to plug into Equations (4.6) and (4.7). The result in this case is $a = -1.34$, $b = 2.01$. The best (least squares) equation for predicting demand for newspapers is thus $y = -1.34 + 2.01x$.

In a similar way, the value of r^2 was computed from Table 4.4, resulting in $r^2 = .97$. This indicates that the straight-line regression equation shown above explains 97 percent of the variation in newspaper demand; only 3 percent of the variation is unexplained or due to chance. As shown by the high value of r^2, population is a very good predictor of newspaper demand. If population can be projected accurately for the future, we can also accurately forecast newspaper demand through the regression equation.

Simple linear regression indicates the principles of causal forecasting. The forecast for demand is related to one or more variables which are hypothesized to be independent in nature. It is the user's responsibility to determine the appropriate causal variables and whether the relationships are linear, nonlinear, additive, or multiplicative. In other words, the form of the forecasting model must be specified by the user.

Single-variable regression can be extended to multiple regression, which utilizes more than one x variable. Because of the additional variables, multiple regression is

TABLE 4.4   **REGRESSION EXAMPLE***

i	y_i	x_i	$x_i y_i$	x_i^2	y_i^2
1	3.0	2.0	6.0	4.0	9.0
2	3.5	2.4	8.4	5.8	12.3
3	4.1	2.8	11.5	7.8	16.8
4	4.4	3.0	13.2	9.0	19.4
5	5.0	3.2	16.0	10.2	25.0
6	5.7	3.6	20.5	13.0	32.5
7	6.4	3.8	24.3	14.4	41.0
8	7.0	4.0	28.0	16.0	49.0
	39.1	24.8	127.9	80.2	205.0

* The demand for newspapers y_i is expressed in thousands of copies. The population x_i is expressed in ten thousands of people.

often more useful than simple regression in practice. For the newspaper example, we might hypothesize that demand for newspapers is related not only to population but also to family income and educational level. These additional variables might help explain more of the variation in newspapers sales, although the single-variable model is already very good in this case.

One example of the use of multiple regression for demand forecasting has been given by Armstrong and Grohman (1972). They developed the following model for predicting U.S. air travel:

$$M_{t+f} = (1.12)^f M_t \left(\frac{P_{t+f}}{P_t}\right)^{-1.2} \left(\frac{S_{t+f}}{S_t}\right)^{0.2} \left(\frac{I_{t+f}}{I_t}\right)^{0.5} \left(\frac{N_{t+f}}{N_t}\right)^{1.0} \left(\frac{D_{t+f}}{D_t}\right)^{-.05}$$

where t = current year
  f = number of years in the future
  M = U.S. domestic revenue passenger miles
  P = price of air travel (cents per passenger mile in constant dollars)
  S = average airborne speed (miles per hour)
  I = measure of income (GNP per capita in constant dollars)
  N = U.S. population
  D = death rate per 100 million revenue passenger miles

In their study, Armstrong and Grohman compared the forecast obtained from the above model to qualitative forecasts and time-series forecasts. The above causal model was found to provide superior forecasts in this case.

Other forms of causal forecasting—econometric models, input-output models, and simulation models—are described in Table 4.5. In general, these models are more complex and more costly to develop than regression models. However, in situations where it is necessary to model a segment of the economy in detail, the econometric or input-output models may be appropriate.

Simulation models are especially useful when a distribution or logistics system is modeled for forecasting purposes. Chambers, Mullick, and Smith (1971) describe such a simulation model for forecasting the demand for TV picture tubes. In this case a simulation model was built representing the distribution pipeline from the glass-tube manufacturer to the TV tube manufacturer to the TV set manufacturer and finally to wholesale and retail distribution chains; all imports, inventories, and exports from the system were included. Through the use of this model, a quite accurate forecast for glass TV tubes several years into the future was obtained.

One of the most important features of causal models is that they can be used to predict turning points in the demand function. In contrast, time-series models can be used only to predict the future demand pattern on the basis of the past; they cannot predict upturns and downturns in the demand level.

Because of this ability to predict turning points, causal models are usually more accurate than time-series models for medium- to long-range forecasts. Causal models are, therefore, more widely useful for facility and process planning in operations.

TABLE 4.5
CAUSAL FORECASTING METHODS

Causal methods	Description of method	Uses	Accuracy			Identification of turning point	Relative cost	References
			Short-term	Medium-term	Long-term			
1. Regression	This method relates demand to other external or internal variables which tend to cause demand changes. The method of regression uses least squares to obtain a best fit between the variables.	Short- to medium-range planning for aggregate production or inventory involving a few products. Useful where strong causal relationships exist.	Good to very good	Good to very good	Poor	Very good	Medium	Neter and Wasserman
2. Econometric model	A system of interdependent regression equations that describes some sector of economic sales or profit activity.	Forecast of sales by product classes for short- to medium-range planning.	Very good to excellent	Very good	Good	Excellent	High	Huang
3. Input-output model	A method of forecasting which describes the flows from one sector of the economy to another. Predicts the inputs required to produce required outputs in another sector.	Forecasts of company- or countrywide sales by industrial sectors	Not available	Good to very good	Good to very good	Fair	Very high	Leontief
4. Simulation model	Simulation of the distribution system describing the changes in sales and flows of product over time. Reflects effects of the distribution pipeline.	Forecasts of company-wide sales by major product groups.	Very good	Good to very good	Good	Good	High	Forrester, Chambers, et al.

Source: Reprinted by permission of the *Harvard Business Review*. Exhibit adapted from John C. Chambers, Satinder K. Mullick, and Donald D. Smith, "How to Choose the Right Forecasting Technique," July–August 1971, pp. 56–57. Copyright © 1971 by the President and Fellows of Harvard College; all rights reserved.

4.5 COMPUTERIZED FORECASTING SYSTEMS

Many computerized systems are available today to assist the manager and forecasting analyst. A few of these systems are briefly described below.

A program called CENSUS X-11 is available from the U.S. Census Bureau. It uses a moving-average method with trends and seasonal factors to decompose and forecast a time series. The CENSUS X-11 program has been found to be quite useful provided that a reasonable amount of historical data is available. See Shiskin, Young, and Musgrave (1967) for more details.

There is also a library of interactive computer forecasting programs called SIBYL/RUNNER; it contains over twenty of the most commonly used forecasting techniques. These programs are divided into those which assist in identifying the underlying patterns in the time series and those which forecast using a given pattern. A complete description is given by Makridakis and Wheelwright (1977).

The IBM software package INFOREM contains a forecasting module which utilizes variable-response exponential smoothing. This package includes a large number of error-detection and control features to assist the user in handling a large number of items. The forecasting routines were specifically designed for input to inventory control applications in retail and wholesale trade, where many thousands of items must be continually forecasted and monitored. Details are contained in the IBM INFOREM manual (1978).

The causal forecasting methods are quite well covered by standard statistical packages such as SPSS and BMDP. These methods will, however, have to be substantially tailored to the individual situation.

4.6 SELECTING A FORECASTING METHOD

In this section we will present a framework for selecting from among qualitative, time-series, and causal methods. The framework is based in large part on the survey conducted by Wheelwright and Clarke (1976), who identified factors that companies consider important when they select a forecasting method. The most important of these factors are as follows:

1. **USER AND SYSTEM SOPHISTICATION.** How sophisticated are the managers who are expected to use the forecasting results? It has been found that the forecasting method must be matched to the knowledge and sophistication of the user. Generally speaking, managers are reluctant to use results from techniques they do not understand.

Another, related factor is the status of forecasting systems currently in use. Wheelwright and Clarke found that forecasting systems tend to evolve toward more mathematically sophisticated methods; they do not change in one grand step. So the method chosen must not be too advanced or sophisticated for its users or too far advanced beyond the current forecasting system.

2. **TIME AND RESOURCES AVAILABLE.** The selection of a forecasting method will depend on the time available in which to collect the data and prepare the forecast. This

may involve the time of users, forecasters, and data collectors. The time required is also closely related to the necessary resources and the costs of the forecasting method. The preparation of a complicated forecast for which most of the data must be collected may take several months and cost thousands of dollars. For routine forecasts made by computerized systems, both the cost and the amount of time required may be very modest.

3. USE OR DECISION CHARACTERISTICS. As was pointed out in the beginning of the chapter, the forecasting method must be related to the use or decisions required. The use, in turn, is closely related to such characteristics as accuracy required, time horizon of the forecast, and number of items to be forecast. For example, inventory and scheduling decisions require highly accurate short-range forecasts for a large number of items. Time-series methods are ideally suited to these requirements. On the other hand, decisions involving process and facility planning are long range in nature; they require less accuracy for, perhaps, a single estimate of total demand. Qualitative or causal methods tend to be more appropriate for those decisions. In the middle time range are aggregate planning and budgeting decisions which often utilize time-series or causal methods.

4. DATA AVAILABILITY. The choice of forecasting method is often constrained by available data. An econometric model might require data which are simply not available in the short run; therefore another method must be selected. The Box-Jenkins time-series method requires about sixty data points (5 years of monthly data).

5. DATA PATTERN. The pattern in the data will affect the type of forecasting method selected. If the time series is flat, as we have assumed in most of this chapter, a first-order method can be used. However, if the data show trends or seasonal patterns, more advanced methods will be needed. The pattern in the data will also determine whether a time-series method will suffice or whether causal models are needed. If the data pattern is unstable over time, a qualitative method may be selected. Thus the data pattern is one of the most important factors affecting the selection of a forecasting method.

Another issue concerning the selection of forecasting methods is the difference between fit and prediction. When different models are tested, it is often thought that the model with the best fit to historical data (least error) is also the best predictive model. This is not true. For example, suppose demand observations are obtained over the last eight time periods and we want to fit the best time-series model to these data. A polynomial model of degree seven can be made to fit exactly through each of the past eight data points.[3] But this model is not necessarily the best predictor of the future.

The best predictive model is one which describes the underlying time series but is not "force fitted" to the data. The correct way to fit models based on past data is to separate model fit and model prediction. First, the data set is divided into two parts.

---

[3] The model would be $y = a_1 + a_2 t + a_3 t^2 + \cdots + a_8 t^7$, where t = time.

Several models based on reasonable assumptions about seasonality, trend, and cycle are then fitted to the first data set. These models are used to predict values for the second data set, and the one with the lowest error on the second set is the best model. This approach utilizes fit on the first data set and prediction on the second as a basis for model selection.

Finally, an interesting question concerning model selection is the accuracy of qualitative human forecasting versus quantitative model-based forecasting. Ebert (1976) compared humans to models for a variety of underlying time-series demand patterns. He found that, when the data included a great deal of random noise or non-linear seasonal patterns, models did better than humans provided that care was taken in fitting the models. However, when simple (first-order) exponential models with an arbitrary value of α were used, the humans often performed better than the models. This research indicates that quantitative models do not always provide better forecasts than humans.

4.7   USING FORECASTS IN ORGANIZATIONS

Every forecasting method must be embedded in an organizational setting. However, some unusual things can happen to forecasts within their organizational contexts. First of all, forecasts are often passed from one manager or group to another through successive levels of the organization. In the process, these forecasts are sometimes modified or information is lost. This may stem from a lack of a clear distinction among goals, performance measures, and forecasts.

When sales forecasts are made by the marketing department, they are sometimes really goals rather than forecasts. These so-called sales forecasts are set on the high side in order to push salespeople on to greater achievement. Such "forecasts" cannot be used by operations as a basis for output or production planning because they are inspirational targets which will probably not be met.

On the other hand, sometimes performance measures are confused with forecasts. When performance measures are being set, it is customary for each manager up the line to reduce the so-called forecast slightly so that it can easily be met or even exceeded. The pessimistic forecasts that result will probably be exceeded at each level and are also not suitable for output planning by operations.

A forecast should be an unbiased projection of what we expect *will* happen. The forecast should not be confused with a plan, a goal, or a performance measure which indicates what we think *should* happen.

One way to avoid this problem is to ask that forecasts be based on probability. This can be done by producing a frequency distribution showing the likelihood of various forecast estimates. Another approach is to forecast pessimistic, most likely, and optimistic demand values which can be defined in terms of percentiles: the pessimistic at the tenth percentile, the most likely at the fiftieth percentile, and the optimistic at the ninetieth percentile. When such a range of values is produced and transmitted through the organization, the confusion between what will happen and what should happen is greatly reduced.

Very few organizations routinely produce probability forecasts for demand. This stems from a failure to recognize uncertainty and to come to grips with the problem. If probability forecasts are produced, one can plan for contingencies and properly assess the risk inherent in a decision. Without such estimates, the plan cannot properly account for uncertainty or, worse yet, will be set at a medium or low level so that it can be exceeded.

A second issue in using forecasts in organizations is the question of who should make the forecasts. There are many possibilities—including marketing, operations, finance, a central corporate forecasting office, and various corporate or division levels depending on the size and type of organization. Forecasts of total sales and sales by major product are often made by marketing. Since it may not be clear whether these ''forecasts'' are goals or performance measures, other departments may modify the marketing forecasts (usually downward) for their own planning purposes.

Operations has a special problem, because the total sales forecasts and forecasts by product lines are too aggregated for inventory and scheduling decisions. Furthermore, if the marketing department's accuracy is questionable (for the reasons already mentioned), separate and more detailed forecasts will need to be made by operations. While accurate sales forecasting is considered desirable by marketing, it is absolutely essential for operations in order to control inventories and production capacity. For these reasons, the time-series methods, including exponential smoothing, have been pioneered by operations and are widely used in industry. It is unfortunate, however, that the communications problems in organizations sometimes lead different departments to use different forecasts.

Ideally, sales forecasts should be made by quantitative methods when possible, and then it makes little difference who makes the forecasts. All users, however, should have an input to and knowledge of the assumptions behind the models. The aggregate and individual forecasts should be additive, resulting in more coordinated planning by the various functions. The forecasting responsibility must also be carefully coordinated and monitored, because otherwise inflated inventories and missed delivery dates can result. When forecasting is really the driving force behind planning, it must be done carefully.

4.8 KEY POINTS

Demand forecasts are crucial inputs to planning decisions within operations and other parts of business. In this chapter, we have highlighted some of the important uses and methods of forecasting. Some of the chapter's main points are the following:

- Different decisions require different forecasting methods, including the following decisions in operations: process design, capacity planning, and inventory management. The available methods may be classified as qualitative, time-series, and causal methods.

- Four of the most important qualitative methods are Delphi, market surveys, life-cycle analogy, and informed judgment. These methods are most useful when historical data are not available or are not reliable in predicting the future. Qualitative methods are used primarily for long- or medium-range forecasting involving process design or facilities planning.
- Time-series forecasting is used to decompose demand data into their principal components and thereby to project the historical pattern forward in time. the primary uses are short- to medium-term forecasting for inventory and scheduling decisions. Some of the best-known time-series techniques are the moving average, exponential smoothing, mathematical models, and the Box-Jenkins method.
- Causal forecasting methods include regression, econometric models, input-output models, and simulation models. These methods attempt to establish a cause-and-effect relationship between demand and other variables. Causal methods can help in predicting turning points in time-series data and are therefore most useful for medium- to long-range forecasting.
- Two types of errors in forecasting are bias and deviation. Both these errors should be monitored routinely to control the accuracy of the forecasts obtained.
- A forecasting method should be selected on the basis of five factors: user and system sophistication, time and resources available, use/decision characteristics, data availability, and data pattern.
- In many organizations, different forecasts are made by different departments and there is no coordinated planning. This may be caused by confusion about goals, plans, performance measures, and forecasts. To help overcome this confusion, probability forecasts can be used.

QUESTIONS

1. Is there a difference between forecasting demand and forecasting sales? Can demand be forecast from historical sales data?
2. What is the distinction between forecasting and planning? How can organizations become confused over forecasting when this distinction is not clear?
3. Define the terms "qualitative method," "time-series method," and "causal forecast."
4. It has been said that qualitative forecasting methods should be used only as a last resort. Comment.
5. Describe the uses of qualitative, time-series, and causal forecasts.
6. How could the Delphi method be used to predict, for 5 years into the future, the demand for hospital beds in a given community? Under what circumstances would you recommend use of the Delphi method?
7. It has been said that qualitative forecasts and causal forecasts are not particularly useful as inputs to inventory and scheduling decisions. Why is this statement true?
8. What type of time-series components would you expect for the following items?
   a. Monthly sales of a retail florist
   b. Monthly sales of milk in a supermarket
   c. Daily demand for telephone calls
   d. Monthly demand for newspapers
9. What are the advantages of exponential smoothing over the moving average and weighted moving average?
10. How should the choice of α be made for exponential smoothing?
11. Describe the difference between "fit" and "prediction" for forecasting models.

12. A request has gone out to all salespeople in a company to make forecasts for their sales territories for next year. These forecasts will be aggregated by product lines, districts, regions, and—finally—at the national level. Describe the problems in using this forecast for planning aggregate levels of operations for the next year and for specific inventory and scheduling decisions.

13. What are the advantages and disadvantages of preparing a probability forecast of demand?

14. In the Stokely Company, marketing makes a sales forecast each year by developing a sales-force composite. Meanwhile, operations makes a forecast of sales based on past data, trends, and seasonal components. The operations forecast usually turns out to be an increase over last year but still 20 percent less than the forecast of the marketing department. How should forecasting in this company be done?

PROBLEMS

1. In the Atlanta area, the number of daily calls for repair of Speedy copy machines has been recorded as follows:

October	Calls
1	132
2	180
3	95
4	100
5	120
6	145
7	190
8	85

   a. Prepare a three-period moving-average forecast for the data. What is the error on each day?

   b. Prepare a three-period weighted-moving-average forecast using weights of $w_1 = .5$, $w_2 = .3$, $w_3 = .2$.

   c. Which of these two forecasts is the best?

2. The Handy-Dandy department store had forecast sales of $110,000 for the last week. The actual sales turned out to be $125,000.

   a. What is the forecast for this week, using exponential smoothing and $\alpha = .1$?

   b. If sales this week turn out to be $115,000, what is the forecast for next week?

3. Using the data in Problem 1, prepare exponentially smoothed forecasts for the following cases:

   a. $\alpha = .1$ and $F_1 = 120$

   b. $\alpha = .3$ and $F_1 = 120$

4. Compute the errors of bias and absolute deviation for the forecasts in Problem 3. Which of the forecasting models is the best?

5. A grocery store sells the following number of frozen turkeys over the 1-week period prior to Thanksgiving:

	Turkeys sold
Monday	50
Tuesday	30
Wednesday	60
Thursday	20
Friday	70
Saturday	90

a. Forecast the sales for each day, starting with $F_1 = 60$ and $\alpha = .2$.

b. Compute the MAD and the tracking signal for the data given above in each period. Use $MAD_0 = 0$.

c. On the basis of the criteria given in the text, are the demand and tracking signal within tolerances?

6. The manager of Redline Trucking Company believes that the demand for tires used on his trucks is closely related to the number of miles driven. Accordingly, the following data covering the past 6 months have been collected.

Month	Tires used	Thousands of miles driven
1	100	1000
2	150	1400
3	120	1200
4	80	800
5	90	900
6	180	1800

a. Calculate the coefficients a and b for the regression line.

b. What percentage of the variation in tire use can be explained by mileage driven?

c. Suppose we plan to drive 1,300,000 miles next month. What is the expected number of tires that will be used?

*7. The daily demand for chocolate donuts from the Donut-Hole Shop has been recorded for a 2-week period.

Day	Demand	Day	Demand
1	80	8	85
2	95	9	97
3	120	10	110
4	100	11	90
5	75	12	80
6	60	13	65
7	50	14	50

a. Forecast the demand using second order exponential smoothing. Use values of $A_0 = 80$, $T_0 = 20$, and $\alpha = \beta = .2$.

b. Does this appear to be a good model for the data?

SELECTED BIBLIOGRAPHY

ADAM, EVERETT E., JR.: "Individual Item Forecasting Model Evaluation," *Decision Sciences,* vol. 4, October 1973, pp. 458–470.

ARMSTRONG, J. SCOTT, and MICHAEL C. GROHMAN: "A Comparative Study of Methods for Long-Range Market Forecasting," *Management Science,* vol. 19, no. 2, October 1972, pp. 211–221.

BASS, FRANK M., CHARLES W. KING, and EDGAR A. PESSEMEIER (eds.): *Applications of the Sciences in Marketing Management,* New York: Wiley, 1968.

BASU, SHANKAR, and ROGER G. SCHROEDER: "Incorporating Judgements in Sales Forecasts: Application of the Delphi Method at American Hoist & Derrick," *Interfaces,* vol. 7, no. 3, May 1977, pp. 18–27.

* This problem requires use of the supplement.

Box, G. E. P., and G. M. Jenkins: *Time Series Analysis, Forecasting, and Control,* San Francisco: Holden-Day, 1970.

Brown, R. G.: *Smoothing, Forecasting and Prediction,* Englewood Cliffs, N.J.: Prentice-Hall, 1963.

Chambers, John C., Satinder K. Mullick, and Donald D. Smith: "How to Choose the Right Forecasting Technique," *Harvard Business Review,* July–August 1971, pp. 45–74.

Chow, W. M.: "Adaptive Control of the Exponential Smoothing Constant," *Journal of Industrial Engineering,* September–October 1965.

Dalrymple, Douglas J.: "Sales Forecasting Methods and Accuracy," *Business Horizons,* December 1975, pp. 69–73.

Ebert, Ronald J.: "A Comparison of Human and Statistical Forecasting," *AIIE Transactions,* vol. 8, no. 1, March 1976, pp. 120–127.

Forrester, Jay W.: *Industrial Dynamics,* Cambridge, Mass.: M.I.T. Press, 1961.

Groff, Gene: "Empirical Comparisons of Models for Short Range Forecasting," *Management Sciences,* vol. 20, no. 1, September 1973, pp. 22–31.

Huang, D. S.: *Regression and Econometric Methods,* New York: Wiley, 1970.

International Business Machines: "INFOREM: Principles of Inventory Management Application Description," GE20-0571-0, January 1978.

Leontief, Wassily W.: *Input-Output Statistics,* New York: Oxford University Press, 1966.

Makridakis, Spyros, and Steven Wheelwright: *Interactive Forecasting,* San Francisco: Holden-Day, 1977.

Nelson, Charles L.: *Applied Time Series Analysis,* San Francisco: Holden-Day, 1973.

Neter, John, William Wasserman, and G. A. Whitmore: *Fundamental Statistics for Business & Economics,* 4th ed., Boston: Allyn and Bacon, 1973.

North, Harper Q., and Donald Pyke: "Probes of the Technological Future," *Harvard Business Review,* May–June 1969, pp. 68–82.

Raine, J. E.: "Self-Adaptive Forecasting Reconsidered," *Decision Sciences,* vol. 2, no. 2, April 1971, pp. 181–191.

Shiskin, Julius, Allan H. Young, and John Musgrave: "The X-11 Variant of the Census Method II Seasonal Adjustment Program," Bureau of the Census, Technical Paper no. 15, February 1967.

Spencer, Milton H., Colin G. Clark, and Peter W. Hoguet: *Business & Economic Forecasting,* Homewood, Ill.: Irwin, 1961.

Thomopoulos, Nick T.: *Applied Forecasting Methods,* Englewood Cliffs, N.J.: Prentice-Hall, 1980.

Trigg, D. W., and A. G. Leach: "Exponential Smoothing with an Adaptive Response Rate," *Operational Research Quarterly,* vol, 18, no. 1, March 1967, pp 53–59.

Vollmann, Thomas E.: *Operations Management: A Systems Model-Building Approach,* Reading, Mass.: Addison-Wesley, 1973.

Wheelwright, Steven, and Darral G. Clarke: "Corporate Forecasting: Promise and Reality," *Harvard Business Review,* November–December 1976, pp. 40–60.

——, and Spyros Makridakis: *Forecasting Methods for Management,* 2d ed., New York: Wiley, 1977.

Whybark, D. C.: "A Comparison of Adaptive Forecasting Techniques," *The Logistics and Transportation Review,* vol. 8, no. 3, 1972, pp. 13–26.

Winters, Peter R.: "Forecasting Sales by Exponentially Weighted Moving Averages," *Management Sciences,* April 1960, pp. 324–342.

SUPPLEMENT: ADVANCED METHODS

This supplement describes two additional exponential smoothing methods for time-series forecasting which have trend and seasonal components. These methods are extensions of first-order exponential smoothing as described in Section 4.3.

When the time-series model has a trend component, a smoothing model can be developed which is based on updating two variables in each time period, an average level and a trend. [See Vollmann (1973).] The average level is computed as an expanded version of the first-order equation to include trend, as follows:

$$A_t = \alpha D_t + (1 - \alpha)(A_{t-1} + T_{t-1})$$

This average is then, in turn, used to update the estimate of trend by taking the difference in averages and smoothing this difference with the old trend. The updated trend is thus

$$T_t = \beta(A_t - A_{t-1}) + (1 - \beta)T_{t-1}$$

In this case, the smoothing constant β, which can be the same or different than the constant α used for level, is used for trend. The model requires initial estimates of A_0 and T_0 to get started. These estimates can be based either on judgment or on past data.

Using the above values, we can compute forecasts for the future. The procedure is now slightly different than the first-order case, because a constant trend is assumed in the time series. The forecast for period $t + K$ in the future is therefore

$$F_{t+K} = A_t + KT_t \quad K = 1, 2, 3, \ldots$$

One unit of trend is added for each period into the future. An example using these formulas is shown in Table S4.1.

Time series having both trend and seasonal components can be forecast by a method developed by Winters (1960). In this case three variables—average, trend, and a seasonal factor—are updated for each time period.

The average is computed for period t as follows:

$$A_t = \alpha\left(\frac{D_t}{R_{t-L}}\right) + (1 - \alpha)(A_{t-1} + T_{t-1})$$

TABLE S4.1   **TREND-ADJUSTED EXPONENTIAL SMOOTHING***

t	D_t (demand)	A_t (average)	T_t (trend)	F_t (forecast)	$D_t - F_t$ (error)
1	85	85	15	85	0
2	105	100.5	15.05	100	5.00
3	112	115.2	15.01	115.55	−3.55
4	132	130.4	15.03	130.21	1.79
5	145	145.4	15.03	145.43	−.43

* Assume $A_0 = 70$, $T_0 = 15$, $\alpha = .1$, $\beta = .1$

In this case the demand is adjusted by the seasonal ratio and smoothed with the old average and old trend. The trend for period t is

$$T_t = \beta(A_t - A_{t-1}) + (1 - \beta)T_{t-1}$$

The seasonal ratio for period t is

$$R_t = \gamma\left(\frac{D_t}{A_t}\right) + (1 - \gamma)R_{t-L}$$

In this case we are assuming that the seasonal cycle is L periods. There are L seasonal ratios, one for each period. If the demand is monthly and the seasonal cycle repeats on an annual basis, then $L = 12$. Each month, one of the seasonal ratios will be updated to a new value, along with the trend and average.

The model requires initial estimates of A_0, T_0, and R_0, R_{-1}, . . . , R_{-L+1}. These initial estimates can be based on judgment or data, if available.

Using the updated values, the forecast for future periods in period t is

$$F_{t+K} = (A_t + KT_t)(R_{t-L+K})$$

An example of this method is shown in Table S4.2.

If there is no trend, Winters's method can also be used with seasonal factors alone. In this case, the above trend equation and T_t values are simply dropped from the method.

TABLE S4.2   **WINTERS'S SEASONAL EXPONENTIAL SMOOTHING***

t	D_t (demand)	A_t (average)	T_t (trend)	R_t (seasonal ratio)	F_t (forecast)	$D_t - F_t$ (error)
1	66	80.5	10.1	.804	64	2.0
2	106	90.1	10.0	1.195	108.7	−2.7
3	78	99.5	9.9	.799	80.4	−2.4
4	135	110.1	10.0	1.201	130.7	4.3

* Assume $A_0 = 70$, $T_0 = 10$, $L = 2$, $R_{-1} = .8$, $R_0 = 1.2$, $\alpha = .2$, $\beta = .2$, $\gamma = .2$.

PART II

PROCESS DESIGN

- PROCESS SELECTION
- CHOICE OF TECHNOLOGY
- PROCESS-FLOW ANALYSIS
- LAYOUT OF FACILITIES

INVENTORY

WORK FORCE

CAPACITY

QUALITY

PROCESS

Among the most important decisions made by operations managers are those involving the design of the physical process for producing goods and services. This series of decisions encompasses process selection, choice of technology, process-flow analysis, and layout of facilities. When these decisions have been made, the process type, degree of automation, physical layout, and design of jobs have largely been determined. Process design is not merely a technical matter but involves social, economic, and environmental choices as well.

The range of processes which can be selected is described in Part II, along with the important factors in process-selection decisions. As discussed in Part I, process selection is highly interactive with product design. To reflect this interaction, process choices and product choices are displayed as two sides of a product-process matrix. A decision requires the selection of a cell in this matrix, thus fixing both the product and the process.

The choice of technology determines the process's degree of automation. This choice is not merely a technical decision but also a social choice which determines jobs and other social factors. This leads to the idea of a decision-making process which considers the environmental, social, and economic implications of technological alternatives. Finally, the choice of technology is shown to be a series of decisions over time requiring a continuous process of technology surveillance, choice of appropriate technologies, and implementation of technology changes.

The design of processes also requires decisions on a micro level concerning process-flow analysis and facility layout. These decisions determine the physical flow of materials, customers, and information through the process. Process-analysis methods describe the flow of the process through use of flowcharts and mathematical models. Layout decisions improve process flow by the arrangement of physical facilities.

There are two themes which underlie and unify Part II: first, the idea of designing a process to enhance the flow of materials, customers, and information and, second, the idea of combining social and technical considerations in process design. These ideas can be used to design a process which is not only efficient but socially and environmentally acceptable as well.

In the first two chapters of Part II, macro process design decisions are treated. These macro decisions have to do with process selection and the choice of technology. The macro decisions are long range in nature, require considerable resources, are irreversible for long periods of time, and involve top management. The last two chapters of this part treat micro decisions of process design. These micro decisions involve process-flow analysis and layout. The micro decisions are made at lower levels in the organization, they require less resources, and they can be changed more easily than the macro decisions.

Process-design decisions interact with decisions in each of the other four decision areas of the operations function. Capacity decisions affect the type of process selected. The type of process design, in turn, affects the jobs available and the type of work force employed. The process also affects the quality of the product produced, because some processes are more easily controlled than others. Thus process decisions are intertwined with most other decisions in operations.

CHAPTER 5
PROCESS SELECTION

Process-selection decisions determine the type of productive process to be used and the appropriate span of that process. For example, the managers of a fast-food restaurant must decide whether to produce food strictly to customer order or to inventory. The managers must also decide whether to organize the process flow as a high-volume line flow or a low-volume batch-production process. Furthermore, they must decide whether to integrate forward toward the market or backward toward their suppliers. All these decisions help define the type of process which will be used to make the product.

Process selection is sometimes viewed as a layout problem or as a series of relatively low-level decisions, but this is a mistake, since process selection is, on the contrary, strategic in nature and of the greatest importance. Process decisions affect the costs, quality, dependability, and flexibility of operations. As Wickham Skinner (1969) points out, process-selection decisions tend to bind the firm with equipment, facilities, and a particular type of labor force. This, in turn, tends to limit future strategic options.

This chapter addresses process-selection decisions from a strategic management point of view. The main emphasis is on the description of different processes and the conditions which might lead to the selection of one process over another.

Before the process-selection decision can be made, the planned volume of product output must be known. Thus a forecast of demand and a decision on the physical capacity of operations must precede process selection. We treat capacity decisions in the next part, however, in order to integrate long-, medium-, and short-range capac-

123

BOX 5.1 TYPICAL DECISION PROBLEM

The microwave oven business has been expanding rapidly over the past 10 years. One of the leading American companies in this industry is Radarwave, Inc., which has captured a 30 percent market share and has rapidly expanded sales and profits over the past 5 years. In viewing this situation, Mary Lipton, the vice president of operations, wondered how long the sales growth would continue and at what point changes in market conditions might require a corresponding change in the manufacturing process.

At the present time, Radarwave has two plants, one in Boulder, Colorado, and the other in Rapid City, South Dakota. These plants have been using a partially connected assembly line, with some parts of the product also being made in a job-shop facility. Because of the rapid growth in sales as well as frequent product changes, the product flow was somewhat irregular; moreover, the assembly line was not engineered to achieve the most efficient process possible. It was highly labor-intensive, and many parts for the microwave ovens were purchased from outside suppliers.

Recently Japanese competition entered the market with a low-priced microwave oven. American manufacturers also standardized their ovens and some of the large appliance manufacturers were considering adding microwave products to their appliance lines.

In view of this situation, Mary decided to analyze the possible effects of moving toward a more standard assembly line, with increased automation and more vertical integration. To conduct the analysis, she called in Roger Kirk, her assistant for operations planning. Mary asked Roger to lay out the various available options and to prepare an analysis of the impact of each of these options on operations. She cautioned Roger to consider not only the costs of the proposed alternatives but also the effect on operations quality, dependability, and flexibility.

ity decisions. For the purposes of this part, we will assume that the long-range capacity decision has already been made.

In this chapter, two main types of process classifications are examined. First, a process is classified by type of product flow: line, intermittent, or project flow. Second, a process is classified by type of customer order: make-to-stock or make-to-order. These dimensions of classification greatly affect costs, volumes, flexibility, and virtually all aspects of operations. Since these classifications are so crucial to operations, they are described in some detail in the first part of the chapter.

After the static case is considered, process-selection decisions are put into a dynamic context. Process selection is portrayed as a dynamic series of decisions over time, where the product and process evolve together. Finally, at the end of the chapter, the scope of process selection is expanded to include forward and backward integration. A typical decision problem of process selection is illustrated in Box 5.1.

5.1 PROCESS-FLOW CHARACTERISTICS

The first dimension of process classification is the product flow or sequence of operations. There are three types of flows: line, intermittent, and project. In manufacturing, product flow is the same as material flow, since materials are being converted into a product. In pure service industries, there is no physical product flow, but there is, nevertheless, a sequence of operations performed in delivering the service. This sequence of service operations is considered as the "product flow" for service industries.

LINE FLOW. Line flow is characterized by a linear sequence of operations used to make the product or service. Examples are assembly lines and cafeterias. For line-flow operations, the product must be well standardized and must flow from one operation or work station to the next in a prescribed sequence. The individual work tasks are closely coupled and should be balanced so that one task does not delay the next. The pattern typical of line flows is shown in Figure 5.1. Notice that the good or service is created sequentially from one end of the line to the other. There may be side flows which impinge on this line, but they are integrated to achieve a smooth flow.

Line-flow operations are sometimes divided into two types of production: mass and continuous. "Mass production" generally refers to an assembly-line type of operation, such as that used in the automobile industry. "Continuous production" refers to the so-called process industries such as the chemical, paper, beer, steel, electricity, and telephone industries. Although both types of operations are characterized by linear flow, continuous processes tend to be more highly automated and to produce more highly standardized products.

Line operations are extremely efficient but also extremely inflexible. The efficiency is due to substitution of capital for labor and standardization of the remaining labor into highly routine tasks. The high level of efficiency requires that a large volume be maintained in order to recover the cost of specialized equipment. This, in turn, requires a standard product line which is relatively stabilized over time. Because of this standardization and the sequential organization of work tasks, it is difficult and expensive to modify the product or volume in line-flow operations; therefore these operations are relatively inflexible.

Of course, line operations can be justified in only a limited number of situations. The general requirements are for high volume and a standardized product. If these conditions are present, competition will usually force the use of a line flow because of its great potential efficiency. Nevertheless, a firm must carefully analyze the deci-

**Figure 5.1
Line flow.**

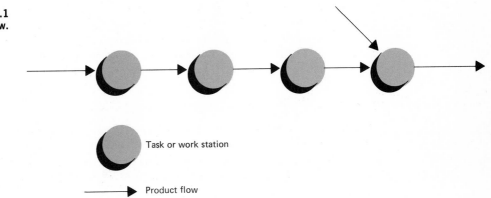

 Task or work station

Product flow

sion to use line operations; this choice should not be based simply on efficiency. Other factors which should be considered are the risk of product obsolescence, possible labor dissatisfaction due to job boredom, and the risk of changing process technology.

INTERMITTENT FLOW (JOB SHOP). An intermittent-flow process is characterized by production in batches at intermittent intervals. In this case, equipment and labor are organized into work centers by similar types of skill or equipment. A product or job will then flow only to those work centers that are required and will skip the rest. This results in a jumbled flow pattern, as shown in Figure 5.2.

Because they use general-purpose equipment and highly skilled labor, intermittent operations are extremely flexible in changing the product or volume; but they are also rather inefficient. At the same time, their flexibility leads to severe problems in controlling inventories, schedules, and quality.

If an intermittent operation is functioning near capacity, high in-process inventories will build up and throughput time for the batches will increase. This is due to job interference when different jobs require the same equipment or the same labor at the same time, leading to much lower utilization of equipment and labor than in a line type of operation.

Constable and New (1976) have suggested a way to measure this loss of efficiency by a ratio they call throughput efficiency or TE:

$$TE = \frac{\text{total work involvement time for the job}}{\text{total time in operations}} \times 100\%$$

In the numerator, total work involvement time for the job is the machine hours or labor hours actually spent working on the job. This does not include the time the job waits because of job interference. The denominator is the total time it takes to complete the job in operations, including all waiting time. Intermittent operations typi-

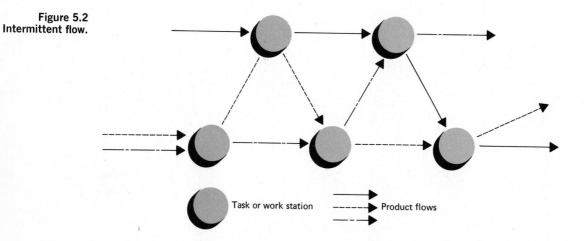

**Figure 5.2
Intermittent flow.**

Task or work station ------▶ Product flows

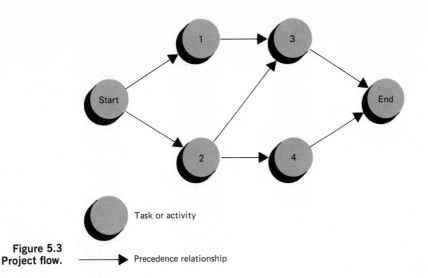

**Figure 5.3
Project flow.**

Task or activity

Precedence relationship

cally have a TE of about 10 or 20 percent, rarely higher than 40 percent. In contrast, the TE of a line-flow operation approaches 90 to 100 percent.

One key characteristic of an intermittent process is that similar equipment and work skills are grouped together. This is also known as a process form of layout. In contrast, the line flow is called a product layout because the various processes, equipment, and labor skills are put into sequence according to the way the product is made.

To further complicate the terminology, intermittent operations are often called job shops. However, sometimes the term "job shop" is reserved for only those intermittent operations that make to customer order. Because of this confusion and the factory connotations of "job shop," we prefer the use of the term "intermittent operation."

Intermittent operations can be justified when the product lacks standardization or the volume is low. In this case, the intermittent operation is the most economical and involves the least risk. Such forms of operations are common in the early life cycles of all products, for products which are customized in nature, and for products with a low-volume market.

PROJECT. The project form of operations is used to produce a unique product such as a work of art, a concert, a building, or a motion picture. Each unit of these products is produced as a single item. Strictly speaking, there is no product flow for a project, but there is still a sequence of operations. In this case, all individual operations or tasks should be sequenced to contribute to the final project objectives. A conceptual sequence of project tasks is shown in Figure 5.3, which indicates precedence among the various tasks required for project completion. A significant problem in project management is the planning, sequencing, and control of the individual tasks leading to completion of the entire project.

The project form of operations is used when there is a great need for creativity and uniqueness. It is difficult to automate projects because they are only done once; nevertheless, general-purpose equipment can sometimes be used to reduce labor requirements. Projects are characterized by high cost and difficulty in managerial planning and control. This is because a project is often hard to define initially, and it may be subject to a high degree of change and innovation.

The characteristics of the processes we have been discussing are summarized in Box 5.2, which makes a direct comparison between process types for each characteristic. For an excellent and more detailed work on this subject, see Marshall et al. (1975), chap. 3.

At this point, examples from the housing industry may help to solidify some of the concepts. At the project end of the continuum is the custom-built house. A unique plan for it may be drawn up by an architect or existing plans may be modified for each house built. Since the construction of the house is customized, planning, sequencing, and control of various construction activities often become major problems. The customer is highly involved in all stages of construction, and sometimes the plans are modified while the house is being built. The operation is labor-intensive, time-consuming, and costly.

The intermittent operation is characterized by the batch production of houses. In this case, the customer can select one of a few standard houses with only minor options on things like colors, fixtures, and carpets. The house is produced with little

BOX 5.2 **PROCESS CHARACTERISTICS**

Characteristics	Line	Intermittent	Project
Product			
Order type	Continuous or large batch	Batch	Single unit
Flow of product	Sequenced	Jumbled	None
Product variety	Low	High	Very high
Market type	Mass	Custom	Unique
Volume	High	Medium	Single unit
Labor			
Skills	Low	High	High
Task type	Repetitive	Nonroutine	Nonroutine
Pay	Low	High	High
Capital			
Investment	High	Medium	Low
Inventory	Low	High	Medium
Equipment	Special purpose	General purpose	General purpose
Objectives			
Flexibility	Low	Medium	High
Cost	Low	Medium	High
Quality	Consistent	More variable	More variable
Throughput time	Low	Medium	High
Control and planning			
Production control	Easy	Difficult	Difficult
Quality control	Easy	Difficult	Difficult
Inventory control	Easy	Difficult	Difficult

reference to blueprints, since identical or very similar houses have been produced elsewhere. The contractor may buy materials in large carload lots and specialized equipment or jigs may be used to speed up construction. A crew which is very familiar with the type of house being built is brought in, and the entire structure—except for final touches—may be put up in only a few days. Such a house is usually less expensive per square foot than the custom-built project house.

The line method of house production is characterized by modular or factory operations. Standard houses are produced in sections, in a factory, by relatively cheap labor. The use of expensive plumbers, carpenters, and electricians is largely avoided by installing complete electrical and plumbing systems at the factory. Special-purpose machines are also used in the factory to cut costs still further. After being built on an assembly line, the house sections are brought to the site and erected in a day or so by a crane. These modular houses are typically the least expensive of all.

Obviously, a contractor faces a major strategic decision in choosing the type of process to use for the construction of houses. All three approaches may be used, but then care must be taken to separate these operations because of their different requirements for labor, management, and capital. If all three types of houses are to be offered, the contractor might form a separate division for each type of process as well as a separate operation for each.

5.2 CLASSIFICATIONS BY TYPE OF CUSTOMER ORDER

Another critical dimension affecting process choice is whether the product is made-to-stock or made-to-order. Each of these processes has its own advantages and disadvantages. While a make-to-stock process will provide fast service at low cost, it offers less flexibility in product choice than a make-to-order process.

A make-to-order process essentially responds to the customer's request for a product. At some point in the make-to-order production process, it must be possible to identify a particular customer order. However, in a make-to-stock process individual orders are not assigned to customers during production. One can then tell whether the process is make-to-order or make-to-stock by examining the work orders in the conversion process.

Even though the process is make-to-order, a wide range of order specification may remain. In some cases, nothing is done until the order is received, and the product is then produced entirely to customer specifications. In other cases, components are built up in advance, and the product is merely assembled at the last minute to meet the customer's choices. In this case, the finished product is standardized but not carried in stock.

In a make-to-order process, the processing activities are keyed to individual customer orders. The order cycle begins when the customer specifies the product that he or she wants. On the basis of the customer's request, the producer will quote a price and delivery time. This quotation may be offered immediately if the order is standard or, for custom orders, it may take a period of time. If the customer accepts the quotation, the product will either be assembled from components or built completely to customer specifications. If the order is built to customer specifications and special materials are needed, they will be placed on order. When the materials arrive, they will be fabricated and assembled as capacity permits. Finally, the product will be delivered to the customer. This sequence of events is essentially the same whether the product is a good or a service.

As far as product availability is concerned, the key operations performance measure for a make-to-order process is the delivery time. Before placing the order, the customer will want to know how long it will take for delivery. If the delivery time is accepted by the customer, then operations should control the order flow to meet the delivery date. This means, of course, that delivery times should be set realistically by operations and marketing working in cooperation. The measures of operations performance will be delivery parameters such as length of delivery time and percentage of orders delivered on time.

A make-to-stock firm has a completely different problem. First, the make-to-stock operation must have a standardized product line. The product availability objective then is to provide the customer with these standard products from inventory at some satisfactory service level, say, 95 percent of orders filled from stock. In meeting the service level, the company will build up inventory in advance of demand. The inventory will then be used to meet demand uncertainty and, possibly, to smooth out capacity requirements. Therefore forecasting, inventory management, and capacity planning become essential for a make-to-stock operation.

In a make-to-stock company, very little in operations is keyed to actual customer orders; rather, the focus is on replenishment of inventory. With the rare exception of back orders, it will not be possible to identify actual customer orders in the production process.

In a make-to-stock operation, the cycle begins with the producer specifying the product. The customer takes the product from stock if the price is acceptable and the product is on hand. Otherwise, a back order may be placed. Quite separately from the actual flow of orders, the production process seeks to replenish inventory. At any particular time, there may be little correlation between actual orders being received and what is being produced. The production system is building stock levels for future orders, not current ones. Current orders are being filled from available stock. This split between the order cycle and the replenishment cycle is illustrated by Appleton (1977) in Figure 5.4. The figure also indicates that such a split does not occur in a make-to-order system, since the production process starts when the order is received.

In a make-to-stock situation, the key performance measures are utilization of production assets (inventory and capacity) and customer service. These measures might include inventory turnover, capacity utilization, use of overtime, and percent of orders filled from stock. The objective of the operation is to meet the desired level of customer service at minimum cost.

In summary, a make-to-order process is keyed to delivery time and control of the order flow. The process must be flexible so as to meet customer orders. A make-to-stock process is keyed to replenishment of inventories and efficiency of operations. The process is streamlined to produce only standard products. The essential differences between these processes are summarized in Box. 5.3.

Classic examples of make-to-stock and make-to-order processes are the

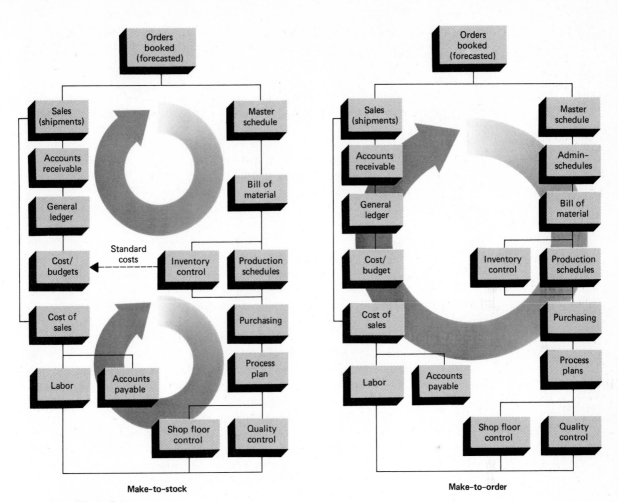

**Figure 5.4
Information flow
comparison.**
*(Source: Daniel S.
Appleton, "A Strategy
for Manufacturing
Automation," Datama-
tion, October 1977,
pp. 65–66.)*

McDonald's and Burger King fast-food chains. The hamburgers at McDonald's are, in some cases, made-to-stock. When the demand is steady, McDonald's will build up inventory of various types of hamburgers. In this case, the operation attempts to forecast demand and replenish inventory.

At Burger King the slogan is "Have it your way." Customers can specify the ingredients they want in their hamburgers or those they don't want. In this case, the exact order cannot be kept in stock, and the measure of performance shifts to delivery time. Burger King is a make-to-order operation.

A third variation on this theme is Burger Chef. There, the customer can customize hamburgers by using the "fixings" bar, but it is also possible to order from stock. In other words, Burger Chef has shifted part of the production process to the customer. You can also "have it your way" at Burger Chef, but you have to do part of the work.

BOX 5.3   **MAKE-TO-STOCK VERSUS MAKE-TO-ORDER**

Characteristics	Make-to-stock	Make-to-order
Product	Producer-specified Small range Inexpensive	Customer-specified Large range Expensive
Objectives	Balance inventory, capacity, and service	Manage delivery lead times and capacity
Main operations problems	Forecasting Planning production Control of inventory	Delivery promises Delivery control

Source: Adapted from Constable and New (1976).

5.3 PROCESS-SELECTION DECISIONS

We have classified processes according to two dimensions: product flow and type of customer order. These dimensions are shown in Table 5.1 on a matrix with six different processes. In a firm, each particular product is produced by one of these six processes; however, a mixture of products often leads to a mixture of process types in the same firm. It is very common for organizations to have several different types of processes within the same physical facility.

All six process combinations shown in Table 5.1 are used in practice. For line flows, it is common to make-to-stock, but a line can also make-to-order. For example, automobile assembly lines put together specific combinations of options requested by customers. To be sure, the product is standardized, but it is nevertheless made-to-order. At the other extreme, projects usually make to order, but the project form of operations can make-to-stock too. For example, a builder who constructs a few speculation houses is making to stock while using a project type of process.

It should also be noted that all six processes apply to services as well as goods. A pure service operation can only produce to order. But as we noted in Chapter 3, most services are delivered as a goods-service bundle with facilitating goods. These facilitating goods can be made-to-stock, as in the case of fast-food hamburgers.

The six-cell process-classification system can be used for several purposes: first, it can be used to categorize different types of decision problems encountered in operations. For example, cost-, quality-, production-, and inventory-control decisions differ greatly among these process types. The second use of the classification matrix is for process selection, which is the main issue discussed in the rest of this section.

In discussing the process-selection decision, we shall begin with an example and generalize from there. Let us consider the contractor, mentioned in Section 5.1, who can choose to build houses using either the project, intermittent, or line process. With any of these processes, the contractor can also choose to make the houses to stock or to order. What, then, are the factors which should be considered in making this choice?

First of all, the contractor should consider capital. The line-flow process will require a great deal more capital than the project or intermittent flow. The line flow requires capital to equip the factory assembly line and to finance the partially com-

TABLE 5.1   PROCESS CHARACTERISTICS MATRIX

	Make-to-stock	Make-to-order
Line flow	I Oil refining Flour milling Cannery Cafeteria	II Automobile assembly line Telephone company Electric utility
Intermittent flow	III Machine shop Fast food Glassware factory Furniture	IV Machine shop Restaurant Hospital Custom jewelry
Project	V Speculation homes Commercial paintings	VI Buildings Movies Ships Portraits

pleted houses. If the houses are built to stock in advance of customer orders, more capital is required to finance finished-goods inventories. By way of contrast, construction of custom project houses would require much less capital, since only one or a few houses are being built at any one time and no factory is needed.

Second, the contractor should consider local market conditions. The line approach requires a mass market for inexpensive houses, the intermittent process requires a lower-volume market for medium-priced houses, and the project process requires a market for expensive houses.

But the market should also be considered from the standpoint of competition. Can the contractor enter the market at the right time and gain an advantageous position? This will depend on competitors' plans and how they react to the contractor's process choice. In the end, matching the process to the market will be a key strategic decision involving considerable costs and risks.

The third factor which should be considered is the availability and cost of labor. The project and intermittent processes require costly skilled labor such as plumbers, electricians, and carpenters. The factory line approach requires relatively cheap low-skilled labor. Unionization may affect both the supply and cost of labor.

The fourth factor the contractor should consider is the management skills required for each process. The project approach can be managed on a small scale without a great deal of sophistication. However, even in this case, certain project planning and control techniques will be helpful, as will the principles of good supervision and quality control. For the intermittent process, the contractor will require operations management skill in forecasting, scheduling, and inventory control. The contractor must also become more concerned with standardization and cost control, since the houses are being made in batches. The line process requires the most sophisticated management skills of all. The contractor will need to manage and coordinate a factory, construction at the site, and a distribution network.

The fifth factor which will be important to the contractor is the availability and price of raw materials. The project form of process is very flexible and can adjust to different materials if necessary. The line approach is much less flexible and may require costly changes if the supply of raw materials is interrupted. For example, a change from copper to plastic plumbing pipes could be a big changeover problem for the line flow but pose little problem for the intermittent or project process.

Finally, the contractor should consider the state of technology for both process and product. Are innovations likely to come along which will make a process obsolete before costs are recovered? Assessment of these conditions is part of risk evaluation for the process. Generally speaking, the risk in order of highest to lowest is line, intermittent, and project.

In summary, six factors appear to influence process selection from among the processes shown in Table 5.1.

1. *Capital requirements.* How much capital is needed for inventory, equipment, and facilities? What is the return on investment?
2. *Market conditions.* What will customer acceptance be? Is there sufficient volume at a price that will ensure a profit? Are competitive conditions favorable at the present time and for the foreseeable future?
3. *Labor.* Is there a sufficient supply of labor at reasonable cost? What are the prospects for the future?
4. *Management skills.* Can the company acquire and maintain the type of management skills needed?
5. *Raw materials.* Are the raw materials available in sufficient supply? What will changes in raw material do to the process?
6. *Technology.* Is the technology of product and process stable enough to support the process for a sufficient period of time to recover costs?

A convenient way to remember these factors is to use the systems view of operations and think in terms of the different types of inputs, transformation technologies, and outputs. All six factors will then be apparent.

A good process-selection decision requires a careful analysis of each of the six factors through several types of studies. A market research study should be done to assess potential demand and other market conditions. Whenever possible, future sales should be projected not only as a single figure but also as a range of possible estimates. For example, three estimates—pessimistic, most likely, and optimistic—might be used, thereby allowing an analysis of risks involved in the decision.

Many of the other factors can be considered by an economic analysis of process alternatives. The key to this is to consider the cash flows for each alternative by determining the investments, revenues, and costs on a year-by-year basis. The net cash-flow streams for each year can then be discounted to present values or a return on invested capital can be computed. The alternative with the largest present value or largest rate of return is then preferred from an economic point of view. The details of these calculations are given in the supplement to Chapter 6.

In our discussion of the economics of process choice, it will also be helpful to

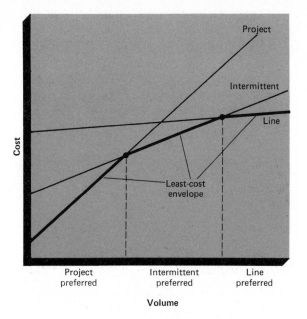

**Figure 5.5
Cost curves
for process
alternatives.**

consider fixed and variable costs. Generally speaking, if the choice were between a project, intermittent, or line process, the cost comparison would appear as in Figure 5.5. The figure shows that the project would have the least cost for a low volume, followed by the intermittent flow at medium volume and the line process at high volume. The project process has the lowest fixed cost and highest variable cost, which makes the project least costly in total for low volumes. The line has the highest fixed cost and the lowest variable cost, which makes the line least costly in total for high volumes. See Chapter 2 for details on this method of cost analysis.

When the marketing and economic studies have been completed, they should be synthesized into the decision process. In some cases, these studies will indicate a definite preference for one process alternative over another. If this is the case, subjective factors are liable to play only a small role in process selection. Usually, however, process selection will require considerable judgment because of the different cost and risk factors involved.

5.4 PRODUCT-PROCESS STRATEGY

We have been treating process selection as a static decision. But it actually is dynamic in nature, since it continues as the process evolves from one stage to another over time. Furthermore, changes in the process are closely related to product changes.

Hayes and Wheelwright (1979) have suggested that process and product be viewed as two sides of a matrix, as in Figure 5.6. On the product side is the product life cycle of a firm whose output ranges from low-volume, one-of-a-kind products through high-volume, standard commodity products. As the product line matures, it moves from the left side of the matrix to the right side.

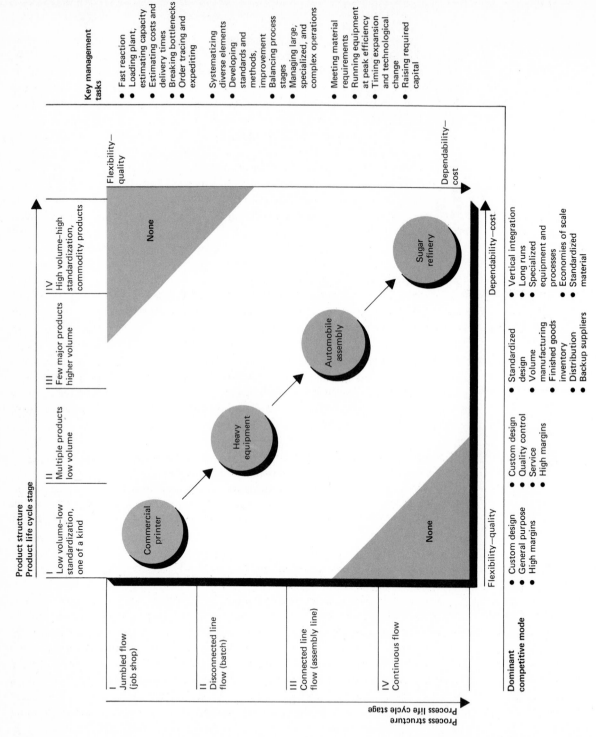

Product structure
Product life cycle stage

	I Low volume–low standardization, one of a kind	II Multiple products low volume	III Few major products higher volume	IV High volume–high standardization, commodity products

Process structure
Process life cycle stage

I Jumbled flow (job shop)

II Disconnected line flow (batch)

III Connected line flow (assembly line)

IV Continuous flow

Commercial printer

Heavy equipment

Automobile assembly

Sugar refinery

None

None

Flexibility— quality

Dependability— cost

Flexibility—quality

Dependability—cost

Dominant competitive mode

- Custom design
- General purpose
- High margins

- Custom design
- Quality control
- Service
- High margins

- Standardized design
- Volume manufacturing
- Finished goods inventory
- Distribution
- Backup suppliers

- Vertical integration
- Long runs
- Specialized equipment and processes
- Economies of scale
- Standardized material

Key management tasks

- Fast reaction
- Loading plant, estimating capacity
- Estimating costs and delivery times
- Breaking bottlenecks
- Order tracing and expediting

- Systematizing diverse elements
- Developing standards and methods, improvement
- Balancing process stages

- Managing large, specialized, and complex operations

- Meeting material requirements
- Running equipment at peak efficiency
- Timing expansion and technological change
- Raising required capital

136

On the process side of the matrix is the type of process, ranging from a job shop (jumbled flow) through a continuous process. Abernathy and Townsend (1975) have observed that processes go through a "process life cycle" similar to the product life cycle. In this case, the process moves from a fluid and flexible process at the top of the matrix to an efficient and highly standardized process at the bottom of the matrix. See Chapter 3 for a complete discussion of this process life cycle.

Firms are often positioned along the diagonal of the matrix. In the upper left-hand corner is the printer who produces many jobs to customer order on general-purpose equipment in a job-shop environment. Further down the diagonal, there is the heavy-equipment manufacturer who makes products in batches. The product flow in this case is higher in volume and more connected, and the product line has been standardized. Still further down the diagonal is the automobile assembly line, which represents a line-flow process with a few major product lines, specialized equipment, and highly structured jobs. Finally, in the lower right-hand corner, there is the sugar refiner, representing the continuous-process type of operation with a high-volume commodity product.

The process-product matrix helps describe the relationship between process and product strategy. In some cases, corporate strategy is developed only in light of products and markets. This limits the firm to a choice along only one dimension of the matrix. By recognizing the process dimension, the firm can also take advantage of competence in operations processes. This considerably expands the strategic options available and allows the use of operations as a "weapon" of corporate strategy.

Hayes and Wheelwright (1979) illustrate this interaction of product and process strategy with the following example from Litton, a manufacturer of microwave ovens.

> As the market leader since the early 1960's, Litton has emphasized flexibility in its production facilities so as to be responsive to the frequent product changes required by a young, rapidly growing market. However, with the maturing market expected in the late seventies and the entry of more traditional appliance manufacturers, Litton recently has been forced to review how far it should move towards vertical integration and more efficient production processes.

Thus, Litton is being forced to consider changing both product and process strategies, thereby moving down the diagonal.

Abernathy (1976) has studied the matter of product and process evolution in great detail. He observes that product and process changes rarely occur simultaneously. Rather, these changes occur in alternating vertical or horizontal steps on the product-process matrix. A change in product strategy may move the firm to the right, off the diagonal, if the old process remains in effect. The competitors who are operating on the diagonal or below it can then produce at lower costs. This forces a change in process technology to move the firm back down to the diagonal or below it. If the firm moves below the diagonal, this could, in turn, force further product changes.

On the basis of the foregoing discussion, one might wonder whether the best strategy is to operate below the diagonal or simply to move down the diagonal ahead of the competition. Although the latter strategy has cost advantages, the firm adopting it can suffer from a lack of flexibility. If product standardization does not occur in line with expectations, changes to the process can be expensive, even forcing the firm back up to the diagonal. Thus, a firm should not venture too far from the diagonal unless this is part of a conscious corporate strategy.

All the members of an industry do not necessarily move down the diagonal together. For example, some producers might choose to be low-volume–intermittent-process companies which stress flexibility and quality products. Meanwhile, other companies might move down the diagonal and stress standard products at low cost. In the hand-calculator business, it appears that Hewlett Packard has chosen to stay in the upper left-hand corner while Texas Instruments operates in the lower right-hand corner. Hayes and Wheelwright (1979) report that for a time, Hewlett Packard attempted to move toward more standard high-volume products without automating their process further. This caused them to operate above the diagonal. Soon after, they retreated to their more traditional end of the matrix rather than competing directly with Texas Instruments.

This story indicates the interesting phenomenon of distinctive competence. A firm defines its distinctive competence by that set of tasks which sets it apart from the competition. Choosing a distinctive competence amounts to choosing a patch on the matrix. If the distinctive competence is defined only in terms of market strategy without regard for process, the firm is missing an important dimension of strategy. Furthermore, a one-dimensional strategy may cause the firm to operate off the diagonal without recognizing the problem and thereby encounter competitive trouble. Wickham Skinner (1974) calls this problem a lack of operations focus. This occurs when the operations process is not properly matched to the marketing concept.

5.5 VERTICAL INTEGRATION

To this point we have been considering the process-selection decision for one particular site or location. For a single site we have considered the inputs and outputs of the productive process as given. But there is a larger question: Should the inputs or outputs of the productive process also be brought under ownership of the same enterprise? This is the vertical-integration decision.

There are two types of vertical integration: backward and forward. Backward integration is concerned with expanding ownership "backward," toward the source of supply. Backward integration may apply to any of the inputs of a productive process, including raw materials, labor, and capital equipment. Backward integration occurs when, for example, a newspaper buys a pulp mill to control one of its critical inputs, newsprint; a steelmaker buys iron mines in northern Minnesota to control the supply of ore; a vegetable canner buys farms and starts raising its own vegetables; or General Motors opens a training institute for its managers and technical employees.

Forward integration is concerned with expanding ownership of the process

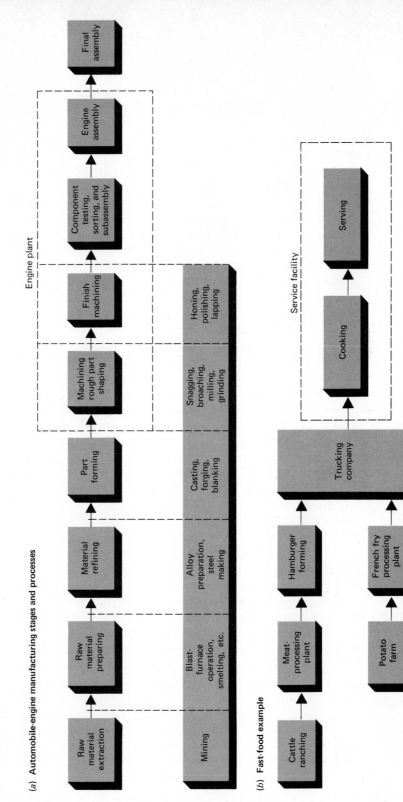

**Figure 5.7
Examples of
vertical integration.**

[*Source of Part (a):
William J. Abernathy,
The Productivity
Dilemma—Roadblock
to Innovation in the
Automobile Industry,
Baltimore: Johns
Hopkins, 1978.*]

(a) Automobile-engine manufacturing stages and processes

(b) Fast-food example

139

"forward," toward the market. Forward integration then brings the distribution channels under the control of the same firm. Forward integration occurs when, for example, a farmers' cooperative buys a processing plant and begins processing the sugar beets grown by the farmers; a maker of solid-state components expands its operations and marketing into the computer-terminal market (after forward integration, it makes not only the components for the terminals but also the terminals themselves); or a maker of basic steel expands into the production of finished steel products as well as iron ingots.

The vertical-integration decision is made in relation to the production-distribution chain. One must first identify the particular inputs and outputs of a firm's process. Backward integration then occurs along the chain toward the firm's suppliers. Forward integration occurs along the chain toward the firm's markets. For any particular point in the chain, one can then easily identify the backward and forward integration paths. If a particular firm owns the entire chain, we say that the firm is completely integrated vertically. Some examples of production-distribution chains are shown in Figure 5.7.

The vertical-integration decision varies depending on whether backward or forward integration is being considered. In the case of backward integration, the key decision factors are costs and reliability of supply. If a firm is a major user of certain inputs, it may be less costly for it to produce its own inputs than to procure them from another supplier. In this case, however, the capital required to purchase from an existing supplier or to start up a business must be considered. The analysis required here is the classic acquisition question involved in deciding on ownership of any business. But even if the economics are not entirely favorable in relation to other uses of capital, a firm may integrate backward to ensure reliability of supply. This might be especially important if the inputs are supplied by only a few firms or are otherwise subject to uncertainties of supply and price.

In the case of the forward-integration decision, the focus shifts to issues of marketing and channels of distribution. In this case, acquisition economics must still be considered in the same way. However, reliability of demand rather than reliability of supply is the crucial factor. A firm may be able to improve its competitive position greatly by integrating forward and thereby controlling more of the distribution chain.

The vertical-integration decision is complex and wide in scope. It is a decision that would usually be made by top management, and it would often involve all the functional areas of business as well. Vertical-integration decisions should support the corporate strategy and be an integral part of operations process planning.

5.6 KEY POINTS

This chapter has emphasized process-selection decisions, including selection of process type and span of vertical integration. Process type was specified in terms of two key dimensions—product flow and type of customer order—leading to six major process types. The process-product matrix was introduced as a way of describing the dynamic nature of process selection and its relationship to market strategy.

Specific points covered in the chapter are as follows:

- There are three types of process flow: line, intermittent, and project. Line flow is characterized by a linear sequence of operations and a product layout. Line processes utilize specialized equipment, are very efficient, and are inflexible in adapting to product or volume changes. Intermittent operations use a process layout with similar equipment or skills grouped together. The resulting flow pattern is jumbled, since the product is made in batches and flows through only the processes needed. Intermittent operations are highly flexible but much less efficient than line processes. The project flow is used to make a unique product. All tasks are sequenced to support the single product being made. Projects provide the most flexibility but are usually quite expensive.

- Operations processes can also be classified as make-to-order and make-to-stock. The make-to-order process is set in motion by customer orders and geared to delivery performance. The make-to-stock process is geared to the replenishment of inventory; it does not respond to specific customer orders. Make-to-stock operations are measured by use of capacity, inventory levels, and stockout performance.

- The combination of product flow with type of customer order yields six types of operations processes. Selection from among these processes is made by considering capital requirements, market conditions, labor, management skills, raw materials, and technology. These factors are evaluated by conducting marketing and economic studies, but the process-selection decision is always strategic in nature.

- The process-product matrix describes stages in the life cycles of products and processes. A firm should define its distinctive competence in terms of both process and product by selecting a patch on the matrix. The matrix helps relate process-selection decisions to product decisions and the market.

- Vertical integration defines the ownership question in process selection. Forward integration extends ownership of the process forward toward the market. Backward integration extends ownership of the process backward toward suppliers. Both types of integration involve economic considerations; however, backward integration is concerned with reliability of supply, while forward integration is concerned with reliability of demand.

QUESTIONS

1. Classify the following types of processes as line, intermittent, or project:
   a. Doctor's office
   b. Automatic car wash
   c. College curriculum
   d. Studying for an exam
   e. Registration for classes
   f. Electric utility
2. Why are line processes so much more efficient but less flexible than intermittent processes? Give three reasons.
3. The rate of productivity improvement in the service industries has been much lower than in manufacturing. Can this be attributed to process-selection decisions? What problems would be involved in using more efficient processes in service industries?

4. The project process is typically used for skyscraper construction. Does this lead to higher costs? Could more efficient processes be used? If so, how?

5. Several industries—including those that produce furniture, houses, sailboats, and clothing—have never progressed down the diagonal of the process-product matrix to become highly standardized and efficient. Why do you think this is so? Is this a serious problem?

6. Compare the expensive restaurant, fast-food restaurant, and cafeteria in terms of process characteristics such as capital, product type, labor, planning, control systems, etc.

7. An entrepreneur is planning to go into the food business. How would he or she decide whether to open a cafeteria, fast-food restaurant, or fine restaurant? What factors should be considered in this decision?

8. A company is in the business of making souvenir spoons to customer order. The customers select the size of the spoons and may specify the design to be embossed on them. One or more spoons may be ordered. The company is considering going into the make-to-stock spoon business for souvenir spoons and everyday tableware as well. What will it have to do differently? How is the business likely to change?

9. What are the possible consequences of defining a marketing strategy independently of the process strategy?

10. What are the distinctive competencies of the following organizations? Is the distinctive competence defined in terms of product or process?
   a. McDonald's
   b. Bell Telephone Co.
   c General Motors
   d. Harvard Business School

11. Identify the following examples as using either forward or backward integration. Explain.
   a. A shoe company going into the leather business
   b. A food processor going into the restaurant business
   c. A paper mill buying a publishing house
   d. A restaurant chain buying a cattle ranch

12. The oil industry is heavily integrated vertically. What are the possible reasons for this? What would be the effects, pro and con, of breaking up the oil companies?

13. Suppose a firm integrates backward quite rapidly while its products are still in the early phase of their life cycles. What could be the possible adverse effects of this strategy?

SELECTED BIBLIOGRAPHY

ABERNATHY, WILLIAM, J.: "Production Process Structure and Technological Change," *Decision Sciences,* vol. 7, no. 4, October 1976, pp. 607–619.

———, and P. L. TOWNSEND: "Technology, Productivity, and Process Change," *Technological Forecasting and Social Change,* vol. 7, August 1975, pp. 377–396.

APPLETON, DANIEL S.: "A Strategy for Manufacturing Automation," *Datamation,* October 1977, pp. 64–70.

BOAS, MAX, and STEVE CHAN: *Big Mac,* New York: Mentor, 1976.

CHASE, RICHARD B., and NICHOLAS AQUILANO: *Production and Operations Management: A Life Cycle Approach,* rev. ed., Homewood, Ill.: Irwin, 1977.

CONSTABLE, C. J., and C. C. NEW: *Operations Management: A Systems Approach Through Text and Cases,* New York: Wiley-Interscience, 1976.

HAYES, ROBERT H., and STEVEN C. WHEELWRIGHT: "Link Manufacturing Process and Product Life Cycles," *Harvard Business Review,* January–February 1979, pp. 133–140.

MARSHALL, PAUL W., et al.: *Operations Management: Text and Cases,* Homewood, Ill.: Irwin, 1975.

SKINNER, WICKHAM: "Manufacturing—Missing Link in Corporate Strategy," *Harvard Business Review,* May–June 1969, pp. 136–145.

———: "The Focused Factory," *Harvard Business Review,* May–June 1974, pp. 113–121.

CHAPTER 6
CHOICE OF TECHNOLOGY

echnology has become a dominant factor in business and in our lives. The relentless advancement of technology has been termed "technological determinism," meaning that technology determines the course of society and seems to leave us no choice in the matter. But people have finally realized that they do have a choice of technologies. This was dramatically illustrated by the decision not to produce the supersonic transport (SST) aircraft.

Peter Drucker argues that we do have a choice and must learn to become aggressive managers of technology by choosing certain technologies and rejecting others. [See Drucker (1969).] He argues that survival on this planet requires intelligent technological decisions; we should not adopt every new "technological advance" regardless of the negative side effects on humans and the environment. We therefore need to become "managers of technology," not only "users of technology."

The responsibility for choice of the technological process almost always resides with the operations manager. It is surprising, therefore, that the operations management literature does not address the issue of technological choice in greater depth. This can, perhaps, be attributed to past assumptions of technological determinism and a technological aversion on the part of some managers. Whatever the reason, it is becoming increasingly important for operations management, and indeed all managers, to address complex issues of technological choice.

In this chapter, two definitions of technology are offered. One is: *the application of knowledge to solve human problems.* This definition is extremely broad and includes almost all human activity. A narrower definition of technology, and one which is used for the remainder of the chapter is: *that set of processes, tools, methods, procedures, and equipment which are used to produce goods or services.* This definition is clearly one of process technology rather than product technology.

In casual conversation, technology is often equated with equipment or machines. The above definition is much broader because it also includes methods or procedures used to produce goods or services. If a surgeon develops a new method for open-heart surgery using the same equipment as before, a new technology has been developed. If a student develops a different method or procedure for studying, the student has developed a new technology, even though no equipment is used.

In the last chapter, process selection was discussed, which, in the broadest sense, is a matter of technological choice. In a more narrow sense, there are also many possible choices of technology within a specific process. For example, a line flow does not require a highly automated machine conversion process, although a great deal of automation is often used. One could choose to use a labor-intensive line flow and still gain considerable efficiencies over intermittent flows. Similarly, an intermittent process can use a range of automation from very low to very high. Until recently, however, managers have not normally used these choices because they have assumed that the most efficient process was the best, resulting in a high level of automation.

The process-selection and technology-choice decisions are closely related and intertwined. One decision does not necessarily precede the other because, in practice, the two decisions are often made together. These decisions have been separated into two chapters simply for the sake of convenience.

The question of technological choice has a great impact on all parts of operations. In particular, job design is greatly affected by the choice of technology. In the past, it was assumed that job design followed choice of technology. In other words, the job is dictated by the technology; this is technological determinism. Job design and choice of technology are now seen by many as simultaneous decisions resulting in a sociotechnical design. In this view, the social and technical systems are jointly

**Figure 6.1
Sociotechnical
system design.**

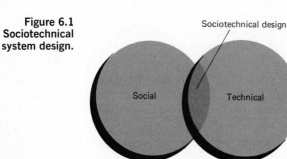

Sociotechnical design

Social   Technical

optimized, as shown in Figure 6.1. The result is not merely the most cost-efficient system but one which considers human and social values as well. A good deal more will be said about this in Chapter 16.

But in addition to jobs, choice of technology affects all aspects of operations, including productivity and product quality. Productivity is, of course, affected through the substitution of capital inputs for labor. Quality is affected, since high-technology systems often have more uniform output than lower-technology systems. The technology decision also affects the corporate strategy by binding it with processes, equipment, facilities, and procedures. Thus, choice of technology is not an isolated decision; it affects all parts of operations and business.

In the first part of this chapter, the role of managers and society in technological choice will be discussed. This part of the chapter essentially deals with the question of who influences a firm's choice of process technology. The second part of the

BOX 6.1

TYPICAL DECISION PROBLEM

Eugene Blake, a recent M.B.A. graduate from the University of Minnesota, and Roberta Clark, a practicing attorney, were discussing, over a cup of coffee, the possibility of starting a new type of legal clinic. According to Roberta, some of the problems encountered in a traditional legal practice were high costs to the customers and the difficulty of delivering fast and professionally competent service, especially for routine legal matters. Gene commented that perhaps the solution to these problems was in the "technology" and process used to deliver services.

Gene went on to describe a legal clinic that would operate something like McDonald's. A set of "standard" legal services such as wills, real estate titles, and divorces would be identified and delivered on a low-cost, consistent-quality basis provided that complications did not occur. A legal clinic would be established to deliver these services on a preset schedule and price basis. Any complications or special cases could be referred to the traditional law practice in another location.

Upon entering the clinic, the client would see a lawyer who would determine whether the client had a standard problem or not. This procedure would help prevent errors in the initial screening. If a standard service were required, the client would be referred to a paralegal assistant who would handle the rest of the visit. The paralegal aide would then explain to the customer exactly what steps were required in the legal procedure and what documents and information the client would have to provide. The time schedule for completion of the process would be established and entered into a computer for later tracking and reference. The customer would be given a copy of the exact schedule and a list of additional information needed. When appropriate points in the schedule were reached, the computer would notify the legal staff to prepare papers or to contact the customer regarding the case. Billing would also be tied in to the computer and explained to the customer in the initial contact meeting.

Roberta and Gene wondered whether this new technology would really result in better service, whether the service would be accepted by the customer, and whether it would be profitable. In an attempt to answer these questions, they decided to develop a proposal for a prototype clinic. The proposal would include an economic analysis and the results of a market survey to gauge customer reaction. The economic analysis would require a variety of assumptions and would culminate in a pro forma projection of revenues, expenses, profitability, and investment required. The market analysis would be based on surveys of potential customers regarding their needs for legal services and willingness to patronize this type of facility. When the study was completed, a basis would be available for deciding whether to develop this new technology.

chapter briefly describes some of the newly emerging technologies, with emphasis on the automatic factory, the automated office, and the service industries. The chapter concludes with sections on the technological decision itself and the problem of managing technological change. A typical technology-choice decision is described in Box 6.1.

6.1 TECHNOLOGY AND THE MANAGER

What should the manager know about technology? After all, shouldn't the matter of technology choice be left to scientists and engineers? How can a manager be expected to master the intricacies of technology when technologists have spent their lifetimes studying the subject? These are important questions and they reflect the fears that some managers have about technology.

All of us make technological choices in everyday life. We purchase color TVs, refrigerators, and automobiles, all of which utilize complex technologies. In making these everyday choices, we concentrate on the performance characteristics of the technology, not the engineering or technical details. When we buy a color TV, we are interested in such performance characteristics as the clarity of the picture, the energy consumption, and the cost. We are not particularly interested in the number of radio frequency stages or the voltage of the picture tube. When we buy an automobile, we are interested in its handling qualities, gas consumption, and possible future repair bills. We are not very interested in the engine's revolutions per minute or the rear-end differential ratio. In the same way, a manager should be concerned with the performance characteristics of a technology, not the technical details.

The decisions of technological choice are of extreme importance and require managerial attention. These decisions, in the end, are not really technical in nature. Technology is only one component of a decision which involves economics, strategy, products, and all aspects of management responsibility. Thus, managers should be willing to understand enough about technology to be able to integrate their technical knowledge with the management factors involved.

Researchers at the Harvard Business School have illustrated the problem of technology choice as follows [see Harvard Business School (1977)].

Consider a simple example of equipment technology, a process for cutting grass, a lawn mower.

A lawn mower could be described to a prospective purchaser as follows: "It costs $128. It has a gasoline engine and cuts a 24-inch wide swath of grass and is well made by a well-known manufacturer."

A technology-aversive prospective buyer might say, "I'll take it," only to get home to the 8-inch grass and find that:

The cutting technology was based on a reel moving past a cutter bar. It could not handle grass much higher than one-half of the reel diameter. It simply pushed the 8-inch crop forward and down.

It was self-propelled but had no effective free-wheeling device, so that it was not possible to work close to and around a formal garden.

It took 30 minutes to change the cutting height so that hillside grass could be cut longer (to cut down on erosion) than lawn grass.

It was not powerful enough to cut wet, thick grass going uphill.

It did not mulch leaves.

It had a two-cycle engine which meant that oil had to be mixed with the gasoline each time the little tank was filled.

This buyer should have purchased an extra-powerful, four-cycle, self-propelled rotary mower with easy handling for tight maneuvering and with a simple height-adjustment mechanism.

Understanding the equipment and process technology of lawn mowing in order to make a wise purchase of machinery would have required the owner-manager to develop an accurate mental concept or picture of the process of cutting grass with the machine operating on the hillside and on the level, under a variety of physical conditions, with consideration for the operator's time, money and skills. The most crucial mistake, of course, was in the choice of a reel mower rather than one with a rotary blade. But for a house with low, big glass windows and with close-by neighbors' houses which were similarly constructed, the buyer would have also needed to consider the danger from flying stones propelled by the rotary mower. In either case, a reasonably good conceptual approximation of the actual grass-cutting action would have suggested enough of the right questions to lead to other useful questions.

Choosing technology in manufacturing or service industry operations has many parallels to the lawn-mower problem. The lawn-mower example illustrates that managers should study the operations process in depth before choosing a technology. The manager should assess the performance characteristics of the technology along with its economic and managerial implications. How this should be done will be illustrated in detail later in the chapter.

6.2 TECHNOLOGY AND SOCIETY

The choice of technology is never neutral with respect to society and the work force. Technology makes implicit assumptions about human values for material outputs, for the quality of working life, and so on. Recently, as people have become more and more concerned about the effects of technology on society, some of these values have been questioned.

In the past few years some sociologists and economists have begun to consider "appropriate technology," "voluntary simplicity," or the notion that "small is beautiful." According to this thinking, modern technology has advanced too far in terms of efficiency and mechanization, to the point where human and environmental values have been sacrificed. These effects are reflected in low job satisfaction, loss of a sense of meaning in work, absenteeism, environmental pollution, and other social ills. According to this thinking, the way to solve many of these problems is to select a more appropriate technology—a lower form of technology which has fewer such social and environmental effects. Writers on appropriate technology do not suggest a return to cottage industry but rather the choice of an intermediate form of technology, between the highest and lowest forms. Some forms of mass production might even be retained, but technological decisions would always be made in light of their environmental and social consequences as well as their economic effects.

Perhaps the best-known proponent of this thinking is E. F. Schumacher, who writes in his book *Small Is Beautiful* (pp. 13–15):

> One of the most fateful errors of our age is the belief that "the problem of production" has been solved. Not only is this belief firmly held by people remote from production and therefore professionally unacquainted with the facts—it is held by virtually all the experts, the captains of industry, the economic managers in the governments of the world, the academic and not-so-academic economists, not to mention the economic journalists. They may disagree on many things but they all agree that the problem of production has been solved; that mankind has at last come of age. For the rich countries, they say, the most important task now is "education for leisure" and, for the poor countries, the "transfer of technology." . . .
>
> The illusion of unlimited power, nourished by astonishing scientific and technological achievements, has produced the concurrent illusion of having solved the problem of production. The latter illusion is based on the failure to distinguish between income and capital where this distinction matters most. Every economist and businessman is familiar with the distinction and applies it conscientiously and with considerable subtlety to all economic affairs—except where it really matters: namely, the irreplaceable capital which man has not made, but simply found, and without which he can do nothing.
>
> A businessman would not consider a firm to have solved its problems of production and to have achieved viability if he saw that it was rapidly consuming its capital. How, then, could we overlook this vital fact when it comes to that very big firm, the economy of Spaceship Earth and, in particular, the economies of its rich passengers?
>
> One reason for overlooking this vital fact is that we are estranged from reality and inclined to treat as valueless everything that we have not made ourselves. . . .

Schumacher goes on to point out that our economic system does not properly consider the cost of using up irreplaceable natural resources. These inputs are considered as free except for the cost of extracting them from the earth. Furthermore, the costs of pollution and human dissatisfaction with work are not accounted for in our economic systems. Schumacher believes the result is technologies which become larger and larger and rapidly consume our national resources.

The solution to these problems which has been suggested by Schumacher and others is to adopt appropriate technologies. Wakefield and Stafford (1977) describe an appropriate technology as one which utilizes a mix of high, intermediate, and low technologies which are in harmony with the environmental and human needs of society.

It is clear that changes in technology will not come easily or quickly or without social and political effects. What is significant about appropriate technology thinking is the realization that managers do have a choice. We can be managers of technology. We should seriously question whether the highest form of technology is the best and whether traditional economics properly reflects today's value systems.

6.3 TECHNOLOGIES AVAILABLE

But one cannot choose a technology without understanding the various technologies available. A brief summary of available technology will be given in this section, beginning with factory technology and proceeding to the office and then to the service industries.

Factory technology

A number of levels of factory technology have been identified on the basis of whether humans or machines provide the power and the control. Table 6.1 shows three such levels. At the hand-made level, humans provide both the power and the control of the tools used. This type of technology includes, for example, cutting lumber with a handsaw and rowing a boat. The technology is characterized by manual labor, hard work, and minimal environmental impacts.

With the machine-made technology shown in Table 6.1, the machine provides the power, but the human still provides control of the tools. Examples of this type of technology include cutting lumber with a chain saw, driving a car, and mowing grass with a rotary mower. This technology eliminates manual labor but still requires the human to control the machine.

On the third level of technology, which is automated, the machine provides both power and control. The human is the programmer and supervisor of machine functions. Examples of this technology are numerically controlled machine tools and automatic transfer lines. In the automobile industry, the Ford Motor Company has an engine transfer line which performs 150 separate machine operations on an engine block. [See Abernathy (1976).] The raw block is fed in at one end of the line and is automatically transferred from one machine to the next as the machines automatically position the block and adjust for tool wear. The role of the operators is to monitor the machine functions and to call maintenance people as needed. Since the machine is so intricate, maintenance people must be very highly trained; however, operators are relatively low-skilled. There are many other examples of this type of technology, including most of the "process" industries (e.g., food, oil, chemicals, and steel).

But automated technology is not confined to line-flow processes. Indeed, numerically controlled (NC) machine tools are used in intermittent processes. NC tools can be programmed, like a computer, to make the particular part wanted. Once the tool has been programmed, the operator's role is to feed material, monitor machine performance, and take away finished products. Even the material-handling function is automated in some cases. Thus both special-purpose and general-

TABLE 6.1   **FACTORY TECHNOLOGY LEVELS**

	Hand-made	Machine-made	Automated
Power	Human	Machine	Machine
Control	Human	Human	Machine

purpose machines and line or intermittent flows can be used at the automated level of technology.

Office technology

Office technology has not advanced very much since the invention of the typewriter. To be sure, there are electric typewriters, electronic copying machines, and dictaphones, but most office work is still labor-intensive (about 80 percent of office costs are for labor). Computerized word-processing technology is now becoming economical and will drastically change offices in the future.

In offices, the transformation process consists of the following activities:

1. Handling messages
2. Typing and retyping paperwork
3. Copying printed materials
4. Filing
5. Keeping a calendar

How will these activities be changed by an automated office?

The automated office will have a computer terminal for each secretary and each manager, connecting them together in a network fashion. When the manager arrives in the office, he or she will use the terminal to obtain all messages from the computer memory—an electronic in-basket. After each message is reviewed, it can be filed in the computer according to date, sender, subject, etc., and a response can be typed into the computer terminal if desired. The response will then be routed electronically to whomever is selected. If some individuals do not have terminals, the computer can be used to type out paper copies for them. The manager can select from a file of standard responses if that is appropriate.

In handling the in-basket, the manager may have occasion to refer to previous messages or correspondence. These can be accessed through the electronic filing system of the computer.

In the automated office, all the office activities previously identified are performed through electronic media. Paperwork is drastically reduced. Repetitive tasks are simplified by electronic filing, on-line correction of errors, and the use of standard responses. This should reduce the cost of secretarial labor, postage, and copying. However, at the present time these cost reductions are not quite sufficient to cover the cost of a completely automated office. They are, however, already sufficient to cover the cost of partial automation through single word-processing stations and electronic mail transfer between some large offices. In the future, as the cost of computer technology is reduced, the fully automated office will become cost-effective. Some companies are already using prototypes of fully automated offices; see, for example, the article by Robert White (1977).

The automated office can also have other impacts on society. For example, offices can be dispersed to outlying sites or even to homes. There is no need to have all office functions centralized in large skyscraper buildings with the attendant transportation and energy costs.

For certain types of businesses, such as life insurance companies, the automated office will provide a reprieve from an avalanche of paperwork. In this type of office of the future, each person will perform his or her task on a computer terminal and then pass the work electronically on to the next work station. With automated offices, managers can easily track the flow of transaction processing to manage and improve the process-flow characteristics. Such an application is very similar to the concept of control of work flow used in factories.

Service industries

Theodore Levitt (1972) has described a new approach to the delivery of services which he calls the "production-line approach to service." With this approach, services are standardized and delivered in an efficient and cheerful manner. The service facility itself is designed so that mistakes are minimized. Various stages of service delivery are automated so that costs are reduced and standardization is achieved.

Levitt uses the McDonald's chain to illustrate these concepts. He points to the special wide-mouth scoop which has been developed to fill French-fry bags to the correct levels more efficiently. All the food inputs at McDonald's are carefully specified to ensure consistency. Procedures for cleaning the restaurants are prescribed. All this is done to standardize the service and to deliver it in a controlled and efficient manner.

In his classic article, Levitt indicates that service people tend to think their problems are different from those of people in manufacturing. Service is often thought of as something which is delivered "out there in the field" under highly variable conditions, while manufacturing is done in a factory under highly controlled and automated conditions. Levitt argues that until the delivery of services is thought of as a transformation process similar to that of manufacturing, little improvement in efficiency or quality will be possible.

Another factor in service thinking is the attitude of personal ministration or servitude. This goes back hundreds of years to when service was equated with obedience, subordination, and subjugation. According to this view, if the service delivered

Figure 6.2
(Reprinted by permission of the Harvard Business Review. Exhibit from Theodore Levitt, "Production-Line Approach to Service," September–October 1972. Copyright © 1972 by the President and Fellows of Harvard College. All rights reserved.)

is low in quality or costly, the solution is to try harder. The solution to service problems is not seen as one of changing the procedures, the task, or the equipment available. Service managers think in humanistic terms and this, according to Levitt, is at the heart of the problem. As long as they are managed in terms of humanistic thinking, services will be inefficient and lacking in quality control. The attitude of servitude distracts management from looking for solutions in the process technology itself.

In contrast, manufacturing problems are often seen in technocratic terms. If there is poor quality or high cost, an analysis is made of the tasks performed, the work flow, and the equipment used. A solution is sought in the technology of the process.

But there are some services which are already being delivered by a "manufacturing approach." Examples are automatic bank tellers, fast-food outlets, supermarkets, car washes, car rentals, and vending machines. At the same time, there are still many services which are delivered on a personal ministration basis. These include health care, legal, educational, life insurance, and repair services. The lack of quality and efficiency in the delivery of these services are among some of the most frustrating problems of society today.

The contrast between technology problems in the service sector and in manufacturing is striking. While some individuals feel that manufacturing should use lower forms of technology which are more appropriate, the service industries appear to be using too little technology. Thus opposite solutions are being prescribed for these two segments of industry.

6.4 TECHNOLOGY CHOICE

Technology choice is often seen as a problem in capital budgeting. One should simply calculate the return on investment (ROI) for various alternatives and choose the one with the best return. Although the ROI calculations are certainly important, they are only part of the decision process.

In the first place, a need or an opportunity for improved technology must be recognized. As we have indicated above, service industries and offices have been slow to recognize such a need. As a greater awareness develops, managers will aggressively pursue these new opportunities for technology.

Once an opportunity for improved technology has been recognized, the alternatives should be subjected to several tests. One test is the ROI provided. The technique of making these calculations is treated in the chapter supplement.

The second test is whether the new technology is compatible with the needs of the work force and the environment. Managers are becoming increasingly aware that ROI is not the only criterion. Furthermore, ROI calculations frequently do not properly reflect the economic effects of higher personnel turnover, absenteeism, and the pollution-control equipment which might be needed. Thus, both quantitative and qualitative effects of the technology must be considered.

Finally, the technology choice itself must be made. In a firm, this decision is likely to involve operations management, top management, and finance, at a minimum. Operations management is deeply involved in this choice because it affects the cost, dependability, quality, and flexibility of operations.

In the public sector, the public and public officials are often involved in questions of technology choice. Electric utilities involve the public in decisions about new generating plants. The public participates in decisions regarding pollution standards for all new technologies and in decisions regarding educational technology. When the public is involved, there will be a great concern about who is affected by the new technology—about public safety and health—in addition to the factors which have already been discussed.

The choice of new process technology is seldom clear cut. While the costs may favor one technology alternative over another, other factors may not. In the end, the decision makers will have to weigh environmental, social, and economic factors in making the choice. In many cases there will be disagreement about the final choice because of the different values and different weights given to the various criteria. The example below illustrates the technology-choice problem.

Example

In this example, assume that a proposal is being evaluated to automate an existing office in a way similar to that described in Section 6.3. Suppose that, at present, the office has eight secretaries doing various clerical tasks such as typing, filing, copying, and message handling. Assume the cost of this office is $8000 per month for clerical labor and $2000 per month for supplies, postage, copying, and equipment.

The proposed automation project will require a computer plus five terminals and memory to handle the current office volume. The equipment will allow all letters and memos to be typed into the computer memory for composition, transmission, copying, and filing purposes. As a result, it is expected that the clerical staff can be reduced to five persons at $5000 per month, and the remaining budget will be $3000 per month. Thus the equipment saves $2000 per month in total operating expenses, but the initial investment cost is $60,000. It is expected that the equipment will last 5 years. The cash-flow stream resulting from this investment is shown in Figure 6.3. Should this technology be used?

Since the savings occur over a future period of time, this problem should utilize discounting to reflect the time value of money. The procedures for discounting are described in the chapter supplement, which should be understood before the remainder of this example is read.

Suppose that a discount rate of 18 percent has been established as a "hurdle rate" for approval of this investment. Using 18 percent, the present value (pv) of the cash-flow stream is as follows:

$$pv = -\$60,000 + \$24,000 \left[\frac{1}{1.18} + \frac{1}{(1.18)^2} + \frac{1}{(1.18)^3} + \frac{1}{(1.18)^4} + \frac{1}{(1.18)^5} \right]$$

$$= -\$60,000 + \$24,000 \ (3.1272)$$

$$= \$15,053$$

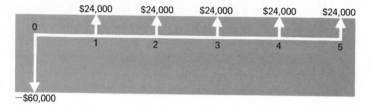

**Figure 6.3
Cash-flow
example.**

Since the present value is positive, the discounted cash savings exceed the investment and the investment is therefore "economically" worthwhile at 18 percent.

This particular decision will involve a number of factors other than the present-value analysis. How can the work force be reduced by three employees? If this reduction is to be achieved through natural attrition, how long will it take? What will be involved in training the present staff to use the new equipment? How will the present employees adjust to the change? How reliable will the equipment be? What type of repair service is available and how will the office operate while the equipment is down? Will the equipment be obsolete in less than 5 years? Should leasing of the equipment be considered instead of buying? All these factors will need to be evaluated as part of the decision process.

The analysis should also incorporate any additional benefits for the automated office. For example, the automated system will do filing of messages and correspondence. As a result, the automated files will probably be in better condition than the current manual files. This improved filing benefit can be reflected in the analysis by adding the cost to provide the same benefit under the current manual system. For example, suppose one additional secretary would have been required to maintain the same file accuracy and cross referencing as the new system will provide. Then $1000 additional savings per month, the cost of one additional secretary, should be added to the savings for the new system. This assumes, of course, that the filing benefit is fully useful and desired in the new system. Similarly, the value of any other additional benefits for the new system should be added to the savings already identified. This procedure will more accurately reflect the value of additional benefits.

6.5 MANAGING TECHNOLOGICAL CHANGE

For the sake of simplicity, we have been treating technological choices as isolated decisions. But the choice of process technology should be viewed as ongoing and evolutionary in nature. Technological choice is not a single decision or a series of separate decisions but a choice process where the decisions are interrelated over time.

In most manufacturing companies, this choice process has been recognized by designating a person or persons within operations who are responsible for process technology. This organizational function—often called "manufacturing engineering" or "process engineering"—is also responsible for other aspects of process design in addition to technological choice. The important thing is that problems of technological choice are under continuous evaluation and supervision. These problems should not be merely left to chance or assigned to someone when a crisis arises.

In contrast, service industries and offices do not usually have someone in operations assigned to process technology choice. Levitt (1972) ascribes this to the fact that service managers think in humanistic, not technological, terms. If services are to be improved through aggressive use of process technology, an organizational function should be established for process design and technology choice. This function would assume the responsibility for technological improvement on an ongoing basis.

Assuming that an operation does have a person (or persons) charged with process technology, possibly as part of a larger responsibility for process design, what then are the critical responsibilities for this person (or persons)? These responsibilities might be categorized as follows:

PROCESS TECHNOLOGY POLICY. An organization should have a policy or strategy for process technology choice which forms a basis for guiding and evaluating individual decisions. The policy might call for evaluating these choices in terms of such criteria as product quality, efficiency, and process flexibility. It might also state what stance the organization expects to take on these criteria in general terms. For example, to what degree does the organization intend to maintain flexibility or cost-efficiency in its processes? Finally, the policy might state whether the organization expects to be a leader in process technology or a follower in the industry. All these parameters are critical in setting the climate and general approach toward process technology decisions.

PRODUCT-PROCESS COORDINATION. A second responsibility might be to coordinate changes in products and process technology within operations. A major cause of change in process technology is product change. When this occurs, there will be a need to integrate product and process changes smoothly so as to minimize the impact on ongoing operations. This responsibility will include ensuring that product designs are made with operations feasibility in mind and that changes in individual processes fit into the overall process policy.

IDENTIFYING PROCESS TECHNOLOGY NEEDS. A third responsibility could be to identify the need for process technology changes. Apart from changes in products, processes may be changed by such other factors as advances in technology, deterioration of equipment, and the replacement of dated procedures and methods. When any of these problems are identified, the need for a change in process technology should be considered. By keeping abreast of the industry and the literature, managers can continually monitor and identify needs for change.

ANALYZING TECHNOLOGICAL DECISIONS. A fourth responsibility might be to analyze the costs and benefits of particular technological-choice alternatives. This analysis would be similar to that described in the example in Section 6.4. Specific responsibilities might include the gathering of all pertinent information and the preparation of a study for management evaluation and approval. The study would usually include a recommendation for a particular process technology alternative.

IMPLEMENTING TECHNOLOGICAL CHANGE. Once a decision is made, the persons responsible for process technology will often be assigned the responsibility for implementing the change in operations. This is perhaps the most difficult responsibility of all because it involves changing not only process but people as well. In writing on the subject of technological innovation, Schoen says,

> In every established organization there exist strong pressures and forces for stability that inevitably make innovation difficult. Management can deal with these most effectively if they are accepted and understood as natural, instead of being treated as annoying aberrations.
>
> The fact of resistance to innovation emerges from nearly all studies of the innovation process. The relationship between the entrepreneur (in an established organization) and resistance sometimes appears almost to follow Newton's third law of motion (action and reaction are equal and opposite). . . . [See Schoen (1969).]

Schoen goes on to indicate that most of the resistance to change can be attributed to normal human fears, including loss of a job, change in social status, failure, added workload, the need to develop new skills, and disruption of the organization. These fears must be effectively overcome if a new technology is to be successfully installed. Most of the problems encountered in using new technologies can be attributed to these human problems rather than to issues of a technical nature.

In summary, all operations should have one or more persons responsible for process technology, possibly as part of a larger responsibility for process design. This will ensure that technology decisions are not fragmented but treated in an integrated and comprehensive manner. The need is particularly critical in the service industries and in offices, where the process technology function does not usually exist. We have also identified some responsibilities this function should assume in viewing process technology as a broad area of management responsibility.

6.6 INTEGRATION OF PROCESS-DESIGN DECISIONS

At this point is might be helpful to emphasize the interaction between process-design decisions and other decisions in operations. A convenient way to describe these interactions is to use the five decision areas in operations.

As we have already noted, the capacity of physical facilities will affect process-selection and technology decisions. If a large capacity is required, a high-volume line process may be warranted. For lower capacities, an intermittent or project form of process may be more appropriate.

The process decisions, in turn, affect the type of production and inventory control system used. A line process generally leads to a more simplified form of production and inventory control than an intermittent process. This is true because the flows in a line process are very regular and consistent, while the flows in an intermittent process are complex and constantly changing.

Process decisions also affect scheduling methods, as we shall see later. When a line process is used, certain types of scheduling methods are appropriate. When an intermittent process is used, other scheduling methods are more appropriate.

The process and technology decisions affect the type of work force employed and the types of jobs designed. A line process which is highly automated calls for relatively low labor skills and repetitive jobs. An intermittent process requires higher skill levels and leads to greater job variety because of the changing requirements of the job.

The line process facilitates quality planning and control. Since the product and process are standardized, quality can be more easily specified and inspections can be carefully planned. For the intermittent process, the high level of product variety and constantly changing requirements make quality more difficult to define and control.

As can be seen, process decisions are interrelated with each of the other four decision categories. If a new process is being designed, the relationship with the existing processes, if any, must also be recognized. These existing processes may affect the type of new process selected, the degree of automation, and the type of technology used.

6.7 KEY POINTS

In this chapter, we have considered the choice of process technology for operations. It was argued that the highest form of technology is not always the best from an economic, social, and strategic point of view; therefore a choice is indeed required.

The key points discussed in this chapter are:

- Technology is that set of processes, tools, methods, procedures, and equipment which is used to produce goods or services. This definition is broader than simply "equipment selection" and includes choice of procedure and methods as part of the technology.
- One of the most important points in the chapter is that technology choice, by fixing jobs and working conditions, also automatically includes social choice. It is, therefore, important to consider the joint social and technical consequences through the concept of a sociotechnical design. Through the use of this concept, technologies are chosen to optimize both social and technical variables.
- Sociologists and economists have proposed the concept that "small is beautiful" and have advocated the adoption of both "appropriate technology" and "voluntary simplicity." According to this thinking, the effects of pollution, job dissatisfaction, and environmental depletion may render intermediate technologies more appropriate than the highest forms of technology for some types of production. In terms of this approach, our analysis must include traditionally noneconomic costs of environmental and social effects. The result could be a mix of high, intermediate, and lower technologies.
- Managers should have knowledge of the performance characteristics of technologies they manage. These performance characteristics include possible effects

on inputs, outputs, process flow, and costs, which can be properly evaluated only by managers.

- In the factory, there has been a great movement from hand-made technologies to machine-made and automated technologies. With the introduction of computers and the interconnection of previously separate office components and offices, office technology is rapidly changing. This new office technology promises to reduce the volume of paperwork, to reduce clerical costs, and to enrich clerical jobs. In a similar way, the automation of service operations offers great potential. As services are viewed in technical rather than humanistic terms, automation and standardization become possible. This can result not only in lower costs but also in more uniform quality.

- The choice of technology should not be based solely on ROI. The effects of technology on operations objectives, on the work force, and on the environment should also be considered.

- Finally, technology choice should not be a single act but rather a well-organized process which includes continuous surveillance of technology, choice of appropriate technologies, and implementation of technology choice. If these functions are to be performed, it will be necessary to designate a manager in operations who will be responsible for staff support of process design and choice of process technology.

QUESTIONS

1. How is the problem of technology choice related to process selection and product design? *all related*
2. Schumacher says that a fateful error of our age is the belief that "the problem of production" has been solved. What are the consequences of this error?
3. How much detailed technical knowledge on the part of managers is required to make a decision regarding the selection of computer hardware?
4. Suppose you need to select a computer terminal to use in your office. What performance characteristics of the technology would you assess? How would you get the necessary information to make the selection?
5. Describe a sociotechnical approach to the selection of computer input devices from among alternatives including the keypunch, on-line terminal, and printed document reader.
6. How do the concepts of a sociotechnical approach and appropriate technology fit in with the profit-making objectives of a business?
7. What does it mean to choose an appropriate technology for the following processes?
   a. Electricity generation
   b. Production of automobiles
8. Do higher forms of technology necessarily result in more pollution, boring jobs, and other societal ills? Discuss.
9. Suppose your boss has asked you to evaluate the possibilities of office automation. How would you approach this problem? What information would you gather?
10. What is meant by a manufacturing or technocratic approach to the delivery of services?
11. Is the success of the McDonald's chain attributable to a marketing concept or an operations concept? Discuss.
12. What is the main obstacle to using a manufacturing approach to the delivery of services?
13. In managing the process of technology choice, why is a separate office or organizational function required?

SELECTED BIBLIOGRAPHY

ABERNATHY, WILLIAM J.: "Production Process Structure and Technological Change," *Decision Sciences,* vol. 7, no. 4, October 1976, pp. 607–619.

BRIGHT, JAMES: "Does Automation Raise Skill Requirements?" *Harvard Business Review,* July–August 1958, pp. 85–98.

DRUCKER, PETER: *The Age of Discontinuity,* New York: Harper & Row, 1969.

HARVARD BUSINESS SCHOOL: "Technology and the Manager," Working Paper 9-671-060, Boston: Intercollegiate Case Clearing House, rev. March 1977.

LEVITT, THEODORE: "Production-Line Approach to Service," *Harvard Business Review,* September–October 1972, pp. 41–52.

SCHOEN, DONALD: "Managing Technological Innovation," *Harvard Business Review,* May–June 1969, pp. 156–162.

SCHUMACHER, E. F.: *Small Is Beautiful,* New York: Harper & Row, 1973.

WAKEFIELD, ROWAN, and PATRICIA STAFFORD: "Appropriate Technology: What Is It and Where Is It Going?" *The Futurist,* April 1977, pp. 72–77.

WHITE, ROBERT B.: "A Prototype of the Automated Office," *Datamation,* April 1977, pp. 83–90.

SUPPLEMENT: FINANCIAL ANALYSIS

Decisions regarding the choice of technology or process design require investment of capital. Therefore, these decisions utilize financial analysis of discounted cash flows or present values to determine economic worth. In this supplement, several methods of financial analysis will be described, particularly as they relate to decisions in operations.

Typical operations decisions which require detailed financial analysis are:

1. The purchase of new equipment or facilities
2. The replacement of existing equipment or facilities
3. The choice between two different technologies or pieces of equipment

An example of each of these decisions will be described later in the supplement.

CONCEPTS

Before methods are described in detail, it is important to discuss several concepts of cost and investment analysis.

Fixed and variable costs. Fixed costs do not vary with the volume of output, while variable costs vary directly with volume. Although the definition of fixed and variable costs is clear cut, several difficulties are encountered in practice. First, all costs are variable in the long run. Thus fixed and variable costs must be defined within the relevant time range of the decision. For example, 2 years may be selected as the appropriate time range for definition of fixed and variable costs. The second difficulty is that costs are fixed or variable only over some range of volume. For example, the fixed cost of a product might be $10,000 and the variable cost $1 per unit for the first 10,000 units. Beyond 10,000 units, another $5000 of fixed cost is required and the variable cost becomes 90 cents a unit. As a result, both time horizon and volume range must be specified for fixed and variable costs.

Sunk costs. Sunk costs are those costs which do not vary with the decision to be made. Sunk costs can therefore be ignored for purposes of decision making. If, for example, a decision is being made to produce 1000 additional tons of flour from an existing flour mill, the cost of the mill can be ignored, since it is a sunk cost. Whether the additional flour is produced or not will have no effect on the cost of the flour mill itself.

Cash flow. One of the principles of investment analysis is to consider only cash flows resulting from the investment. This means that all allocated costs from previous investments, all allocated overhead costs, and depreciation charges are irrelevant for purposes of the investment decision. Only the direct cash flow, or out-of-pocket cost, resulting from the investment is considered. In any given situation, one must then carefully separate cash flows from other costs.

Depreciation. Depreciation is a way of allocating investment costs to the units produced. Depreciation costs represent consumption or usage of the capital investment during production. In investment analysis, depreciation has an effect on taxes paid. Since depreciation is an expense, it reduces taxes; but depreciation itself is not a cash-flow expense. Depreciation is merely a book-keeping charge which reduces taxes.

There are several methods of depreciation, the simplest being straight-line depreciation. If, for example, the life of an investment is 5 years, the initial cost is $10,000, and the salvage value is $2000 at the end of 5 years, then the annual depreciation charge D is $1600 per year.

$$D = \frac{\$10,000 - \$2000}{5} = \$1600$$

Straight-line depreciation assumes that capital is consumed on a uniform basis. This is the least advantageous method of depreciation from a tax standpoint.

Another method of depreciation is sum-of-the-years digits (SYD). With this method, greater depreciation is allowed in the early years of an investment and less in the later years. The precise amount of depreciation is obtained by first adding the digits for the life of the investment. On the basis of a 5-year life, the sum of the digits is:

$$5 + 4 + 3 + 2 + 1 = 15$$

In the first year, the depreciation is $5/15$ of the value of the investment (investment − salvage); the second year the depreciation is $4/15$ of the investment value, and so on until the fifth year, when the depreciation is $1/15$ of the value of the investment. With this approach, the fraction taken each year should add up to 1 as follows:

Year	Fraction	Investment value		Annual depreciation
1	5/15	× 8000	=	$2667
2	4/15	× 8000	=	2133
3	3/15	× 8000	=	1600
4	2/15	× 8000	=	1067
5	1/15	× 8000	=	533
	$\overline{1}$			$\overline{\$8000}$

Notice how the amount of depreciation starts high, with $1/3$ in the first year, and drops off rapidly to $1/15$ in the last year. From a tax standpoint, less taxes will be paid in early years, which is advantageous from a cash-flow standpoint.

Another form of accelerated depreciation is the declining-balance method. Using double declining balance, twice the straight-line rate is used, although other multiples (e.g., 150 percent) may be used too. With the declining-balance method, the original investment is depreciated without regard for salvage value. For example, suppose the above investment is depreciated using a double-declining balance. Since the straight-line rate is 20 percent (for 5 years), the double-declining rate is 40 percent. Using the 40 percent rate on the remaining balance in each year, the depreciation is:

Year	Rate (%)	Remaining balance	Depreciation
1	40	10,000	4000
2	40	6,000	2400
3	40	3,600	1440
4	40	2,160	160
5	40	2,000	—

Notice how only $160 in depreciation is taken in year 4, because the remaining balance cannot decrease below the salvage value of $2000.

The depreciation method which may be used is determined by the U.S. Internal Revenue Service. Whenever they are permitted, the accelerated methods are advantageous to the investor because they permit a greater cash flow after taxes in the earlier years.

Taxes

Investments should always be evaluated on an after-tax basis. This provides a true return to the investor. There are two considerations for tax purposes: the first is depreciation, which we have already described, and the second is the investment tax credit, which is a direct deduction from taxes. For example, if a 10 percent investment tax credit is in effect and the investment is $10,000, then the investor is allowed to deduct $1000 (10 percent of the $10,000) from the taxes due in the first year.

For medium and large companies, the tax rate is about 50 percent. In terms of this tax rate, we will illustrate how depreciation and tax credits affect the investor's cash flow. Suppose an investment of $10,000 is made which results in a pretax cash flow of $1500 a year for 10 years. This annual cash flow is the net of revenues over actual out-of-pocket expenses in each year. Also assume that in this case straight-line depreciation is used for a 10-year economic life. The depreciation will be $1000 a year assuming no salvage value at the end of 10 years. The net income of the investment for tax purposes is therefore $500.

Cash flow	$1500
Depreciation	1000
Net income	$ 500

On its net income, the company will pay $250 in taxes at the 50 percent rate. The cash flow is therefore reduced to $1250 ($1500 − $250) on an after-tax basis. An investment tax credit of 10 percent will increase the cash flow by $1000 to a total of $2250 in the first year *only*.

In some cases, depreciation can increase rather than decrease the cash flow after taxes. For example, suppose the cash flow from the above investment is only $500 instead of $1500 a year. Then we have:

Cash flow	$ 500
Depreciation	1000
Net loss	$ 500
Tax savings	250

The after-tax cash flow would be $500 + $250 = $750 a year due to the tax savings of $250 a year. We would also have the additional investment tax credit of $1000 in the first year.

TIME VALUE OF MONEY

In evaluating investments, we should consider the time value of money. We would rather have a dollar now than a dollar a year from now be-

cause we could invest the current dollar and earn a return on it for a year. Therefore, any future cash flows have less value to us than current cash flows. As a result, future cash flows must be discounted or reduced in value to their present values in order for future dollars to be comparable to present dollars.

Discounting of future cash flows is based on the idea of compound interest. If we have P dollars at the present time and invest it at an interest rate of i, the future value in one year will be

$$F_1 = P + iP = P(1 + i)$$

In n years, at compound interest, the value of our P dollars will be

$$F_n = P(1 + i)^n$$

This assumes that the interest is reinvested each year as it is earned.

If we divide the above equation by $(1 + i)^n$, we will have:

$$P = \frac{F_n}{(1 + i)^n}$$

By turning the compound interest equation around, we see that the present value of an amount F_n paid in n years is simply P. We can, therefore, discount F_n to its present value by multiplying by the quantity $\frac{1}{(1 + i)^n}$. This quantity is known as the discount factor of the present value of $1 in year n. Values of the discount factor are tabulated in Appendix C. These factors can be used to convert any future cash flow to a present-value amount.

For example, suppose an investment has an annual cash flow of $1000 after taxes for 5 years. The present value of this cash stream at 10 percent interest is $3790.

n Year	Return	$\frac{1}{(1 + .1)^n}$	Present value
1	$1000	.909	$ 909
2	1000	.826	826
3	1000	.751	751
4	1000	.683	683
5	1000	.621	621
			$3790

In this case, each future cash amount was converted to a present value and the present values were then added. As a result, if we want to earn 10 percent on our money, we would be willing to invest $3790, the present value, now so as to get the future earnings of $1000 a year for 5 years.

In discounting future cash flows, it is also convenient to know the present value of a $1 annuity each year for n years. The annuity's present value is:

$$P = \frac{1}{1 + i} + \frac{1}{(1 + i)^2} + \cdots + \frac{1}{(1 + i)^n}$$

Here we have discounted $1 each year back to the present time and added. The resulting values of P are tabulated in Appendix D for various interest rates and numbers of years.

We can solve the above problem directly by using the annuity's present values. For example, the present value of $1 a year for 5 years at 10 percent interest, from Appendix D, is 3.791. If $1000 is earned each year for 5 years, the present value is:

$$P = \$1000 \, (3.791) = \$3791$$

This is the same figure we arrived at above by adding the present values for each year.[1] The annuity table, therefore, saves time when uniform annual payments are present. The modern calculator, however, may be even more convenient than the table.

In some investment problems, it is necessary to calculate an internal rate of return (IROR). The IROR is the interest rate which will just make the present investment equal to the future stream of earnings. In mathematical notation, suppose that an investment I has after-tax cash flows C_1 in year one, C_2 in year two, . . . , C_n in year n. The IROR is obtained by solving the following equation for i:

$$I = \frac{C_1}{1 + i} + \frac{C_2}{(1 + i)^2} + \cdots + \frac{C_n}{(1 + i)^n}$$

[1] With the exception of roundoff error in the last digit.

In general, the value of i is obtained by trial and error or iteration using the above equation. Suppose, for example, that we invest $5000 and earn $3000 in the first year, $2000 in the second year, and $2500 in the third year. Arbitrarily, assume $i = 20$ percent and solve the equation

$$I = \frac{\$3000}{1 + .20} + \frac{\$2000}{(1 + .20)^2} + \frac{\$2500}{(1 + .20)^3}$$

$$= \$5335$$

Since $5335 is larger than the $5000 investment, we need a larger value of i to reduce the right-hand side. Assuming $i = .30$, we have:

$$I = \frac{\$3000}{1 + .30} + \frac{\$2000}{(1 + .30)^2} + \frac{\$2500}{(1 + .30)^3}$$

$$= \$4629$$

Since $I = \$4629$ is smaller than the investment of $5000, the true value of i lies between 20 and 30 percent. Using linear interpolation, we can estimate that

$$i = .30 - .10 \left(\frac{\$5000 - \$4629}{\$5335 - \$4629} \right) = .2475$$

Using $i = .2475$ in the equation to check the result, we have:

$$I = \frac{\$3000}{1 + .2475} + \frac{\$2000}{(1 + .2475)^2} + \frac{\$2500}{(1 + .2475)^3}$$

$$= \$4977$$

Since this result, $I = \$.4977$, is slightly below $5000, we should reduce the interest rate a little more, perhaps to .24. By successive approximation, we will finally arrive at the interest rate to any desired degree of approximation.

In cases where the annual payments are equal, we can use the annuity tables (Appendix D) to find the IROR directly. For example, if the $5000 investment earns $2500 each year for 3 years, the following equation must be solved:

$$\$5000 = \$2500 \left[\frac{1}{1 + i} + \frac{1}{(1 + i)^2} + \frac{1}{(1 + i)^3} \right]$$

The annuity factor is therefore $5000/2500 = 2.0$. From Appendix D, the interest rate for 3 years will be between 22 and 24 percent. The estimated figure, by interpolation, is 23.4 percent.

CHOOSING INVESTMENT PROJECTS

Now that we know how to calculate present values and internal rates of return, we can apply these ideas to choosing investment projects. Suppose there is a portfolio of investment alternatives. How should we choose among these alternatives or rank them in order of preference?

In general, there are three ways to make the choice; payback, present value, and IROR.

Payback. According to the payback method, a payback period for each investment is calculated as follows:

$$N = \frac{I - S}{A}$$

where N = payback period in years
I = investment
S = salvage value
A = annual cash flow after tax

The investments in the portfolio are then ranked in order of their payback periods.

For example, suppose a $10,000 investment will earn $2000 a year after taxes, and there is no salvage value. The payback period for this investment is then 5 years.

The payback method has several shortcomings. First, the length of the earning period of the investment is not taken into account. Two investments could have the same payback period but drastically different lifetimes. The second problem with the payback method is that it does not consider the time value of money. Thus different earnings streams are not evaluated dif-

ferently. Finally, the above formula requires a constant annual cash flow. This assumption could easily be relaxed, however, by determining the time required for earnings to equal the investment.

Although the payback method has serious weaknesses, it is still quite popular because it gives a sense of time to recover the investment. Nevertheless, it is being replaced by the next two methods as ways to rank investment alternatives.

Net present value. Whenever a hurdle rate or cost of capital is specified for investment comparisons, the investments can be compared through the use of present values. The given hurdle rate is used as the "interest" rate, and all future cash flows are discounted to the present time. The net present value (NPV) is then computed as follows:

$$NPV = -I + \sum_{j=1}^{N} P_j$$

where I = investment required
P_j = present value of cash flow for year j

Whenever the net present value exceeds zero, the investment is worthwhile at the specified hurdle rate. If capital is limited, the investments can be ranked in terms of NPV from largest to smallest and funded in order of priority until capital is exhausted.

Internal rate of return. The IROR can also be used to rank investments and select those for funding from the portfolio. Figure S6.1 shows several investments ranked by IROR and the cost of capital as a function of the amount invested. Notice how the cost of capital increases when large amounts of investment are required. As a result, the IROR falls below the cost of capital for alternatives E and F. In this case, alternatives A, B, C, and D should be funded because their IROR exceeds the cost of capital, and alternatives E and F should not be funded.

The NPV and IROR methods are the opposite of each other. With NPV, the "interest" rate

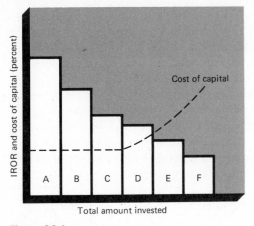

Figure S6.1
Investment projects.

or cost of capital is used to compute NPVs; a positive NPV indicates a worthwhile investment. For IROR, the "interest" rate is not given but is computed and compared with the cost of capital. An IROR greater than the cost of capital is considered a worthwhile investment.

If two investments have equal lifetimes, both IROR and NPV methods will yield the same result. If investment lifetimes vary, however, these methods require additional assumptions to yield a correct answer. The additional assumptions must specify what is done after the lifetime of the shortest investment. Is the capital invested in a riskless investment, a like investment, a technologically superior alternative, or what? The answer to these questions will affect the ranking of the alternatives.

A series of applications of the above investment methods will be described next. In each case, not only the numerical analysis but also other factors in the decision will be discussed.

PURCHASE OF A NEW MACHINE

The operations department is considering the installation of a machine to reduce the labor required in one of its processes. The machine will

cost $50,000 and have a 5-year life, with a salvage value of $10,000 at the end of 5 years. The pretax cash-flow savings in labor which will accrue over the cost of operating the machine is $11,000 per year. Assume a 50 percent bracket, straight-line depreciation, and a 10 percent investment tax credit. What is the NPV of the investment at a 15 percent hurdle rate after tax? What IROR does the investment provide?

In all investment problems, the cash flow must, first, be determined on an annual basis. In this case, the annual cash flow is:

Cash flow—pretax	$11,000
Depreciation	8,000
Net income	$3,000
Additional taxes	1,500

Since the additional taxes paid are $1500 per year, the cash flow after tax is $9500 per year ($11,000 − $1500). In the first year, there is an additional tax credit of $5000 (10 percent of $50,000). The net cash flow in the first year is therefore $14,500 ($9500 + $5000). The after-tax cash flows—assuming that all of these occur at the end of the year—are shown in Figure S6.2. Here, investments and cash outflows are shown as negative numbers while cash inflows and salvage values are shown as positive numbers. It is always helpful to draw one of these cash-flow diagrams prior to making NPV or IROR calculations.

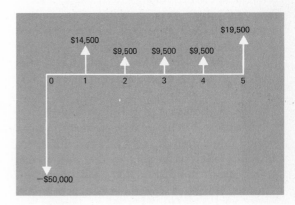

Figure S6.2
Cash flow, example 1.

The NPV at 15 percent cost of capital is:

$$\text{NPV} = -\$50,000 + \left[\frac{\$14,500}{1 + .15} + \frac{\$9500}{(1 + .15)^2} \right.$$

$$+ \frac{\$9500}{(1 + .15)^3} + \frac{\$9500}{(1 + .15)^4}$$

$$\left. + \frac{\$19,500}{(1 + .15)^5} \right]$$

$$\text{NPV} = -\$50,000 + \$41,165$$

$$\text{NPV} = -\$8835$$

Since the NPV is negative, the investment is not worthwhile at 15 percent.

The IROR is obtained by inserting i in place of .15 in the above equation and solving for an NPV = 0. Thus the IROR must satisfy the following equation:

$$0 = -\$50,000 + \left[\frac{\$14,500}{1 + i} + \frac{\$9500}{(1 + i)^2} \right.$$

$$\left. + \frac{\$9500}{(1 + i)^3} + \frac{\$9500}{(1 + i)^4} + \frac{\$19,500}{(1 + i)^5} \right]$$

Since the NPV at 15 percent was negative, we know that $i < .15$. As a trial value select $i = .10$ and plug into the right-hand side of the above equation. At $i = .10$, we have NPV = $-\$3232$. Since NPV is still negative, try a smaller interest rate, say 5 percent, which yields an NPV of $3727. Since this NPV is positive, the interest rate must lie between 5 and 10 percent. By interpolation:

$$i = 5 + \frac{\$3727}{\$3232 + \$3727} (10 - 5) = 7.7\%$$

The IROR is thus estimated to be 7.7 percent.

In this case, there are other factors to be considered in the decision, such as a possible loss of flexibility after converting to the machine and more consistent quality due to the machine. Since the ROI is so low, these factors will probably not be overriding.

MACHINE REPLACEMENT

The second example is the well-known machine-replacement problem, where the decision is whether or not to replace a current machine with a new model. Suppose for the sake of this example that we have a 3-year-old car and are considering whether to replace it with a new one. If the car is not replaced now, assume it will be driven for another 3 years. For each alternative, the following costs are given:

	Year		
Keep old car	**1**	**2**	**3**
Maintenance	$ 200	$250	$ 300
Tires	200	—	—
Gas and oil	600	600	600
Insurance and license	150	125	100
Total	$1150	$975	$1000
Buy new car			
Maintenance	$ 50	$150	$200
Tires	—	—	—
Gas and oil	400	400	400
Insurance and license	250	200	150
Total	$700	$750	$750

The new car is expected to get better gas mileage, as reflected in the above costs of gas and oil. The new car will have higher insurance and license costs but lower maintenance and tire costs, also as shown in the above numbers. The net result is that the new car will be less expensive to operate than the old one.

Assume that the new car will cost $5000 ($2000 with the trade-in) and it will be worth $3000 at the end of 3 years. Also assume that the old car is worth $3000 now and will be worth $1400 in 3 more years.

The cash-flow pattern for the difference between these two alternatives is shown in Figure S6.3. The new-car alternative requires a net investment of $2000 at time zero, including the trade-in. The new-car alternative will save $450 in the first year, $225 in the second year, and $250

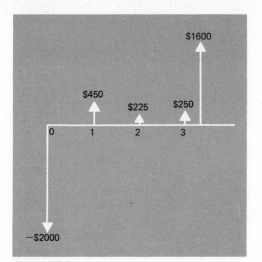

Figure S6.3
Cash flow, example 2. The cash flows reflect the net difference between purchasing the new car and keeping the old car.

in the third year. In addition, the salvage value of the new car will be $1600 ($3000 − $1400) more than the old car's salvage value at the end of 3 years. Since this is a personal decision, there will be no depreciation and no tax consequences.

As in the previous example, there are two questions which can be asked: (1) is the new car worth the investment at some given rate of interest, perhaps 15 percent and (2) what rate of interest does the investment earn? The first question can be answered by computing the net present value of the cash flow shown in Figure S6.3.

$$NPV = -\$2000 + \frac{\$450}{1.15} + \frac{\$225}{(1.15)^2}$$

$$+ \frac{\$250}{(1.15)^3} + \frac{\$1600}{(1.15)^3}$$

$$NPV = -\$2000 + \$1778 = -\$222$$

Since the net present value of the investment is negative, it is not worthwhile to buy the new car at 15 percent return on capital.

The IROR is the interest rate which makes the above net present value equal to zero. By iteration, we find that IROR = 9.6 percent.

In this example, there are several additional questions of interest. First, what is the value of capital to the car buyer? If the buyer takes the money out of a savings account, the after-tax value of capital might be about 7 or 8 percent. At this rate the investment would clearly be worthwhile, since the IROR is 9.6 percent. If the capital were diverted from other personal investments which could earn, say, 15 percent after tax, then the investment would not be worthwhile.

The new-car buyer would also want to consider the intangible value of having a new car. The buyer might have fewer repair problems, there might be less squeaks and rattles, and there would be an aesthetic value to owning the new car. It would be difficult to put a dollar figure on such intangible benefits, and they would probably have to be incorporated subjectively in the decision. One way to evaluate these intangibles, however, is to compute their dollar value. If capital is worth 15 percent, the intangibles would have to be worth more than $222 (the negative amount of present value) to go ahead with the decision.

Similar problems are encountered in process technology choice when a current machine is being replaced by a new one. The new machine will require additional investment, but it will probably reduce annual operating costs. The new machine will also provide intangible benefits, as does the new car, such as less production disruptions through greater reliability.

CHOICE BETWEEN TWO DIFFERENT TECHNOLOGIES

The third example is the most complicated of all. Assume that two alternative technologies are being considered for a *new* process. There is no existing manual or automatic process. The first technology has a higher investment cost but a lower annual operating cost than the second. A situation such as this may be encountered where special-purpose and general-purpose machines

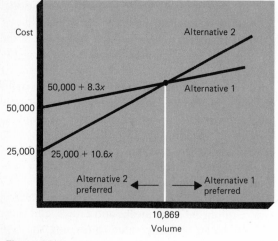

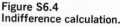

Figure S6.4
Indifference calculation.

are being considered. The special-purposes machine costs more to buy but less to operate per unit produced. To further complicate the example, assume that the first technology will last for 6 years while the second has only a 3-year life.

In comparing these technologies, one might first do a break-even analysis without discount-

ing (see Chapter 2 for details). For this calculation, we need the following information:

Alternative 1: Initial investment = $50,000
Variable cost = $8.30 per unit

Alternative 2: Initial investment = $25,000
Variable cost = $10.60 per unit

A cost-volume graph for these two alternatives is shown in Figure S6.4. The graph indicates that alternative 2 is least costly for a volume of less than 10,869 units and alternative 1 is least costly above that volume. The break-even volume or crossover point may be calculated algebraically as follows:

$$50,000 + 8.30x = 25,000 + 10.60x$$
$$x(2.30) = 25,000$$
$$x = 10,869 \text{ units}$$

This comparison does not consider either the time value of money or the different lifetimes of the two investments. If these factors are to be considered, a cash-flow analysis is needed. This will require an estimate of annual volume, which

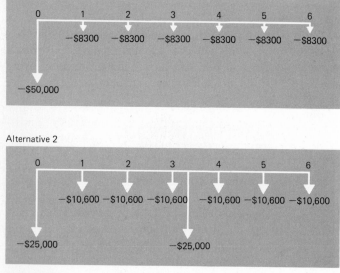

Figure S6.5
Cash flow, example 3.

is assumed to be the same for both alternatives, since the costs of these alternatives are being compared to produce the same output level. (If different output levels were involved, revenue would be brought into the picture through a profit analysis.)

Suppose the annual volume is estimated at 1000 units per year for each of the next 6 years. In this case, the after-tax cash flows for each alternative are shown in Figure S6.5; all of them are costs (negative values). Notice that a 6-year pattern of costs is assumed to make the two investment lifetimes equal for comparison purposes. In the case of alternative 2, this will require a second investment of $25,000 after the first 3 years. At the end of 6 years, both investments will have zero salvage values.

Assuming an interest rate of 12 percent, the net present value of each alternative is then as follows:

$$NPV_1 = -\$50,000 + \frac{-\$8300}{1.12} + \frac{-\$8300}{(1.12)^2}$$

$$+ \frac{-\$8300}{(1.12)^3} + \frac{-\$8300}{(1.14)^4}$$

$$+ \frac{-\$8300}{(1.12)^5} + \frac{-\$8300}{(1.12)^6}$$

$$NPV_1 = -\$84,124$$

$$NPV_2 = -\$25,000 + \frac{-\$10,600}{1.12} + \frac{-\$10,600}{(1.12)^2}$$

$$+ \frac{-\$10,600}{(1.12)^3} + \frac{-\$25,000}{(1.12)^3} + \frac{-\$10,600}{(1.12)^4}$$

$$+ \frac{-\$10,600}{(1.12)^5} + \frac{-\$10,600}{(1.12)^6}$$

$$NPV_2 = -\$86,375$$

Since alternative 1 costs the least, it is preferred at a 12 percent interest rate.

If the interest rate is increased, then eventually alternative 2 will be preferred. By successive calculation, we find that alternative 2 is preferred for interest rates above 15.2 percent. In this case, there is no discounted IROR calculation because the alternatives involve only costs; the object is to find the least-cost alternative.

Another way to look at this problem is to compare the annual cost for each alternative. In this case, for alternative 1, the initial investment of $50,000 is converted into an annual payment of $\frac{\$50,000}{4.111} = \$12,162$ for 6 years.[2] In other words, paying $50,000 now is equivalent to paying $12,162 a year for 6 years at 12 percent compounded. Similarly, for alternative 2, the $25,000 is converted into an annual payment of $\frac{\$25,000}{2.4018} = $ $10,409 for 3 years at 12 percent interest. The total annual cost of each alternative is thus:

	Alternative 1	Alternative 2
Investment annualized	$12,162	$10,409
Operating annual	8,300	10,600
Total annual	$20,462	$21,009

The result is the same: alternative 1 is least costly.

This method of converting investment costs to an annual basis has the advantage that any two lifetimes can easily be compared. For example, suppose one alternative has a lifetime of 3 years and another a lifetime of 7 years. With the first method, a 21-year time horizon would be required to equalize the cash flows. With the second, the 7-year and 3-year cash flows can be compared directly by converting these investments to an equivalent annual basis.

In this case, there might also be intangible considerations. For example, alternative 2 is exposed to less technological risk because it must last for only 3 years, not 6. Alternative 2 is also less risky from a volume standpoint if volume is less than expected. For example, if volume is only half that projected, then alternative 2 would

[2] The factor of 4.111 may be found in Appendix E, or the factor may be computed as the sum of $\frac{1}{1.12} + \frac{1}{(1.12)^2} +$ $\frac{1}{(1.12)^3} + \frac{1}{(1.12)^4} + \frac{1}{(1.12)^5} + \frac{1}{(1.12)^6}$.

be less expensive. So alternative 2 might be favored if the volume estimates appear optimistic or if technology is rapidly changing. Lower investment cost and flexible technology are often preferred in the early life cycles of products and processes.

The three examples illustrate three different types decisions on choice of process technology.

The first example was a choice between an existing manual technology and a proposed new automated technology. The second problem was one of technology replacement, and the third was a choice between two different technologies for a new facility. In practice, there are other variations of these problems, but the basic principles still apply.

QUESTIONS

1. What are the advantages and disadvantages in using the payback method?
2. Under what conditions would you use the IROR or NPV method?
3. What problems are created by unequal investment lives? How are these problems handled?
4. Precisely how does depreciation affect cash flows?
5. What is the advantage of using SYD or declining-balance depreciation over the straight-line method?
6. Under what conditions would you choose an investment which does not meet the hurdle rate?

PROBLEMS

1. A factory is considering the installation of a new machine which will replace three workers who have been doing the job by manual methods. The combined wages and benefits of the three workers are $50,000 per year. The new machine will be run by a single operator paid $15,000 a year in wages and benefits; it will also require $5000 a year for maintenance and utilities expense. The machine will provide the same output as the manual method, but the investment and installation cost will be $50,000. For tax purposes, the machine can be depreciated over a 5-year period using a double declining balance. Assume a 50 percent tax rate, a 10 percent investment tax credit, and no salvage value. *STRAIGHT LINE DEP*
   a. Is the machine a good investment at a 20 percent interest rate? Use a 10-year machine life.
   b. Calculate the IROR for this decision.
   c. What other issues are important in this process technology decision?
2. A laundromat is considering replacing its washers and dryers. Two options are available.
   Option A: The new machines will cost $10,000 initially and $12,000 per year to operate. Expected life for taxes and operations purposes is 5 years.
   Option B: The new machines will cost $14,000 initially and $11,000 per year to operate. Expected life for taxes and operations purposes is 10 years.
   a. Using straight-line depreciation, which option is the best at a 15 percent interest rate? Assume a 50 percent tax rate.
   b. What is the break-even interest rate, where the two options have equal present values?
3. A machine has been used in production for 5 years and is being considered for replacement. At the present time the machine is fully depreciated but could be sold for $5000. The firm pays tax on half of all capital gains. The new machine being considered will cost $20,000 and will have a 5-year life for both tax and cash-flow considerations. The new machine will require one less operator at a savings of $10,000 per year in wages and benefits. Assume no salvage value, a 50 percent corporate income tax, a 10 percent investment tax credit, and straight-line depreciation. *50% TAX BCKT*
   a. What is the NPV of the investment at 15 percent?
   b. What is the IROR?
   c. What additional factors would you consider in this decision?

4. The ABC Company is considering whether to lease or own its automobiles. If an automobile is purchased, it will cost an average of $8000. It will be driven for 20,000 miles a year and can be sold for $3000 at the end of 3 years. Assume that the out-of-pocket expenses for gasoline, oil, and repairs are 20 cents per mile. Also assume that the SYD method is used for depreciation with a 3-year life and $3000 salvage value. If the leasing option is used, the lease will cost 30 cents per mile driven. This cost includes the car plus all gas, oil, and repairs.
   a. If the cost of capital is 20 percent, should the company buy or lease the cars? Assume a 50 percent tax rate.
   b. What is the IROR of this investment?
   c. What are the intangible factors in this decision?

SELECTED BIBLIOGRAPHY

ANTHONY, ROBERT N., and GLENN A. WELSCH: *Fundamentals of Management Accounting,* Homewood, Ill.: Irwin, 1974.

GRANT, EUGENE L., and W. GRANT IRESON: *Principles of Engineering Economy,* 5th ed., New York: Ronald, 1970.

VAN HORNE, JAMES C.: *Financial Management and Policy,* 3d ed., Englewood Cliffs, N.J.: Prentice-Hall, 1974.

WELSCH, GLENN A., and ROBERT N. ANTHONY: *Fundamentals of Financial Accounting,* Homewood, Ill.: Irwin, 1974.

CHAPTER 7
PROCESS-FLOW ANALYSIS

In the last two chapters, we dealt with macro-level decisions in process design. These macro decisions determine the type of process selected and the type of technology used. Once the macro design decisions are made, we can proceed with the micro-level process-design decisions, which are process–flow analysis and facilities layout.

These micro-level decisions affect decisions in other parts of operations, including scheduling decisions, inventory levels, the types of jobs designed, and the methods of quality control used. Therefore, micro process-design decisions should always be made with the effects on other parts of operations in mind.

The study of process flows deals directly with the transformation process itself, since most transformation processes can be viewed as a series of flows connecting inputs to outputs. In studying process flows, we will be analyzing how a good is manufactured or how a service is delivered. When the sequence of steps used in converting inputs into outputs is analyzed, better methods or procedures can usually be found.

At the heart of process-flow analysis is the flowchart. Although flowcharting techniques are easily understood, the idea of describing process flows in flowchart form is quite powerful and aids the search for better procedures and methods.

BOX 7.1   **TYPICAL DECISION PROBLEM**

In Chapter 2, we read about the First City Bank's effort to decide whether to install a new automatic teller. In connection with this decision, Sally Jones, manager of cashier operations, decided to conduct a process-flow analysis. This analysis required Sally to trace the flow of paperwork for the new teller and the flow of customers through the bank.

The decision concerning the automatic teller will affect the waiting time of customers as they stand in line for service. Sally reasoned that the average time a customer waits in line will depend on both the arrival rate of customers and the service time of the automatic teller. If customers arrive at a fast rate, there will be more waiting time than in slack periods. If the automatic teller can handle customers rapidly, the waiting time will be reduced. To evaluate these effects quantitatively, Sally decided to construct a queueing model of the automatic teller and the waiting line. This model would provide estimates of waiting times and teller capacity for typical bank conditions.

As part of the process-flow analysis, Sally also decided to trace the flow of paperwork required to operate the automatic teller. To do this, she constructed a flowchart and documented the procedures required at each step of the way. Although much of the procedure was the same as for the human teller, a few steps were different. This flowchart helped Sally to understand how the new automatic teller would affect daily cashier operations, and she felt more confident that she could describe the effect to others.

Throughout the first part of this chapter, different types of flowchart methods will be described.

In the second part of the chapter, flowchart analysis is extended to the mathematical modeling of process flows. A model can be used to describe a transformation process in more precise terms than is possible with a simple flowchart. Thus mathematical models are an extension of the flowchart analysis described in the first part of the chapter. A typical example of process-flow analysis is given in Box 7.1.

7.1 FLOWCHART ANALYSIS

Flowcharts are used to describe and improve the transformation process in productive systems. In improving the effectiveness or efficiency of productive processes, some or all of the following process elements might be changed:

1. Raw materials
2. Product (output) design
3. Job design
4. Processing steps used
5. Management control information
6. Equipment or tools

Process analysis can, therefore, have a wide effect on all parts of operations.

Process-flow analysis is heavily dependent on systems thinking, which was described in Chapter 2. In order to analyze process flows, a relevant system is selected and the inputs, outputs, boundaries, and transformations are described. In effect, the process-flow problem is described as a system.

Using the systems approach, the following steps are taken in a process flowchart analysis:

1. Decide on the objectives of the analysis, e.g., to improve efficiency, effectiveness, capacity, or worker morale.
2. Select a relevant productive process (or system) for study, e.g., the whole operation or some part of it.
3. Describe the existing transformation process by means of flowcharts and efficiency measurements.
4. Develop an improved process design by revising the process flows and/or inputs used. Usually the revised process is also described by a flowchart.
5. Gain management approval for the revised process design.
6. Implement the new process design.

Notice that this method assumes an existing process. If there is no existing process, steps 3 and 4 are combined to describe the desired process, but the rest of the method is still used. This general method of flowchart analysis will be illustrated below for specific situations.

In Section 7.2, material flows will be treated in detail. This will be followed by analysis of information flows. One of our objectives is to show how these two types of process flows can be analyzed by the same procedure even though they are often thought of as being different.

7.2 MATERIALS-FLOW ANALYSIS

The analysis of materials flows in factories was one of the first applications of process-flow-analysis ideas. These ideas were developed in the early 1900s by industrial engineers applying the principles of Taylor's scientific management. First they broke down the manufacturing process into detailed elements, and then they carefully studied each element and the interrelationship between elements in order to improve overall process efficiency.

As part of materials-flow analysis, it is necessary to describe the flow of materials in great detail. This is done in manufacturing through four principal types of documents: assembly drawings, assembly charts, routing sheets, and flow–process charts.

An assembly drawing is used to specify how the parts in a manufactured item should be assembled. These drawings are developed by the engineering department and given to manufacturing. An example of an assembly drawing for a child's tricycle is shown in Figure 7.1.

In order to show the exact sequence of operations used to assemble a product, an assembly or "Gozinto" (goes into) chart is prepared from the assembly drawing. This chart shows each step in the assembly process and the parts which go into the final product, as illustrated for the tricycle in Figure 7.2.

A routing sheet (or operations process sheet) is even more detailed than an as-

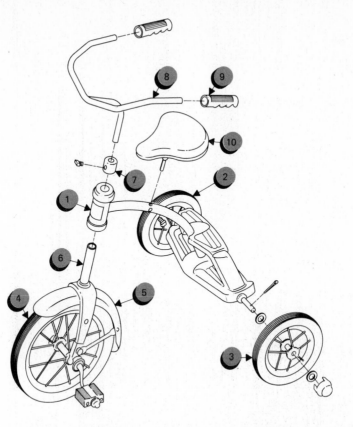

**Figure 7.1
Assembly drawing
for a tricycle.**
*(Source: The Murray
Ohio Manufacturing
Company, Lawrenceburg,
Tenn.)*

sembly chart because it shows the operations and routing required for an individual part. Each machine or labor operation is listed, along with the tools and equipment needed. In some cases the production times for each operation are also listed. A routing sheet for the rear wheel of the tricycle is shown in Figure 7.3.

Taken together, the assembly drawings, assembly charts, and routing sheets will completely specify how a product is to be manufactured. These documents are all derived from the blueprints and the bill of materials which specify the original design of the product.

One would expect to find assembly drawings, assembly charts, and routing sheets as part of normal manufacturing documentation. Although these documents help describe the process flow, they do not provide all that is needed for analysis and improvement. For analysis purposes, a flow-process chart (or, more simply, a process chart) is usually constructed; it breaks the process down in terms of the elements and symbols shown in Figure 7.4.

The flow-process chart is illustrated by an operation in which groceries are selected, assembled, and delivered in response to customer telephone orders. [See Tuzcu (1978).] As the first step in the process, orders are received by phone from

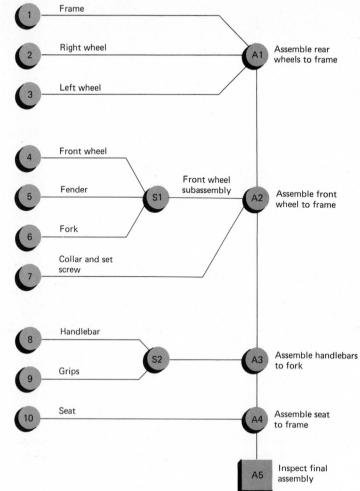

Figure 7.2 Tricycle assembly chart.

customers and punched directly into a computer. The computer then generates picking lists for each of the various aisles (dry groceries, produce, meat, dairy, etc.) in the grocery warehouse. The items are picked by employees in each aisle and then assembled into a complete order for delivery to the customers.

Figure 7.5 is a flow-process chart for a portion of this operation, which includes the groceries that are picked from the produce, dairy, and meat aisles. Notice the use of the special symbols for operations, transportation, inspection, delays, and storage. In this example, the time and the distance are not noted on the chart, but these quantities were measured in the study in order to identify and assess possible improvements.

The flow-process chart is a key tool for improving the flow of materials. After examining it, the manager may be able to combine certain operations, eliminate others, or simplify operations to improve overall efficiency. This may, in turn, re-

Part Name	Rear Tricycle Wheel		Date	9/8/78
Assembly	A2936		Issued by	RGS
Part Number	261982			

Operation	Description	Dept.	Tools/Equipment
1	Cut wires for spokes (10 qty.)	06	E10 Shear
2	Cut tubing for axle	06	F2 Hacksaw
3	Cut flat steel for rim	02	F1 Shear
4	Stamp end caps for spokes	03	A7 Press
5	Form steel for rims	03	A4 Press
6	Weld rim together	01	U9 Welder
7	Weld caps to axle tube	01	U9 Welder
8	Weld spokes to axle and rim	01	U7 Welder
9	Cut rubber tire to size	06	E7 Shear
10	Fix rubber tire on rim	09	C6 Press

**Figure 7.3
Routing (opera-
tions-process)
sheet.**

quire changes in layout, equipment, and work methods and possibly even changes in product design.

But it is not enough simply to draw flow-process charts. A key to analyzing these charts is to ask the following types of questions:

1. *What:* What operations are really necessary? Can some operations be eliminated, combined, or simplified? Should the product be redesigned to facilitate production?

**Figure 7.4
Flow-process-chart
symbols.**

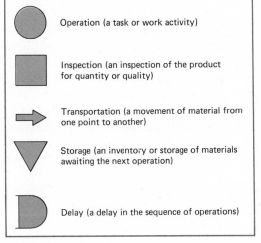

Operation (a task or work activity)

Inspection (an inspection of the product for quantity or quality)

Transportation (a movement of material from one point to another)

Storage (an inventory or storage of materials awaiting the next operation)

Delay (a delay in the sequence of operations)

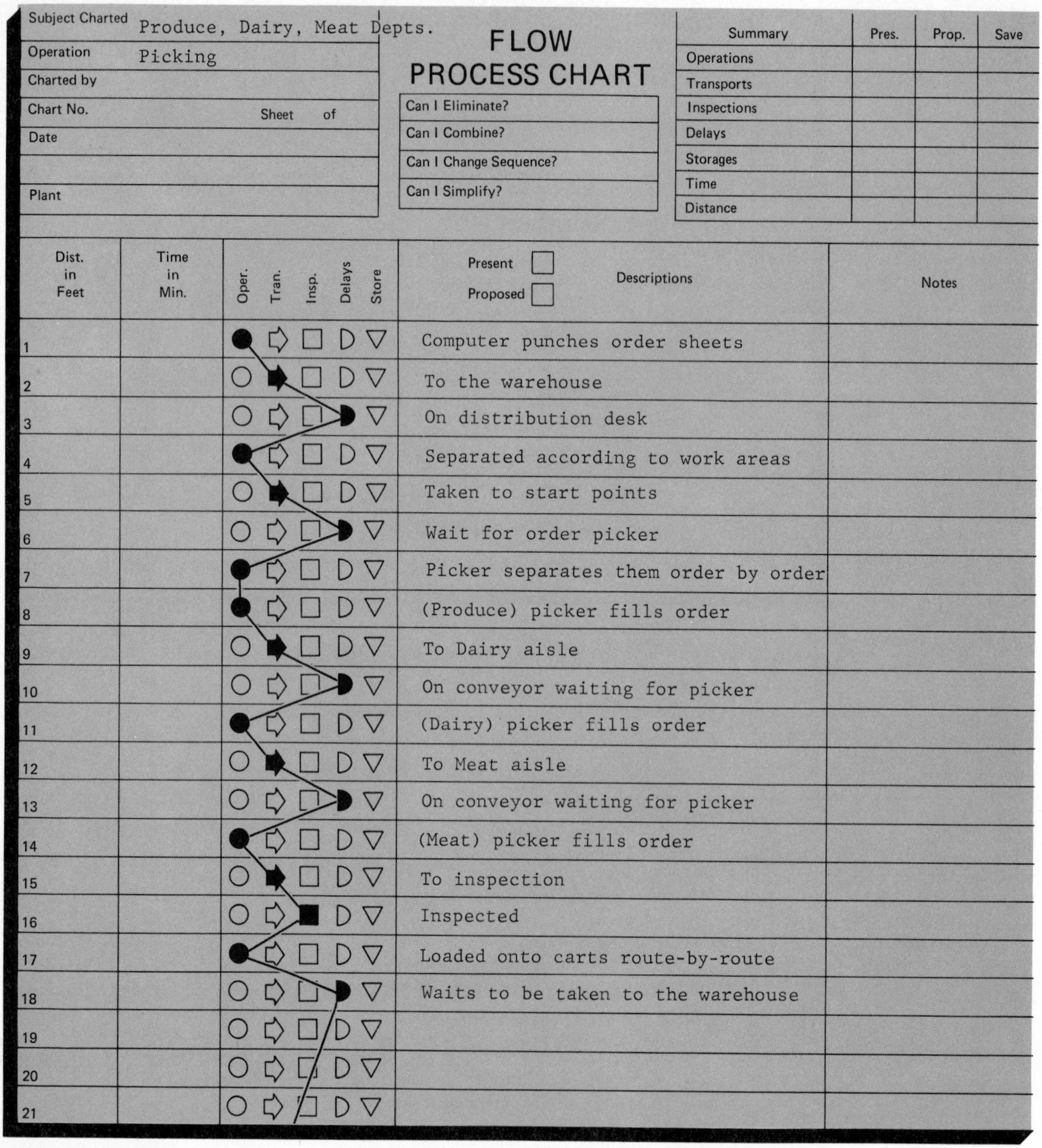

Subject Charted	Produce, Dairy, Meat Depts.	FLOW PROCESS CHART		Summary	Pres.	Prop.	Save
Operation	Picking			Operations			
Charted by		Can I Eliminate?		Transports			
Chart No.	Sheet of	Can I Combine?		Inspections			
Date		Can I Change Sequence?		Delays			
Plant		Can I Simplify?		Storages			
				Time			
				Distance			

Dist. in Feet	Time in Min.	Oper.	Tran.	Insp.	Delays	Store	Present ☐ Proposed ☐ Descriptions	Notes
1		●	⇨	☐	D	▽	Computer punches order sheets	
2		○	◣	☐	D	▽	To the warehouse	
3		○	⇨	☐	◣	▽	On distribution desk	
4		●	⇨	☐	D	▽	Separated according to work areas	
5		○	◣	☐	D	▽	Taken to start points	
6		○	⇨	☐	◣	▽	Wait for order picker	
7		●	⇨	☐	D	▽	Picker separates them order by order	
8		●	⇨	☐	D	▽	(Produce) picker fills order	
9		○	◣	☐	D	▽	To Dairy aisle	
10		○	⇨	☐	◣	▽	On conveyor waiting for picker	
11		●	⇨	☐	D	▽	(Dairy) picker fills order	
12		○	◣	☐	D	▽	To Meat aisle	
13		○	⇨	☐	◣	▽	On conveyor waiting for picker	
14		●	⇨	☐	D	▽	(Meat) picker fills order	
15		○	◣	☐	D	▽	To inspection	
16		○	⇨	■	D	▽	Inspected	
17		●	⇨	☐	D	▽	Loaded onto carts route-by-route	
18		○	⇨	☐	◣	▽	Waits to be taken to the warehouse	
19		○	⇨	☐	D	▽		
20		○	⇨	☐	D	▽		
21		○	⇨	☐	D	▽		

Figure 7.5 Flow-process chart.

2. *Who:* Who is performing each operation? Can the operation be redesigned to use less skill or less labor hours? Can operations be combined to enrich jobs and thereby improve productivity or working conditions?

3. *Where:* Where is each operation conducted? Can the layout be improved to reduce distance traveled or to make the operations more accessible?

4. *When:* When is each operation performed? Is there excessive delay or storage? Are some operations creating bottlenecks?

5. *How:* How is the operation done? Can better methods, procedures, or equipment be used? Should the operation be revised to make it easier or less time-consuming?

The application of these questions can be illustrated by using the grocery warehouse example. In that case, two more items of information in addition to the flow-process chart were collected as part of the analysis: a flow diagram of the facility and time-study data. The flow diagram, shown in Figure 7.6, illustrates the layout of the facility and the major flow of groceries for each order. Extensive data were also collected on the time it took, both for current methods and the suggested new methods, to perform each type of picking operation.

**Figure 7.6
Initial layout of grocery warehouse.**

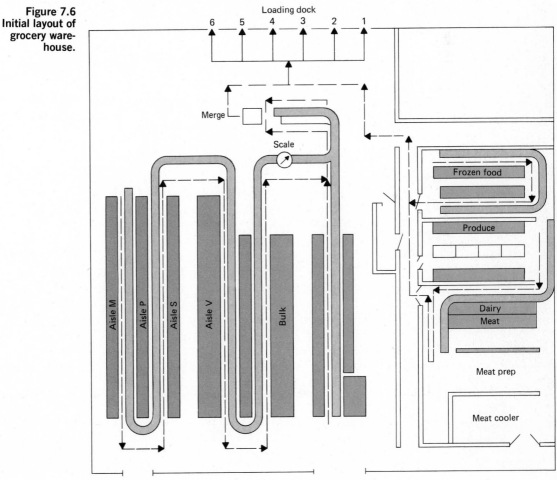

After the data were collected and the above questions were asked, the following types of changes were made:

1. *Layout:* The layout of the facility was revised to be more efficient and compact. Some aisles were moved from one part of the warehouse to another.
2. *Methods and jobs:* Methods of picking groceries were revised to reduce bottlenecks and labor.
3. *Equipment:* Special carts were designed to make loading of the delivery vans easier and faster. An overhead conveyor was also installed to consolidate orders and speed up the flow of materials.

These changes contributed significantly to better materials flow and improved efficiency.

It should be noted that analysis of materials flow extends far beyond manufacturing. The grocery warehouse example was a service operation. Other examples of service operations with substantial material flows are restaurants, laundries, the U.S. Postal Service, warehousing, and retail trade.

7.3 INFORMATION-FLOW ANALYSIS

Information flows can be analyzed in a manner analogous to that used for the flow of materials. Although information flows are sometimes recorded on a flow-process chart using the standard symbols, different forms of flowcharting are also used for information flows. However, the purpose of information-flow analysis is the same as for the analysis of materials flow: to improve the efficiency and effectiveness of the process.

There are two types of information flows. In the first, information is the product of the operation. This is typical, for example, of clerical processing in offices, where the office can be thought of as a "paperwork factory" converting the paperwork from "raw material" to "finished goods."

In the second case, the information flow is used for management or control purposes. Examples of this are order entry, purchasing documents, and paperwork used in manufacturing. In this case the paperwork is used to control the flow of materials. Although the methods of analysis are the same, the purposes of these two types of information flow are quite different.

It is usually insufficient to analyze a materials-flow process without also analyzing the flow of information. This is because the materials flow may be improved but management control of the process may still be lacking. To illustrate this concept, we have shown in Figure 7.7 the information flow from the grocery warehouse example. (See Figure 7.8 for an explanation of the symbols used. Although these are not the only symbols used in flowcharting, they illustrate the concepts involved.)

Figure 7.7 (Opposite) Information flows in grocery warehouse.

As Figure 7.7 indicates, three key types of information are used to control the flow of groceries: (1) route maps, (2) drivers' manifests, and (3) pick sheets. A route map tells the driver which route to follow in delivering the groceries for a particular run. The computer constructs the routes for each delivery on the basis of the loca-

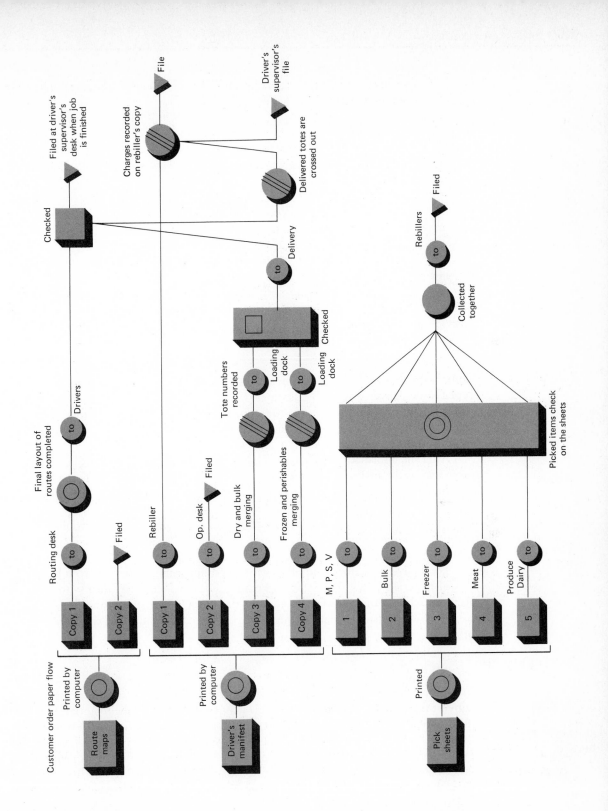

Customer order paper flow

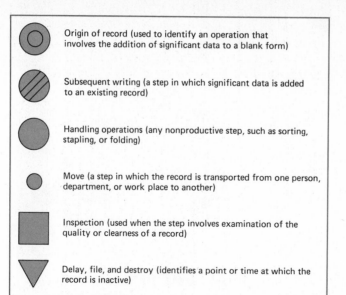

Origin of record (used to identify an operation that involves the addition of significant data to a blank form)

Subsequent writing (a step in which significant data is added to an existing record)

Handling operations (any nonproductive step, such as sorting, stapling, or folding)

Move (a step in which the record is transported from one person, department, or work place to another)

Inspection (used when the step involves examination of the quality or clearness of a record)

Delay, file, and destroy (identifies a point or time at which the record is inactive)

Figure 7.8 Information-processing symbols.

tions of the customers' homes. The driver's manifest is simply a listing of the groceries to be delivered to each customer. Finally, the pick sheets are used to list the groceries by warehouse aisle so as to facilitate picking. In this case, all these types of information are used to control the delivery of grocery services. The paperwork flow itself is not the "product."

After the information flowchart is completed, the analysis proceeds in much the same way as the analysis of materials flows. The analysis should include the five key questions of "what," "who," "where," "when," and "how." It might also include some recording of times and information-flow volumes.

As a result of the analysis, it should be possible to consolidate or simplify information flows. This may result in changes in equipment (perhaps involving the computer), in jobs, and in procedures.

The analysis of information flows is sometimes seen as different from the analysis of materials flows. This may be because industrial engineers deal with materials flows while computer systems analysts deal with information flows. As we have seen, however, systems analysts might be considered as "industrial engineers of the office."

7.4 USING PROCESS-FLOW ANALYSIS

In summary, process flowchart analysis describes the transformation process used to convert inputs into outputs. The analysis may be used to describe materials flows or information flows. After a flowchart of the process is constructed, questions of "what," "who," "where," "when," and "how" are asked to improve the process. From the answers to these questions, improvements might be made in procedures, tasks, equipment, raw materials, layout, or management control information. As we have shown in the examples, a variety of processes can be improved by following this relatively simple form of analysis.

To this point, process-flow analysis has been presented as primarily technological in nature. But this type of analysis also affects the design of jobs and social aspects of the work environment. Process-flow analysis can be viewed as a sociotechnical problem, but only limited work along these lines has been done to date.

In an attempt to address this problem, the author developed a combined sociotechnical approach for an office of the state of Minnesota.[1] This approach included both a traditional analysis of process flow and a diagnosis of job and organizational attitudes, as shown in Figure 7.9. With this approach, process-flow information and psychological data on workers' attitudes toward their jobs were collected. The analysis was then merged in a sociotechnical design of the new system.

It is clear that much attention needs to be given to the human element in process-flow analysis—not only in designing the new system but also in gaining accept-

[1] Further details are contained in Management Analysis Division (1978).

Figure 7.9
A sociotechnical approach to process-flow analysis.

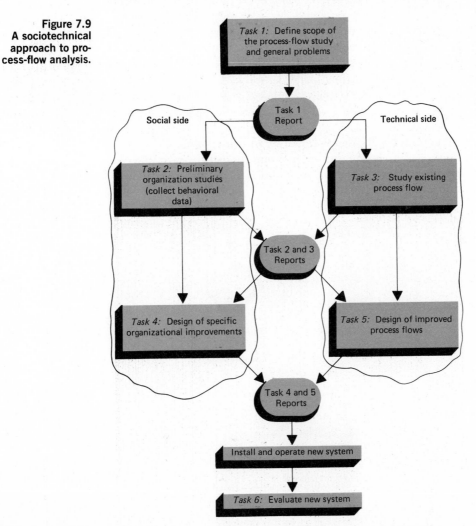

ance for changes. Research has shown that the best way to accomplish this is to involve the persons affected in every stage of diagnosis and design. This tends to suggest individual ownership of the new system and therefore to reduce fears associated with change. It is difficult to overemphasize the need for user and worker involvement in process-flow design.

In the remainder of this chapter, we will describe a more sophisticated form of process-flow analysis which utilizes mathematical models. The basic idea is to express the process flow in terms of one or more mathematical relationships. These models can then be manipulated to analyze the effects of alternative management decisions.

7.5 MODELING OF PROCESS FLOWS

A great many models—including linear programming, simulation, and queueing—are used to describe process flows. Our purpose in this section is not to explain any of these particular methodologies but rather to describe the general approach to the modeling of process flows and to show how this is useful in process-design decisions. For the remainder of this chapter, however, it is assumed that the reader is familiar with simulation methods; see the supplement to Chapter 2 to review these.

The first step in modeling process flows is to draw a flowchart of the process or the information flows used to control the process. Frequently, a block-diagram flowchart is useful. A block diagram consists of a series of three types of blocks: processing blocks, decision blocks, and feedback blocks, as in Figure 7.10. The processing block is represented by inputs, transformation, and outputs. It is, in effect, a small system used to convert inputs into outputs. In a decision block, the output is

**Figure 7.10
Types of blocks.**

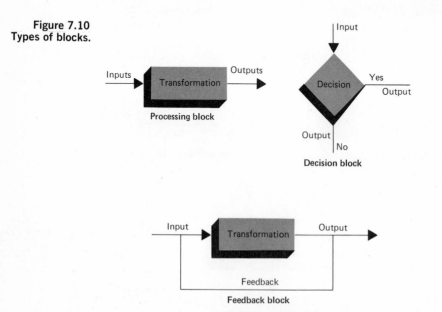

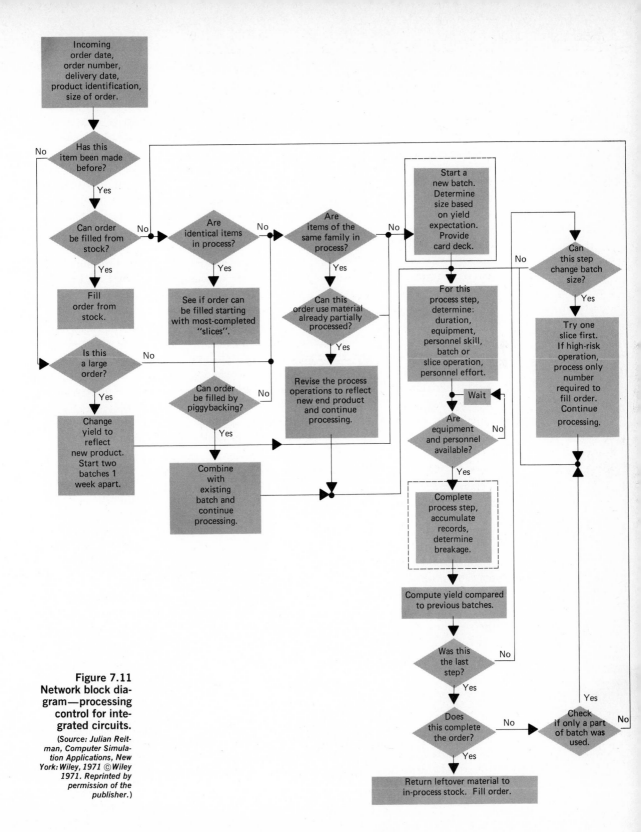

**Figure 7.11
Network block diagram—processing control for integrated circuits.**

(Source: Julian Reitman, Computer Simulation Applications, New York: Wiley, 1971 ©Wiley 1971. Reprinted by permission of the publisher.)

the result of a decision made during processing. Branches can be taken in the logic of the model depending on the decisions made. The last type of block is a feedback block; here information on the output level is fed back to control or change input values. Feedback blocks are most often used for management control purposes.

An operations process can be described as a network of processing blocks, decision blocks, and feedback blocks. Actually, a very complex system can be represented by interconnecting a large number of different blocks. As a first step in modeling, a network block diagram is drawn to isolate the processing system and the various subsystems of interest. Once this has been done, mathematical relationships for each of the blocks in the diagram can be defined. In this way a very complex system can be built up from a set of relatively simple blocks.

We will illustrate below the development of a block diagram and the subsequent use of a simulation model to improve decision making. The example is a classical job-shop simulation study.

Job-shop simulation was one of the early applications of process-flow modeling by simulation; an excellent example from the production of integrated circuits is given by Reitman (1971). In Reitman's example, batches of silicon slices are processed through a number of steps including polishing, chemical etching, heating, photoengraving, and testing. The number of steps, up to a maximum of 24, varied for different circuits. The integrated circuits are microscopic in size—up to 1000 circuits may be placed on a small silicon wafer 1½ inches in diameter.

Production yields of these circuits were often quite low and unpredictable. As a result, a great deal of reprocessing was required and it was difficult to meet delivery schedules.

The sequence of events was as follows. After a new order had been taken, a check was made to see whether the order could be filled from inventory. If this could not be done, the order was added to existing batches in process before the new order was separately scheduled. Once it was in production, the order was processed at some stations in batches and at other stations as single wafers.

The decision process used to plan and control this job shop is shown by a network block diagram in Figure 7.11. Notice that this is the information-control system and not the flow process itself.

After drawing the network block diagram, the information-control system was tested by simulation. Incoming orders were accepted by the simulation model, and the resulting effect on work-in-process inventories and production schedules was determined. As a result, different scheduling rules and processing steps could be tested on the simulation model before putting them into effect.

7.6 SIMULATION OF PROCESS FLOWS

While the above example illustrates the use of a block diagram to model process flows, the next example will concentrate on issues of data collection and model validation. The example is an outpatient obstetric-care facility studied by Glenn and Roberts (1973) to determine the effects of resource allocations (doctors, nurses, and rooms) on patient service. The simulation started with the flowchart shown in Figure 7.12, which describes the steps each patient goes through in the clinic.

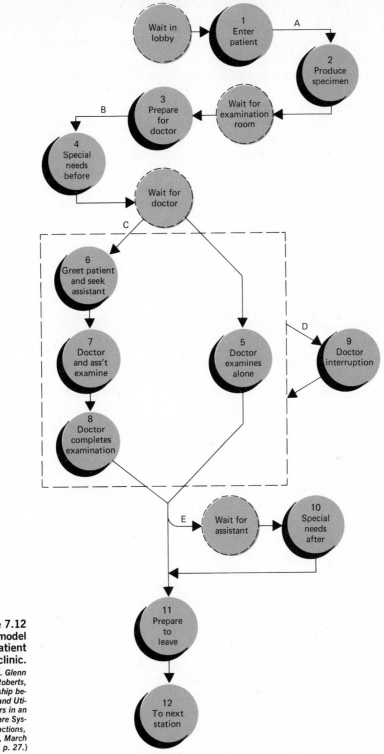

**Figure 7.12
Flowchart model
of outpatient
clinic.**

(Source: John K. Glenn
and Stephen Roberts,
"The Relationship be-
tween Resource and Uti-
lization Factors in an
Outpatient Care Sys-
tem," AIIE Transactions,
vol. 5, no. 1, March
1973, p. 27.)

Patients reported to the appointment station when they entered the clinic. They then waited in the lobby until they were taken by a nurse's assistant for laboratory tests, if required, and then to an examination room where they prepared for the prenatal exam. When the doctor became available, the examination was conducted, sometimes with the assistance of a nurse's assistant. The patient then left the examining room and received information about caring for herself during pregnancy, including dietary information if needed. Finally, the patient made another clinic appointment and then left the clinic. This process is summarized in Figure 7.12.

For this simulation model, a given patient load was assumed, using levels of 20, 50, and 80 patients per day. It also was assumed that patients' visits would be scheduled to supply a continuous input to the first processing step in the flowchart. Thus, patient scheduling was not part of the model.

Management decided to use two measures of patient service: total time to process a given number of patients (clinic duration) and average time in the clinic per patient (mean transit time). Resource utilization was measured by three variables, room utilization (percent), physician utilization (percent), and assistant utilization (percent). The purpose of the study was to determine the relationship between the amount of resources available (rooms, physicians, and assistants), the resulting utilization of resources, and the measures of patient service.

After the flowchart was drawn, the next step was to collect data on the process. Over a 7-day period, some 303 patients were observed by three data collectors at various locations in the clinic. These observers collected data on all processing times and tasks for each patient. The observers also collected data for 2 additional clinic days; these data were reserved for validation of the model.

A simulation model was developed and programmed on the computer. The user of the model specified four input variables: number of patients to be treated, number of physicians assigned, number of examining rooms assigned, and number of assistants assigned. The model used the empirical data for processing times and processing steps, along with a first-come-first-serve scheduling rule to process all the hypothetical "patients" one at a time. When the last one had been processed, the computer reported statistics on clinic performance: clinic duration, mean patient transit time, and utilization of rooms, physicians, and assistants.

The model was validated using three methods. First, a logical check was made. For example, when the number of physicians was increased, with all other variables held constant, did physician utilization decrease? Second, an intuitive check of model performance was made on "standard" clinic conditions of 50 patients, 9 rooms, 3 doctors, and 5 assistants. The output of the simulation for these conditions was checked by clinic personnel to see if the results appeared reasonable. The third validity check utilized data for the 2 additional days which were observed. The outputs of the simulation were compared to figures actually observed and tested statistically for differences. The model passed all three of these validation tests.

The next step in the analysis was to use the simulator to develop relationships between inputs and outputs. Rather than simply running a large number of trials and plotting graphs, the investigators developed an experimental design to test different levels of each variable systematically and to develop a series of equations relating input to output.

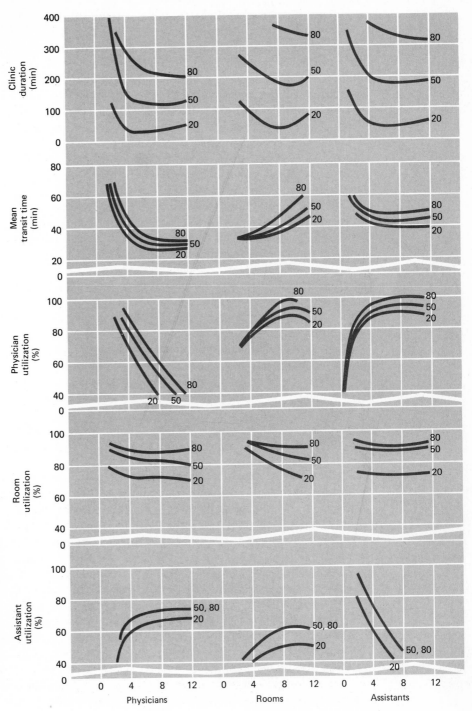

Figure 7.13 Outpatient clinic results. Numbers identifying curves indicate patient load (patients per session).

(Source: John K. Glenn and Stephen Roberts, "The Relationship between Resource and Utilization Factors in an Outpatient Care System." AIIE Transactions, vol. 5, no. 1, March 1973, p. 30.)

From this part of the analysis, it was determined that outputs varied nonlinearly with inputs and that various resources interacted in affecting outputs. These results can be seen quite clearly in Figure 7.13, along with the general results of the study. The graphs in Figure 7.13 indicate the relationship between each input and all outputs. In effect, we have described the production function[2] of the clinic through the simulation of process flows.

Clinic managers can use the information in Figure 7.13 to answer several questions. For example, what will be the effect of increasing the number of assistants from four to six? What will be the effect of an increasing patient load in the clinic if no additional resources are added? What will be the effect on clinic hours of adding two more physicians? Can the entire patient load be processed in 2 hours instead of 3?

In summary, the two examples given above have indicated several things about the simulation of process flows. First, process-flow simulations almost always start with a flowchart or block diagram. Second, the collection of data is difficult and often expensive. The relevant data are usually not available and must therefore be specially collected. Third, it is necessary to validate a process-flow model before using it to make sure that it is reasonably accurate. Several methods of validation were noted. Finally, these process-flow models result in a description of the production function which transforms input into output. By using the process-flow model, one can investigate changes in the inputs, the transformation itself, or the outputs. This kind of analysis can support many types of process-design decisions.

Models of process flows can often be described as queueing models. The general definition of a queueing model and some analytic results are described in the chapter supplement.

7.7 KEY POINTS

This chapter has emphasized the analysis of transformation processes used to produce goods or services. Two main types of analysis were stressed; descriptive analysis through the use of flowcharts and mathematical analysis through the use of process-flow models. Both these forms of analysis can be used to improve the dependability, costs, quality, and/or flexibility of the productive process.

Some of the key points stressed in the chapter are as follows:

- Both materials and information flows can be analyzed by a common framework and common procedure: that is, to describe the flows as a system through the use of flowcharts and to ask questions regarding what is done, who does it, and where, when, and how it is done. The result of this analysis may lead to changes in any or all elements of the process (output, raw materials, tools, equipment, jobs, methods, and information).

- In analyzing materials flows, four types of documents are typically used: assembly drawings, assembly ("Gozinto") charts, routing sheets, and flow-process

---

[2] The term "production function" is used here in the classic economic sense as a transformation function between input and output.

charts. These documents together describe exactly how the product is made and how it flows through the production process.

- Information flows can be analyzed as either the product itself or as management information used to plan and control production of the product. In the same way as materials flows, information flows are depicted in flowcharts which are then analyzed to find ways of improving the process.
- A sociotechnical approach is needed to consider physical flow design simultaneously with the design of jobs. This approach should result in processes which are both economically and humanly rewarding.
- Mathematical models can be used to study the design of production processes described in terms of input, transformation, and output. A model is used to study process-design alternatives before putting them into practice. Classical applications of process design through process-flow modeling are the job-shop simulation and flows through facilities such as hospitals, restaurants, and warehouses.

QUESTIONS

1. In the following operations, what services are produced and what are the primary process flows?
   a. A college
   b. A fast-food restaurant
   c. A library
2. How is the analysis of material similar to and different from the analysis of information?
3. Give three reasons why the flow of materials and the flow of control information should be analyzed together, at the same time.
4. What is meant by a sociotechnical approach to process analysis? Under what circumstances should such an approach be used?
5. What kinds of problems are presented by the redesign of existing processes which are not encountered in the design of a new process?
6. How can a job shop be viewed as a "network of queues"?
7. Why are block diagrams needed to study process flows? How are they useful?
8. Describe the differences between a simulation model used to design a process initially and a simulation model used to operate and redesign the process on an ongoing basis.
9. What is meant by the statement, "A simulator describes the production function of an operation."
10. How is the flowcharting of a process related to simulation or optimization models of the same process?
11. Discuss the methods and problems of validating process-flow models.

PROBLEMS

1. Draw a flowchart of the following processes:
   a. The procedure used to keep your checkbook
   b. College registration
   c. Obtaining a book from the library
2. Using the special symbols, draw a flow-process chart of the processes listed in Problem 1.
3. Use the key questions of "what," "who," "where," "when," and "how" on Problem 1 or 2 to suggest improvements in the process.
4. Draw an assembly chart for a double-decker hamburger.
5. Develop a routing sheet (operations process sheet) for all operations required to:
   a. Cook a hamburger
   b. Prepare a term paper

SELECTED BIBLIOGRAPHY

EMSHOFF, JAMES R., and ROGER L. SISSON: *Design and Use of Computer Simulation Models,* New York: Macmillan, 1970.

GLENN, JOHN K., and STEPHEN ROBERTS: "The Relationship between Resource and Utilization Factors in an Outpatient Care System," *AIIE Transactions,* vol. 5, no. 1, March 1973.

MANAGEMENT ANALYSIS DIVISION, Department of Administration, State of Minnesota, "Operations Assessment Methodology and Training Manual," October 1978.

NAYLOR, THOMAS H.: *Computer Simulation Experiments with Models of Economic Systems,* New York: Wiley, 1971.

REITMAN, JULIAN: *Computer Simulation Applications,* New York: Wiley, 1971.

TUZCU, ERTUGRUL: "Methods Improvement and Design of an Existing Plant," Minneapolis: University of Minnesota. Spring 1978, Plan B paper.

SUPPLEMENT: WAITING LINES

In many operations, waiting lines for service are formed, as when customers wait in a checkout lane at a grocery store, machines wait to be repaired in a factory, or airplanes wait to land at an airport. The common characteristic of these apparently diverse examples is that a number of physical entities (the arrivals) are attempting to receive service from limited facilities (the servers). As a consequence, the arrivals must sometimes wait in line for their turn to be served.

Waiting-line situations are also called queuing problems, after the British term "queue." A tremendous number of queuing problems occur in operations, including the design of facility layouts, staffing decisions, and physical capacity problems. Queuing theory is useful in analyzing many of the problems associated with process design.

A queuing problem may be solved by either analytic formulas or simulation methods. The usefulness of analytic formulas, however, is limited by the mathematical assumptions which must be made to derive the formulas. As a result, analytic queuing models sometimes do not closely match the real situation of interest, although they do have the advantage of being simpler and less costly than simulation methods. Analytic queuing models may be used to obtain a first approximation to a queuing problem or to make a low-cost analysis. The simulation method is used to solve queuing problems that are more complex and require a more precise solution.

In this supplement, general ideas about queuing problems and analytic solution methods are developed. Simulation methods for solving queuing problems are described in the supplement to Chapter 2.

QUEUING CHARACTERISTICS

Every queuing problem can be described in terms of three characteristics: the arrival, the queue, and the server.

1. The arrival. The arrivals are described by their statistical arrival distribution, which can be specified in two ways: by arrivals per unit of time or by the interarrival time distribution. If the arrival distribution is specified in the first way, the numbers of arrivals that can occur in any given period of time must be described. For example, one might describe the number of arrivals in one hour. When arrivals occur at random, the information of interest is the probability of n arrivals in a given time period, where $n = 0, 1, 2, \ldots$

If the arrivals are assumed to occur at a constant average rate and are independent of each other, then they occur according to the Poisson probability distribution. In this case the probability of n arrivals in time T is given by the formula:

$$P(n,\ T) = \frac{e^{-\lambda T}\ (\lambda T)^n}{n!} \qquad n = 0, 1, 2, \ldots$$

where λ = mean arrival rate per unit of time
T = time period
n = number of arrivals in time T
$P(n,\ T)$ = probability of n arrivals in time T

193

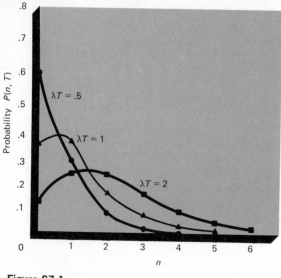

Figure S7.1
Poisson probability distribution.

of the distribution changes dramatically to a more symmetrical ("normal") form and the probability of a larger number of arrivals increases. It has been found that Poisson distributions can be used in practice to approximate many actual arrival patterns.

The second method of arrival specification is the time between arrivals. In this case one specifies the probability distribution of a continuous random variable which measures the time from one arrival to the next. If the arrivals follow a Poisson distribution, it can be shown mathematically that the interarrival time will be distributed according to the exponential distribution.

$$P(T \leq t) = 1 - e^{-\lambda t} \qquad 0 \leq t < \infty$$

where $P(T \leq t)$ = probability that the interarrival time T is $\leq$ a given value t
λ = mean arrival rate per unit time
t = a given value of time

The exponential probability distribution is shown in Figure S7.2. Notice that as the time t increases, the probability that an arrival has occurred approaches 1.

The Poisson and exponential distributions

Three typical Poisson probability distributions are shown in Figure S7.1 Notice that for small values of $\lambda T = .5$, there is a high probability of zero arrivals in the time interval T, and that most of the probability is concentrated on 0, 1, 2 arrivals. As the value of λT increases, the shape

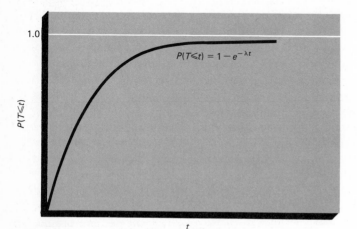

Figure S7.2
Exponential distribution.

are entirely equivalent in their underlying assumptions about arrivals. Therefore, either can be used to specify arrivals, depending on whether the time between arrivals or the number of arrivals in a given time is desired. Which of these specifications is used depends strongly on the form of arrival data available.

There are other distributions which can be used to specify arrivals. One of the most common is the Erlang distribution. The Erlang provides more flexibility than the Poisson distribution, but it is also more complicated. [See Saaty (1961) for details.]

A factor which affects the choice of arrival distribution is the size of the calling population. For example, if a repairer is tending six machines, the calling population is limited to the six machines. In this case it is unlikely that the arrival distribution will be Poisson in nature because the failure rate is not constant. If five machines have already failed, the arrival rate is lower than when all machines are operating.

2. The queue. The nature of the queue also affects the type of queuing model formulated. For example, a queue discipline must be specified to describe how the arrivals are served. One queue discipline is the well-known first-come-first-served rule. Another queue discipline is one where certain arrivals have a priority and move to the head of the line.

When the queue is described, the length of the line must also be specified. A common mathematical assumption is that the waiting line can reach an infinite length. In some cases this assumption causes no practical problems. In other cases, a definite line-length limit may cause arrivals to leave when the limit is reached. For example, when more than a certain number of aircraft are in the holding pattern at an airport, new arrivals are diverted to another field.

Finally, customer behavior in the queue must be defined. How long will the customers wait for service before they leave the line? Some customers may not even join the line if they observe a congested situation when they arrive. The customer behavior assumed in simple queuing models is that customers wait until they are served.

For analytic purposes, the most common queuing assumptions are that there is a first-come-first-served discipline, that the line length is infinite, and that all arrivals wait in line until served. These assumptions lead to mathematically tractable models. When the assumptions are changed, however, the mathematics of the queuing model quickly becomes complex.

3. The server. There are also several server characteristics which affect the queuing problem. One of these characteristics is the distribution of service time. Just like the arrival time, the service time may vary from one customer to the next. A common assumption for the distribution of service time is the exponential distribution. In this case, the service time will vary as shown in Figure S7.2. Other distributions of service times also used in queuing problems are a constant service time, normal service times, and uniform service times.

The second characteristic of the server which should be specified is the number of servers. There may be a single server or multiple servers, depending on the amount of capacity needed. Each server is sometimes called a channel.

The service may also be rendered in one phase or in multiple phases. A multiple-phase situation is one where the customer must go through two or more servers in sequence to complete the service. An example of multiphase service is where each patient sees a nurse and then a doctor before leaving a clinic.

The combination of multiple servers and multiple phases gives rise to the four queuing problems shown in Figure S7.3. In addition to these problems, the multiple-channel queues can also have more than one line. As a result, a great variety of queuing problems are possible.

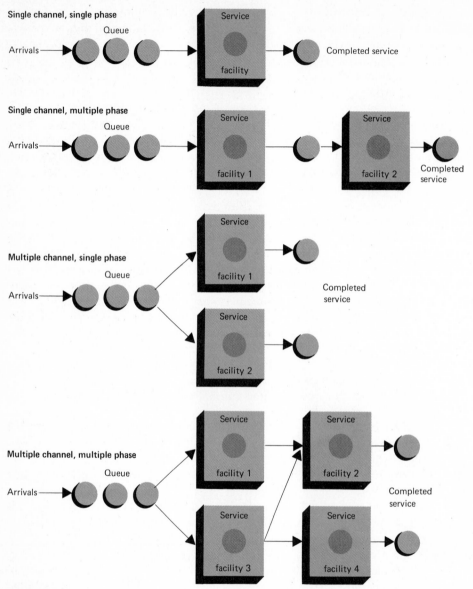

Figure S7.3
Different queuing situations.

FORMULATING QUEUING PROBLEMS

Given assumptions about arrivals, the queue, and the servers, we wish to predict the performance of a specific queuing system. The predicted per-formance of the system may be described, for ex-ample, by the average number of arrivals in the queue, the average waiting time of an arrival, and the percentage of idle time of the servers. These performance measures can be used to decide on the number of servers which should be provided, changes which might be made in the service rate, or other changes in the queuing system.

When queuing performance measures are being evaluated, total costs should be determined whenever possible. This is done by adding the cost of the arrival waiting time and the cost of the servers. In cases such as the repair of machines, the machine waiting time can be equated to the cost of lost production. In cases where the arrivals are customers, however, it is very difficult to estimate the cost of waiting time. As a result, total costs of queuing systems cannot always be determined and surrogate objectives are used instead. One surrogate objective, for example, is that no customer should wait more than an average of 5 minutes to get service. With this service objective, a required number of servers can be determined without reference to the cost of waiting time.

Performance measures and parameters for queuing models are specified by the following notation:

λ = mean arrival rate (the number of arrivals per unit time)

$1/\lambda$ = mean time between arrivals

μ = mean service rate (the number of units served per unit time when the server is busy)

$1/\mu$ = mean time required for service

ρ = server utilization factor (the proportion of the time the server is busy)

P_n = probability that n units (arrivals) are in the system

L_q = mean number of units in the queue (length of the queue)

L_s = mean number of units in the system

W_q = mean waiting time in the queue

W_s = mean waiting time in the system

In the above notation, "in the system" refers to units that may be in the queue or in service. Thus W_q refers to waiting time of a unit in the queue before service starts and W_s refers to the total waiting time in the queue plus the time spent being served.

Queuing model formulas are derived for the last six variables specified above, given input values of λ and μ. These formulas are derived for steady-state conditions, which represent the long-run equilibrium state of the queuing system. In steady state, initial starting conditions do not affect the performance measures. The steady state will be achieved, however, only when $\mu > \lambda$; the service rate must be greater than the arrival rate for steady state to occur. Whenever $\mu \le \lambda$, the queuing system is unstable and the line can potentially build up to an infinite length because the units are arriving faster than they can be served. We will thus assume that $\mu > \lambda$ for the remainder of this supplement.

SIMPLE QUEUING MODEL

The simplest queuing model which has been defined in the literature is based on the following assumptions:

1. Single server and single phase
2. Poisson arrival distribution with λ = mean arrival rate
3. Exponential service time with μ = mean service rate
4. First-come-first-served queue discipline, all arrivals wait in line until served, and infinite line length

From these assumptions, the following performance statistics can be derived:

$$\rho = \lambda/\mu$$
$$P_0 = 1 - \lambda/\mu$$
$$P_n = P_0(\lambda/\mu)^n$$

$$L_q = \frac{\lambda^2}{\mu(\mu - \lambda)}$$

$$L_s = \lambda/(\mu - \lambda)$$

$$W_q = \frac{\lambda}{\mu(\mu - \lambda)}$$

$$W_s = 1/(\mu - \lambda)$$

Example. Suppose a bank teller can serve customers at an average rate of 10 customers per hour ($\mu = 10$). Also, assume that the customers arrive at the teller's window at an average rate of 7 per hour ($\lambda = 7$). Arrivals are believed to follow the Poisson distribution and service time follows the exponential distribution. In the steady state, the queuing system will have the following performance characteristics:

$\rho = 7/10$; the server will be busy 70 percent of the time.

$P_0 = 1 - 7/10 = .3$; thirty percent of the time there will be no customers in the system (in line or being served).

$P_n = .3 \ (7/10)^n$; a formula for finding the probability of n customers in the system at any time: $n = 1, 2, 3, \ldots$; $P_1 = .21$; $P_2 = .147$; $P_3 = .1029$; etc.

$L_q = \dfrac{7^2}{10(10 - 7)} = 1.63$; on average, 1.63 customers will be in the queue.

$L_s = 7/(10 - 7) = 2.33$; on average, 2.33 customers will be in the system (queue and server).

$W_q = \dfrac{7}{10(10 - 7)} = .233$; the customer spends an average of .233 hour waiting in the queue.

$W_s = 1/(10 - 7) = .333$; the customer spends an average of .333 hour in the system (queue and service).

If customers walk away from the teller whenever there are three customers ahead of them in the

system, the proportion of customers lost is:

$$1 - (P_0 + P_1 + P_2 + P_3)$$
$$= 1 - (.3 + .21 + .147 + .1029) = .2401$$

In this case, 24 percent of the customers will be lost because the wait is too long.

The performance of the queuing system can now be evaluated. The manager will have to consider the idle time of the server (30 percent), the time the customer waits (.233 hour), and the length of the line which forms (1.63 customers). If this performance is unacceptable, a second server might be added or other changes in arrival, queue, or server characteristics can be made.

MULTIPLE SERVERS

The simple model with Poisson arrivals and exponential service times can be extended to multiple servers without too much difficulty. If we let s equal the number of servers, the performance measures of the multiple-server queuing system are:

$$\rho = \frac{\lambda}{s\mu}$$

$$P_0 = \frac{1}{\left[\displaystyle\sum_{n=0}^{s-1} (\lambda/\mu)^n/n!\right] + \dfrac{(\lambda/\mu)^s}{s!} (1 - \lambda/s\mu)^{-1}}$$

$$P_n = P_0[(\lambda/\mu)^n/n!] \qquad 1 \le n \le s$$

$$P_n = P_0 \left[\frac{(\lambda/\mu)^n}{s!(s)^{n-s}}\right] \qquad n \ge s$$

$$L_q = \frac{P_0(\lambda/\mu)^s\rho}{s!(1 - \rho)^2}$$

$$L_s = L_q + \lambda/\mu$$

$$W_q = L_q/\lambda$$

$$W_s = W_q + 1/\mu$$

These formulas are for the steady-state conditions and assume Poisson arrivals, exponential service time, first-come-first-served queue discipline, all arrivals wait in line until served, and infinite line length.

Example. Suppose we add a second bank teller to the example described above. How much will service be improved? The performance calculations for $s = 2$ are as follows:

$$\rho = \frac{7}{2(10)} = .35 \text{ (the servers are utilized 35 percent of the time)}$$

$$P_0 = 1/\{(1 + \lambda/\mu) + \frac{(\lambda/\mu)^2}{2!}(1 - \lambda/2\mu)^{-1}\}$$

$$= 1/\{(1 + 7/10) + \frac{(7/10)^2}{2}(1 - 7/20)^{-1}\}$$

$= .4814$ (the probability that no customers are in the system)

$P_1 = .3369$ (the probability that one customer is in the system)

$P_2 = .1179$ (the probability that two customers are in the system)

$P_3 = .0413$ (the probability that three customers are in the system)

$P_4 = .0145$ (the probability that four customers are in the system)

etc.

$$L_q = \frac{.4814(7/10)^2(.35)}{2!\,(1 - .35)^2}$$

$= .0977$ (an average of .0977 customer will be in line)

$L_s = L_q + 7/10 = .7977$ (an average of .7977 customer will be in the system)

$W_q = L_q/7 = .0139$ (the customer spends an average of .0139 hour in the queue)

$W_s = W_q + 1/10 = .1139$ (the customer spends an average of .1139 hour in the system)

With two servers, the customer statistics have improved dramatically. Now an average of only .0977 customer is in line, and the average customer waits for only .0139 hour for service (less than a minute). The price for this good service is that the servers are busy only 35 percent of the time. Unless extraordinarily good service is desired, the bank would probably not want to incur the cost of the second teller. Other approaches, such as cutting the average service time or reducing services offered during peak hours, might be considered. In queuing terms, the distribution of service time might be changed by eliminating the long service times.

COMMENTS ON QUEUING MODELS

One use of queuing models is to study the relationship between capacity and customer service. In Figure S7.4, for example, customer service is measured on the y axis by waiting time or length

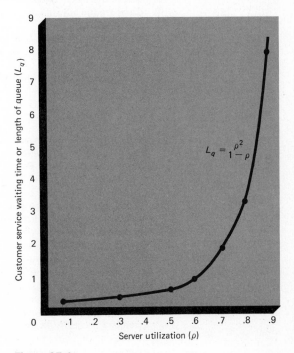

Figure S7.4
Capacity and customer service.

of the queue. On the x axis is ρ, the server-utilization factor. The value of ρ is a measure of relative capacity, since it is a ratio of average arrival rate to average service rate.

As Figure S7.4 indicates, waiting time increases rapidly as the service-utilization factor ρ approaches 1. For example, in Figure S7.4, utilization above 70 to 80 percent will have an adverse effect on waiting time and queue length. It is important to recognize the nonlinear effect of the service-utilization factor on customer service. As the facility becomes saturated (ρ approaches 1), customer service rapidly deteriorates. For good customer service, it is therefore prudent to operate at somewhat less than full ca-

pacity. If the cost of customer waiting time and the cost of servers can be estimated, an optimal decision can be made regarding the amount of capacity provided. If these costs are not available, the curve in Figure S7.4 can still be used to examine the tradeoff between customer service and capacity provided. From Figure S7.4, capacity utilization objectives which are related to customer service levels can also be established.

Although we have treated only the simplest cases of queuing models in this supplement, many more elaborate models are available in the literature. See, for example, Saaty (1961) or Hillier and Lieberman (1974) for additional models.

QUESTIONS

1. What are the two major costs in any queuing study?
2. What are the three basic elements of any queuing system?
3. What is meant by "steady-state conditions"?
4. What characteristics of the arrivals, the queue, and the server must be specified in a queuing problem?
5. Define the term "queue discipline."
6. Compare the advantages and disadvantages of an analytic queuing solution and a simulation solution.
7. What is the difference between waiting time in the system and waiting time in the queue?
8. How are the Poisson and exponential distributions related for arrivals?
9. Why must we have $\mu > \lambda$ for queuing problems?
10. Describe the queuing characteristics of a barber shop.

PROBLEMS

1. A tugboat serves ships arriving in a harbor. The average time between ship arrivals is 2 hours. The average time required to tow a ship to its berth is 1 hour. Studies have shown that ship arrivals are nearly Poisson and service time is exponentially distributed.
   a. Calculate all the queuing performance statistics for this case.
   b. If ships call another tugboat service whenever there are more than two ships in the harbor, what percentage of the ship arrivals are lost?
2. A gas station currently has two pumps and is considering adding a third. A vehicle arrives at the system on an average of once every 10 minutes. Each vehicle requires an average of 5 minutes for servicing. Assume that the vehicles arrive in a Poisson fashion and that service times are exponentially distributed.
   a. What would be the effect on waiting time of adding the third pump?
   b. How would you evaluate the costs in this situation?
3. Two accountants have an office and each has his own secretary. The accountants are considering pooling their secretaries to gain efficiency in office operations. Currently, a task is given to a secretary on the average of once every 15 minutes. It takes an average of 10 minutes to complete the task. On the basis of available data, the task arrival times are Poisson distributed and service times are exponentially distributed.

a. What effect will the pooling of secretaries have on task waiting time and secretary utilization?
b. What advantages or disadvantages, other than those in *a*, are to be gained from pooling secretaries?
4. A computer processes jobs on a first-come-first-served basis. The jobs have Poisson arrival times with an average of 5 minutes between arrivals. The objective in processing these jobs is that no job spend more than 6 minutes on average in the system being processed. How fast does the processor have to work to meet this objective?
5. A barber shop has three barbers to handle customers. At the present time, customers arrive at an average rate of six customers per hour. Each barber can cut hair at a rate of four customers per hour. Arrivals appear to follow the Poisson distribution, and service times follow the exponential distribution.
a. How long will the waiting line be on average?
b. How long does the average customer wait until service begins?
c. What is the utilization of the barbers?
6. A clerk handles phone calls for an airline reservation system in an average of 3 minutes per call, with an exponential distribution of service time. The calls arrive on an average of 10 minutes apart with a Poisson distribution. Recently, some of the customers have complained that the line is busy when they call. Investigate this complaint by means of queuing theory.

SELECTED BIBLIOGRAPHY

COOPER, ROBERT B.: *Introduction to Queuing Theory,* New York: Macmillan, 1972.
GROSS, DONALD, and CARL M. HARRIS: *Fundamentals of Queuing Theory,* New York: Wiley, 1974.
HILLIER, FREDERICK S., and GERALD J. LIEBERMAN: *Operations Research,* 2d ed., San Francisco: Holden-Day, 1974.
MORSE, PHILLIP M.: *Queues, Inventories, and Maintenance,* New York: Wiley, 1958.
PANICO, J. A.: *Queueing Theory,* Englewood Cliffs, N.J.: Prentice-Hall, 1969.
SAATY, T. L.: *Elements of Queueing Theory,* New York: McGraw-Hill, 1961.
WAGNER, HARVEY: *Principles of Operations Research,* 2d ed., Englewood Cliffs, N.J.: Prentice-Hall, 1975.

CHAPTER 8
LAYOUT OF FACILITIES

In the last chapter we considered the analysis and modeling of process flows. One type of modeling, however, has been reserved for this chapter—modeling for decisions on the layout of physical facilities. In this chapter we will be discussing layout decisions and models for all types of facilities: those using line, intermittent, and project processes. Box 8.1 outlines a typical layout-decision problem.

In Chapter 5 the process-selection decision from among line, intermittent, and project processes was discussed. Because the pattern of flow is so different in each type of process, the layout decisions will also differ for each. In this chapter we will assume that the process-selection decision has been made and that we are dealing with the layout of a specific type of process.

In Section 8.1, layout decisions for intermittent processes are discussed. Following sections deal with line-flow and project layouts. As the chapter develops, exactly how these layout decisions are related to one another and how they differ will become clear.

BOX 8.1   TYPICAL DECISION PROBLEM

Sherry Stahl, manager of operations analysis for Pizza U.S.A., was considering the layout of the company's stores. She wondered whether a better design could be developed. Was the traffic flow the best from both the customers' viewpoint and that of operations efficiency? Where should the tables be located? How many tables can effectively be put in a store of a certain size? Is the store laid out to promote efficient travel of the waitresses and waiters?

To get at these questions, Sherry decided to propose a layout study to her boss, Ted Hickford, vice president of operations. The objective of the study would be to improve both the efficiency of operations and customer reaction. The efficiency objective would be measured by employees' travel time within the facility. Customer reaction would be measured by showing a panel of customers mockups of alternate layout designs. When this data was assembled, it would be used to evaluate certain layout features and to arrive at the best overall layout plan.

Ted Hickford was pleased with this approach to layout analysis and gave his approval to the study. After beginning the study, Sherry ran into several difficulties she had not expected. First, the company's architecture department was not particularly helpful. They had certain architectural standards which they wanted to maintain, and they did not entirely agree with the study's objectives. Sherry was sorry that she had not involved the architecture department earlier in the study to obtain their full cooperation. She also encountered problems in data collection. To study the efficiency of operations, it was necessary to know the number of trips per day made by various personnel. She also needed to know the present distances traveled. Since these data were not available, they had to be collected in the field.

Sherry was frustrated since she could not find a way to combine, quantitatively, the objectives of operations efficiency and customer reaction. Therefore, the results of the study would depend heavily on judgments regarding the relative importance of these two objectives. Since this problem could not be overcome, Sherry decided to lay out the final report format in such a way that different managers could apply different judgments and arrive at different conclusions. Her recommendations would also be couched in conditional terms, i.e.: "Under this set of conditions and assumptions, layout A is the best;" "Under a second set of assumptions and conditions, layout B is the best." Although she wanted to make a positive recommendation, she did not feel that she could do so on an entirely objective basis.

8.1   LAYOUT OF INTERMITTENT PROCESSES

It will be recalled that in intermittent operations, the flow pattern is jumbled because different products or customers flow through the facility along different paths. From a layout standpoint, the intermittent operation is called a process layout because similar equipment processes or similar worker skills are grouped together by department (or work center). Each product or customer being processed then flows through some departments and skips others, depending on processing requirements. If these concepts are not clear, they can be reviewed in Chapter 5, Section 5.1.

In the intermittent-flow layout problem it is likely that flows between some departments may be very heavy, while those between others are very light. In a hospital, for example, the flow of patients between the orthopedic and x-ray departments may be very heavy because most bone fractures require an x-ray before treatment.

Other departments, such as pediatrics and geriatrics, may have very little patient or doctor flow between them. Because of such differences in flow volumes, an economical flow of traffic can be obtained by locating departments with a heavy flow of traffic adjacent to each other while those with light traffic are placed farther apart.

In a nutshell, the intermittent-flow layout decision determines the relative location of processing centers (departments) to achieve a stated decision criterion within certain layout constraints. Examples of decision criteria for the layout decision include minimizing materials-handling costs, minimizing distance traveled by customers, minimizing employee traveling time, and maximizing the proximity of related departments. The most common constraints include limitations of space, the need to maintain fixed locations for certain departments (e.g., shipping and receiving), the limited weight-bearing capacity of certain floor areas, safety regulations, fire regulations, and aisle requirements. The problem is to find the best layout or at least a satisfactory layout which meets all the applicable constraints.

Intermittent-flow layout problems fall into two basic categories: (1) those involving quantitative decision criteria and (2) those involving qualitative criteria. The quantitative-criteria problems call for decisions which can be expressed in measurable terms such as materials-handling costs, travel time of customers, or distances. In qualitative-criteria layout decisions, it may not be possible to identify a specific, measurable flow of materials, customers, or employees. Instead, qualitative criteria may be stated. For example, it may be highly desirable to locate the washrooms near the cafeteria for sanitation purposes, or it may be desirable to keep the welding and paint departments apart for fire-safety reasons. These relationships are qualitative in nature and cannot be handled by the same methods used to solve quantitative problems.

Quantitative criteria

Various types of intermittent layout problems can be formulated with quantitative criteria. These include the minimization of materials-handling costs in factories and warehouses and the minimization of employee or customer traveling time in service operations. A choice of criteria, of course, always requires a decision on the objectives of the operation; i.e., is it more important to minimize doctor or patient traveling time in a hospital, or should the sum of both times be minimized?

Many quantitative-criteria problems concerning the location of facilities can be expressed in the following form:

$$C = \sum_{i=1}^{N} \sum_{j=1}^{N} T_{ij} C_{ij} D_{ij} \tag{8.1}$$

where T_{ij} = trips between department i and department j
C_{ij} = "cost" per unit distance per trip traveled from i to j
D_{ij} = distance from i to j
C = total cost
N = number of departments

Notice that T_{ij} and C_{ij} are fixed constants and do not depend on the location of departments i and j. Thus, D_{ij} is the only variable in Equation (8.1) which depends on location decisions. In concept, then, we are searching for the particular D_{ij} combination, or layout plan, which results in a minimum value of C.

The "cost" in Equation (8.1) can be considered in dollars or time units, to accommodate either materials-handling or traveling-time criteria. Actually any resource-based criteria can be handled by considering the "cost" as some scarce resource which is being conserved or minimized by the layout decision.

From Equation (8.1), it is apparent that the cost criterion has been expressed as a linear function of distance.[1] This has mathematical advantages, but it also has practical disadvantages. For example, the layout of a school district which has 50 students each of whom lives a mile from the school is considered equivalent to a layout with one student living at a distance of 50 miles and 49 students at zero distance.[2]

The mathematical location problem is to minimize C by determining the values of D_{ij} in Equation (8.1). To illustrate this problem, consider a factory which makes snow blowers and lawn mowers using the departments shown in Figure 8.1. Assume that the objective in this problem is to minimize the cost of moving materials from one department to the next as the products are made in the intermittent operation. In describing this example, we will simply list the steps required to define T_{ij}, C_{ij}, and D_{ij} for Equation (8.1).

The first step in solving this problem is to determine the number of trips between each pair of departments. This number can be estimated from the routing sheets for each of the various product types and estimates of future product volumes. The information on number of materials-handling trips is shown in Figure 8.2, where the entries in the matrix are interpreted as the total number of trips per week between department i and department j *in both directions*.[3] The weekly volume was

[1] Cost is a linear function, since T_{ij} and C_{ij} are constants, the D_{ij} variables are to the first power, and the terms are additive.

[2] The solution methods described in this section can easily be extended to nonlinear functions if desired.

[3] It is also possible to formulate the problem by separating trips between i and j from those between j and i. The formulation presented here combines trips in both directions simply for convenience.

FIGURE 8.1   **DEPARTMENT IN A LAWNMOWER/SNOWBLOWER FACTORY**

Department number	Department name	Area (m^2)
1	Painting	500
2	Metal shearing	350
3	Welding	600
4	Small engines	225
5	Metal working	600
6	Controls	275
7	Tires and wheels	500
8	Final assembly	600

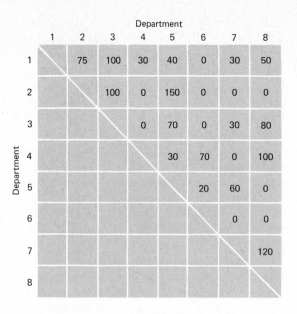

Department

		1	2	3	4	5	6	7	8
	1		75	100	30	40	0	30	50
	2			100	0	150	0	0	0
	3				0	70	0	30	80
Department	4					30	70	0	100
	5						20	60	0
	6							0	0
	7								120
	8								

**Figure 8.2
Trip matrix.
Matrix entry T_{ij} is
the number of
materials-handling
trips per week be-
tween department
i and department j
in both directions.**

simply chosen for convenience; any time period—such as daily, monthly, or yearly—could be used.

The next step is to determine the cost of materials handling per unit of distance traveled on each trip. This cost might vary between department pairs because of different materials-handling methods. For example, forklifts might be used to move materials between the engine department and the final assembly department, while material might be moved by handcarts between controls and welding. For the sake of this example, the materials-handling costs per meter per trip are shown in Figure 8.3.

The next step in the analysis is to determine the distances between each pair of departments. These distances will depend on the layout chosen; we will assume the layout shown in Figure 8.4 as an initial solution. With this layout, the distances between each pair of departments can be found, as shown in Figure 8.5.

We have now specified the number of trips (T_{ij}) matrix, the cost (C_{ij}) matrix, and the distance (D_{ij}) matrix for a particular layout. With these data, it is possible to compute the total materials-handling cost for each pair of departments. In Figure 8.6, each cell in the total-cost matrix is computed by multiplying $T_{ij}D_{ij}C_{ij}$ from each of the three previous matrices. For departments 1 to 2, for example, the cost of materials handling is $(75)(.05)(30) = \$112.50$. After these costs have been calculated, all cells in Figure 8.6 are added to yield $C = \$3668.50$ per week. This completes the evaluation of Equation (8.1) for a particular layout plan.

Given the total cost of an initial layout, we might wonder whether improvements can be made to reduce C. This question can be answered by considering exchanges in pairs of departments. Suppose, for example, that departments 4 and 5

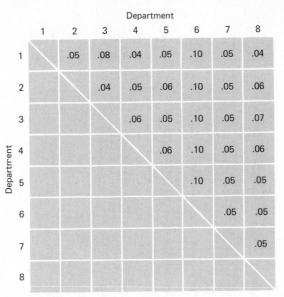

		1	2	3	4	5	6	7	8
	1		.05	.08	.04	.05	.10	.05	.04
	2			.04	.05	.06	.10	.05	.06
	3				.06	.05	.10	.05	.07
Department	4					.06	.10	.05	.06
	5						.10	.05	.05
	6							.05	.05
	7								.05
	8								

Figure 8.3
Unit materials-handling costs.
Matrix entry C_{ij} is the materials-handling cost in dollars per meter per trip between department i and department j.

were exchanged in the initial layout. Recalculating the cost matrix in Figure 8.6 (or evaluating the cost changes), we get $C = \$3144.50$, a reduction of $524 per week. The revised costs of the affected cells are shown in Figure 8.7. By considering other possible exchanges of departments, we might be able to reduce cost even further. However, one cannot expect to arrive at an optimal solution by this method unless every possible combination of departments is evaluated.

For small problems it may be feasible to enumerate all possible layout combinations. For example, if there are nine departments, there are $9! = 362,880$ possible location combinations, since there are nine choices of location for the first department, eight for the second, seven for the third, and so on. However, some of these 9! locations are mirror images of the others. There are only $9!/8 = 45,360$ layout combinations which differ in relative locations. For 20 departments, for example, there are 608 trillion different combinations of layouts, which is too many to enumerate

Figure 8.4
Initial layout.

Painting 1	Small engines 4	Metal working 5	Tires and wheels 7	*Receiving dock*
		Aisle		
Metal shearing 2	Welding 3	Controls 6	Final assembly 8	*Shipping dock*

Figure 8.5
Initial interdepart-
mental distances.
Matrix entry D_{ij} is
the materials-han-
dling distance
(per trip) between
department i and
department j in
meters.

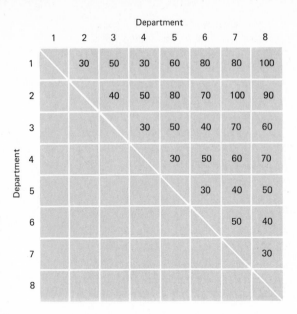

Department

	1	2	3	4	5	6	7	8
1		30	50	30	60	80	80	100
2			40	50	80	70	100	90
3				30	50	40	70	60
4					30	50	60	70
5						30	40	50
6							50	40
7								30
8								

Department

Figure 8.5
Initial interdepart-
mental distances.
Matrix entry D_{ij} is
the materials-han-
dling distance
(per trip) between
department i and
department j in
meters.

even by the fastest computer. [See Buffa (1977), p. 262.] There are, however, computer methods for approximating a solution to these larger problems; these will be discussed later.

In summary, then, the quantitative layout problem for intermittent operations can often be expressed as a linear function of distance between departments. The

Figure 8.6
Total cost matrix.
Each matrix entry
is the product of
$T_{ij}\,C_{ij}\,D_{ij}$ from Fig-
ures 8.2, 8.3, and
8.5. The resulting
entries are the
cost in dollars of
materials flows be-
tween each pair of
departments.

Department

	1	2	3	4	5	6	7	8
1		112.5	400	36	120	0	120	200
2			160	0	720	0	0	0
3				0	175	0	105	336
4					54	350	0	420
5						60	120	0
6							0	0
7								180
8								

Department

Total cost = $3668.50 per week ($190,762 per year)

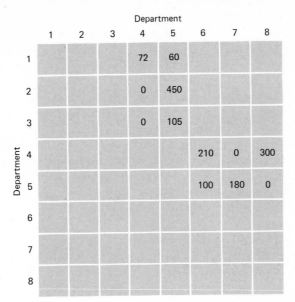

**Figure 8.7
Adjusted costs
due to department
4/5 swap.**

required data are the number of trips between departments per time period, the "cost" per unit of distance traveled on each trip, and the distance between departments for any particular layout. These data permit the total cost of a particular layout plan to be evaluated. Improved layouts can then be determined by considering exchanges between pairs of departments. However, in most cases of practical interest, there are so many possible exchanges that all possibilities cannot be evaluated; therefore special methods are needed to arrive at an optimal or near-optimal (minimum cost) solution for these problems.

Qualitative criteria

Layout problems involving qualitative criteria occur when relationships between departments in intermittent-flow facilities are specified in qualitative terms (e.g., the desirability of locating one department near another or at a distance from another). In some cases, these qualitative criteria may be more readily available or more appropriate than quantitative criteria.

The qualitative location problem has been studied in depth by Muther (1962), who has proposed a method of formulation and solution called SLP (systematic layout planning). According to Muther's approach, the desirability of locating a given department next to any other department is rated by one of the following terms: "absolutely necessary," "especially important," "important," "ordinary closeness okay," "unimportant," and "undesirable." These qualitative ratings may be based on safety considerations, customer convenience, or approximate flows between departments. For example, it might be desirable to locate the baby food department near the milk department in a supermarket for convenience of shopping; it might also be desirable to locate the heavy items near the supermarket door to reduce carrying distance; and expensive items should perhaps be located near the cash registers to reduce pilferage. These kinds of qualitative relationships can be specified using SLP, as shown in Figure 8.8 for a typical supermarket example. Notice how the relationships are arranged in a matrix format similar to that for the quantitative layout problem.

After the qualitative relationships are specified, it is necessary to find a way to solve the problem. For small problems, this can be done by visual inspection, as shown in Figure 8.8. One simply attempts to locate all the absolutely essential departments next to each other; the especially important relationships are also satisfied by adjacent departments, if possible, or by departments at a separation of one department, and so on, until the undesirable departmental relationships are satisfied by departments as far apart as possible. The solution shown in Figure 8.8 is not necessarily an "optimal" solution but simply a good solution chosen for purposes of illustration.

When the relationships have been decided, the layout problem is still not solved. This is because the entire layout must usually fit within a rectangular or other geometric shape. Figure 8.8 shows how the layout is converted from a block diagram to a final layout plan. At this point, it may be helpful for the reader to study all the steps used in Figure 8.8 to arrive at a solution.

For larger problems, the solution cannot be obtained by inspection but must depend on computerized methods which attempt to consider all of the specified relationships and arrive at an optimal (or satisfactory) solution. These methods require that qualitative relationships be converted to a numerical scale; the resulting problem is then solved by a mathematical algorithm. The solution obtained may not accurately reflect the qualitative relationships originally specified; it must then be adjusted to do so. Some of these computerized methods will be described below.

The qualitative layout formulation has been applied to many types of situations including factories, warehouses, offices, and service operations [Francis and White (1974), p. 37]. This method can be used for any layout problem because qualitative relationships between departments can always be specified. Qualitative layout problems are frequently encountered in the service industries, where customers interact with the facilities. In this case, customer preference for relative location of facilities becomes an important qualitative consideration.

Computerized layout planning

Computerized layout planning of intermittent-process facilities has been evolving since 1963 when CRAFT, the first practical program, was developed. Today, as catalogued by the Center for Environmental Research, some eighty computer programs are available. [See Kaiman (1970, 1971).] We will examine the three most widely known programs: CRAFT for quantitative criteria and CORELAP and ALDEP for qualitative criteria.

1. CRAFT (Computerized Relative Allocation of Facilities). CRAFT was developed by Armour and Buffa (1963) and later refined by Buffa, Armour, and Vollmann (1964). It

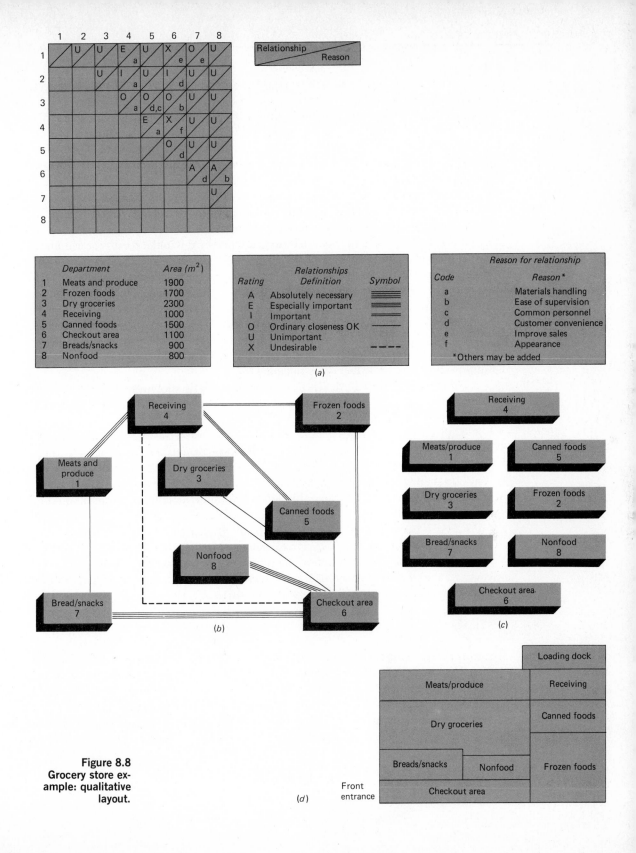

**Figure 8.8
Grocery store example: qualitative layout.**

uses a quantitative-criterion layout formulation and can solve problems with up to 40 departments or activity centers.

The input to CRAFT is a matrix of unit costs and an initial layout plan. The unit-cost matrix is the product of the T_{ij} and C_{ij} matrices described earlier. The initial layout plan may be an existing layout or an arbitrary starting layout. Then, using the initial layout provided, the computer determines the distances between centroids of departments.

The next step in the program is to calculate the cost of the initial layout by using the unit-cost matrix and the computed distances from the initial layout. In effect, the CRAFT program evaluates Equation (8.1), just as in the previous example.

The CRAFT program then determines whether the initial total cost can be reduced by exchanging departments in pairs.[4] Each possible pair of departments is exchanged and the resulting cost, whether an increase or a decrease, is computed and stored in the computer's memory. When all pairs of exchanges have been considered, the lowest cost exchange is selected and these departments are exchanged in the initial layout.[5] If the cost is reduced, the resulting cost and the new layout are then printed out, and the procedure is repeated for a second exchange of departments. A new layout and lower cost are printed out on each successive round of exchanges until no further cost reduction is obtained.

An example of a CRAFT printout for one step is shown in Figure 8.9. Each letter represents a different department; together, the letters outline the shape of the departments on the layout plan.

With CRAFT, it is possible to fix the location of certain departments. This is extremely important, since it allows the revision of existing floor plans without moving special equipment or violating constraints which must be met.

The final solution reached by CRAFT is often sensitive to the initial layout input. Thus, to reduce the effect of bias, several different starting layouts should be selected.

CRAFT has been applied in practice to a large number of different layout problems. According to Buffa (1977), it has been used by four aircraft plants, two of the largest automobile companies, two computer manufacturing operations, a pharmaceutical manufacturer, a meat packer, a precision machine shop, a movie studio, and a hospital. Since the program is in wide circulation, it has, no doubt, been used for other applications as well.

There are, however, several limitations regarding CRAFT. One is that cost must be a linear function of distance. The second is that all flow of materials is assumed to occur between the centroids of departments. As a result, long, thin departments are sometimes selected by the program because their centroids are close together, even though the actual materials-flow pattern may be quite long. The third limitation is that CRAFT does not provide a minimum-cost solution. CRAFT is a heuristic program which provides a very good solution but not a guaranteed optimal

---

[4] In a more advanced version of CRAFT, departments are also exchanged three at a time.

[5] All together, $\binom{n}{2} = \dfrac{n(n-1)}{2}$ pairs of exchanges are considered on each round for n departments.

	1	2	3	4	5	6	7	8	9	10	11	12	13	14	15
1	T	T	T	T	T	V	V	V	V	V	V	V	V	V	V
2	T				T	V									V
3	T				T	V									V
4	T				T	V									V
5	T				T	V	V	V	V	V	V	V	V	V	V
6	T	T	T	T	T	N	N	N	N	N	B	B	B	A	A
7	P	P	P	P	P	N				N	B		B	A	A
8	P				P	N	N	N		N	B		B	A	A
9	P	P	P	P	S	M	L	L	N	N	B		B	A	A
10	R	R	R	S	S	L			L	L	B		B	A	A
11	R	R	R	S	S	L			L	B	B	B	A	A	
12	Q	Q	S		S	L			L	L	D	D	D	C	C
13	Q	Q	S		S	L	L	L	K	K	D		D	C	C
14	Q	Q	S	S	S	K	K	K		K	D		D	C	D
15	O	O	O	O	O	K			K	D			D	D	
16	O			O	K	K	K	K	K	D				D	
17	O		O	U	U	U	U	U	U	D				D	
18	O		O	U				U	D				D		
19	O		O	U				U	D				D		
20	O		O	U	U	U	U	U	D	D	D	D	D		
21	O		O	E	E	E	E	E	E	E	E	E			
22	O		O	E	E	E	E	E	E	E		E			
23	O		O	I	I	I	I	I	J	J	E	E			
24	O		O	I				I	J	J	J	J			
25	O		O	I	I	I	I	I	F	F	F	F			
26	O		O	H	H	H	H	F				F			
27	O		O	G	G	G	G	F				F			
28	O	O	O	O	O	O	G	G	G	G	F	F	F	F	F

TOTAL COST 3126.24   EST. COST REDUCTION 168.74

MOVEA   P   MOVEB   S   MOVEC

**Figure 8.9
Example of CRAFT printout.
The letters on the computer printout outline the physical boundaries of each department.**

(Reprinted by permission of the Harvard Business Review. Exhibit from E. S. Buffa, G. C. Armour, and T. E. Vollmann, "Allocating Facilities with CRAFT," vol. 42, no. 2, 1964. Copyright © 1964 by the President and Fellows of Harvard College. All rights reserved.)

solution. (See Box 8.2 on heuristics.) In practice, however, the lack of a truly optimal solution is not a severe limitation—any improvement over the present layout or over other layout methods is useful. Despite its limitations, CRAFT has been quite helpful in reaching better layout decisions.

2. ALDEP (Automated Layout Design Program). ALDEP was developed by IBM in 1967 and originally described by Seehof and Evans (1967). The ALDEP program and CORELAP, described next, handle only qualitative-criteria layout problems.

The inputs to ALDEP include a relationship matrix, as shown in Figure 8.8, and constraints such as building size, fixed locations of departments, stairwells, etc. The ALDEP program begins by randomly selecting a department and placing it in the layout plan. In the second step, all remaining departments are scanned and one with a high closeness-relationship rating (such as A or E) is selected and placed in the layout next to the first department. If a high closeness rating cannot be found, a department is selected at random and placed in the layout. This selection process continues until all departments have been placed in the layout plan. A total score for the layout is then computed by converting each closeness relationship to a numerical scale and adding the values of those relationships in the layout plan. The entire process is then repeated by starting with another random department as the first step.

The ALDEP program is useful for generating a large number of good layouts for examination. The program can be controlled so that only layouts with a specified score or better are printed out. This has the effect of reducing the number of layouts which must be examined. While ALDEP is a useful heuristic for generating good layouts, it does not produce optimal solutions except by accident.

ALDEP saves much of the tedious work involved in layout, but it still requires judgment to arrive at a final solution. The ALDEP program is designed to handle up to 63 departments and a three-story building.

3. CORELAP (Computerized Relationship Layout Planning). CORELAP is also a qualitative-criteria layout program. It was originally developed by Lee and Moore (1967) and subsequently improved by Sepponen (1969). An interactive computer version has also been developed by Moore (1971). CORELAP handles up to 70 departments.

BOX 8.2   **HEURISTIC DECISION RULES**

The word "heuristic" is derived from the Greek *heuriskein,* meaning "to discover." Heuristics are decision rules which are discovered, usually by trial and error, to solve problems. Sometimes these rules come very close to providing an optimal solution to mathematical problems and sometimes the rules are not so good.

We use heuristics, or rules of thumb, in everyday life. For example, we decide to start looking for a gas station when the tank reaches ¼. We decide to invest in the stock market when the price of our favorite stock stops dropping and rises for the second day in a row.

Heuristics are used to solve decision problems when optimal techniques are not available or too cumbersome or too expensive to use. In this chapter we will use such heuristic rules of thumb to solve both layout problems and assembly-line balancing problems. In practice, these heuristics are sometimes quite good and lead to improved solutions for decision problems even though the optimal or best solution may not be reached.

The input to CORELAP includes a relationship matrix and restrictions on layouts such as size of departments, building length-to-width ratio, and fixed department locations. The relationship matrix is converted to numerical values for closeness ratings, as follows:

A = 6, E = 5, I = 4, O = 3, U = 2, X = 1

These numerical values are then used to compute a total closeness rating (TCR) for each department by summing the values of all relationships for that department.

Assuming that there are no preassigned departments, CORELAP first selects the department with the highest TCR score and places it in the layout. Call this department number 1. The CORELAP program then scans the relationship matrix and selects a department with an A rating with department 1, if available. Otherwise, it selects an E rating, an I rating, or an O rating, in order of preference. If a tie develops—for example, if several departments have an A rating—the department with the highest TCR is selected. If there is no department with an O rating or better, the department with the highest TCR is selected.

Now a second department which is located next to department 1 in the layout plan is selected. Call this department number 2. The CORELAP program then scans the relationship matrix and selects a department with an A rating with department 1, if available. If not, an A rating with department 2 would be sought. If an A rating cannot be found with either department, the procedure is repeated with E ratings for departments 1, 2, and so on until the U rating is reached. If no department is found to enter with a U rating or better, the department with the highest TCR is selected. We have now entered three departments in the layout. A similar procedure is then repeated for the remaining departments until all of them have been entered into the layout plan. When this process is complete, the CORELAP program prints out the final layout plan.

It is interesting to note that if CORELAP were run a second time, it would arrive at exactly the same solution. Unlike ALDEP, the CORELAP procedure is completely deterministic.

A serious limitation of both CORELAP and ALDEP is that qualitative relationships are converted to a numerical scale. The effect of this is to introduce a more precise mathematical relationship than was originally specified by the input. For example, an A rating is assigned a value of 6 and a B rating a value of 5. But the original specification of A and B ratings did not imply that A is one-fifth better than B. These numerical relationships were defined for the computer programs in order to achieve a numerical solution. Because of this feature, one must intepret the output very carefully and possibly adjust the final output for unwanted effects introduced by the numerical conversion process.

Layout decisions

We have been emphasizing layout principles, concepts, and methods which are applicable to a wide variety of decision problems. There are, however, a number of other factors which must be considered in the layout decision.

First, while layout *analysis* might be done by technical specialists such as engineers, architects, and operations staff, the assumptions and the final layout decisions are made by managers. It is therefore important for all managers to recognize good layout analysis and to be able to guide technical specialists in making appropriate analyses of layout problems.

Although we have emphasized computerized methods, many layouts are still done by visual inspection. One reason for this is that many technical specialists and managers are still not aware of the methods available. A second reason is that sometimes visual methods are more appropriate, especially for small-layout problems or those with low complexity. A research study by Scriabin and Vergin (1975) indicates that some layout problems can be solved as well or better by visual inspection than by computerized methods of the type discussed above. In their research, layout problems were sized from 5 to 20 departments and human solutions were compared to the best computer solutions. In all cases the humans did as well as or better than the computer. Unfortunately, the experiment utilized equal-sized departments with concentrated flow patterns. These problems tend to favor the human problem solver to some extent. Nevertheless, the research showed that humans were better than computers at solving layout problems of a certain type.

In practice there is undoubtedly much room for expanded use of the computer as an aid in making layout decisions. The challenge is to make greater use of the computer in those situations where it does apply.

It is best to think of computerized layout methods as aids to human decision making rather than single-point problem solvers. The computer programs should be used iteratively to suggest layout solutions which are then studied and perhaps solved again with different assumptions. When such a combination of human and computer problem solving is used, the best capabilities of both humans and computers are utilized.

It is obvious that, with the iterative method of problem solving, the manager cannot be removed entirely from the analysis process because analysis and decision making are iterative and interactive. The manager and analyst must, therefore, work closely together in arriving at a decision. It also becomes apparent that managers should know something about the analytic methods of solving layout problems and that analysts should know something about management decision making.

8.2 LAYOUT OF LINE PROCESSES

The layout of line processes differs greatly from the layout of intermittent processes. These differences arise because the sequence of processing activities in the line processes is fixed by the product design; the product is made sequentially from one step to the next along the line of flow. While the layout of line flows does not affect the direction of flow of the product, it does affect the efficiency of the line and the jobs assigned to individual workers.

The classic case of line-flow operations is the moving assembly line. This form of production results in great efficiency, as we noted in Chapter 5. At the same time, the assembly line seems to have serious side effects in terms of job boredom, absenteeism, and turnover. Thus the design of assembly lines and alternatives to the traditional assembly line should be carefully considered by management.

In the first part of this section it is assumed that a traditional moving assembly line is being used, and we will consider the problem of assigning tasks (operations) to workers along the assembly line so that the work is evenly divided among workers. This is the classic problem of assembly-line balancing. In the second part of this section, we will consider alternative forms of assembly-line layout including two or more smaller lines and work-group or team assembly. These alternatives may solve some of the human problems related to single-paced assembly lines.

Assembly-line balancing

The problem of assembly-line balancing can best be described by example. Suppose an assembly line is being designed where the maximum time that any worker on the line can spend on the product is specified to be 60 seconds (this is called the cycle time). Now visualize a number of workers along this line, each working on the product for a maximum of 60 seconds and then passing the product along to the next worker.

In balancing the assembly line we ask: How should individual operations (or tasks) be assigned to these workers? If we assign the first worker on the line a discrete number of operations, the total time assigned may add up to slightly less than the 60 seconds available, because there may be no combination of operations which need to be done at the first work station that add up exactly to the cycle time. Similarly, the second worker may also be assigned less than 60 seconds of work, and so on down the line. It is very possible that, due to the product structure and the discrete nature of operation times, some workers may have substantially less than 60 seconds of work.

Therefore the problem of assembly-line balancing is as follows: given a cycle time, find the minimum number of work stations or workers required. In this case each worker will have a minimum amount of idle time consistent with the product structure and the line will use as few people as possible. In rare cases, a perfect balance will be achieved, where each worker has no idle time and the line is 100 percent efficient.

Another way to state the assembly-line balancing problem is to minimize the cycle time for a given number of work stations. These problems are mirror images of each other. It just depends on whether we are given the cycle time or the number of work stations to start with.

The following symbols and definitions will be used in discussing the assembly-line balancing problem:

N = number of work stations along the line. Usually a work station is the space occupied by a single worker. A work station could, however, have more than one worker assigned, or one worker could handle more than one work station. We will assume, however, that each work station has exactly one worker unless otherwise noted.

C = cycle time, the maximum time allowed at any one work station. The cycle time will also be the time between production of successive finished units by the line.

t_i = operation time for the ith operation on the product. Each operation is assigned to one and only one work station.

Σt_i = total work content of the product. This is the total labor required to produce one unit.

There are some important relationships between these variables. First of all, it is common for output rate (units per day) to be given. The cycle time can then be derived from the output rate by the equation C = 420/output rate, C being expressed in minutes. This formula assumes there are 420 productive minutes (7 hours) in a day.

Once C is known, we can derive the minimum number of stations required on the line (assuming 100 percent efficiency, or perfect balance).[6]

$$N_{\min} = \left\langle \frac{\Sigma t_i}{C} \right\rangle$$

This formula is based on the idea that the total work-content time must be provided by workers who put in a time of C units each with perfect balance. Whether a balance can then be found with the minimum number of stations depends on the particular precedence constraints and task times in the problem under consideration.

After balancing the line, the efficiency of the balance is computed as follows:

$$\text{Efficiency} = \frac{\Sigma t_i}{NC}$$

This formula is based on the notion that NC is the actual time spent on each product including idle time, but Σt_i is the productive time spent. The opposite of efficiency has been termed "balance delay" in the literature of assembly-line balancing.

Balance delay = 1 − efficiency

The following example will illustrate the procedure used for assembly-line balancing and also the calculation of the above quantities. Suppose that a line is being designed to assemble the tricycle shown in Figure 7.1. To start, we would need assembly drawings and an assembly chart of the type shown in Figures 7.1 and 7.2. As a matter of fact, because operations will be grouped into work stations, we will need to have the operations defined at the most detailed level possible, as in Figure 8.10. This figure defines each assembly operation required and the associated operation times (t_i). As can be seen, the maximum t_i is 18 seconds. Since these operations cannot be subdivided further, 18 seconds will be the minimum cycle time unless two workers are assigned to some work station. Furthermore, the cycle time cannot exceed the total work content of the product. Thus we have:

Max $[t_i]$ ≤ cycle time ≤ Σt_i

---

[6] The symbol < > denotes the next integer greater than the quantity in brackets. The minimum number of stations is thereby rounded up to an integer value.

FIGURE 8.10   TRICYCLE ASSEMBLY OPERATIONS

Operation number	Description*	Time (seconds)
1	Starting point	0
	Left wheel	
2	Fit washer on left axle	10
3	Fit left wheel on axle	18
4	Fit washer on left axle	10
5	Insert and fasten cotter key	15
6	Insert and fasten hub cap	17
	Right wheel	
7	Fit washer on right axle	10
8	Fit right wheel on axle	18
9	Fit washer on right axle	10
10	Insert and fasten cotter key	15
11	Insert and fasten hub cap	17
12	Dummy operation	0
	Front-wheel assembly	
13	Insert front wheel fork in frame	18
14	Fit collar on front wheel fork	11
15	Insert handle bars into fork	15
16	Tighten front wheel collar	18
17	Attach left handle grips	12
18	Attach right handle grips	12
	Seat assembly	
19	Insert seat into frame	9
20	Tighten seat set screw	18
21	End point	0
	Total	253

* Operations 1, 12, and 21 are added for purposes of computer convenience. The computer requires a single beginning and ending point in the diagram.

Suppose we decide initially to balance this tricycle line at 20 seconds. Notice that this will be a very fast line made up of exceedingly boring and repetitive tasks (e.g., putting the left wheel on the axle).

At this cycle time of 20 seconds, 1260 tricycles (420/.333) will be produced per day. The minimum number of stations is 13.

$$N_{min} = \langle 253/20 \rangle = \langle 12.65 \rangle = 13$$

Certain technological constraints must be observed in assembling the tricycle; e.g., the inside washer must be put on before the wheel, and the seat must be inserted before the seat bolt is tightened. The technological constraints are shown in Figure 8.11. Actually, these constraints are slightly more restrictive than necessary. For example, the seat can be put on the tricycle at the same time as the rear wheels. This

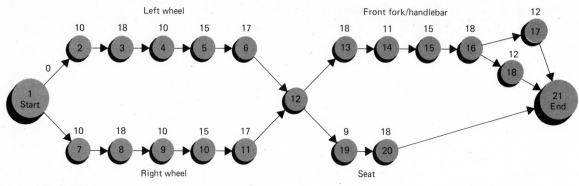

**Figure 8.11
Tricycle prece-
dence diagram.**

might result, however, in a work station which inserts one washer on a rear axle, inserts the seat, and puts one handle grip on the handle bar. To avoid such mixed jobs Figure 8.11 requires that both rear wheels be put on before proceeding to the seat and front fork assemblies.

The precedence diagram in Figure 8.11 shows which operations must precede other operations. In the diagram, all tasks at the tail of an arrow must be completed before tasks at the head of the arrow. Thus, the sequence of assembly operations required on the left rear wheel is washer, wheel, washer, cotter key, hubcap. However, these operations can be intermixed between the left and right rear wheels since the two rear-wheel sequences are in parallel. Assembly of the seat and front fork can also be intermixed, but—according to the diagram—not with assembly of the rear wheels.

With the 20-second cycle time, the operations times, and the precedence diagram, operations can be assigned to work stations to minimize the number of work stations required. There are a great number of possible assignments to consider. If precedence constraints are ignored, there are 18! ways of assigning the 18 operations to work stations. Since we cannot enumerate all possibilities in real-world cases, assembly-line balancing methods have been devised to solve this problem.

The best methods currently available are heuristic methods, which do not necessarily find the minimum number of work stations but do usually find solutions which are close to the optimum. It is not our intention to present all the various heuristic assembly-line balancing methods here. Rather, we will simply present two methods for illustrative purposes.

One way to solve the problem at hand is to begin the assignment of operations with the one that has the least number of predecessors and then to move on to those with more predecessors.[7] In Figure 8.12, the tricycle operations are rank-ordered in terms of their number of predecessors, starting with the least number of predecessors. The operations are then assigned to work stations, moving down the list until a maximum of 20 seconds is reached. If there is a tie in precedence, the longest operation time is assigned first so as to save short operations until the end and to pack stations as tightly as possible in the beginning. If an operation with the next-highest precedence does not fit in the work station's available time, then we

[7] This method was first suggested by Kilbridge and Wester (1961).

FIGURE 8.12   TRICYCLE OPERATIONS RANKED BY
                     NUMBER OF PREDECESSORS

Operations	Number of predecessors	t_i
1	0	0
2	1	10
7	1	10
3	2	18
8	2	18
4	3	10
9	3	10
5	4	15
10	4	15
6	5	17
11	5	17
12	11	0
13	12	18
19	12	9
14	13	11
20	13	18
15	14	15
16	15	18
17	16	12
18	16	12
21	20	0

move down the precedence list to find an operation that does fit in the available time. If none is found, the work station is left partly idle.

As a result of applying this rule, 15 stations are required, as shown in Figure 8.13. The resulting efficiency of this balance is 84 percent or a balance delay of 16 percent.

$$\text{Efficiency} = \frac{\Sigma t_i}{NC} = \frac{253}{15(20)} = .84$$

In solving practical assembly-line balancing problems, computer methods are necessary. Hoffmann's method, for example, requires three types of inputs common to all assembly-line balancing problems: precedence relationships, operations time, and cycle time. [See Hoffmann (1963).] The output is an assignment of operations to work stations, the theoretical minimum number of stations, and the efficiency of the balance. A sample output from Hoffman's method is shown in Figure 8.14.

Hoffmann's method attempts to assign to the first station those operations which would result in the least idle time at that station. This is done by enumerating all feasible solutions from the precedence graph. If a solution with no idle time is found, the enumeration is stopped. A similar procedure is followed for the second station, the third station, and so on, until all operations have been assigned. The assembly line is then also balanced backward on the precedence graph, and the best forward and backward solution is taken as the final balance.

FIGURE 8.13 **LEAST PREDECESSOR RULE LINE BALANCE**

20-second cycle time		
Stations	Operations	Idle
1	1, 2, 7	0
2	3	2
3	8	2
4	4, 9	0
5	5	5
6	10	5
7	6	3
8	11	3
9	12, 13	2
10	19, 14	0
11	20	2
12	15	5
13	16	2
14	17	8
15	18, 21	8

We could go on to describe several of the other methods available, but this is not our main objective. Rather, our purpose is to describe the principles of assembly-line balancing and the implications for management. Other methods have been surveyed and compared in the literature by Ignall (1965), Mastor (1970), Gehrlein and Patterson (1978), and Tonge (1965).

One of the implications of assembly-line balancing is that efficiency varies greatly with cycle time, as shown in Figure 8.15 for the tricycle example. From a management standpoint, it therefore seems prudent to investigate a range of cycle times rather than a single number. The result may be a slightly higher or lower cycle time (and output) than originally desired, but at a much greater efficiency of operation (see Figure 8.15).

The assembly-line balancing problem has been greatly simplified in our discussion. In practice, there are several considerations which complicate the problem and sometimes require more sophisticated solutions. Some of these include:

1. *Variability of operations times.* The time required for humans to perform a task will often vary depending on such factors as materials problems, fatigue, and improper alignment. As a result, buffers of materials may be required between stations, the whole assembly line may be slowed down to accommodate these variations, or some items may be only partially completed on the line.

2. *Multiple products.* It is quite common for mixed models or products to be made on the same assembly line. The result of this is a balance which is not optimal for any one of these products.

3. *Zoning constraint.* In some cases certain operations must be done together because similar skills are required or certain operations, such as painting and sanding, must be separated. To reflect these conditions, zone constraints are added to

```
TOTAL ELEMENT TIME =253.ØØØØ
NUMBER OF ELEMENTS IS   21
NUMBER OF PRECEDENCE RESTRICTIONS IS   23
 WHAT IS THE CYCLE TIME        ? 2Ø
                       ASSEMBLY LINE BALANCE
                       CYCLE TIME = 2Ø.ØØØØ


 STATION              SLACK
 NUMBER               TIME        ELEMENT NUMBERS

    1                    Ø    1    2   7
    2               2.ØØØØ     3
    3               2.ØØØØ     8
    4                    Ø     4    9
    5               5.ØØØØ     5
    6               3.ØØØØ     6
    7               5.ØØØØ    1Ø
    8               3.ØØØØ    11   12
    9               2.ØØØØ    13   12
   1Ø                    Ø    14   19
   11               2.ØØØØ    2Ø
   12               5.ØØØØ    15
   13               2.ØØØØ    16
   14               8.ØØØØ    17
   15               8.ØØØØ    18   21

 TOTAL SLACK TIME =47.ØØØØ          EFFICIENCY = 84.33  PER CENT

 THEORETICAL MINIMUM NUMBER OF STATIONS IS    13
```

**Figure 8.14
Sample assembly-
line balancing pro-
gram.**

*(Source of program:
Thomas R. Hoffman,
"Assembly Line Balanc-
ing with a Precedence
Matrix," Management
Science, vol. 9, no. 4,
July 1963, pp. 551–
562.)*

the precedence diagram and operations must be completed within their assigned zones.

4. *Social factors.* The effect of short cycle times on worker attitudes and job performance has already been noted. Some alternatives for addressing this problem will be described below.

Despite all the work which has been done on assembly-line balancing, these methods are not widely used in practice. In an excellent survey of 90 companies,

**Figure 8.15
Efficiency versus
cycle time.**

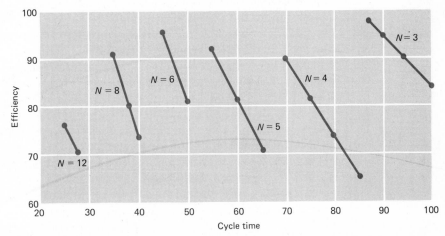

Chase (1974) found that 80 used manual methods, 7 used computer methods, and 3 used combined computer and manual methods. Chase attributes lack of use primarily to unfamiliarity with formal published methods (57 percent of the respondents were unfamiliar with these techniques). For those who were familiar with the methods, the lack of use was attributed to the time it takes to use them and their perceived inflexibility. From an educational and management perspective, there remains a great deal of room for improvement of practice in industry.

One of the most important implications of our discussion on assembly-line balancing is that output rate cannot be varied up and down in line-flow operations. If management decides to change the output rate or model mix, the line must be rebalanced. After the balance is changed, it will take a period of time for the workers to learn their new jobs and for efficiency to return. Therefore the output rate and product mix are kept as stable as possible while demand variations are absorbed by a buffer of finished-goods inventory. In his survey, Chase (1974) noted that the average assembly line was rebalanced three times per year and that it took an average of 5.4 days to reach full production after a major rebalance.

Alternatives to traditional assembly lines

The study by Chase (1974) also gathered some information on the effects of assembly lines on the work force, as shown in Table 8.1. The table indicates that personnel turnover averages 28.9 percent per year, with a range from 3.5 to 46.3 percent. The average number of formal grievances per 100 workers per year is 51.9. This is evidence of considerable turmoil on the part of at least some assembly-line workers. It behooves management, therefore, to consider alternatives to traditional, rigidly paced assembly lines. [See also Chase (1975).]

When the subject of assembly lines is discussed, it is often thought that assembly-line balancing is the only problem. This attitude assumes that a single-paced line flow is the only possible type of assembly line. But, there is a wide range of alternatives, including:

1. Several assembly lines producing the same product, each with longer cycle times and thus more task variety than a single line.
2. Assembly lines which permit group organization and teamwork, thus allowing more social interaction between workers while on the job.
3. Assembly lines which permit more self-pacing through buffers of materials between work stations. The product in this case would not be rigidly fixed to the assembly line but would move along at variable rates.

The use of the first type of assembly-line alternative would be rather expensive in capital-intensive industries because it requires the duplication of equipment and tools. There are, however, many highly labor-intensive assembly lines which could easily adopt this approach. For example, in the assembly of the tricycle, which is primarily labor-intensive, several small lines could be used.

The second approach has been tried in Europe by Volvo [Gyllenhammar (1977)]

TABLE 8.1 **EFFECTS OF ASSEMBLY LINES ON THE WORK FORCE***

	All companies surveyed	Small appliances	Light manufacturing	Automobile parts	Lawn and garden	Large appliances	Tractors and engines
Absenteeism (average number of days per worker per year)	5.9	7.3	4.8	4.3	6.2	6.5	6.1
Turnover (average percentage of line work force per year)	28.9	3.5	46.3	9.4	25.6	40.1	42.3
Formal grievances (per 100 line workers per year)	51.9	63.1	39.5	54.4	66.7	46.1	44.2
Age of average line worker	33.2	31.8	36.9	41.0	31.9	28.1	32.0
Percentage of female workers	39.3	70.2	83.1	30.0	20.7	16.6	0
Grouped percentage of unionized shops	79.3	72.7	61.5	85.7	85.9	78.5	100.0
Percentage of firms using utility workers	70.6	63.6	46.1	71.4	85.7	78.5	83.0
Percentage of firms using job rotation on the lines	27.0	20.0	46.1	14.3	42.8	21.4	14.0
Percentage of firms attempting job enlargement	38.2	60.0	45.5	14.3	14.2	50.0	29.0

Source: Richard B. Chase, "Survey of Paced Assembly Lines," *Industrial Engineering,* vol. 16, no. 2, February 1974.

* Based on a survey of 90 companies.

for the assembly of automobiles. In their plan, a group of employees is assigned the automobile for a block of time. For example, an upholstery group might work as a team to install all the interior upholstery. The team decides who does what jobs, and they can rotate work assignments provided the team completes the upholstery in the assigned block of time. This approach enriches the social interaction between workers and allows job rotation and job variety.

The third approach has also been tried by Volvo. In this case, the automobiles are fixed to dollies which can be pushed about the factory. These dollies are not fixed to a rigid moving track, allowing more flexibility in scheduling work as well as some margin for variability in work pace. The flexibility is provided by buffers of partly completed automobiles between work stations.

As can be seen, there are many ways to organize assembly work once some of the traditional assumptions are brought into question. These options can be illustrated a little more clearly by again using the tricycle example.

Suppose we want to assemble 575 tricycles per day (in 8 hours). This amounts to a 50-second cycle time if a single-paced line is used. Using Hoffmann's method, we will need six stations. The first person's job will involve putting the left wheel and three washers in place, the second person will complete the left wheel assembly and put on the right wheel, and so on for the other workers. These are obviously quite finely divided jobs.

Another way to organize assembly of 575 tricycles a day is to set up two-person teams. In this case, one person can put on the right wheel while the other puts on the left wheel. One person can put on the seat while the other inserts the front fork, and they can both complete the front fork and put on handle grips. As a matter of fact, each team could organize its own work in precisely the fashion they wished. A manager should expect the same productivity, perhaps more, from these teams as from the single assembly line. For the same productivity, there should be three two-person teams and each team should produce 192 tricycles per day with a cycle time of 150 seconds per tricycle. For many workers, this method of assembly might be much more desirable than the single-paced line with shorter cycle time and less opportunity for human interaction. From an efficiency standpoint, it makes no difference to management as long as the same number of tricycles are produced by the same number of employees.

Another way to organize the assembly of tricycles would be to have two small assembly lines, each with three work stations. These smaller assembly lines would have a cycle time of 100 seconds, thus permitting more job variety for each worker.

We could go on with still other alternatives, but the point should be clear. There are many options which need to be considered carefully if management is to design assembly lines from both the social and technical viewpoints. The problem of assembly-line layout is not merely one of balancing single-paced lines.

8.3 LAYOUT OF PROJECTS

A project is a one-time activity which produces a unique product. The uniqueness of the product is one of the primary reasons why project layouts are different from intermittent or line layouts. Some examples of project-layout problems may be helpful at the outset. After reviewing these examples, we will summarize the key principles of project layout.

One category of projects is the construction of buildings, highways, dams, and so on. In construction projects, materials-handling cost is an important consideration; therefore much attention is paid to the efficient layout and staging of materials during construction. An attempt will usually be made to locate high-usage materials near the construction site and lower usage materials at greater distances. This materials-handling problem can be formulated in a manner similar to that of the CRAFT model used for intermittent layouts.

Another key factor in determining the layout of construction projects is technological precedence. Materials will be staged according to whether they are used early or later in the project. This factor is especially important when space is limited. A related factor here is scheduling, which also determines the timing of project activities and thus establishes a basis for layout of the construction facility.

A second category of projects is manufacturing in fixed position. Large items are usually manufactured in this way, including ships, aircraft, locomotives, and space vehicles. In this type of project, materials are often located in concentric circles, with the product at the center. On the inner rings of the circle are those items used most often—such as rivets, bolts, or fasteners—while unique items are located further out from the center. This principle of concentric circles is used by both construction and fixed-manufacturing projects to reduce materials-handling costs.

The third category is multiple projects undertaken at the same site. Examples are projects for advertising agencies, research and development departments, movie lots, etc. Each project executed by these operations is unique, but the same type of project is repeated by using an intermittent process. For example, movie lots are organized by wardrobe shop, scenery shop, prop shop, and so on. The multiple-project layout problem can thus be thought of as intermittent production with a batch size of one unit each. Therefore the principles of intermittent-process layout apply in this case. There will, however, be difficulty in forecasting flows of materials because of the uniqueness of projects.

What, then, do these operations have in common? First of all, materials handling is often an important consideration; however, a regular flow pattern cannot easily be established for project layouts. The second feature is that layout is dictated to a large extent by technological and scheduling considerations. This is especially relevant as the timing of a project process becomes an important factor in the staging of materials. In summary then, materials handling, technological considerations, and scheduling are all important factors in project layouts.

Although we have considered project layouts in general terms, there is not a great deal of research on the subject. Perhaps the layout of project operations is difficult to study because of project uniqueness. Furthermore, there has been a preoccupation with scheduling problems in project operations which may have precluded the study of other problems, such as layout.

8.4 KEY POINTS

We have seen in this chapter that layout decisions are highly dependent on the process selection decision which we assumed has been made prior to layout decisions. Layout is then concerned with the arrangement of the physical processing facilities within a given type of process (intermittent, line, or project). Service and manufacturing layout decisions are treated within a common framework. Thus, the same general principles, concepts, and methods are used for both services and manufacturing; but the application of these ideas may be slightly different, as we have noted.

Key points covered in the chapter are as follows:

• Intermittent operations present a challenging layout problem. In this case, the physical arrangement of departments or processing activities must be determined to achieve stated criteria within physical constraints. We have discussed both quantitative decision criteria and qualitative criteria and the different methods used to solve each case.

- Intermittent-process layout problems of practical size usually require computer-assisted solutions. CRAFT, CORELAP, and ALDEP are heuristic methods used in practice to solve intermittent-process layout problems. As noted, these methods should receive wider use in practice through an iterative process involving both analyst and manager.

- The line-flow layout problem is quite different from that involving intermittent flows because the direction of the flow of product has already been decided. The physical arrangement of processing facilities is dictated for line flows by the product technology. There does remain, however, a problem of assigning operations (processing tasks) to workers.

- In the single-paced assembly line, the primary problem of layout is assembly-line balancing. Here the objective is to minimize the number of workers for a given cycle time or vice versa. The solution to this problem can be approximated by various heuristic methods which assign individual operations to workers. Management should not arbitrarily specify cycle times because small changes in cycle time can greatly affect the efficiency of the balance.

- With regard to assembly-line layout, perhaps the greatest problems facing operations management today are the high levels of boredom, turnover, absenteeism, and dissatisfaction among workers. A possible solution is to consider alternative types of assembly lines. For example, cycle time can be increased by using two or more assembly lines instead of one. If the process is labor-intensive, this is a practical alternative and can reduce the problems mentioned. Management should also consider various forms of group or team assembly and assembly using flexible, buffered lines which allow more individual pacing.

- The third type of layout problem is the project process. For projects, the product is unique, but similar projects can be conducted at the same site. The layout problem is highly dependent on technological precedence and project scheduling, since this determines the order in which materials and skills are used. A principle of concentric circles was described for fixed-location manufacturing and construction, where the product is in the center and material with high usage is staged on inner circles while materials with lower usage are placed in the outer circles.

- Layout decisions still present a substantial challenge for management. Many layout decisions have long-term effects which cannot be easily reversed. These decisions determine the efficiency of operations as well as the design of jobs. It is thus important to improve the practice of layout by using the best approaches available.

QUESTIONS

1. In considering layout decisions, why do we assume that the process-choice decision has already been made?
2. Consider a layout decision which has been made in your residence or at work. How was the decision made? What were the important factors?

3. What relationships exist between layout decisions, capacity decisions, and scheduling?
4. How, specifically, do layout problems differ between intermittent, line, and project flows?
5. Suppose you were asked to lay out a department store.
   a. What questions would you ask management?
   b. What data would you need to collect, and where do you think you would get the data?
   c. How would you analyze the data to arrive at a recommendation?
6. In a few sentences state the intermittent-process layout problem.
7. In laying out a hospital, do you think it is appropriate to minimize the sum of distances walked by all patients and staff? Suggest some other criteria that you might use.
8. What type of decision criterion do you think would be appropriate for the following types of layout situations?
   a. Cafeteria line
   b. Hotel rooms
   c. Golf course
   d. Office
   e. Factory
   f. School rooms
9. Compare and contrast the quantitative and qualitative layout problem for intermittent-process facilities. Which type of criterion is best?
10. What differences are there between the layout design of a new facility and the revised layout of an existing facility?
11. Identify behavioral factors which may be important in making layout decisions. Do these factors differ between the various types of layout problems?
12. Compare and contrast CRAFT, ALDEP, and CORELAP.
13. While the departments in a factory were being located, the comment was overheard that CRAFT would not be a suitable method because it considers only materials-handling costs and ignores other tangible and intangible factors. Comment on this statement.
14. In a few sentences, define the assembly-line balancing problem.
15. Suppose a cycle time of 1 minute has been given for assembly-line balancing. It has been said that slightly lower and higher cycle times should also be investigated. Why?
16. Several alternatives to single-paced assembly lines were suggested. Which of the alternatives might be appropriate for:
   a. Capital-intensive operations
   b. Labor-intensive operations
17. Should managers and analysts work together on layout problems? Why? How?

PROBLEMS

1. Suppose that four departments (A, B, C, and D) are located on a grid, as shown in the diagram. Show that there are 24 possible locations of departments but only three location plans with different relative locations of departments. [Adapted from Buffa (1977).]

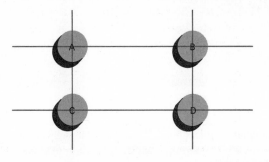

2. A small manufacturing company has four departments between which the following loads are transported:

	To			
	A	B	C	D
A		20	40	60
From B	10		20	35
C	30	30		45
D	50	15	24	

Assuming that all departments are the same size and that materials-handling cost is a linear function of distance, find the location plan which minimizes total materials-handling cost. (Hint: See Problem 1.)

3. A manager is trying to determine the best layout for her office. The following information has been collected on the average number of trips per day by various types of persons from and to their own offices. It is also known that executives are paid $150 per day, staff people are paid $90 per day, and secretaries are paid $50 per day. The manager would like to minimize the cost of lost time due to trips between various locations in the office.

$150 $50 $90

Department	From/to trips per day		
	Executives	Secretaries	Staff
A. Mail room	0	40 ×10	10×15
B. Secretarial office	10 ×10	0	30×10
C. Conference room	20 × 10	10×5	20×10
D. Coffee room	5×15	20 × 10	20×5
E. Executive offices	0	40 × 10	40×15
F. Staff offices	20 ×15	30 × 10	0

675 min. 1360 1350

Assume that a trip between adjacent offices takes 5 minutes traveling time in both directions. If the trip is between nonadjacent offices, the traveler must move in rectangular directions along the hallways between offices. Thus, the traveling times for the layout shown are given below.

210.94 140.63 253.13

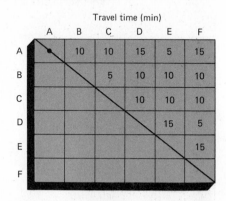

Travel time (min)

	Executives E	Mail A
	Secretaries B	Conference Room C
	Coffee D	Staff F

	A	B	C	D	E	F
A	•	10	10	15	5	15
B			5	10	10	10
C				10	10	10
D					15	5
E						15
F						

a. Evaluate the total cost of this layout plan.
b. Develop a layout plan with lower cost.
c. What additional factors other than travel cost might be important in this problem?

4. For the layout problem given in Figures 8.1 to 8.6, find the cost of an exchange between departments 7 and 8.

5. In an outpatient clinic, the relative desirability of locating departments near each other has been rated as shown below. These ratings are based on such factors as patient travel, staff travel, safety and fire hazards, preference of doctors and nurses, etc.

	X-ray	Orthopedics	Pediatrics	Gynecology	Lab	General
X-ray		A	U	I	U	O
Orthopedics			U	E	U	O
Pediatrics				U	E	O
Gynecology					I	I
Lab						E
General						

A = Absolutely necessary
E = Especially important
I = Important
O = Ordinary closeness OK
U = Unimportant
X = Undesirable

a. Using ALDEP, generate a layout for the clinic.

b. Using CORELAP, generate a layout for the clinic.

6. An enterprising college student has received a contract to deliver 200 submarine sandwiches per day to a cafeteria. The student expects to assemble these sandwiches on an assembly line using the following times and precedence relationships.

Task	Description	Seconds	Precedences
A	Spread both buns (butter)	20	—
B	Put on lettuce	15	A
C	Put on meat	10	A
D	Put on cheese	15	A
E	Put on tomato	12	A
F	Wrap finished sandwich	20	A, B, C, D, E

a. For a 35-second cycle time, balance the assembly line using the least-number-of-predecessors rule. How many stations are required and what operations are assigned to each?

b. What is the minimum number of stations for a 35-second cycle time? What is the efficiency of the balance obtained in part *a*? How long will it take to produce the 200 sandwiches a day?

c. Suggest alternative ways to organize the assembly of these sandwiches using the same amount of labor. Which method do you perfer?

7. Develop your own heuristic rule to balance the line given in Problem 6.

8. The following precedence diagram and times are given for the assembly of a hydraulic valve. (Times are shown above the circles.)

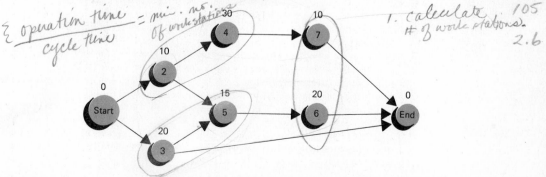

a. Given a cycle time of 40 seconds, balance the line using the least-number-of-predecessors rule.
b. How many valves are produced in 7 hours? *630*
c. If you were given three stations to use, what cycle time would be best?
d. Use Hoffmann's method to balance the line with a cycle time of 40 seconds.

SELECTED BIBLIOGRAPHY

ARMOUR, G. C., and E. S. BUFFA: "A Heuristic Algorithm and Simulation Approach to Relative Location of Facilities," *Management Science,* vol. 9, no. 1, 1963, pp. 294–309.

BUFFA, ELWOOD S.: *Modern Production Management: Managing the Operation Function,* 5th ed., New York: Wiley, 1977.

——, G. C. ARMOUR, and T. E. VOLLMANN: "Allocating Facilities with CRAFT," *Harvard Business Review,* vol. 42, no. 2, 1964, pp. 136–159.

CHASE, RICHARD B.: "Strategic Considerations in Assembly Line Selection," *California Management Review,* Fall 1975, pp. 17–23.

——: "Survey of Paced Assembly Lines," *Industrial Engineering,* vol. 6, no. 2, February 1974, pp. 14–18.

——, and Nicholas Aquilano: *Production and Operations Management: A Life Cycle Approach,* rev. ed., Homewood, Ill.: Irwin, 1977.

DAR-EL (MANSOOR), E. M.: "MALB—A Heuristic Technique for Balancing Large Single Model Assembly Lines," *AIIE Transactions,* vol. 5, no. 4, 1973, pp. 343–356.

——: "Solving Large Single-Model Assembly Line Balancing Problems—A Comparative Study," *AIIE Transactions,* vol. 7, no. 3, September 1973, pp. 302–310.

DENHOLM, D. H., and G. H. BROOKS: "A Comparison of Three Computer Assisted Plant Layout Techniques," *Proceedings of the American Institute of Industrial Engineers, 21st Annual Conference and Convention,* Cleveland, 1970.

FRANCIS, RICHARD L., and JOHN A. WHITE: *Facility Layout and Location: An Analytical Approach,* Englewood Cliffs, N.J.: Prentice-Hall, 1974.

FRYER, J. S.: "Organizational Segmentation and Labor Transfer Policies in Labor and Machine Limited Production Systems," *Decision Sciences,* vol. 7, October 1976, pp. 725–738.

GEHRLEIN, WILLIAM, and JAMES PATTERSON: "Balancing Single Model Assembly Lines: Comments on a Paper by E. M. Dar-El (Mansoor)," *AIIE Transactions,* March 1978, pp. 109–112.

GYLLENHAMMAR, PEHR: "How Volvo Adapts Work to People," *Harvard Business Review,* July–August 1977.

HELGESON, W. B., and D. P. BIRNIE: "Assembly Line Balancing Using the Ranked Positional Weight Technique," *Journal of Industrial Engineering,* vol. 12, no. 6, November–December 1961, pp. 394–398.

HOFFMANN, THOMAS R.: "Assembly Line Balancing with a Precedence Matrix," *Management Science,* vol. 9, no. 4, July 1963, pp. 551–562.

IGNALL, EDWARD: "A Review of Assembly Line Balancing," *Journal of Industrial Engineering,* vol. 16, no. 4, July–August 1965, pp. 244–252.

KAIMAN, LEE: *Computer Architecture Programs,* Boston: Center For Environmental Research, 1970 (3 vols., looseleaf).

——: "Computer Programs for Architects and Layout Planners," *Proceedings of the American Institute of Industrial Engineers, 22nd Annual Conference and Convention,* Boston, 1971.

KILBRIDGE, MAURICE, and LEON WESTER: "A Heuristic Method of Assembly Line Balancing," *Journal of Industrial Engineering,* vol. 12, no. 4, July–August 1961, pp. 292–298.

LEE, R. C., and J. M. MOORE: "CORELAP—Computerized Relationship Layout Planning," *Journal of Industrial Engineering,* vol. 18, no. 3, March 1967, pp. 195–200.

MASTOR, ANTHONY: "An Experimental Investigation and Comparative Evaluation of Production Line Balancing Techniques," *Management Science,* vol. 16, no. 11, July 1970, pp. 728–746.

MOORE, J. M.: "Computer Program Evaluates Plant Layout Alternatives," *Industrial Engineering,* vol. 3, no. 8, 1971, pp. 19–25.

MUTHER, RICHARD: *Practical Plant Layout,* New York: McGraw-Hill, 1955.

————, and JOHN D. WHEELER: "Simplified Systematic Layout Planning," *Factory,* vol. 120, nos. 8, 9, 10, August, September, October, 1962, pp. 68–77, 111–119, 101–113.

SCRIABIN, M., and R. C. VERGIN: "Comparisons of Computer Algorithms and Visual Based Methods for Plant Layout," *Management Science,* vol. 22, October 1975, pp. 172–181.

SEEHOF, J. M., and W. O. EVANS: "Automatic Layout Design Program," *The Journal of Industrial Engineering,* vol. 18, no. 12, December 1967, pp. 690–695.

SEPPONEN, R.: *CORELAP 8 User's Manual,* Boston: Department of Industrial Engineering, Northeastern University, 1969.

SOMMERS, M. S., and J. B. KERNAN: "A Behavioral Approach to Planning Layout and Display," *Journal of Retailing,* Winter 1965–66, pp. 21–27.

STARR, MARTIN K.: *Operations Management,* Englewood Cliffs, N.J.: Prentice-Hall, 1978.

TONGE, FRED M.: "Assembly Line Balancing Using Probabilistic Combinations of Heuristics," *Management Science,* vol. 11, no. 7, May 1965, pp. 727–735.

VOLGYESI, A. S.: "Toronto General: The Hospital That Computers Built," *Computer Decisions,* September 1969.

VOLLMANN, THOMAS E., and ELWOOD BUFFA: "The Facilities Layout Problem in Perspective," *Management Science,* vol. 12, no. 10, June 1966, pp. B450–B458.

————, C. E. NUGENT, and R. L. ZARTLER: "A Computerized Model for Office Layouts," *Journal of Industrial Engineering,* vol. 19, July 1968, pp. 321–327.

WILD, RAY: *Mass Production Management,* New York: Wiley, 1972.

CAPACITY PLANNING AND SCHEDULING

WORK FORCE

QUALITY

INVENTORY

PROCESS

- FACILITIES DECISIONS
- AGGREGATE PLANNING
- SCHEDULING OPERATIONS
- PROJECT SCHEDULING

CAPACITY

perations managers are responsible for providing sufficient capacity to meet their firm's needs. Capacity decisions should be made by forecasting demand and by developing plans to provide sufficient capacity for the long, medium, and short time ranges. The disaggregation of capacity plans from long-range facility planning through medium-range aggregate planning and then to short-range scheduling provides the organizing principle for Part III. One chapter is devoted to each of the long-, medium-, and short-range capacity decisions.

Long-range facilities decisions typically extend 2 years or more into the future and constrain all shorter-range capacity decisions. Facilities planning naturally leads to questions of how much capacity is needed, when is it needed, and where the facilities should be located.

The term "aggregate planning" is used to describe planning for all product lines aggregated together over approximately one year into the future. As a result of aggregate planning, decisions should be made regarding the size of the work force, overtime, subcontracting, and overall inventory levels. In the chapter on aggregate planning, a variety of methods are reviewed for making this decision in both manufacturing and service industries.

Scheduling involves short-range capacity decisions allocating available resources to jobs, orders, activities, or tasks. While facility planning and aggregate planning are resource-acquisition decisions, scheduling allocates available resources. The result of scheduling is a time schedule which describes exactly when each activity will be started and completed. Scheduling should also be used to help predict the load on facilities and to control the relationships between the operation's input and output. An organizing principle of the scheduling chapters is the separation of line, intermittent, and project scheduling problems.

As a result of the entire range of capacity decisions, the output of the operations function should closely match the customer needs. This will require accurate demand forecasting and numerous tradeoffs between the conflicting goals of good customer service, low inventories, and low costs of operations. It will also require a hierarchy of interlocked capacity decisions from long to medium to short range.

The decision-making framework can be used to describe the interaction between capacity decisions and all other decisions in operations. As we have already noted, capacity decisions affect the type of process used and the degree of process automation as well as the details of process design. Capacity decisions also affect the level of inventory through capacity-inventory tradeoffs. Scheduling decisions are of great importance in managing the work force; they affect output, quality, and the morale of workers. Capacity decisions should, therefore, be made with the impact on other parts of operations in mind.

CHAPTER 9
FACILITIES DECISIONS

Facilities decisions are of great importance to the business and to the operations function. These decisions place physical constraints on the amount that can be produced and they require investment of scarce capital. Therefore, facilities decisions are often made at the highest corporate level, including top management and the board of directors.

Facilities decisions occur at one end of a hierarchy of capacity decisions ranging from long-term to short-term. The facilities commitment is the longest-range in nature and thus constrains all the other capacity decisions. After the facilities decisions have been made, the remaining capacity decisions must be made within the facilities available. These remaining short- and medium-range capacity decisions are discussed in the next two chapters.

Because of construction lead times, facilities decisions often require up to 5 years of lead time, but they can also require as little as 1 year. The 1-year time frame refers to buildings and equipment which can quickly be constructed or leased. The 5-year time frame refers to large and complex facilities such as oil refineries, paper mills, steel mills, and electricity generating plants.

In facilities decisions, there are three crucial questions:

1. How much capacity is needed?
2. When is the capacity needed?
3. Where should the capacity be located?

Although these questions can be separated conceptually, they are often intertwined. As a result, facilities decisions are often exceedingly complex and difficult to analyze.

In this chapter a framework will be developed for making facilities decisions, including simultaneous consideration of all three of the above questions. The facili-

BOX 9.1 TYPICAL DECISION PROBLEM

The U.S. Tractor Company is one of the country's major tractor manufacturers. At present, the company has three major plants—in Moline, Illinois; Los Angeles, California; and Newark, New Jersey. The company also has 11 distribution centers located at various points throughout the United States. The tractors are shipped from the plants, through the distribution centers, and then on to the dealers around the country.

Recently Gregory Taylor, president of the company, attended the Minnesota Executive Program, where he was exposed to distribution planning and the transportation method. Since two of the plants were getting old and would have to be replaced over the next 10 years, Mr. Taylor was particularly anxious to evaluate the location of plants, distribution centers, and the entire distribution network. The company was highly centralized, but Taylor wondered whether this practice should be continued.

Explaining his concerns to Sam Appleby, the vice president of manufacturing operations, Taylor said, "Sam, we need a study of plant and distribution location in the company. I want you to develop a plan for the study and report back to me in two weeks. Include in the plan a suggested methodology, data-collection needs, personnel required, a study budget, and a timetable for completion."

Sam was not sure what the appropriate methodology for this study would be. He called LeeAnn Telzer, the corporate vice president of operations research. She agreed to investigate this situation but indicated that the problem had to be more clearly defined before a methodology could be selected. LeeAnn said, "I will need to understand the objectives of the study, the types of alternatives to be considered, the constraints, and the assumptions. If you want a 'quick-and-dirty' analysis, we can select a few different distribution plans, perhaps ten or twenty, and simply cost them out. This type of study can be done rapidly and inexpensively, but we will, no doubt, miss some potentially good location options because of the limited number of alternatives considered. A more elaborate analysis can be constructed using the transportation method, with fixed site costs and variable transportation costs. This method will, however, require much more data collection, extensive use of the computer, and outside consulting help to obtain a suitable computational algorithm." LeeAnn agreed to investigate the various options in more detail and to report back in a few days.

ties-planning framework will be described next, followed by a detailed discussion of facilities-location decisions. To provide an orientation to these decisions, a typical facilities-location decision is described in Box 9.1.

9.1 A FRAMEWORK FOR FACILITY PLANNING

A general framework for facilities planning can be developed around the steps required for any facility decision. [Also see Marshall et al. (1975).] These steps are quite simple to describe, as listed below, but difficult to implement in practice. The steps are:

1. Develop a measure of facility capacity.
2. Prepare a forecast of future demand.
3. Determine facility needs.
4. Generate alternatives.
5. Evaluate alternatives.
6. Decide.

Measuring facility capacity

The first step in facilities decisions is quite challenging in its own right and requires a clear definition of capacity. *Capacity is the maximum output rate of an operation*. As a rate of output, capacity should always be measured in units of output per time period. Some examples of capacity measures are:

> Barrels of beer per day
> Tons of steel per year
> Patients treated per month
> Customers served per day
> Cubic yards of gravel moved per day
> Students graduated per year

One common mistake in measuring capacity is to ignore the time dimension. For example, erroneous measurements of capacity are the number of beds in a hospital, seats in a restaurant, or pupils in a school building. The number of beds in a hospital represents facilities size, not a rate of output. The number of beds should be combined with an estimated length of hospital stay to arrive at a capacity measure, such as patients treated per month. Similarly, the restaurant and school examples represent only facility size and not the maximum rate of output.

Another common mistake in measuring capacity is to confuse capacity and volume. Volume is the actual output rate over some time period, while capacity is the maximum output rate. Thus if 10,000 students were graduated from the University of Minnesota last year, this figure—unless volume happened to equal capacity—is merely a volume figure. The actual graduation volume by itself does not tell us how many students *could* have been graduated.

After capacity has been correctly defined, there are still two important measurement problems. First, an aggregate unit of capacity must be specified for facility-planning purposes. In cases where there is a single product or there are a few homogenous products, such as beer or flour, the aggregate measure is easily defined. When a complex product mix is produced from the same facility, however, capacity is more difficult to measure. As an example of a complex product mix, suppose we want to measure the capacity of a restaurant which produces hamburgers, French fries, shakes, etc. In this case, meaningful measures of aggregate capacity are customers served per day or dollars of sales per day. Most other measures one could think of would not reflect the great diversity of products. Using this same line of reasoning, airlines often measure their capacity in available seat miles (ASMs) per month.[1] This measure incorporates the effects of different types of planes, different turnaround times for maintenance, different flying speeds, etc.

In general terms, if all other measures fail, one can express capacity in terms of dollars of sales. However, more convenient physical units, such as those mentioned above, are available in many cases. In any event, the capacity will be affected by product mix; this cannot be avoided.

The second problem in measuring capacity is to assess the effect of management policy variables. One of these variables is the number of hours worked per week. This figure will vary from a normal week of 40 hours to three shifts for 7 days a week. The correct number of hours to use depends on the operating policies in effect. In a steel mill, it would be normal to base capacity on around-the-clock operations 7 days a week. In other operations, such as public schools, the normal school day might be used, although it should be noted that evening classes add to the capacity available. To handle this problem, nominal capacity is sometimes defined as the maximum output rate possible under normal operations policies. This might be one shift, two shifts, or three shifts, whatever is normal. Nominal capacity would not, however, include overtime, extra subcontracting, or crowding of the facilities.

In measuring capacity, there is one final distinction which must be made: peak capacity versus sustained capacity. Peak capacity can be sustained for only a short period of time, such as a few hours in a day or a few days in a month. Peak capacity represents the surge capability of the operation, considering, perhaps, overtime, extra workers, and special surge policies. On the other hand, the sustained capacity is a level which can be maintained over long periods of time with no adverse effects.

In planning facilities, it is often necessary to consider both peak and sustained capacities. For service industries, however, it should be noted that the peak capacity is often more important than sustained capacity, e.g., electricity generating, golf courses, restaurants, and telephone service. The greater emphasis on planning for peak capacity in service industries arises because the product cannot be stored.

---

[1] An available seat mile is one seat flown for a distance of 1 mile. Multiplying the number of seats in each plane by the number of miles which can be flown will yield total ASM.

In summary, measurement of capacity will require resolution of the following issues:

1. An aggregate measure
2. Product-mix effects
3. Operations policies (e.g., hours per week)
4. Sustained and peak capacity

Forecasting demand

While the first step in facilities planning is concerned with defining an appropriate measure of capacity, the second step takes the measure as given and proceeds to develop a forecast of demand. As noted in Chapter 4, a long-range forecast will often be made by qualitative methods or causal models, the time-series models being less useful.

In facilities planning, great care is often taken in making the forecast, since the forecast will drive the decision. Furthermore, it is good practice to develop a probability forecast for facilities so that the risk of the decision can be evaluated. Since forecasting was discussed at length in Part I, we will not dwell on it further here.

Determining facility needs

The third step in facilities planning is to determine the capacity needs over time. The need can be thought of as the gap between required and available capacity in the future. The required capacity, in turn, can be related to the forecast and to the degree of management risk taken in meeting the forecast.

For example, suppose that the probability forecast of demand 2 years in the future is as follows:

Demand (units per year)	Cumulative probability
≤ 10,000	.1
≤ 12,000	.3
≤ 14,000	.5
≤ 16,000	.7
≤ 18,000	.9

Management will need to study this forecast to determine the required capacity. If a 30 percent chance of demand exceeding capacity can be accepted, then the required capacity can be set at 16,000 units. If only a 10 percent risk can be taken, 18,000 units of capacity should be planned. The level of risk accepted should depend on the means available to expand capacity and the consequences of demand exceeding capacity. Thinking in these terms requires assignment of a "cost" to running out of capacity and a cost of having too much capacity. The relative values of these two costs will determine the proper level of capacity.

After the requirement has been decided upon, the available capacity can be projected into the future, deducting for worn-out facilities or other reductions in capacity which will occur. The difference between the required and projected available capacity then represents the needed capacity. This need should be time-phased over several years into the future so that various alternatives for meeting future needs can be considered.

Generating alternatives

This is perhaps the most creative step in the entire decision process and will certainly require management judgment and input. The generation of alternatives can be complex because combinations of the three basic questions ("how much," "when," and "where located") may be used. For example in a particular situation the following alternatives might be considered:

1. Build a 40,000-unit-per-year facility now in Los Angeles.
2. Build a 40,000-unit-per-year facility now in Denver.
3. Build a 20,000-unit-per-year facility now and a 20,000-unit-per-year facility in 2 years in Los Angeles.
4. Build a 30,000-unit facility a year from now in Chicago.

Because of the combinations possible, a large number of alternatives may have to be considered. In some cases, however, management may constrain the alternatives to make the decision more manageable. This could be done by deciding on capacity, location, or timing first and thereby reducing the size of the problem. Such decisions not only constrain the number of alternatives but can make the alternatives more readily comparable for evaluation purposes.

In some cases, the number of alternatives cannot easily be enumerated. This quite commonly occurs in plant- or warehouse-location problems where a very large number of alternatives are available. In these cases, a mathematical model may be formulated which implicitly constrains the alternatives without enumerating each one. An example of this procedure will be given later.

In other cases, it is difficult to find one feasible alternative (to say nothing about the optimal or best alternative). This situation quite commonly occurs in public decisions involving compromise and in consensus decisions. Here the problem is to develop simply one alternative which all parties can accept.

Whether one or many alternatives present themselves, the quality of the decision will be defined in relation to the alternatives available. It is, therefore, important to expend creative effort on the generation of alternatives.

Evaluating alternatives

The most crucial step in evaluating alternatives is to select the relevant criteria. These criteria usually include benefits and costs. If costs and benefits both vary between the alternatives, it will be difficult to evaluate them; it is much easier if the alternatives generated are either equal cost or equal benefit. For example, if all the alternatives provide the required capacity which is considered the benefit, then the evaluation is simply a cost comparison. If the alternatives generate different revenues, the most convenient evaluation measure may then be profit or return on investment. In still other cases, response time or service delivered may be an important measure of benefit.

In many facility-evaluation problems, the benefits can be stated in terms of cash flows over time. If this is the case, present values, discounted cash flows, or internal rate-of-return calculations can be used as a basis for evaluation. Since we have already discussed these methods in the Supplement to Chapter 6 we will use them freely in this chapter without further comment.

If the alternatives include a large number of location options, it may be necessary to construct a mathematical model of the problem. These models, to be discussed later in the chapter, provide a framework for the formal evaluation of alternatives and for extensive analysis of the decision alternatives.

Although the evaluation step often receives a great deal of attention, it should be kept in perspective as only one element of the decision-making process. It should be further emphasized that managers make decisions—models do not. Therefore, the evaluation step will not automatically lead to the decision and, furthermore, the decision will sometimes be inconsistent with the evaluation conducted. If this is the case, the inconsistency can usually be explained by management's rejection of one or more key assumptions. To maintain reality in the evaluation process, close contact between the decision makers and evaluators is, of course, desirable. Indeed, the evaluation should be an integral part of the decision makers' personal decision process.

The facilities decision

In the end, facilities decisions will often be made by the chief executive and board of directors in consultation with operations and other departments in the firm. The facility decision should be seen as one which affects all parts of the organization and not just operations. Facilities decisions require capital and are thus of concern to financial managers. Facilities decisions also affect the future ability of the firm to meet customer needs and are thus of interest to marketing. Because of these multiple effects, facilities decisions are often made at the level of top management, where all facets of the problem can be properly evaluated and the decision can be integrated with corporate strategy.

In the end, the decision maker must determine whether the decision meets the objectives of the firm. If the objectives are to provide superb customer service, then some excess capacity may be provided. If the competitive situation and the firm's objectives require strict cost control, then a more conservative stance on capacity may be taken. In cases where products are rapidly changing, flexibility may be an important objective. The decision should ultimately be guided by management's assessment of how the decision meets these conflicting objectives.

9.2 FACILITY DECISION EXAMPLE

In January 1981, Mary Daws was considering whether she should add to her very successful Golden Fork Restaurant in Melrose Park, Illinois. In 1971, the restaurant was started with a kitchen, a bar, and dining rooms which seated 50 people. The restaurant had been expanded in 1976 to its present configuration: a kitchen, two bars, and 100 seats in the dining rooms.

Over the years, profits had been very good and business continued to grow. The income statement for 1980, the year just ended, is shown in Figure 9.1. Although Mary was pleased with the results, she felt that business had once again reached capacity and that further improvement in profits would require another building addition. For the moment Mary had ruled out expansion to a new site.

The history of revenues for the Golden Fork is shown in Figure 9.2. Mary estimated that this pattern of growth in sales would continue for the next several years if capacity were available and economic conditions remained good.

Mary decided to analyze this situation using the steps described in the last section. Her first task was, therefore, to develop a measure of capacity. She considered the number of dining seats as one measure of capacity. However, she realized this did not represent throughput or velocity of output but only the physical size of the restaurant. This left two other measures: revenue per time period and number of customers per time period. Since she did not have good data on the number of customers served, Mary decided to use revenue per unit of time as an aggregate measure of capacity. In annual terms, the capacity is now $630,000 per year.

In using revenue per year as a measure of capacity, Mary realized she could increase the nominal capacity in several ways besides building more space. One way would be to encourage dining at off-peak times, perhaps by offering price discounts or other incentives. Another way would be to try to speed up dining at peak times by offering a more limited menu or perhaps adding more waitresses. This tactic, however, would run the risk of reducing apparent service to the customer and thus causing a loss of business. Putting these possibilities aside for the moment, Mary

FIGURE 9.1   **GOLDEN FORK RESTAURANT INCOME STATEMENT, YEAR ENDED DECEMBER 31, 1980**

Revenue	$630,000
Costs	
Labor	$180,000
Food	168,000
Other	99,000
Total direct cost	$447,000
Depreciation	70,000
Total cost	$517,000
Profit before taxes	$113,000
Taxes	56,000
Profit after taxes	$ 57,000

FIGURE 9.2   **REVENUE HISTORY ($000)**

	1974	1975	1976	1977	1978	1979	1980
Revenue	310	350	400	450	500	560	630

decided to concentrate on the building addition, using revenue per year as the aggregate measure of capacity.

Mary's next step was to develop a demand forecast for the future. Theoretically, she needed a forecast through the life of the building addition. For practical purposes, the forecast might be made for about 5 years into the future or until the new addition again reached capacity. Over the past 4 years, revenue had been increasing at an annual rate of 12 percent per year, and Mary considered this a good forecast of the most likely outcome for the future. On the pessimistic side, she thought that revenues might increase by as little as 8 percent per year. The most optimistic estimate she could foresee was a 15 percent annual increase.

The third step in Mary's facility analysis was to determine the capacity needed. She felt that requirements could be expressed as the most likely revenue forecast of a 12 percent increase per year, since operations are now at 100 percent capacity and no facilities will be retired from use. Mary did, however, want to analyze the situation for only an 8 percent growth rate to help assess the risk inherent in this decision.

Next, Mary decided to generate alternatives. At this stage she realized that there were really three types of capacity in this problem: kitchen, dining, and bar. Mary estimated that the present kitchen had 25 percent extra capacity, so a kitchen addition could be delayed 2 years. In this case, however, it was expected that construction would cost more and the site would be disrupted again when the later addition was built. The two bars had sufficient capacity to handle more diners by adding bartenders, but more people could not be seated in the bar due to limitations of space. Considering this situation, Mary defined two alternatives for close analysis.[2]

1. Expand the bar, kitchen, and dining facilities by 50 percent.
2. Expand the dining facilities now by 50 percent but do not expand the kitchen facilities until 2 years from now. Do not expand the bar.

The next step for Mary was to evaluate these alternatives. She thought about the criteria to use. Since the alternatives involved different revenues, costs, and investments, Mary decided to use return on investment as a criterion. (See the Supplement to Chapter 6 for details on the calculation of return on investment.)

The cash-flow streams for each alternative were computed as shown in Figure 9.3. The first alternative was based on a $500,000 investment with a 20-year life. This investment permitted Mary to expand capacity and revenue by 50 percent, which is reached in the fourth year. The cash flows from this investment are $37,000 in the first year, increasing to $104,000 in the fourth year as sales increase by 12 percent per

[2] In practice, more alternatives would, no doubt, be studied, but the situation is being kept simple here for discussion purposes.

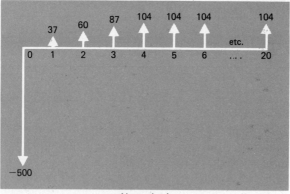

Alternative 1

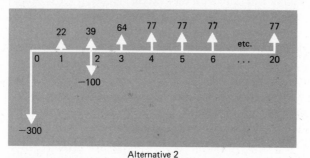

**Figure 9.3
Cash flows.**

Alternative 2

year. Other assumptions used to calculate these figures are cost increases at 8 percent per year (two-thirds variable, one-third fixed), depreciation is $35,000 per year, and taxes are 50 percent of profits.

The second alternative is more conservative. The expansion of the dining facilities is based on a $300,000 investment, followed by a $100,000 investment for the kitchen 2 years from now. The revenue from the dining facilities, which is 75 percent of the total (excluding the bar sales), is assumed to increase at 12 percent per year to a maximum of 50 percent more capacity in the fourth year. For this alternative, cash flow is $22,000 in the first year, increasing to $77,000 in the fourth year as sales increase.

The internal rate of return was calculated for both alternatives, with the following results:

Alternative 1 = 16.5%

Alternative 2 = 15.9%

When the sales were assumed to increase at only 8 percent a year instead of 12 percent, the internal rate of return figures were:

Alternative 1 = 14.9%

Alternative 2 = 14.3%

Now that the facts are available, what should Mary decide? First of all, she needs to determine her cost of capital, which depends on financing considerations. If the cost of capital is low enough, below 15.9 percent, either alternative could be attractive. If the cost of capital is high, neither alternative may be selected.

Mary should also consider strategic factors in this decision. By adding to the restaurant, she may be able to prevent competition from moving into the area. She may also be able to improve the appearance of the facility, relieve crowded conditions, or offer new services. All these strategic factors must be considered along with the economic considerations.

If capital is freely available, Mary might choose alternative 1, since it provides a higher internal rate of return. However, a shortage of capital may make alternative 2 more desirable, since only $300,000 is required initially instead of $500,000. The rate of return on alternative 2, even though it is lower, may still be attractive in the face of capital constraints.

Finally, Mary should consider risk in her decision. We have quantified risk to some extent by calculating the internal rate of return at the 8 percent growth rate. If this return is acceptable, Mary may decide to go ahead and take the risk. A greater risk, which has not been quantified, is the risk that the new capacity will exceed total needs. However, this risk could easily be calculated as another dimension of the analysis.

In summary, the keys to Mary's facility decision are economic, strategic, and risk factors. Whatever the decision, the facilities expansion should help Mary achieve her objectives as the operator of the restaurant.

9.3 ECONOMIES OF SCALE

One of the common justifications for capacity expansion is economy of scale. As Schmenner (1976) points out, however, the term "economy of scale," which has different meanings to different individuals, is far too vague to be used as a basis for capacity decisions. The most commonly accepted notion is that unit costs will decline for larger facilities simply due to their size. But the operations manager should go beyond the general notion of size to determine how costs and other operations objectives are affected.

Consider an example of a capacity decision based on the rationale of economies of scale. Company A, a large automobile manufacturer, centralized all its engine production in one location. As sales expanded, the engine plant grew larger and larger. Despite the supposed economies of scale, transportation costs were larger from the centralized facility, flexibility was reduced, and it was difficult to obtain fast deliveries. Thus, while unit production costs were lower for the large plant, transportation costs were higher, deliveries were slower, and flexibility suffered.

When considering economies of scale, managers should include volume, capacity, and process considerations. It is far too simplistic to lump all these factors under one general heading. As an example, see Table 9.1, which includes four facilities with different volumes, capacities, and process technologies. Facility A is the base case; it has a capacity of 100 units per week, a volume of 100 units per week, a process technology of type X, and costs of $1 per unit produced. Facility B is the same

TABLE 9.1   **FACILITIES COMPARISON**

Facility	Capacity	Volume produced	Process technology	Cost per unit produced
A	100	100	X	$1 per unit
B	100	40	X	Higher than $1 per unit
C	200	200	X	Lower than $1 per unit
D	200	200	Y	Much lower than $1 per unit

Source: Roger W. Schmenner, "Before You Build a Big Factory," *Harvard Business Review,* July–August 1976, p. 102.

as A, but it is operating at a volume of only 40 units per week. As a result, the fixed costs of operations are spread over fewer units and the average unit cost for B is higher than $1. This situation represents different economies of scale due to volume considerations.

Facility C differs from A in having twice as much capacity and twice as much volume. As a result, we ordinarily expect average unit costs of facility C to be lower than those of A because of C's larger size. But why does this cost reduction occur? No change in process technology is indicated, therefore any cost reductions for facility C must be due to differences in scheduling and inventory. For example, suppose two products were made in both facilities A and C. Facility A, which uses a single production line, must switch over from one product to the other. Therefore, finished-goods inventories are built up to cover the times during which one product is not in production. In the larger facility C, a separate line might be devoted to each product, thus allowing for smaller finished-goods inventories. If "scale" means "capacity," then facility C enjoys greater economies of scale.

Facility D differs from C in that it uses a different process technology. In this case, any economies of scale are attributed to the substitution of capital for labor and to increased division of labor. As a result of these economies, facility D is expected to have a lower average unit cost than facility C. Once again, the reasons for these economies are different than in the preceding cases.

As illustrated above, the term "economy of scale" is ambiguous. Rather than using this phrase to justify capacity decisions, managers should carefully think in terms of volume, capacity, or process economies. The reasons for economies of scale will then be apparent.

In addition to costs, managers should be concerned with quality, dependability, and flexibility insofar as these objectives are affected by the scale of facilities. As we noted in the example above, flexibility and schedule are often adversely affected by large, centralized facilities. At some point, objectives other than cost may become more important and result in a smaller scale.

9.4 FACILITY LOCATION PROBLEMS

In Sections 9.1 through 9.3 we have been treating facilities decisions in general terms, including how much, when, and where located. The methodology described is useful in many contexts, but it is limited when complex location problems are presented. We shall, therefore, expand specifically on location problems in the remainder of this chapter.

Location problems can be characterized by a choice among multiple sites. Apart from this common feature, each location decision tends to be different. In some cases, the decision criterion is cost; in others it is revenue, vehicle response time, or multiple criteria. Some location problems involve the consideration of only a few sites; others involve many. Some location problems include distribution costs from muliple plants and warehouses, other do not.

Since there are many different types of location problems, the following classification framework has been developed.

1. SINGLE-FACILITY LOCATION. In this type of location problem, only one facility which does not interact with the firm's other facilities is located. Examples include a single factory or warehouse, a government facility, and a single retail store. This type of location problem typically has multiple criteria such as labor costs, labor supply, union atmosphere, community services, and taxes. The problem is to consider all these criteria objectively.

2. LOCATION OF MULTIPLE FACTORIES AND WAREHOUSES. In this type of location problem, total distribution costs and perhaps total production costs will be affected by the location decision. The new facility may necessitate adjustment in the shipping patterns and production levels of all other facilities. This problem is usually formulated by considering a production-distribution network of plants and warehouses with the criterion of minimizing costs.

3. LOCATION OF COMPETITIVE RETAIL STORES. In this location problem, the revenue obtained from the retail store is affected by the relative location of competing stores. This problem is typically encountered in selecting sites for department stores, supermarkets, restaurants, etc., where the sales level is assumed to be affected by the distance customers have to travel to the new location versus the locations of competitors. Revenue is a variable that depends on where the facility is located in relation to competition.

4. LOCATION OF EMERGENCY SERVICES. The decision criterion in locating emergency services is often related to response time. Such problems occur in the location of police, fire, and ambulance stations. In this case the criterion has shifted from revenue to a direct measure of the service delivered.

As can be seen from Box 9.2, different operations tend to formulate their location problems in different ways. Manufacturing companies tend to fall into category 1 or 2, depending on whether single or multiple facilities are involved. Retail stores and emergency services also fall into category 1 if there is only a single site; otherwise they fall into categories 3 or 4, respectively.

In the remainder of the chapter, these various types of location problems will be considered. In each case a methodology will be presented, along with examples of how the methodology can be used.

BOX 9.2   **EXAMPLES OF LOCATION PROBLEMS**

1. Single-facility problems (multiple criteria)
   A factory or warehouse
   Government facility
   Hospital
   Electric power plant
2. Location of multiple factories and warehouses (minimize production and distribution cost)
   Multiple factories
   Multiple warehouses
   Multiple factories and warehouses
3. Location of competitive retail stores (maximize revenue)
   Banks
   Department stores
   Supermarkets
   Restaurants
4. Emergency-service location (minimize response time)
   Ambulance
   Fire station
   Police station

9.5 SINGLE-FACILITY LOCATION

Many location problems require the selection of a site for a single facility. These include the location of a factory, a warehouse, and a government office. A crucial assumption in these problems is that the revenue, costs, or other facility characteristics do not depend on the location of other facilities of the firm or competitors. When this is the case, the facility can be isolated for location purposes and analyzed by the methods described in this section.

Most facility location problems involve multiple criteria. In the case of the single-facility problem, several criteria can be dealt with directly. In other cases, a single criterion is often selected to simplify the analysis.

Multiple decision criteria can be simplified into two types: cost and noncost factors. The cost factors can be measured objectively even though substantial uncertainties may be involved. The noncost factors include various intangibles such as community attitudes, labor relations, and government relations. Even though these factors may be intangible, they can be systematically evaluated and logically considered together with the cost factors. [For further details see Student (1976) and Fulton (1971).]

The types of tangible costs usually involved in a location problem include:

1. Costs of land, buildings, and equipment
2. Transportation costs
3. Utilities costs
4. Taxes and insurance
5. Labor cost

The noncost factors which should be considered include:

1. Supply of labor
2. Labor and union relations
3. Community attitudes
4. Government regulations
5. Quality of life (climate, schools, living, recreation, etc.)
6. Environmental impact
7. Corporate strategy

One way to combine all these factors is to develop a rating scale for each one which reduces management judgment to a quantifiable score. The noncost factors can then be combined with the cost factors to arrive at one overall score for each location alternative. This method will be more completely described below by an example; see also Brown and Gibson (1972).

Suppose we are considering two different cities—Richmond, Virginia, and Birmingham, Alabama—for the location of a medium-sized bakery. The bakery will produce an assortment of bakery goods on site and will sell directly to retail customers as well as wholesale to grocery stores, restaurants, etc. It is expected that the bakery will employ 20 people ranging from a store manager to clerks, bakers, truck drivers, and custodians. The factors shown in Table 9.2 have been evaluated for these two sites.

A total score can be computed for each site. This is done by first converting the rating for each noncost factor to a numerical score. The conversion for the example is shown in Table 9.3, using a 10-point scale.

The next step is to develop a weighting scheme among the factors by rating, subjectively, the importance of each factor in relation to the others, as shown in Table 9.3. In this case, 100 points have been assigned to all the factors. However, it is not necessary that the weights add to 100 in every case; any total score can be used. If an additive scale is used, it is appropriate to multiply the weight by the factor scores to arrive at a total score for each factor. The location with the highest total score is then the best choice.

The procedure which has been described can be summarized as follows:

$$S_j = \sum_{i=1}^{m} W_i F_{ij} \qquad j = 1, \ldots, n$$

where S_j = total score for location j
W_i = weight for factor i
F_{ij} = factor score for factor i on location j
n = number of locations
m = number of factors

In the example we have been using in Table 9.3, the total scores are as follows:

$$S_1 = 15(8) + 5(6) + 5(10) + 5(2) + 10(8) + 60(6) = 650$$

$$S_2 = 15(10) + 5(4) + 5(8) + 5(6) + 10(6) + 60(10) = 900$$

TABLE 9.2   **BAKERY LOCATION EXAMPLE**

	Richmond	Birmingham
Supply of labor	Very good	Excellent
Labor and union relations	Good	Fair
Community attitudes	Excellent	Very good
Government regulations	Poor	Good
Quality of life	Very good	Good
Annual return on investment	9%	15%

This scoring system, therefore, indicates that alternative 2, Birmingham, is preferred.

There are some aspects of the scoring system which need discussion. First, in the model used, several assumptions are being made to quantify and combine factor ratings. It is assumed that subjective ratings can be converted to a "ratio interval" scale where excellent (10), for example, is five times better than poor (2). It is also assumed that a linear combination of factor scores is appropriate in arriving at the total score. In this way, a low score on one factor can be "made up" by a higher score on another factor.

Some managers might argue that such assumptions cannot be defended and that therefore subjective ratings should not be converted to a quantitative score. The other side of the argument is that subjective factors cannot be meaningfully incorporated into the decision unless some basis for quantification is developed. It is better, therefore, to quantify the subjective factors even though the result may be imprecise.

In some decision settings, it is important that *all* factors have relatively high ratings for the alternative selected. In this case, a multiplicative model might be more appropriate than an additive scoring model. The score for factor j can then be computed as follows:[3]

$$S_j = \prod_{i=1}^{n} F_{ij}{}^{W_i} \qquad j = 1, \ldots, n$$

With this model, any single factor with a low score will cause a low overall product score. Furthermore, the weighting is nonlinear in emphasizing the effect of a factor score through the exponent weights used. In choosing the product scoring model over the additive model, one must remember that the product model will tend to favor alternatives which do not have a low rating on any of the factor scales.

The methods which have been defined in this section can be used on almost any single-facility location problem. [See Brown and Gibson (1972).] They have been applied to location problems for factories, hospitals, office buildings, retail stores, etc. We will turn next to location problems involving interaction and dependence between the facilities.

---

[3] The Π sign in the equation denotes the *product* of the factors.

TABLE 9.3   **COMPUTATION OF LOCATION SCORE**

Weight		Richmond	Birmingham
15	Supply of labor	8	10
5	Labor and union relations	6	4
5	Community attitudes	10	8
5	Government regulations	2	6
10	Quality of life	8	6
60	Annual return on investment	6	10
100			

Excellent = 10, very good = 8, good = 6, fair = 4, poor = 2. Return on investment is normalized to a ten-point maximum scale, the same as the subjective ratings.

9.6 LOCATION OF MULTIPLE FACTORIES AND WAREHOUSES

In many plant and warehouse location problems, the primary objective is to minimize the costs of providing a given amount of supply. In other words, the capacity has been fixed and the best location plan from a distribution point of view is being sought. A simple version of this problem will be presented below, followed by a more general discussion of it.

The H. G. Hicks Company supplies lumber to three market areas from two warehouses in Chicago and Atlanta. The company is considering locating an additional warehouse either in Kansas City or Minneapolis, and they would like to evaluate these two sites based on the minimum cost of transportation. It is assumed that the new warehouse may alter the current distribution plan from the two existing warehouses. In this case, all present shipments may be rerouted to take advantage of the new warehouse configuration.

The approach used in evaluating these sites will be to consider two distribution problems. The first will assume that the Minneapolis site is used along with Chicago and Atlanta. The second will assume that the Kansas City site is used along with Chicago and Atlanta. The best of these two plans, based on minimum cost, will then be selected.

The situation using the new Minneapolis warehouse and the warehouses in Chicago and Atlanta is shown in Figure 9.4. The matrix indicates the amount available from each warehouse (per month), the amount required in each of the three markets, and the unit costs of shipping from each warehouse to each market. The data are shown in the form of a transportation matrix using a "from-to" shipment convention. In this case the product is shipped from the warehouses in the rows to the markets in the columns. Each cell in the matrix represents a possible distribution channel from a particular warehouse to a particular market.

If the total supply requirements are met, the amounts shipped through all cells in a column must add to the total required at the bottom of the column. This will ensure that each market requirement is met by shipments from one or more warehouses. If we let X_{ij} represent the amount shipped from warehouse i to market j, then the column requirement which has just been stated can be written:

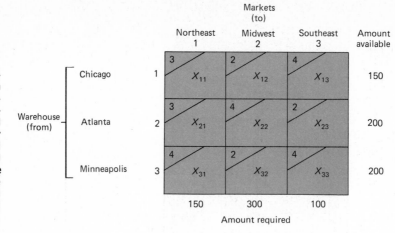

Figure 9.4 Transportation matrix. The number above the diagonal of each cell is the cost per unit shipped through the cell (C_{ij}). The X_{ij} value in the cell is the amount shipped through the cell (unknown).

$$\sum_{i=1}^{m} X_{ij} = b_j \tag{9.1}$$

where b_j = total amount required by market j.

Notice that the summation is over all rows ($i = 1, \ldots, m$) for each column j. Physically we are summing over all warehouses i for each market area j.

In a similar manner, the total amount shipped from each warehouse must be sent to some market. In this case, when we sum the amount shipped across the columns for each particular row, we will obtain the total amount shipped from each warehouse. Thus we have

$$\sum_{j=1}^{n} X_{ij} = a_i \tag{9.2}$$

where a_i = total amount available at warehouse i.

The total amount shipped to all markets must equal the amount available at each warehouse. We also require that the amount shipped be nonnegative.

$$X_{ij} \geq 0 \tag{9.3}$$

Our objective is to minimize the costs of transportation. To formulate this objective, we let C_{ij} represent the cost of shipping one unit from warehouse i to market j. By multiplying these unit costs by the amount shipped and then adding, we will arrive at the total transportation cost C. Thus we have

$$C = \sum_{i=1}^{m} \sum_{j=1}^{n} C_{ij} X_{ij} \tag{9.4}$$

The mathematical problem then is to minimize the cost given by Equation (9.4) subject to the restrictions in Equations (9.1), (9.2), and (9.3).

The problem originally given in Figure 9.4 can be written in mathematical terms as shown below:

$$\text{Min } 3X_{11} + 2X_{12} + 4X_{13} + 3X_{21} + 4X_{22} + 2X_{23} + 4X_{31} + 2X_{32} + 4X_{33}$$

Subject
to:

$$
\begin{aligned}
X_{11} + X_{12} + X_{13} &= 150 \\
X_{21} + X_{22} + X_{23} &= 200 \\
X_{31} + X_{32} + X_{33} &= 200 \\
X_{11} \qquad\qquad + X_{21} \qquad\qquad + X_{31} &= 150 \\
X_{12} \qquad\qquad + X_{22} \qquad\qquad + X_{32} &= 300 \\
X_{13} \qquad\qquad + X_{23} \qquad\qquad + X_{33} &= 100 \\
X_{ij} &\geq 0
\end{aligned}
$$

This is just a linear programming problem with a special structure. It can be solved by using either the simplex method described in the Supplement to Chapter 3 or the special transportation algorithm described in the Supplement to this chapter. The transportation algorithm is generally somewhat more efficient because it takes advantage of the special structure in the problem. It does, however, require a separate computer program.

The problem in Figure 9.4 has been solved and the optimal solution is shown in Figure 9.5. The solution tells us that the new warehouse in Minneapolis should ship entirely to the midwest market and the Chicago and Atlanta warehouses should each split up their shipments to the two remaining markets. The total cost of this distribution plan is $1250, which is the minimum possible cost using the Minneapolis warehouse.

The result for the Kansas City warehouse is also shown in Figure 9.5. In this case the new warehouse in Kansas City ships both to the midwest and the southeast, while the Chicago warehouse ships only to the midwest and the Atlanta warehouse ships to the northeast and southeast. The cost of this optimal solution is $1400.

Since the cost of using the Minneapolis warehouse is lower, it should be given preference over the Kansas City location. We have thus solved our original location problem by using the transportation method to find the least-cost solution for each alternative. While this simple example illustrates the principles involved, it does not provide a feel for the complexities encountered in real plant and warehouse location problems. These complexities will be described below and illustrated by two real-world examples.

Some of the typical complexities encountered in the location of plants and warehouses are as follows:

1. There may be many plants, many warehouses, and many customer locations, leading to a very large number of variables and constraints. It would not be unusual, for example, to have 20 plants, 50 warehouses, and 150 markets, resulting in 150,000 variables and 220 constraints.
2. The number of plants and warehouses to be used may not be fixed in advance. This produces a very large number of combinations of locations to consider.
3. There may be fixed charges at each plant and warehouse plus a variable cost

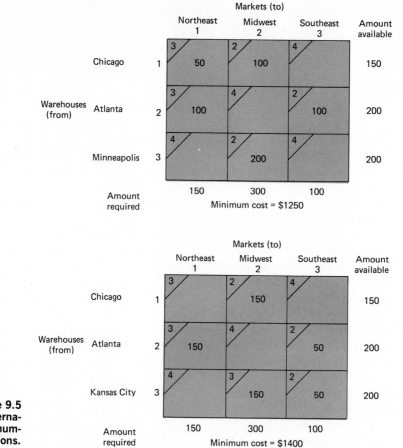

Figure 9.5
Location alternatives: minimum-cost solutions.

depending on the amount produced and shipped. This cost structure is nonlinear and therefore requires a special algorithm for solution.

4. There are usually multiple products, which increases the size of the problem.
5. It may be necessary to consider alternate inventory levels at various locations. In this case the service level is not fixed but depends on the decision parameters selected.
6. Different modes of transportation may be possible (air freight, truck, train, etc.).
7. Various customer-service policies may be stated, such as, "The customer must be served from the closest warehouse."
8. The demand may be probabilistic in nature.

These complexities all serve to make the problem more difficult to formulate and solve. Nevertheless, many of these conditions have been represented in models used in practice. The state-of-the-art in solving distribution problems has been very highly developed.

Arthur Geoffrion (1976) formulated and solved a complex distribution problem for Hunt-Wesson Foods. The original distribution system involved national distribution of several hundred distinct products from 14 plants through 12 regional distribution centers (warehouses). The purpose of the study was to determine how many distribution centers were needed, whether some of the 12 centers should be relocated, and how customers should be assigned to them. As a result of the study, five changes in the location of distribution centers were made (including movement of existing facilities to new locations and the opening of new facilities). Geoffrion reports annual cost savings from these changes to be in the millions of dollars.

This problem was formulated as a multiple-product transportation problem with 17 product classes, 14 plants, 45 distribution-center sites, and 121 customer zones defined by zip codes. A minimum-cost solution for the resulting problem was found using Bender's decomposition method and the transportation algorithm. Recent advances in operations research methods made it possible to solve such a large problem within reasonable computer cost and time. It was also possible to solve many variations on the problem for purposes of sensitivity analysis.

Another application of sophisticated modeling to real-world distribution problems was reported by Markland (1973). In this case the problem was to determine the number of warehouses, warehouse locations, and inventory service levels for the Ralston Purina Company. The distribution network in 10 midwestern states consisted of 4 factories with associated factory warehouses, 5 field warehouses, and 137

TABLE 9.4
DISTRIBUTION COST SUMMARY (3-MONTH PERIOD)—
ALTERNATIVE WAREHOUSE LOCATIONS (thousands of dollars)

Type of cost	Warehouse configuration					
	Five field ware-houses	Four* field ware-houses	Three* field ware-houses	Two* field ware-houses	One* field ware-house	Zero field ware-houses
Transportation costs†						
Manufacturing facility → customer	$514	$530	$525	$567	$574	$665
Manufacturing facility→field warehouse	36	30	20	17	10	0
Field warehouse→customer	60	51	42	20	28	0
Subtotal	610	611	587	604	612	665
Warehousing costs						
Field warehouses	30	25	16	13	6	0
Manufacturing facility warehouses	303	304	310	313	316	320
Subtotal	333	329	326	326	322	320
Penalty costs						
Order shifting costs	12	8	9	7	5	22
Back ordering costs	4	2	4	4	3	4
Subtotal	16	10	13	11	8	26
Total distribution cost	$959	$950	$926	$941	$942	$991

Source: Robert E. Markland, "Analyzing Geographically Discrete Warehousing Networks by Computer Simulation," *Decision Sciences,* vol. 4, 1973.

* Minimum-cost combination for the particular warehouse configuration.

† Transportation costs associated with interplant and interwarehouse shipments are not shown, for the sake of brevity. They were of small magnitude and did not vary significantly between the various simulation runs.

TABLE 9.5
DISTRIBUTION COST SUMMARY (3-MONTH PERIOD)—ALTERNATIVE INVENTORY LEVELS (thousands of dollars)

Type of cost	Inventory level										
	100%	95%	90%	85%*	80%	75%	70%	65%	60%	55%	50%
Transportation costs†											
Manufacturing facility → customer	$ 460	$ 660	$ 594	$ 543	$ 559	$ 575	$ 614	$ 638	$ 694	$ 736	$ 761
Manufacturing facility → field warehouse	147	45	40	36	41	36	38	39	41	43	44
Field warehouse → customer	235	64	50	58	58	58	61	71	60	50	52
Subtotal	842	769	684	637	658	669	713	748	795	829	857
Warehousing costs											
Field warehouse	318	28	27	26	26	25	25	24	24	24	23
Manufacturing facility warehouses	71	303	304	305	306	307	308	309	310	310	312
Subtotal	389	331	331	331	332	332	333	333	334	334	335
Penalty costs											
Order shifting costs	0	11	9	11	12	11	12	13	14	15	16
Back ordering costs	0	3	3	3	3	3	3	3	3	4	4
Subtotal	0	14	12	14	15	14	15	16	17	19	20
Total distribution cost	$1231	$1114	$1027	$982	$1005	$1015	$1061	$1097	$1146	$1182	$1212

Source: Robert E. Markland, "Analyzing Geographically Discrete Warehousing Networks by Computer Simulation," *Decision Sciences,* vol. 4, 1973.

* Minimum-cost inventory level.

† Transportation costs associated with interplant and interwarehouse shipments are not shown for the sake of brevity. They were of small magnitude, and did not vary significantly between the various simulation runs.

customer shipping zones. It was possible to ship from factory warehouses or field warehouses to customers and also to transship between factory warehouses or field warehouses, depending on inventory availability and the closest point of demand.

This problem was modeled by using simulation. Since inventory levels and random demands were involved, it was necessary to use simulation rather than the transportation method. The simulation was conducted by generating demands for each product type and filling them by the closest warehouse with inventory available. If a demand could not be filled, a back order was placed and an associated back-order-cost assigned. Penalty costs were also assigned to demands not filled from the closest warehouse. Once the location of the source of shipment had been determined, the mode of transportation (truck or rail) was simulated from previously known probability distributions. Transportation costs were then charged and the inventory was reduced by the amount shipped. This process was then continued for all products, customers, and time periods. Costs were accumulated for transportation, warehousing, and penalties to arrive at a total distribution cost.

At Ralston-Purina, the costs for 5, 4, 3, 2, 1, and 0 field warehouses were computed. (See Table 9.4.) As a result of these calculations, it was found that 3 field warehouses was the least-cost alternative, resulting in a large annual savings over the existing 5 field warehouses. The costs were also computed for various inventory service levels, as shown in Table 9.5. This table indicates that an 85 percent service level is the least-cost alternative, with a 100 percent service level costing significantly more per year.

This simulation model illustrates how one can handle nonlinear cost structures, random demands, and combined capacity and location problems. It is a classical application of simulation analysis to the study of complex management problems.

9.7 LOCATION OF COMPETITIVE RETAIL STORES

Many retail location problems can be formulated with the criterion of maximizing revenue. These problems typically occur for grocery stores, department stores, and fast-food restaurants, where the revenue of a particular site depends on the intensity of competition from other competitors' locations nearby. Notice how the location chosen for these service facilities has become a determinant of revenue, which was not a factor for manufacturing facilities.

Most retail location models are based on the assumption that revenue is proportional to the size of the facility and inversely proportional to the time the customer has to travel to the facility. Huff (1962) developed a model in which revenue was proportional to the ratio S/T^A, where S is the size of the retail facility in square feet, T is the travel time, and A is a parameter estimated empirically to reflect the effect of travel time on shopping preferences. [Also see Buffa (1976).] Huff cites evidence that travel time and store size influence consumer behavior and may be sufficient by themselves to predict consumer preferences.

To reflect the effect of competition in a given trade area, the following model is formulated:

$$N_{ij} = P_{ij}C_i = \frac{\dfrac{S_j}{T_{ij}^A}}{\displaystyle\sum_{j=1}^{n} \dfrac{S_j}{T_{ij}^A}} C_i \qquad (9.5)$$

where N_{ij} = number of customers in region i that are likely to travel to site j
$\quad\; P_{ij}$ = probability that an individual customer in region i will travel to site j
$\quad\; C_i$ = number of total customers residing in region i
$\quad\; S_j$ = size of the facility at site j (ft²)
$\quad\; T_{ij}$ = customer time required to travel from region i to site j
$\quad\; A$ = parameter used to reflect effect of travel time on customer shopping behavior

To use this model, a trade region is first divided into customer zones. Census tracts or zip codes might be used as a convenient base to identify the number of likely customers in each zone i. The existing competitive sites in the trade area are then identified, along with their sizes, the travel times from each site to every customer zone, and an estimate of the number of customers served by each site. Using the above model, we select a value of A to "tune" the model to the data collected. Notice that all values except A are known for existing sites. In a study by Huff (1962), values of A in the range of 2.1 to 3.2 were found to work quite well for furniture stores.

After "tuning" the model to the existing sites, a new proposed site is inserted in the trade area. Travel time and the size for this new site are inserted into the model along with the previously determined value of A and the values for the existing sites. The model is solved to estimate the number of customers for the new site. Notice that the model assumes a gain of customers for the new site at the expense of the old sites through relative drawing power based on size of facilities and travel times. The model thus predicts how the available customers will be "divided up" among the stores.

As an example of this procedure, consider the situation shown in Figure 9.6. In this case there are two stores, four customer zones, and 3800 total customer trips per day for shopping purposes. Using the model given by Equation (9.5) with $A = 2$, we find that store 1, the smaller store, is expected to draw 1526 customers per day that the new store takes customers from both the small store and the large store. The new store also draws the greatest proportion of its customers (72.7 percent) from the zone in which it is located.

What will happen if a new store is located at site 3 in zone 2? Using Equation (9.5) once again, this time with three stores, we find that store 1 is expected to draw 1045 customers per day, store 2 will draw 1606 customers per day, and the new store, store 3 will probably serve 1149 customers per day. The result is interesting in that the new store takes customers from both the small store and the large store. The new store also draws the greatest proportion of its customers (72.7 percent) from the zone in which it is located.

Retail location models are quite useful, since they apply to a large number of

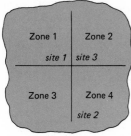

Zone i	Customers C_i	Travel times, minutes		
		T_{i1}	T_{i2}	T_{i3}
1	1000	5	15	10
2	500	10	10	5
3	1500	10	10	15
4	800	15	5	10

Store j	Size S_i(ft^2)
1	200,000
2	400,000
3	400,000

Computed P_{ij}

	Store 1	Store 2	Store 3
Zone 1	.580	.130	.290
Zone 2	.091	.182	.727
Zone 3	.257	.515	.228
Zone 4	.0425	.7665	.191

Figure 9.6
Simulation of distribution alternatives.

situations. These models also indicate the problems faced by service industries in locating dispersed facilities. While distribution cost is not a significant factor in these cases, the effect of competition on revenue is a significant problem. In the next section we shall consider another service location problem where the criterion is not revenue but rather the service delivered. Such problems are commonly encountered in the public sector.

9.8 EMERGENCY-SERVICE LOCATION

A significant class of location problems concerns the delivery of emergency services —fire, police, and ambulance. These problems often have minimum response time as a decision criterion, since time is of the essence in delivering emergency service. As a result, these problems illustrate location decisions where a measure of service, such as response time, is the most important location criterion.

The location of emergency units can have a great impact on cost. Chaiken and Larson (1972) estimate that it takes about five people on the payroll to fill a single post around the clock. Thus the direct labor costs of operating a two-person patrol car in New York are approximately $150,000 per year; a single fire engine may cost over $500,000 per year to operate. If only one or two emergency units can be eliminated by the choice of location, a substantial reduction in cost will result.

Decisions regarding the location of fire, police, and ambulance units have often been made on the basis of geographical coverage. These decisions have been reinforced by government and insurance standards. For example, the American Insurance Association standard is used in most communities to establish fire insurance rates. In certain "high-value districts" the standard requires every point to be within 1 mile from an engine company and no further than 1.25 miles from a ladder company. Furthermore, there must be at least three engine companies within 1.5 miles of any point and at least two ladders within 2 miles. [See Chaiken and Larson (1972).]

Geographic coverage standards do not, however, consider the density of calls for emergency service. If an area has many calls, the response time will be reduced. The standard also does not consider the speed of travel possible and the availability of direct roads. Geographic standards are, therefore, poorly correlated with response time. But, even response time is a surrogate measure when the purpose of emergency units is to save lives, reduce property damage, or deter crime.

Emergency response time can be estimated for different location sites by using simulation models. These models permit the incorporation of factors such as density of calls, speed of travel, dispatching rules, and number of vehicles available. Through the use of these models, it is possible to evaluate not only location sites but other operations decisions as well. For information on the exact models available, see Fitzsimmons (1973), Savas (1969), and Rider (1976).

9.9 KEY POINTS

This chapter has described facilities decisions concerned with the amount of capacity, when it is needed, and where it should be located. These decisions are on the long-range end of a hierarchy of capacity decisions which successively constrain the capacity available to operations. Facilities decisions are crucial because they determine future availability of output and require the organization's scarce capital.

Some of the chapter's key points are:

- A procedure was suggested for analyzing facilities decisions, including (1) measurement of capacity, (2) forecasting of demand, (3) determination of capacity needs, (4) generation of alternatives, (5) evaluation of alternatives, and (6) deciding. This procedure can be used to analyze any capacity decision including "how much," "when," and "where located."
- Facilities decisions are often made by the chief executive and the board of directors. Because these decisions are so encompassing, they require the input not only of operations but of all other functional areas as well.
- Economy of scale can be a misleading basis for capacity decisions. Managers should determine the role of process, volume, or capacity economies in any given decision.
- Location problems can be classified into four basic categories: single-facility location, plant and warehouse location, retail store location, and emergency-service location. Each of these problems typically has different decision criteria and utilizes a different type of modeling approach.
- Single-facility location problems are those which do not interact with existing facilities and can therefore be isolated for purposes of analysis. These problems are also characterized by multiple criteria, and either additive or multiplicative scoring models can be used.
- Plant and warehouse location problems are often formulated to minimize distribution and production costs while providing a given amount of supply capacity. These problems can be analyzed by either the transportation method or simulation models.
- Location of retail stores may affect revenues as well as costs. The revenue can be estimated by a drawing-power model which relates travel time and store size to store revenues. The resulting model estimates the effect of competition at any given location.

- Emergency units can be located on the basis of response time rather than revenue. There are a variety of models which can be used to locate these services.

QUESTIONS

1. Approximately how long would one need to plan ahead for the following types of facilities?
   a. Restaurant
   b. Hospital
   c. Oil refinery
   d. Toy factory
   e. Electric power plant
   f. Public school
   g. Private school

2. What problems are created by mixing the capacity questions of "how much," "when," and "where located"?

3. How could capacity be measured for the facilities listed in Question 1? What assumptions are needed about product mix, nominal capacity, and peak versus sustained capacity?

4. A school district has forecast student enrollment for several years into the future and predicts excess capacity for 2000 students. The school board has said that the only alternative is to close a school. Evaluate.

5. Why is it difficult to evaluate both costs and benefits at the same time? How does the single-facility scoring model handle this problem?

6. For each of the facilities listed in Question 1, specify one or more decision criteria which might be used.

7. Why will the facility decisions made not necessarily agree with the analysis? In this a problem? Why?

8. Why are facilities decisions often made by top management? What is the role in these decisions of operations, marketing, finance, and personnel?

9. What are the strengths and weaknesses associated with scoring models for facility location?

10. Discuss the interactive nature of multiple facilities in plant-and-warehouse environments. How is this interaction represented by a transportation matrix?

11. How does the location problem for retail stores differ from that for factories?

12. Why is a scoring model inappropriate for the location of multiple emergency-service units?

13. How do facilities decisions for public firms differ from those for private firms?

14. In what ways does corporate strategy affect location decisions?

PROBLEMS

1. The Quickfix Hairdressing Salon is considering expanding its capacity to handle 100 more hairdos per week. Two options, both of which provide the same capacity, have been identified:

   Alternative A: Build a new salon at a separate location. The cost of the building is estimated to be $100,000 with a 20-year life. The cost of the equipment is $50,000 with a 10-year life. Property taxes would be $4000 per year. Use straight-line depreciation and assume a 50 percent income tax bracket.

   Alternative B: Lease a building for 5 years. The annual lease payments would be $8000. In this case the equipment would cost $60,000 and would last 10 years.

   It is expected that the operating costs of these two options—including labor, supplies, and utilities—would be the same.

   a. Compare the two alternatives on an after-tax basis using 15 percent cost of capital.
   b. What additional factors should be considered in this case?

2. Suppose that we are considering the question of how much capacity to build in the face of uncertain demand. Assume that the cost is $10 per unit of lost sales due to insufficient capacity. Also assume that there is a cost of $4 for each unit of capacity built. The probabil-

ity of various demand levels is as follows:

Demand— X units	Probability of X
0	.05
1	.10
2	.15
3	.20
4	.20
5	.15
6	.10
7	.05

a. How many units of capacity should be built to minimize the total cost of providing capacity plus lost sales?

b. State a general rule regarding the amount of capacity to build.

c. What principle does this problem illustrate?

3. The Goodfeel Shirt Company is considering a new plant location for either Denver or Phoenix. The existing plants are located in New York City and San Francisco; they ship to four national warehouses in Chicago, Atlanta, Kansas City, and Los Angeles. The unit costs of transportation, the availability of goods, and the requirements are show below:

City of origin	Shipping costs per unit to warehouse in				Units available
	Chicago	Atlanta	Kansas City	Los Angeles	
New York	$ 4	$ 3	$ 5	$ 7	100
San Francisco	5	8	5	2	150
Denver	3	6	2	4	100
Phoenix	5	7	3	2	100
Units required	75	50	125	100	

a. To minimize the costs of transportation, where should the new plant be located—Denver or Phoenix?

b. What other factors should be considered in making this plant location decision?

4. Two locations for the new Bay City Hospital are being considered. These locations have been rated on a number of factors, as shown below.

	Site 1	Site 2	Percent weight
Miles per month traveled			
Patients over 55	20,000	15,000	10
Patients under 55	18,000	17,000	10
Doctors and nurses	10,000	15,000	15
Costs of land and building	$4 million	$4.5 million	25
Average miles traveled per emergency	6.7	5.6	10
Support of community groups	Fair	Very good	15
Doctors' and nurses' preference	Excellent	Poor	10
Room for future expansion	Fair	Excellent	5

In brief, site 1 is closer for doctors and nurses but further away for patients; it is cheaper but has less room for future growth.

a. Using an additive scoring model, which site is preferred? (Use excellent = 5, very good = 4, fair = 3, poor = 2.)

b. When a multiplicative scoring model is used, which site is preferred?

    c. Which model (additive or multiplicative) is the best for this case?

    d. What role do you think models of this type can play in actual hospital location decisions?

5. The Hurryback Department Store is considering a new site (site 3) in a trade area where two other stores are already located. The following data for these stores are given:

Customer zone	Time to store site (minutes) 1	2	3	Customer visits per day
1	8	4	12	1000
2	12	8	8	1500
3	4	8	8	1200
4	8	12	4	1600
Site size in square feet	200,000	400,000	300,000	

a. If management locates the new store at site 3, how many customer visits per day can they expect? Use $A = 2$.

b. Suppose the average customer spends $4 per visit and the store is open 300 days per year. Also assume that it costs $3 million to build the store, that $1.5 million per year is needed to operate it, and that the store will last 20 years. What internal rate of return on the investment can the store expect before taxes?

c. What additional factors might be important in this decision?

SELECTED BIBLIOGRAPHY

ATKINS, ROBERT J., and RICHARD H. SHRIVER: "New Approach to Facilities Location," *Harvard Business Review*, May–June 1968.

BROWN, P. A., and D. F. GIBSON: "A Quantified Model for Facility Site Selection: Application to a Multiplant Location Problem," *AIIE Transactions*, vol. 4, no. 1, March 1972, pp. 1–10.

BUFFA, ELWOOD S.: *Operations Management*, New York: Wiley, 1976.

CHAIKEN, JAN M., and RICHARD C. LARSON: "Methods for Allocating Urban Emergency Units: A Survey," *Management Science*, vol. 19, no. 4, part 2, December 1972, pp. 110–130.

FITZSIMMONS, JAMES: "A Methodology for Emergency Ambulance Development," *Management Science*, vol. 19, no. 6, February 1973, pp. 627–636.

FULTON, MAURICE: "New Factors in Plant Location," *Harvard Business Review*, May–June 1971, pp. 4–17, 166–168.

GEOFFRION, ARTHUR M.: "Better Distribution Planning with Computer Models," *Harvard Business Review*, July–August 1976, pp. 92–99.

HUFF, D. L.: "Determination of Intra-Urban Retail Trade Areas," Los Angeles: UCLA Graduate School of Management, 1962.

MARKLAND, ROBERT E.: "Analyzing Geographically Discrete Warehousing Networks by Computer Simulation," *Decision Sciences*, vol. 4, 1973, pp. 216–236.

MARSHALL, PAUL W., et al.: *Operations Management: Text and Cases*, Homewood, Ill.: Irwin, 1975.

RIDER, KENNETH LLOYD: "A Parametric Model for the Allocation of Fire Companies in New York City," *Management Science*, vol. 23, no. 2, October 1976, pp. 146–158.

SAVAS, E. S.: "Simulation and Cost-Effectiveness Analysis of New York's Emergency Ambulance Service," *Management Science,* vol. 15, no. 12, August 1969, pp. B-608–B-627.

SCHMENNER, ROGER W.: "Before You Build a Big Factory," *Harvard Business Review,* July–August 1976, pp. 100–104.

STUDENT, KURT R.: "Cost vs. Human Values in Plant Location," *Business Horizons,* April 1976, pp. 5–14.

SULLIVAN, WILLIAM G., and W. WAYNE CLAYCOMBE: "The Use of Decision Trees in Planning Plant Expansion," *SAM: Advanced Management Journal,* vol. 40, no. 1, Winter 1975.

SUPPLEMENT: TRANSPORTATION METHOD

In Chapter 9, we treated location problems that involve the distribution of goods from one location to another. These problems can be formulated as transportation models where the objective is to find the lowest-cost location alternative. Even when location is not an issue, the transportation method can be used to find the best shipping routes.

In this supplement we will develop methods for solving the transportation problem. But first the transportation problem must be formulated. The general transportation problem can be described in the form of a matrix with shipments from one location to another. Suppose, for ex-

ample, we have shipments from factories to warehouses, with factories represented by the rows and warehouses by the columns of the matrix. In Figure S9.1, there are three factories and four warehouses. Each cell in the matrix represents a route from a particular factory to a particular warehouse. In all there are 12 routes in this problem.

Listed on the right-hand side of the matrix are the amounts available at each factory. These amounts must be shipped to one or more warehouses. Listed on the bottom of the matrix are the amounts required at each warehouse. These amounts required must be supplied from one or

Figure S9.1
Transportation problem.

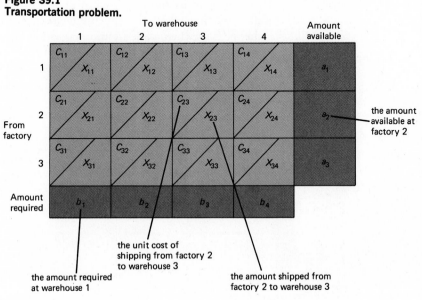

more factories. We assume that the total amount available at all factories just equals the total amount required at all warehouses.

The objective of the transportation problem is to find the shipping routes from factories to warehouses which will minimize the total cost of transportation. In each cell of the matrix the unit cost of shipping one unit through the cell or route is shown. The total cost of transportation is then the sum of the amounts shipped through each cell multiplied by the unit costs of shipping through that cell.

To describe the transportation problem mathematically, we let:

X_{ij} = amount shipped from factory i to warehouse j

C_{ij} = unit cost of shipping from factory i to warehouse j

Then the total transportation cost is:

$$C = \sum_{i=1}^{m} \sum_{j=1}^{n} C_{ij}X_{ij}$$

We wish to find the values of X_{ij} which will minimize the value of C subject to the constraints:

$$\sum_{i=1}^{m} X_{ij} = b_j$$

The total shipped to each warehouse j must equal the amount required at the warehouse.

$$\sum_{j=1}^{n} X_{ij} = a_i$$

The total amount shipped from each factory i must equal the amount available at the factory.

$$X_{ij} \geq 0$$

All shipments must be nonnegative.

In Figure S9.2, a particular set of costs, requirements, and availabilities is given for the three factories and four warehouses. The objective is to find a set of shipments through the cells (values of X_{ij}) which will minimize the total cost of transportation subject to the constraints on the row and column totals.

To solve a transportation problem, we first find an initial solution (values of X_{ij}) and then improve the initial solution by reducing the cost through successive iterations until the minimum-cost solution is found. The transportation method is an iterative method, like the simplex method, which reduces the cost of the solution on each successive iteration.

THE INITIAL SOLUTION

One way to find an initial solution is to use the northwest corner rule. Using this rule, the maximum amount is shipped through the northwest cell of the matrix. Maximum shipments through other cells are then made by moving to the right and down in the matrix until all row and column requirements are met. The northwest corner assignment for the sample problem is shown in Figure S9.3.

Figure S9.2
Transportation example.

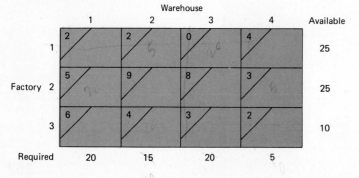

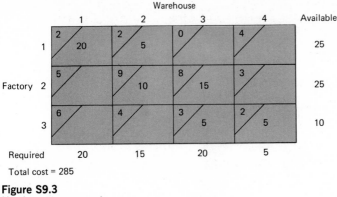

Total cost = 285

Figure S9.3
Northwest corner rule.

Although the northwest corner rule results in a feasible solution to the transportation problem, the solution is often quite costly because no attention is given to costs as the solution is constructed. Therefore Vogel has developed a better method which does consider costs.[1]

The Vogel approximation method (VAM) begins by computing the difference between the lowest cost and the next-lowest cost in each row and column. The row or column with the largest cost difference is then selected for a shipment. As much as possible is shipped through the minimum-cost cell in the selected row or column. The row or column which is filled is then deleted from further consideration and the method is repeated. Because of the row or column deletion, at least some of the row and column differences must be recomputed at each step.

Application of the VAM to the sample problem is shown in Figure S9.4. In step 1, the largest difference between the lowest cost and next-lowest cost was found in columns 1 and 3. Since there is a tie, column 3 is selected arbitrarily for an assignment. The lowest cost in column 3 is zero in cell (1, 3); thus as much as possible should be shipped through that cell. The assignment of a value of 20 through cell (1, 3) satisfied the requirement for column 3; therefore column 3 is

deleted from further consideration. The VAM differences are recomputed in step 2 and the procedure is repeated. After five steps, an initial feasible solution is found.

The VAM method uses an opportunity-cost principle. At each step the difference between the lowest cost and next-lowest cost is the opportunity cost of not making an assignment in a particular row or column. By choosing the largest difference, the largest opportunity cost is avoided. The result of the VAM method is usually a good approximation to the optimal solution; in some cases, the optimal solution itself may be found. The VAM method produces a much better starting solution than the northwest corner rule.

EVALUATION AND IMPROVEMENT

Given a starting solution, the next step in the transportation method is evaluation of the solution for optimality. The evaluation is done by assigning row and column numbers to the initial solution. This is done by selecting an arbitrary row or column and assigning a zero (or other value) to that row or column. In Figure S9.5, we have assigned a zero arbitrarily to row 1.

For each cell with a positive shipment value, the row-plus-column numbers must equal the unit cost in the cell. As a result of applying this

[1] N. V. Reinfeld and W. R. Vogel, *Mathematical Programming,* Englewood Cliffs, N.J.: Prentice-Hall, 1958.

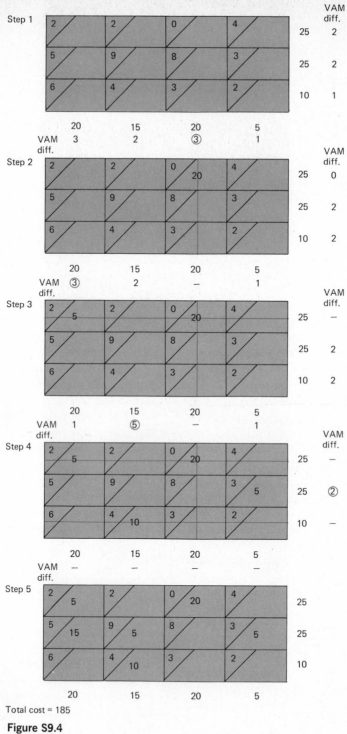

Total cost = 185

**Figure S9.4
VAM method.**

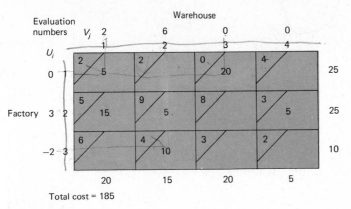

Figure S9.5
Evaluation of the initial solution.

rule, a 2 can be assigned to column 1 and a zero can be assigned to column 3. Using the 2 assigned to column 1, a 3 must be assigned to row 2 so the sum equals 5. This procedure is then continued until all row and column numbers are assigned.

A condition for optimality of a solution is:

$$U_i + V_j \le C_{ij}$$

where U_i = evaluation number for row i
V_j = evaluation number for column j
C_{ij} = unit cost of shipping via cell (i, j)

To check for optimality, we test whether the above optimality condition is satisfied for all cells. Notice that we have already assigned $U_i + V_j = C_{ij}$ for the cells with positive shipment values.

In Figure S9.5, the optimality condition is satisfied for all cells except cell (1, 2). Therefore, the initial solution is not optimal. Furthermore, we should consider cell (1, 2) for a shipment to reduce the cost of the present solution.

To revise the solution, we ship as much as possible through cell (1, 2). This change will require an adjustment of the other shipments in our

Figure S9.6
Revised solution.

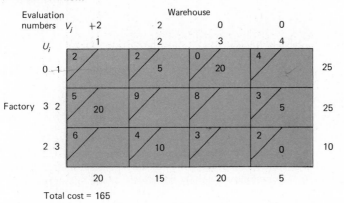

solution to maintain row and column constraints. From Figure S9.5, the most we can ship through cell (1, 2) without driving one of the current shipments negative is five units. When we set $X_{12} = 5$, both X_{11} and X_{23} will be reduced to zero. The revised solution resulting from these changes is shown in Figure S9.6.

The revised row-and-column numbers are also shown in Figure S9.6. These numbers were obtained in the same way as before. Assign a zero to row 1, then make the row-plus-column sum equal to the cost in each cell with a positive shipment. In this case, we find that a zero must be assigned to one of the cells in order to continue with the evaluation procedure. A zero can be assigned arbitrarily to any cell whenever it is needed to continue the evaluation algorithm. In this case we selected cell (3, 4) for a zero assignment.

The row-and-column numbers in Figure S9.6 indicate that an optimal solution has been reached, since for every cell we have:

$$U_i + V_j \leq C_{ij}$$

The cost of this optimal solution is $165. This is a substantial reduction from the northwest corner solution, which cost $285.

COMMENTS ON THE TRANSPORTATION PROBLEM

To this point we have assumed that the total amount available at the factories equals the total amount required at the warehouses. Whenever the two amounts are not equal, the problem can be solved by adding a dummy row or a dummy column. If the total amount available at the factories exceeds the total requirements at the warehouses, a dummy warehouse (column) should be added to absorb the excess supply. The costs of shipping to this dummy warehouse from any factory should be set equal to zero. The dummy warehouse serves exactly the same purpose as slack variables in an LP formulation.

If the total amount required at the warehouses exceeds the amount available, a dummy factory (row) should be added. The amount supplied by the dummy factory should just meet the shortage, and the shipping costs from the dummy factory should be zero.

The transportation problem can also be solved by the simplex method, since the transportation problem is an LP problem. The simplex method, however, is not as efficient as the transportation method. The special transportation method takes advantage of the structure in the transportation problem and thus provides a more efficient solution procedure.

The transportation problem has been particularly important in operations and logistics management. Applications include efficient location of warehouses and plants, optimal shipping patterns from existing plants to warehouses, and optimal shipping patterns from existing warehouses to markets. Some of the advanced applications have included variations on the basic transportation method, including fixed charges, nonlinear cost structures, and other refinements.

PROBLEMS

1. The Staytight Door Company ships doors from three factories to three warehouses located in the Midwest. The amounts available for an average month, the amounts required, and the unit shipping costs are shown below. Find a shipping schedule that will minimize the total transportation cost.

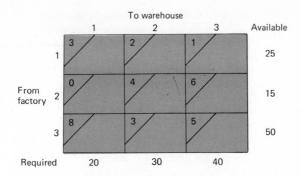

2. The Staytight Door Company in Problem 1 is considering adding a new warehouse, number 4, due to expanding sales. The new transportation problem is shown below.

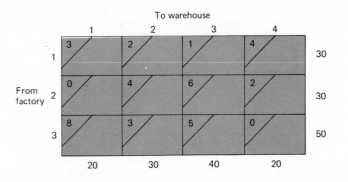

   a. Find the optimal shipping plan.
   b. What effect will the new warehouse have on the optimal shipping routes found in Problem 1?

3. The ABC Freight Company ships freight from three warehouses to four markets. The transportation costs and the total amounts shipped are shown below.

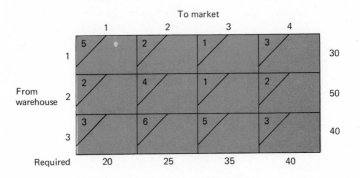

   a. How much should be shipped from each warehouse to each market?
   b. What is the effect of changing C_{12} from 2 to 3?
   c. What is the effect of changing C_{22} from 4 to 2?

4. The Best Wooden Pencil Company is considering revising its current transportation routings to reduce costs. At present, the company has extra capacity at its factories as shown below.

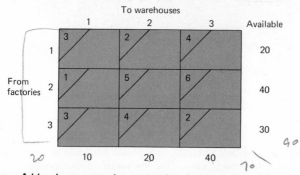

To warehouses

	1	2	3	Available
From factories 1	3	2	4	20
2	1	5	6	40
3	3	4	2	30

20 10 20 40

90
70

a. Add a dummy warehouse to absorb the slack in this problem.
b. How much should be shipped from each factory to each warehouse?
c. What is the effect on the optimal solution of changing the amount required at warehouse 1 from 10 to 30 units?

CHAPTER 10
AGGREGATE PLANNING

Aggregate planning is concerned with matching supply and demand of output over the medium time range, up to approximately 12 months into the future. The term "aggregate" implies that the planning is done for a single overall measure of output or, at the most, a few aggregated product categories. The aim of aggregate planning is to set overall output levels in the near to medium future in the face of fluctuating or uncertain demand.

As a result of aggregate planning, decisions and policies should be made concerning overtime, hiring, firing, subcontracting, and inventory levels. Aggregate planning determines not only the output levels planned but also the appropriate resource input mix to be used.

Aggregate planning might seek to influence demand as well as supply. If this is the case, variables such as price, advertising, and product mix might be used. If changes in demand are considered, then marketing, along with operations, will be intimately involved in aggregate planning.

In this chapter, we will be using a broad definition of the term "aggregate planning." There are also narrow definitions which limit aggregate planning to particular types of mathematical formulations. These formulations might include, for example, supply variables only, a specific objective of cost minimization, or particular mathematical forms.

In the broad sense of the definition, the aggregate planning problem has the following characteristics:

1. A time horizon of about 12 months, with updating of the plan on a periodic basis (perhaps monthly).
2. An aggregate level of product demand consisting of one or a few categories of product. The demand is assumed to be fluctuating, uncertain, or seasonal.
3. The possibility of changing both supply and demand variables.
4. A variety of management objectives which might include low inventories, good labor relations, low costs, flexibility to increase future output levels, and good customer service.
5. Facilities that are considered fixed and cannot be expanded.

Aggregate planning forms an important link between facilities planning on the one hand and scheduling on the other. Facilities planning determines the physical capacity which cannot be exceeded by aggregate planning. Thus facilities planning extends further into the future than aggregate planning and constrains the aggregate planning decisions.

Scheduling, on the other hand, refers to the short range (a few months or less) and is constrained by aggregate planning decisions. While aggregate planning deals with the acquisition of resources, scheduling is concerned with allocating available resources to specific jobs and orders. Thus a basic distinction should be made between acquiring resources through aggregate planning and later allocating them through scheduling.

This hierarchy of capacity decisions is shown in Figure 10.1 and is discussed in more detail in the introduction to this part of the book. Notice that the decisions proceed from the top down and that there is also a feedback loop from the bottom up. Thus, scheduling decisions often indicate a need for revised aggregate planning, and aggregate planning may also uncover facility needs.

Aggregate planning is closely related to other corporate decisions, involving, for

Figure 10.1 Hierarchy of capacity decisions.

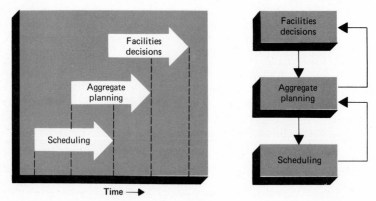

Time →

example, budgeting, personnel, and marketing. The relationship to budgeting is a particularly strong one. Most budgets are based on assumptions about aggregate output, personnel levels, inventory levels, purchasing levels, etc. An aggregate plan should thus be the basis for initial budget development and for budget revisions as conditions warrant.

Personnel planning is also greatly affected by aggregate planning because the results of aggregate planning include hiring, firing, and overtime decisions. In the service industries, where inventory is not a factor, aggregate planning is practically synonymous with budgeting and personnel planning.

Marketing must always be closely related to aggregate planning because the future supply of output, and thus customer service, is being determined. Furthermore, cooperation between marketing and operations is required when both supply and demand variables are being used to determine the best *corporate* approach to aggregate planning. Aggregate planning should be seen as an activity which is the primary responsibility of the operations function but which requires coordination and cooperation with all parts of the firm. The coordination problem in a typical aggregate planning decision is illustrated in Box 10.1.

BOX 10.1

TYPICAL DECISION PROBLEM

In January 1980, a meeting was held at the corporate offices of Farwell Enterprises, a major manufacturer of furnaces and furnace equipment. In attendance at the meeting were Marlene Lenton, president, Gretchen Davidson, vice president of operations, and Tom Christopherson, marketing vice president. Christopherson began, "I've just returned from our national sales meeting, and it appears that sales will be up even beyond my previous forecast. Last year we lost sales because of stockouts of certain key furnace models, and this hurt us more than we expected. As a result, I'm raising the forecast for fiscal 1981 (June 1980 to June 1981) from 100,000 units to 110,000 units."

Gretchen interrupted, "Tom, you've got to be kidding. Just two months ago we sat here in this office and agreed on the forecast of 100,000 units. We simply do not have the plant capacity to produce 110,000 units. And what are we going to do with all the inventory if we add the capacity and the forecast does not materialize?"

Marlene changed the subject by asking, "Suppose for a moment the forecast is correct, what are our options for more plant capacity?" Gretchen replied, "We don't have time to build a new plant. That leaves us with four options: (1) add a night shift in the present plant, (2) work the present work force on overtime, (3) add a second assembly line using some of the present warehouse space, or (4) build up more inventory in advance of the selling season. At the present time, the demand for furnaces is extremely seasonal, with a peak during the late summer and early fall and much lower sales the rest of the year. To meet this demand pattern, we've been using a level work force with some layoffs in the off season and some overtime in the peak season."

Marlene wanted to see these options properly evaluated and a better job of forecasting done. Accordingly, she directed Tom to prepare a detailed analysis of probable sales for each product line, using as much hard data as possible. This report would be due in 3 weeks, and the group would meet again to decide on the forecast. Marlene put Gretchen on notice that if the forecast were increased as a result of the study, she would ask for a new aggregate production plan considering all the options already outlined along with a supporting analysis and recommendation. The aggregate plan would have to specify the costs of inventory, labor, and capital equipment for each of the options. In addition, the effects on other operations objectives, dependability, flexibility, and quality would have to be evaluated.

The next section contains a detailed discussion of the options available to modify demand and supply for aggregate planning. This will be followed by the development of specific decision rules which can be used to plan aggregate output for both manufacturing and service industries. The chapter is completed with examples of aggregate planning and an evaluation of its use in practice.

10.1 DECISION OPTIONS

The aggregate planning problem can be clarified by a discussion of the various decision options available. These will be divided into two types: (1) those modifying demand and (2) those modifying supply. For a more detailed discussion, see Galbraith (1969).

Demand can be modified or influenced in several ways:

1. **PRICING.** Differential pricing is often used to reduce peak demand or to build up demand in off-peak periods. Some examples are matinee movie prices, off-season hotel rates, factory discounts for early- or late-season purchases, nighttime telephone rates, and two-for-one prices at restaurants. The purpose of these pricing schemes is to level demand through the day, week, month, or year.

2. **ADVERTISING AND PROMOTION.** This is another method used to stimulate or in some cases smooth out demand. Advertising is generally timed so as to promote demand during slack periods and to shift demand from the peak periods to the slack times. For example, ski resorts advertise to lengthen their season, and turkey growers advertise to stimulate demand outside the Thanksgiving and Christmas seasons.

3. **BACKLOG OR RESERVATIONS.** In some cases demand is influenced by asking customers to wait for their orders (backlog) or by reserving capacity in advance (reservations). Generally speaking, this has the effect of shifting demand from peak periods to periods with slack capacity. However, the waiting time may result in a loss of business. This loss can be desirable when the aim is to maximize profit, although most operations are extremely reluctant to turn away customers; backlogs or reservations are preferred.

4. **DEVELOPMENT OF COMPLEMENTARY PRODUCTS.** Firms with highly seasonal demands sometimes try to develop products which have countercyclic seasonal trends. The classic example of this approach is a lawn-mower company that begins building snow-blowers. In the service industry, an example is provided by fast-food restaurants that begin to offer breakfast so as to smooth out demand and utilize capacity more fully.

The service industries, using all the mechanisms cited above, have gone much further than their manufacturing counterparts in influencing demand. This can probably be attributed to one crucial difference—the inability of service operations to inventory their product.

There are also a large number of variables available to modify supply through aggregate planning. These include:

1. **HIRING AND FIRING EMPLOYEES.** The use of this variable differs a great deal between companies and industries. Some companies will do almost anything before reducing the size of the work force through layoffs. Other companies routinely increase and decrease their work forces as demand changes. These practices affect not only costs but also labor relations, productivity, and worker morale. As a result, company hiring and firing practices may be restricted by union contracts or company policies. One of the purposes of aggregate planning, however, is to examine the effect of these policies on costs or profits.

2. **USING OVERTIME AND UNDERTIME.** Overtime is sometimes used for short- or medium-range labor adjustments in lieu of hiring and firing, especially if the change in demand is considered temporary. Overtime usually costs 150 percent of regular time, with double time on weekends or Sundays. Because of its high cost, managers are sometimes reluctant to use overtime. Furthermore, workers are reluctant to work more than 20 percent weekly overtime for a duration of several weeks. "Undertime" refers to planned underutilization of the work force rather than layoffs or perhaps a shortened work week. Undertime can be thought of as the opposite of overtime. Another term for undertime is "idle time."

3. **USING PART-TIME LABOR.** In some cases it is possible to hire part-time employees in order to meet demands. This option may be particularly attractive because part-time employees are often paid significantly less in wages and benefits. Unions, of course, frown on the use of part-time employees, because the latter often do not pay union dues and may weaken union influence. Part-time employees are, however, essential to many service operations, such as restaurants, hospitals, supermarkets, and department stores. These operations are highly dependent on their ability to attract and utilize part-time workers for periods of peak demand.

4. **CARRYING INVENTORY.** In manufacturing companies, inventory can be used as a buffer between supply and demand. Inventories for later use can be built up during periods of slack demand. Inventory thus uncouples supply from demand in manufacturing operations, thereby allowing for smoother operations. Inventory can be viewed as a way to store labor for future consumption. This option is, of course, not available for service operations and leads to a somewhat different and more difficult aggregate planning problem for them.

5. **SUBCONTRACTING.** This option, which involves the use of other firms, is sometimes an effective way to increase or decrease supply. The subcontractor may supply the entire product or only some of the components. For example, a manufacturer of toys may utilize subcontractors to make plastic parts during certain times of the year. The manufacturer may furnish the molds and specify the materials and methods to be used. Service operations may subcontract for secretarial help, catering services, or facilities during peak periods.

6. **MAKING COOPERATIVE ARRANGEMENTS.** These arrangements are very similar to subcontracting in that other sources of supply are used. Examples include electric utilities which are hooked together through power-sharing networks, hospitals which send their patients to other hospitals for certain specialized services, and hotels or airlines which shift customers among one another when they are fully booked.

In considering all these options, it is clear that the aggregate planning problem is extremely broad and affects all parts of the firm. The decisions which are made must, therefore, be strategic and reflect all the firm's objectives. If aggregate planning is considered narrowly, suboptimization may occur and inappropriate decisions may result. Some of the multiple tradeoffs which should be considered are customer service level (through back orders or lost demand), inventory levels, stability of the labor force, and costs. All these conflicting objectives and tradeoffs are sometimes combined into a single cost function. A method for doing this will be described in the next two sections.

10.2 BASIC STRATEGIES

Two pure operations strategies can be used, along with many combinations in between, to meet fluctuating demand over time. One pure strategy is to *level* the work force and the other is to *chase* demand with the work force. With a perfectly level strategy, the rate of regular-time output will be constant. Any variations in demand must then be absorbed by using inventories, overtime, part-time workers, subcontracting, cooperative arrangements, or any of the demand-influencing options. What has essentially been done with the level strategy is to fix the regular work force by using one of the above 10 variables available for aggregate planning.

With the pure chase strategy, the work-force level is changed to meet demand. In this case, it is not necessary to carry inventory or to use any of the other variables available for aggregate planning; the work force absorbs all the changes in demand.

Of course, these two strategies are extremes; one strategy makes no change in the work force and the other varies the work force directly with demand changes. In practice, many combinations are also possible, but the pure strategies help focus on the basic issues.

Consider, for example, the case of a brokerage firm which utilized both strategies. The data processing department maintained a capacity to process 17,000 transactions per day, far in excess of the average load of 12,000. This capacity allowed the department to keep a level work force of programmers, systems analysts, computer operators, and keypunchers, even though capacity exceeded demand on many days. Because of the skilled work force, the high capital investment, and the low marginal cost of additional capacity, it made sense for the data processing department to follow this strategy.

Meanwhile, in the cashiering department, a chase strategy was being followed. As the transaction level varied, part-time workers, hiring, and layoffs were used. This department was very labor-intensive, with a high personnel turnover and a low skill level. The manager of the department commented that the high turnover level

BOX 10.2   **COMPARISON OF CHASE VERSUS LEVEL STRATEGY**

	Chase demand	Level capacity
Level of labor skill required	Low	High
Job discretion	Low	High
Compensation rate	Low	High
Working conditions	Sweatshop	Pleasant
Training required per employee	Low	High
Labor turnover	High	Low
Hire-fire costs	High	Low
Error rate	High	Low
Amount of supervision required	High	Low
Type of budgeting and forecasting required	Short-run	Long-run

Source: W. Earl Sasser, "Match Supply and Demand in Service Industries," *Harvard Business Review*, November–December 1976, p. 135.

was an advantage, since it helped facilitate the reduction of work force in periods of low demand.

It can be seen from this situation that the characteristics of the operation seem to influence the type of strategy followed. Sasser (1976) has generalized this observation to the factors shown in Box 10.2. While the chase strategy may be more appropriate for low-skilled labor and routine jobs, the level strategy seems more appropriate for highly skilled labor and complex jobs.

These strategies, however, cannot be properly evaluated unless specific decision criteria are stated. One way to do this is to reduce all the most important criteria to cost, as described in the next section.

10.3 AGGREGATE PLANNING COSTS

Most aggregate planning methods determine a plan which minimizes costs. These methods assume that demand is fixed; therefore strategies for modifying demand are not considered. If both demand and supply were simultaneously modified, it would be more appropriate to maximize profit.

When demand is considered given, the following costs should be considered.

1. HIRING AND FIRING COSTS. The hiring cost consists of the recruiting, screening, and training costs required to bring a new employee up to full productive skill. For some jobs, this cost might be only a few hundred dollars; for more highly skilled jobs, it might range up to several thousand. The firing cost includes employee benefits, severance pay, and other costs associated with layoff. The firing cost may also range from a few hundred dollars to several thousand dollars per person. In some cases, where an entire shift is hired or fired at one time, a "shift" cost can be included.

2. OVERTIME AND UNDERTIME COSTS. The overtime costs often consist of regular wages plus 50 to 100 percent premium. The cost of undertime is often reflected by use of employees at less than full productivity.

3. **INVENTORY CARRYING COSTS.** Inventory carrying costs are associated with maintaining the product in inventory; they include the cost of capital, variable cost of storage, obsolescence, and deterioration. These costs are often expressed as a percentage of the dollar value of inventory, ranging from 15 to 35 percent per year. This cost can be thought of as an "interest" charge assessed against the dollar value of inventory held in stock. Thus, if the carrying cost is 20 percent and each unit costs $10 to produce, it will cost $2 to carry one unit in inventory for a year.

4. **SUBCONTRACTING COSTS.** The cost of subcontracting is the price that is paid to a subcontractor to produce the units. It is often more expensive to subcontract than to produce units in house.

5. **PART-TIME LABOR COSTS.** Because of differences in benefits, the cost of part-time labor will probably be less than that of regular labor. Although part-time workers often get no benefits, a maximum percentage of part-time labor may be specified by operational considerations or by union contract. Otherwise, there might be a tendency to use all part-time labor. However, the regular labor force is essential to the effective utilization of part-time personnel.

6. **COST OF STOCKOUT OR BACK ORDER.** The cost for taking a back order or for a stockout should reflect the effect of reduced customer service. This cost is extremely difficult to estimate, but it can be related to the loss of customer goodwill and the possible loss of future sales. Thus we may think of stockout or back-order costs in terms of foregone future profits.

Some or all of these costs may be present in any particular aggregate planning problem. The applicable costs will be used to "price out" alternative strategies. In the example below, only a few strategies will be priced out. In later mathematical models, a very large number of strategies will be considered.

10.4 EXAMPLE OF COSTING

The Hefty Beer Company is constructing an aggregate plan for the next 12 months. Although several types of beers are brewed at the Hefty plant and several container sizes are bottled, management has decided to use gallons of beer as the aggregate measure of capacity.

The demand for beer over the next 12 months is forecast to follow the pattern shown in Figure 10.2. Notice how this demand usually peaks in the summer months and is decidedly lower in the winter.

The management of the Hefty brewery would like to consider three aggregate plans:

1. *Level work force.* Use inventory to meet peak demands.

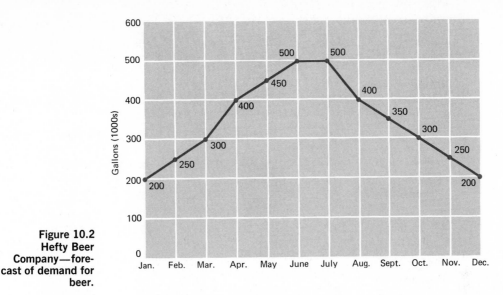

**Figure 10.2
Hefty Beer
Company—fore-
cast of demand for
beer.**

2. *Level work force plus overtime.* Use 20 percent overtime along with inventory as necessary in May, June, and July to meet peak demands.
3. *Chase strategy.* Hire and fire workers each month as necessary to meet demand.

To evaluate these strategies, management has collected the following cost and resource data:

1. Each worker can produce 2000 gallons of beer per month on regular time. On overtime, the same production rate is assumed; but overtime can be used for only 3 months during the year.
2. Each worker is paid $1500 per month on regular time. Overtime is paid at 150 percent of regular time. A maximum of 20 percent overtime can be used in any of the 3 months.
3. It costs $500 to hire a worker, including screening costs, paperwork, and training costs. It costs $200 to fire a worker, including all severance and benefit costs.
4. For inventory valuation purposes, beer costs $1 a gallon to produce. The cost of carrying inventory is assumed to be 2 percent a month (or 2 cents per gallon of beer per month).
5. Assume that the starting inventory is 300,000 gallons. The desired ending inventory, a year from now, is also 300,000 gallons. All forecast demand must be met; no stockouts are allowed.

The next task is to evaluate each of the three strategies in terms of the costs which have been given. The first step in this process is to construct charts like those shown in Tables 10.1 through 10.3, which show all the relevant costs: regular work force, hiring/firing, overtime, and inventory. Notice that subcontracting, part-time labor, and back ordering/stockouts have not been allowed as variables in this case.

TABLE 10.1   **AGGREGATE PLANNING COSTS—STRATEGY 1***

Level work force	Jan.	Feb.	Mar.	Apr.	May
Resources					
Regular workers	171	171	171	171	171
Overtime (percent)	—	—	—	—	—
Units produced	342	342	342	342	342
Sales forecast	200	250	300	400	450
Inventory (end of month)	442	534	576	518	410
Costs					
Regular time	$256.50	$256.50	$256.50	$256.50	$256.50
Overtime	—	—	—	—	—
Hire/fire	—	—	—	—	—
Inventory	8.84	10.68	11.52	10.36	8.20
Total cost	$265.34	$267.18	$268.02	$266.86	$264.70

* All costs are expressed in thousands of dollars. All production, inventory, and sales figures are in thousands of gallons. Starting inventory is 300,000 gallons in each case.

TABLE 10.2   **AGGREGATE PLANNING COSTS—STRATEGY 2***

Use of overtime	Jan.	Feb.	Mar.	Apr.	May
Resources					
Regular workers	163	163	163	163	163
Overtime (percent)					20
Units produced	326	326	326	326	391
Sales forecast	200	250	300	400	450
Inventory (end of month)	426	502	528	454	395
Costs					
Regular time	$244.50	$244.50	$244.50	$244.50	$244.50
Overtime					73.35
Hire/fire	—	—	—	—	—
Inventory	8.52	10.04	10.56	9.08	7.90
Total cost	$253.02	$254.54	$255.06	$253.58	$325.75

* All costs are expressed in thousands of dollars. All production, inventory, and sales figures are in thousands of gallons. Starting inventory is 300,000 gallons in each case.

TABLE 10.1 (*Continued*)

June	July	Aug.	Sept.	Oct.	Nov.	Dec.	Total
171	171	171	171	171	171	171	
—	—	—	—	—	—	—	
342	342	342	342	342	342	342	4104
500	500	400	350	300	250	200	4100
252	94	36	28	70	162	304	
$256.50	$256.50	$256.50	$256.50	$256.50	$256.50	$256.50	$3078.00
—	—	—	—	—	—	—	—
—	—	—	—	—	—	—	—
5.04	1.88	.72	.56	1.40	3.24	6.08	68.52
$261.54	$258.38	$257.22	$257.06	$257.90	$259.74	$262.58	$3146.52

TABLE 10.2 (*Continued*)

June	July	Aug.	Sept.	Oct.	Nov.	Dec.	Total
163	163	163	163	163	163	163	
20	20						
391	391	326	326	326	326	326	4107
500	500	400	350	300	250	200	4100
286	177	103	79	105	181	307	
$244.50	$244.50	$244.50	$244.50	$244.50	$244.50	$244.50	$2934.00
73.35	73.35						220.05
—	—	—	—	—	—	—	—
5.70	3.54	2.06	1.58	2.10	3.62	6.14	70.84
$323.55	$321.39	$246.56	$246.08	$246.60	$248.12	$250.64	$3224.89

TABLE 10.3   **AGGREGATE PLANNING COSTS—STRATEGY 3***

Chase demand	Jan.	Feb.	Mar.	Apr.	May
Resources					
Regular workers	100	125	150	200	225
Overtime (percent)	—	—	—	—	—
Units produced	200	250	300	400	450
Sales forecast	200	250	300	400	450
Inventory (end of month)	300	300	300	300	300
Costs					
Regular time	$150.00	$187.50	$225.00	$300.00	$337.50
Overtime	—	—	—	—	—
Hire/fire	—	12.50	12.50	25.00	12.50
Inventory	6.00	6.00	6.00	6.00	6.00
Total cost	$156.00	$206.00	$243.50	$331.00	$356.00

* All costs are expressed in thousands of dollars. All production, inventory, and sales figures are in thousands of gallons. Starting inventory is 300,000 gallons in each case.

In evaluating the first option, we must calculate the size of the work force required to meet the demand and inventory goals. Since ending and beginning inventories are assumed to be equal, the work force must be just large enough to meet total demand during the year. When the monthly demands from Figure 10.2 are added, the annual demand is 4,100,000 gallons. Since each worker can produce $2000(12) = 24,000$ gallons in a year, a level work force of $4,100,000/24,000 = 171$ workers is needed to meet the total demand. On the basis of this work-force figure, the inventories for each month and the resulting costs have been calculated in Table 10.1.

The second strategy is a bit more complicated, since some overtime can be used. If X is the work-force size for option 2, we must have:

$$9(2000X) + 3[(1.2)(2000X)] = 4,100,000$$

For 9 months we will produce at $2000X$ gallons per month and for 3 months we will produce at 120 percent of this rate including overtime. When the above equation is solved for X, we have $X = 163$ workers on regular time. In Table 10.2 we have once again calculated the inventories and resulting costs for this option.

The third option requires that the work force be varied in each month to meet the demand by hiring and firing workers. Straightforward calculations produce the number of workers and associated costs for each month. In this case, notice that a constant level of 300,000 units in inventory is maintained as the minimum inventory level.

The annual costs of each strategy are collected and summarized in Box 10.3.

TABLE 10.3 (*Continued*)

June	July	Aug.	Sept.	Oct.	Nov.	Dec.	Total
250	250	200	175	150	125	100	
—	—	—	—	—	—	—	
500	500	400	350	300	250	200	4100
500	500	400	350	300	250	200	4100
300	300	300	300	300	300	300	
$375.00	$375.00	$300.00	$262.50	$225.00	$187.50	$150.00	$3075.00
—	—	—	—	—	—	—	—
12.50	—	10.00	5.00	5.00	5.00	5.00	105.00
6.00	6.00	6.00	6.00	6.00	6.00	6.00	72.00
$393.50	$381.00	$316.00	$273.50	$236.00	$198.50	$161.00	$3252.00

Based on the assumptions used, strategy 1 is the least-cost strategy, but cost is not the only consideration. For example, alternative 1 has more flexibility to respond to higher demands since no overtime has been planned. Alternative 2, on the other hand, has less down-side risk, since planned overtime can be cancelled. If prospects for higher-than-forecast demand are good, alternative 1 may be preferred; if lower-than-forecast demand is more likely, alternative 2 may be preferred.

BOX 10.3   **COST SUMMARY**

	Annual cost
Strategy 1	
Regular-time payroll	$3,078,000
Inventory carrying	68,520
Total	$3,146,520
Strategy 2	
Regular-time payroll	$2,934,000
Overtime	220,050
Inventory carrying	70,840
Total	$3,224,890
Strategy 3	
Regular-time payroll	$3,075,000
Hire/fire	105,000
Inventory carrying	72,000
Total	$3,252,000

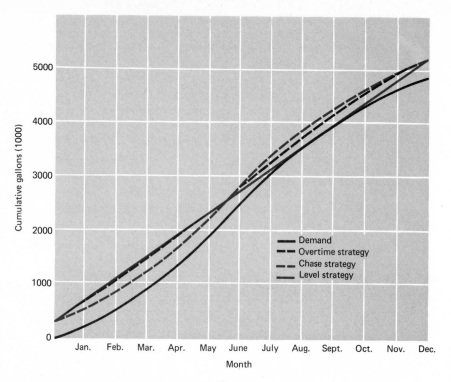

**Figure 10.3
Cumulative de-
mand and produc-
tion.**

In aggregate planning, it is sometimes useful to compare cumulative demand against cumulative production plus initial inventory, as shown in Figure 10.3. The difference between these curves will then be the inventory (or backlog) at any given time. The inventory buildup rates and inventory levels can be seen at a glance from these cumulative curves.

We have shown how to compare costs in a very simple case of aggregate planning for a few strategies. In Section 10.5, many other strategies and more complex cost structures will be considered by formulating the aggregate planning problem as a series of mathematical models.

10.5 MATHEMATICAL MODELS

A wide variety of aggregate planning models have been developed over the years. In this section the general model formulation will be described. This formulation will be followed by a discussion of linear decision rules and a survey of the entire range of modeling approaches available.

To formalize the aggregate planning problem, the following symbols will be used:

P_t = production level during period t, output in units
W_t = work-force level during period t, in number of workers

I_t = inventory at the end of period t, in units
F_t = demand forecast for period t, in units

Assume that demand forecasts are given for each period, F_1, F_2, . . . , F_T, over the future planning horizon T. Also assume the initial production level P_o, workforce level W_o, and inventory level I_o are given. The problem is to find the values of P_t and W_t which will meet management's objectives, usually assumed to be minimum cost, while meeting the given demand.

In using an aggregate planning model, only the values of P_1 and W_1 for the first period are implemented. Although the succeeding values of P_2, P_3, . . . , P_n and W_2, W_3, . . . , W_n are specified by the model, these subsequent values will not be implemented unless conditions remain exactly the same for the next period. The model is thus used sequentially, with decisions from only one period at a time being implemented.

In addition to providing the best decisions, aggregate planning models often provide decision rules which can be used to calculate optimal decisions in successive time periods. Typically two decision rules are provided, one for P_t and another for W_t. The cost parameters, initial values, and demand forecasts serve as input for these decision rules and are used to calculate P_t and W_t in any time period. We will illustrate several decision rules below by using P_t as an example.

One decision rule for P_t would be to simply let

$$P_t = F_t$$

In this case the production level would fluctuate with forecast demand. This is the chase rule which has been described previously.

Another decision rule for P_t would be to let

$$P_t = P_{t-1} + A(F_t - P_{t-1})$$

where A is a smoothing constant, $0 \leq A \leq 1$. This decision rule would smooth the value of P_t depending on the choice of A in a manner exactly analogous to exponential smoothing. If $A = 0$, we will have a level strategy, with no response to demand, and if $A = 1$, we will have the chase strategy. Thus a variety of smoothed responses can be obtained simply by choosing a value for A.

Perhaps the value of P_t should also be affected by inventory levels. In this case let

$$P_t = P_{t-1} + A(F_t - P_{t-1}) + B(I_n - I_{t-1})$$

where I_n = normal inventory level and B = smoothing constant, $0 \leq B \leq 1$. Here, P_t will be decreased if inventories are above the normal level; otherwise P_t will be increased. Again, the rate of response can be controlled by choosing B.

Finally, the decision rule can be enhanced by considering not only F_t but all future demand forecasts, F_{t+1}, F_{t+2}, etc. At this point, the decision rule will approximate rules derived from actual aggregate planning models. By adjusting the coefficients in these rules, one can achieve any desired response between a chase and a level strategy. A cost structure is needed, however, in order to choose the "best" rule; this will be described next.

10.6 LINEAR DECISION RULES

The aggregate planning problem was first formulated by Holt, Modigliani, and Simon in 1955. Their formulation utilized quadratic costs and resulted in the so-called linear decision rule (LDR), which was applied to a paint factory problem.

The LDR formulation assumed four types of costs:

1. **REGULAR PRODUCTION COSTS.** The cost of regular-time production in period t was assumed to be

$$C_1(t) = C_1 W_t$$

Notice that the cost of regular production was linearly related to the size of the work force, as shown in Figure 10.4a.

2. **HIRING AND FIRING COSTS.** The cost of increasing or decreasing the work force in period t was assumed to be

$$C_2(t) = C_2(W_t - W_{t-1})^2$$

Figure 10.4 Costs for linear decision rule. (*a*) Regular production cost. (*b*) Hiring and firing cost. (*c*) Cost of overtime. (*d*) Cost of inventories/back orders.

(Source: Charles C. Holt, Franco Modigliani, and Herbert Simon, "A Linear Decision Rule for Production and Employment Scheduling," Management Science, vol. 2, no. 1, October 1955.)

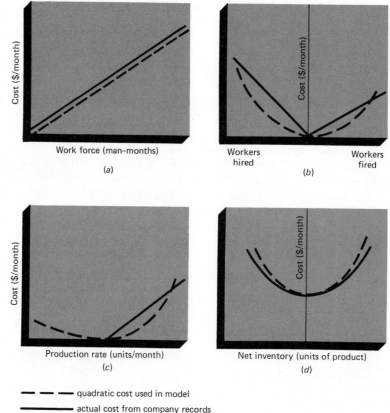

(a) Cost ($/month) — Work force (man-months)

(b) Cost ($/month) — Workers hired / Workers fired

(c) Cost ($/month) — Production rate (units/month)

(d) Cost ($/month) — Net inventory (units of product)

– – – quadratic cost used in model

——— actual cost from company records

The cost of changing the work force was a squared function of the amount of increase or decrease in the work force. This function was an approximation to the costs observed in the paint factory, as shown in Figure 10.4*b*. The quadratic form was chosen for mathematical convenience, as an approximation.

3. OVERTIME COSTS. The overtime cost was expressed as zero cost up to 100 percent utilization of the work force and then as a linear cost for overtime production beyond 100 percent. See Figure 10.4*c*. Through the use of quadratic functions, this overtime cost was approximated as follows:

$$C_3(t) = C_3(P_t - C_4 W_t)^2 + C_5 P_t - C_6 W_t$$

4. COST OF INVENTORIES AND BACK ORDERS. In the LDR formulation, back orders were treated as negative inventory. The following inventory/back-order cost function for the paint factory was used, also see Figure 10.4*d*.

$$C_4(t) = C_7(I_t - C_8 - C_9 F_t)^2$$

The total cost in each period was just the sum of the above four costs:

$$C(t) = C_1(t) + C_2(t) + C_3(t) + C_4(t)$$

and the cost over the planning horizon T was the sum of the period costs:

$$C = \sum_{t=1}^{T} C(t)$$

The LDR problem is to minimize the total cost C by choosing W_t and P_t for each period. These variables are connected from period to period by the inventory balance.

$$I_t = I_{t-1} + P_t - F_t$$

When I_t is substituted in the above cost equations, the resulting problem is an unconstrained minimization problem which can be solved by using calculus.

Since all cost functions are quadratic, the optimal solution to this problem is a linear decision rule for P_t and W_t. In general, these rules may be expressed in the following form:

$$P_t = A_0 F_t + A_1 F_{t+1} + \cdots + A_T F_{t+T} + b_1 W_{t-1} - d_1 I_{t-1} + e_1$$
$$W_t = A_0' F_t + A_1' F_{t+1} + \cdots + A_T' F_{t+T} + b_1' W_{t-1} - d_1' I_{t-1} + e_1'$$

where A_i, A_i', b_1, b_1', d_1, d_1', and e_1, e_1' are constants. As may be noted, the two decision rules have exactly the same form, only the coefficients vary in magnitude. Each of these rules is linear in the variables F_t, W_t, and I_t; hence the name "linear decision rule."

In the paint factory, several interesting results were observed. The production level was greatly affected by the sales forecast for the next 3 months; the remaining 9 months had little effect. The work-force level was much less affected by short-term sales forecasts; instead, it depended on the entire 12-month forecast. Thus short-range changes in demand were absorbed by changing the production rate, while long-range changes were absorbed by work-force changes. These rules, therefore, had a great deal of intuitive appeal.

The advantage of the LDR formulation is its simplicity and ease of use. There are, however, several disadvantages.

1. The LDR is restricted to the use of quadratic cost approximations. More general cost forms cannot be used.
2. The LDR reacts gradually to changed forecasts, hiring or firing a few people each month. Management sometimes prefers to hold off changes in the work force and then, when changes are required, to make them in larger increments.
3. Since no limitations are placed on the variables, a negative work force could be employed, or inventory could be carried beyond warehouse capacity. This result, however, is remote when the decision rules are used in their normal range.

Despite these limitations the LDR has considerable historical value and continues to be used as a benchmark for comparison with other methods.

10.7 SURVEY OF METHODS

Since 1955, the aggregate planning problem has been a rich source of research aimed at removing restrictions in the LDR formulation. To provide a historical perspective, eight of the methods will be summarized in the order of their development. The purpose of these summaries is not to concentrate on the details of any particular method but to provide an appreciation for the wide variety of possible approaches. More complete surveys are given by Silver (1967) and Eilon (1975).

1. TRANSPORTATION METHOD. In 1956 Bowman suggested that the transportation method be used to solve a special case of the aggregate planning problem. In his formulation, the rows represented the available supply of regular time, overtime, and subcontracting in each month. The columns represented the demand required. Production could be scheduled in a current month to satisfy demand in a later month by carrying the production in inventory. Although the problem was easy to solve through the transportation method, it did not include hiring or firing costs or back-order costs. The lack of these costs could result in indiscriminate hiring and firing, which is unrealistic in practice.

2. LINEAR PROGRAMMING. In 1960 Haussmann and Hess formulated the aggregate planning problem in a linear programming format. The problem is similar in every aspect to the LDR except that linear costs are used in place of quadratic costs. This formulation also allowed the use of constraints, such as a maximum amount of overtime and inventory and it allowed the use of the powerful simplex method for solution and sensitivity analysis. The major restriction is the requirement that linear or piecewise linear costs be used. Nevertheless, this approach relieves the restrictions of the transportation method, and it will yield better results than the LDR when the costs are approximately linear. See the Supplement to this chapter for details.

3. MANAGEMENT COEFFICIENTS. In 1963 E. H. Bowman suggested that past management behavior be used to determine the appropriate coefficients of the production-level and work-force decision rules. This was quite a departure from previous thinking, which utilized costs to set the value of these coefficients. Bowman's logic was based on the assumption that management makes good decisions but could perhaps make them more consistent by using a mathematical decision rule. His rule has been criticized by Eilon (1975) and others for being second-order in nature and self-defeating, since a good rule is obtained only when management decisions *have* been consistent, and this is exactly the case where the rule is not needed. Because of these difficulties, all other formulations have continued to use cost, profit, or multiple objectives—rather than past management performance.

4. SIMULATION. Vergin (1966) supplied an example of how simulation can be used to select parameters for aggregate planning decision rules. Through the use of simulation, any desired cost structure or other objectives can be evaluated. A disadvantage is that only a limited number of rules can be evaluated, since each rule requires a separate simulation run. A heuristic search method can be used, however, to provide a systematic basis for selecting alternate runs. Historically the use of simulation represents a step away from the highly restrictive linear and quadratic cost formulations of previous methods. The simulation method should be considered when complex cost structures are required.

5. PARAMETRIC PRODUCTION PLANNING. This method was developed by Jones in 1967, also to allow more general cost functions to be used. In it, the two LDR rules are generalized by the introduction of two smoothing parameters in each rule. The method utilizes a grid search over the four-dimensional parameter space to choose the parameter values which minimize costs. The resulting rules work quite well when tested against the LDR or linear programming methods.

6. SEARCH DECISION RULE (SDR). In 1968 Taubert introduced his SDR method to find the best rule for generalized cost structures. This method represents a refinement of previous formulations in that any desired cost function and decision rules can be used. The resulting cost function is minimized by using the Hookes-Jeeves pattern-search method. This method establishes a search procedure based on past patterns of step size and direction which have reduced the cost function. Through successive steps, the procedure can arrive at an approximate local minimum of the cost function. Taubert used the procedure to evaluate decision rules with 20 variables and obtained very good results in a reasonable amount of computer time (less than 20 seconds).

7. GOAL PROGRAMMING. Lee and Moore (1974) suggested a goal-programming formulation for aggregate planning. In this formulation, multiple goals such as the following are specified in priority order:

P_1 = operate within the limits of productive capacity
P_2 = meet the contracted delivery schedule
P_3 = operate at a minimum level of 80 percent of regular-time capacity
P_4 = keep inventory to a maximum of three units
P_5 = minimize total production and inventory costs
P_6 = hold overtime production to a minimum

The solution procedure seeks satisfaction of these goals, starting with P_1 and proceeding to P_2, P_3, etc. Through the use of this approach, tradeoffs can be made between the goals of capacity, delivery schedule, stable work force, production, inventory, and overtime cost. This makes it possible to consider a framework that is broader than the simple cost structures of the past.

8. PRODUCTION-SWITCHING HEURISTIC. About the time that some authors thought that all methods had been exhausted, Mellichamp and Love (1978) developed the production-switching heuristic. Their method is based on the observation that managers seem to favor one large change in work force over a series of smaller and more frequent changes. Accordingly, a three-level—low, medium, and high—production (and work-force) rule was formulated. Production is switched from one level to another depending on the level of inventory and sales forecasts. The production-switching points are based on minimization of any given cost function through the use of a search procedure. The advantage of this method is that fluctuations in period-to-period production are held to a minimim.

10.8 AGGREGATE PLANNING APPLICATION

To illustrate the use of the above methods, an application of aggregate planning will be reviewed. The application was done by Taubert (1968) in a research laboratory which employed approximately three hundred scientists and a hundred support employees. Research for both company projects and outside government contracts was done. However, there was considerable fluctuation in the load on the laboratory due to the changing nature of government contracts.

The aggregate planning problem was to determine each month the size of the scientific and support staffs as well as an allocation of the scientific staff to government contracts, company research programs, and overhead. The purpose of the overhead allocation was to retain scientists temporarily until future work developed. The aggregate planning problem was therefore formulated in terms of the following four variables for each month of a 6-month planning horizon:

1. Staff allocated to government contracts
2. Staff allocated to corporate research programs
3. Staff allocated to overhead
4. Size of support staff

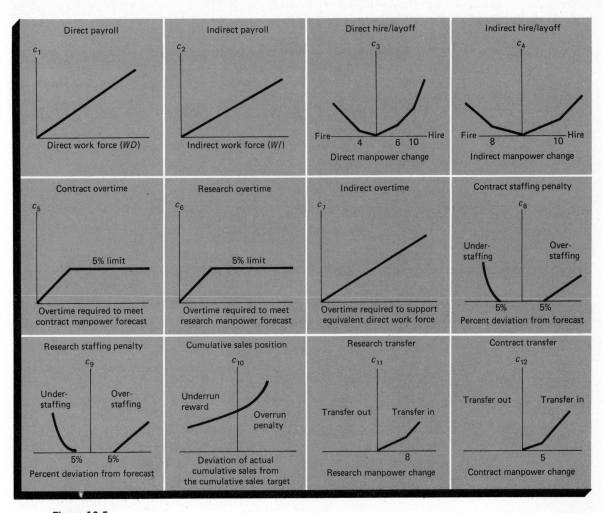

**Figure 10.5
Search laboratory
cost model.**
*(Source: W. H.
Taubert, "The
Search Decision Rule
Approach to Operations
Planning," Ph.D. disser-
tation, University of
California at Los
Angeles, 1968.)*

Taubert formulated the cost structure of this laboratory in terms of the 12 cost functions, shown in Figure 10.5. These cost functions included linear, piecewise linear, and nonlinear costs. The objective was to choose the 24 variables which would minimize the overall cost. The minimization was achieved by using the search methodology described above.

Taubert validated the model over a 5-year period. When compared to management decisions, the model's results showed fewer fluctuations in the work-force level from month to month. More importantly, the analysis indicated that costs could have been reduced by 12 percent through use of the model.

It should be noted that Taubert's search model is very similar to the manufacturing problem except that it has no inventory and it uses multiple manpower categories. It is interesting that four types of staff were used instead of one overall aggregate manpower category. This example illustrates the need to tailor a model to the specific decision problems faced by management.

10.9 EVALUATION OF AGGREGATE PLANNING

Now that a large number of methods have been reviewed, what can be said about these methods and their use in business? First, it should be observed that most of the methods incorporate the concept of a decision rule. This concept is fundamental to aggregate planning and should be clearly understood.

Second, there has been a tendency over time for the methods to become more powerful in handling general cost structures. While the early methods were restricted to quadratic and linear costs, more recent methods can handle any desired cost function. The more recent methods have also been designed to handle multiple criteria through goal programming or simulation methods.

Finally, there have been changes in decision rules. While the early rules were strictly of a smoothing nature, more general decision rules are now possible. Examples of the more general rules are the parametric production-planning formulation and the production-switching heuristic.

Although there has been a vigorous development of methods, there have been only a few studies of how well these methods perform in practice. One study of note is the original LDR paint factory study, which showed a possible cost reduction of 8.5 percent. Twenty years later, however, Schwarz and Johnson (1978) showed that much of this reduction was attributable to aggregate inventory policy, not detailed aggregate planning rules.

In three companies, Bowman (1963) showed that the LDR could have reduced costs by 1.5 to 3.3 percent over management performance. Lee and Khumawala (1974) report on a study comparing several decision rules with management practice in a job shop. The results, shown in Table 10.4, indicate that profits could have been improved 13.6 percent by the best decision rule. This was an impressive saving of over $600,000 per year.

Although there is good evidence that aggregate planning methodologies can improve profits or reduce costs in practice, the implementation record has been poor. An *ongoing* use of aggregate planning methods is rarely reported in the literature. Even in the original paint company, only a part of the LDR was implemented. In most other cases, the company was used as an example of what could have been done, not what actually was done over a period of time. Why has this occurred with a methodology which is rather well developed and apparently has the potential to

TABLE 10.4   **COMPARATIVE PROFIT PERFORMANCE**

	Imperfect forecast	Perfect forecast
Company decisions	$4,420,000	—
Linear decision rules	4,821,000	$5,078,000
Management coefficients model	4,607,000	5,000,000
Parametric production planning	4,900,000	4,989,000
Search decision rule	5,021,000	5,140,000

Source: W. B. Lee and B. M. Khumawala, "Simulation Testing of Aggregate Production Planning Models in an Implementation Methodology," *Management Science,* vol. 20, February 1974, p. 906.

improve profits substantially? Shouldn't management be anxious to adopt these methods?

A study done by Shearon (1974) helps to shed some light on these questions. [Also see Colley, Landel, and Fair (1977), chapters 7 and 8.] In his survey of aggregate planning in industry, Shearon surveyed 100 companies from which he received 48 replies. These companies were all included in the Fortune 500 listing of the largest industrial companies in the United States.

The results of Shearon's survey indicate that production managers are typically responsible for aggregate planning decisions but general managers often review and approve large changes in inventories or work force. The study also indicates that the aggregate decisions are fragmented, with marketing controlling variables which influence demand and operations controlling supply variables. There is little coordination between marketing and operations strategies.

Of the 48 firms surveyed, 42 indicated that they preferred to maintain a level work force whether demand was fluctuating, seasonal, or uncertain. This preference seemed to be influenced by continuing efforts from labor unions to make labor a fixed cost. In half the cases, the unionized firms were required to pay supplemental unemployment benefits. These benefits ranged up to 90 percent of take-home pay for up to 26 weeks while a worker was on layoff, making layoff and rehire very expensive propositions.

Operations managers were also asked how they were evaluated on job performance. Meeting schedules was clearly the most important criterion, followed in order of importance by controlling direct costs, controlling indirect costs, inventory turnover, and labor relations. These criteria seemed to help explain the types of aggregate decisions which were made. In periods of increasing demand, operations managers added overtime first, followed by increases in the work force. The typical manager will use up to 8 hours overtime per week for 12 weeks before adding employees. Reductions in inventories or increased back orders are clearly secondary options when demand increases. On the other hand, when demand decreases, inventories are allowed to increase and layoffs in labor are considered only as a last resort. This behavior can perhaps be explained by the greater emphasis on schedule than on costs or inventory turnover.

It is interesting to note that management behavior on the up side of demand is different than on the down side. It is also interesting to observe the fragmented nature of aggregate decisions with multiple criteria rather than a single criterion such as cost.

Vollmann (1973) also sheds some light on aggregate planning in industry by his study of a furniture manufacturer. In this case Vollmann was part of a research team which developed an aggregate planning model similar to the Search model. Although management was very pleased with the results, they were not inclined to use the model. It appeared to management that other short-range scheduling problems were more pressing. To gain user support, the research team then shelved the aggregate planning model and proceeded to develop a computerized scheduling system. After some time, this scheduling system was successfully implemented.

Upon returning to the aggregate planning problem, Vollmann and his associates discovered that the managers still did not want to use the original model. The company did not really do aggregate planning in the classical sense. First of all, planning was done by several major product groups, since these groups were produced on separate assembly lines. Planning was not done by one overall measure of aggregate capacity. Second, management did not think that all their objectives could be combined into a single cost objective; they felt, instead, that the objectives should be treated separately. As a result, the research group developed a simulation model which was tailor-made for the problem faced by management.

The model projected inventories and back orders into the future for 36 months by each product line, using demand forecasts and current work-force, overtime, and subcontracting levels. The model permitted management to evaluate suggested changes in capacity variables in terms of their effect on projected inventory and back-order levels, and the model was programmed for computer time sharing so that the user could easily manipulate the variables and receive the results. Management found this model useful because it clearly addressed the decisions they had to make.

In summary, these studies seem to indicate some guidelines for using aggregate planning in industry:

1. Management may not perceive the existence of an aggregate planning problem. The decisions on work force and inventories may be made on a reactive week-by-week basis through scheduling. If this is the case, management will need to establish an aggregate planning function and assign the responsibility to some manager before quantitative techniques will be useful.

2. Management may not understand the value of a quantitative approach. In Vollmann's case study, the lack of familiarity with quantitative approaches required solution of the scheduling problem before the more general aggregate planning problem was attacked. Vollmann argues that modeling efforts must be oriented toward user problems if implementation is to succeed.

3. Aggregate planning models should be tailor-made for the particular situation. It may be necessary to include more than one aggregate product type in the model, or to consider product allocation decisions between plants, or to work with multiple objectives—not only costs. The management problem should always be considered carefully first and alternate formulations should be explored, rather than force-fitting a particular model to the situation.

4. In some companies, aggregate planning is highly constrained by a policy such as maintenance of a level work force. In some cases, the aggregate planning problem might be viewed as a one-time policy-evaluation effort rather than an ongoing model for making monthly decisions.

5. Before a company accepts an aggregate planning approach, the model's capacity to provide better decisions should be demonstrated. This can often be done by comparing past management performance with the results which could have been achieved by the model. If the results are not improved, a better model should be built or the present methods continued in use.

It should be possible to improve aggregate planning practice in many companies. The potential improvement has been shown in a few cases. A vast array of standard techniques have been developed. The opportunity and challenge is to demonstrate that practice can, in fact, be broadly improved.

10.10 KEY POINTS

Aggregate planning serves as a link between facilities decisions and scheduling. The aggregate planning decision sets overall output levels for the medium time range. As a result, decisions regarding aggregate inventory levels, work-force size, subcontracting, and back-order levels are also made. These decisions must fit within the level of facilities available, and they constrain the resources which will be available for scheduling.

The following key points are made in the chapter:

- Aggregate planning is concerned with matching supply and demand over the medium time range. In the aggregate planning problem, the overall output level is planned so as to use the best possible mix of resource inputs.
- Supply variables which may be changed by aggregate planning are hiring, firing, overtime, idle time, inventory, subcontracting, part-time labor, and cooperative arrangements. Variables which are available to influence demand are pricing, promotion, backlog or reservations, and complementary products.
- When demand is given, two pure strategies are available for adjusting supply: the chase strategy and the level strategy. There are also many mixed strategies between these two extremes. A choice of strategy can be made by determining the total cost of each of the strategies available.
- Many models for aggregate planning have been proposed. The first model to be developed was the linear decision rule, which minimized a quadratic cost function by using two decision rules: one for work force and the other for production level. Since then, the new models have generalized the cost structures which can be used and have included various other types of decision rules.
- Despite the number of models available and the favorable results in a few cases, aggregate planning models have not gained widespread acceptance in industry. A more concerted implementation effort may be needed which includes careful definition of the decision problem in each case, tailor-made models, and demonstration of improved planning results.

QUESTIONS

1. A definition of aggregate planning by another author is given here. Contrast and compare this definition to the one given in the text. "*Aggregate* planning or scheduling refers to planning in general terms—considering product groups, special promotions, trends in workforce availability, changes in resource suppliers, etc. The objective of aggregate planning is to effectively allocate system capacity—men, materials, and equipment—over

some time horizon." (Richard B. Chase and N. J. Aquilano, *Production and Operations Management,* rev. ed., Homewood, Ill.: Irwin, 1977, p. 227.)

2. Aggregate planning is sometimes confused with scheduling. What is the difference?

3. The XYZ Company manufactures a seasonal product. At the present time, they use a level labor force as a matter of company policy. The company is afraid that, if they lay off workers, they will not be able to rehire them or to find qualified replacements. Does this company have an aggregate planning problem? Discuss.

4. It has been said that aggregate planning is related to personnel planning, budgeting, and market planning. Describe the nature of the relationship between these types of planning.

5. Every company has multiple objectives such as good labor relations, low operations costs, high inventory turnover, and good customer service. What are the pros and cons of treating these objectives separately in an aggregate planning problem versus combining them all into a single measure of cost?

6. How is the choice between a level strategy and a chase strategy influenced by the skill level of the work force and the degree of automation? After all, isn't the choice between these strategies just a matter of the lowest cost?

7. What factors are important in choosing the length of the planning horizon for aggregate planning?

8. What are the cost factors that should be included in calculating the total cost of an aggregate strategy?

9. Provide a definition of a decision rule. Is a decision rule always required in an aggregate planning model?

10. What assumptions are used in deriving the LDR model?

11. What are the advantages and disadvantages of the following aggregate planning methods?
    a. Linear decision rule (LDR)
    b. Transportation method
    c. Linear programming
    d. Management coefficients
    e. Simulation
    f. Parametric production planning
    g. Search decision rule (SDR)
    h. Goal programming
    i. Production-switching heuristic

12. What problems are being experienced in using aggregate planning in industry? How can these problems be overcome?

13. A barbershop has been using a level work force of barbers 5 days a week, Tuesday through Saturday. The barbers have considerable idle time on Tuesday through Friday, with certain peak periods during the noon hours and after 4 p.m. each day. On Friday afternoon and all day Saturday, all the barbers are very busy, with customers waiting a substantial amount of time and some customers being turned away. What options should this barbershop consider for aggregate planning? How would you analyze these options? What data would be collected and how would the options be compared?

PROBLEMS

1. The Zoro Company manufactures fast-cutting lawn mowers. The company has devised the following decision rules based on the LDR methodology:

$$P_t = 1.5F_t + .9W_{t-1} - .4I_{t-1}$$

$$W_t = .8W_{t-1} + .2F_t - .1I_{t-1} + 3$$

If, at the present time, Zoro has 100 workers and an inventory of 1000 units, what will be the production and work-force levels for the next 3 months with forecast sales of 800, 1000, and 1200 units?

2. The Chewy Candy Company would like to determine an aggregate production plan for the next 6 months. The company makes many different types of candy but feels it can plan its

total production in pounds provided the mix of candy sold does not change too drastically. At the present time, the Chewy Company has 50 workers and 10,000 pounds of candy in inventory. Each worker can produce 100 pounds of candy a month and is paid $5 an hour (use 160 hours regular time per month). Overtime, at a pay rate of 150 percent of regular time, can be used up to a maximum of 20 percent in addition to regular time in any given month. It costs 50 cents to store a pound of candy for a year, $200 to hire a worker, and $500 to fire a worker. The forecast sales for the next six months are 8000, 10,000, 12,000, 8000, 6000, and 5000 pounds of candy.

    a. Determine the costs of a level production strategy for the next 6 months, with an ending inventory of 10,000 pounds.

    b. Determine the costs of a chase strategy for the next 6 months.

    c. Calculate the cost of using the maximum overtime for the 2 months of highest demand.

    *d. Formulate this as a linear programming problem.

3. Draw a cumulative graph of demand and of the three production strategies given in Problem 2.

4. A company produces to a seasonal demand, with the forecast for the next 12 months as given below. The present labor force can produce 500 units per month. Each employee added can produce an additional 20 units per month and is paid $1000 per month. The cost of materials is $20 per unit. Overtime can be used at the usual premium of time and a half for labor up to a maximum of 10 percent per month. Inventory carrying cost is $50 per unit per year. Changes in production level cost $2000 per additional 20 units due to hiring, firing, line changeover costs, etc. Assume 100 units of initial inventory. Extra capacity may be obtained by subcontracting at an additional cost of $15 per unit over and above producing them yourself on regular time. What plan do you recommend? What is the incremental cost of this plan?

Month	J	F	M	A	M	J	Jy	A	S	O	N	D
Demand	600	700	800	700	600	500	600	700	800	900	700	600

5. Approximately 40 percent of a medical clinic's weekly incoming calls for doctor's appointments occur on Monday. Due to this large workload, 30 percent of the callers receive a busy signal and have to call back later. The clinic now has one clerk for each two doctors to handle incoming calls. Each clerk handles calls for the same doctors all week long and thus is familiar with the doctors' hours, scheduling practices, and idiosyncrasies. Consider the following alternatives to solve this problem:

- Continue the present system, which results in some customer inconvenience, loss of business, and perceived poor service. About 1000 patients attempt to call the clinic on Mondays. The clinic has 50,000 patients in all.
- Expand the phone lines and add more people to handle the peak load. Estimated cost to add five more lines and five clerks is $50,000 per year.
- Install a computer to speed up appointments. In this case, the peak load could be handled with present personnel. Estimated cost to lease and maintain the equipment and programs is $25,000 per year.
- Expand the phone lines and ask people to call back later in the week for an appointment. Add five lines and five phone-answering clerks part time at $30,000 per year.

    a. Analyze these options from the standpoint of an aggregate planning problem. What are the pros and cons of each option?

    b. Which option do you recommend? Why?

    c. How does this problem differ fom the other aggregate planning problems given above?

6. The Restwell Motel in Orlando, Florida, would like to prepare an aggregate plan for the next year. The motel has a maximum of 200 rooms which are fully utilized in the winter months

* Advanced problem skills are required.

but largely vacant in the summer, as shown by the forecast below. The motel requires one employee, paid $600 per month, for each 20 rooms rented on regular time. It can utilize up to 20 percent overtime at time and a half and can also hire part-time workers at $700 per month. The regular-time workers are hired at a cost of $500 and fired at a cost of $200 per worker. There is no hiring and firing cost for the part-time workers.

Month	J	F	M	A	M	J	Jy	A	S	O	N	D
Demand (rooms)	185	190	170	160	120	100	100	80	100	120	140	160

a. With a regular work force of six employees and 20 percent overtime when needed, how many part-time workers are required in each month and how much does this strategy cost per year?

b. What is the best strategy to follow if a level work force of six regular workers is used? You may use various amounts of overtime and part-time workers.

*c. Formulate this as a linear programming problem.

SELECTED BIBLIOGRAPHY

ABERNATHY, WILLIAM J., et al.: "A Three-Stage Manpower Planning and Scheduling Model—A Service Sector Example," *Operations Research,* vol. 21, May–June 1973, pp. 693–711.

BOWMAN, E. H.: "Consistency and Optimality in Managerial Decision Making," *Management Science,* vol. 9, January 1963, pp. 310–321.

———: "Production Scheduling by the Transportation Method of Linear Programming," *Operations Research,* vol. 4, February 1956, pp. 100–103.

BUFFA, ELWOOD S.: *Modern Production Management,* 5th ed., New York: Wiley, 1977.

COLLEY, JOHN L., JR., ROBERT LANDEL, and ROBERT R. FAIR: *Production Operations Planning & Control,* San Francisco: Holden-Day, 1977.

EILON, SAMUEL: "Five Approaches to Aggregate Production Planning," *AIIE Transactions,* vol. 7, no. 2, June 1975, pp. 118–131.

FULLER, JACK A.: "A Linear Programming Approach to Aggregate Scheduling," *Academy of Management Journal,* vol. 18, no. 1, 1975, pp. 129–137.

GALBRAITH, JAY R.: "Solving Production Smoothing Problems," *Management Science,* vol. 15, no. 12, August 1969, pp. B665–B673.

HAUSSMANN, F., and S. W. HESS: "A Linear Programming Approach to Production and Employment Scheduling," *Management Technology,* vol. 1, January 1960, pp. 46–52.

HOLT, C., et al: *Planning Production Inventories and Work Force,* Englewood Cliffs, N.J.: Prentice-Hall, 1960.

———, FRANCO MODIGLIANI, and HERBERT SIMON: "A Linear Decision Rule for Production and Employment Scheduling," *Management Science,* vol. 2, no. 1, October 1955, pp. 1–30.

JONES, CURTIS H.: "Parametric Production Planning," *Management Science,* vol. 13, no. 11, July 1967, pp. 843–866.

KRAJEWSKI, L. J., and H. E. THOMPSON: "Efficient Employment Planning in Public Utilities," *The Bell Journal of Economics and Management Science,* Spring 1975.

LEE, S. M.: "An Aggregative Resource Allocation Model for Hospital Administration," *Socio-Economic Planning Sciences,* vol. 7, 1973, pp. 381–395.

———and L. J. MOORE: "A Practice Approach to Production Scheduling," *Production and Inventory Management,* 1st quarter, 1974, pp. 79–92.

LEE, W. B., and B. M. KHUMAWALA: "Simulation Testing of Aggregate Production Planning Models in an Implementation Methodology," *Management Science,* vol. 20, February 1974, pp. 903–911.

MELLICHAMP, JOSEPH, and ROBERT LOVE: "Production Heuristics for the Aggregate Planning Problem," *Management Science,* vol. 24, no. 12, August 1978, pp. 1242–1251.

SASSER, W. EARL: "Match Supply and Demand in Service Industries," *Harvard Business Review*, November–December 1976, pp. 133–140.

SCHROEDER, ROGER G.: "Resource Planning in University Management by Goal Programming," *Operations Research,* vol. 22, July–August 1974, pp. 700–710.

SCHWARZ, LEROY B., and ROBERT E. JOHNSON: "An Appraisal of the Empirical Performance of the Linear Decision Rule for Aggregate Planning," *Management Science,* vol. 24, no. 8, April 1978, pp. 844–849.

SHEARON, WINSTON T.: "A Study of the Aggregate Planning Production Problem," Ph.D. dissertation, the Colgate Darden Graduate School of Business Administration, University of Virginia, 1974.

SILVER, EDWARD A.: "A Tutorial on Production Smoothing and Work Force Balancing," *Operations Research,* November–December 1967, pp. 985–1011.

TAUBERT, W. H.: "A Search Decision Rule for the Aggregate Scheduling Problem," *Management Science,* vol. 14, no. 6, February 1968, pp. B343–B359.

———: "The Search Decision Rule Approach to Operations Planning," Ph.D. dissertation, University of California at Los Angeles, 1968.

VERGIN, R. C.: "Production Scheduling under Seasonal Demand," *Journal of Industrial Engineering,* vol. 17, May 1966,

VOLLMANN, THOMAS E.: "Capacity Planning: The Missing Link," *Production and Inventory Management,* 1st quarter, 1973, pp. 61–73.

SUPPLEMENT: LINEAR PROGRAMMING FORMULATION

One of the most useful methods for aggregate planning is the linear programming model. In this supplement the L.P. model is described in detail, along with the underlying assumptions and conditions.

In brief, the L.P. formulation for aggregate planning finds the minimum-cost strategy which meets the given demand forecast for n future periods. In each period the level of regular production, overtime production, and subcontracting are specified by the L.P. solution in order to minimize total costs. We assume that back orders and stockouts are not permitted, although the formulation could be modified to relieve this assumption.

The variables in the L.P. formulation are as follows:

R_t = production on regular time in period t (units)

O_t = production on overtime in period t (units)

S_t = units subcontracted in period t (units)

I_t = inventory at the end of period t (units)

H_t = units of regular production added during period t (hiring)

F_t = units of regular production subtracted during period t (firing)

For purposes of the L.P. formulation, the following constants are assumed given:

d_t = demand during period t (units)

M = maximum regular time capacity in any period (units)

N = maximum overtime capacity as a proportion of regular production time

L = maximum subcontracted capacity in any period (units)

a = cost per unit produced on regular time ($/unit)

b = cost per unit produced on overtime ($/unit)

c = cost per unit subcontracted ($/unit)

g = cost per unit held in inventory per period ($/unit/period)

h = cost of adding one unit of production ($/unit)

f = cost of subtracting one unit of production ($/unit)

Of course, any of the above constants could be made a function of time t if so desired.

The constraints which must be met are:

$$I_t = I_{t-1} + R_t + O_t + S_t - d_t$$
$$t = 1, \ldots, n$$

This is an inventory balance constraint. The inventory at the end of period t is equal to the inventory at the end of the previous period, $t - 1$, plus the production ($R_t + O_t + S_t$) minus the demand. We assume the starting inventory I_0 is given.

Another set of constraints which must be met is:

$$R_t = R_{t-1} + H_t - F_t \qquad t = 1, \ldots, n$$

These constraints relate the regular work-force levels to the hiring and firing variables. The L.P. solution automatically guarantees that H_t and F_t will not both be positive in the same period at optimality. This ensures that people will not be simultaneously hired and fired in the same period. We assume the starting value R_0 is given.

We also specify upper bounds on each of the production variables:

$$R_t \leq M \qquad t = 1, \ldots, n$$
$$O_t \leq NR_t \qquad t = 1, \ldots, n$$
$$S_t \leq L \qquad t = 1, \ldots, n$$

Finally, we require nonnegative variables:

$$R_t, O_t, S_t, I_t, H_t, F_t \geq 0$$

The objective function in the L.P. problem is to minimize the sum of the following costs:

$$\text{Min} \sum_{t=1}^{n} aR_t + bO_t + cS_t + gI_t + hH_t + fF_t$$

The L.P. objective function includes the costs of the various types of production (regular time, overtime, and subcontracting), the costs of holding inventory, and the costs of hiring and firing. Notice that the L.P. formulation utilizes a linear-cost structure, since the costs are a linear function of the corresponding levels of activity.

The L.P. formulation provides a powerful solution methodology when the assumptions of the problem are met. All possible strategies, including the chase and the level strategy, are examined by the L.P. model. The model finds the resulting strategy in terms of R_t, O_t, and S_t, which minimizes the total cost.

CHAPTER 11
SCHEDULING OPERATIONS

Scheduling decisions allocate available capacity or resources (equipment, labor, and space) to jobs, activities, tasks, or customers. Since scheduling is an allocation decision, it uses the resources made available by facilities decisions and aggregate planning. Therefore scheduling is the last and most constrained decision in the hierarchy of capacity planning decisions.

In practice, scheduling results in a time-phased plan (or schedule) of activities. The schedule indicates what is to be done, when, by whom, and with what equipment.

Scheduling should be clearly differentiated from aggregate planning. The purpose of scheduling is to ensure that available capacity is efficiently and effectively used to achieve the organization's objectives. The purpose of aggregate planning is to determine the resources (labor, equipment, and space) that should be acquired for scheduling. As these resources are acquired, certain estimates of costs, demand, and desired service levels will be made. When the resulting resources have become fixed and demand is either known or more accurately forecasted, scheduling is used to allocate the resources in the best manner possible. Therefore a distinction should be

BOX 11.1	**TYPICAL DECISION PROBLEM**

Dr. Jerome Preston, Chief of Surgery for the Crestview Hospital, faced a continual problem in scheduling the 12 operating rooms in the hospital. Sometimes all the operating rooms were busy and patients were waiting to get in; at other times all or almost all the rooms were empty. The problem was compounded by the need to reserve a certain part of the schedule for emergency operations, the difficulty of predicting how long any given operation would take, and the preferences of doctors to work only certain hours. For the doctors' convenience, it was common practice to schedule most surgery in the morning and to have the operating rooms empty during much of the afternoon.

Faced with this problem, Dr. Preston met with Sally Ames, his assistant in charge of operating room scheduling. "Sally, isn't there something we can do to improve the scheduling of operating rooms? It seems to be either feast or famine. How can the work load be predicted or leveled to achieve better utilization of the operating rooms? If this isn't done, it's possible that we'll have to add more operating rooms in the near future."

Sally proposed that several measures be taken. First, she suggested that a committee of surgeons be formed to study the situation and suggest changes in scheduling practices. She would act as a staff assistant to the committee. The committee would be shown utilization figures for the operating rooms by time of day, day of the week, and month of the year. Suggestions for changes in scheduling practice would then be taken from the committee members and evaluated by Sally as to their potential impact on operating room utilization. To do this, Sally would simulate the use of the suggested rules and practices. After reviewing the results of the simulations, the committee would suggest changes to Dr. Preston, who would then decide on actions to be taken. Dr. Preston agreed to form the committee to begin work on the problem.

made between acquiring resources through aggregate planning and allocating available resources through scheduling.

Scheduling seeks to achieve several conflicting objectives: high efficiency, low inventories, and good customer service. Efficiency is achieved by a schedule which mantains high utilization of labor, equipment, and space. Of course, the schedule should also seek to maintain low inventories, which—unfortunately—may lead to low efficiency due to lack of available material or high setup times. Thus a tradeoff decision in scheduling between efficiency and inventory levels is required. Customer service can be measured by the speed with which customer demands are met, either through available stock or short lead times. Fast customer service is in conflict, too, with low inventories and high efficiency. The primary aim of scheduling is, therefore, to make tradeoffs between conflicting objectives so as to arrive at a satisfactory balance. One example of the conflicting objectives faced in a scheduling decision is given in Box 11.1.

It is not possible to treat scheduling for all types of operations as a single subject. In order to highlight the differences, scheduling can be classified by type of process: line, intermittent, and project. This chapter addresses the scheduling of ongoing line and intermittent operations. Chapter 12 addresses the scheduling of projects.

11.1 LINE PROCESSES

The scheduling of line processes is required for both assembly lines and the so-called process industries. For these line processes the scheduling problem is, at least partly, solved by the design of the process, since the product flows smoothly from one work station to another. For a single product made in one facility, there is no scheduling problem, because the flow of materials is completely determined by the design of the process. Such a problem exists only when multiple products are made in a single facility.

When several different products are made on the same line, each product is typically produced in a large batch and a line changeover is required for the next product. The changeover may be fairly simple, or it may be complex enough to require extensive retooling and modification of work stations. One example of line scheduling is the production of air conditioners, where a changeover from one model to another may cost several thousand dollars. Other examples include refrigerators, microwave ovens, stoves, electronic devices, tires, and most mass-produced products. These changeover problems involve scheduling, since they require the allocation of line capacity to several different products.

The first concern in scheduling the multiple-product line is to calculate economic lot sizes. This calculation requires a tradeoff between setup cost and inventory carrying cost. If the setup is done often, small lots are produced and frequent setup costs are incurred, but inventories are held down. If setups are done infrequently, the opposite situation occurs, leading to less setup but more inventory. Thus the economic (least-cost) lot size can be determined by a balance between setup costs and inventory carrying costs. Lots which are either too large or too small are expensive. The exact formula for calculating these lot sizes is explained in Chapter 13.

Once the lot sizes for each product have been determined, on strictly economic grounds or otherwise, there is still a question of when each product should be produced. This gets to the heart of the scheduling problem, which is the sequencing of products on the line, one after another.

Sometimes the best sequence can be calculated by means of a mathematical model. However, the available mathematical formulations do not consider demand uncertainty, which is a serious problem in line scheduling. To solve this problem, a dynamic method of scheduling and continually rescheduling products is needed.

In addressing the line-scheduling problem, we will assume that the line is pro-

TABLE 11.1   **RUNOUT-TIME CALCULATIONS**

	Demand data			Supply data		
Product	Inventory units	Weekly demand, units	Runout time, weeks	Lot size, units	Production rate, units per week	Production time, weeks
A	2,100	200	10.5	1500	1500	1.0
B	550	100	5.5	450	900	.5
C	1,475	150	9.8	1000	500	2.0
D	2,850	300	9.5	500	1000	.5
E	1,500	200	7.5	800	800	1.0
F	1,700	200	8.5	1200	800	1.5
Total	10,175	1150				

ducing to inventory, and we will develop a scheduling rule which considers current inventory levels as well as future demand rates. If the inventory for a particular product is low relative to future demand, that product will be scheduled ahead of products with larger relative inventories. A way to formalize this idea is to schedule lots on the basis of runout times.

The runout time for product i is defined to be

$$r_i = \frac{I_i}{d_i} \qquad i = 1, \ldots, n$$

where r_i = runout time, weeks
  I_i = inventory, units
  d_i = weekly demand, units

The scheduling rule is to schedule first one lot of the product with the lowest value of r_i. This will ensure that the product with the smallest runout time is placed first in the schedule. The next step is to reevaluate the runout times assuming the first lot has been completed and to repeat the process until several lots have been scheduled. By this process of simulation, a schedule can be developed for as far into the future as desired.

The following example illustrates the idea of runout-time calculations. An assembly line makes six different products to stock. The lot sizes, production rates, inventories, and forecast demand for these products are shown in Table 11.1. The runout time is calculated for each product by taking the ratio of inventory to forecasted weekly demand. The product with the lowest runout time—in this case product B with a runout time of 5.5 weeks—should be scheduled first.

We then continue to develop the entire production schedule. The lot size for product B is 450 units and the production rate is 900 units per week. Thus product B should be scheduled for 0.5 week to produce one lot. The inventories and runout times are projected forward to the end of 0.5 week, as shown in Table 11.1. Product E now has the lowest runout time at 7.0 weeks, so it is scheduled for a lot of pro-

TABLE 11.1 (*Continued*)

End of week 0.5		End of week 1.5		End of week 3.0		End of week 3.5	
Inventory	Runout time	Inventory	Runout time	Inventory	Runout time	Inventory	Runout time
2,000	10.0	1800	9.0	1500	7.5	1400	7.0
950	9.5	850	8.5	700	7.0	650	6.5
1,400	9.3	1250	8.3	1025	6.8	950	(6.3)
2,700	9.0	2400	8.0	1950	(6.5)	2300	7.7
1,400	(7.0)	2000	10.0	1700	8.5	1600	8.0
1,600	8.0	1400	(7.0)	2300	11.5	2200	11.0
10,050		9700		9175		9100	

duction. This lot will take 1.0 week, so the status is projected forward again until the end of week 1.5.

Now product F has the lowest runout time, so product F is scheduled next. This time the lot size will require 1.5 weeks to produce, so the status is projected forward to the end of week 3.0. Continuing this process as shown in Table 11.1, the production sequence will be B, E, F, D, C for the next 5.5 weeks.

As the calculations indicate, we should not simply make up the entire schedule from the initial runout times but rather schedule the lots one at a time while simulating the process forward. Furthermore, this schedule should be revised as actual demand data are accumulated and new forecasts are made. The runout calculation is, therefore, dynamic and continually adjusts to changing conditions.

After the scheduling is done, one should look carefully at the resulting projected inventories to see whether inventory is building up too fast or being reduced to low levels. If this is the case, a change in capacity may be needed to bring the schedule into conformity with objectives. From the example in Table 11.1, it can be seen that inventories are being reduced somewhat over the scheduling period from a starting level of 10,175 units to an ending level of 9100 units. Unless inventories were too high in the beginning, this calculation would indicate a need for aggregate planning to provide more capacity through overtime, subcontracting, hiring, etc. If an aggregate decision is made to change capacity, we would then recalculate the schedule by using the new production rates. This example illustrates clearly the interaction between scheduling and aggregate planning.

The runout method is a very simple heuristic which does not take into account inventory carrying costs, stockout costs, different demand variances, and so on. It can be improved by formulating a model which takes specific management objectives into account. Nevertheless, the runout-time calculation has intuitive appeal because it clearly illustrates the line-scheduling problem.

Whatever scheduling rule is utilized, it must be imbedded in a production scheduling and control system. Often the concept of a well-structured system is more important than the particular scheduling rule utilized. Later in the chapter, we will be discussing some general principles for the design of such scheduling systems.

11.2 INTERMITTENT PROCESSES

In this section much of the terminology ("shop," "job," "work center") comes from traditional manufacturing job shops. The concepts, however, apply equally to intermittent operations of all types, including factories, hospitals, offices, and schools. For service operations, the term "job" can be replaced by "customer," "patient," "client," "paperwork," or whatever flows through the process instead of materials or jobs. Furthermore, the term "work center" can be replaced by the words "room," "office," "facility," "skill specialty," or whatever the processing centers are. Although the terminology we use has manufacturing connotations, the concepts apply equally well to all types of intermittent operations.

The intermittent scheduling problem is quite different from that for line processes. First of all, each unit flowing through an intermittent process typically moves along with many starts and stops, not smoothly. This irregular flow is due to the layout of the intermittent process by machine group or skills into work centers. As a result, jobs or customers wait in line as each unit is transferred from one work center to the next. Work-in-process (WIP) inventory builds up or people wait in lines, and scheduling becomes complex and difficult.

The intermittent scheduling problem can be thought of as a network of queues. A queue of WIP inventory is formed at each work center as jobs wait for the facilities to become available. These queues are interconnected through a network of material or customer flows. The problem in intermittent scheduling is to manage these queues.

It should be noted at the outset that one of the characteristics of an intermittent operation is that jobs or customers spend most of their time waiting in line. The amount of time spent waiting will, of course, vary with the load on the process. If the process is highly loaded, a job may spend as much as 95 percent of its total production time waiting in queues. Under these circumstances, if it takes a week to actually process an order, it will take 20 weeks to deliver it to the customer. On the other hand, if the process is lightly loaded, the waiting time will be reduced, since all the jobs flow through the process more rapidly. Regardless of the load on the process, the challenge is to develop scheduling procedures that will effectively manage the flow of jobs, customers, and work.

The scheduling of intermittent processes in manufacturing is highly related to materials-requirements planning (MRP) systems, which are discussed in Chapter 14. Since MRP deals with a variety of topics—inventory, scheduling, and manufacturing control—the discussion of MRP is deferred until later. Much of the material discussed in this section, however, can be considered as a component of an MRP system, in addition to the broader scheduling and service-industry applications.

There are a number of scheduling problems for intermittent processes: input-output analysis, loading, sequencing, and dispatching. Each of these problems and their interrelationships will be described below.

11.3 INPUT-OUTPUT CONTROL

The purpose of input-output control is to manage the relationship between a work center's inputs and outputs. Before discussing these relationships, a definition of terms will be helpful.

1. *Input*. The amount of work (jobs) arriving at a work center per unit of time. Input may be measured in such units as dollars, number of orders, standard hours of work, or physical units (tons, feet, cubic yards) per unit of time.
2. *Load*. The level of WIP inventory or back orders in the system. Load is the total volume of work still to be processed. It may be measured in the same units as input, but load is not expressed as a rate per unit of time.
3. *Output*. The rate at which work is completed by a work center. Output rate depends on both capacity and load.
4. *Capacity*. The maximum rate of output which can be produced. Capacity is de-

termined by a combination of physical factors and management policy, as described in Chapter 9.

The relationships between these four terms may easily be visualized by the hydraulics analogy in Figure 11.1. Input is represented by the rate at which water flows into the tank and is controlled by the input valve. Load is represented by the level of water in the tank and corresponds to WIP inventory or back orders. Output is the rate at which water flows out of the tank. Capacity is the size of the output pipe, not the size of the tank. While capacity limits the maximum rate of flow, the actual output rate may be less than capacity if the water level is low. The proper way to control this tank system is to regulate the input valve so that the output and load achieve the proper levels. One cannot push more water through the tank simply by opening up the input valve, although this tactic is frequently attempted in factories and service operations. Once capacity is reached, the *only* way to get more output is to increase the size of the output pipe.

Managers are well aware of the consequences of too little input: low machine utilization, idle labor, and high unit costs. What is often not understood are the consequences of too much input. In this case working capital will rise due to a larger WIP inventory, the average processing time to complete an order will increase as orders spend more time in queues, and system performance will generally decline. It is often better to control input by backlogging orders or even turning business away, if necessary, than to make futile attempts to push more through the system.

One popular way to attempt to increase output without increasing capacity is to expedite the work in progress. Expediting is done by identifying critical jobs and

**Figure 11.1
Hydraulic analogy
to input-output
control.**

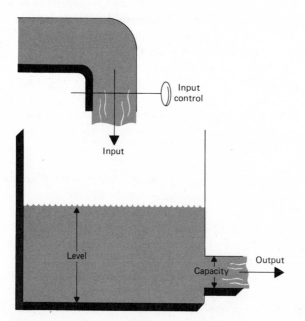

rushing them through the facility. For example, an expeditor may place red tags on critical jobs which should be worked on first. This is a shortsighted solution which often does more harm than good. Every job expedited today may cause two jobs to be late tomorrow. Expediting destroys a smooth flow of work; it is the antithesis of planning. Even in the best-managed operations, a little expediting may be needed when things go wrong; but expediting should not be substituted for proper planning, scheduling, and control. One way to tell whether an operation is out of control is to count the number of jobs carrying rush stickers, red tags, or other expediting messages. Expediting indicates a failure to manage the relationships between input and output.

Some basic calculations will help explain input-output relationships. Figure 11.2 shows an input rate to an operation of $100,000 per week or about $5 million per year. The output rate is also $100,000 per week, and WIP inventory is $2 million. Notice that the system is in steady state, with the input rate equal to the output rate. In this condition, the average processing time for an order will be $\frac{\$2,000,000}{\$100,000} = 20$ weeks. It would be interesting to know, in this case, what amount of time the average order spends in actual processing—perhaps 1 or 2 weeks out of the 20-week total.

There is also a relationship between utilization and WIP inventory level, but this must be expressed through complicated formulas or simulation models. Such a simulation of a typical job shop was done by Colley et al. (1977), with the results shown in Figure 11.3. In this case, various levels of WIP inventory were selected and the resulting utilization of labor and equipment was calculated. When initial levels of utilization were low, they were greatly increased by even a small increase in WIP. This occurred because machines and people—not jobs—were waiting. When utilization was high (in the 90 percent range), only a very large increase in WIP inventory could raise utilization still higher.

The tradeoff between utilization and WIP inventory can be illustrated by the following simple example. Suppose that WIP inventory can be reduced by 10 percent while utilization of labor declines by only 1 percent. Is this tradeoff worthwhile? To answer this question, we need to know that WIP inventory = $2 million, 200 people are employed at $5 per hour, and it costs 20 cents to carry $1 of inventory for

**Figure 11.2
Input-output calculations.**

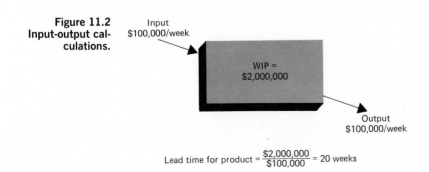

Input
$100,000/week

WIP =
$2,000,000

Output
$100,000/week

Lead time for product $= \frac{\$2,000,000}{\$100,000} = 20$ weeks

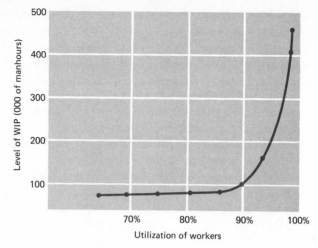

Figure 11.3
WIP inventory versus labor utilization.

a year. The annual cost of decreased utilization is then

$$(.01)(200)(40)(52)(\$5) = \$20,800$$

The annual savings in inventory is

$$(.1)(.20)(\$2,000,000) = \$40,000$$

Since the inventory savings is greater than the cost due to lower labor utilization, it would pay to reduce inventories. This can be done, of course, by holding input

Figure 11.4
Input-output relationship.

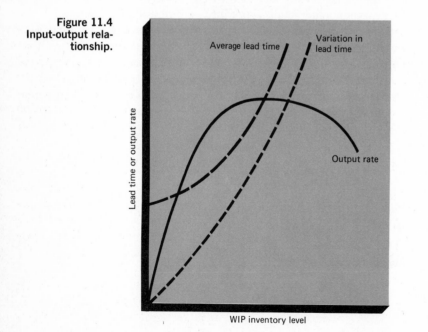

below output for a period of time and clearing the system of some of the partially completed orders.

This discussion of input-output control can be summarized by Figure 11.4. In this case, increasing levels of WIP are seen to help in increasing throughput (output rate) to a point where the curve actually decreases because WIP inventory finally "gets in the way." At the same time, increasing WIP can also be expected to increase the average lead time (processing time) and the variance of processing time as jobs spend more time in the queues. A key to controlling lead times, utilization, and inventories is to control input to the intermittent process. In some industries, too little attention is paid to input control; the result is high WIP inventories and long lead times.

11.4 LOADING

Loading is a type of scheduling used to develop a "load" profile by work center. In loading, the total hours or number of jobs is used to obtain a rough idea of when orders can be delivered or whether capacity will be exceeded. A precise schedule or sequence for each job is not developed.

Loading uses an *average* waiting time for jobs at each work center to determine the progress of jobs through the facility. This is in contrast to detailed scheduling or sequencing, where job interference is taken into account and the waiting time of each job in each queue is precisely calculated. This type of exact sequencing will be covered in Section 11.5. Remember, the purpose of loading is to obtain a rough idea of the load on the facilities and not an exact work schedule.

There are two types of loading: backward and forward.

1. *Backward loading* begins with the due date for each job and loads the processing-time requirements against each work center by proceeding backward in time. The capacity of work centers may be exceeded if necessary. The purpose of backward loading is to calculate the capacity required in each work center for each time period. As a result, it may be decided that capacity should be reallocated between work centers or that more total capacity should be made available through revised aggregate planning. Due dates of jobs are always given for backward loading.

2. *Forward loading* begins with the present date and loads jobs forward in time. The processing time is accumulated against each work center, assuming infinite capacity. In this case, however, due dates may be exceeded if necessary. Since average waiting times are used in queues, the resulting job completion date is only an approximation of the date which might be calculated by more precise scheduling. The purpose of forward loading is to determine the approximate completion date of each job and the capacity required in each time period.

The techniques of backward and forward loading are best illustrated by example. Suppose we have a very simple shop with three work centers (A, B, C) consisting of one machine each and five jobs (1, 2, 3, 4, 5) to be loaded. The processing

Job	Work center/machine hours	Due date
1	A/2, B/3, C/4	4
2	C/6, A/4	3
3	B/3, C/2, A/1	4
4	C/4, B/3, A/3	4
5	A/5, B/3	2

**Figure 11.5
Job data for
loading.**

time of each job in each work center is shown in Figure 11.5. These times will be
accumulated to form the load on each work center in machine hours. One could
also accumulate labor hours, but that would complicate the example. We are thus assuming that machine hours is the scarce resource in this example.

A job will spend a great deal of its production time being moved and waiting in
line. We will assume that wait-move time is an average of 8 hours per work center in
addition to the machine processing time. The wait/move time will be incurred each
time a job changes from one work center to the next. A job thus alternates between
processing and waiting as it moves from one work center to the next.

In backward loading, we start with the due dates, given in Figure 11.5, and work
backward in time. In converting days to hours, we will use 8 hours in a day and
assume a one-shift operation. Thus job 1, for example, is due on day 4, which is 32
hours from now. In backward loading job 1, start at the end of day 4 and load 4
hours in work center C, as shown in Figure 11.6. After subtracting 8 hours
move/wait time, load 3 hours in work center B during day 3. After subtracting another 8 hours of move/wait time, load 1 hour in work center A for day 2 and 1 hour
for day 1. Notice that in this case the 2 hours required for work center A do not fit
entirely in a single day. This completes the loading of job 1. Next we load job 2 in a

**Figure 11.6
Backward loading
example.**

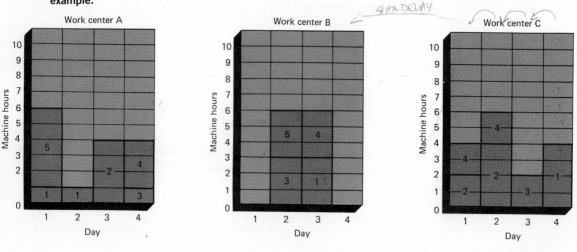

similar way, beginning with the due date of day 3 and working backward. The profiles resulting when this has been done for all jobs are given in Figure 11.6. It would be good practice to work through this example in detail to obtain the complete load.

The backward load defines the capacity requirements in each week, assuming that the due dates must be met. If the resulting load is unsatisfactory, either capacity or due dates will have to be changed. For example, there are several problems in Figure 11.6. First, work center B has no work load on day 1. It would be desirable to move some work into this day if possible or to assign the people and machines to other jobs. Similarly, work center A is underloaded on day 2. In solving these two problems, we could start job 1 up to 7 hours earlier (32 to 25), job 2 up to 6 hours earlier, and so on. In this case, the jobs would be finished before they were really due, but the people and machines would be utilized. We are thus making a tradeoff between finishing the job earlier for inventory and machine/labor utilization.

The data given in this example can also be used to develop a forward load. In this case we will assume that the start dates of all jobs are time zero (now). The jobs will be loaded in order 1, 2, 3, 4, 5, although the order of loading does not affect the capacity required or the delivery dates. Job 1 is loaded first in work center A for 2 hours. After 8 hours of move/wait time, job 1 requires 3 hours on day 2 in work center B. After another 8 hours move/wait time, 3 hours are used in work center C on day 3 and 1 hour on day 4. Notice that in this case there is not enough time on day 3 to complete the job. Jobs 2, 3, 4, and 5 are also loaded by the same procedure, with the result shown in Figure 11.7.

The load obtained from forward loading is also rather irregular. The machine utilization, however, is high in the early periods, since the jobs are produced as soon as possible. Furthermore, the delivery dates calculated by the forward-loading procedure are the earliest possible. This may result in some orders being delivered before they are due or held in finished-goods inventory until the customer is ready.

Figure 11.7
Forward loading
example.
The numbers 1, 2,
3, 4, 5 within the
bars are job
numbers.

If the forward load is not satisfactory, then load leveling can be used. In this case the start dates for some jobs are delayed to yield a more desirable load. There is no exact method to determine which jobs should be delayed; this can be done only by

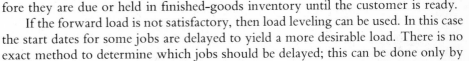

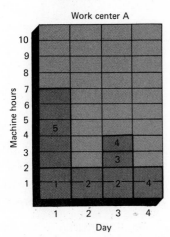
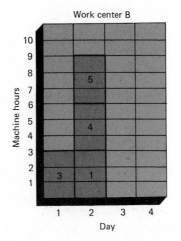
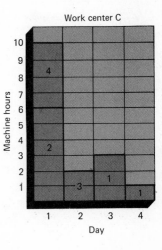

inspection and heuristic analysis. Without missing the due dates, the possible delay in starting date for each job is as follows:

Job	Possible delay
1	7
2	6
3	10
4	6
5	0

Figure 11.7 suggests that it might be desirable to move jobs 1 and 4 forward in time to achieve a more nearly uniform work load. When the start date for jobs 1 and 4 is deferred until the second day, the resulting load is shown in Figure 11.8.

This is the best load achieved so far since it yields a compromise between leveling work centers and meeting due dates, but jobs 1 and 4 will be a day late. If the customers will accept these delays we will have achieved a much more efficient loading of the facilities.

This example indicates how loading can be used to achieve the multiple objectives of an intermittent operation. Backward loading is done first. If a level load is obtained, there will be low WIP inventory and efficient utilization, and all due dates will be met. If the backward load is not efficient, we can load the jobs forward. If this is still not satisfactory, we can unload some of the jobs and reload them with later start dates until a satisfactory load on work centers and acceptable due dates are achieved.

It is easy to see from an understanding of loading why close liaison should be maintained between marketing and operations. Marketing should not promise arbitrary delivery dates simply on the basis of the customer's request because of the possible adverse effect on the intermittent facility's load. Perhaps a few days' difference in the delivery promise will make it possible to level out the peaks and valleys in

Figure 11.8
Load-leveling example.

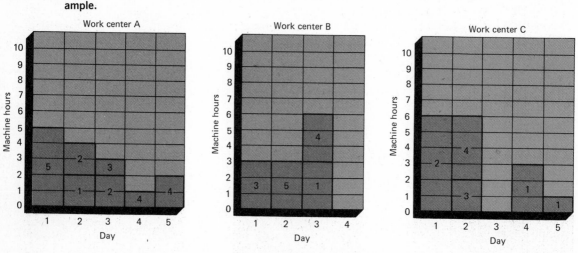

load. Thus marketing should check with operations before making delivery promises, and operations should then live up to its commitments to deliver on time. This procedure is often not followed in practice, leading to a great deal of friction and poor delivery performance.

In this section we have been loading to "infinite" capacity with subsequent use of load leveling to reflect actual capacities. Forward loading can also be done to finite capacity. In this case, capacities are never exceeded, but due dates may be. Since forward loading to finite capacity is very similar to sequencing, we will discuss it in the next section.

11.5 SEQUENCING

Sequencing is concerned with developing an exact order (or sequence) of job processing. In sequencing, job interference and queuing times are computed by laying out a schedule for each job. An average queuing (or waiting) time is *not* assumed, as in the case of loading.

One of the oldest sequencing methods, the Gantt chart, was proposed by Henry L. Gantt in 1917. Although there are many variations of the Gantt chart, we shall restrict its use in this chapter to the sequencing problem.

The Gantt chart is a table with time across the top and a scarce resource along the side. The scarce resource may be machines, people, machine hours, or any other. In the example below, we shall assume that machines are the scarce resource to be scheduled.

For the sake of contrast, we will take the previous example and sequence the jobs with the Gantt chart. In doing this it will be assumed, as before, that each work center contains exactly one machine. Then the jobs are scheduled forward in time within the finite capacity of the one machine of each type (A, B, and C). We also assume, arbitrarily, that the jobs should be scheduled in the sequence 1, 4, 5, 2, 3.

The Gantt chart resulting from these assumptions is shown in Figure 11.9. This chart is constructed by first scheduling job 1 on all three machines. Job 1 starts on machine A for 2 hours, then is placed on machine B for 3 hours (time 2 to time 5), and is finally processed on machine C for 4 hours (time 5 to time 9). There is no idle time for the first job scheduled, since there can be no job interference. Next, job 4 is scheduled on the Gantt chart for machines C, B, and then A. Job 4 can begin immediately on machine C, since the machine is open until time 5 and only 4 hours are needed. After an idle time of 1 hour, job 4 can start on machine B. Job 4 can finally be scheduled on machine A from time 8 to 11. This process of scheduling is continued until all jobs have been placed in the Gantt chart.

After a Gantt chart has been constructed, it should be evaluated with respect to both job and machine performance. One way to evaluate machine performance is on the basis of the time it takes to complete all work—the make span. In Figure 11.9 the make span is 20 hours, since it takes 20 hours to complete all the jobs.

Another measure of the Gantt chart performance is machine utilization. Utilization may be measured in Figure 11.9 by adding up the idle time for each machine (5 + 8 + 4 = 17) and computing a utilization or idle percentage. The idle-time percentage

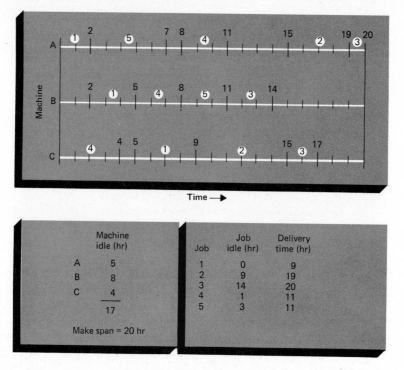

Figure 11.9 Gantt chart. Jobs are sequenced in order 1, 4, 5, 2, 3.

Machine	idle (hr)
A	5
B	8
C	4
	17

Make span = 20 hr

Job	Job idle (hr)	Delivery time (hr)
1	0	9
2	9	19
3	14	20
4	1	11
5	3	11

is $^{17}/_{60} = 28.3$ percent, and the utilization percentage is $^{43}/_{60} = 71.7$ percent. Notice that utilization is closely related to make span. In the five jobs a total of 43 hours of processing time is required (simply add machine times for all jobs from Figure 11.5). The 43 hours of processing time is a constant regardless of the schedule used. Notice also that we have: idle time = 3 (make span) − 43. Therefore, minimizing make span will also minimize machine idle time.

A measure of job performance is the sum of the delivery times for each job. Minimizing this measure would also be equivalent to minimizing job waiting time, since the two times are complementary. In Figure 11.9 the delivery times and job waiting times are listed for each job. These figures are obtained directly from the Gantt chart. The delivery time and waiting times will, of course, depend greatly on the job sequence used. Since job 1 was scheduled first, it has no waiting time and is completed as soon as possible, ahead of due date. Jobs 2 and 3, which were scheduled last, have considerable waiting time.

It can be seen from this example that the waiting time for jobs is highly variable and not a constant 8 hours, as we assumed for loading purposes. Loading is therefore a very rough procedure which approximates only total load and delivery times for jobs. Gantt chart scheduling is more precise, since it considers job interference and computes the waiting times for each job. Despite the advantage of precision, however, Gantt charts are more difficult to construct than loading charts.

A great deal of attention has been given in the literature to optimal job-sequencing algorithms. These algorithms typically optimize one or more measures of schedule performance, such as make span, but they utilize a highly restrictive set of assumptions, such as constant processing times, no passing of jobs, no lot splitting, etc. One particular problem is called the $m \times n$ machine-scheduling problem, where m is the number of machines and n is the number of jobs. To suggest the nature of the research which has been done on this problem we will review a few of the simpler algorithms below.

The $m \times n$ machine-scheduling problem has been solved for $m = 1, 2, 3$ and arbitrary values of n. Efficient algorithms have not been developed for $m \geq 4$ because of the extremely large number of possible sequences. However, fairly good heuristics which seem to develop "good" solutions for any values of m and n are available. See Campbell, Dudek, and Smith (1970).

The simplest $m \times n$ machine-scheduling problem is for $m = 1$ and any n. In this simple case, the make span and utilization are fixed, since all jobs must be processed through the single facility. Make span will be the sum of the processing times and machine utilization will be 100 percent. We can, however, minimize the sum of the delivery dates or the *job* idle times. This is accomplished by scheduling the job with the shortest processing time first. By doing this, we are getting work done as fast as possible and thus reducing the time that other jobs wait for processing.

Let us assume that there are four jobs to schedule on a single machine, with processing times A = 3, B = 6, C = 2, D = 1, and that the jobs are sequenced in the order D, C, A, B. This sequencing uses shortest processing time first, then next-shortest processing time, etc. The resulting job waiting times will be D = 0, C = 1, A = 3, and B = 6, for a total of 10 hours. This is the minimum waiting time of all possible job sequences.

The $m = 2$ machine-scheduling problem is slightly more complicated. First, assume that all jobs go through machine 1 and then machine 2 in the same order. Also assume that the processing times are given for each job on each machine, as shown in Figure 11.10.

The algorithm for solving this problem was first developed by S. M. Johnson (1954) and has been called the left-hand–right-hand rule by Woolsey (1975). According to the method, the job timetable is first searched for the shortest processing time. In Figure 11.10, the shortest time is 1 hour and is on the right under machine 2. Since this time is on the right, job A is placed on the right side of the sequence and is crossed off the table. The next-shortest time is 2, which is also on the right under job C, so job C is placed on the right of the sequence next to job A and is crossed off the table. The next-shortest time is 3, which is on the left, so job B is placed on the left of the sequence and crossed off the table. The remaining jobs D and E are tied for shortest time, so we select job D arbitrarily and place it on the right. Job E remains and is placed on the left, according to its shortest time.

The resulting job sequence is B, E, D, C, A. If the jobs are processed in this order, we will achieve the minimum make span. This sequence will, of course, also minimize machine idle time, as noted above.

To compute the value of the minimum make span for this particular sequence, a Gantt chart should be constructed, as shown in Figure 11.10. The minimum make

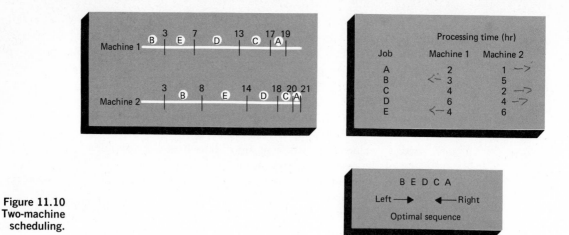

Figure 11.10
Two-machine
scheduling.

span is 21 hours. According to S. M. Johnson, this is the shortest make span among all possible job sequences (5 ! = 120 sequences in this case).

In studying the Gantt chart, one can see intuitively what is happening with Johnson's rule. A short time is scheduled first on machine 1, so that machine 2 is not kept waiting too long in the beginning. Since the shorter times in the beginning are on machine 1, on the left, machine 2 probably can be kept busy once it starts processing. At the end of the sequence the situation reverses, and the shortest times are on machine 2. This helps in the "end game" in quickly processing the remaining jobs through the second machine.

Although these sequencing rules and others have a great deal of theoretical interest, they have not been applied much in practice. This is because real sequencing problems involve a great deal of variability in processing times, multiple objectives, and other complicating factors. Nevertheless, the rules are useful for gaining insight into scheduling problems and for suggesting heuristics which might possibly be of value in practice. Some of these heuristics are reviewed in detail in Section 11.6.

11.6 DISPATCHING RULES

In practice, schedules are difficult if not impossible to maintain because conditions often change; a machine breaks down, a qualified operator becomes ill, materials do not arrive on time, and so on. As a result, some operations are run without a detailed schedule. In this case, dispatch rules are used.

A dispatch rule specifies which job should be selected for work next from among a queue of jobs. When a machine or worker becomes available, the dispatch rule is applied and the next job selected. A dispatch rule is thus dynamic in nature and continually adjusts to changing conditions. Unlike a schedule, a dispatch rule cannot be out of date, and it answers the worker's immediate question: "What should I do next?"

A classic study of dispatch rules by Earl LeGrande (1963) evaluated six rules at Hughes Aircraft in El Segundo, California. The Hughes fabrication shop had 1000 machines, 400 to 500 workers, and 1800 to 2500 orders in process; it completed 100 to 150 shop orders per day. The performance of the rules was evaluated by simulating the shop in detail. As each job was completed on a machine, the dispatching rule was used to select the next job. [For another simulation study, see Jones (1973).]

The following six rules were evaluated:

1. MINPRT (minimum processing time per operation). For this rule the job with the shortest processing time on the machine is selected. This rule is based on the idea that when a job is finished quickly, other machines downstream will receive work, resulting in a high flow rate and high utilization.
2. MINSOP (minimum slack time per operation). "Slack time" is defined as time remaining until the due date minus processing time remaining. Thus a job with zero slack would have just enough time to be completed if there were no waiting time in queues. In this rule, the slack is divided by the number of operations to normalize the slack time.
3. FCFS (first come, first served). This rule is based on the familiar "fairness" criterion, where the job which arrives first at the work center is also processed first.
4. MINSD (minimum planned start date per operation). This rule uses the results of a previous schedule to determine the planned start date for each job. The job with the minimum planned start date is processed first.
5. MINDD (minimum due date per order). By this rule, the job with the earliest due date is processed first.
6. RANDOM (random selection). This rule selects the next job to be processed at random. The rule would not be used in practice; it is simply a benchmark for comparison with other rules.

In order to evaluate these rules, it is necessary to develop criteria for shop performance. As previously mentioned, there are three types of criteria: efficiency of machines and labor, work-in-process inventory, and customer service. Although there are only three criteria, there are many ways to measure them. In the Hughes Aircraft simulation, 10 measures were selected, as shown in Table 11.2. The table also indicates how each rule performed on each measure. In this table, a value of 1.00 indicates the best performance on each measure, while the other values are relative measures.

The table indicates that the MINPRT rule does best on efficiency and flow-rate measures, while the MINSOP rule does best on meeting due dates. This result should be expected because the MINSOP rule incorporates due date in the rule while MINPRT does not. It should also be noted that the FCFS rule, which is quite popular in practice, performs poorly on all criteria. As a matter of fact, FCFS performs about the same as the RANDOM rule.

Since the Hughes study was completed, two additional rules which are quite useful have been proposed:

1. MINPRT WITH TRUNCATION. In this rule the job with minimum processing time is selected next, just as in MINPRT, except when a job has waited for a specified pe-

TABLE 11.2 COMPARISON OF DISPATCHING RULES

Criteria*	1	2	3	4	5	6	7	8	9	10	Total relative rank
Relative weights	1	1	1	1	1	1	1	1	1	1	
MINPRT	1.00	.83	1.00	.20	1.00	1.00	.76	.91	1.00	1.00	8.70
MINSOP	.87	1.00	.63	1.00	.73	.52	.96	.99	.92	.92	8.54
FCFS	.80	.54	.54	.20	.73	.38	.84	.98	.93	.93	6.93
MINSD	.84	.48	.46	.22	.68	.36	.91	1.00	.91	.91	6.77
MINDD	.94	.62	.64	.24	.84	.51	1.00	.99	.87	.87	7.52
RANDOM	.84	.68	.79	.20	.67	.66	.80	.93	.92	.91	7.40

Source: Earle LeGrande, "The Development of a Factory Simulation System Using Actual Operating Data," *Management Technology,* vol. 3, no. 1, May 1963, p. 17.

* Key to criteria:
 1. Number of orders completed
 2. Percent of orders completed late
 3. Mean of the distribution of completions
 4. Standard deviation of the distribution of completions
 5. Average number of orders waiting in the shop
 6. Average wait time of orders
 7. Yearly cost of carrying orders in queue
 8. Ratio of inventory carrying cost while waiting to inventory cost while on machine
 9. Percent of labor utilized
10. Percent of machine capacity utilized

riod of time. The rule is then truncated and the job that has been waiting longest is done next. The result of this truncation is to process the long jobs sooner, with some sacrifice in efficiency. This reduces the adverse effect of the MINPRT rule, which is that long jobs wait in the queue and do not get processed.

2. **CRITICAL RATIO.** The critical ratio is computed as:

$$CR = \frac{\text{remaining time until due date}}{\text{remaining processing time}}$$

The job with the minimum value of CR is scheduled next. This rule calculates the ratio of demand time to supply time. When the ratio exceeds a value of 1, there is sufficient time available to complete the job if the queue times are properly managed. If the ratio is less than 1, the job will be late unless processing times can be compressed. The performance of the CR rule is similar to that of MINSOP, since they both explicitly account for due dates. However the CR rule has slightly more intuitive appeal, since the CR itself has a precise meaning; e.g., a ratio = 2 means that there is twice as much time remaining as the processing time.

Rules such as MINSOP and the CR rule are the most widely used in practice, since due dates seem to have more importance than efficiency and flow time. This is understandable because of the emphasis placed on schedule performance in industry.

In using dispatching rules, a shop-floor control system which updates the status of each job in process is needed. Using the feedback on job status, the supervisor receives a priority report each morning (or in real time). The priority report ranks all jobs waiting in that work center (or due to arrive that day) in priority order. These priorities can be calculated with any of the dispatching rules available. The supervisor then schedules work on the jobs in the work center on the basis of the priorities given. If the highest-priority job can not be done (due to machine breakdown, operator illness, or other reasons), the second job is done, and so on down the list. The priority list does not specify a rigid schedule and thus allows flexibility for local work-center conditions.

The use of priority rules in dispatching illustrates a very important principle stated by George Plossl (1978): "Lead time is what you say it is." If a job is given a very tight due date, perhaps just a little greater than total processing time, a rule such as CR or MINSOP will speed the job through the shop because of the high priority. Of course, too many of these high-priority jobs will ruin the system. According to Plossl's rule, if a long lead time is promised, the entire time will be used, since the job has a relatively low priority. With dispatching rules, lead time can be expanded or contracted by a large factor. This is one of the problems with loading calculations which assume that lead time is fixed when it is not.

When loading is used in conjunction with input-output control and a dispatching rule, an effective dynamic scheduling system can be designed. The loading rule will serve to make the required capacity available in the work centers; the input-output rule will control the release of work to the shop so that the shop is not overloaded; and the dispatching rule will serve to manage the jobs through the operation to meet desired due dates. Notice that, in this case, a Gantt chart schedule is not maintained on individual jobs. There are cases, however, where Gantt chart sequencing is quite valuable. These cases include intermittent-process operations with relatively stable conditions. In this situation, a Gantt chart can be used to represent current conditions and thus to answer the worker's question, "What do I do next?"

11.7 PLANNING AND CONTROL SYSTEMS

As a popular TV advertisement says, "The system is the solution." This principle applies to scheduling operations, where an adequate planning and control system is needed. This scheduling system should not only facilitate the development of good schedules (planning) but also ensure that schedules are implemented and corrected as needed (control). These scheduling systems will usually incorporate some of the methods which have been described above. But without the system, the methods are useless. For a classic study in this area see Bulkin, Colley, & Steinhoff (1966).

There are several questions that every scheduling system should answer:

1. *What delivery date do I promise?* As discussed above, the promised delivery date should be based on both marketing and operations considerations. These considerations include available capacity, the customer's work requirements, and efficiency of operations. We have seen how the promised date can be derived for intermittent-process operations through loading or Gantt chart scheduling.

2. *How much capacity do I need?* A scheduling system can answer this question by forecasting and developing workloads for individual activities. For line-process

operations, the question is answered by using runout times and projecting inventories into the future. For intermittent-process operations, this question is answered by backward loading of the available jobs.

3. *When should I start on each particular activity or task?* This question too should be answered by all scheduling systems, but the methods used vary. In intermittent-process operations, the question is answered by using dispatching rules or a Gantt chart schedule. In line-process operations, the question is addressed directly by runout times.

4. *How do I make sure that the job is completed on time?* We have not discussed this question yet, but it is crucial in all planning and control systems. The answer requires feedback on job status and constant monitoring of activity. If progress is continually or periodically evaluated, corrective action can be taken as needed to make sure that deliveries are made on time. In manufacturing, this question is answered by a shop-floor control system.

In order to illustrate the principles of scheduling and control, three examples that cover a wide range of scheduling problems will be discussed.

Courtroom scheduling[1]

Courtroom scheduling urgently requires more systematic scheduling and control systems. Sometimes court calendars are overloaded, with the result that police officers, witnesses, lawyers, and defendants spend long times waiting. After a day in court without being heard, some witnesses will not return.

On the other hand, the same court may also suffer from case underload, with judges kept waiting and inefficient use of courtrooms. This condition occurs when cases finish early or cases scheduled to appear are delayed.

In an attempt to correct these problems, a court scheduling system was developed for the New York City Criminal Court. The system was designed to achieve the following five objectives: (1) there should be a high probability that judges will be kept busy, (2) there should be a high probability that cases will be heard when scheduled, (3) several cases should be batched together for a police officer on the same day, (4) high-priority cases should be scheduled as soon as possible, (5) and a maximum waiting-time limit should be set for all cases.

The heart of the system was a priority dispatching rule. The rule determined priorities for cases based on such factors as seriousness of the charge, whether the defendant was in or out of jail, and elapsed time since arraignment. When the priority of a case reached a certain threshold, it was inserted into the court calendar; otherwise it was returned to the unscheduled pool.

When a case was scheduled, the time required was predicted by a multiple regression equation which utilized causal variables such as plea of the defendant, seriousness of the offense, number of witnesses, and presiding judge. The predicted time was then scheduled for the first available spot on the calendar. Some slots, however, were kept open for emergencies and future rescheduling.

[1] This discussion is based on a study by Shapiro (1971) and an abstract of the study by Shore (1973).

Each day the priorities were revised on the basis of the current conditions. Any new cases with a high enough priority were placed on the schedule with the required amount of predicted time.

The example illustrates how a service operation can use a dispatching rule as part of a logical scheduling and control system. The methods used were embedded in an informative system which provided overall planning and control of the schedule. The system helped answer the crucial questions required to develop and implement the schedule.

Production scheduling and control system

The production scheduling and control (PSC) system was developed by Honeywell for use in intermittent-process manufacturing facilities. The computerized PSC system performs the following functions: (1) developing a capacity requirement plan, (2) scheduling and dispatching individual orders, and (3) shop-floor control reporting. The general outline of the system is shown in Figure 11.11.

In order to perform its functions, the system maintains several files. A work-center file is maintained for each group of similar machines. This file contains information such as maximum machine hours available, length of workday, cost of operations per hour, average queue time, and average move time.

A routing file is also maintained for each job or order. This file contains a description of all operations required, the sequence of operations, setup times, and run times per piece (or per batch).

Finally, a work-in-process file is maintained for each order which is planned or released. This file contains information on the status of the order, such as current operation being worked on, expected completion date, and required completion date.

A key part of the system is a set of turnaround cards or shop-feedback cards which are punched when each order is released to the shop. Normally there will be one computer card for each operation required. This pack of cards is placed in a shop packet along with shop paperwork authorizing work on the job. When each operation is completed, the card is returned to the central control office, along with information on time taken, number of pieces produced, scrap, and other items of importance.

This information is used by the PSC system to perform scheduling, dispatching, and production reporting functions. The scheduling function is done through forward and backward loading to infinite capacity. Backward loading is done on the basis of given due dates, and forward loading is done from given start dates. The times used for loading include setup time (if required), run time per piece times number of pieces, average queue time for each work center, and average move time. Orders that fall behind schedule are reloaded by the system. The result of loading is a schedule for each order plus a load profile for each work center.

PSC performs the dispatching function by means of the critical-ratio rule (the ratio of total work time available to processing time remaining). These priorities are then listed for the supervisor of each work center to use in selecting jobs. In order to provide a measure of user control, the calculated ratios may be multiplied by user-

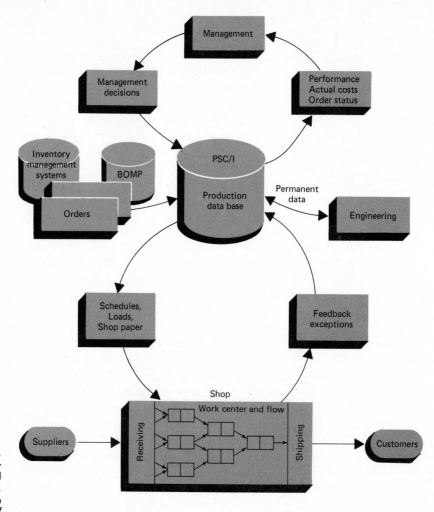

**Figure 11.11
Production sched-
uling and control
system.**
*(Reprinted with
permission of
Honeywell, Inc.)*

supplied priorities. The user priorities will alter the priority of the order as the user specifies.

The production reporting function of PSC consists of a variety of status and management reports, work-center utilization records and shop paperwork. These reports allow management to monitor the status of the system and the performance of the loading and dispatching functions.

Like the courtroom scheduling system, the PSC system provides the information environment for scheduling. The various rules and methods are the heart of the system, and the information ties the parts together into a logical whole.

Telephone study

Buffa, Cosgrove, and Luce (1976) scheduled telephone operators at the General Telephone Company of California. The operators numbered 2600 in 43 different locations throughout the state. They handled directory assistance, coin-telephone dialing, and toll-call assistance.

The first step in designing the telephone scheduling system was to analyze the demand for calls. Profiles of demand on a yearly, monthly, daily, and hourly basis are shown in Figure 11.12. For the yearly demand pattern, the busiest hour per week is plotted in Figure 11.12a. The two busiest times of the year are at Mother's Day and Christmas Day and the lowest demand is in week 28. The peak-to-minimum demand ratio is 1.38, so 38 percent more capacity must be provided on Christmas Day than in week 28 to maintain the same service level.

Monthly demand is shown in Figure 11.12b. The pattern indicates very clearly that Saturdays and Sundays are low-demand days, despite price discounts offered for weekend calls. The day of the week, therefore, also greatly influences staffing schedules.

Figure 11.12c shows the demand by each half hour of a typical day. The demand curve shows a very pronounced peak from 10 a.m. through 6 p.m. and then low evening demand. Daily work shifts must be devised to accommodate this daily demand pattern also.

Finally, Figure 11.12d shows the demand in 1-minute intervals for a portion of one day. This demand was found to be essentially random and therefore, could not be predicted in advance.

The strategy adopted for this scheduling problem was to predict demand within half-hour segments for each day and each office. The work force would then be scheduled to meet these demand requirements.

To implement this strategy, a three-level system was developed, as shown in Figure 11.13. The heart of the system was the daily load forecast by half-hour period. This forecast was converted to operators required, shift schedules, and assignment of operators to shifts. Within a particular day, the intraday cycle operated to adjust for illness or emergency-call load levels. On a monthly basis, the daily performance was assessed by management and aggregate work-force and policy decisions were made. It is interesting to note this relationship between monthly aggregate planning, daily scheduling, and intraday control.

The scheduling part of the system relied on two heuristic algorithms, one to schedule work shifts for each particular day of the week and another to assign operators to the shifts which were available. The first algorithm took account of state regulations, federal regulations, union contracts, company policies, and practical considerations, which all affect work-shift choice. For example, each shift had to have at least a half-hour rest break near the middle and two additional 15-minute rest breaks. The length of the shifts was also required to be either 5, 6, 7, or 8 hours. Operators were assigned to these shifts on the basis of seniority, preference, and weekend rotations.

General Telephone Company of California has been using the integrated work-shift scheduling system since 1973. Each day the 2600 operators in 43 locations are scheduled by the computerized systems. As a result, savings of over $170,000 were reported for 1974 in clerical and supervisory costs plus a 6 percent increase in work-force productivity.

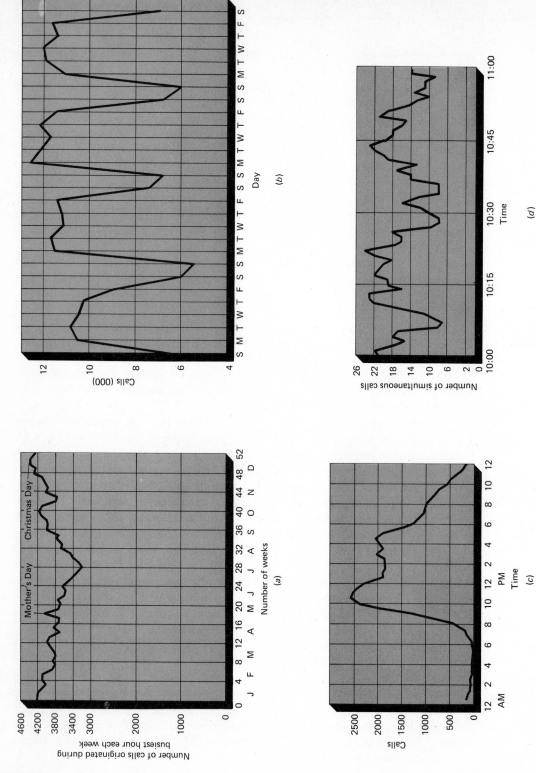

Figure 11.12
General Telephone demand profiles. (a) Typical distribution of calls during the busiest hour for each week during a year. (b) Daily call load for Long Beach, January 1972. (c) Typical half-hourly call distribution. (d) Typical intrahour distribution of calls, 10:00–11:00 a.m.

(*Source: Elwood S. Buffa, Michael J. Cosgrove, and Bill J. Luce, "An Integrated Work Shift Scheduling System," Decision Sciences, vol. 7, no. 4, October 1976, pp. 621–622.*)

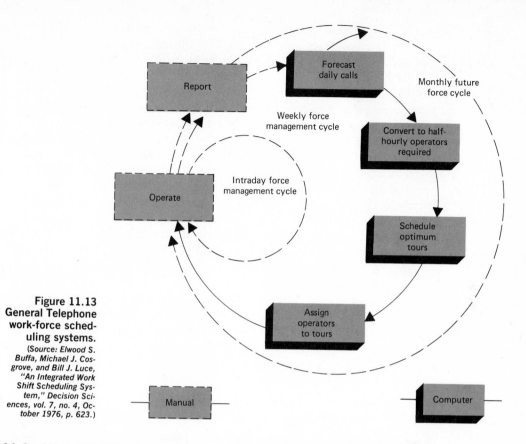

**Figure 11.13
General Telephone
work-force sched-
uling systems.**
(*Source: Elwood S.
Buffa, Michael J. Cos-
grove, and Bill J. Luce,
"An Integrated Work
Shift Scheduling Sys-
tem," Decision Sci-
ences, vol. 7, no. 4, Oc-
tober 1976, p. 623.*)

11.8 KEY POINTS

In this chapter, we have treated scheduling decisions for line- and intermittent-process operations. The chapter's theme is that all scheduling decisions deal with the allocation of scarce resources to jobs, activities, tasks, or customers. We assume, for scheduling purposes, that resources are fixed as a result of aggregate planning and facilities decisions.

The following are among this chapter's key points:

- Within the available resources, scheduling seeks to satisfy the conflicting objectives of low inventories, high efficiency, and good customer service. Thus, trade-offs are always implicitly or explicitly made whenever a schedule is developed. Scheduling, however, differs between line, intermittent, and project forms of operations.
- The scheduling of line-process operations is concerned with producing multiple items on a single line. If only one product is produced on a line, there is no scheduling problem because the line is utilized to the extent needed for the single product. For multiple products, runout-time calculations are used to determine a schedule which allocates line capacity among the products.

- There are a variety of scheduling decisions for intermittent-process operations. One of these involves regulating the input to the intermittent process. Too little input will result in low inventories, low utilization of labor and machines, and fast customer service. Too much input will result in high inventories, high utilization, and long customer delivery times. The concepts of input-output control are used to regulate inputs in relation to outputs and available capacity.

- A second scheduling decision for intermittent-process operations is the loading of work centers. Both backward and forward loading are used to determine capacity needs, delivery due dates, and a smooth work flow. Loading utilizes average queue times and thus only approximates the aggregate load on facilities.

- For scheduling individual jobs, either sequencing or dispatching rules may be used. If sequencing is used, a Gantt chart is developed which shows exactly when each operation is planned for each job. When dispatching rules are used, jobs are selected for the next operation on the basis of prescribed priority rules. These priority rules are used to control the flow of work dynamically as it progresses through a facility. When dispatching rules are used, a Gantt chart or sequence is not constructed in advance.

- To be useful, scheduling methods must be embedded in an information system. Scheduling systems, in general, should answer the following questions: (1) what delivery date do I promise? (2) how much capacity do I need? (3) when should I start each particular activity or task? (4) how do I make sure that the job is completed on time? In order to handle constantly changing situations, these systems are usually computerized, and they require constant feedback on job status.

QUESTIONS

1. What types of scheduling decisions is management likely to encounter in the following operations?
   a. Hospital
   b. University
   c. Movie making
   d. Military campaign
   e. Appliance factory
   f. Railroad
2. Specify the kinds of objectives that might be appropriate for each of the situations listed in Question 1.
3. What is the role of costs in the changeover and scheduling of assembly lines?
4. In making runout calculations, how far should one plan into the future?
5. Why is it important to view an intermittent-process operation as a network of interconnected queues?
6. How is the scheduling of patients in a doctor's clinic similar to or different from the scheduling of jobs in a factory?
7. What is meant by input-output control for intermittent-process operations? How is input-output control handled for line-process operations?
8. What are the effects of too little input and of too much input?
9. Under what circumstances is a combination of input-output control, loading, and dispatching more effective than precise sequencing through Gantt charts?
10. Describe the differences between forward loading and sequencing.
11. Why are there so many different types of dispatching rules?
12. What is the purpose of forward loading and backward loading?
13. How can production lead time be managed in operations? Why isn't lead time a constant value?

14. Why do you suppose that $m \times n$ machine-scheduling algorithms are not widely used in practice? Should optimal rules be more widely used?
15. What is the purpose of a shop-floor control system? Can effective scheduling be done without shop-floor control?

PROBLEMS

1. An assembly line is used to make products A, B, and C. The scheduling information for these products follows:

Product	On-hand inventory, units	Production rate, units per week	Demand rate, units per week	Lot size, units
A	10,000	2000	1000	1000
B	6,000	1500	500	1500
C	9,000	4000	1500	2000

   a. Calculate the production sequence (schedule) for the next 6 weeks using the runout method. Only one product can be produced at a time.
   b. What is the projected inventory at the end of 6 weeks? Should capacity be adjusted?
   c. Suppose capacity is reduced by 25 percent for each product. What is the effect on the production sequence calculated in part a?
2. In an intermittent-process operation, work-in-process inventory can be reduced by 20 percent with a corresponding 5 percent reduction in labor utilization. Should the inventory reduction be made? The current level of WIP inventory is $5 million, carrying cost is 30 percent per year, and labor cost is $10 million per year. If the input to this operation is $1 million per week, what is the production lead time? How much will customer service be improved by the proposed inventory reductions?
3. The following information is given for four jobs and three work centers:

Job	Work center/machine hours	Due date, days
1	A/3, B/2, C/1	3
2	C/2, A/4	2
3	B/6, A/1, C/3	4
4	C/4, A/1, B/2	2 3

JOB 4 REQUIRES 3 DAYS

   Assume there are <u>6 hours of move and queue time between work centers for each job.</u>
   a. Perform a backward load of all jobs.
   b. Forward load all jobs.
4. Sequence the jobs given in Problem 3 using a Gantt chart. Assume that the move time between machines is 1 hour. Sequence the jobs in priority order 1, 2, 3, 4.
   a. What is the make span?
   b. How much machine idle time is there?
   c. When is each job delivered compared with its due date?
   d. How much idle time (waiting time) is there for each job?
   e. Devise a better job sequence for processing.
5. Students must complete two activities in order to register for class: registration and payment of fees. Because of individual differences, the processing time (in minutes) for each of

these two activities varies as shown below for five students:

	Minutes	
Student	Registration	Pay fees
A	10	⑤
B	7	④
C	⑤	7
D	③	8
E	②	6

E D C A B

a. What sequence should be used to process the students in order to minimize student waiting time? Hint: Use the left-hand–right-hand rule.
b. Construct a Gantt chart to determine the total time required to process all five students.
c. What problems might be encountered in using this approach for registration in colleges?

6. Several dispatching rules are being considered by a secretary for purposes of typing term papers. The following information is given on jobs which are waiting to be typed.

Paper	Hours until due date	Total remaining processing time, hours*	Processing time, typing hours	Remaining number of operations	Order of arrival
A	20	15	12	2	4th
B	19	12	10	1	3d
C	15	8	5	3	2d
D	10	5	3	1	1st
E	18	11	7	2	5th

* Includes typing corrections, and copying.

Use the following dispatching rules to determine the order of processing by the typing activity.
a. MINPRT
b. MINSOP
c. FCFS
d. MINDD
e. CR

SELECTED BIBLIOGRAPHY

BUFFA, ELWOOD S., MICHAEL J. COSGROVE, and BILL J. LUCE: "An Integrated Work Shift Scheduling System," *Decision Sciences,* vol. 7, no. 4, October 1976, pp. 620–630.

BULKIN, MICHAEL L., JOHN L. COLLEY, and HARRY W. STEINHOFF, JR.: "Load Forecasting, Priority Sequencing, and Simulation in a Job Shop Control System," *Management Science,* vol. 13, no. 2, October 1966, pp. B29–B51.

CAMPBELL, H. G., R. A. DUDEK, and M. L. SMITH: "A Heuristic Algorithm for the *n* Job *m* Machine Sequencing Problem," *Management Science,* vol. 16, no. 10, June 1970, pp. B630–B637.

COLLEY, JOHN L., ROBERT LANDEL, and ROBERT FAIR: *Production Operations Planning and Control,* San Francisco: Holden-Day, 1977.

CONSTABLE, C. J., and C. C. NEW: *Operations Management: A Systems Approach through Text and Cases,* New York: Wiley, 1976.

CONWAY, R. W., WILLIAM L. MAXWELL, and LOUIS W. MILLER: *Theory of Scheduling,* Reading, Mass.: Addison-Wesley, 1967.

FETTER, R. B., and J. D. THOMPSON: "The Simulation of Hospital Systems," *Operations Research,* vol. 13, no. 5, September–October 1965, pp. 689–711.

HONEYWELL INFORMATION SYSTEMS, INC.: *Production Scheduling and Control System I: Functional Description,* AE37, 1972.

JOHNSON, S. M.: "Optimal Two-Stage and Three-Stage Production Schedules with Setup Times Included," *Naval Research Logistics Quarterly,* vol. 1, no. 1, March 1954, pp. 61–68.

JONES, C. H.: "An Economic Evaluation of Job Shop Dispatching Rules," *Management Science,* vol. 20, no. 3, November 1973, pp. 293–307.

LEGRANDE, EARL: "The Development of a Factory Simulation System Using Actual Operating Data," *Management Technology,* vol. 3, no. 1, May 1963, pp. 1–18.

MABERT, VINCENT A., and ALAN R. RAEDELS: "Detail Scheduling of a Part-Time Work Force," *Decision Sciences,* vol. 8, no. 1, January 1977, pp. 109–120.

MATHER, HAL, and GEORGE PLOSSL: "Priority Fixation versus Throughput Planning," *Production and Inventory Management,* vol. 19, no. 3, 3d quarter, 1978.

SHAPIRO, SAMUEL: "An Automated Court Scheduling System," presented at the 12th American Meeting of the Institute of Management Sciences, Detroit, Mich., September 1971.

SHORE, BARRY: *Operations Management,* New York: McGraw-Hill, 1973.

WIEST, JEROME, and FERDINAND LEVY: *A Management Guide to PERT/CPM,* 2d ed., Englewood Cliffs, N.J.: Prentice Hall, 1977.

WOOLSEY, R. D., and H. S. SWANSON: *Operations Research for Immediate Application, A Quick & Dirty Manual,* New York: Harper & Row, 1975.

CHAPTER 12
PLANNING AND SCHEDULING PROJECTS

In the last three chapters, we have discussed capacity planning and scheduling for ongoing operations, but we have omitted one important type of operation—the project. As originally defined in Chapter 5, the project form of operations is used to produce the unique product, a single unit. Because of this, the management of a project is quite different from that of an ongoing operation.

Although there are many decisions in projects that differ from those in ongoing operations, our main concern in this chapter will be with project planning and scheduling decisions. In the first part of the chapter, a broad framework for project planning will be established; this will include the objectives of projects and the planning and control activities they require. In the last part of the chapter, specific scheduling methods—PERT and CPM—will be described in detail.

Projects include a wide range of manufacturing and service activities. Large objects such as ships, passenger aircraft, and missile launchers are manufactured on a project basis. Each unit is made as a unique item, and the manufacturing process is often stationary, so that materials and labor must be brought to the project. The construction of buildings is typically organized on a project basis. Services such as movies, R&D, and fund raising are also delivered on a project basis. Table 12.1 lists a wide range of manufacturing and service activities which are managed as projects. Box 12.1 describes a typical project scheduling decision for a movie studio.

12.1 OBJECTIVES AND TRADEOFFS

In projects, there are usually three distinct objectives; cost, schedule, and performance. The project cost is the sum of direct and allocated costs assigned to the project. The project manager's job is to control those costs which are directly controllable by the project organization. These costs typically cover labor, material, and some support services. Ordinarily, the project manager will have a project budget which includes the costs assigned to the project. The project manager should control costs within the project budget.

BOX 12.1	TYPICAL DECISION PROBLEM

Carrie James, a recent MBA graduate from a prestigious eastern business school, had just been hired by International Pictures Studio to work in the project management area. Her boss, Arthur Broberg, director of the studio, was describing the current method of project management used. "Carrie, as you know, each movie we produce is established as a separate project. In the beginning, the producer determines an overall schedule and budget for the picture. The producer then develops a detailed work breakdown and a bar-chart schedule of all activities required to produce the movie. Although these activities and schedules are unique for each movie, they bear some resemblance to those for other movies which we have produced in the past. A detailed budget is also established by the producer and time-phased to correspond to the time schedule. When these planning and scheduling activities are completed, the project begins, with initial casting and work on the script, the scenery, and the costumes."

Mr. Broberg continued by discussing several problems that he had with the present project management system: "The individual movie schedules do not consider the load on common facilities such as scenery shops, the film editing department, and costume shops. As a result, these shops are frequently overloaded and the schedules cannot be met."

Mr. Broberg also observed that "the schedule we set initially is often out of date. We try to revise the schedules for each movie monthly, but due to changing priorities and time estimates, we cannot seem to stay on schedule. Carrie, as you know, movie stars are sometimes fickle and difficult to work with; therefore, certain shots may take longer than expected. On other occasions, we shoot a scene successfully the first time, and then we are ahead of schedule. We need a better method to handle the variability in schedule times."

Broberg went on to describe the method used to run the weekly schedule. "Each Monday morning, we have a meeting of all the shop superintendents and directors. All the scheduling problems that directors are having are discussed at the meeting and decisions are made on the spot. Sometimes these meetings last for three or four hours. There must be a better way to handle these problems. Frequently a crisis atmosphere prevails. Would you please review these problems and give me your analysis and suggestions in writing by a week from Friday? We will then meet again to discuss your report."

As she left the meeting, Carrie wondered whether the problems could be solved with a better project scheduling technique such as PERT or whether a completely fresh approach was required.

TABLE 12.1 **EXAMPLES OF PROJECTS**

Building construction
New-product introduction
Research and development
Computer system design
Installation of equipment
Space shots
Fund raising
Movie making
Teaching a course
Designing an advertising campaign
Startup or shutdown of a plant
Manufacture of aircraft, ships, and large machines
Auditing accounts
Planning a military invasion

The second objective in managing projects is schedule. Frequently a project completion date and intermediate milestones are established at the outset. Just as the project manager must control the project costs within budget, so the project manager must control the schedule to meet established dates. Frequently, the budget and schedule conflict. For example, if the project is behind schedule, overtime may be needed to bring it back on. But there may be insufficient funds in the budget to support the overtime costs. Therefore, a tradeoff decision between time and cost must be made. Management must determine whether the schedule objective is of sufficient importance to justify an increased cost.

The third objective in project management is performance, that is, the performance characteristics of the product or service being produced by the project. If the project is research and development on a new type of machine, "performance" refers to the performance specifications of the new machine. If the project is a movie, "performance" refers to the quality of the movie produced and its subsequent box-office receipts. In this case, performance may be specified by a variety of movie standards regarding casting, sound, filming, and editing. Performance for a service project, such as a movie, is ordinarily much more difficult to specify than for a manufactured product.

Performance may also require tradeoffs with both schedule and cost. In a movie, for example, if the picture is not meeting performance expectations, additional shots or script revisions may be required. These performance requirements may, in turn, cause cost and schedule changes. Since it is rarely possible to predict performance, schedule, and cost requirements accurately before a project begins, numerous tradeoffs may be required while the project is underway. These tradeoff decisions are a specific example of the general notion of operations tradeoffs first described in Chapter 2.

12.2 PLANNING AND CONTROL IN PROJECTS

A general sequence of management decisions required in all projects is planning, scheduling, and control decisions. "Planning" refers to those decisions, required in the beginning of a project, which establish its general character and direction. Generally speaking, project planning establishes the major project objectives, the resources required, the type of organization used, and the key people who will manage and implement the project. Project planning is usually a function of top and middle managers. When completed, project planning should be documented by a project authorization form or letter which is used to initiate further project activities. The project authorization form should specify all the planning decisions listed in Table 12.2.

The scheduling phase of project management specifies the project plan in more detail. This phase begins with the construction of a detailed list of project activities, called a work-breakdown structure. A detailed time schedule for each activity in the work-breakdown structure is then established, using the methods described later in this chapter. When the time schedule is completed, a time-phased budget, which is keyed to the start and completion times of each of the project activities, can be developed. Finally, the project personnel can be assigned to individual project activities.

Project control is maintained by monitoring each activity as the work is performed on the project. Activities should be monitored for time, cost, and performance in accordance with the project plan. When a significant discrepancy exists between actual results and the plan, corrective action should be taken. These corrective actions might include revision of the plan, reallocation of funds, personnel changes, or other changes in resources. As a result of corrective actions, the plan should once again be feasible and realistic.

The study of project management should ideally treat all aspects of planning,

---

TABLE 12.2   **PROJECT MANAGEMENT ACTIVITIES AND DECISIONS**

A. Planning

Identify the project customer
Establish the end product or service
Set project objectives
Estimate total resources and time required
Decide on the form of project organization
Make key personnel appointments (project manager, etc.)
Define major tasks required
Establish a budget

B. Scheduling

Develop a detailed work-breakdown structure
Estimate time required for each task
Sequence the tasks in the proper order
Develop a start/stop time for each task
Develop a detailed budget for each task
Assign people to tasks

C. Control

Monitor actual time, cost, and performance
Compare planned to actual figures
Determine whether corrective action is needed
Evaluate alternative corrective actions
Take appropriate corrective action

scheduling, and control, including both behavioral and quantitative issues. Due to space limitations, however, the remainder of this chapter will be restricted primarily to quantitative scheduling methods.

12.3   SCHEDULING METHODS

Several types of scheduling methods are in use. These may be generally classified as Gantt chart or network methods. The Gantt chart methods utilize a bar or milestone chart as shown in Figure 12.1. The network methods use a graph or network to show precedence relations.

The Gantt chart method of scheduling has a great deal in common with Gantt chart scheduling for intermittent processes, described in Chapter 11. In each case, the activity durations are shown on the chart by a bar or line. These charts also show when each activity is scheduled to begin and when it will be completed.

Figure 12.1 is a simplified Gantt chart for the construction of a house. Time is shown across the top and activities are shown down the side. Each activity in the project is shown as a bar on the chart over the period of time for which the particular activity is scheduled. Notice that activities 1, 2, and 3 must be performed in a sequence. Activity 1 must be completed before activity 2 can begin and activity 2 must be completed before activity 3 can begin. The chart also indicates that activities 7, 8, and 9 can be done in parallel, at the same time. The Gantt chart, therefore, shows not only the time required for each activity but also when each activity takes place.

In addition to activities, Gantt charts can also show milestones (or events). A milestone is an instant in time, while an activity is a task with a certain duration of

**Figure 12.1
Gantt chart
project example.**

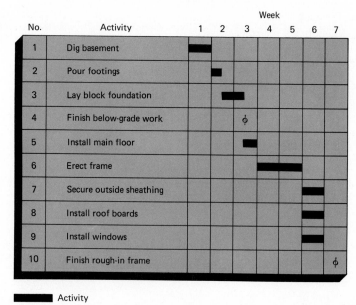

No.	Activity	Week 1	2	3	4	5	6	7
1	Dig basement	▬						
2	Pour footings		▪					
3	Lay block foundation			▬				
4	Finish below-grade work			φ				
5	Install main floor			▪				
6	Erect frame					▬▬		
7	Secure outside sheathing						▬	
8	Install roof boards						▬	
9	Install windows						▬	
10	Finish rough-in frame							φ

▬ Activity

φ Milestone

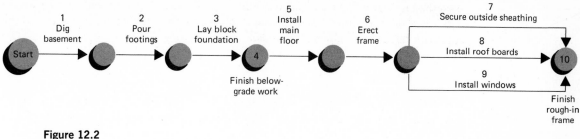

**Figure 12.2
Network project
chart.**

time. A milestone is often used to signal the beginning or end of one or more activities. In Figure 12.1, one milestone indicates the completion of all below-grade work and another milestone indicates the completion of all rough-in framing.

Gantt charts are very commonly used in project scheduling because they are easy to use and quite widely understood. In complex projects, however, a Gantt chart becomes inadequate because it does not show the interdependencies and relationships between activities. For complex projects, it is difficult to schedule the project initially and even more difficult to reschedule it when changes occur. The network method of project scheduling overcomes these difficulties.

Figure 12.2 is a network diagram for the same house construction project shown in Figure 12.1. In the network chart, activities are shown as arrows, while milestones (or events) are shown as circles.[1] Notice that the network diagram clearly shows precedence relationships between the activities. The convention used in drawing these network diagrams is that all arrows leading into a circle (event) must be completed before any arrows leading out of the circle can begin. All arrows leading into a circle are then called predecessors, and all arrows leading out of the circle are called successors. All predecessor activities must be completed before any of the successors can begin.

The advantage of the network methods over the Gantt chart is that the precedence relationships in network scheduling are explicitly shown on the network. This permits development of a scheduling algorithm which accounts for all precedence relations when the schedule is developed. With Gantt charts, the precedence relations must be kept in the scheduler's head. On complex projects, this cannot easily be done, and Gantt charts become unwieldy. Furthermore, when a single activity time changes on the Gantt chart, the entire chart must be rescheduled by hand. Rescheduling can be done automatically by a network algorithm. On the other hand, networks are more complex, more difficult to understand, and more costly to use than Gantt charts. Thus networks should be used in complex projects, where they are needed provided the additional cost is justified.

Network scheduling methods involve the use of some important scheduling concepts, such as critical path and slack. These network scheduling concepts will be

---

[1] This notation is called the activity on arrow (AOA) convention. There is also the activity on node (AON) convention, which is the opposite. When the AON convention is used, the activities are denoted by circles (or nodes) and the precedence relationships between activities are indicated by arrows.

described in Section 12.4 by means of the constant-time network. More complicated networks, using random times and cost-time tradeoffs, will be developed later in the chapter.

12.4 CONSTANT-TIME NETWORKS

In constant-time networks, the time for each activity is assumed to be a constant. This is the simplest case from the standpoint of scheduling. Other, more complicated methods are then derived from these constant-time network methods.

A simple constant-time network is shown in Figure 12.3. In this example, the events are numbered in sequential order, so that the head of each arrow has a larger number than the tail. This will ensure that all successor activities and events have larger numbers than their predecessors. Through the use of this numbering scheme, scheduling computations can proceed in order of the numbers, and the predecessors will all be scheduled ahead of successors.

The event numbers shown in Figure 12.3 allow each activity to be identified by its tail and head number pair. Thus activity 1-2 identifies the activity or arrow going from event 1 to event 2. Other activities are also identified in a similar manner.

Some of the precedence relationships indicated in Figure 12.3 are as follows: Activity 1-2 must be completed before activity 2-4 or 2-3 can begin. Activities 1-2, 2-3, and 1-3 must all be completed before activity 3-4 can begin. In general, all predecessors must be completed before any successor activity can begin. Figure 12.3 also shows, immediately next to the arrow, the time required for the completion of each activity. For example, activity 1-2 requires 3 days, and activity 1-3 requires 4 days.

With the help of the above information, the scheduling calculations can be made. Actually there are two types of calculations; one for event times and the other

**Figure 12.3
Network diagram.**

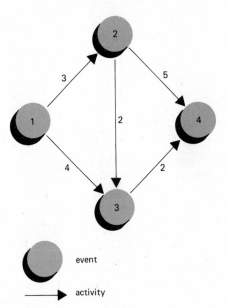

event

activity

for activity times. For the sake of simplicity, event calculations will be presented first.

Event calculations

To calculate event times, the following notation is needed:

t_{ij} = time to complete activity from event i to event j
E_j = earliest time event j can occur based on completion of all predecessor activities
L_j = latest time event j can occur without delaying the project's completion

The forward computational pass will be used to calculate the earliest event times (E_j) for each event j. This is done by means of the following algorithm:

1. Set $E_1 = 0$ for the starting event.[2]
2. Set $E_j = \max_i (E_i + t_{ij})$ where the maximization occurs over all events i which are immediate predecessors of event j.

This algorithm proceeds sequentially from one event to the next beginning with event number 1.

As the algorithm proceeds, each event j is labeled with the value of its earliest start time E_j. In Figure 12,4, the values of E_j are shown above each event, using the example from Figure 12.3. In this example, event 1 is labeled with time zero as the starting time. Event 2 is then labeled with the time $0 + 3 = 3$ by using the activity time from 1 to 2. To label event 3, both activity times 2-3 and 1-3 must be considered. In this case we have:

$$E_3 = \max (3 + 2, 0 + 4) = 5$$

[2] Arbitrary starting times other than zero can also be used.

**Figure 12.4
Network forward
pass.
Early occur-
rence, E_j, values
shown above each
event j.**

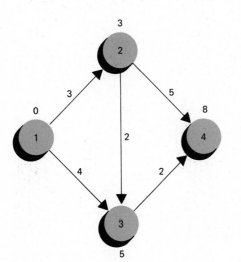

The earliest occurrence time of event 4 is computed by taking the maximum of event 2 plus activity 2-4 and event 3 plus activity 3-4. Thus we have

$$E_4 = \max (3 + 5, 5 + 2) = 8$$

We label event 4 with the value 8. Since event 4 is the last event in the network, the earliest completion of the entire project will also be 8 days. This is the earliest completion time of the project considering the precedence and times of all activities in the network.

In network calculations, a backward pass is also made to derive the latest time that each event can occur without delaying completion of the project. The algorithms for computing these latest times is:

$$L_n = E_n$$

where n represents the last event in the network,

$$L_i = \min_j (L_j - t_{ij})$$

where the minimization occurs over all events j which are immediate successors of event i.

The above times are computed by starting with the last event in the network, representing completion of the project, and proceeding in reverse order, backward, through the network.

The latest event times for the example are shown in Figure 12.5. In this example, we set $L_4 = E_4 = 8$ for the last event. Then there is only one successor for event 3, so:

$$L_3 = L_4 - t_{34} = 8 - 2 = 6$$

We label event 3 with a 6 for its latest occurrence time. For event 2, we have two

Figure 12.5
Network backward pass.
Latest occurrence,
L_i**, values shown above each event** i**.**

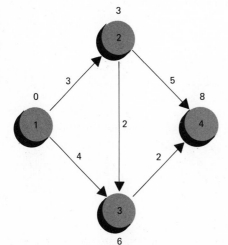

successor events, 3 and 4. Therefore we have:

$$E_2 = \min (8 - 5, 6 - 2) = 3$$

We have taken the minimum in this case, rather than the maximum on the forward pass, because all the successor events must occur before their latest times. Event 2 is labeled with a latest time of 3 days.

The latest time for event 1 is computed in a similar way as that for event 2. Since event 1 has two successor events:

$$E_1 = \min (3 - 3, 5 - 4) = 0$$

It should always turn out that the latest and earliest occurrence time of the first event is zero. This fact can be used as a partial check on the arithmetic used in the calculations.

The information calculated from the forward and backward pass can be used for several managerial purposes: (1) identifying the critical path, (2) calculating slack, and (3) determining the final completion date of the project. A path is any sequence of activities which connects the starting and ending events of the network. The critical path is defined as the *longest-time* path through the network. The critical path, therefore, constrains the completion date of the project, since it is the longest path of activity times from the start to the end of the network.

In the example from Figure 12.3, there are only three paths through the network 1-2-4, 1-2-3-4, and 1-3-4. The length of these paths is 8,7, and 6 respectively. These lengths are obtained by adding the times along the activities on each path. It is apparent from these calculations that path 1-2-4 is the longest of the three and is therefore the critical path. Notice that the length of the critical path is 8, which is also the earliest completion time (E_4) of the project that we have just computed. The forward pass, therefore, immediately provides the length of the critical path as the project completion time.

In large examples, it is not possible to evaluate all paths, as we have just done, to find the longest path, because there are simply too many. Therefore, the forward and backward passes are used directly to find the critical path. In general, the critical path connects those events with $E_i = L_i$. These events are critical since their earliest and latest occurrence times are the same. In the example, events 1, 2, and 4 have $E_i = L_i$; therefore the critical path is 1-2-4.

In managing a project, all activities and events on the critical path must be carefully monitored. If any of the critical activities slips (takes more time than planned), the completion date of the project will slip by a like amount. In a typical project, only 5 to 10 percent of all activities are on the critical path. Therefore the monitoring of critical activities and events provides a significant reduction in managerial effort.

The information computed from the forward and backward passes also allows for the calculation of event slack. The slack for event i, S_i, is defined as follows:

$$S_i = L_i - E_i$$

The slack is, therefore, the precise amount that the event occurrence time can slip before affecting the project completion date. Observe that all events on the critical path should have slack equal to zero. This is another, equivalent way of defining the critical path.

In the example we have been using, the event slack = 0 for events 1, 2, and 4, and slack = 1 for event 3. Thus the occurrence time of event 3 can slip by 1 day before the completion time of the project is affected. This slip of 1 day could occur by either an increase of 1 day in activity 2-3 or 2 days in activity 1-3. In this case there are two different activities which can consume the event slack.

The third use of the forward and backward pass computations is to establish a completion date for the project. If the date calculated from the forward pass is not satisfactory, perhaps activities along the critical path can be extended or shortened to obtain an acceptable date. In this case, tradeoffs may have to be made between cost, performance, and time. The network calculations help to evaluate these tradeoffs since they provide a precise determination of the effect of each proposed change on the completion date of the project.

It is now apparent that network calculations have several advantages over the Gantt chart. Networks allow precise determination of the critical path and slack, and they allow the rapid evaluation of proposed schedule changes. In addition, the ideas of critical path and slack are important conceptual notions in their own right.

Activity calculations

Up to this point we have concentrated on calculating event times. But there are similar calculations for activity start and finish times. In managing networks, it is sometimes important to know the scheduled times for both activities and events.

To calculate activity start and finish times, the following notation is needed:

$ES(a)$ = early start of activity a
$EF(a)$ = early finish of activity a
$LS(a)$ = late start of activity a
$LF(a)$ = late finish of activity a

Each activity has four scheduled times, as defined above. These times may be calculated by a forward and backward pass of the type used for event times, or they may be calculated directly from the event schedule.

To calculate the four activity times directly from the network, a forward activity pass is made by the following method:

$ES(a)$ = 0 for starting activities
$EF(a)$ = $ES(a) + t(a)$
$ES(a)$ = max [EF (all predecessors of a)]

where $t(a)$ denotes the duration of activity a.

On the basis of the example from Figure 12.3, the forward-activity pass computations are made; they are shown in Figure 12.6. The early start and early finish for each activity are placed on the top of each arrow, as shown.

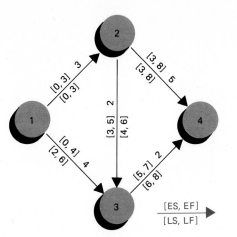

Figure 12.6
Activity start and
finish times.

As an example, the earliest start time of activity 3-4 is computed as the maximum of the earliest finish of activities 2-3 and 1-3. The maximum is used because both these predecessors must be completed before activity 3–4 can begin. The early start time of activity 3–4 is therefore the maximum of (4, 5) = 5. The earliest finish of activity 3–4 is just its early start time of 5 plus the duration of 2 days. In a similar way, the ES and EF times for all other activities are computed.

A backward pass is also needed to calculate the late start and late finish times. The backward-activity pass is based on the following calculations:

$$LF(a) = \min \, [LS \, (\text{all successors of a})]$$
$$LS(a) = LF(a) - t(a)$$

These late times are computed by starting with the last activities in the network and proceeding backward through the entire network in numerical order. The project completion time is set equal to 8, based on the forward pass, and used as the LF times for all ending activities.

In the example in Figure 12.6, the LS and LF times are placed on the bottom of each activity arrow, as shown. To illustrate the computations, the latest finish for activity 2-3 is time 6, since there is only one successor of activity 2-3 which has a latest start of 6. In the case of activity 1-2, there are two successors; the latest finish of activity 1-2 is therefore the minimum of the latest starts for the two successors.

The start and finish times for each activity are summarized in Table 12.3, along with two types of activity slack (or float)—total slack and free slack. The definitions of these activity slack times are:

$$\text{Total slack} = LS(a) - ES(a) = LF(a) - EF(a)$$
$$\text{Free slack} \; = \min \, [ES \, (\text{all successors of a})] - EF(a)$$

The total slack is the amount of time that an activity duration can be increased without delaying the project completion. All activities on the critical path will, therefore, have a total slack of zero.

TABLE 12.3   **ACTIVITY TIMES**

Activity	ES	EF	LS	LF	Total slack	Free slack
1–2	0	3	0	3	0	0
1–3	0	4	2	6	2	1
2–3	3	5	4	6	1	0
2–4	3	8	3	8	0	0
3–4	5	7	6	8	1	1

Free slack is the amount of time that an activity time can be increased without delaying the start of the *very next activity*. The slack is free in the sense that the next activity is not delayed due to other precedence relationships in the network. On the other hand, use of the total slack early in a project network will reduce the slack in successor activities later in the project. Use of total slack in one activity may therefore affect the start dates of successor activities throughout the network, but the final completion date of the project will not be affected. Use of free slack will not affect any of the start dates in the network.

The results of the activity-time calculations are used in the same way as the event-time calculations. The critical path can be identified, the slack times are available, the total project completion date is known, and one can identify the effect on the project completion of reducing or increasing the time for any particular activity. In principle, then, the management information available from activity or event computations is the same.

In summary, it is possible to define early occurrence time, late occurrence time, and slack for each event. These quantities are calculated by a forward and backward pass on event times. We have also shown how it is possible to compute early start, late start, early finish, late finish, total slack, and free slack for each activity. These activity times are computed by a forward and backward pass on activity times. Actually it is possible to compute all these times with only one forward and backward pass. In this case, the activity times ES, LS, EF, LF can be computed directly from the early occurrence and latest occurrence times of the event without doing a separate forward and backward pass. While this procedure is easier computationally, it is more difficult to understand conceptually.

12.5 PERT NETWORKS

Program evaluation review technique (PERT) is a network method for project scheduling that was first developed in the mid 1950s for the Polaris submarine project. [See PERT (1958).] The technique was used to schedule over 3000 contractors, suppliers and agencies, and it is credited with bringing the Polaris submarine project in ahead of schedule by up to two years.

PERT, as originally defined, required three time estimates for each activity; an optimistic time estimate T_o, a most likely time estimate T_m, and a pessimistic time estimate T_p. These three estimates recognize the uncertainty in activity time which is typical of R&D projects. The PERT technique also assumes that the actual activity times are distributed according to the beta probability distribution. The beta distribution is skewed to the right with time estimates that are more likely to exceed the average than to be less than the average (see Figure 12.7).

From the beta distribution, it is possible to convert the PERT network into a constant-time network. This is done by using the expected times T_e for each activity. According to a beta distribution, the average or expected time can be computed as follows:

$$T_e = \frac{T_o + 4T_m + T_p}{6}$$

In this formula, the most likely time is weighted four times more heavily than the optimistic or pessimistic times. The value of T_e is then used as the single constant-time value for each activity. With these expected times, the constant-time methods of the last section can be used in forward and backward passes to compute all event and activity times.

But one cannot eliminate the problem of uncertainty in activity times so easily. When the individual activity times are uncertain, the total project completion time will also be uncertain. To deal with this problem, PERT calculations assume that the variance in total project completion time can be computed by adding the variances along the critical path. This is a reasonable assumption when there are no other near critical paths in the network. In this case, the variance (var_i) for each activity i on the critical path is estimated as follows:

$$var_i = \left(\frac{T_p - T_o}{6}\right)^2$$

This formula is based on the assumption that the pessimistic and optimistic times

**Figure 12.7
PERT activity
times.**

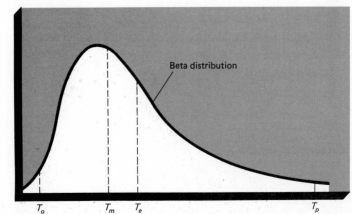

Beta distribution

T_o T_m T_e T_p

BOX 12.2   PERT EXAMPLE

The PERT network and three time estimates for each activity are given below. Compute the probability that the project will be completed by time 13.

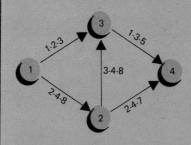

Using the formulas given in the text, the expected time and variance for each activity are computed as follows:

Activity	T_e	Activity variance
1-2	4.33	1.000
2-3	4.50	0.694
1-3	2.00	0.111
2-4	4.17	0.694
3-4	3.00	0.444

Using the values of T_e, a forward pass is made to calculate the expected project completion time of 11.83 as follows:

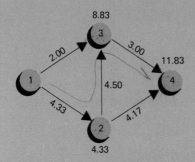

The variance of project completion time (2.138) is the sum of the variances along the critical path.

$$\text{var} = 1.0 + .694 + .444 = 2.138$$

The project completion time is assumed to have a normal distribution with mean = 11.83 and standard deviation = $\sqrt{2.138}$ = 1.462. The probability that the project completion time will be 13 days or less is obtained by calculating the standard normal variate, which is

$$Z = \frac{13 - 11.83}{1.462} = .8002$$

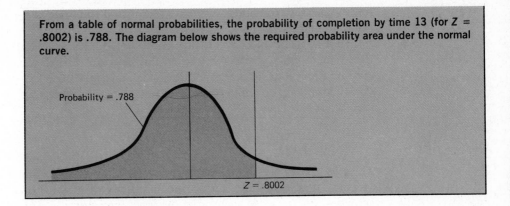

From a table of normal probabilities, the probability of completion by time 13 (for $Z = .8002$) is .788. The diagram below shows the required probability area under the normal curve.

Probability = .788

$Z = .8002$

will cover six standard deviations on the beta distribution.[3] The variance is then the square of the standard deviation.

If we let T be the total completion time of the project, we can then compute:

$$E(T) = \sum_{\substack{\text{critical} \\ \text{path}}} T_e$$

$$\text{var}(T) = \sum_{\substack{\text{critical} \\ \text{path}}} \text{var}_i$$

where $E(T)$ denotes the expected value of T and $\text{var}(T)$ denotes the variance of T.

We also assume that the distribution of project completion times is normal. This assumption is based on the central limit theorem, which assures us that the sum of random times will tend to a normal distribution under rather general conditions. Since we know the mean and variance of the normal distribution of project completion times, it is possible to compute the probability of completing the project by any given date. This is done by standardizing the normal variable and using a table of normal probabilities. See Box 12.2 for an example of these calculations.

Dealing with the uncertainty or randomness of individual time estimates is the essence of the PERT network. When the individual activity times are random, the project time will also be random. It is therefore not appropriate, in this case, to set concrete project completion dates. Each completion date will have a certain probability of being met, which is a function of the uncertainties in the individual activities and the precedence relationships. From a management standpoint it is much better to recognize the uncertainty in completion dates than to force the problem into a constant time framework.

Another concept which emerges from the PERT network is the idea of a probabilistic critical path. Following PERT logic, there is no critical path. Rather, each activity has a probability of being on the critical path; some activities having proba-

---

[3] This assumption, in turn, implies that T_o should be set at about the first percentile, while T_p is set at the 99th percentile.

bilities near zero and others near one. The critical path itself is random when activity times are uncertain.

PERT calculations have been extended to reduce the assumptions inherent in the PERT methodology. One way to do this is to simulate the network by sampling random times for each activity. As a result, an exact distribution of project completion time and a probability that each activity is on the critical path can be computed. [See Wiest and Levy (1977) for more details.]

12.6 CRITICAL PATH METHOD

The critical path method (CPM) was developed by E. I. du Pont de Nemours & Co. as a way to schedule the startup and shutdown of major plants. Since these plant activities were repeated frequently, the times were fairly well known. However, the time of any activity could be compressed by expending more money. Thus CPM assumes a time-cost tradeoff rather than the probabilistic times used in PERT.

The CPM method of project scheduling uses a time-cost function of the type shown in Figure 12.8 for each activity. The activity can be completed in proportionally less time if more money is spent. To express this linear time-cost relationship, four figures are given for each activity: normal time, normal cost, crash time, and crash cost.

The project network is solved initially by using normal times and normal costs for all activities. If the resulting project completion time and cost are satisfactory, all activities will be scheduled at their normal times. If the project completion time is too long, the project can be completed in less time at greater cost.

For any given project completion time that is less than the normal time, a great number of network possibilities exist, each at a different total cost. This occurs because a variety of different activity times can be decreased to meet any specified

**Figure 12.8
CPM time-cost
tradeoff.**

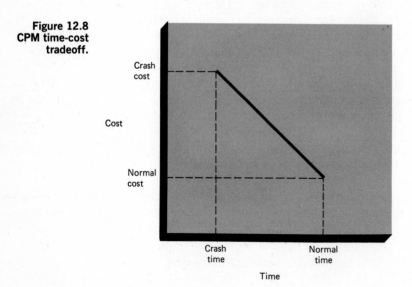

BOX 12.3 **CPM EXAMPLE**

A project network—along with activity times and costs—is given below. Calculate the normal project time and normal cost. Also calculate the least-cost way to reduce the normal project completion time by 1 day.

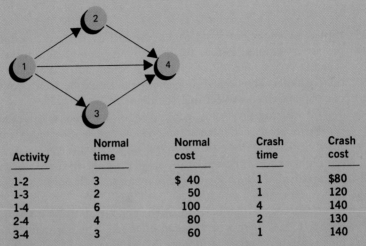

Activity	Normal time	Normal cost	Crash time	Crash cost
1-2	3	$ 40	1	$80
1-3	2	50	1	120
1-4	6	100	4	140
2-4	4	80	2	130
3-4	3	60	1	140

The normal project completion time is computed by setting all activities at their normal times and making a forward pass. The resulting normal project completion time = 7. See the event time calculations below.

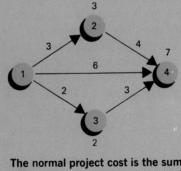

The normal project cost is the sum of normal costs for all activities, which equals $330. The project completion time can be reduced to 6 days by crashing either activity 1-2 or 2-4 by one day. It costs $20 per day to crash activity 1-2 and $25 per day to crash activity 2-4. Therefore it is less costly to crash activity 1-2 by 1 day in order to achieve an overall project completion time of 6 days.

project completion time. All these possibilities can be evaluated by means of a linear programming problem. The LP problem is used to find the solution representing the minimum total project cost for any given project completion time. [For details on this formulation, see Wiest and Levy (1977).]

To illustrate the principles involved, an example is shown in Box 12.3. The example shows how to calculate normal times and normal costs and how to determine the best way to reduce project completion by 1 day. Although this simple example is easily evaluated, it will, as the network becomes more complex, be necessary to use linear programming to evaluate all the combinations.

12.7 USE OF PROJECT MANAGEMENT CONCEPTS

Project management requires a great deal more than scheduling. Planning for the project is required before the scheduling begins and control is required after the schedule is developed. Project management requires a blend of behavioral and quantitative skills. Thus scheduling methods should be seen as only one part of a complete approach to project management.

In selecting project scheduling methods, a conscious tradeoff should be made between sophisticated methods and cost. Gantt chart methods should not be seen as outdated or naive. Rather, Gantt charts are justified for projects where the activities are not highly interconnected or for small projects. In these cases where the Gantt chart is warranted, a network method may not provide enough additional benefits in relation to its costs.

If a network method is justified, a choice must be made between constant time, PERT, CPM, or more advanced methods. The constant-time method is adequate for cases where activity times are constant or nearly so. If activity times are random, a PERT network should be chosen to reflect the uncertainty directly. PERT may therefore be applied to situations such as R&D, computer system design, and military invasions, where activity times are expected to vary.

CPM methods, on the other hand, should be used where activity times are fairly constant but can be reduced by spending more money. CPM might apply in cases such as construction projects, installation of equipment, and plant startup and shutdown. More advanced network methods include generalized networks and resource-constrained situations. These methods are still in development and have not been widely used in practice. See Davis (1976) for more details on advanced scheduling methods.

Network scheduling methods are usually computerized in practice. A large number of different standard software packages are available to cover the entire range of scheduling methods. These packages not only support scheduling but also assist in project accounting and in controlling progress.

12.8 KEY POINTS

The planning and scheduling of projects is concerned with the unique, one-time production activity. Because projects are unique, the scheduling problem is quite different from that of ongoing operations.

The key points covered in this chapter include the following:

- The three objectives in projects are time, cost, and performance. Because these objectives are conflicting, tradeoffs between them must constantly be made in the course of managing projects.

- All projects go through three phases: planning, scheduling, and control. The planning phase establishes the objectives, organization, and resources for the project. The scheduling phase establishes the time schedule, cost, and personnel assignments. The control phase monitors the progress of the project in cost, time, and performance; it also corrects the plan as necessary to achieve project objectives.
- The Gantt chart is a scheduling method for displaying project activities in a bar-chart format. The Gantt chart is useful for small projects or projects where activities are not highly interrelated.
- There are three network scheduling methods; constant-time, PERT, and CPM. All these methods rely on a network or graph to represent the precedence relationship between activities.
- A network allows one to identify the critical path, slack, and activities which need to be rescheduled. The critical path is the longest time path of activities from the beginning to the end of the network. Activities on the critical path have zero slack—they must be completed on time to prevent slippage of the project completion date. Slack is the amount of time that an activity or event can be extended, while still allowing the project to be completed on time.
- The earliest and latest occurrence time for each event is computed by means of a forward and backward pass through the network. The early start, late start, early finish, and late finish time for each activity can also be computed by means of a forward and backward pass.
- PERT is a network-based project scheduling method which requires three time estimates for each activity: optimistic, most likely, and pessimistic. Using these three time estimates, a probability of project completion by any specified date can be computed, along with the standard start and finish times for each activity or event.
- CPM is a network-based method which uses a linear time-cost tradeoff. Each activity can be completed in less than its normal time by crashing the activity for a given cost. Thus if the normal project completion time is not satisfactory, certain activities can be crashed to complete the project in less time.

QUESTIONS

1. How, precisely, does project scheduling differ from the scheduling of ongoing operations?
2. How would you, after the fact, audit a project to determine whether it was successful or not?
3. Give three examples of projects not given in the text. Are these projects entirely unique or are they repeated in some way?
4. Contrast and compare CPM and PERT as project scheduling techniques.
5. Define the terms "critical path," "event slack," "free slack," and "early start."
6. What is the management significance of finding the critical path through a network?
7. What statistical assumptions are made in PERT? Under what conditions are those assumptions realistic?
8. An R&D manager has told you that the statistical part of PERT seems complicated and perhaps too complex for scheduling R&D. What would your response be?
9. What cost-time assumptions are made for the CPM method?

10. How is the Gantt chart used as a scheduling tool? When should the Gantt chart be used in preference to network-based methods?
11. Is it possible to have multiple critical paths in the CPM method? How will this occur?
12. Suppose a particular activity has a very high variance in a PERT chart. How will this affect the result?

PROBLEMS

1. A public accounting firm requires the following activities for an audit.

Activity	Immediate predecessor	Immediate successor	Activity time
a	—	b, e	3
b	a	d	2
c	—	d	4
d	b, c	g	4
e	a	g	2
f	a	—	6
g	e, d	—	5

a. Prepare a Gantt chart for this project.
b. Draw a network for this project. Label the events in sequential order.
c. Make a forward and backward pass for events.
d. What is the critical path and the project completion time?
e. If the project completion must be reduced by 2 days, which activities might be affected?

2. A construction project has the following network and activity times.

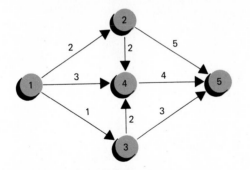

a. Prepare a Gantt chart for this project.
b. Make a forward and backward pass on the activity times.
c. Find the total slack and free slack for each activity.
d. Activity 1-4 will be delayed by 1 day. What effect will this have on the project?

3. An advertising campaign uses a PERT network as shown below.

Activity	T_o	T_m	T_p
1-2	4	5	6
1-3	3	4	8
2-4	1	2	5
2-5	2	3	4
3-4	5	6	9
3-5	2	3	6
4-6	4	5	6
5-6	3	4	8

a. Draw a network and label each activity with its expected time and variance.
b. Calculate the expected completion time and variance for the entire project.
c. What is the probability that the project is completed in 14 days?
d. Are the PERT assumptions used to calculate the probability in part c realistic in this case? Why or why not?
e. What is the effect of the large variance in activity 1-3?

4. A plant startup is based on the following CPM network:

Activity	Immediate predecessor	Immediate successor	Normal time	Normal cost	Crash time	Crash cost
a	—	d, e	4	$100	2	$150
b	—	g	6	80	2	140
c	—	f	2	40	1	60
d	a	g	3	60	1	90
e	a	—	5	80	3	140
f	c	—	4	60	1	100
g	b	—	6	100	2	160

a. Draw the network for this project and label the events.
b. What is the normal project completion time and normal cost?
c. Identify the critical path.
d. How much will it cost to crash the project completion by 1 day? by 2 days?
e. What is the minimum time for project completion?

5. An entrepreneur is starting a new business. The activities and times required are given below.

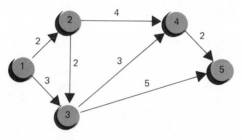

a. Find the critical path and the project completion time.
b. What is the ES, LS, EF, and LF for each activity?
c. How much total slack and free slack is there in activity 2-4?
d. Suppose the project completion must be reduced by 1 day. The costs of expediting various activities are shown below. What should be done and how much will it cost?

Activity	Expediting cost per day
1–2	$50
2–3	30
2–4	40
3–4	20
4–5	20
3–5	50

6. In preparing to teach a new course, the professor has estimated the following expected activity times and variances. On each arrow, the expected time is given, followed by the variance.

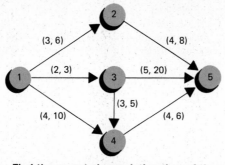

a. Find the expected completion time of the project and the variance of completion time.
b. What is the probability that the class will be ready by time 12?
c. What will the effect of the large variance be on activity 3-5?
d. Are the PERT assumptions justified in this case? Explain. What is the effect of the PERT assumptions on the probability calculated in part c?

SELECTED BIBLIOGRAPHY

DAVIS, EDWARD W. (ed.): *Project Management: Techniques, Applications, and Managerial Issues,* monograph no. 3, Production Planning and Control Division, American Institute of Industrial Engineers, 1976.

KELLY, JAMES E., JR., and MORGAN R. WALKER: "Critical Path Planning and Scheduling," *Proceedings of the Eastern Joint Computer Conference,* Boston, Mass., 1959, pp. 160–173.

MACCRIMMON, K. R., and C. A. RYAVEC: "Analytic Studies of the PERT Assumptions," *Operations Research,* vol. 12, no. 1, January–February 1964, pp. 16–37.

MALCOLM, DONALD G., et al.: "Applications of a Technique for Research and Development Program Evaluation," *Operations Research,* vol. 7, no. 5, September–October 1959, pp. 646–669.

MARTIN, CHARLES C.: *Project Management: How to Make It Work,* New York: AMACOM, a division of American Management Associations, 1976.

PERT, Program Evaluation Research Task, Phase I Summary Report, Special Projects Office, Bureau of Ordnance, Department of the Navy, Washington, D.C., July 1958, pp. 646–669.

WIEST, JEROME D., and FERDINAND LEVY: *A Management Guide to PERT/CPM,* 2d ed., Englewood Cliffs, N.J.: Prentice Hall, 1977.

PART IV
INVENTORY MANAGEMENT

QUALITY

PROCESS

WORK FORCE

CAPACITY

- **INDEPENDENT DEMAND**

- **MATERIALS REQUIREMENTS PLANNING**

INVENTORY

One of the oldest decision areas addressed by operations managers is the scientific management of inventories. In a manufacturing company, inventory and capacity are two sides of the same coin; they must be managed together. In Part III, the primary focus was on capacity, with inventory treated as a related variable. In Part IV, the primary focus will be on inventory, with capacity as a related variable.

The basis for organizing Part IV is the distinction between independent- and dependent-demand inventories. Independent demand is subject to market forces and is thus independent of operations. All finished goods and spare parts are independent-demand inventories. Dependent demand is derived from the demand for another part or component; thus all work-in-process inventory and raw-materials inventories have dependent demand. In automobile production, the demand for finished automobiles is independent, and the demand for parts which go into the automobile is dependent (e.g., one steering wheel, four wheels, and one engine per car).

Chapter 13, on independent-demand inventory, focuses on the different types of models which can be used to replenish inventories. These models help the inventory manager answer the questions of how much and when to order to meet customer service goals at the lowest possible cost. Some examples of computer systems for controlling independent-demand inventories are also given.

Dependent-demand inventories are controlled by materials requirements planning (MRP) systems described in Chapter 14. These systems support the planning and control of inventories and capacity in manufacturing companies. This is done by developing a master schedule of planned output and exploding it into all the parts and components required in a time-phased materials plan. As a result, purchase orders and shop orders are released at the right time and capacity is managed to meet delivery promises.

The distinction between independent and dependent demand has yielded a great improvement in the management of inventories and in production control. By utilizing the concepts in Part IV, the manager will find it possible to meet customer service goals while holding down the costs of inventory and production.

CHAPTER 13
INDEPENDENT-DEMAND INVENTORY

Inventory management is among the most important operations management functions because inventory requires a great deal of capital and affects the delivery of goods to customers. Inventory management has an impact on all business functions, particularly operations, marketing, and finance. Inventories provide customer service, which is of vital interest to marketing. Finance is concerned with the overall financial picture of the organization, including funds allocated to inventory. And operations needs inventories to assure smooth and efficient production.

361

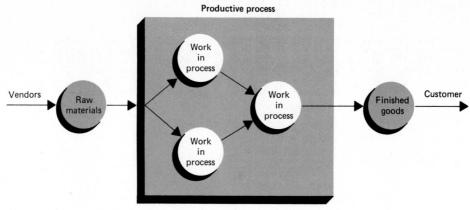

Productive process

**Figure 13.1
A materials-flow
process.**

There are, however, conflicting inventory objectives within the firm. The finance function generally prefers to keep the level of inventories low to conserve capital, marketing prefers high levels of inventories to enhance sales, while operations prefers high inventories for long production runs and smooth employment levels. Inventory management must balance these conflicting objectives and manage inventory levels in the best interests of the firm as a whole. This chapter provides a basis for such an overall approach to inventory management.

It is, perhaps, best to begin our discussion with a definition of inventory. An *inventory* is a stock of materials used to facilitate production or to satisfy customer demands. Inventories typically include raw materials, work in process, and finished goods. This definition fits nicely with the view of operations as a transformation process. In Figure 13.1, an operation is shown as a materials-flow process with raw-materials inventories waiting to enter the productive process, work-in-process inventories in some intermediate stage of transformation, and finished-goods inventories already completely transformed by the production system.

Our definition of inventory as a stock of materials is narrower than that given by some. Shore (1973) defines inventory as "an idle resource of any kind which has potential economic value." Shore's definition allows one to consider equipment or

**Figure 13.2
A water tank anal-
ogy for inventory.**

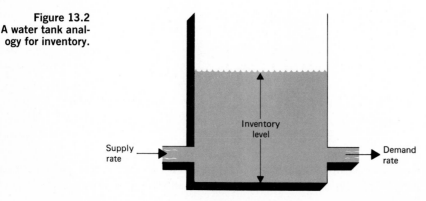

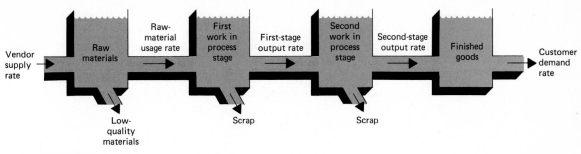

**Figure 13.3
A water tank system analogy.**

idle workers as inventory, but we consider all idle resources other than materials as capacity. From a management and accounting perspective, it is important to distinguish between inventory and capacity. Capacity provides the potential to produce, while inventory, as defined here, is the product at some point in the conversion and distribution process.

Inventory stocks are located at various points in the productive process, with flows connecting one stock point to another. The rate at which a stock can be replenished is the supply capacity and the rate of stock depletion is demand. Inventory acts as a buffer between the different demand and supply rates.

The water tank shown in Figure 13.2 is a good analogy for these concepts of flows and stocks. In this figure, the level of water in the tank corresponds to inventory. The rate of flow into the tank is analogous to supply capacity and the rate of flow out corresponds to demand. The water level (inventory) is thus a buffer between supply and demand. If demand exceeds supply, the water level will drop until the demand and supply rates come back into balance or until the water is depleted. Likewise, if supply exceeds demand, the water level will rise.

Imagine a number of these tanks connected together, each with varying inputs and outputs. This situation, illustrated in Figure 13.3, is a good analogy to a single-product inventory-management problem. Here, one tank represents raw materials, while there are two tanks for work in process and one for finished goods. The tanks serve as buffers to absorb variations in flow rates within the system.

13.1 PURPOSE OF INVENTORIES

The primary purpose of inventories is to uncouple the various phases of operations. Raw-materials inventory uncouples a manufacturer from its vendors; work-in-process inventory uncouples the various stages of manufacturing from each other; and finished-goods inventory uncouples a manufacturer from its customers.

Within the overall uncoupling purpose, there are four reasons to carry inventory:

1. TO PROTECT AGAINST UNCERTAINTIES. In inventory systems, there are uncertainties in supply, demand, and lead time. Safety stocks are maintained in inventory to protect against those uncertainties. If customer demand were known, it would be feasible—although not necessarily economical—to produce at the same rate as consumption. In this case, no finished-goods inventory would be needed; however, every change in demand would be immediately transmitted to the productive system in order to maintain customer service. Instead of such tight coupling, safety stocks of finished goods are maintained to absorb changes in demand without immediately changing production. In a similar way, safety stocks of raw materials are maintained to absorb uncertainties in delivery by vendors, and safety stocks of in-process inventories are maintained to allow for fast schedule changes. In general, inventory carried to absorb uncertainty is called safety stock.

2. TO ALLOW ECONOMIC PRODUCTION AND PURCHASE. It is often economical to produce materials in lots. In this case, a lot may be produced over a short period of time, and then no further production is done until the lot is nearly depleted. This makes it possible to spread the setup cost of the production machines over a large number of items. It also permits the use of the same productive equipment for different products. A similar situation holds for the purchase of raw materials. Due to ordering costs, quantity discounts, and transportation costs, it is often economical to purchase in large lots, even though part of the lot is then held in inventory for later use. The inventory resulting from the purchase or production of material in lots is often called cycle inventory, since the lots are produced or purchased on a cyclic basis.

3. TO COVER ANTICIPATED CHANGES IN DEMAND OR SUPPLY. There are several types of situations where changes in demand or supply may be anticipated. One case is where the price or availability of raw materials is expected to change. Companies often stockpile steel prior to an expectd steel industry strike. Another source of anticipation is a planned market promotion where a large amount of finished goods may be stocked prior to a sale. Finally, companies in seasonal businesses often anticipate demand in order to smooth employment, as discussed in Chapter 10. For example, a producer of air conditioners may select a nearly uniform rate of production, although a great deal of the product is sold in the summer. Any inventories carried in anticipation of demand or supply are quite naturally called anticipation inventories.

4. TO PROVIDE FOR TRANSIT. Transit inventories consist of materials that are on their way from one point to another. These inventories are affected by plant location decisions and by the choice of carrier. Technically speaking, inventories moving between stages of production, even within a plant, can also be classified as transit inventories. Sometimes the inventory in transit is called pipeline inventory because it is in the "distribution pipeline."

The first two categories of inventory will be treated extensively in this chapter, while the remaining two categories are treated in other parts of the book. The reasons for carrying inventory will influence the methods used for inventory management. This will become clearer as the chapter develops.

13.2 DECISION PROBLEMS

There are a number of different decision problems in inventory management:

1. Which items should be carried in stock?
2. How much should be ordered?
3. When should an order be placed?
4. What type of inventory control system should be used?

Question 1 deals with whether the item will be made to stock or made to order. It also deals with the issue of whether existing items should be continued in stock or discontinued. Many inventories include numerous obsolete or "insurance" items for which there is very little demand. Should these items be kept, salvaged, written off the books, or replenished?

Question 2 and 3 are the classical inventory questions. There have probably been more papers published on these two questions than any other topics in business administration. Question 2 is concerned with the order quantity, given that an order is placed. Question 3 is concerned with the timing of the order—when it should be

BOX 13.1   **TYPICAL DECISION PROBLEM**

Marlene Lenton, president of Farwell Enterprises, was glad that she had increased capacity of operations in response to the aggregate planning problem presented in Box 10.1. Sales had once again increased and the additional capacity was already being used. Problems were now cropping up in the mix of individual furnace products. While some products were in good supply, others were out of stock.

Farwell's products were distributed through a factory warehouse and through several field warehouses. Each of these distribution sites placed orders with the factory for individual stock-keeping units (furnaces, furnace parts, and furnace equipment). All together, there were 10,000 different stock-keeping units which could be ordered by the distribution sites. At each distribution site, inventory was controlled by a reorder-point system. When the inventory on hand plus that on order dropped to the reorder point, an order for a predetermined economic order quantity was placed to the factory. The factory then accumulated these orders and filled them as soon as it could.

In discussing this situation with Gretchen Davidson, vice president of operations, Marlene noted two problems: "First, we need to study the reorder points at the distribution sites. Some reorder points may be set too high and others too low, leading to an oversupply of some items and shortages of others. The second problem we need to study is the interaction between the aggregate capacity available and the warehouse inventory systems. In developing the aggregate plan, we decide on total inventory levels and total capacity by month. We need to synchronize the individual orders coming from the warehouses with the overall aggregate plan. In periods of slack demand, we will be building more inventory than we need at the warehouses, and in periods of high demand, we will be building less than needed."

Marlene asked Gretchen to look into these two problems and to report back within 2 weeks. Marlene observed, "We must find a better way to coordinate production planning in the factories with the distribution system. I am willing to change our reorder-point system at the warehouses or the way we do production planning in order to integrate these two systems."

placed. Answers to both of these questions provide a decision rule which specifies when to order and how much to order. Several decision rules will be examined later.

To make sure that the right amount is ordered at the right time, an inventory control system is needed. This system should keep accurate records, trigger orders when needed, and track the flow of materials in and out of inventory. An answer to Question 4 matches the right kind of computer or manual system to the inventory problem.

A typical inventory decision problem is given in Box 13.1. Notice how this problem is related to the aggregate planning problem discussed in Chapter 10.

13.3 INVENTORY COST STRUCTURES

Many inventory decision problems can be solved by using economic criteria. One of the most important prerequisites, however, is an appropriate cost structure. Many of these cost structures incorporate the following four types of costs:

1. **ITEM COST.** This is the cost of buying or producing the individual inventory items. The item cost is usually expressed as a cost per unit multiplied by the quantity procured or produced. Sometimes item cost is discounted if enough units are purchased at one time.

2. **ORDERING (OR SETUP) COST.** The ordering cost is associated with ordering a batch or lot of items. Ordering cost does not depend on the number of items ordered; it is assigned to the entire batch. This cost includes typing the purchase order, expediting the order, transportation costs, receiving costs, and so on. When the item is produced within the firm, there are also costs associated with placing an order which are independent of the number of items produced. These so-called setup costs include paperwork costs plus the costs required to set up the production equipment for a run. In some cases, setup costs can amount to thousands of dollars, leading to significant economies for large runs.

3. **CARRYING (OR HOLDING) COSTS.** The carrying or holding cost is associated with keeping items in inventory for a period of time. The holding cost is typically charged as a percentage of dollar value per unit time. For example, a 15 percent annual holding cost means that it will cost 15 cents to hold $1 of inventory for a year. In practice, holding costs typically range from 15 to 30 percent per year.

The carrying cost usually consists of three components:

Cost of capital. When items are carried in inventory, the capital invested is not available for other purposes. This represents a cost of foregone opportunities for other investments, which is assigned to inventory as an opportunity cost.

Cost of storage. This cost includes variable space cost, insurance, and taxes. In some cases, a part of the storage cost is fixed, for example, when a warehouse is owned and cannot be used for other purposes. Such fixed costs should not be included in the cost of inventory storage. Likewise, taxes and insurance should be included only if they vary with the inventory level.

Costs of obsolescence, deterioration, and loss. Obsolescence costs should be assigned to items which have a high risk of becoming obsolete; the higher the risk, the higher the costs. Perishable products should be charged with deterioration costs when the item deteriorates over time, e.g., food and blood. The costs of loss include pilferage and breakage costs associated with holding items in inventory.

4. STOCKOUT COST. Stockout cost reflects the economic consequences of running out of stock. There are two cases here. First, suppose items are back ordered or backlogged for the customer and the customer waits until the material arrives. There may be some loss of goodwill or future business associated with each back order because the customer had to wait. This opportunity loss is counted as a stockout cost. The second case is where the sale is lost if material is not on hand. The profit is lost from the sale and goodwill, in the form of future sales, may also be lost.

Inventory costs are often difficult to assess, but with persistence they can be estimated accurately enough for most decision-making purposes. The item cost can usually be estimated directly from historical records. Item cost is one inventory cost on which estimation accuracy is normally good.

The ordering (setup) cost can also be determined from company records. However, difficulties are sometimes encountered in separating fixed and variable ordering-cost components. The ordering cost should include only the costs which vary with the number of orders placed. Fixed ordering costs should be ignored for inventory decision-making purposes.

The carrying cost is more difficult to determine accurately. First of all, the cost of capital is an opportunity cost which cannot be derived from historical records. One can, however, determine an appropriate cost of capital on the basis of financial considerations. The rest of the carrying costs—storage, deterioration, obsolescence, and losses—can be based on company records plus special cost studies.

Stockout cost is the most difficult of all inventory costs to estimate. Estimates can be based on the concept of foregone profits; in practice, however, the problem is often handled indirectly by specifying an acceptable stockout risk level. This practice can be costly; it may imply very high stockout costs, as will be demonstrated later. The problem of stockout-cost measurement does not have a satisfactory solution. More theoretical and practical research work is needed.

13.4 INDEPENDENT VERSUS DEPENDENT DEMAND

A crucial distinction in inventory management is whether demand is independent or dependent. *Independent demand* is influenced by market conditions outside the control of operations; it is therefore independent of operations. Finished-goods inventories and spare parts for replacement have independent demand. *Dependent demand* is related to the demand for another item and is not independently determined by the market. When products are built up from parts and assemblies, the demand for these components is dependent on the demand for the final product.

A toy wagon can be used to illustrate the difference between independent and dependent demand. The demand for wagons is independent because it is influenced by the market. The demand for wagon wheels is dependent because it is mathematically related to the demand for wagons; it takes four wheels to complete each wagon produced. Likewise, the demand for wagon handles is dependent on the demand for finished wagons. In general, therefore, the demand for finished products and spare parts is independent while the demand for component parts, assemblies, and raw materials is dependent.

Independent and dependent demands exhibit very different usage or demand patterns. Since independent demand is subject to market forces, it often exhibits some fixed pattern while also responding to random influences which usually stem from a great many different customer preferences. On the other hand, dependent demand exhibits a lumpy, on-again, off-again pattern because production is typically scheduled in lots. A quantity of parts is required when a lot is made; then no parts are required until the next lot is made. These demand patterns are shown in Figure 13.4.

Different demand patterns call for different approaches to inventory management. For independent demand, a *replenishment* philosophy is appropriate. As the stock is used, it is replenished in order to have materials on hand for customers. Thus, as inventory begins to run out, an order is triggered for more material and the inventory is replenished.

For dependent-demand items, a *requirements* philosophy is used. The amount of stock ordered is based on requirements for higher-level items. As one begins to run out, additional raw material or work-in-process inventory is *not* ordered. More material is ordered only as required by the need for other higher-level or end items.

The nature of demand, therefore, leads to two different philosophies of inventory management. These philosophies, in turn, generate different sets of methods and computer software systems. In this chapter, the independent demand case will be covered, including the following types of inventories:

1. Finished-goods inventories and spare parts in manufacturing companies
2. Retail and wholesale finished goods
3. Service-industry (e.g., hospitals, schools, etc.) inventory

In Chapter 14, we will study the management of dependent-demand inventories.

Figure 13.4 Demand patterns.

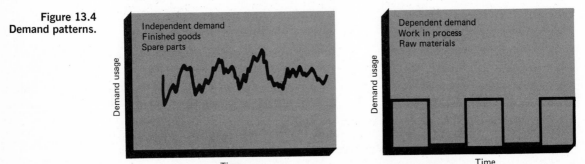

13.5 ECONOMIC ORDER QUANTITY

In 1915, F. W. Harris developed the famous economic order quantity (EOQ) formula. Later, this formula gained wide use in industry through the efforts of a consultant named Wilson. Thus, the formula is often called the Wilson EOQ even though it was developed by Harris. The EOQ is still widely used in industry for independent-demand inventory management.

The derivation of the EOQ model is based on the following assumptions:

1. The demand rate is constant, recurring, and known. For example, demand (or usage) is 100 units a day with no random variation, and demand is assumed to continue into the indefinite future.
2. The lead time is constant and known. The lead time, from order placement to order delivery, is therefore always a fixed number of days.
3. No stockouts are allowed. Since demand and lead time are constant, one can determine exactly when to order material to avoid stockouts.
4. Material is ordered or produced in a lot or batch and the lot is placed into inventory all at one time.
5. A specific cost structure is used as follows: The unit item cost is constant and no discounts are given for large purchases. The carrying cost depends linearly on the average inventory level. There is a fixed ordering or setup cost for each lot which is independent of the number of items in the lot.
6. The item is a single product; there is no interaction with other products.

Under these assumptions, the inventory level over time is shown in Figure 13.5. Notice that the figure shows a perfect "sawtooth" pattern, because demand is constant and items are ordered in fixed lot sizes.

In choosing the lot size, there is a tradeoff between ordering frequency and inventory level. Small lots will lead to frequent reorders but a low average inventory level. If larger lots are ordered, the ordering frequency will decrease but more inventory will be carried. This tradeoff between ordering frequency and inventory level can be represented by a mathematical equation using the following symbols:

D = demand rate, units per year
A = cost per order placed, dollars per order
C = unit cost, dollars per unit

**Figure 13.5
EOQ inventory
levels.**

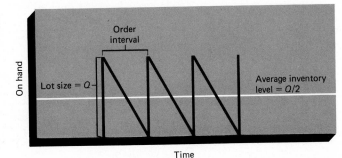

i = carrying "interest" rate, percent of dollar value per year

Q = lot size, units

$C(Q)$ = total of ordering cost plus carrying cost, dollars per year

The annual ordering cost is:

$$\text{Ordering cost per year} = (\text{cost per order})(\text{orders per year}) = A\frac{D}{Q}$$

In the above equation, D is the total demand for a year, and the product is ordered Q units at a time; thus D/Q orders are placed in a year.

The annual carrying cost is:

$$\text{Carrying cost per year} = (\text{annual carrying rate})(\text{unit cost})(\text{average inventory})$$
$$= \frac{iCQ}{2}$$

In this equation, the average inventory is $Q/2$. A maximum of Q units is carried just as a batch arrives; the minimum amount carried is zero units. Since the stock is depleted at a constant rate, the average inventory is $Q/2$. The carrying rate per year i times the unit cost C gives the cost of holding *one* unit in inventory for a year. This unit charge multiplied by the average inventory level gives the total carrying cost on an annual basis.

The total annual cost of inventory is then:[1]

$$\text{Total cost per year} = \text{ordering cost per year} + \text{carrying cost per year}$$

$$C(Q) = \frac{AD}{Q} + \frac{iCQ}{2} \tag{13.1}$$

---

[1] Notice that the item cost of procurement is the constant CD, which is independent of Q and can therefore be ignored from further consideration. It will not affect the minimum of $C(Q)$.

**Figure 13.6
Total cost of inventory.**

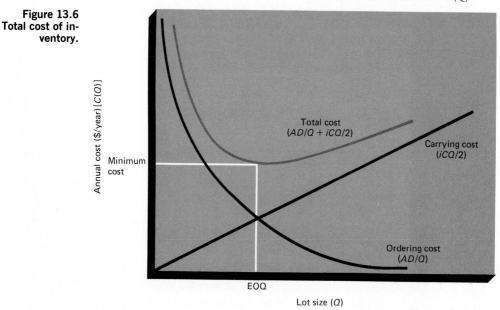

Figure 13.6 is a plot of $C(Q)$ versus Q, with each component of $C(Q)$ shown separately along with the total. As Q increases, the ordering-cost component decreases because less orders are placed per year; at the same time, however, the carrying-cost component increases because more average inventory is held. Thus, ordering and carrying costs are offsetting; one decreases while the other increases. This is precisely the tradeoff between ordering and carrying costs which we mentioned earlier. Because of this tradeoff, the function $C(Q)$ has a minimum.

Finding the value of Q which minimizes $C(Q)$ is a classic problem in calculus.[2] We take the derivative of $C(Q)$, set it equal to zero, and then solve for the resulting value of Q.

$$C'(Q) = -\frac{AD}{Q^2} + \frac{iC}{2} = 0$$

$$\frac{AD}{Q^2} = \frac{iC}{2}$$

$$Q^2 = \frac{2AD}{iC}$$

$$Q = \sqrt{\frac{2AD}{iC}} \tag{13.2}$$

Equation (13.2) is the classic Wilson economic order quantity, which minimizes the cost of operating the inventory. Although we have minimized cost on an annual basis, any unit of time can be used provided the demand rate and interest rate are compatible. For example, if demand is expressed on a monthly basis, the interest rate must also be expressed on a monthly basis.

To illustrate the use of the EOQ formula, suppose we were managing a carpet store and wanted to determine how many yards of a certain type of carpet to buy. The carpet has the following characteristics:

D = 360 yards per year
A = \$10 per order
 i = 25% per year
C = \$8 per yard

Thus

$$Q = \sqrt{\frac{2(10)(360)}{.25(8)}} = \sqrt{3600} = 60$$

The manager should order 60 yards of carpet at a time. This will result in 360/60 = 6 orders per year, or one order every 2 months.

The minimum cost of operating this inventory will be \$120 per year.

$$C(60) = 10(^{360}/_{60}) + .25(8)\,(^{60}/_2) = 60 + 60 = 120$$

[2] Without the use of calculus, the EOQ formula can be rationalized as follows: Observe from Figure 13.6 that the minimum of $C(Q)$ occurs where the two curves intersect. Determine this intersection by setting $AD/Q = iCQ/2$ and solve for the resulting value of Q.

Notice that the minimum cost occurs when the ordering-cost component equals the carrying-cost component.

Table 13.1 shows that the total-cost curve for the carpet inventory is very flat in the neighborhood of the minimum. For example, if 50 or 70 units instead of 60 are ordered, the cost change is very slight, about a 1 percent increase. Even if 80 units are ordered instead of 60, the cost increase is about 4 percent. Thus the manager can adjust the order quantity by a fair amount if necessary, with little effect on the cost of operating the inventory.

Likewise, the cost of ordering and holding need not be exact because the EOQ is fairly insensitive to these parameters. For example, if the cost of ordering is increased by 50 percent, the EOQ only increases by 22.5 percent due to the square-root effect.

The EOQ formula has many limitations. Some of the most serious ones are the following:

1. Demand is assumed constant, while in many real situations demand varies substantially. In the next sections, random demand will be considered.
2. The unit cost is assumed to be constant, but in practice there are often quantity discounts for large purchases. This case requires a modification of the basic EOQ model and is treated in the chapter supplement.
3. The material in the lot is assumed to arrive all at once, but in some cases material will be placed in inventory continuously as it is produced. This case is also treated in the supplement.
4. A single product is assumed, but sometimes multiple items are purchased from a single supplier and they are all shipped at the same time. This case is treated later in the chapter.

Even though the EOQ formula is derived from rather restrictive assumptions, it is a useful approximation in practice. The formula at least "puts you in the ball

TABLE 13.1

INVENTORY COST VERSUS ORDER QUANTITY

Q	C(Q)
10	$370
20	200
30	150
40	130
50	122
60	120
70	121.4
80	125
90	130
100	136

park." Furthermore, the total-cost curve is rather flat in the region of the minimum; thus the EOQ can be adjusted somewhat to conform to reality without greatly affecting the costs.

The EOQ formula can also provide insight into economic behavior of inventories. For example, traditional turnover arguments suggest that inventory should increase directly with sales if a constant turnover ratio is desired. Since turnover is the ratio of sales to inventory, a doubling of sales will allow a doubling of inventory if the turnover rate is held constant. But the EOQ formula suggests that inventory should increase only with the square root of sales. This indicates that it is not economic to maintain a constant turnover ratio as sales increase; a higher turnover is indeed justified.

Despite this caveat, managers continue to place undue reliance on turnover criteria. Although turnover may "suggest" that inventories are too high or too low, inventory policy should *not* be based on turnover ratios. In Section 13.8 a rational basis for inventory policy which considers both costs and desired service levels will be discussed.

13.6 CONTINUOUS REVIEW SYSTEM

In practice one of the most serious limitations of the EOQ model is the assumption of constant demand. In this section, we will relax this assumption and allow random demand. The result will be a model which is sufficiently flexible to use in practice for independent-demand inventory management. All other EOQ assumptions except constant demand and no stockouts will remain in effect. In this section, we will be assuming that the stock level is reviewed continuously; in Section 13.7, a periodic review model will be developed.

In inventory work, decisions to reorder stock are based on the total on-hand plus on-order quantity. On-order material is counted the same as on-hand for reorder decisions because the on-order material is scheduled to arrive, even if nothing more is done. The total of on-hand and on-order material is called stock position (or available stock). One should be careful on this point. A common mistake in inventory problems is failure to consider amounts already on order.

In a continuous review system, the stock position is monitored after each transaction (or continuously). When the stock position drops to a predetermined order point (or reorder point), a fixed quantity is placed on order. Since the order quantity is fixed, the time between orders will vary depending on the random nature of demand. The continuous review system is sometimes called the Q system or the fixed-order-quantity system.

A formal definition of the Q-system decision rule follows:

Continually review the stock position (on hand plus on order). When the stock position drops to the reorder point R, a fixed quantity Q is ordered.

A graph of the operation of this system is shown in Figure 13.7. The stock position drops on an irregular basis until it reaches the reorder point R, where an order for Q

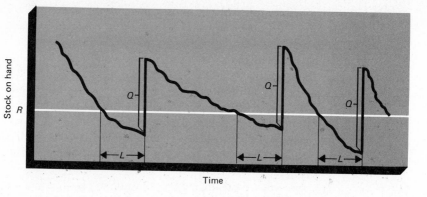

Figure 13.7
A continuous re-
view (Q) system.
(R = reorder
point; Q = order
quantity; L = lead
time.)

units is placed. The order arrives later, after a lead time L, and the cycle of usage, reorder, and stock receipt is then repeated.

The Q system is completely determined by the two parameters Q and R. In practice, these parameters are set by using certain simplifying assumptions. First, Q is set equal to the EOQ value from Equation (13.2) by using the average demand for D. In more complicated models, Q and R must be determined simultaneously. Using the EOQ formula for Q is, however, a reasonable approximation provided that demand is not highly uncertain.

The value of R can be based on either stockout cost or stockout probability. Formulations which utilize stockout cost, however, become quite complicated mathematically and the stockout cost is difficult to estimate. Therefore, stockout probability is commonly used as a basis to determine R.

A widely used term in inventory management is service level, which is the percentage of customer demands satisfied from inventory. A 100 percent service level thus represents meeting all customer demands from inventory. The stockout percentage is equal to 100 minus service level.

There are several different ways to express service level:

1. Service level is the probability that all orders will be filled from stock during the lead time.
2. Service level is the percentage of demand filled from stock during a given period of time (e.g., a year).
3. Service level is the percentage of time the system has stock on hand.

Each of these definitions of service level will lead to different reorder points. Furthermore, one must determine whether to count customers, units, or orders when applying any of these definitions. In this text, for the sake of simplicity, only the first definition of service level will be used.[3]

The reorder point is based on the notion of a probability distribution of demand over the lead time. When an order has been placed, the inventory system is exposed

---

[3] In this case the percentage of orders filled from stock during a given period of time will be a function of the reorder frequency.

to stockout until the order arrives. Since the reorder point is usually greater than zero, it is reasonable to assume that the system does not run out of stock unless an order has been placed; the only risk of stockout is during replenishment lead time.

Figure 13.8 shows a typical probability distribution of independent demand over lead time. The reorder point in the figure can be set sufficiently high to reduce the stockout probability to any desired level. However, in calculating this probability, it will be necessary to know the statistical distribution of demand over the lead time. In the remainder of this discussion, we will assume a normal distribution of demand. This assumption is quite realistic for many independent-demand inventory problems.

The reorder point is defined as follows:

$$R = m + s \qquad\qquad (13.3)$$

where R = reorder point
   m = mean (average) demand over the lead time
   s = safety stock (or buffer stock)

We can express safety stock as:

$$s = z\sigma$$

where z = safety factor
   σ = standard deviation of demand over the lead time

Then we have:

$$R = m + z\sigma$$

Thus the reorder point is set equal to the average demand over lead time m plus a specified number of standard deviations σ to protect against stockout. By controlling z, the number of standard deviations used, one can control not only the reorder

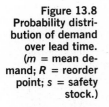

**Figure 13.8
Probability distri-
bution of demand
over lead time.
(m = mean de-
mand; R = reorder
point; s = safety
stock.)**

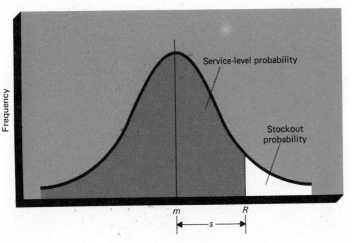

Demand over lead time

point but also the service level. A high value of z will result in a high reorder point and a high service level.

The percentages in Table 13.2 are from the normal distribution. These percentages represent the probability that the demand will fall within the specified number of standard deviations from the mean. Given a particular service level desired, it will be possible to determine z and then the reorder point from Table 13.2.

An example might help cement some of these ideas. Suppose we are managing a warehouse which distributes a certain type of breakfast food to retailers. The breakfast food has the following characteristics:

Average demand = 200 cases per day
Lead time = 4 days for resupply from the vendor
Standard deviation of daily demand = 150 cases
Desired service level = 95%
A = $20 per order
i = 20% per year
C = $10 per case

TABLE 13.2   NORMAL DEMAND PERCENTAGES

z	Service level, percent	Stockout, percent
0	50.0	50.0
.5	69.1	30.9
1.0	84.1	15.9
1.1	86.4	13.6
1.2	88.5	11.5
1.3	90.3	9.7
1.4	91.9	8.1
1.5	93.3	6.7
1.6	94.5	5.5
1.7	95.5	4.5
1.8	96.4	3.6
1.9	97.1	2.9
2.0	97.7	2.3
2.1	98.2	1.8
2.2	98.6	1.4
2.3	98.9	1.1
2.4	99.2	.8
2.5	99.4	.6
2.6	99.6	.5
2.7	99.6	.4
2.8	99.7	.3
2.9	99.8	.2
3.0	99.9	.1

Assume that a continuous review system will be used and also assume that the warehouse is open 5 days a week, 50 weeks a year, or 250 days a year. Then average *annual* demand = 250(200) = 50,000 cases per year.

The economic order quantity is:

$$Q = \sqrt{\frac{2(20)(250)(200)}{10(.20)}} = \sqrt{10^6} = 1000 \text{ cases}$$

The average demand over the lead time is 200 cases a day for 4 days; therefore $m = 4(200) = 800$ cases. The standard deviation of demand over the lead time is $\sqrt{4}(150) = 300$ units.[4]

The 95 percent level requires a safety factor of $z = 1.65$ (see Table 13.2). Thus we have:

$$R = m + z\sigma = 800 + 1.65(300) = 1295$$

The Q-system decision rule is to place an order for 1000 cases whenever the stock position drops to 1295 cases. On average, 50 orders will be placed per year, and there will be an average of 5 working days between orders. The actual time between orders will vary, however, depending on demand.

[4] The standard deviation of demand over the 4-day lead time can be computed from the daily standard deviation by assuming that the daily demands are independent. In this case the variance is additive and the variance for 4 days is four times the daily variance. This equates to $\sigma^2 = 4(150)^2$ or $\sigma = \sqrt{4}(150)$.

| BOX 13.2 | A Q-SYSTEM EXAMPLE* |

A Q-SYSTEM EXAMPLE*

Day	Demand	Beginning period on hand	Beginning period on order	Beginning period stock position	Amount ordered	Amount received
1	111	1100	—	1100	1000	—
2	217	989	1000	1989	—	—
3	334	772	1000	1772	—	—
4	124	438	1000	1438	—	—
5	0	1314	—	1314	—	1000
6	371	1314	—	1314	—	—
7	135	943	—	943	1000	—
8	208	808	1000	1808	—	—
9	315	600	1000	1600	—	—
10	0	285	1000	1285	1000	—
11	440	1285	1000	2285	—	1000
12	127	845	1000	1845	—	—
13	315	718	1000	1718	—	—
14	114	1403	—	1403	—	1000
15	241	1289	—	1289	1000	—
16	140	1048	1000	2048	—	—

* For this box we have used Q = 1000 and R = 1295.

To complete this example, Box 13.2 simulates the operation of the Q-system decision rule. Here a series of random demands were generated on the basis of an average of 200 cases per day and a standard deviation of 150 cases per day. It is assumed that 1100 units are on hand at the beginning of the simulation and none are on order. An order for 1000 cases is placed whenever the stock position reaches 1295 units. The stock position is reviewed each day, as demands occur, for a possible order. The result is that orders are placed in periods 1, 7, 10, and 15. The lowest inventory level is 285 units at the beginning of day 10. It will be good practice to verify the numbers in part of the box.

13.7 A PERIODIC REVIEW SYSTEM

In some cases the finished-goods stock position is reviewed periodically rather than continuously. Suppose a supplier will only take orders and make deliveries at periodic intervals, for example, every 2 weeks, as his truck makes the rounds to your store. In this case, the stock position is reviewed every 2 weeks and an order is placed if material is needed.

In this section we are assuming that the stock position is reviewed periodically and the demand is random. All EOQ assumptions in Section 13.5 except constant demand and no stockouts will remain in effect.

In a periodic review system, the stock position is reviewed at fixed intervals. When the review is made, the stock position is "ordered up" to a target inventory level. The target level is set to cover demand until the next periodic review plus the delivery lead time. A variable quantity is ordered depending on how much is needed to bring the stock position up to target. The periodic review system is often called the P system of inventory control, the fixed-order-interval system, the fixed-order-period system, or simply the periodic system.

A formal definition of the P-system rule follows:

> Review the stock position (on hand plus on order) at fixed periodic intervals P. An amount equal to target inventory T minus the stock position is ordered after each review.

A graph of the operation of this system is shown in Figure 13.9. The stock position drops on an irregular basis until the fixed review time is reached. At that time, a quantity is ordered to bring the stock position up to the target level. The order arrives later, after a lead time L; then the cycle of usage, reorder, and stock receipt repeats.

The P system functions in a completely different manner than the Q system because (1) it does not have a reorder point but rather a target inventory; (2) it does not have an economic order quantity, since the quantity varies according to demand; and (3) in the P system, the order interval is fixed, not the order quantity.

The P system is completely determined by the two parameters, P and T. An approximation to the optimal value of P can be made by using the EOQ formula in Equation (13.2). Since P is the time between orders, it is related to the EOQ as follows:

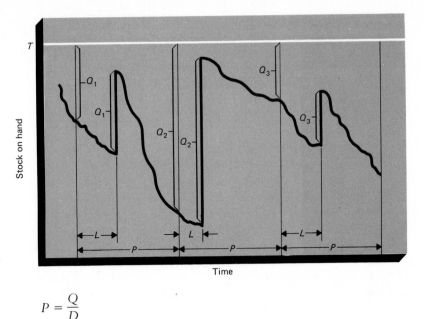

**Figure 13.9
A periodic review
system.**

$$P = \frac{Q}{D}$$

Then, substituting the EOQ formula for Q, we have:

$$P = \frac{Q}{D} = \frac{1}{D}\sqrt{\frac{2DA}{iC}} = \sqrt{\frac{2A}{iCD}} \tag{13.4}$$

Equation (13.4) provides an approximately optimal review interval P.[5]

The target inventory level can be set by a specified service level. In this case the target inventory is set high enough to cover demand over the lead time plus review period. This coverage time is needed because stock will not be ordered again until the next review period, and that stock will take the lead time to arrive. To achieve the specified service level, demand must be covered over the time $P + L$ at the average level plus a safety stock. Thus we have:

$$T = m' + s' \tag{13.5}$$

where T = target inventory level
m' = average demand over $P + L$
s' = safety stock

The safety stock should be set high enough to assure the desired service level. For safety stock, we have:

$$s' = z\sigma'$$

where σ' = the standard deviation over $P + L$
z = safety factor

---

[5] When demand is highly uncertain, the approximation may be quite poor. See Starr and Miller (1962), p. 129.

By controlling z, we can control the target inventory and the resulting service level provided.

To illustrate, we will use the breakfast food example from the last section. Recall that the EOQ was 1000 cases and the daily demand 200 cases. The optimal review interval is then:

$$P = \frac{Q}{D} = \frac{1000}{200} = 5 \text{ days}$$

The formula for target inventory is:

$$T = m' + z\sigma'$$

In this case, m' is the average demand over $P + L = 5 + 4 = 9$ days. Thus we have $m' = 9(200) = 1800$. The standard deviation σ' is for the period $P + L = 9$ days. Thus we have $\sigma' = \sqrt{9}(150) = 450$, where 150 is the daily standard deviation and 9 the number of days.

Therefore,

$$T = 1800 + z(450)$$

For a service level of 95%, we need $z = 1.65$. Thus,

$$T = 1800 + 1.65(450) = 2542$$

BOX 13.3 **A P-SYSTEM EXAMPLE***

Day	Demand	Beginning period on hand	Beginning period on order	Beginning period stock position	Amount ordered	Amount received
1	111	1100	—	1100	1442	—
2	217	989	1442	2431	—	—
3	334	772	1442	2214	—	—
4	124	438	1442	1880	—	—
5	0	1756	—	1756	—	1442
6	371	1756	—	1756	786	—
7	135	1385	786	2171	—	—
8	208	1250	786	2036	—	—
9	315	1042	786	1828	—	—
10	0	1513	—	1513	—	786
11	440	1513	—	1513	1029	—
12	127	1073	1029	2102	—	—
13	315	946	1029	1975	—	—
14	114	631	1029	1660	—	—
15	241	1546	—	1546	—	1029
16	140	1305	—	1305	1237	—

* For this box we have used $P = 5$ and $T = 2542$.

The P-system decision rule is to review the stock position every 5 days and order up to a target of 2542 cases.

It is interesting to note, at this point, that the P system requires 1.65(450) = 742 units of safety stock, while the same service level is provided by the Q system with only 1.65(300) = 495 units of safety stock. A P system always requires more safety stock than a Q system for the same service level. This occurs because the P system must provide coverage over a time of $P + L$, while the Q system must protect against stockout only over the time L.

This example is completed by Box 13.3, which uses the same demand figures as Box 13.2. Here, however, the review is periodic instead of continuous. A review is made in periods 1, 6, 11, and 16—that is, every five periods. The amounts ordered are 1442, 786, 1029, and 1237. While the review period is fixed, the amount ordered is not.

13.8 USING P AND Q SYSTEMS IN PRACTICE

In industry, both Q and P systems as well as modifications of them are in wide use for independent-demand inventory management. The choice between these systems is not a simple one and may be dictated by management practices as well as economics. There are, however, some conditions under which the P system may be preferred over the Q system:

1. The P system should be used when orders must be placed and/or delivered at specified intervals. An example is weekly order and delivery of canned goods to a grocery store.
2. The P system should be used when multiple items are ordered from the same supplier, and delivered in the same shipment. In this case the supplier would prefer consolidation of the items into a single order. An example is different colors of paint which might be ordered from a paint supplier. The supplier would then deliver at fixed times instead of delivering the different colors of paint at different times.
3. The P system should be used for inexpensive items which are not maintained on perpetual inventory records. An example is nuts or bolts used in a manufacturing process. In this case, the bins may be filled up daily or weekly. The bin size determines the target inventory and the bin is filled up to target at fixed time intervals. No records need be kept of each disbursement and receipt into inventory.

In sum, the P system provides the advantage of scheduled replenishment and less record keeping. It requires, however, a somewhat larger safety stock than the Q system, as the last example illustrates. Because of this larger safety stock, the Q system is often used for expensive items where it is desirable to hold down the investment in safety stock inventory. The choice between the Q and P systems should, however, be made on the basis of timing of replenishment, the type of record-keeping system in use, and the cost of the item.

In practice, one also finds hybrid systems which are a mixture of P and Q inventory rules. One of these systems is characterized by min/max decision rules and periodic review. In this case, the system has both a reorder point (min) and a target (max). When the periodic review is made, no order is placed if the stock position is above the min. If the stock position is below min, an order is placed to raise the stock position to the max level.

Use of forecasts

The issue of forecasting is important for both the P and Q systems. These systems have been derived under the assumption of a constant average demand level with random variation around the average. When this is the case, it is only necessary to forecast the average demand level and to monitor the actual demands for a possible change in the average. When such a change is detected (by statistical methods), the model should be reset on the basis of the new average demand observed. If no change in average is detected, the model should remain in effect.

In many cases, however, independent demand is subject to either a trend or a seasonal pattern, i.e., the average demand is not constant. Then the P and Q formulas from the last section are inadequate and must be modified. Equation (13.3) for the reorder point is modified by using *forecast* demand over lead time for m in place of *average* demand over lead time. The forecast demand for the future lead-time period will include a trend or seasonal adjustment. Thus the reorder point will be dependent on the forecast and will change after each new forecast is made. Conceivably, the reorder point could change after each inventory transaction, when a new demand is observed and a new forecast is computed. In the same way the order quantity should be recomputed after each new forecast is made.

In the case of the P model, a modification to the target inventory equation— Equation (13.5)—is needed. In this case, the *forecast* demand over $P + L$ should be substituted for the *average* demand over $P + L$. This change will have the effect of introducing a changing target level each time a new forecast is made.

The simple example in Box 13.4 illustrates these ideas. In this case, a P system with a review interval of two periods and a lead time of one period is being used. Upon review of inventory levels, a forecast is made for three periods ($P + L$) and this forecast is used to set the new target level. The forecast utilizes second-order exponential smoothing with $\alpha = .2$, a starting level of 50, and a starting trend of 50.[6] The changing target level is needed because finished-goods demand is clearly exhibiting an upward trend of about 50 units per period. As indicated, the revised target adjusts quickly to the changing demand levels. The low point reached is five units in week nine. For practice, one might construct a similar table using the Q method of inventory control.

In addition to expected demand, one must also forecast the standard deviation of

---

[6] See Chapter 4 for details on second-order exponential smoothing.

CHAPTER 13 / INDEPENDENT-DEMAND INVENTORY **383**

BOX 13.4   **P SYSTEM FOR INCREASING DEMAND**

Period	Demand	Three-period second-order forecast	Target*	Beginning on hand	End on hand	Amount ordered	Amount received
1	100	450	500	200	100	300	—
2	140	—	—	400	260	—	300
3	200	742	792	260	60	532	—
4	230	—	—	592	362	—	532
5	290	1027	1077	362	72	715	—
6	350	—	—	787	437	—	715
7	410	1325	1375	437	27	938	—
8	460	—	—	965	505	—	938
9	500	1649	1699	505	5	1194	—
10	535	—	—	1199	664	—	1194
11	590	1940	1990	664	74	1326	—

* Target = three-period forecast + s', s' = 50, review interval = 2, lead time = 1 period.

demand σ. Recall that the standard deviation is used to set the safety stock in both the P and Q systems. The forecast standard deviation is also sometimes called the "forecast error." These forecasts of error or standard deviation are automatically made by exponential-smoothing systems. The forecast standard deviation is, however, produced for the same period of time as the demand interval. For example, with daily demand data, the forecast standard deviation will be for one day. This standard deviation must be adjusted to L periods, since we need the standard deviation over the lead time ($L + P$ in the case of the P model). The adjustment can be made by using the procedure described above.

Service level and inventory level

There is an important tradeoff between service level and inventory level. In the management of independent-demand inventories, one of the key considerations is customer service levels. But service levels must be balanced against investment in inventory, since higher service levels require higher inventory investments.

The average inventory level I is given by:

$$I = \frac{Q}{2} + z\sigma$$

The reasoning behind this formula is that $Q/2$ units are carried on average due to ordering in lots of size Q, and $z\sigma$ units are carried on average due to safety stocks. (In the case of the P system, use σ' in place of σ.) Thus the inventory level is the sum of cycle stock and safety stock components.

For a fixed Q, the inventory level will be a function of z, which, in turn, also determines the service level. Thus, for given values of z, one can plot service level versus the average inventory required. Such a plot is shown in Figure 13.10.

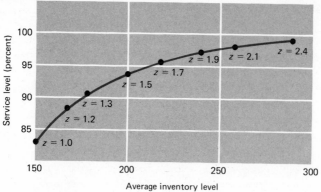

**Figure 13.10
Service level
versus inventory
level. (Q = 100,
σ = 100.)**

The figure indicates that an increasing inventory level is required to achieve higher service levels. As the service level approaches 100 percent, very large inventories are required. This happens because we are assuming normally distributed demand over the lead time, and we must cover very unlikely events as the probability approaches 100 percent.

Due to the highly nonlinear relationship, it is crucial for management to compare the service-level graph with that of the inventory level before setting a service level. Selection of an arbitrary service level may be very costly, since the difference of a few percentage points in service level could substantially increase the required inventory level. For instance, in Figure 13.10, an increase in service level from 95 to 99 percent (four percentage points) requires a 32 percent increase in inventory. It is, therefore, essential that management study the service level and inventory tradeoffs in each situation.

The relationship between service level and inventory level helps to determine appropriate inventory turnovers. Suppose a firm is compared with its industry or with itself over time and turnover is now low. This lower turnover could be explained by either higher service levels or different ordering and holding costs. Management should look beyond turnover to the service-level policy or the cost structure inherent in the situation. On the basis of better customer service or different cost structures, management may prefer a policy which leads to turnovers that are lower than the industry norm.

Multiple items

Most inventory situations involve multiple items. If P and Q systems are used for these, the resulting inventories could exceed available space or the quantities required could exceed purchasing budgets. On the other hand, if no constraints, budgets, or inventory policies are violated, then the P and Q models derived in the earlier discussion can be used directly for multiple items. In this case, the multiple-item inventory problem is simply a composite of all the single items considered one at a time.

If constraints are violated, then adjustments must be made to the P or Q model in use. There are two cases of interest here. First, assume that a budget, investment level, or space constraint has been violated. In this case, a higher value of carrying cost i should be used to reduce the values of Q, or lower service levels should be used. Whether one or both of these adjustments should be used will depend on the types of constraints violated and the effect of each adjustment. Higher-level management should then be made aware of the resulting service levels and required value of carrying cost. This could result in a reassessment of the situation and perhaps a change in the constraints.

This discussion indicates that the inventory carrying charge i can be viewed as a policy variable. If management specifies certain constraints on space or budget, they have in fact implicitly set a value of i (or service level). Such constraints should not be applied blindly but always evaluated in light of their effect on inventory. [See Schroeder (1974) for more details on this subject.]

The second case, where multiple items may interact, is the case of a single supplier of multiple items. In this case the supplier may offer substantial discounts if a truckload lot is ordered at one time, due to the transportation economics involved. The question then becomes: Under what circumstances would it be economical to place a single order for all the different items to take advantage of the lower freight rate? This question can be answered by comparing the total cost of ordering the items together, in one shipment, with the sum of the total cost for ordering them separately. The option with the lower total inventory cost is preferred.

A similar problem occurs when several items can be produced from a single machine setup. In this case it may cost a great deal to set up the machine for the group of items but only a small amount to shift over from one item to the next. The question in this case is the same: When is it economical to schedule the group of items together rather than independently? The answer here also depends on a comparison of total setup plus holding costs for the two options.

Multiple items may, therefore, require modification of the basic inventory formulas to reflect the interaction between items. Although we have not presented the new formulas in detail, they are available in the literature for many different cases. [See Peterson and Silver (1977).]

13.9 INVENTORY CONTROL SYSTEMS

To this point, we have been concentrating on decision rules which can be used to determine when and how much to order. In operations, these rules need to be embedded in an inventory control system. In addition to calculation of the decision rules, the system should include a way to record inventory transactions and a way to monitor inventory management performance.

An inventory control system can be either manual or computerized or a combination of the two. Nowadays many inventory systems are computerized, the exceptions being those with a small number of items or inexpensive items. For these cases, the cost of a computerized system may be greater than its benefits.

Regardless of whether a control system is computerized or not, the following functions should be performed:

TRANSACTION COUNTING. Every inventory system requires a method of record keeping, which must support both the accounting needs of the organization and the inventory management function. Sometimes this requires that perpetual records be kept by recording every disbursement and receipt. In other cases, periodic (e.g., annual) counts of the inventory will suffice. Whatever the exact method used, every inventory control system requires a suitable transaction subsystem.

The accuracy of inventory records is of such importance that it can hardly be overemphasized. Many systems simply do not respond properly because the records of on-hand or on-order inventory are inaccurate. In Chapter 14, we will discuss cycle counting as a way to control the accuracy of inventory records.

INVENTORY DECISION RULES. An inventory system should incorporate decision rules to determine when and how much to order. In this chapter, we have developed the periodic and continuous decision rules at length. Whatever rules are used, the system should implement them automatically. In many systems, the computer can also automatically generate purchase orders based on the decision rules in use.

EXCEPTION REPORTING. When inventory decision rules are automatically incorporated in a system, exceptions should be reported to management. These exceptions might include situations in which the forecast is not tracking accurately with demand, a very large purchase order has been generated, stockouts have reached an excessive level, and so on. The purpose of exception reporting is to alert management to changing assumptions. In practice, however, some systems do not incorporate sufficient exception reporting. Such systems have a tendency to run out of control and to generate inventory orders which are not economical.

FORECASTING. Inventory decisions should be based on forecast demand. In Chapter 4 we developed exponential smoothing, which is a useful technique for forecasting inventory demands. Inventory decisions should not be based purely on hunches from the marketing department or the inventory manager; a quantitative technique should be incorporated into the system. Judgment should play a role in forecasting, however, to modify the quantitative forecasts for unusual events.

TOP-MANAGEMENT REPORTING. An inventory control system should generate reports for top management as well as for inventory managers. These reports should measure the overall performance of inventory and they should assist in making broad inventory policy. Such reports should include service level provided, costs of operating the inventory, and investment levels as compared with other periods. Too much reliance is often placed on turnover ratios as the only performance measure, resulting in inadequate information for inventory policy making. In practice, most systems provide very poor information for top management.

As can be seen, a good inventory control system should go far beyond mere record keeping. It should provide for management decision making while also controlling inventory levels.

Types of control systems

Many types of inventory control systems are in use. These four are typical:

1. SINGLE-BIN SYSTEM. In a single-bin system, the bin or shelf is filled up periodically. Examples of this are shelves in retail stores, automobile gas tanks, and small-parts bins in factories. The single-bin system is a P system. The size of the bin is the target, and the inventory is brought up to target periodically by filling the bin. In this type of system, records of each receipt or disbursement are not kept. However, purchase orders are usually kept, so that usage between any two physical counts of inventory can be determined.

2. TWO-BIN SYSTEM. To understand the two-bin system, visualize a bin with two compartments. The front compartment contains material which is issued and the back compartment is sealed. When the material in the front compartment is gone, the back compartment is opened for use and an order for new material is placed. Thus the back compartment must contain enough material to last throughout the replenishment lead time with high probability. This is a Q system of inventory control with the back compartment containing stock equal to the reorder point. The record-keeping aspects of this system are the same as those of the one-bin system.

BOX 13.5 **IBM INFOREM INVENTORY SYSTEM**

The Inventory Forecasting and Replenishment Modules (INFOREM) is a set of programs which operate on an IBM System/370. These programs forecast item sales and generate ordering instructions for optimum replenishment of inventory items. The programs are designed to interface with the user's record-keeping system.

The INFOREM system consists of a series of program modules performing these major functions:

- Monitoring and measuring the average current demand for items at the stockkeeping unit (SKU) level.
- Producing forecasts of future SKU demand with allowances made for seasonality and trend.
- Developing ordering decision rules for the optimum restocking of an item for various types of merchandising and replenishment situations. This includes the calculation of order points; order-up-to levels; and specific order quantities. INFOREM can also project future item order requirements, where minimum order size restrictions require this.
- Maintaining an accurate and updated measurement of lead time at the item or vendor level, based upon current ordering experience.
- Simulating the performance of the system through a month, a season, or a full year. This simulation will show the expected performance for groups of items in terms of sales, level-of-service and inventory requirements by week for the duration of the simulation. Users may experiment with different policy decisions; such as desired service level objectives, review time frequency, etc. via the simulator and observe the changes that will result from such actions.

Source: INFOREM: Principles of Inventory Management: Application Description, 2d ed., IBM, GE20-0571-1, May 1978.

3. **CARD-FILE SYSTEM.** With this system, a card file—usually containing one card for each inventory item—is kept. As items are sold, the corresponding cards are located and updated. Similarly, the cards are updated when new material arrives. They may also contain decision rules for either the P or Q system. The card-file system is appropriate for small inventories with not too many transactions.

4. **COMPUTERIZED SYSTEM.** A record on computer-readable storage is maintained for each item. Transactions are posted against this record as items are disbursed or received. The computer applies either the P or Q decision rules, forecasts demand, and monitors performance of the inventory system. The computer system reduces clerical effort and also provides better management control of inventories. Because computer systems are very important for inventory management, a typical system is described in Box 13.5.

The choice between these four systems depends on the relative costs and benefits. Generally speaking, the cost-benefit ratio for medium and large inventories favors the computer. Still, there are many smaller inventory systems which can be managed by one of the manual systems. One should resist the conclusion that "all inventories should be managed by the computer in this day and age."

ABC inventory management

In 1906, Vilfredo Pareto observed that a few items in any group constitute the significant proportion.[7] At that time he was concerned that a few individuals in the economy seemed to earn most of the income. It can also be observed that a few products in a firm result in most of the sales and that, in volunteer organizations, a few people do most of the work. The law of the significant few can be applied to inventory management as well.

In inventories, a few items usually account for most of the inventory value as measured by dollar usage (demand times cost). Thus, one can manage these few items intensively and control most of the inventory value. In inventory work, the items are usually divided into three classes: A, B, and C. Class A typically contains about 20 percent of the items and 80 percent of the dollar usage. It therefore represents the most significant few. At the other extreme, class C contains 50 percent of the items and only 5 percent of the dollar usage. These items contribute very little of the dollar value of inventory. In the middle is class B, with 30 percent of the items and 15 percent of the dollar usage. The classification of inventory in this way is often called ABC analysis or the 80-20 rule. [See Dickie (1951).]

Table 13.3 is an example of an inventory with 10 items. In this case, items 3 and 6 account for a great deal of the dollar usage (73.2 percent). On the other hand, items 1, 5, 7, 8, and 10 are low in dollar usage (10.5 percent). The ABC principle, therefore, applies to this small example. The percentages in each category are summarized in Table 13.4.

[7] Vilfredo Pareto, *Manual of Political Economy*, Ann A. Schwier (trans.), New York: A. M. Kelly, 1971.

TABLE 13.3   ANNUAL USAGE OF ITEMS BY DOLLAR VALUE

Item	Annual usage in units	Unit cost	Dollar usage	Percentage of total dollar usage
1	5,000	$ 1.50	$ 7,500	2.9
2	1,500	8.00	12,000	4.7
3	10,000	10.50	105,000	41.2
4	6,000	2.00	12,000	4.7
5	7,500	0.50	3,750	1.5
6	6,000	13.60	81,600	32.0
7	5,000	0.75	3,750	1.5
8	4,500	1.25	5,625	2.2
9	7,000	2.50	17,500	6.9
10	3,000	2.00	6,000	2.4
Total			$254,725	100.0

The designation of three classes is arbitrary; there could be any number of classes. Also, the exact percentage of items in each class will vary from one inventory to the next. The important factors are the two extremes: a few items which are significant and a large number of items which are relatively insignificant.

Most of the dollar usage in inventory (80 percent) can be controlled by closely monitoring the A items (20 percent). For these items, a tight control system including continuous review of stock levels, less safety stock, and close attention to record accuracy might be used.

On the other hand, looser control might be used for C items. A periodic review system could be used to consolidate orders from the same supplier and less record accuracy might be sufficient. Even manual systems might be used for C items. The B items require an intermediate level of attention and management control.

With computerized systems, a uniform level of control is sometimes used for all items. Nevertheless, the management of inventories still requires the setting of priorities, and the ABC concept is often useful in doing this.

TABLE 13.4   ABC CLASSIFICATION

Class	Item numbers	Percentage of total items	Percentage of total dollar usage
A	3, 6	20	73.2
B	2,4,9	30	16.3
C	1, 5, 7, 8, 10	50	10.5
Total		100	100.0

13.10 KEY POINTS

Inventory management is a key operations responsibility because it greatly affects capital requirements, costs, and customer service. This chapter provides an overview of inventory management together with specific methods for the management of independent-demand inventories.

The chapter's major points include the following:

- There are conflicting inventory objectives among the marketing, finance, and operations functions. The role of inventory management is to balance these conflicting objectives in the best interests of the firm as a whole.
- Inventory is a stock of materials used to facilitate production or to satisfy customer demands. Inventories include raw materials, work in process, and finished goods.
- Decision problems in inventory management include what to carry, how much to order, when to order, and the type of control system to use. A decision rule specifies how much to order and when. In the calculation of decision rules, there are four types of inventory costs to consider: item cost, ordering (or setup) cost, carrying (or holding) cost, and stockout cost. The relevant costs to include are those which vary with the decision to be made.
- The economic order quantity (EOQ) assumptions include a constant demand rate, constant lead time, no stockouts, lot ordering, no discounts, and a single product. Within the assumptions made, the EOQ formula minimizes both holding and ordering cost.
- A continuous review system provides one way to handle random demand. When the stock position drops to the reorder point R, a fixed quantity Q is ordered. The time between orders will vary depending on actual demand. The value of Q is set equal to the EOQ. The value of R is based on the service level desired.
- A periodic review system provides another way to handle random demand. The stock position is reviewed at fixed intervals P, and an amount is ordered equal to the target inventory T minus stock position. The amount ordered at each review period will vary depending on actual demand. The value of P is set by use of the EOQ and the value of T is based on the service level desired.
- The choice between P and Q systems should be based on the timing of replenishment, type of record keeping, and cost of the item. A periodic system should be used when inventory orders must be regularly scheduled.
- Forecasting and inventory are interrelated, with forecasts being used to set initial decision-rule parameters and to adjust them dynamically as conditions change. Forecasts should also be used to predict the standard deviations of demand for the determination of service level.
- High service levels require high investment levels. Management should, therefore, study the service level and investment relationship before setting the service levels desired. The optimal turnover in inventory should be based on the service level desired and the problem's cost structure. Comparisons of turnover ratio do not, by themselves, provide an adequate basis for decisions on inventory level.

- An inventory control system should do five things: count transactions, implement inventory decision rules, report exceptions, forecast, and report to top management. There are four basic types of inventory control systems: single-bin, two-bin, card-file, and computerized. The choice between the systems should be based on a cost-benefit comparison.
- The ABC inventory concept is based on the significant few and the insignificant many. The concept should be used to carefully control the significant A items and to spend less effort and cost on the B and C items.

QUESTIONS

1. Identify the different types of inventories (raw-materials, work-in-process, and finished-goods) carried in the following organizations: gas station, hamburger stand, clothing store, and machine shop. What functions (purposes) do these inventories perform?
2. Consider the following types of items carried in a retail store: light bulbs, phonograph records, and refrigerated drugs. Discuss the probable cost structure for each of these items including item cost, carrying cost, ordering cost, and stockout cost.
3. Why is stockout cost difficult to determine? Suggest an approach which might be used to estimate it.
4. Why can the item cost be dropped from the simple EOQ formula? Are item costs important when quantity discounts are given? Why?
5. What is the difference between a requirements philosophy and a replenishment philosophy of inventory management? Why is this difference important?
6. Compare and contrast the management of finished-goods inventory in a manufacturing company with that in a retail or wholesale firm.
7. For a given service level, why will a P system require a larger inventory investment than a Q system? What factors affect the magnitude of the difference?
8. Suppose you were managing the Speedy Hardware Store. Give examples of items which might be managed by a P system and other items which might use a Q system. How do these items differ?
9. How should a manager decide on the appropriate service level for finished-goods items? Should some items have a 100 percent service level?
10. A manager was heard to complain, "I have some items which have a two-week review interval, and it takes four weeks for resupply. Every two weeks, I place orders based on the on-hand quantity in stock. Now I seem to have too much inventory." What went wrong?
11. A student was overheard saying, "The EOQ-model assumptions are so restrictive that the model would be hard to use in practice." Is it necessary to have a different model for each variation in assumptions? Why or why not?
12. What is the appropriate role of turnover criteria for managing inventory? Under what circumstances is high turnover detrimental to the firm?
13. How should forecasting be used in an inventory control system? Under what circumstances would forecasts be unnecessary?
14. Suppose you were managing a chain of retail department stores. The inventory in each store is computerized, but there are a large number of different items. As a top manager, how would you measure the overall inventory-management performance of each store? How would you use this information in your relationship with the individual store managers?
15. Why should exception reporting be included in an inventory control system? What types of exceptions would you want reported?
16. Visit a department store, a local garage, or a fast-food outlet. Determine the type of inventory control system used, including forecast methods, decision rules, exception reporting, record keeping, and management reports.

PROBLEMS

1. The Speedy Grocery Store carries a particular brand of coffee which has the following characteristics:
   Sales = 10 cases per week
   Ordering cost = $20 per order
   Carrying charge = 30 percent per year
   Item cost = $60 per case
   a. How many cases should be ordered at a time?
   b. How often will coffee be ordered?
   c. What is the annual cost of ordering and carrying coffee?
   d. What factors might cause the company to order a larger or smaller amount than the EOQ?

2. The Grinell Machine Shop makes a line of metal tables for customers. Some of these tables are carried in finished-goods inventory. A particular table has the following characteristics:
   Sales = 200 per year
   Setup cost = $500 per setup (this includes machine setup for all the different parts in the table)
   Carrying cost = 20 percent per year
   Item cost = $25
   a. How many of these tables should be made in a production lot?
   b. How often will production be scheduled?
   c. What factors might cause the company to schedule a different lot size than you have computed?

3. What is the effect on EOQ and total cost of the following types of errors for the data in Problem 1?
   a. A 50 percent increase in demand
   b. A 50 percent increase in carrying charge
   c. What conclusions can you draw from studying these effects?

4. An appliance store carries a certain brand of TV which has the following characteristics:
   Average annual sales = 50 units
   Ordering cost = $25 per order
   Carrying cost = 25 percent per year
   Item cost = $400 per unit
   Lead time = 4 days
   Standard deviation of daily demand = .1 unit
   Working days per year = 250
   a. Determine the EOQ.
   b. Calculate the reorder point for a 95 percent service level, assuming normal demand.
   c. State the Q rule for this item.
   d. How far apart would orders be placed on average?

5. For the data given in Problem 4:
   a. Determine a P system of inventory control for a 95 percent service level. Compute the values of P and T.
   b. Compare the inventory investment required for the P system and the Q system from Problem 4.
   c. Why does the P system require a higher inventory investment?

6. The Suregrip Tire Company carries a certain type of tire with the following characteristics:
   Average annual sales = 500 tires
   Ordering cost = $10 per order
   Carrying cost = 20 percent per year
   Item cost = $40 per tire
   Lead time = 5 days
   Standard deviation of daily demand = 1 tire

    a. Calculate the EOQ.

    b. For a **Q** system of inventory control, calculate the safety stock required for service levels of 85, 90, 95, 97, and 99 percent.

    c. Construct a plot of inventory investment versus service level.

    d. What service level would you establish on the basis of the graph in part c? Discuss.

7. For the data in Problem 6:

    a. Calculate the optimum annual turnover as a function of service level.

    b. If sales were to increase by 50 percent, what would happen to the optimal turnover at a 95 percent service level?

8. Assume that the Suregrip Tire Company described in Problem 6 faces an increasing demand trend. They have been using second-order exponential smoothing, which has predicted a current daily average of 2 units, with an increasing trend of ½ unit per day.

    a. Calculate the reorder point for a 99 percent service level.

    b. What service level would be obtained if the reorder point were calculated by ignoring the trend?

9. The Easyfoot Carpet Company carries three types of carpet with the following characteristics:

Type	Annual demand, yards	Item cost per yard
A	200	$10
B	200	8
C	250	6

Assume that the items are to be ordered together from the same supplier at an ordering cost of $20 per order and an annual carrying cost of 25 percent. Also assume 300 working days in a year.

    a. Using a P system, what is the optimal ordering interval in days?

    b. How much of each type carpet would be ordered when a combined order is placed?

    c. Suppose that carpet can only be ordered in minimum quantities of 30 yards. What would you do?

    d. Why can't these carpets be ordered by a Q system?

*10. Suppose that, for Problem 1, the Speedy Grocery Store is offered a discount if more than 50 cases are ordered at a time. The unit item costs are $60 a case for 0 to 49 cases and $57 a case for 50 cases or more. This price of $57 applies to the entire order.

    a. Should the grocery store take the discount offer?

    b. What discount is required before the store is indifferent between taking the discount or ordering the EOQ?

*11. For Problem 2, suppose the Grinell Machine Shop produces its tables at a rate of 2 per day. (250 working days per year.)

    a. What is the optimal lot size?

    b. Draw a graph of on-hand inventory versus time.

    c. What is the maximum value of inventory?

SELECTED BIBLIOGRAPHY

BROWN, ROBERT G.: *Decision Rules for Inventory Management,* New York: Holt, 1967.

BUFFA, E. S., and W. H. TAUBERT: *Production-Inventory Systems: Planning and Control,* rev. ed., Homewood, Ill.: Irwin, 1972.

CHASE, RICHARD B., and NICHOLAS AQUILANO: *Production and Operations Management: A Life Cycle Approach,* rev. ed., Homewood, Ill.: Irwin, 1977.

* The supplement is required to work these problems.

DICKIE, H. FORD: "ABC Inventory Analysis Shoots for Dollars Not Pennies," *Factory Management and Maintenance,* July 1951.

GREEN, JAMES H.: *Production and Inventory Control,* Homewood, Ill.: Irwin, 1974.

PETERSON, R., and E. A. SILVER: *Decision Systems for Inventory Management and Production Planning,* New York: Wiley, 1977.

SCHROEDER, ROGER G.: "Managerial Inventory Formulations with Stockout Objectives and Fiscal Constraints," *Naval Research Logistics Quarterly,* vol. 21, no. 3, September 1974, pp. 375–388.

————: "Return on Investment as a Criterion for Inventory Models," *Decision Sciences,* vol. 7, no. 4, October 1976, pp. 697–704.

SHORE, BARRY: *Operations Management,* New York: McGraw-Hill, 1973.

STARR, M. K., and D. W. MILLER: *Inventory Control: Theory and Practice,* Englewood Cliffs, N.J.: Prentice Hall, 1962.

VOLLMANN, THOMAS E.: *Operations Management: A Systems Model-Building Approach,* Reading, Mass.: Addison-Wesley, 1973.

SUPPLEMENT: ADVANCED MODELS

This supplement presents two additional models which are useful for independent inventory demands. The first model applies to outside procurement where price discounts are given, while the second applies to a gradual fill of inventory when the lot arrives uniformly over time—not all at once.

PRICE BREAKS

Outside suppliers often offer price discounts for large purchases. These discounts may be given at different procurement levels and they may apply either to the whole order or only to the increment purchased. In this supplement, we assume that the price discounts apply to the entire procurement order. For example, the procurement price may be $2 per unit for 0 to 99 units and $1.50 per unit for 100 units and up. The cost of the units thus exhibits a jump or discontinuity at 100 units. For 99 units, the cost of the procurement order is $198, and for 100 units the cost is $150.

In order to solve for the economic order quantity, the procedure is to first calculate the EOQ for each different procurement price. Some of these EOQs may not be feasible because the EOQ falls outside the range of the price used to compute it. The infeasible EOQs are eliminated from further consideration. The total procurement and inventory operating cost for each feasible EOQ and each price-break quantity is then computed. The feasible EOQ or price break which results in the lowest total cost is then selected as the order quantity.

Consider the following example:

$$D = 1000 \text{ units per year}$$
$$i = 20 \text{ percent per year}$$
$$A = \$10 \text{ per order}$$
$$C_1 = \$5 \text{ per unit for 0 to 199 units}$$
$$C_2 = \$4.50 \text{ per unit for 200 to 499 units}$$
$$C_3 = \$4.25 \text{ per unit for 500 units or more}$$

First, calculate the three EOQs corresponding to the three values of C_i. We then obtain $Q_1 = 141$, $Q_2 = 149$ and $Q_3 = 153$. In this case, Q_2 and Q_3 are infeasible, and they are eliminated from further consideration. We then compute the total cost of procurement and inventory at the remaining EOQ and at the two price breaks. These total costs are as follows:[1]

$$C(Q) = A(D/Q) + iC(Q/2) + CD$$

$$C(141) = 10(^{1000}/_{141}) + .20(5)(^{141}/_2) + 5(1000)$$
$$= 5141$$

$$C(200) = 10(^{1000}/_{200}) + .20(4.50)(^{200}/_2)$$
$$+ 4.50(1000) = 4640$$

$$C(500) = 10(^{1000}/_{500}) + .20(4.25)(^{500}/_2)$$
$$+ 4.25(1000) = 4482$$

Since $C(500)$ is the lowest annual cost, 500 units should be ordered.

The cost behavior for the example is shown in Figure S13.1. Notice that at each price break the total cost is reduced. Therefore the quantity at the highest price break is selected.

---

[1] Note that the annual cost CD of buying the units has been added to this cost equation, since this cost will be affected by the discount.

395

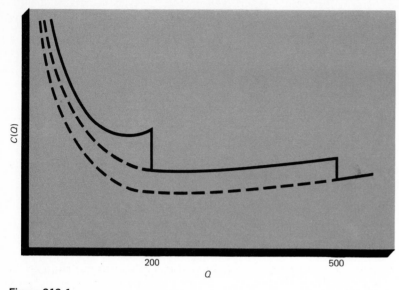

Figure S13.1
Inventory cost with price breaks.

It is not always necessary to calculate all the EOQs and the cost at each point. A more efficient procedure is to first calculate the EOQ for the lowest cost per unit (the largest price-break quantity). If this EOQ is feasible, i.e., above the price break, then the most economical quantity has been found. If the EOQ is not feasible, use the next-lowest price and continue calculating EOQs until a feasible EOQ is found or until all prices have been used. Then calculate the total cost of the EOQ, if found, and the total cost at all the *higher* price breaks. The minimum of these total costs indicates the most economic order quantity. In the above example, this procedure would have resulted, by coincidence, in the same amount of calculation.

UNIFORM LOT DELIVERY

In some cases, the entire lot is not placed in inventory at one time but is delivered gradually. An example is a manufacturer who builds inventory at a constant production rate. Another example is a retailer who takes the lot in several shipments over a period of time.

The effect of this delivery condition on inventory is shown in Figure S13.2. The inventory level builds up gradually as both production and consumption occur. Then the inventory level is depleted as only consumption takes place.

The effect of gradual delivery is to reduce the maximum and average inventory level over that obtained in the simple EOQ case. Suppose units are produced at a rate of p units per year and consumed at a rate of D units per year (where $p > D$). Then the average inventory level will be:

$$\frac{Q}{2}\left(1 - \frac{D}{p}\right)$$

This formula can be derived with the use of geometry by reference to Figure S13.2.

The above expression for average inventory is used in place of $Q/2$ in Equation (13.1). By minimizing the resulting expression for $C(Q)$, the following EOQ formula is obtained:

$$Q = \sqrt{\frac{2AD}{iC(1 - D/p)}}$$

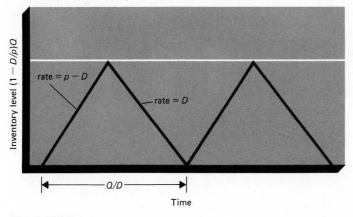

Figure S13.2
Uniform lot delivery.

The EOQ in this case will always be somewhat larger than the ordinary EOQ because the factor $(1 - D/p)$ is less than 1. As p approaches D, the EOQ becomes very large, which means that production is continuous. When p is very large, the above EOQ formula approaches the ordinary EOQ. In deriving the ordinary EOQ, we assumed the entire lot arrived in inventory at once, which is equivalent to an infinite production rate p.

CHAPTER 14
MATERIALS REQUIREMENTS PLANNING

Some manufacturing operations are managed in a more or less chaotic way. We might find that inventories are swollen, parts are being expedited to get orders out on time, and a pressure-cooker atmosphere prevails. It is now possible to remedy this situation through use of a new computerized planning and control system called materials requirements planning (MRP).

MRP derives its power from the very important distinction between independent- and dependent-demand inventories. In Chapter 13 we defined independent-demand inventories as those which are subject to market conditions and are thus independent of operations. Examples of independent-demand inventories are finished goods and spare parts in a manufacturing company that are used to satisfy final customer demand. These inventories should be managed by the order-point methods described in the last chapter.

Dependent-demand inventories, on the other hand, are not subject to market conditions. They are dependent on demand for higher-level parts and components up to and including the master production schedule. Examples of dependent-demand inventories are raw-materials and work-in-process inventories used in manufacturing companies to support the manufacturing process itself. These inventories should be managed by an MRP system.

An MRP system is driven by the master schedule which specifies the "end items" or output of the production function. All future demands for work in process

BOX 14.1   **TYPICAL DECISION PROBLEM**

After solving the inventory distribution problems at Farwell Enterprises, Gretchen Davidson turned her attention to internal manufacturing problems. Beginning 3 years ago, she had developed an MRP system in conjunction with Tom Trader, the materials manager. The MRP system was not, however, working to her satisfaction.

After a particularly heavy weekend, Tom arrived at Gretchen's office on Monday morning. Gretchen observed, "Our work-in-process inventories have been too high during the past month. Art Jacobson, our controller, met with me on Friday, and we decided that these inventories must be cut. I am also concerned that we are still meeting only 70 percent of our delivery promises, and our raw-materials inventory levels are creeping upward. Before long, Art is going to be seeing me again about the raw-materials inventories. When we installed the MRP system, I thought it would solve these problems. What has happened?"

After the weekend, Tom didn't need this problem, but he tried to get his thoughts together as best he could. He replied, "As I see it, there are three problems with our current MRP system. First, the master schedule is inflated. Even though the inventory distribution changes which you made last week will help this problem somewhat, we are going to need more cooperation from marketing. When changes are made in the master schedule, marketing refuses to inform the customer or the warehouse. As a result, we are late on the delivery promise to one customer while we are trying to satisfy marketing's requirements on another customer. Marketing does not seem to understand fully the need for tradeoffs in customer delivery dates. The result is an inflated master schedule and too much work-in-process inventory as materials are brought in house before they are needed. I suggest that we plan the master schedule to stay within our actual production capacity. I will need your support and the support of the president to implement this policy, because some orders will be turned down and some customers will not get their requested delivery dates."

"The second problem we have in using our MRP system is inaccurate bills of materials. Because of these inaccuracies, we sometimes order the wrong parts, and customer deliveries are subsequently delayed. We are working with the engineering department on this problem, but it will take another six months before the bills are reasonably accurate."

"Our third problem area is in vendor deliveries. We are simply getting too much variability in lead times from vendors. For example, last week one vendor delivered a part three weeks late. Expediting in purchasing does not really work. The vendors are used to the pressure from purchasing. We have got to start taking drastic action, such as canceling orders, when vendors do not deliver on time. I am asking you to resolve this issue with our purchasing manager. He doesn't seem to listen to me."

Tom concluded, "We in manufacturing are really trying to make the MRP system work, but we still do not have enough cooperation from other departments. It is simply going to take a long time before everyone understands what they must do to help us improve manufacturing performance. We cannot do it alone."

and raw materials should be dependent on the master schedule and derived by the MRP system from the master schedule. When raw-materials and work-in-process inventories are being planned, all past history of demand is irrelevant unless the future is exactly the same as the past. Since conditions are usually changing, the master schedule is a far better basis than past demand for planning raw-materials and work-in-process inventory.

Using MRP, the master schedule is "exploded" into purchase orders for raw materials and shop orders for scheduling the factory. For example, suppose the product in the master schedule is a hand-held calculator. The process of parts explosion will determine all the parts and components needed to make a specified number of calculator units. This process of parts explosion requires a detailed bill of materials which lists each of the parts needed to manufacture any given end item in the master schedule. The required parts may include assemblies, subassemblies, manufactured parts, and purchased parts. Parts explosion thus results in a complete list of the parts which must be ordered and the shop schedule required.

In the process of parts explosion, it is necessary to consider inventories of parts which are already on hand or on order. For example, an order for 100 end items may require a new order of only 20 pieces of a particular raw material because 80 pieces are already in stock.

Another adjustment made during parts explosion is for production and purchasing lead times. Starting with the master schedule, each manufactured or purchased part is offset (i.e., ordered earlier) by the amount of time it takes to get the part (the lead time). This procedure ensures that each component will be available in time to support the master schedule. If sufficient manufacturing and vendor capacity is available to meet the orders resulting from parts explosion, the MRP system will produce a valid plan for procurement and manufacturing actions. If sufficient capacity is not available, it will be necessary to replan the master schedule or to change the capacity. Methods for doing this will be described in detail later. Some of the typical decision problems encountered in operating an MRP system are described in Box 14.1.

14.1 DEFINITIONS OF MRP SYSTEMS

Although MRP is easy to understand conceptually, it can be used in a variety of different ways. This leads to the different types of MRP systems described below:

TYPE I: AN INVENTORY CONTROL SYSTEM. The type I MRP system is an inventory control system which releases manufacturing and purchase orders at the right time to support the master schedule. This system launches orders to control work-in-process and raw-materials inventories through proper timing of order placement. The type I system does not, however, include capacity planning.

TYPE II: A PRODUCTION AND INVENTORY CONTROL SYSTEM. The type II MRP system is an information system used to plan and control inventories and capacities in manufacturing companies. In the type II system, the orders resulting from parts explosion are checked to see whether sufficient capacity is available. If there is not enough capacity, either the capacity or the master schedule is changed. The type II system has a feedback loop between the orders launched and the master schedule to adjust for capacity availability. As a result, this type of MRP system is called a closed-loop system; it controls both inventories and capacity.

TYPE III: A MANUFACTURING RESOURCE-PLANNING SYSTEM. The type III MRP system is used to plan and control all manufacturing resources: inventory, capacity, cash, personnel, facilities, and capital equipment. In this case the MRP parts-explosion system also drives all other resource-planning subsystems in the company.

All the above types of MRP systems are used in practice, leading to a confusion of terminology. In a survey of 679 industrial companies, respondents were asked how the term "MRP" was used in their company. [See Anderson et al. (1980).] Fifty-seven percent indicated they used a type I definition, 34 percent said they used a type II definition, and 9 percent used "other" definitions. Thus usage of the term "MRP" is nonstandard, and one must carefully determine the user's definition in any discussion of the subject.

The range of definitions of MRP can probably be attributed to the evolution of MRP systems in practice. In the installation of an MRP system, a sequential approach is required, starting with the most elementary type I system and proceeding to more elaborate type II and type III systems. Since many companies see MRP in terms of their own installed systems, a range of definitions occurs.

A closed-loop (type II) MRP system can conveniently be described by Figure 14.1. At the top of the figure is the master production schedule, which is determined by customer's orders and forecasts of future demand. The parts-explosion process, at the heart of the system, is driven by three inputs: master production schedule, bill of materials, and inventory records. The result of the parts-explosion process is two types of orders: purchase orders which go to vendors and shop orders which go to the factory. Before shop orders are sent to the factory, however, a check is made on whether sufficient capacity is available to produce the parts required. If capacity is available, the shop orders are placed under control of the shop-floor control system. If capacity is not available, a change must be made in the capacity or in the master schedule through the feedback loop shown in Figure 14.1. Once the shop orders are under the shop-floor control system, the progress of these orders is managed through the shop to make sure that they are completed on time.

Figure 14.1 on the next page represents MRP as an *information system* used to plan and control inventories and capacity. Information is processed through the various parts of the system to support management decisions. If the information is accurate and timely, management can use the system to control inventories, deliver customer orders on time, and control the costs of manufacturing. In this way the materials conversion process will be continually managed in a dynamic and changing environment.

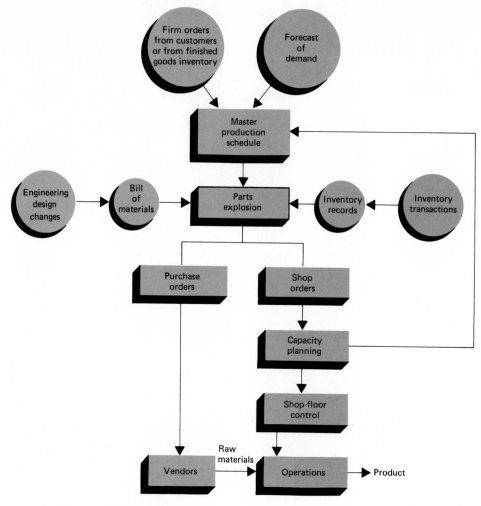

Figure 14.1
A closed-loop MRP
system.

Joseph Orlicky, in his pioneering book on MRP [(1975), p. 158], has defined three principal functions of MRP as follows:

Inventory
Order the right part
Order in the right quantity
Order at the right time

Priorities
Order with the right due date
Keep the due date valid

Capacity
A complete load
An accurate (valid) load
An adequate time span for visibility of future load

BOX 14.2   **LONG-HELD ATTITUDES IN MANUFACTURING COMPANIES**

- "You can't forecast our business out that far."
- "We in Sales are not interested in your Manufacturing problems; we have enough of our own."
- "Don't ask me which customer order I want shipped first. I want them all now."
- "You can't lock up any part of this master production schedule" [sales talking]. Or, "You can't change any of this schedule within the first six months" [manufacturing talking].
- "That new system just can't react fast enough. We need Ed to ramrod through extra orders from time to time."
- "If I want 100 units a month out of this plant, I know from long experience I have to ask for 150."

Source: G. W. Plossl, *Newsletter # 18,* September 1975.

If the closed-loop system in Figure 14.1 is used properly, all of Orlicky's three functions can be achieved.

Since MRP is a simple and logical concept, one might wonder why it was not introduced earlier. The chief reason was the lack of computer technology until the mid 60s. Today, further advances in computer technology are making MRP systems practical even for the small business. Although the technology is in hand, substantial implementation problems still exist in industry. These problems will be discussed in detail later in the chapter; also see Box 14.2.

14.2 MRP VERSUS ORDER-POINT SYSTEMS

MRP calls into question many of the traditional concepts used to manage inventories. The order-point systems discussed in Chapter 13 do not work well for the management of inventories which are subject to dependent demand. Prior to the advent of MRP, however, there was no choice; the typical manufacturing company managed *all* inventories with order-point systems.

Some of the key distinctions between MRP and order-point systems are summarized in Table 14.1. One distinction is the requirements philosophy used in MRP systems versus a replenishment philosophy used in order-point systems. A replenishment philosophy indicates that material should be replenished when it runs low. An MRP system does not do this. More material is ordered only when a need exists as directed by the master schedule. If there are no manufacturing requirements for a particular part, it will not be replenished, even though the inventory level is low. This requirements concept is particularly important in manufacturing because demand for component parts is "lumpy." When a lot is scheduled, the component parts are needed for that lot, but demand is then zero until another lot is scheduled. If order-point systems are used for this type of lumpy demand pattern, material will be carried on hand during long periods of zero demand.

Another distinction between the two systems is in the use of forecasting. For

TABLE 14.1   **COMPARISON OF MRP AND ORDER-POINT SYSTEMS**

	MRP	Order point
Demand	Dependent	Independent
Order philosophy	Requirements	Replenishment
Forecast	Based on master schedule	Based on past demand
Control concept	Control all items	ABC
Objectives	Meet manufacturing needs	Meet customer needs
Lot sizing	Discrete	EOQ
Demand pattern	Lumpy but predictable	Random
Types of inventory	Work in process and raw materials	Finished goods and spare parts

order-point systems, future demand is forecast based on the past history of demand. These forecasts are used to replenish the stock levels. In MRP systems, past demand for component parts is irrelevant. The ordering philosophy is based on requirements generated from the master schedule. MRP is future-oriented; it derives the future demand for component parts from higher-level demand forecasts.

The ABC principle also does not work well for MRP systems. In manufacturing a product, C items are just as important as A items. For example, an automobile cannot be shipped if it lacks a fuel line or radiator cap, even though these items are relatively inexpensive C items. Therefore it is necessary to control all parts, even the C items, in manufacturing.

The time honored square-root EOQ is not useful in MRP systems, although modified EOQ formulas are available. The assumptions used to derive the traditional EOQ are badly violated by the lumpy demand patterns for component parts. Lot sizing in MRP systems should be based on discrete requirements. For example, suppose that the demand for a particular part by week is 0, 30, 10, 0, 0, 15. Further assume that the EOQ is calculated to be 25 parts. With the EOQ or multiples of the EOQ, we could not match the requirements exactly and would, therefore, end up with remnants in inventory. These remnants from the EOQ cause unnecessary inventory carrying costs. It would be far better to base lot sizes on the discrete demand observed. For example, with a lot-for-lot policy, we could order 30 units for the second week, 10 for the third week, and 15 for the sixth week, resulting in three orders and no carrying costs. We could also order 40 units for the second and third weeks combined, thereby saving one order but incurring a small carrying cost. With MRP systems, various discrete lot sizes need to be examined. [See Orlicky (1975) for further details.]

The objective in managing independent-demand inventories with reorder-point rules is to provide a high customer service level at low inventory operating costs. This objective is oriented toward the customer. On the other hand, the objective in managing dependent-demand inventories with MRP is to support the master production schedule. This objective is manufacturing-oriented—it focuses inward rather than outward.

no unnecessary inventory accumulations or wasted time waiting for materials in the shop, and the orders for delivery of finished tables will be shipped on time.

As an exercise, the projected inventories which will result from this materials plan have been calculated and are shown in Table 14.4. Notice that the initial inventory of parts and finished product is worked off as the plan progresses. The only inventory provided by this materials plan is due to initial on-hand inventory, previously scheduled orders, and planned work-in-process inventories. If this plan does not provide sufficient inventory to cover future demand uncertainty, inventory can be added to the plan in the form of safety stocks. Methods for doing this will be discussed later.

14.4 MRP ELEMENTS

Although parts explosion is the heart of MRP, it takes a good deal more to make an MRP system work. The other MRP system elements are described in this section.

MASTER SCHEDULING. The purpose of master scheduling is to specify the output of the operations function. Master scheduling drives the entire materials planning process. The master schedule has been described by George Plossl as "top management's handle on the business" [Plossl (1974)]. By controlling the master schedule, top management can control customer service, inventory levels, and manufacturing costs. Top managers cannot perform the master-scheduling task by themselves because there are too many details. However, top management can review the master schedule that has been created and they can set master-scheduling policy, thereby controlling the materials-planning function.

The parts-explosion process assumes that the master schedule is feasible with respect to capacity. Using the master schedule as input, parts are exploded to produce shop orders and purchase orders. In type II and III systems, the shop orders are put into a capacity planning routine to determine whether sufficient capacity is available. If sufficient capacity is not available, then either capacity or the master schedule must be changed until the master schedule is feasible.

One of the functions of master scheduling is to make sure that the final master schedule is not inflated and reflects realistic capacity constraints. All too often the master schedule is inflated in practice on the assumption that operations will produce more output if the pressure is kept on. (This is not unlike the approach of some college professors who assign students too much homework in hopes that the students will learn more.) As a result of an inflated master schedule, the order priorities (due dates) are no longer valid. The formal MRP system then quickly breaks down and the informal planning and control system takes over. The result is many past-due orders, expediting, and stock chasing to get the product out the door. Nothing is more insidious than an inflated master schedule which leads to invalid order due dates. [See Smolens (1977).]

The master schedule is often developed in terms of weekly output requirements or so called weekly time buckets. In this case an entire week's production is represented by one column of the materials plan.

The master schedule is also frequently updated on a weekly basis. Each week after the new master schedule is developed, the parts-explosion program is run to generate new requirements. This is a so-called regenerative MRP system.

Another form of MRP is the net-change system, where changes can be made as they occur on a real-time basis. The net-change systems are continually kept up to date; this is done in preference to using a massive regeneration run. Although net-change systems have more current data, they are sometimes "nervous" in terms of constant order changes.

The master schedule might extend into the future for a year or more. It must extend at least beyond the longest cumulative production lead time to ensure that sufficient time is available to order all parts. Generally speaking, the master schedule should be frozen inside the production lead time to prevent unnecessary scrap and expediting due to changes during the production cycle.

Rarely is the master schedule a reflection of future demand forecasts. Rather, the master schedule is a forecast of what will be produced. It is a "build" schedule. Finished-goods inventory is a buffer between the master schedule and final customer demand, smoothing out workloads and providing fast customer service.

BILL OF MATERIALS (BOM). The BOM is a structured list of all the materials or parts needed to produce a particular finished product, assembly, subassembly, manufactured part, or purchased part. The BOM serves the same function as a recipe used for cooking: it lists all the ingredients. It would be foolish to allow errors to creep into your favorite cooking recipes. The same is true for a BOM. If there are errors in the BOM, the proper materials will not be ordered and the product cannot be assembled and shipped. As a result, the other parts which *are* available will wait in inventory while the missing parts are expedited. Management must, therefore, insist that all BOMs are 100 percent accurate.

Some companies have several BOMs for the same product. Engineering has one BOM, manufacturing has a different version, and cost accounting has still another. An MRP system requires a single BOM for the entire company. The BOM in the computer must be the correct one, and it must represent how the product is manufactured. In companies where the BOM has been used as a reference document and not a materials-planning tool, this concept of a single bill is very difficult to implement.

BOMs are constantly undergoing change as products are redesigned. Thus, an effective engineering-change-order (ECO) system is needed to keep the BOMs up to date. Usually an ECO coordinator must be appointed and charged with the responsibility for coordinating all engineering changes with the various departments involved.

INVENTORY RECORDS. The contents of a typical computerized inventory record are shown in Figure 14.4. The item master data segment contains the part number, which is the unique item identifier, and other information such as lead time, standard cost, and so on. The inventory status segment contains a complete materials plan for each item over time. Finally, the subsidiary data segment contains information con-

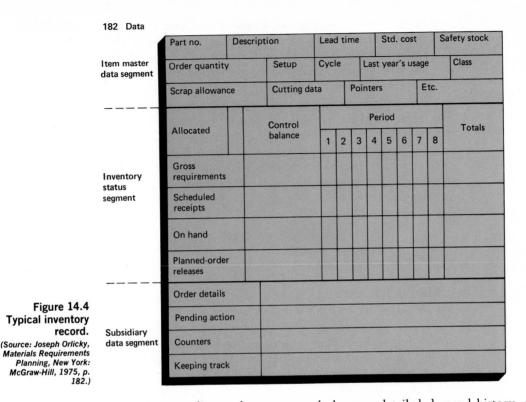

**Figure 14.4
Typical inventory
record.**
*(Source: Joseph Orlicky,
Materials Requirements
Planning, New York:
McGraw-Hill, 1975, p.
182.)*

cerning outstanding orders, requested changes, detailed demand history, and the like.

In practice, constant effort is required to keep inventory records accurate. Traditionally, inventory accuracy has been assured by the annual physical inventory count, where the plant is shut down for a day or two and everything is counted from wall to wall. It has been found that, because inexperienced people are doing the counting, as many errors are introduced by this procedure as are corrected. After the inventory is taken, the total inventory in dollars is accurate for financial purposes because the plus and minus errors cancel out. But the counts of individual items are usually not accurate enough for MRP purposes. As a result, cycle counting has been developed as a substitute for the annual physical inventory.

With cycle counting, a small percentage of the items are counted each day by storeroom personnel. Errors are corrected in the records and an attempt is made to find and correct the procedure which caused them. By developing a high regard for accuracy and adopting daily cycle counting, most errors in inventory records can be eliminated. [See Tallman (1976).] The result is so reliable that many auditors no longer require a physical inventory when an effective cycle-counting system is in place.

CAPACITY PLANNING. The necessary elements for an order-launching MRP system (type I) have been described above. This system requires master scheduling, a BOM, inventory records, and parts explosion. The resulting order-launching system will determine correct due dates (order priorities) if sufficient capacity is available. If sufficient capacity is not available, inventories will rise, past-due orders will build up, and expediting will be used to pull orders through the factory. To correct this situation, a capacity planning subsystem is needed.

The purpose of capacity planning is to check on the validity of the master schedule. There are two ways this can be done: rough-cut capacity planning (also called resource planning) and shop loading. In rough-cut capacity planning, approximate labor hours and machine hours are calculated directly from the master schedule to project future capacity needs without going through the parts-explosion process. When sufficient capacity is not available, the master schedule is adjusted or capacity is changed to obtain a feasible schedule. When the master schedule is feasible, then the full parts explosion is run.

When shop loading is used, a full parts explosion is run prior to capacity planning. The resulting shop orders are then loaded against work centers through the use of detailed parts-routing data. As a result, work force and machine hours for each work center are projected into the future. If sufficient capacity is not available, either capacity or the master schedule should be adjusted until the master schedule is feasible. At this point a valid materials plan is available.

Rough-cut capacity planning requires less detailed calculation but is not as accurate as shop loading. Either of these methods or both of them can be used, depending on individual conditions and circumstances. The important point is that capacity planning should be used to close the loop in the MRP system. [See also APICS (1975).]

PURCHASING. The purchasing function is greatly enhanced by the use of an MRP system. First, past-due orders are largely eliminated because MRP generates valid due dates and keeps them up to date. This permits purchasing to develop credibility with vendors, since the material is really needed when purchasing says it is.

By developing and executing a valid materials plan, management can eliminate much of the order expediting which is usually done by purchasing. This allows the purchasing managers to concentrate on their prime function: qualifying vendors, looking for alternate sources of supply, and maintaining low purchasing costs.

With an MRP system, it is possible to provide vendors with reports of planned future orders. This gives vendors time to plan capacity before actual orders are placed. The practice of giving vendors planned orders more closely interlocks them with the company's own materials plan. [See Papesch (1978).] Some firms have gone so far as to insist that their vendors also install MRP systems so that the vendors' delivery reliability can be more readily assured.

SHOP-FLOOR CONTROL. The purpose of the shop-floor control subsystem is to manage the orders on their way through the factory to make sure that they are completed on time. The shop-floor control system helps management adjust to all the day-to-day things which go wrong in manufacturing: absenteeism among workers, machine breakdowns, loss of materials, and so on. When these unplanned complications arise, decisions must be made about what to do next. Good decisions require information on job priorities from the shop-floor control system.

Job priorities are frequently calculated by dispatching rules of the type discussed in Chapter 11. When these rules are used as part of the shop-floor control system it is possible to adjust to changing conditions and still get the work out on time. Through the use of dispatching rules, a job's production lead time can be drastically cut or increased as it goes through the shop. This is possible because a job normally spends as much as 90 percent of its time waiting in queues. If a job is behind schedule, its priority can be increased until it gets back on schedule. Similarly, a job can be slowed down if it is ahead of schedule. It is the function of the shop-floor control system to provide information to managers so that they can manage production lead time dynamically.

The old notion of an accurate or good lead time must be discarded. Lead times can be managed by expanding or contracting them on the basis of priority. George Plossl has expressed this by saying, "Lead time is what you say it is." This is a very difficult concept to accept when managers are used to thinking in terms of fixed lead time or lead times as random variables.

It is possible through a shop-floor control system to deexpedite orders—that is, to slow them down. This is not done in normal manufacturing, where orders are expedited but never deexpedited. Orders should be slowed down when the master schedule is changed or when other parts will not be available on time. This results in the minimum inventory consistent with MRP timing requirements.

To do its job properly, a shop-floor control system requires feedback reports on all jobs as they are processed. Typically, a worker notifies the system as each processing step is completed. This may be done through a computer terminal on the shop floor or by information submitted to a central office. The computer system then produces a dispatching list for each supervisor each day. The list shows the priority of each job in the work center, and—if possible—the supervisor works on the highest-priority job. If materials, labor, or machines are not available for the highest-priority job, then the job that is next-highest in priority is done, and so on down the list.

A shop-floor control system requires valid due dates on orders. If the master schedule is inflated and the shop is overloaded, no shop-floor control system will get the work out on time. The shop-floor control system is highly dependent on proper priority and capacity planning.

14.5 OPERATING AN MRP SYSTEM

There is much more to MRP than just installing the proper computer modules. Management must operate the system in an intelligent and effective way.

One of the decisions management should make is how much safety stock to carry. To the surprise of many managers, little safety stock is needed if MRP is properly used. This is due to the concept of lead-time management, where both purchasing and shop lead times are effectively controlled within small variances. In purchasing, this is done by developing relationships with vendors who provide reliable deliveries. In the shop, lead times can be managed by a shop-floor control system as described above. Once the uncertainty in lead time is reduced, there is much less need for safety stock.

If safety stock were carried at the component level, a great deal of it would be needed to be effective. Suppose, for example, that 10 parts are required to make an assembly and each part has a 90 percent service level. The probability of having all 10 parts on hand when needed is only 35 percent.[1] It is much better, therefore, to plan and control the timing of the 10 parts than to try to cover all contingencies with safety stock.

When safety stock is carried, it is often added at the master-schedule level. This ensures that matched sets of components, not simply an assortment of various parts, are available for final products. The purpose of safety stock at the master-schedule level is to provide flexibility to meet changing customer requirements.

Safety lead time is a concept that should be considered for component parts. If a vendor is unreliable and the situation cannot be remedied, then the planned lead time can be lengthened by adding safety lead time. This will add to inventories, however, when the vendor delivers the parts earlier than planned.

Another problem in operating an MRP system is the constant danger that the informal system will drive out the formal system. If the formal MRP system is not used by management, the informal system will rapidly take over as material is expedited, past-due orders build up, and an atmosphere of crisis develops. The informal system is always "lurking in the wings" to take over. It is necessary, therefore, that management strive to maintain data accuracy, user education, and system integrity so that the formal MRP system is used to manage the company.

If an MRP system is operating properly, it can be more than just a production and inventory control tool. The MRP system can support planning and control in all parts of the company (a type III system). For example, it can be used to drive financial planning systems—to project future total inventories, forecast purchasing budgets, and plan needs for equipment and facilities. An MRP system used for the physical control of materials can be expanded to provide the basis for financial planning and control. MRP users are beginning to realize that detailed physical planning can be the basis for improved financial planning.

An MRP system can also be extended to support product costing and cost accounting. When an accurate bill of material is in the computer, it is a realitively simple matter to calculate product costs from the labor and materials costs of the component parts. As a matter of fact, a costing module is sometimes provided as part of the MRP software.

An MRP system can also be expanded into personnel planning by using a bill of labor. In this case all the labor skills for each product are listed on the bill of labor. The labor requirements are then exploded from the master schedule in a similar way as materials requirements. This makes it possible to forecast labor requirements and to tie together labor and materials needs.

---

[1] Probability = $(.9)^{10}$ = .35, assuming independent demands.

The possibilities for making MRP more than just a tool for production and inventory control are appealing. These possibilities have not been achieved in very many companies to date because most companies are still in the first phases of MRP implementation. Once these organizations have achieved materials control, they can widen the applicability of their MRP systems to the planning and control of other resources.

14.6 THE CHANGING ROLE OF PRODUCTION AND INVENTORY CONTROL MANAGERS

The advent of MRP systems has drastically changed the role of production and inventory control managers in industry. Traditionally, there has been a split between inventory managers and production control managers. The inventory manager was in charge of issuing orders for more material, usually by means of order-point systems. This amounted to pushing material into the factory. The production control manager determined the real priorities through expediting and pulling material through to final assembly.

MRP is a combined push and pull system. It launches orders at the correct time and then pulls them through to meet the promised due dates. The MRP system, however, does not make decisions. Orders are still released by the inventory control manager based on the MRP system's advice. More importantly, the inventory control manager is responsible for seeing that the assumptions and information in the system are accurate. For example, is the lot size for a particular order correct or have conditions changed? Has an engineering change order been properly entered into the system, so that the new materials are ordered? Has a new vendor lead time taken effect? As long as all the information in the system is current, orders will be placed by the system at the right time.

Similarly, the production control manager should have much less expediting to do in the shop. More time should be spent by the production control manager on master scheduling and capacity planning and on keeping the shop-floor control system up to date.

With the advent of MRP, production and inventory control managers have become planners and users of information systems rather than order writers, stock chasers, and expediters. As Oliver Wight (1974), a noted consultant, has said: "The job of production and inventory management is to generate plans that other people can be held responsible for executing. Plans are made and performance is monitored against these plans in order to manage production and inventories." This role requires a great deal more education and a change toward professionalism in the production and inventory control field.[2]

In some organizations, MRP has led to a new management position called the materials manager. In the organizational hierarchy, purchasing, inventory control, and production control all report to the materials manager, thereby improving the

---

[2] The transition to professionalism has been greatly aided by the American Production and Inventory Control Society, a national professional organization of some 38,000 members (in 1980).

integration of materials flow. The materials manager's position represents an attempt to apply the systems philosophy of integration across the entire materials conversion process. [For further details, see Miller and Gilmore (1979).]

14.7 THE SUCCESSFUL MRP SYSTEM

It takes a great deal of effort to make MRP successful. As a matter of fact, research indicates that four elements are required for success:

1. Adequate computer support
2. Accurate data
3. Management support
4. User knowledge

An adequate computer system is probably one of the easiest elements of MRP to implement. Today, there are over twenty MRP software packages on the market. Many companies use these standard packages rather than writing their own computer programs. A flowchart for a typical software package is shown in Figure 14.5.

An MRP system requires accurate data, which are very difficult to obtain. Many companies are accustomed to lax record keeping in manufacturing because the company has always been managed by the informal system. But accurate data are required when decisions are made from information supplied by the computer.

A company that does not have an MRP system will need to create accurate BOMs as a first step. In some cases, the BOMs are in such poor condition that the company literally has to start over from the beginning. In other cases, the BOMs may be relatively accurate and require only some updating.

Once the BOMs are accurate, a system will be needed to keep them that way. This will require an engineering change coordinator who is in charge of all changes to the BOM.

Inventory records must also be accurate to support the MRP system. The initial accuracy of inventory records may be somewhat better than the BOMs, but inventory record keeping will need improvement too. The best way to improve and maintain the accuracy of inventory records is to install a system of cycle counting.

All other MRP system data—such as shop routings, shop-floor status, and costs —must be initially screened for errors and then maintained in an acceptable state of accuracy. Keeping MRP data accurate for system integrity is one of the most important tasks in operating an MRP system. (See Box 14.3.)

The importance of management support to the successful MRP system can hardly be overemphasized. Many studies have shown that top-management support is the key to successful implementation of systems. [See, for example, Hall and Vollmann (1978) and Hall (1977).] But management support requires more than lip service and passive support on the manager's part. "Management participation" would be a better phrase. Top managers must be actively involved in installing and operating the MRP system. They must give their time and they must change the way they operate the company. If top managers change, then the climate is set for other man-

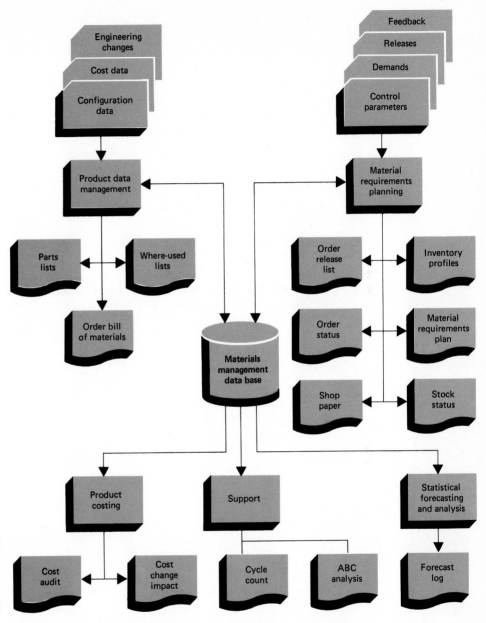

**Figure 14.5
Honeywell IMS
systems flowchart.**
*(Source: Honeywell,
"Manufacturing IMS/66
(Extended) Systems
Handbook," DE80, Rev
1, June 1977.)*

agers also to make the changes required by the MRP system. The ultimate change required by managers at all levels is to use the system and not to override it by using the informal system.

The final requirement for the successful MRP system is user knowledge at all levels of the company. An MRP system requires an entirely new approach to manufacturing. All company employees must understand how they will be affected and

BOX 14.3   MISCONCEPTIONS ABOUT MRP

1. *MRP is a computer system.* It's really a *people* system made possible by the computer. The computer does nothing but generate paper or put an image on the tube; it's what people do with that information that makes things happen in a factory.

2. *MRP primarily affects production and inventory control people.* We call it *Manufacturing Resource Planning* today because it is a company plan, a way to tie together the activities of marketing, manufacturing, and engineering so that schedules for all of these activities can be coordinated to get the best overall results for the company. Obviously, a company game plan isn't going to work very well if all of the players aren't tuned in to it.

3. *Each company requires a unique "system"* designed for them to solve their unique problems. In practice the problems of scheduling a factory, scheduling the vendors, and coordinating the activities of marketing, engineering, manufacturing, and finance are not particularly unique company to company. There is a standard logic for MRP, and we have yet to see a company that had to reinvent this logic, or, for that matter, one that tried to reinvent it and made it work.

4. *The MRP installation problems are going to be in the computer area.* The computer end of MRP installation is usually the most straightforward. The real problems come in getting basic data like inventory records and bills of material accurate enough to support MRP. Under the informal system—the shortage list—accurate bills of material were not particularly significant. If the formal system is going to work for people, these numbers have to be right. And that involves instilling a new set of values in a large group of people in the organization. And, of course, that's the real problem. MRP can provide the tools to run a business differently. The trick is in teaching people to install and use these tools effectively.

Source: Newsletter from Oliver Wight, 1977.

grasp their new roles and responsibilities. [See Walker and Hills (1977).] In beginning the installation of MRP, only a few key managers need to be educated. But as the system begins to be used, all supervisors, middle managers, and top managers need to understand MRP, including managers inside and outside of manufacturing. As the MRP system is broadened in scope, the level of education within the company must be broadened too.

If an effective MRP system is installed according to the above guidelines, what

TABLE 14.5   MRP BENEFITS

	"Pre-MRP" estimate	Current estimate	Future estimate
Inventory turnover	3.2	4.3	5.3
Delivery lead time (days)	71	59	44
Percentage of delivery promises met	61%	76%	88%
Percentage of orders requiring "splits" because of unavailable material	32%	19%	9%
Number of expediters	10	6	5

Source: Schroeder et al. (1980), p. 28.

benefits and costs can be expected? Table 14.5 helps answer this question by showing the benefits from a survey by Schroeder et al. (1980). The average company reported an improvement in inventory turnover from 3.2 to 4.3, while future improvement to 5.3 is expected when the MRP system is fully implemented. Similarly, benefits are shown in the table for reduced delivery lead time, increasing the percentage of delivery promises met, reducing the percentage of orders split because of unavailable material, and reducing the number of expenditures needed. It should be noted that these are average benefits; some companies obtain fewer benefits and others obtain more.

The benefits obtained from MRP are quite substantial. Since the average company in the above study had $11.8 million invested in inventory, the current improvement in inventory turnover represents a reduction of $4 million in inventory with another $2.2 million reduction expected when MRP is fully implemented. This improvement in inventory is matched by equally impressive gains in customer service and in efficiency of operations.

As far as the cost of MRP is concerned, the average company in the study by Schroeder et al. reported spending $375,000 on MRP system installation to date, with an eventual cost of $618,000 when the MRP system is fully developed. These installation costs included people, software, hardware, and training for development of the system. The installation costs were found to be highly variable by size of company, as shown in Table 14.6.

Many companies apparently believe that the cost of MRP is worthwhile, since the number of MRP companies has rapidly expanded from only a few in 1965 to about 1000 in 1979. This number is still, however, only a small fraction of the manufacturing industry. As more managers become aware of MRP in the future, the number of MRP companies can be expected to grow.

There are some MRP companies that are not gaining the maximum benefit

TABLE 14.6   ESTIMATED COST OF MRP INSTALLATION

	Average	Standard deviation
	$375,000	$ 600,000
	618,000	1,137,000

	Cost of MRP installation (thousands of dollars)	
Annual sales	Current cost	Eventual cost
Under $10 million	$ 93	$ 194
$ 11–25 million	210	385
$ 26–50 million	298	560
$ 51–100 million	511	912
$101–500 million	565	800
Over $500 million	1633	2237

Source: Schroeder et al. (1980), p. 32.

from their MRP systems or who have failed in implementing MRP. The reasons for this are usually a lack of management support for the system and a failure in communications within the company. As a result, the informal system is in use and the formal MRP system is in danger of failing or has already failed. Some companies are even considering reimplementing their MRP systems because the formal systems provide so little benefit.

14.8 WHO CAN BENEFIT FROM MRP?

It has been demonstrated in practice that most manufacturing companies can benefit from an MRP system *if it is properly installed and utilized*. Successful companies range from the small single-plant manufacturer to the large multiple-plant conglomerates. There are successful companies in all industries—including automobiles, metalworking, electronics, and the process industries.

While some companies may benefit from a very elaborate MRP system, others may need only a simple system. [See Miller and Sprague (1975).] Each company should determine the scope of the MRP system needed on the basis of the incremental costs and benefits. Starting with a minimum system, a company can add features and determine whether the additional cost is justified by the additional benefits. By using this approach, each company can arrive at the type of MRP system which is best suited to its needs.

Some people feel that a company must have a fixed master schedule and fixed lead times to use MRP. Change does not destroy an MRP system, since MRP is designed to adjust to changing conditions. However, those companies that have a fixed master schedule or fixed lead times can operate their MRP systems with less inventory than those that must add safety lead time or safety stock to cover uncertainties in supply or demand. Therefore variable lead time does not destroy MRP, but it does require more inventory and results in less benefit.

Users of MRP systems can be classified by the type of BOM they have. Figure 14.6*a* shows a BOM for a process company, where a given input is split into several different outputs. This occurs, for example, during the cracking and distillation of petroleum and during food processing. Figure 14.6*b* shows a BOM for a company which is in the assembly business. All parts are purchased, and the company is not vertically integrated. Finally Figure 14.6*c* is a BOM for a company which has both

**Figure 14.6
Types of BOM
structures.**

*(Source: Adapted from
Elwood S. Buffa and Jeffrey Miller, Production
Inventory Systems: Planning and Control, 3d ed.,
Homewood, Ill.: Irwin,
1979.)*

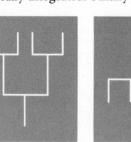

(a)
Process industry

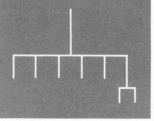

(b)
Assembly only

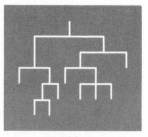

(c)
Assembly and
fabrication

fabrication and assembly operations. This company—which might be a machinery or appliance manufacturer—is vertically integrated through all stages of manufacturing. Generally speaking, the most benefit from MRP is achieved by companies of the third type, which have the most complex bills of materials.

There is tremendous room for the application of MRP concepts in the service industry. If the bill of materials is replaced by a bill of labor or a bill of activities, one can explode the master schedule of output into all the activities and personnel required to deliver a particular mix of services. Some service operations will also require a bill of materials where materials are an important part of the goods-services bundle.

As an example, one electric utility has been using the MRP concept for several years in the electric hookup part of its business. When a new customer requests electrical service, a planner enters the request into a computer system for the type of service required. The computer then explodes this service request into detailed labor, material, and work activities. Each of these requirements is time-phased and accumulated over all jobs to determine whether sufficient capacity is available. When the time comes, the utility hookup crews are given work orders from the computer system, and work accomplishment is reported back to the computer. The "MRP" system then drives billing, labor-reporting, and other accounting systems.

The MRP concept is only beginning to be applied to service industries. There is potential in every phase of service operations including restaurants, hotels, legal offices, health care, and many others.

14.9 INTEGRATION OF MATERIALS PLANNING AND CONTROL

In a manufacturing company, one of the most important problems is the integration of all facets of materials planning and control. This integration can be achieved through a comprehensive information system; through a materials manager position, as described above; and through coordinated decision making. Figure 14.7 shows how the decisions described in past chapters are interrelated in a manufacturing environment.

At the top of the figure, facilities planning and aggregate planning set physical capacity and inventory levels over the medium- to long-range time frame. These decisions constrain the amount of capacity available to the master schedule and the aggregate amount of finished-goods inventory available.

Demand is entered into the master schedule through finished-goods inventory when finished goods exist. Demand also drives forecasting, which may be used at any of three levels; facilities, aggregate planning, and master scheduling. Master scheduling is followed by the parts-explosion process, described in this chapter. Detailed or rough-cut capacity planning (or loading) is then done to determine whether or not sufficient capacity exists at the level of the master schedule. If insufficient capacity is available, the master schedule is adjusted through a feedback loop which may, in turn, affect aggregate planning or facilities planning. If sufficient capacity is available, the operations are scheduled and purchasing actions take place. The orders are then monitored through the shop-floor control system.

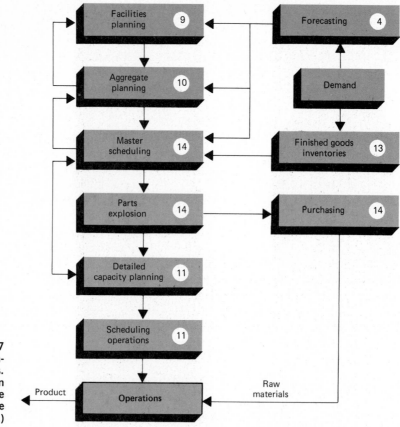

Figure 14.7 Integration of materials decisions. (Numbers within circles indicate chapters in the text.)

The chapters in the text which deal with each of these integrated decisions are shown in circles in Figure 14.7. As the figure indicates, each of these decisions exist within the context of an overall materials-management system and the decisions should be integrated accordingly.

14.10 KEY POINTS

Materials requirements planning is based on the concept of dependent demand. By exploding the master schedule through the BOM, it is possible to derive demand for component parts and raw materials. The MRP system can then be used to plan and control capacity, and it can be extended to resource planning throughout a manufacturing firm.

This chapter's key points include the following:

- MRP is an information system used to plan and control manufacturing. There are three types of MRP systems: type I, an inventory control system (order launching); type II, a production and inventory control system (closed loop); and type

III, a manufacturing resource planning system. Each of these systems expands the scope and use of MRP.

- The parts-explosion process has three principal inputs: master schedule, BOM, and inventory records. There are two principal outputs: purchase orders and shop orders. Parts explosion is the heart of the MRP system.
- MRP uses a requirements philosophy where parts are ordered only as required by the master schedule. Past demand for parts is irrelevant, and component inventories are *not* replenished when they reach a low level.
- Master schedules should be based on both marketing and production considerations. They should represent a realistic build plan within factory capacity. Top management should use the master schedule to plan and control the business.
- The BOM contains the list of parts used to make the product. To maintain the accuracy of the bill of materials, an engineering-change-order (ECO) system is needed.
- The accuracy of inventory records should be maintained through cycle counting. Daily cycle counting can be used in place of annual physical inventories.
- Shop-floor control is used to control the flow of materials through the factory. This is done by managing lead times dynamically as the product is manufactured. If lead times are properly managed, much safety stock can be eliminated.
- A successful MRP system requires (1) adequate computer support, (2) accurate data, (3) management support, and (4) user knowledge. Both system and people problems must be solved to use MRP successfully. When this is done, benefits include reduced inventory, increased customer service, and improved efficiency.
- All manufacturing and service companies can benefit from MRP if it is properly installed and operated. This includes large and small companies and all industries.

QUESTIONS

1. In what ways do independent-demand inventories differ from dependent-demand inventories?
2. Why is demand history irrelevant for the management of raw materials and work-in-process inventories?
3. A vendor has quoted a lead time of 10 weeks for delivery of a part. Your purchasing manager says the part can be delivered in 3 weeks if necessary. Of course, the vendor disagrees. Who is correct? Explain.
4. It has been said that MRP is an information system which does not rely on sophisticated mathematical models. Discuss the historical significance of this statement.
5. With regard to inventory management, discuss the difference between a replenishment philosophy and a requirements philosophy.
6. Can the ABC principle be applied to manufacturing component inventories? Discuss.
7. How much safety stock should be carried in an MRP system? What is the role of safety stock in MRP systems? Where should safety stock be carried?
8. What are the potential effects of an inflated master schedule?
9. Describe the advantages of cycle counting over an annual physical inventory.
10. Under what circumstances is a shop-floor control system needed?
11. Is it possible to control financial totals without physical control of materials in manufacturing?
12. How is the role of the production and inventory control manager changed by an MRP system?

13. A company president said his company was too small to afford an MRP system. Discuss.
14. A materials manager said that her company needed only an order-launching system. Should the loop be closed?
15. Describe how MRP concepts could be used for the following service operations:
    a. Hotel
    b. Legal office

PROBLEMS

1. The following information is given for a particular part. Using a lead time of 2 weeks, complete the table.

	Week				
	1	2	3	4	5
Gross requirements			100	200	100
On-hand/scheduled receipts	80	50			
Net requirements					
Planned order releases					

2. The Old Hickory Furniture Company manufactures chairs on the basis of the BOM shown below. At the present time, the inventories of parts and lead times are as follows:

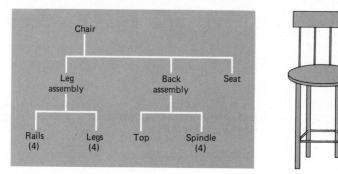

	On hand	Weeks lead time
Chairs	100	1
Leg assembly	50	2
Back assembly	25	1
Seat	40	3
Rails	100	1
Legs	150	1
Top	30	2
Spindles	80	2

The company would like to produce 300 chairs in week five and 200 chairs in week six.
a. Develop a materials plan for all the parts.
b. What actions should be taken now?

c. Suppose rails and legs are made on the same machine. Rails take .1 hour each and legs take .2 hour each. How many hours of machine time are needed in each week?

d. Suppose it takes 1 hour to assemble backs, 1 hour to assemble legs, and 2 hours to finish completed chairs. Also assume that total assembly time for all three types of assembly is limited to 1000 hours per week. Will this capacity constraint cause a bottleneck in assembly? If it does, what can be done?

3. Product A consists of subassemblies B and C. Subassembly B requires two parts of D and one part of E. Subassembly C requires one part of D and one part of F.

   a. Draw a product structure tree (BOM) for this product.
   b. How many parts are needed to make 100 units of finished product?

4. The BOM for product A is given below:

Part	On hand	Weeks lead time
A	50	1
B	100	2
C	50	1
D	100	2

(A tree: A → D, C(2); C → D(2), B)

Assume that the master schedule calls for 200 units of product A in week five and 100 units in week six.

a. Develop a materials plan for this product.
b. What actions should be taken immediately?
c. Project the inventory ahead for each part.
d. If you were suddenly notified that part D will take 3 weeks to get instead of 2 weeks, what actions would you take?

SELECTED BIBLIOGRAPHY

ANDERSON, JOHN C., ROGER G. SCHROEDER, SHARON E. TUPY, and EDNA M. WHITE: "Material Requirement Planning Systems: The State of the Art," working paper. Minneapolis: University of Minnesota, April 1980.

APICS: "Capacity Planning and Control Study Guide," *Production and Inventory Management,* vol. 16, no. 1, 1975, pp. 1–16.

BELT, BILL: "The New ABC's of Lead-Time Management," *Production and Inventory Control Management,* vol. 15, no. 2, 1974, pp. 81–91.

BEVIS, GEORGE E.: "A Management Viewpoint on the Implementation of a MRP System," *Production and Inventory Management,* vol. 17, no. 1, 1976, pp. 105–116.

BUFFA, ELWOOD S., and JEFFREY MILLER: *Production Inventory Systems: Planning and Control,* 3d ed., Homewood, Ill.: Irwin, 1979.

HALL, ROBERT: "Getting the Commitment of Top Management," *Production and Inventory Management,* vol. 18, no. 1, 1977, pp. 1–9.

——— and Thomas E. Vollmann: "Planning Your Material Requirements," *Harvard Business Review,* September–October 1978, pp. 105–112.

HONEYWELL INC., "Manufacturing IMS/66 (Extended) Systems Handbook," DE80, Rev 1, June 1977.

HOYT, JACK: "Dynamic Lead Times That Fit Today's Dynamic Planning," *Production and Inventory Management,* vol. 19, no. 1, 1978, pp. 63–70.

MILLER, JEFFREY G., and PETER GILMORE: "Materials Managers: Who Needs Them," *Harvard Business Review,* July–August 1979, pp. 143–153.

——— and LINDA G. SPRAGUE: "Behind the Growth in Materials Requirements Planning," *Harvard Business Review,* September–October 1975, pp. 83–91.

ORLICKY, JOSEPH: *Materials Requirements Planning,* New York: McGraw-Hill, 1975.

PAPESCH, ROGER M.: "Extending Your MRP System into Your Vendor's Shop," *Production and Inventory Management,* vol. 19, no. 2, 1978, pp. 47–52.

PLOSSL, G. W.: *Manufacturing Controls—The Last Frontier for Profits,* Reston, Va.: Reston Publishing Co., 1973.

———: "Tactics for Manufacturing Control," *Production and Inventory Management,* vol. 15, no. 3, 1974, pp. 21–34.

SCHROEDER, ROGER G., JOHN C. ANDERSON, SHARON E. TUPY and EDNA M. WHITE: "A Study of MRP Benefits and Costs," working paper, Minneapolis: University of Minnesota, August 1980.

SMOLENS, R. W.: "Master Scheduling: Problems and Solutions," *Production and Inventory Management,* vol. 18, no. 3, 1977, pp. 32–38.

TALLMAN, JACK: "A Practical Approach to Installing a Cycle Counting Program," *Production and Inventory Management,* vol. 17, no. 4, 1976, pp. 1–16.

WALKER, JOHN, and FREDERICK HILLS: "The Key to Success or Failure of MRP: Overcoming Human Resistance," *Production and Inventory Management,* vol. 18, no. 4, 1977, pp. 7–16.

WIGHT, OLIVER W.: *Production and Inventory Management in the Computer Age,* Cahners Books International, 1974.

PART V
WORK-FORCE MANAGEMENT

PROCESS

CAPACITY

QUALITY

INVENTORY

- MANAGING
  WORK FORCE
  IN OPERATIONS
- JOB DESIGN
- WORK MEASUREMENT
- PRODUCTIVITY

WORK FORCE

Part V deals with one of the most important responsibilities of operations managers: managing the work force. A broad view is taken toward the subject, beginning with a discussion of managing people for performance and proceeding through job design, work measurement, and productivity issues. The discussion is based on the idea that work should be managed from a sociotechnical perspective and that such management should include the process considerations first described in Part II as well as the behavioral considerations developed here. The combined management of both technical and behavioral aspects of work can result in operations which are socially stimulating as well as productive.

Chapter 15 presents an approach to managing the people assigned to operations. The performance objective of operations is described and some management principles which should lead to improved performance in operations are defined. The chapter ends with examples of how these principles of work-force management have been applied in practical situations.

Chapter 16 focuses on job design decisions related to managing the work force. A sociotechnical approach is utilized which combines the technical and human aspects of job design. The principles of Frederick Taylor's scientific management approach are described in some detail, as are the various approaches to job enrichment. By properly combining these two approaches, a sociotechnical job design can be achieved.

After jobs are designed, a critical element in managing the work force is the measurement of work. In Chapter 17, various approaches to work measurement and methods improvement are described. It is suggested that the selection of an appropriate work-measurement technique should depend on its intended use, its cost, and the behavioral reactions of the workers. The conditions under which one work-measurement approach or another might be preferred are explained.

Part V is completed by a comprehensive treatment of productivity. Chapter 18, which focuses on this subject, addresses not only the measurement of productivity but also the question of how it might be improved in operations. Although the improvement of productivity extends far beyond work-force considerations, the work force is involved or affected by it. Thus Chapter 18 integrates work-force issues and other decisions in operations within a productivity framework.

Managing the work force is always a central responsibility of the operations function. How well it is managed determines the quality, flexibility, dependability, and cost of operations. It is only through the effective management of people that goods and services are produced and the objectives of operations met.

CHAPTER 15
MANAGING THE WORK FORCE IN OPERATIONS

When operations managers are asked, "What is your greatest responsibility or your most important problem?" the usual reply is, "Management of our people." Yet the work force is one of the most poorly managed resources in operations.

In the past, the literature of operations management has paid little attention to management of the work force in operations. Instead, the attention has been directed to quantitative models and the technical aspects of operations. At the same time, psychologists and organizational theorists have conducted a great deal of research on how humans behave in organizations. There is now a need for more application of this behavioral research in the operations function, along with an operations management point of view regarding management of the work force. Such a viewpoint will necessarily draw heavily on psychology and organizational behavior as underlying disciplines.

The purpose of this chapter is to develop a broad perspective regarding management of the work force in operations. It will also provide a point of departure for the more detailed issues of job design and work measurement to be discussed in the next

429

BOX 15.1   **TYPICAL DECISION PROBLEM**

In addition to its problems concerning the installation of an automatic teller, as described in Chapters 2 and 7, the First City Bank is having some work-force management problems. The 20 employees in the bank are unionized, and a contract has recently been signed giving the workers good pay and benefit increases; the workers, however, are still unhappy and restless. Their feelings have been spilling over into increasing absenteeism, higher personnel turnover, and some problems of accuracy in the bank's accounts.

George Andrews, the vice president of bank operations, was very concerned about this problem, but he was unsure of what action to take. In discussing the matter with Ted Blaine, the bank's president, George said, "Ted, the problems we are having with our work force are difficult to diagnose. I do feel, however, that a quick fix will not work. The problems have been building up for some time, and a comprehensive solution is now needed."

Ted agreed and mentioned a few things he had been considering. "Most of our complaints have come from the tellers and accounting personnel, about the boring jobs they have. Some of these employees find it difficult to concentrate on their work, and they get little enjoyment from the work itself. On the other hand, if they try hard and do a good job, they are not paid more. Pay is based strictly on seniority and job classification."

George replied, "I think the solution to this problem may lie in giving the employees something to look forward to. First, I would like to see if we can institute a merit pay or bonus system to reward our people for extra effort. I also feel we need to establish career paths for the employees, so that those who want to advance know they are not stuck in their current jobs forever. And I would like to establish some type of recognition system. Although it may seem a little corny, perhaps we could select an employee of the month, who would be rewarded by being taken out to lunch or would receive some other form of recognition. Little things like this may make a difference. What I think I am really saying is that we should reward people for performance. If we do this, I think many of the petty complaints—and the dissatisfaction—will disappear. What do you think?"

two chapters. Finally, the chapter shows how decisions regarding management of the work force are linked to other decisions in operations and to general personnel policy in the firm. A typical work-force decision is presented in Box 15.1.

15.1 OBJECTIVES IN MANAGING THE WORK FORCE

Since many of the controversies regarding specific approaches to managing the work force are related to differences concerning objectives, our discussion begins with the objectives of work-force management. In operations, the most important objective of work-force managers must be achievement of performance. The performance objective is sometimes stated as productivity, but the term "productivity" is too narrow. Performance includes all the objectives in operations including cost, quality, dependability, and flexibility, as originally defined in Chapter 2.

The mention of performance in operations sometimes conjures up the image of a "slavedriver" who cares little about people. This image implies that the best way to get performance from people is to drive them. But the objective of performance in operations implies nothing about how the objective is to be achieved. As a matter of fact, a "people-oriented" approach *may* result in more performance than the "slavedriver" approach.

It should also be stated, at the outset, that the objective of work-force management is not to *maximize* performance. Rather, the objective of the work-force manager is to maximize performance within the applicable constraints. The constraints tend to prevent the operations work-force manager from pursuing undesirable social, psychological, or environmental solutions which may not be represented by the performance objective itself.

Another view of the work-force objective is that of satisfactory performance rather than maximum performance; Herbert Simon (1960) calls this "satisficing." Satisfactory performance can be defined as that level of performance which permits the organization to stay in business and attract the people, capital, governmental support, and customers that it needs to survive. Satisfactory performance is therefore related to long-run survival of the organization rather than to maximum performance per se.

It should be clear that the satisfaction or happiness of the work force is not the organization's *primary* objective. If the work force is happy but the organization ceases to survive, there will be no jobs. This is not to say that both objectives —performance and satisfaction—cannot be achieved simultaneously. As a matter of fact, in many cases this can be done by a proper management approach. But satisfaction of the work force should be viewed as a means, not as an end in itself.

For many years, a satisfaction-performance controversy has been reported in the literature of organizational behavior. Some have theorized that satisfaction caused performance, and that therefore satisfaction could be pursued as an end in its own right. This thinking led to the cliché that "a happy worker is a productive worker."

More recent behavioral research suggests that satisfaction does not cause performance and that probably the reverse is true. It follows that operations managers should not pursue satisfaction of the work force as an objective, hoping that performance will automatically follow. Rather, the manager should pursue an acceptable performance level, and satisfaction will follow if the worker is properly rewarded for the performance achieved. [See Lawler (1977) for a review of this issue.]

15.2 WHO MANAGES THE WORK FORCE?

The immediate answer to the question "Who manages the work force" is "The supervisor." But the full answer is somewhat more complicated. The personnel office has a great deal of influence on what can and cannot be done in managing the work force, top management often becomes involved in work-force management decisions, and all levels of operations managers are involved (top, middle, and lower). Thus, while the supervisor may be *responsible* for managing the work force, many others are also involved.

The responsibility of the supervisor is to manage the work force within the constraints imposed by the organization. Because of multiple and conflicting constraints, the supervisor's role may be nearly impossible to fulfill. As a result, the first-level supervisor has been described by Roethlisberger (1965) as a person caught in the middle. Roethlisberger argues that in some cases, top management has become the worker's manager by usurping the supervisor's authority. Unions are the first to recognize this. They view supervisors as powerless and realize that they must bypass the supervisory level to get things done. This is a reflection of the fact that top management is making the crucial decisions in managing the work force. In these cases, top management has failed to properly delegate responsibility to lower levels of work-force management. As a result, the supervisor is caught in the middle between top management and the worker.

The number of staff specialists has been continually increasing in business. These specialists include engineers, accountants, lawyers, personnel staff, quality-control staff, and data processing staff. The role of the staff should be to support and assist the line managers. However, staff specialists who have channels to top or middle management can cause problems for first-line supervisors rather than helping them. For example, staff reports may be developed without the knowledge or participation of supervisors. When these reports are given to upper management, supervisors are asked to explain or defend themselves to their bosses. The supervisor is once again caught in the middle between the staff and upper management.

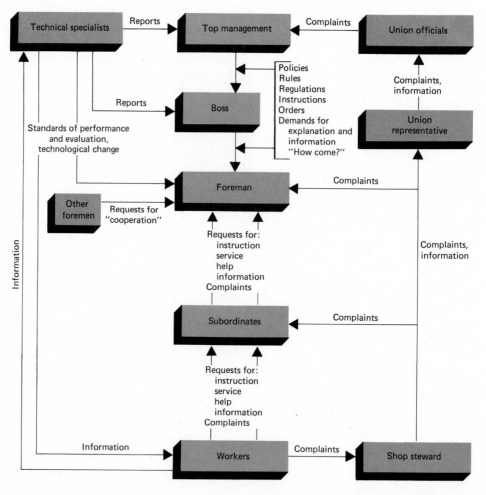

**Figure 15.1
Forces impinging
on the supervisor.**
(Source: F. J. Roethlisberger, "The Foreman: Master and Victim of Double Talk," Harvard Business Review, September–October 1965.)

The role of the supervisor as described by Roethlisberger is shown in Figure 15.1. It is a role where the supervisor is hemmed in on all sides. On the top, the supervisor is restricted by management edict, policies, rules, and regulations. The supervisor is circumvented and restricted by the staff specialists through standards which are set for quality, time, performance, and costs. And the supervisor is hemmed in by the unions through contracts and grievance procedures. Under these conditions, the supervisor is expected to produce results and to deal effectively with the work force, but this is sometimes an impossible assignment.

This situation is, of course, not typical of all organizations. Many managers, recognizing the pressures on first-level supervisors, have aligned responsibility and authority at the first level of supervision. Thus the first-level supervisor's role is expanded to a professional management job which is respected and viewed as a key managerial position. Under these circumstances, a proper relationship between line and staff is established and the work-force managers are given the authority they need to achieve the expected results. Such a supervisor's job is demanding and can lead to a position in general management.

The answer to the question of who is the worker's manager, posed at the opening of this section, should be "The supervisor." Authority and ultimate responsibility for results should rest at the supervisory level, but the supervisor should be assisted and sometimes constrained by others in the organization. When constraints are applied, they should be imposed with the objectives of operations and the business in mind. These constraints should not then be reflected in the evaluation of the work-force managers' performance. If there are too many constraints, the work-force manager's job will become meaningless and the performance level of operations may be reduced.

15.3 DECISIONS IN WORK-FORCE MANAGEMENT

Now that we have identified the objectives and managers involved in managing the work force, we will turn to work-force decisions. These decisions, normally made by operations managers, will be described along with their relationships to other organizational functions. The work-force decisions will be grouped in a logical sequence. First, the job must be designed and a position made available. Then, a specific worker must be selected and trained for the job. Finally, the worker should be evaluated and rewarded for performance.

1. JOB DESIGN. Job design determines the specific job that each worker will perform. As we have emphasized in Part II of this book, job design occurs simultaneously with process design. Job design is of extreme importance to the work-force manager because job design determines the performance and satisfaction of the worker. Work-force managers should, therefore, have a strong role in job design because of its great effect on the worker. More details on this subject will be covered in Chapter 16.

2. STAFFING LEVELS. Before workers can be selected or assigned, a decision on staffing levels must be made. These decisions have already been discussed in Part III, as part of capacity planning and control. Although staffing decisions are often made at the highest levels of the organization, work-force managers are also involved and may have a key role in determining how many work-force positions are required.

3. SELECTION. Once the job has been defined and one or more positions have been identified, the task of selecting an individual from outside or inside can proceed. If a worker is hired from outside, the personnel (or human resources) office will often perform a staff role in screening and selecting candidates. In all cases, the final hiring decision should be reserved for the worker's immediate supervisor, perhaps with the approval of higher-level supervisors or managers. This is done to make sure that the supervisor's responsibility and authority are aligned with respect to the new employee.

If an employee is selected from inside the organization, either a lateral transfer or a promotion is required. The personnel office may or may not have a role in this case, but the factors involved in the decision are similar to those of hiring.

4. TRAINING AND CAREER DEVELOPMENT. The work-force manager should be held accountable for the development of human resources. Workers may be trained for existing jobs or new jobs as the organization evolves. Workers should have an opportunity to pursue other jobs in the organization as part of a career. Sometimes workers start in jobs which are not entirely suited to their talents and aspirations. In these cases, workers who desire advancement can use promotion and career development as routes to a better job. Work-force managers, who are held responsible for developing human resources, often depend on the personnel office for training and career development programs.

5. APPRAISAL. Finally, the work-force managers must appraise the performance of each worker. Appraisal should be related to standards of performance for the job. Various work-measurement methods, described in Chapter 17, can be used to set performance standards. Once appraisal is completed, it should lead to rewards consistent with performance. These might include pay, promotion, or other forms of compensation that the organization can offer. It is important to reward performance in order to provide positive reinforcement for future achievement. An organizational theory which supports this view is described by Nadler and Lawler (1977).

Due to space limitations, it is not possible to provide more detail regarding all work-force decisions. Some of these decisions—for example, those regarding selection, training, motivation, and appraisal—are covered in detail in organizational behavior or management courses. Other work-force decisions, those involving job design and the setting of production standards, will be treated in more detail in Chapters 16 and 17.

The above discussion indicates the main responsibilities and decisions of work-force managers who are supported or constrained by other managers or staff. The general principles of work-force management described in the next section will be helpful in guiding these decisions.

15.4 PRINCIPLES OF WORK-FORCE MANAGEMENT

In managing the work force, there has been a tendency to follow fads, such as those identified by Sirota (1973):

> Human relations of the 1930s and 1940s
> Participative management of the 1950s
> T groups of the 1960s
> Job enrichment of the 1970s

This is not to say that such approaches to work-force management are not useful. On the contrary, each of these approaches is useful under a particular set of circumstances. The problem is that some managers have applied these behavioral methods when they were not appropriate.

Rather than advocating any specific behavioral approach to work-force management, we shall propose a broad set of principles that can be used in a wide variety of situations. These principles are derived from organizational theory and modern management thinking. In practice, many work-force managers follow them instinctively.

The proposed principles of good work-force management are as follows:

1. **MATCH THE WORKER AND THE JOB.** This principle implies that people should be selected for jobs on the basis of their individual differences and preferences for work. It also implies that jobs should be designed for the work force that is available. If the work force is well educated, intelligent, and able to accept responsibility, broad jobs should be designed. Individuals should also be counseled to accept jobs which meet their personal needs.

This principle implies that jobs can be overdesigned as well as underdesigned. In other words, some people might be asked to accept too much responsibility while others are asked to accept too little. How the worker and the job can be matched is described in Chapter 16.

2. **SET STANDARDS OF PERFORMANCE.** Standards of performance should be developed for all jobs. These specify what the worker is expected to accomplish and make it possible to decentralize more control to the worker on the basis of performance. When performance standards are not set, workers can become confused about their responsibilities and overly dependent on the supervisor for job direction. Several techniques for standard setting and work measurement are described in Chapter 17.

3. **REWARD PEOPLE FOR PERFORMANCE.** When performance standards are set, it is possible to reward people on the basis of performance. According to behavioral theory, this leads to further performance in expectation of further rewards. [See Nadler and Lawler (1977).] Since the work-force manager's primary responsibility is to obtain results, the giving of rewards for performance constitutes the prime method of motivating people toward goals. Rewards can include all forms of compensation

(pay, promotion, status, a pat on the back, etc.). Several incentive schemes are described in Chapter 18.

4. **ENSURE GOOD SUPERVISION.** There is nothing more fundamental to the worker than good supervision. A supervisor should be competent in both technology and management skills and should possess a sense of fairness in dealing with people. The supervisor should also be genuinely concerned with the welfare of each individual employee while also emphasizing performance and results. According to behavioral theory, when the workers know what performance is expected and participate in developing those expectations, they will be motivated to perform. The supervisor should make sure that this type of performance climate exists.

It is middle management's job to ensure that good supervisors are developed and selected. All supervisors should have knowledge of behavioral theories and practice. They should be professional managers who are given the responsibility for results and the authority needed to achieve them.

5. **CLEARLY DEFINE RESPONSIBILITIES OF THE WORKER.** When job responsibilities are unclear or constantly changing, workers feel frustrated. The result can be poor quality, low productivity, and conflict between individuals. Therefore, one of the principles of good work-force management is to define job responsibilities clearly for all workers. This would normally be done through written job descriptions or statements of objectives which are kept up to date.

The above principles do not establish a foolproof procedure for good work-force management. Rather, they attempt to summarize what organizational theorists consider the important decisions leading to both high performance and high worker satisfaction.[1] In any given situation, the principles must be properly applied to be useful. Some applications of these ideas will be described in the remainder of the chapter.

15.5 THE IBM STORY

IBM was one of the first companies to put modern principles of work-force management into practice. The following story which goes back to the 1940s, is told to show that these basic principles have been developing for a long time.

When Thomas J. Watson, the president of IBM, was in the factory one day, he observed a woman machine operator sitting idle.[2] He asked her why she was idle, and she replied that she was waiting for the machine setup man, who was required to change a tool for the next job. When asked whether she could make the setup herself, she replied, "Of course, but I am not permitted to make setups." Upon further inquiry, Mr. Watson discovered that each operator spent several hours a week waiting

[1] See, for example, Raymond E. Miles, *Theories of Management: Implications for Organizational Behavior and Development,* New York: McGraw-Hill, 1975.
[2] This section is derived from Drucker (1954), chap. 19, and Walker and Richardson (1948).

for setup men. It was also determined that only a few days of training would be required to qualify each operator for all setup work. As a result, setup work was added to the machine operator's job. The change was so successful that inspection was also soon added. Over the years, this principle of job enlargement has continually been expanded throughout IBM.

Another IBM innovation was to assign one or two lead workers in each department to part-time training duties. These "job instructors" were responsible, in addition to their regular jobs, for improving the training of other workers throughout the department. This innovation also improved productivity and provided a means whereby workers could move into supervisors' jobs. The "job instructor's" role was highly coveted and carried prestige in the department.

Almost by accident, IBM also developed another innovation in new-product introduction. As the story goes, a new-model computer was being rushed into production but there was not enough time to work out the final design before manufacturing on the shop floor began. As a result, engineers worked closely with production people to get the new product started. The production people had a role in designing their own jobs, and the engineers saw design changes that would make the computer easier to produce. The product introduction actually went more smoothly than previous efforts, where final design was completed in engineering before going to manufacturing. As a result of this success, a standard practice was developed where the design project was turned over to a supervisor in the final stages before production began. This allowed production people and engineers to work out the problems together.

IBM has been equally innovative in its approach to standards and pay. In 1936, the company did away with incentive pay in favor of a fixed hourly wage and flexible standards. In the new approach, each production worker was asked to set his or her own production goals in consultation with the supervisor. It was felt that each worker and supervisor would have a good idea of the amount of output which could be achieved. Employees were asked to set their own goals as a way of obtaining their commitment to results. But the main benefit of this approach was that a great deal more attention was given to training and job placement. If a worker set a relatively low goal, a discussion naturally ensued on how output could be improved through training or how the employee might be shifted to a more suitable job. The resulting joint effort toward improved productivity was the key to success.

But none of the IBM innovations would have worked without a commitment to stable employment, because workers might have feared that improvements in productivity might lead to the loss of jobs. The key to stable employment was IBM's aggressive marketing practices, for which the company is well known. What is not so well known is IBM's commitment to innovative work-force management practices and to stable employment.

The IBM story illustrates several of the principles of good work-force management. The machine operator's job was initially not matched to the worker's abilities and interests. When the job was broadened, improved performance was obtained. The approach to new-product introduction shows how a change in job definition can increase performance—in this case, by allowing the production people to have a role in product design. Finally, IBM adopted an innovative approach to setting standards of performance, which once again improved output.

15.6 JAPANESE WORK-FORCE MANAGEMENT

Another example of the application of work-force management principles is the Japanese management approach. Although limited space does not allow us to discuss the entire Japanese approach to management, some of the concepts that are most relevant to management of the work force will be described.[3]

The Japanese have evolved a very interesting concept of worker responsibility. In Japan, the worker is directly responsible for the work methods used. For example, after an industrial engineer has studied a job, the final decision on whether or not the job should be changed rests with the worker. The industrial engineer is a consultant and an adviser to the worker. Because of this relationship, industrial engineers in Japan complain that they are too busy. The workers willingly call the industrial engineers to study their jobs because they are not threatened by change.

A second tradition in Japanese society is lifelong employment. With few exceptions, an employee stays with the same company for his or her entire lifetime. As a result, the commitment to the company is clear. If employees are not productive, they cannot receive wage increases simply by moving to another company. Management also knows that each employee must be helped to perform, since the company cannot simply replace an unsatisfactory worker. Although lifelong employment has disadvantages too, it establishes a clear relationship between the employees' welfare and that of the company.

Another interesting Japanese practice involves the idea of continuous training. Each Japanese worker is assigned to a group or circle which meets periodically to discuss work-related matters. These training circles are run by the workers, not management. The purpose of the circle is to facilitate communications within the work force, not to solve problems or make decisions. At one meeting, a worker may describe new products which are being developed. At another meeting, a worker might describe scheduling practices used in the company. And at yet another meeting, a worker might describe his or her own job. These circles help expand the worker's vision of the work place, they provide knowledge outside the worker's specialty, and they help integrate the organization. The Japanese also have separate training sessions to enhance and improve each worker's particular specialty. But the chief aim of continuous training is to teach the worker more about other jobs in his or her circle.

We are not suggesting that these Japanese practices be adopted by American companies. They would probably not work any better here than American practices would work in Japan. We *are* suggesting that Japanese practices be studied to see whether they might be modified and adapted by United States companies. Although it is difficult to see how the idea of lifelong employment could be used in the Amer-

---

[3] The material in this section is largely derived from Drucker (1954) and Drucker (1971).

ican system without massive social changes, the ideas of worker responsibility and continuous training could more easily be adopted. The Japanese practices are another illustration of the principles of work-force management described earlier in this chapter.

15.7 WORK-FORCE MANAGEMENT IN PRACTICE

In order to use the ideas suggested in this chapter and to avoid falling prey to "solution fixation," the following actions are suggested:

1. Work-force managers should determine the current impediments to performance in each individual work situation and for each person. Is the problem a lack of technology, too much technology, poor job design, lack of pay-performance relationship, incorrect job placement, or what? This problem analysis should be done by observation and formal surveys of employees. A continuing survey of employees should also be instituted to determine how conditions are changing over time.

2. Work-force managers should formulate a plan to improve performance. The plan may extend one or more years into the future and will require management to set measures of performance in conjunction with employees. The focus of the improvement effort should be on performance: better quality, lower costs, improved adherence to schedules, or more flexibility. The objective should not be to enrich jobs or to change technology; these are only means to an end.

3. Work-force managers should reward performance. Current theories of motivation hold that proper rewards lead to motivation, which, in turn, produces effort and desirable work outcomes. In some cases, work-force management is hamstrung in rewarding performance. If this is the case, top management needs to act to return reward and incentive control to the work-force managers. The rewards given should be tailored to each individual worker and they should be visible, so that all employees are aware of the reward-performance relationship.

If the above actions are taken, a proper relationship between work and performance will be established. It is only through progressive work-force management that an organization's human resources can be properly managed.

15.8 KEY POINTS

The thrust of this chapter is to provide a broad perspective regarding management of the work force in operations. The key points are as follows:

- The work-force manager's primary objective should be performance (quality, cost, flexibility, and dependability). Worker satisfaction is not, by itself, a primary objective, but satisfaction may be achieved along with performance.
- Many people are involved in managing the work force: top managers, supervisors, middle managers, unions, and staff specialists. As a result, the supervisor

can be caught in the middle between opposing interests. To prevent this situation, work-force managers should have authority consistent with the responsibility assigned to them.

- Decisions are made by work-force managers on such matters as job design, staffing levels, selection, training, and appraisal. These decisions may be made in conjunction with others in the organization.

- The principles of work-force management are: match the worker and the job, set standards of performance, reward people for performance, ensure good supervision, and clarify the responsibility of the worker. These principles are derived from behavioral theory and management practice.

- The Japanese style of work-force management utilizes worker responsibility for production, lifetime employment, and continuous training. If some of these approaches were considered and modified as necessary, they might be useful to United States work-force managers.

- To apply the ideas in this chapter, work-force managers should (1) determine the impediments to performance in the work place, (2) formulate an approach to remove those impediments, and (3) reward the workers for performance.

QUESTIONS

1. Why is the happy worker not necessarily the most productive worker?
2. Should the work-force manager be concerned about worker satisfaction? Discuss.
3. The teachers' union in a local school district has advocated that all teachers be paid on the basis of seniority and education. Is this a good basis for rewarding teachers?
4. Susan works in a typing pool. What kinds of rewards might be available for her? How could Susan's performance be measured? Suggest some possible measures.
5. In the ABC Tire Company, the production workers are highly dissatisfied (50 percent say they do not like their jobs). Productivity has been dropping (10 percent decrease last year) and many tires are rejected due to poor quality. As a work-force manager, what approach would you take to rectify the situation?
6. East-West Airlines would like to set up a continuous training program for its aircraft maintenance workers. Describe how such a program might work. What would the expected results be?
7. How does the Japanese relationship between line and staff differ from the line-staff relationship in the United States?
8. The employees in the XYZ Company have asked you, as their supervisor, to explain their responsibilities. What would you tell them?
9. Would the answer to Question 8 be any different if the employees were professors, doctors, or lawyers? Explain.
10. For a work-force management situation that you are familiar with, describe the important work-force management decisions and who makes each of them.

SELECTED BIBLIOGRAPHY

DRUCKER, PETER F.: *Management: Tasks, Responsibilities, Practices,* New York: Harper & Row, 1973.
————: *The Practice of Management,* New York: Harper & Row, 1954.
————: "What We Can Learn from Japanese Management," *Harvard Business Review,* March–April 1971.
DYER, JAMES S., ROBERT MILLEN, and JOHN MORSE: "A Framework for the Study of Work Settings," *Management Science,* vol. 24, no. 13, September 1978.

HERZBERG, FREDERICK: "One More Time: How Do You Motivate Employees?" *Harvard Business Review,* vol. 46, no. 1, 1968, pp. 53–62.

LAWLER, EDWARD E. III: "Satisfaction and Behavior," in J. Richard Hackman, Edward E. Lawler III, and Lyman W. Porter (eds.): *Perspectives on Behavior in Organizations,* New York: McGraw-Hill, 1977.

NADLER, DAVID A., and EDWARD E. LAWLER III: "Motivation: A Diagnostic Approach," in J. Richard Hackman, Edward E. Lawler III, and Lyman W. Porter (eds.): *Perspectives on Behavior in Organizations,* New York: McGraw-Hill, 1977.

PORTER, LYMAN W., and EDWARD E. LAWLER III: "What Job Attitudes Tell About Motivation," *Harvard Business Review,* January–February 1968.

ROETHLISBERGER, F. J.: "The Foreman: Master and Victim of Double Talk," *Harvard Business Review,* September–October 1965.

SASSER, W. EARL, and STEPHEN P. ARBEIT: "Selling Jobs in the Service Sector," *Business Horizons,* June 1976.

SIMON, HERBERT A.: *The New Science of Executive Decision Making,* New York: Harper & Row, 1960.

SIROTA, DAVID: "Job Enrichment—Is It for Real?" *S.A.M. Journal,* vol. 38, no. 2, April 1973, pp. 22–27.

STEERS, RICHARD M., and LYMAN W. PORTER: *Motivation and Work Behavior,* New York: McGraw-Hill, 1975.

TAYLOR, RONALD, and MARK THOMPSON: "Work Value Systems of Young Workers," *Academy of Management Journal,* vol. 19, no. 4, December 1976.

WALKER, CHARLES R., and R. L. RICHARDSON: *Human Relations in an Expanding Company,* New Haven: Yale University Press, 1948.

CHAPTER 16
JOB DESIGN

In 1973 a special task force to the Secretary of Health, Education and Welfare published a report entitled *Work in America*. The report documented the lack of satisfaction of workers with their jobs, especially assembly-line workers, and it called for a massive enrichment of jobs to make work in America more meaningful. Job design has been a popular topic in the press and in academic journals because people see it as a solution to boredom on the job and sagging productivity. In this chapter several different approaches to job design will be explored.

Job design can be defined as the synthesis of individual tasks or activities into a job which is assigned to an individual worker or to a group of workers. The job design should specify what tasks will be done, who will do them, and what results are expected. The job design completely specifies the work content and the worker's job responsibilities.

Before job design begins, the product is generally specified. Sometimes the technology or the process is given as well. When this is the case, very little flexibility remains, since the job is almost completely specified by the process technology. In our discussion below, we will assume that the technology or process is not specified prior to job design but rather that the technology and the job are designed together.

Job design is a complex subject because it requires an understanding of both technical and human (social) variables. All too often in the past, either the human or the technical variables have been ignored, leading to jobs which were boring or did not utilize the proper technology. One of the aims of this chapter is to emphasize the

BOX 16.1   TYPICAL DECISION PROBLEM

Roger Kirk, the assistant for operations planning at Radarwave, Inc., had just completed his analysis of the proposed assembly-line process for Radarwave's microwave oven (see Box 5.1). Upon receiving Roger's report, Mary Lipton, the vice president of operations, congratulated Roger on the depth of his analysis and the presentation of the results. She observed, "It appears that the proposed assembly-line process will be much more efficient than our current production process, leading to a 20 percent reduction in unit costs of production. While this reduction is significant, I am concerned about the effects that the proposed change will have on our workers. I do not want to turn this plant into an 'automobile' type of factory with problems of job boredom, absenteeism, and 'blue-collar blues.' We have very good labor relations now and I want to maintain them intact. Toward this end, would it be possible to devise a modified assembly-line process that will improve efficiency but also maintain social values and meaningful jobs? Please develop some alternatives and report back to me in three weeks."

Roger was really stuck. He had heard about Volvo of Sweden and wondered whether some of their ideas about job design could be adapted to the production of microwave ovens. He had also heard about several new plants being designed in the United States and wondered whether their experience would be helpful. As he thought the problem through, several possibilities emerged. Instead of one fast assembly line, maybe two or three slower lines could be developed. Although this plan would require more capital, improved productivity might compensate for part or all of the capital costs. Roger also developed several options which permitted individual work pacing by using a more disconnected version of the assembly line as well as variable worker speeds. Perhaps the line could be designed to facilitate job rotation and to allow conversation between workers on the line.

After thinking about these possibilities, Roger decided to put together several alternative assembly-line concepts, each with increasing degrees of job enrichment. Both the capital and operating costs of the alternatives would then be determined. This analysis would permit management to select the best combination of social and technical conditions while also considering costs and return on investment. Although Roger was not familiar with the jargon, he was conducting a *sociotechnical* job design by considering this range of alternatives.

sociotechnical approach to job design, which requires joint optimization of both social and technical variables. Box 16.1 illustrates a typical sociotechnical decision problem.

16.1 SOCIOTECHNICAL APPROACH

The sociotechnical approach to job design was originated by Eric Trist and his associates in studies of coal mining in England. [See Trist (1963).] They discovered that new coal mining technologies which were being considered did not dictate the type of work organization required. Rather, there were a variety of social and organizational choices that could be made for any given technology. Furthermore, there were a variety of technical alternatives which could be used to achieve both economic and social objectives. This realization led to the development of sociotechnical theory as a basis for job design.

The sociotechnical concept is described in Figure 16.1. The left-hand circle represents the set of all jobs which are feasible from a technical viewpoint. Similarly, the

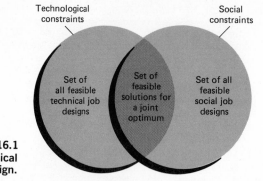

Figure 16.1 Sociotechnical design.

right-hand circle represents all feasible job designs from a social point of view, considering both the psychology and the sociology of the human worker. The intersection of these two circles then contains the set of all job designs which satisfy both social and technical requirements. The best sociotechnical design lies somewhere within this intersection.

The value of sociotechnical theory lies in its emphasis on both technical and social variables in relation to job design. This approach leads to the development of jobs that do not merely represent the most economic technology under the assumption that humans are a part of the machine. Instead, this view takes into account the possible costs of turnover, absenteeism, and boredom in relation to the choice of technology, so that the human factor is not overlooked.

Scoville (1969) proposed a model that permits the determination of the best sociotechnical solution within the feasible intersection set. His model considers the economic costs of job design from both the manager's and worker's point of view. In Figure 16.2 Scoville indicates that the manager's costs are a function of job breadth. Narrow jobs are those which are both highly specialized and repetitive, requiring

Figure 16.2 Management costs of job design.
(Source: James G. Scoville, "A Theory of Jobs and Training," Industrial Relations, vol. 9, 1969, p. 43.)

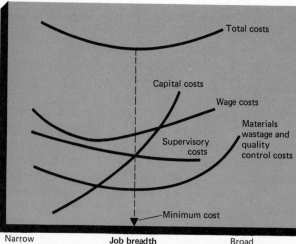

little worker discretion. Broad jobs are enriched to demand more skills, judgment, and decision-making ability.

Scoville identified the following types of costs from the manager's point of view:

1. *Wage costs,* which are high for narrow jobs due to high turnover and absenteeism. Wage costs are also high for broad jobs due to the high cost of training the workers.
2. *Supervisory costs,* which decline as jobs are broadened because the worker assumes more and more of the responsibilities of the supervisor.
3. *Materials wastage and quality control costs,* which are high for narrow jobs because workers tend to be careless when they suffer from boredom and monotony. These costs are also high for enriched jobs because the advantages brought by the division of labor are lost.
4. *Capital costs per worker,* which increase as jobs are broadened because more investment in equipment and inventory will be needed.

When these four costs are added together as in Figure 16.2, the total-cost curve is U-shaped. Therefore, from the management point of view, there is an optimum amount of job breadth where the total-cost curve is minimized.

Scoville also postulated the cost curves in Figure 16.3 from the worker's point of

Figure 16.3 Worker costs of job design.
(Source: James G. Scoville, "A Theory of Jobs and Training," Industrial Relations, vol. 9, 1969, p. 47.)

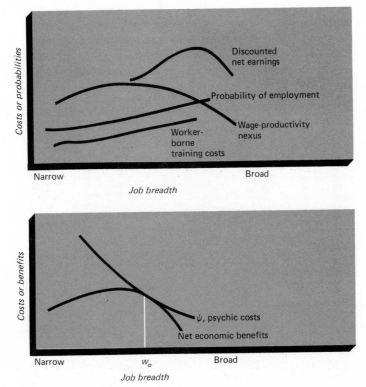

view. In this case the probability-of-employment curve is multiplied by the wage curve to arrive at expected earnings. When the worker-borne training costs are deducted, the result is the discounted net earnings curve. This curve has a maximum at w_0 which is slightly to the right of the curve for management. Workers may, therefore, prefer a slightly broader job than would be provided by management.

Scoville's theory tells us that management and labor must compromise to arrive at a jointly optimal solution within the set of social and technical constraints. Therefore, an appropriate model is an equilibrium model which balances the costs to both workers and management. This model is likely to produce a solution within the joint sociotechnical region shown in Figure 16.1.

When a job is designed from a strictly technological point of view, ignoring the social constraints, the result is called technological determinism. In this case the technology determines not only the task to be done but the social system as well. Then job designers have also become, in effect, social designers.

The sociotechnical design approach does not only involve jobs but also includes the design of the entire organization, as shown in Figure 16.4. The technical variables available for design purposes are shown on the left-hand side of the figure and the social variables on the right. Connecting them are various organizational design mechanisms which can affect the productivity and the quality of working life.

The broad view of organizational design shown in Figure 16.4 is particularly important when alternatives to changes in job design are being considered. When productivity or the quality of work life is too low, they might be improved by changes in supervision, in the type of workers selected, in the reward structures, or in any of the other variables. Thus, job design is only one of the many available design mechanisms which can be used to reach the same result.

The sociotechnical approach will be used as a framework for job design in this chapter. In Section 16.2, the technical approach as exemplified by scientific manage-

Figure 16.4 Organizational design.

(Source: Raymond E. Miles, Theories of Management: Implications for Organizational Behavior and Development, New York: McGraw-Hill, 1975.)

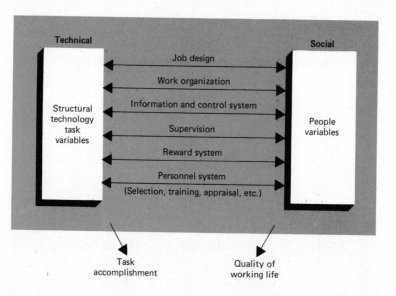

ment will be discussed. This will be followed by a discussion of the social approach, exemplified by job enrichment. The entire discussion will demonstrate how the two approaches can be linked together under the sociotechnical umbrella.

16.2 SCIENTIFIC MANAGEMENT

Scientific management is the oldest method of job design, but it is still widely applied in today's world. It is also a method which has aroused a great deal of controversy and misconception. Because of these misunderstandings, scientific management will receive a detailed discussion here.

Scientific management was developed by Frederick W. Taylor starting in 1882 at the Midvale Steel Company. The method was later refined and applied by Frank and Lillian Gilbreth and Henry L. Gantt, along with hundreds of other managers and scientists. The initial period of active development and application of scientific management extended until about 1912, by which time it had become a widely established practice.

In industry, there is almost universal acceptance among both workers and management of restricted output. When a person first begins work, other workers generally make clear to the new worker the norm or socially acceptable rate of work output. Workers who exceed this unwritten norm often receive group reprisals and are soon conditioned to conform to it.

Taylor believed that restriction of output was due to two reasons: the workers' fear of loss of their jobs and management's unwillingness to pay for higher output levels. Workers are understandably afraid of losing their jobs or of imposing such a loss on fellow workers. It is therefore the responsibility of management and society to make sure that higher output does not result in the permanent displacement of workers. Although it has been shown in many cases that increased productivity creates more jobs, not less, the worker's fear of unemployment persists.

In the second place, management has not always shared increased productivity directly with the workers. Workers, therefore, may restrict their output because their efforts benefit the company by improved profits but bring no gains to the workers themselves. To resolve this problem, Taylor advocated a wage incentive (piecework) system so that workers were automatically paid higher wages for higher output. Taylor believed that workers would not increase their productivity unless they were sure they would benefit from it economically.

There are many misconceptions about scientific management. Some people view it as a piece-rate system, time study, or use of efficiency experts. However, none of the particular techniques or factors, by themselves, are the essence of scientific management.

Taylor saw the essence of scientific management as a revolutionary change in the mental attitude of workers and management. He argued that both sides must join together and eliminate waste in order to boost output. The best method for each job must be developed on the basis of scientific study of the work, and management and workers must cooperate in using the new method to boost output without demanding increased effort from the workers. The additional output is achieved by improved methods, not harder work. As a result of applying this approach, both profits and wages are increased. According to Taylor, if economic benefits do not flow to both workers and management, scientific management will fail.

Taylor specified four principles for the application of scientific management.

1. Study the job scientifically. This requires experimentation, time study, and a search for the best method of work. Workers' suggestions are solicited and tested along with suggestions from industrial engineers and management. The resulting method is not based on opinion but on research to discover the most economical method of work.

2. Select and train workers in the new method. It is known that all workers do not perform equally well on a given job. Each job makes its own peculiar demands on the individual and each individual has his or her own preference and ability for work. This principle of scientific management, therefore, requires the selection of a worker who is matched to the type of work designed, and this must be followed by the careful training of each worker in the new method. If a given worker is not well suited for the new method, it is management's responsibility to find alternative work for him or her. If workers are not carefully selected, productivity will fall to the lowest common denominator rather than reaching a high level.

3. Install the new method in operations. This principle calls upon both management and the workers to change procedures and methods as needed to make the new method work. Careful attention must be paid to following the method or adjusting it as required in order to install it over a period of time. The new method will not be accepted automatically; the change process itself must be carefully managed.

4. Develop teamwork between management and the workers. Taylor stressed that scientific management requires close coordination and cooperation to improve output. He used the example of a baseball team to illustrate the point. Each player may know his own job, but if the team does not work together, a winning record cannot be achieved. This principle is the hardest for management to implement because management must become the facilitator for the worker. Management must accept responsibility for proper planning, timing, and work coordination to remove unnecessary restrictions to output.

An example from the early days of scientific management may help to illustrate how these four principles are applied. One of the jobs Taylor studied was shoveling in the coal yards at Bethlehem Steel, where various types of iron ore, coal, and other materials were shoveled by hand from one place to another. Prior to the application of scientific management, each worker brought his own shovel to work, and the pace of shoveling was more or less dictated by group norms. Upon studying this job, Taylor discovered that work output was maximized (in terms of tons shoveled per day) when the shovel held a certain weight of material (21 pounds). If only 10 to 15 pounds were lifted per shovel, the worker had to shovel too fast to maintain the same output. If 30 to 40 pounds per shovel were moved, the load was too heavy and output also dropped. Although shoveling had been done for hundreds of years, no one had discovered the "science of shoveling" prior to Taylor's experiments.

In using this science at Bethlehem Steel, Taylor found it necessary to have different-size shovels for different types of materials. For example, when heavy iron ore was shoveled, a small shovel was used to handle 21 pounds of material. When light ashes were shoveled, a large scoop shovel was used to equal the 21-pound weight. When workers used their own shovels for all materials, as little as 4 pounds per shovel was moved for light material and 40 pounds per shovel for heavy material.

To facilitate control of shoveling, management built a large tool shed in the yard and supplied different-size shovels for different types of materials. In addition to weight per shovel, other aspects of the job were also studied to arrive at a total job specification.

After the new shoveling method was specified, workers were trained in it. Those workers who could not adjust to the new method were transferred to other jobs. After selection and training, each shoveler was put on a piece-rate system and the amount shoveled per day was recorded. When the amount fell below the standard, the worker was notified and wages were reduced. When the amount shoveled was above the standard, wages were increased. Management was also reorganized to provide centralized planning and control of the shoveling yard. The central control office kept track of schedules and the amount produced by each worker each day. The results of this application of scientific management were striking. Wages increased by 63 percent per worker and the average cost of handling a ton of coal dropped by 54 percent. See Box 16.2.

It is interesting to note that Taylor developed his method as a result of labor-management strife. As a supervisor, Taylor saw the conflict between managers who wanted to drive the workers toward more output and workers who restricted output levels. This resulted in constant tension between management and labor because the only way that productivity could be improved was by pushing the workers to try harder. Taylor saw that both productivity and wages could be significantly improved and labor-management tensions reduced through the use of scientific management.

Scientific management has come under much criticism, some of it justified by inherent weaknesses in the method or by its misapplication. One such criticism is

BOX 16.2   **RESULTS OF CHANGES IN SHOVELING METHOD AT BETHLEHEM STEEL WORKS**

	Old plan	New plan
Number of yard workers	400–600	140
Average tons per worker per day	16	59
Average earnings per worker per day	$1.15	$1.88
Average cost of handling a ton	$.072	$.033

Source: Frederick Winslow Taylor, *Scientific Management*, New York: Harper, 1911.

that scientific management creates boring, repetitive, and highly specialized jobs. Repetitive jobs, however, are created by work specialization and division of labor, which started well before Taylor's time. Automation, advancing technology, and the economics of the division of labor are the chief causes of boring and repetitive work. Scientific management had nothing to do with the division of labor.

Another criticism is that scientific management treats people like machines. This criticism is at least partly justified because scientific management does not consider psychological or social variables in the search for a better method. There is an implicit assumption in scientific management of the economic individual; that people work purely for economic rewards. The sociotechnical approach to work design is intended to correct this defect and broaden Taylor's theory.

Scientific management is sometimes criticized by labor as a speedup campaign. This reflects a misunderstanding of the method. The emphasis is to eliminate wasted motions and thereby accomplish work in a more efficient manner without calling upon people to work harder. In the study of pig-iron handling by Taylor, for example, it was shown that workers required an optimum amount of rest after lifting heavy pig-iron bars. Some workers tended to try to work too fast and thus reduced their output over an entire day. It is clear, therefore, that scientific management does not make people work harder. It attempts to get the most from a given labor input.

Students often wonder whether scientific management is still applicable today. The answer is that the principles still apply, but some modifications must be made in their application. No longer can jobs be merely the result of technology. Meaningful jobs should be synthesized after using Taylor's method to study the individual work elements. Work should still be divided into its basic elements and each element studied scientifically to eliminate wasted motion. But, after the basic elements have been studied, jobs should be synthesized from these elements through the consideration of economic, social, and technical requirements. A worker may, for example, be assigned more work elements than are dictated by strict economic efficiency; thus the skill variety or the wholeness of the job might be improved. The work place may be designed so that people can converse while at work and develop stronger social relationships. These psychological and social considerations can result in greater productivity because of a better-balanced job design. In Taylor's time, economic reward was considered the only motivator. Now, social and psychological factors are known to affect worker motivation also. A theory of job design which emphasizes these social and psychological factors is described next.

16.3 JOB-ENRICHMENT APPROACHES

In 1959, Frederick Herzberg and his associates published a famous research study which showed that intrinsic job factors (e.g., achievement, responsibility, and work itself) are potential satisfiers, while extrinsic job factors (e.g., supervision, pay, and working conditions) are potential dissatisfiers. Herzberg argued that satisfaction and dissatisfaction are not opposites on a single continuum but two distinct scales. The opposite of satisfaction is no satisfaction, and the opposite of dissatisfaction is no dissatisfaction. By this reasoning, improvement in an extrinsic factor such as pay might reduce dissatisfaction but not produce satisfaction. According to Herzberg, the only things that would satisfy workers were factors intrinsic to the job itself. Since Herzberg and his colleagues associated satisfaction with motivation, they argued that jobs should be enriched by adding intrinsic factors. Presumably this would increase not only job satisfaction but productivity as well.

Herzberg used the term "job enrichment" to refer to vertical loading—increasing the intrinsic factors in a job. Vertical loading adds decision-making responsibility, autonomy, and planning to the job. He also used the term "horizontal loading" to refer to adding skill variety to the job but not including additional decision-making responsibilities. Horizontal loading adds more skills by rotation among jobs at the same organizational level. Some psychologists, however, use the term "job enlargement" to refer to both vertical and horizontal loading. Others use the term "job enrichment" to refer to both types of loading. We shall follow the latter convention in the rest of this chapter.

Job enrichment has been carefully specified in a theoretical framework proposed by Hackman and Oldham (1975). In Figure 16.5, the framework begins on the right with a listing of certain personal and work outcomes which result from job enrichment. Proceeding to the left we find critical psychological states, core job dimensions, and implementing concepts. According to the theory, all these factors are linked together in a causal chain.

As far as personal and work outcomes are concerned, high internal work moti-

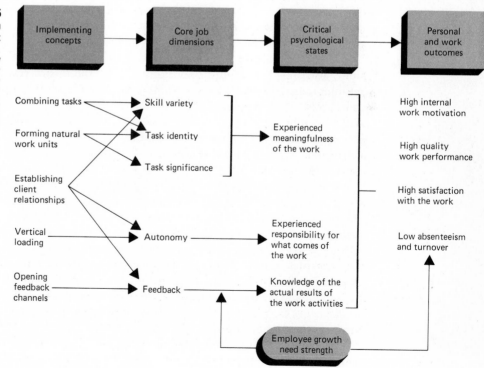

Figure 16.5 Hackman-Oldham job-enrichment framework.
(Source: J. Richard Hackman et al., "A New Strategy for Job Enrichment," California Management Review, Summer 1975, reprinted by permission of the regents.)

vation means that the worker will put a great deal of effort into the job. High-quality work performance means that productivity will be high and quality will meet the standards. High satisfaction with the work, low absenteeism, and low turnover are self-explanatory as work outcomes. Of course, all these outcomes are desirable as the ultimate result of work.

According to the framework, the work and personal outcomes are determined by the following three critical psychological states:

Experienced meaningfulness of work. The work must be perceived as important by a system of values accepted by the worker.

Experienced responsibility for work outcomes. The worker must accept personal responsibility for work outcomes.

Knowledge of results. The worker must be able to determine on some fairly regular basis whether or not the work outcomes are satisfactory.

According to the Hackman–Oldham theory, when these three psychological states are present in the worker, there will be high internal motivation; the worker will be "turned on." The result should be greater performance in terms of personal and work outcomes. Hackman and Oldham use the example of a golfer to describe the three psychological states. The golfer experiences meaningfulness, since the golfer considers the game important by a system of values he or she accepts. If this psychological state is not present, the golf clubs will soon be put away or sold and other activities pursued. The golfer experiences responsibility for the outcome even though the weather and the course are sometimes blamed for poor results. And, the golfer has knowledge of actual good or bad results.

The three critical psychological states can be achieved by five core job dimensions, also shown in Figure 16.5. For example, the theory states that experienced meaningfulness of work results from skill variety, task identity, and task significance. Skill variety is job enlargement—working at a number of different tasks which require different skills. This produces less boredom and less repetition. Task identity is associated with wholeness in the job, producing an identifiable end product or unit which the worker can identify with. In the golf game, task identity is assured because the golfer plays all strokes on all holes. Task significance is associated with a task the worker considers valuable and important to the customer or client. Surgeons tend to perceive high task significance. A person who packs parachutes would tend to feel a greater sense of task significance than another worker who packs ordinary parcels. If these three core dimensions appear in a job, the worker should experience a high degree of meaningfulness in the work.

Hackman and Oldham also postulate that autonomy in a job will affect the workers' feeling of responsibility for work outcomes. Autonomy can be achieved by giving the worker more decision-making authority. This can be done, for example, in the case of keypunching by providing more scheduling authority, more authority for error correction, and so on.

Feedback is the fifth core job dimension; it provides knowledge of actual results. The best feedback is that which is built into the job itself. If the keypuncher works directly with the user, feedback on errors or good performance will come directly to the keypuncher from the user. This type of feedback allows the worker to assess job performance continually.

The five core job dimensions have been combined into a motivating potential score (MPS). If skill variety, or task identity, or task significance is high, and autonomy is high, and feedback is high, then the MPS will be high. Jobs such as those of doctors, lawyers, and professors tend to have high MPS scores. Jobs such as those of keypunchers, assembly-line workers, and toll collectors tend to have very low MPS scores.

The MPS score is formally defined by the following formula:

$$MPS = \left(\frac{\text{skill variety} + \text{task identity} + \text{task significance}}{3} \right) (\text{autonomy})(\text{feedback})$$

Hackman and Oldham (1974, 1975) have also developed a questionnaire, the Job Diagnostic Survey (JDS), which can be used to determine the MPS for any job. The instrument has been validated by use on over 1000 different workers from 100 different jobs in a dozen organizations. When the MPS score is high, it indicates a high motivating potential for the job; and when the MPS is low, a low motivating potential is indicated. In one study, for example, computer programmers had an MPS of 157, while data entry workers had an MPS of only 55. [See Couger and Zawacki (1979).]

Is job enrichment good for everybody? Apparently not. The motivating effect of a job is dependent on the individual's growth need. This is shown by the moderating arrows on the bottom of Figure 16.5. When a job has a low MPS *and* the individual has high growth needs, then job enrichment is likely to produce favorable outcomes. If the worker has low growth needs, the job should not be enriched. In the Hackman-Oldham theory individual differences in growth needs are considered. Many of the earlier theories implied that job enrichment was for everybody.

One of the major contributions of Hackman and Oldham to the job-enrichment literature is the idea that jobs should be carefully diagnosed prior to enrichment through use of the JDS. They suggest that diagnosis proceed along the following lines:

STEP 1: DETERMINE WHETHER THERE IS A PROBLEM WITH MOTIVATION AND JOB SATISFACTION. Sometimes job-enrichment efforts are undertaken when the problem does not lie with motivation and satisfaction but rather with the technical system (task, equipment, work flow, etc.). Prior to job enrichment, a questionnaire such as the JDS should be given to all employees to measure motivation and satisfaction on the job. If these measures are low, proceed to step 2; otherwise, look for problems in the technical system or sociotechnical system interface.

STEP 2: IS THE JOB LOW IN MOTIVATING POTENTIAL? To answer this question, the JDS should be used to compute an MPS for each job under consideration for enrichment. If the MPS is high, the manager should look outside of job design for possible problems in supervision, pay, and so on. If the MPS is low, continue to step 3.

STEP 3: WHAT SPECIFIC ASPECTS OF THE JOB ARE CAUSING THE DIFFICULTY? In order to answer this question, scores should be computed for each of the five core job dimensions. The resulting score can be plotted in a job profile as shown in Figure 16.6. This figure shows two jobs; one high in motivating potential and the other low. Job A is an engineering maintenance job which is high on all core dimensions and has an overall MPS of 260 (out of 350 possible). It would probably not pay to enrich job A. Job B is the repetitive processing of checks in a bank and has an overall MPS of 30, which is quite low (an MPS of 125 is average). Further examination of job B in Figure 16.6 indicates that it is low on all core job dimensions except task significance. The clerks handle a great deal of money and apparently this is the cause of the high task-significance score. The check-processing job, however, is low in autonomy, feedback, task identity, and skill variety because the work is highly fragmented and specialized. Job B is a candidate for enrichment provided that the workers have a high growth need.

STEP 4: ARE THE EMPLOYEES READY FOR THE CHANGE? The JDS has a section which helps determine each employee's growth need. This information can be used to plan who should be first, whether the whole idea should be scrapped, whether some employees should be transferred out of the unit, and so on. Although the determination of growth need is the last step, it is the key to matching the individual's needs to the job design plan.

If all the four steps are completed, the situation is likely to benefit from job enrichment. The job can then be enriched by using the five implementing concepts for job enrichment: (1) forming natural work units, (2) combining tasks, (3) establishing client relationships, (4) vertical loading, and (5) opening feedback channels. As shown in Figure 16.5, the implementing concepts affect the core job dimensions, which in turn affect the psychological states, which finally affect personal and work outcomes. It is through this series of links that jobs are enriched and improved.

Figure 16.6 Job diagnostic survey (JDS) profiles.

(Source: J. Richard Hackman et al., "A New Strategy for Job Enrichment," California Management Review, Summer 1975, pp. 57–71, reprinted by permission of the regents.)

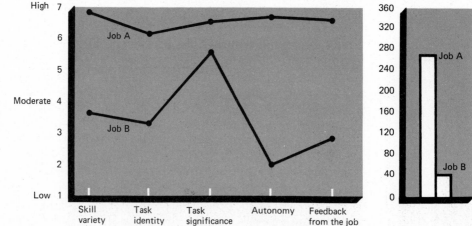

Work is sometimes assigned to individuals in a highly fractionalized and specialized way. For example, several different typists might work on the same report. As a result, the individual typist may have difficulty identifying with the final product and seeing the significance of the entire result. An implementing concept which corrects this situation is the formation of natural work units. In this case, a typist would be assigned the entire report or a specific section of the report. In this way the typist would be able to identify directly with the end product. The arrows in Figure 16.5 indicate that task identity and task significance should result when this is done.

The second implementing concept is combining tasks. This is traditionally a part of job enlargement, where the worker is given more task variety through horizontal loading. Typing-pool jobs, for example, could be enriched by eliminating the pool concept and designing jobs that require more than one skill. According to the classical economic theory of division of labor, breakup of the typing pool may result in less efficiency. But the classical theory ignores the effect of boredom and dissatisfaction on the workers' output and the costs of turnover and absenteeism. When *all* the costs are considered, less job specialization may be more efficient and at the same time more satisfying to the individual.

Another consequence of extreme division of labor is that workers have little contact with the client, user, or customer. This can be corrected by the third implementing concept: establishing client relationships. The result can be simultaneous improvement in three core job dimensions: feedback increases because the employee receives feedback directly from the customer instead of through a supervisor or intermediary; skill variety increases because the worker must develop interpersonal skills; and autonomy increases because the worker is often given discretion in dealing with the customer. The contact between the worker and the customer should be as frequent as necessary to do the job. Any form of contact is desirable: face to face, through letters, or by telephone.

Traditionally, the split between planning and doing has been designed into jobs. The implementing concept of vertical loading can be used to reverse this trend and give more decision-making responsibility to the worker. Vertical loading is perhaps the most important of all the implementing concepts because it leads to autonomy, responsibility, and a high degree of internal work motivation. If none of the other implementing concepts can be used in a particular situation due to technological considerations, vertical loading would still do a great deal to enrich the job. Vertical loading can be increased through a variety of actions such as assigning scheduling responsibility to the worker, assigning troubleshooting responsibility (most workers are told to contact their supervisor immediately if something goes wrong), or assigning responsibility for training new workers.

The last implementing concept is to open feedback channels and thereby improve knowledge of the actual results of the work activity. Feedback information is already available in many organizations, but it is not routinely given to the workers. For example, performance reports are sent to the supervisor and up the chain of command. Only indirectly does the worker learn about these reports. Quality control information is kept separate from the workers, errors are reported directly to the supervisor, and sometimes the supervisor even corrects errors without telling the employee. A great deal more can be done to ensure self-control of workers by giving feedback directly to them and by using feedback from the work itself whenever possible.

The Hackman-Oldham theory has been verified and tested by several research studies. It provides not only a conceptual view of job enrichment but also a practical method of job diagnosis to determine whether job enrichment is needed and how to go about enriching the job.

16.4 AN EXAMPLE OF JOB ENRICHMENT

Hackman and Oldham have tested their theory on keypunching jobs at the Travelers Insurance Company. The enrichment took place in a data processing unit that consisted of 98 keypunchers, 7 assignment clerks, and a supervisor. The keypunchers prepared punched cards for jobs ranging from a few cards to 2500 cards, and they operated verifying machines which checked each card punched.

The work came into the office from a user and was checked for errors and omissions by an assignment clerk. After correction, the job was given to the first keypuncher who was available at the time with the instructions, "punch only what you see." After keypunching and verification, the job was given to the supervisor for error checking and transmittal to the computer. The results of the computer run were given to the user, and errors or problems were handled by the supervisor. Keypunching errors were assigned to the first available keypuncher to correct.

There was much evidence of low motivation, high error rates, low productivity, and higher-than-normal turnover in this work group. The jobs were thus ideal candidates for enrichment. A careful diagnosis of the keypunching jobs indicated that they were low on all five core job dimensions as follows:

Skill variety: None. The keypunchers only operated the keypunch machines.

Task identity: None. Batches of work were randomly assigned to keypunch operators. The keypunchers could not identify with the work as "something of their own."

Task significance: Not apparent. Data entry was one step in providing data processing services. Since the keypuncher was isolated from the user by the assignment clerk and the supervisor, there was little opportunity to see the effect of the work on the user.

Autonomy: None. The worker had no control over the work schedule and the job required little judgment, since the workers were told, "punch only what you see."

Feedback: None. The worker had no knowledge of how many errors were being produced and no feedback on the productivity level achieved.

As a result of the diagnosis, it was decided to enrich the jobs through the use of all five implementing concepts. To determine the effect of the job-enrichment experiment, a control group—a keypunch department at another site—was set up.

Baseline data on absenteeism, turnover, productivity, error rates, and job satisfaction were collected from both groups. In the experimental group, the following changes in job design were made:

Natural work units. Each keypuncher was assigned responsibility for a group of accounts representing one or more users. The keypuncher handled all transactions over a period of time for these accounts.

Combining tasks. The keypunchers were asked to handle error checking, planning, control, and other tasks which were previously handled by the assignment clerks and the supervisor.

Establishing client relationships. Each keypuncher handled all communications with the user. The jobs were received by the keypuncher and any errors or omissions were corrected in consultation with the user. After the computer runs were made, the users also dealt directly with the keypunchers in correcting errors and discussing work-related matters.

Vertical loading. The keypuncher was given complete authority to work out the schedule with the user and to plan and control the available time. Some competent operators were given the option to eliminate verification on certain jobs.

Feedback. In addition to feedback directly from the user, each keypuncher received a weekly computer report on productivity and errors discovered. These reports were given directly to the keypunchers and a summary also went to the supervisor.

The results of the job-enrichment experiment were very good in this case. Productivity increased by 40 percent, allowing a reduction in personnel from 98 to 60. In the control group, productivity increased by only 8 percent over the same period of time. Over the course of the experiment, the error rate dropped from 1.5 percent to 1 percent, while the control group's error rate remained the same. Absenteeism dropped by 24 percent in the experimental group and increased by 29 percent in the control group. Job satisfaction rose by 16.5 percent in the experimental group, while it stayed about the same in the control group. All the measures of work and personal outcomes were improved by job enrichment. The Travelers company estimated that they saved $64,305 during the first year, and they expected to achieve savings of $92,000 per year by further application of the changes.

Job enrichment created a great deal of change in the supervisor's job. The supervisor was no longer a fire fighter but rather a manager. After job enrichment, the supervisor's time was spent forming work modules, designing feedback systems, monitoring the overall performance of the unit, and occasionally dealing with problems which the workers could not handle on their own. The supervisor became much more concerned with overall planning and control and much less involved in daily problems.

There have been many other examples of job enrichment, a few of which are summarized in Table 16.1. For more information on experiments, see U.S. Department of Health, Education and Welfare (1973), Davis and Cherns (1975), Ford (1973), Walton (1972), and Gyllenhammar (1977).

TABLE 16.1   **SELECTED EXPERIMENTS IN JOB ENRICHMENT**

1. Establishment(s) or employee groups	General Foods: Pet food plant, Topeka, Kans.—all plant employees	Texas Instruments, Inc.—group electronic instrument assemblers	Oldsmobile Division, GM—engineering and assembly employees	Norsk Hydro, Oslo, Norway—production workers
2. Year initiated	1971	1967	1970	1966
3. Number of employees affected	70	600	Two plants	About 50
4. Problem	In designing this new plant, management sought to solve problems of frequent shutdowns, costly recycling, and low morale that plagued an existing plant making the same product.	Top management wanted better utilization of human resources.	High absenteeism and turnover.	Competition was becoming tougher and profits were declining.
5. Technique used	Workers were organized into relatively autonomous work groups with each group responsible for a production process. Pay is based on the total number of jobs an employee can do.	The group was asked to set its own production goal and given more information concerning costs and terms of the government contract on which it was working.	A volunteer hourly employee task force held meetings with supervisors and other employees, conducted surveys, and made broad recommendations to improve employee relations.	Autonomous work groups were established without first hands (supervisors). A group bonus plan was installed based on productivity.
6. Human results	Job attitudes a few months after the plant opened indicated "positive assessments" by both team members and leaders. Increased democracy in the plant may have led to more civic activity.	A survey revealed that employees were deriving more satisfaction from their work and had fewer complaints about so-called maintenance items.	"The results included more positive employee relations."	The percentage of workers expressing overall job satisfaction increased from 58 to 100.
7. Economic results	The plant is operated by 70 workers rather than the 110 originally estimated by industrial engineers. Also, there were "improved yields, minimized waste, and avoidance of shutdowns."	During the experiment, assembly time per unit decreased from 138 to 32 hours. Absenteeism, turnover, leaving time, complaints, and trips to health center decreased.	Absenteeism decreased 6% in engineering and 6.5% in assembly, while rising 11% in the rest of Oldsmobile. There were "improved product quality . . . and reduced costs."	Production costs per ton decreased 30% over the first six months of the project, but other factors were also involved. Absenteeism was 4% in the experimental factory versus 7% for the control factory.
8. Reference(s)	Richard E. Walton, *Workplace Alienation and the Need for Major Innovation*, May 1972 (unpublished).	F. K. Foulks, *Creating More Meaningful Work*, AMA 1969, pp. 56–96.	General Motors, *Oldsmobile's Action on Absenteeism and Turnover*, November 1971.	A. Bregard, et al., *Norsk Hydro, Experiment in the Fertilizer Factories*, Work Research Institute, January 1968.

Source: U.S. Department of Health, Education and Welfare, *Work in America*, Report of a Special Task Force. MIT Press, 1973, pp. 188–201.

16.5 NEW PLANT DESIGNS

Job enrichment is sometimes constrained to a great extent by the existing technology. The design of new plants and offices provides the opportunity to choose the technology and the social system together. These opportunities have been utilized by some companies, including General Foods, PPG Industries, Proctor and Gamble, Sherwin Williams, TRW, H. J. Heinz, Dana Corporation, Rockwell, General Motors, The Mead Corporation, and Cummings Engines. [See Lawler (1978).] Some of these organizations have started not only one new plant but two, three, or

TABLE 16.1 *(Continued)*

Texas Instruments, Inc., Dallas, Tex.—maintenance personnel	Netherlands PTT—clerical workers in data collection	Kaiser Aluminum Corporation, Ravenswood, W. Va.—maintenance workers in reduction plant	Operations Division, Bureau of Traffic, Ohio Department of Highways—six field construction crews	Philips Electrical Industries, Holland—assembly workers
1967	Not specified	1971	Not specified	1960
120	100	60	Not specified	240–300
100% quarterly turnover and failure to get buildings clean.	Jobs were routine. Workers and supervisors were both "notably uninterested" in their work.	Productivity was low; there were walkouts and slowdowns.	Low productivity and poor quality of performance.	Not specified
Workers were organized into 19-member cleaning teams. Each member had a voice in planning, problem solving, goal setting, and scheduling.	Jobs were enlarged to comprise a whole collaborative process (e.g., listing, punching, control punching, corrections, etc.) instead of a single stage of this process.	Time clocks were removed and supervision virtually eliminated. Workers now decide what maintenance jobs are to be done and in what priority, and they keep their own time cards.	Three experimental groups were established, each with a different degree of self-determination of work schedules. Crews were unaware that they were participating in an experiment.	Independent work groups were formed and made responsible for job allocations, material and quality control, and providing delegates for management talks.
Not specified.	88% of the workers in the experimental group said the work had become more interesting.	"Morale has improved along with pride in workmanship," says the maintenance chief.	Data showed that as participation increased, so did morale.	The members of semi-autonomous groups derived more satisfaction from their work compared with workers in the old situation.
Quarterly turnover dropped from 100% to 9.8%. Personnel requirements dropped from 120 to 71. Cost savings averaged $103,000 annually between 1967 and 1969. Building cleanliness ratings increased from 65% to 85%.	There was a 15% increase in output per labor hour.	Tardiness is now "nonexistent." Maintenance costs are down 5.5%. Maintenance work is done with more "quality."	There was no significant change in productivity.	By 1967, waste and repairs decreased by 4% and there was an unspecified savings of lower managerial personnel.
Harold M. F. Rush, *Job Design for Motivation,* Report from the Conference Board, 1971, pp. 39–49.	N. A. B. Wilson, *On the Quality of Working Life,* a personnel report to the NATO Committee on Challenges of Modern Society, p. 36.	Donald B. Thompson, "Enrichment in Action Convinces Skeptics," *Industry Week,* Feb. 14, 1971.	Reed M. Powell and John L. Schlacter, "Participative Management: A Panacea?" *Academy of Management Journal,* June 1971, pp. 165–173.	Davis and Trist, "Work in America, Approaches to Improving Quality of Working Life," June 1972, p. 18.

four. No one knows for sure how many new plant designs there are, but in 1978, Lawler estimated the number to be about fifty.

The new plants differ in almost every major respect from traditional factories. Some of the main differences, according to Lawler, are as follows:

EMPLOYEE SELECTION. In the new plants, a process of matching the employee and the work group is used. The prospective employee is interviewed by the work group, and both the employee and the work group decide whether there is a good match. The employees in the work group make the final decision on who will be hired.

DESIGN AND LAYOUT. Employees participate in plant layout and in the selection of equipment and machines. The emphasis is on ensuring that the technical and social systems are coordinated. There is also much more emphasis on equal facilities for workers and managers. There is usually one set of bathrooms, one cafeteria, and one parking lot with equal access to all. This is done to promote an atmosphere of team-work between management and the workers.

JOB DESIGN. Every effort is made to use the job enrichment principles described in the last section. A great deal of emphasis is placed on teams or work groups. Each person is expected eventually to learn all the jobs in the group. The group is expected to function on a semiautonomous basis by making most of its own decisions, e.g., who does what on a given day. The group is also designed to be responsible for its own purchasing, quality control, and other staff functions. This reduces overhead and integrates the support needed into each group. Often the groups are designed to mix interesting and boring jobs, e.g., maintenance and warehousing. This ensures that everyone must share in the undesirable work. In one new plant, for example, there were no janitors; everyone took their turn at sweeping the floor.

PAY. In traditional plants, pay is often based on a job evaluation. In new design plants pay is based on the number of different jobs learned. This encourages each employee to keep learning on the job, and it creates a flexible labor force. In some of the new plants, group wage incentives or group profit sharing is used as a direct incentive to encourage productivity.

ORGANIZATIONAL STRUCTURE. The flat organizational structure used in the new plants represents perhaps the most striking difference by comparison with traditional plants. In some cases, there is no supervisor, merely an elected group leader. One supervisor may handle several groups, and there are often only two levels between the worker and the plant manager. In other cases, there may be a group supervisor, but he or she acts more as a facilitator and group leader. Whenever possible, the groups tend to be organized on a product basis so that they can identify with a whole unit of work. This contrasts sharply with the traditional functional organization of maintenance, quality, and so forth.

MANAGEMENT STYLE. There is a definite effort to decentralize decision making to the work-group level whenever possible. There is less staff and more line responsibility, since the line people carry out some of their own staff functions. There is much less division of labor, more group decision making, and more responsibility placed on the workers themselves.

It is too early to tell exactly how the new plants are doing. It appears there have been some successes and some failures. One new plant which was a very great success for the first few years was finally changed back to a traditional plant. It appeared that the corporate staff in this case had difficulty in working with the new plant, which was so different from the rest. Proctor and Gamble has closed its new plants to researchers, apparently because they feel they have a competitive advantage. At

General Motors, the company and the union have decided not to discuss the new plants because of the adverse effect of too much publicity. Therefore it is difficult to determine how well these plants are doing and how they will fare in the long run. [See Lawler (1978).]

16.6 EVALUATION OF JOB ENRICHMENT

There has been considerable debate about the effectiveness of job enrichment. The advocates have argued that it improves motivation, satisfaction, and productivity. The critics argue that job-enrichment research is not well controlled, that workers are carefully selected, and that job enrichment will not work for a broad segment of society. In this section, an attempt will be made to present both sides of the controversy.

Reif, Ferrazzi, and Evans (1974) studied the application of job enrichment in industry by mailing a questionnaire to a random sample of 300 of Fortune's top 1000 industrial firms. Responses were received from 125 companies. As shown in Table 16.2, only 5 companies had formal job enrichment programs (4 percent of the sample), another 32 companies had informal programs (25 percent), 29 companies said they plan to use job enrichment in the future (23 percent), and 59 companies said they do not plan to use job enrichment (48 percent).

In the companies that had formal or informal programs, only a small percentage of the work force was affected. Of all the workers in the 10 firms that provided information, fewer than 7 percent were doing enriched work. From this it is possible to conclude that less than 1 percent of the employees in the entire sample were working on enriched jobs. One would therefore have to conclude that the extent of job enrichment in industry is quite low.

Some of the comments of those who did not use job enrichment were quite interesting:

"I would like to see more research prior to adopting job enrichment."
"It has limited applicability."
"Problems in routine jobs are solved more efficiently by automation and technical improvements."

TABLE 16.2   **SURVEY OF JOB ENRICHMENT**

Response category	Responding firms	
	No.	Percent
Formal job-enrichment program	5	4
Informal job-enrichment program	32	25
Plan to use job enrichment	29	23
Do not plan to use job enrichment	59	48
Total	125	100

Source: William E. Reif, David N. Ferrazzi, and Robert J. Evans, Jr., "Job Enrichment: Who Uses It and Why?" *Business Horizons,* February 1974, p. 74.

"It is used reluctantly, but increasingly, and it is accepted with limited success."

"We have other things of a more immediate nature to worry about."

One classic response was:

"As an applied concept, job enrichment is probably here to stay. As a formalized program I view it as a passing fancy created by unions for purposes of disruption and featherbedding, by consultants to create more clients, and seized by publishers and educators as a current fad to talk and write about!"

The study by Reif et al. also asked respondents to report benefits of their programs; these are shown in Table 16.3. One-third of the programs indicated productivity improvements, 20 percent reported quality improvements, and so on. About 30 percent of the programs also reported improved attitudes of workers or improved satisfaction. These results are generally less glowing than those of job-enrichment experiments reported in the general literature.

Even the advocates of job enrichment are concerned about the implementation

TABLE 16.3   BENEFITS OF JOB ENRICHMENT*

Benefits	Formal programs (5)	Informal programs (13)	Total (18)†
Performance			
Productivity	3	3	6
Improved quality of work	3	1	4
Reduced costs	1	1	2
Prevention of problems	1	2	3
Reduced turnover	—	2	2
Improved service	1	—	1
Improved control	—	1	1
Profit	—	1	1
Job satisfaction			
Improved attitudes and morale	1	4	5
Autonomy	1	3	4
Job satisfaction	1	1	2
More interesting and challenging work	—	2	2
Developing abilities of workers	—	2	2
Enhancing esteem	—	1	1
Improved work environment	—	1	1

Source: William E. Reif, David N. Ferrazzi, and Robert J. Evans, Jr., "Job Enrichment: Who Uses It and Why?" *Business Horizons*, February 1974, p. 77.

The numbers in the table represent the number of firms which have achieved the indicated benefit.

* The question provided for multiple responses.

† The number in parentheses represents the number of firms that answered the question.

record. Hackman (1975) says that "despite the recent fervor, job enrichment seems to be failing at least as often as it is succeeding." He goes on to give six major reasons why things go wrong when organizations redesign work:

1. Rarely are the problems in the work system diagnosed before jobs are redesigned.
2. Sometimes the work itself is not actually changed.
3. Even when the work itself is substantially changed, anticipated gains are sometimes diminished or reversed because of unexpected effects on the surrounding work system.
4. Rarely are the work redesign projects systematically evaluated.
5. Line managers, consulting staff members, and union officers do not obtain appropriate education in the theory, strategy and tactics of work redesign.
6. Traditional bureaucratic practice creeps into work redesign activities.

Hackman concludes that job enrichment may become just a passing fad unless managers use the technique more carefully in properly selected cases. Perhaps there has been overselling of job enrichment as a panacea to solve organizational problems. See Fein (1974) for an elaboration of this view.

Even though there have been failures, many people are convinced that job enrichment can be a useful approach under the *right* circumstances. Therefore, considerable effort has been devoted to identifying those conditions where job enrichment is an appropriate strategy. Some of the conditions appear to be those in which

1. The employee has a high growth need for enriched work.
2. The employees are satisfied with the work context (pay, supervision, job security, and coworkers).
3. There are problems in such areas as turnover, absenteeism, productivity, or employee morale.
4. There is sufficient flexibility in the technology for job-enrichment alternatives to be feasible and not prohibitively expensive.
5. The jobs have a low MPS in the beginning.
6. There is top-management support for the job-enrichment effort.
7. The benefits of increased productivity are shared by both workers and management.

To determine whether these conditions exist, it is necessary to make a *formal* diagnosis using an instrument such as the JDS. When the conditions are favorable, a properly controlled job-enrichment effort can be successful. Notice, however, that these conditions will exist for only a limited percentage of American jobs.

16.7 KEY POINTS

- This chapter presents a sociotechnical view of job design. Under the sociotechnical approach, several technical alternatives are examined for their social impacts and the best alternative considering both social and technical constraints is selected. As a result, the job should provide higher productivity and satisfaction than when only one set of constraints is considered.

- "Job design" refers to the assignment of specific tasks and activities to an individual or group of workers. The job or jobs involved should be completely specified as to content and responsibilities by job design.

- Job design is only one organizational design mechanism which affects productivity and the quality of working life. Thus, one should examine the possible effects of supervision, pay, personnel selection, and other factors before redesigning jobs.

- Scientific management, a method for designing jobs, stresses research to discover the best work method, worker selection, training, and management and labor cooperation to install the new method. To utilize the scientific management approach, management must share productivity gains with the workers and must ensure job security. Under these conditions, workers will usually no longer restrict output and will accept scientifically developed methods.

- Job enrichment is an approach to job design which stresses the motivating potential in the work itself. According to Hackman and Oldham, several different implementing concepts can be used to improve personal and work outcomes provided that the individual has a sufficiently high growth need. The implementing concepts are: combining tasks, forming natural work units, establishing client relationships, vertical loading, and opening feedback channels. The use of these implementing concepts should lead to changes in core job dimensions, critical psychological states, and—finally—personal and work outcomes.

- Prior to job enrichment, a formal job diagnosis should be made. The diagnosis should determine whether job enrichment is needed and if so, what implementing concepts should be used.

- Job enrichment has met with mixed success and sometimes failure. In one study, less than 1 percent of the employees were working on enriched jobs, and job-enrichment experiments had only a fifty-fifty chance of success. More attention must be paid to the proper use of job-enrichment techniques in carefully selected situations.

QUESTIONS

1. From your own experience, describe a job which is boring and repetitive. What could be done to enrich this job?
2. Rate the following jobs in terms of skill variety, task identity, task significance, autonomy, and feedback.
   a. Highway toll collector
   b. Bank guard
   c. Surgeon
   d. High school teacher
   e. Truck driver
3. At the Midwest Telephone Company, telephone books are prepared in an assembly-line fashion. One person is in charge of receiving changes in name and address, another person checks the input forms for errors, a third person keypunches the information on computer cards, a fourth checks for computer errors, etc. Describe how these jobs could be enriched by using the five implementing concepts of Hackman and Oldham.
4. How would you use scientific management principles to improve your own study habits?

5. A person works in a cafeteria serving food to customers. Describe how scientific management principles could be used to improve this job.
6. According to Scoville, what are the costs associated with jobs which are too specialized?
7. A typing pool contains extremely specialized jobs. Describe how these jobs could be enriched.
8. What are the advantages of a new plant design over enrichment of present jobs?
9. A consultant has suggested that typing-pool jobs be enriched. What questions would you ask prior to approval of this project?
10. What organizational design mechanisms are available for improving productivity and the quality of working life other than job design?
11. At Volvo, the assembly line is broken up into a number of semiautonomous work groups. Each car is placed on an individual conveyor which is moved from group to group. Individuals rotate jobs within these groups from time to time. A group is responsible for a particular phase of automobile assembly such as body, upholstery, etc. Describe the core job dimensions which are affected in this case.
12. It has been said that scientific management leads to "robot" type jobs. Discuss.
13. Scientific management is sometimes viewed as the opposite of job enrichment. Comment.
14. To what degree do workers restrict their output in the following types of jobs?
    a. Government bureaus
    b. College teaching
    c. Assembly lines
    d. Construction
15. To what degree does a baseball player experience each of the three critical psychological states defined by Hackman and Oldham?
16. Compute the MPS score for the following job: skill variety = 3, task identity = 4, task significance = 6, autonomy = 5, feedback = 6. Is this a highly motivating job?
17. It has been said that scientific management should not deal with job synthesis. What is meant by this statement?

SELECTED BIBLIOGRAPHY

Bostrom, Robert P., and J. Stephen Heinen: "MIS Problems and Failures: A Socio-Technical Perspective," MISRC working paper, Minneapolis: University of Minnesota, March 1976.

Couger, J. Daniel, and Robert A. Zawacki: "Something's Very Wrong with DP Operations Jobs," *Datamation,* March 1979, pp. 149–158.

Davis, Louis E., and Albert Cherns (eds.): *The Quality of Working Life,* New York: The Free Press, 1975, vols. 1 and 2.

Fein, Mitchell: "Job Enrichment: A Reevaluation." *Sloan Management Review,* vol. 15, no. 2, Winter 1974, pp. 69–88.

Ford, Robert N.: "Job Enrichment Lessons from AT&T," *Harvard Business Review,* January–February 1973, pp. 96–106.

Gyllenhammar, Pehr G.: "How Volvo Adapts Work to People," *Harvard Business Review,* July–August 1977, pp. 102–113.

Hackman, J. Richard: "Is Job Enrichment Just a Fad?" *Harvard Business Review,* September–October 1975, pp. 129–138.

—— and Greg R. Oldham: "Development of the Job Diagnostic Survey," *Journal of Applied Psychology,* vol. 60, 1975, pp. 159–170.

—— and ——: "The Job Diagnostic Survey: An Instrument for the Diagnosis of Jobs and the Evaluation of Job Redesign Projects," Technical Report no. 4, New Haven, Conn.: Yale University, May 1974.

—— and ——: "Motivation through the Design of Work: Test of a Theory," *Organizational Behavior and Human Performance,* vol. 16, 1976, pp. 250–279.

——, Jane L. Pearce, and Jane Caminis: "Effects of Changes in Job Characteristics on Work Attitudes and Behaviors: A Naturally-Occurring Quasi-Experiment," Technical Report no. 13, New Haven, Conn.: Yale University, December 1976.

———— et al: "A New Strategy for Job Enrichment," *California Management Review,* Summer 1975, pp. 57–71.

HERZBERG, F.: "One More Time: How Do You Motivate Employees." *Harvard Business Review,* January–February 1968, pp. 53–62.

————, B. MAUSNER, and B. SNYDERMAN: *The Motivation to Work,* New York: Wiley, 1959.

LAWLER, EDWARD E., III: "The New Plant Revolution," *Organization Dynamics,* Winter 1978, pp. 3–12.

MIRVIS, PHILLIP H., and DAVID BERG (eds.): *Failures in Organization Development and Change,* New York: Wiley, 1977.

MORSE, JOHN J.: "A Contingency Look at Job Design," *California Management Review,* vol. 16, no. 1, Fall 1973, pp. 67–75.

OLDHAM, GREG R., J. RICHARD HACKMAN, and JONE L. PEARCE: "Conditions under Which Employees Respond Positively to Enriched Work," *Journal of Applied Psychology,* vol. 61, no. 4, 1976, pp. 395–403.

PETERSON, RICHARD B.: "Swedish Experiments in Job Reform," *Business Horizons,* June 1976, pp. 13–22.

REIF, WILLIAM E., and FRED LUTHANS: "Does Job Enrichment Really Pay Off?" *California Management Review,* vol. 15, no. 1, Fall 1972, pp. 30–37.

————, DAVID N., FERRAZZI, and ROBERT J. EVANS, JR.: "Job Enrichment: Who Uses It and Why?" *Business Horizons,* February 1974, pp. 73–78.

SCOVILLE, JAMES G.: "A Theory of Jobs and Training," *Industrial Relations,* vol. 9, 1969, pp. 36–53.

SIROTA, DAVID: "Job Enrichment—Is It for Real?" *S.A.M. Journal,* vol. 38, no. 2, April 1973, pp. 22–27.

TAYLOR, FREDERICK WINSLOW: *Scientific Management,* New York: Harper, 1911.

TRIST, E. L., et al.: *Organization Choice,* London: Tavistock Institute, 1963.

UMSTAT, DENIS, CECIL BILL, JR., and TERENCE MITCHELL: "Effects of Job Enrichment and Task Goals on Satisfaction and Productivity: Implications for Job Design," *Journal of Applied Psychology,* vol. 61, no. 4, 1976, pp. 379–394.

U.S. DEPARTMENT OF HEALTH, EDUCATION AND WELFARE, *Work in America,* Report of a Special Task Force, MIT Press, 1973.

WALTON, RICHARD E.: "How to Counter Alienation in the Plant," *Harvard Business Review,* November–December 1972, pp. 70–81.

WANOS, JOHN P.: "Who Wants Job Enrichment?" *S.A.M. Advanced Management Journal,* Summer 1976, pp. 257–263.

WHITSETT, DAVID A.: "Where Are Your Unenriched Jobs?" *Harvard Business Review,* January–February 1975, pp. 74–80.

WOODMAN, RICHARD W., and JOHN SHERWOOD: "A Comprehensive Look at Job Design," *Personnel Journal,* August 1977, pp. 384–390.

CHAPTER 17
WORK MEASUREMENT

Dost thou love life? Then do not squander time, for that's the stuff life is made of.''[1] Benjamin Franklin admonishes us to conserve time, to use it wisely. This can be done by measuring the work that we do and by devising better work methods. As a result, our efforts should be more productive and efficient.

Work measurement and methods study have their roots in the scientific management movement. Frederick Taylor improved work methods through detailed motion studies, and he was the first to use the stopwatch for work measurement. Another of Taylor's contributions was the idea that a standard of output (e.g., minutes per piece) should be set for each job. A standard determines the amount of output expected of a worker and is used to plan and control direct labor costs.

Work measurement continues to be a useful but controversial practice. For example, work measurement is often a point of friction between labor and management. If the standards are "too tight," they can result in grievances, strikes, or poor

---

[1] Benjamin Franklin, *Poor Richard's Almanac,* June 1746

BOX 17.1   TYPICAL DECISION PROBLEM

After further study, Radarwave, Inc., decided to install a modified assembly line that would meet both social and technical considerations. This presented a new problem to Mary Lipton, in the work-measurement area. In order to design the new process in detail, time standards would be needed for each job. Accordingly, Mary contacted Ronald Belfy in the industrial engineering department. She asked Ron to develop a system of time standards by working together with Roger Kirk. She specifically wanted Roger involved in this effort in order to preserve the sociotechnical concepts which had already been incorporated in the design.

The first problem that confronted Ronald and Roger was how to develop standards for nonexistent jobs. The work could not be timed with a stopwatch in the usual fashion. To solve this problem, Ronald suggested that predetermined time data be used. With the help of tables listing predetermined data, time standards could be "built up" from elementary motions to the complete job. Ronald observed, "Predetermined time data should be sufficiently precise to permit a complete design of the line, and the resulting time standards can also be used during actual production." Since the speed of the line and the general types of jobs had already been determined by Roger's analysis, work could proceed on the careful definition of each job and development of the associated time standard. The work content and time standard would be specified so that each worker could complete the job in the assigned time while working at a normal pace. No worker would be asked to produce more than could be expected from a "normal" person working under the prescribed conditions. Although these standards did not allow a great deal of individual variation, some slack time was included in each job, and buffers between work stations were provided to allow some variability in time. As a result, the time standard was an average time which did not have to be precisely met on each unit.

labor relations. On the other hand, if standards are "too loose," they can result in poor planning and control, high costs, and low profits.

In an age where more and more control is being given to the workers, new ways must be found to measure work and to improve methods. No longer can management simply set standards for a job which may lack motivating potential. While we must continue to measure work and improve methods, the responsibility for these activities is shifting toward the work-force managers and away from the industrial engineers. As the chapter proceeds, we will be examining some of these issues more carefully; but first a complete description of methods study is given and different approaches to work measurement are reviewed. A typical decision problem which utilizes work measurement is described in Box 17.1.

17.1 PURPOSES OF WORK MEASUREMENT

Work measurement can be used for a variety of different purposes. As a result, controversies about techniques and standards are often rooted in the very purpose of work measurement. It is the operations manager's responsibility to define this purpose and to ensure the use of appropriate work-measurement techniques.

Work-measurement techniques can be used for the following purposes:

1. *Evaluate a worker's performance.* This is done by comparing actual output over a given period of time to the standard output determined from work measurement.

2. *Plan work-force needs.* For any given level of future output, work measurement can be used to determine how much labor input is required.
3. *Determine available capacity.* For a given level of work-force and equipment availability, work-measurement standards can be used to project available capacity. This purpose is just the reverse of the one listed in number 2.
4. *Determine price or cost of a product.* Labor standards, obtained through work measurement, are one ingredient of a costing or pricing system. In most organizations, the successful pricing of products is crucial to the survival of the business. This activity, in turn, rests on work measurement whenever cost is a basis for pricing.
5. *Compare work methods.* When different methods for a job are being considered, work measurement can provide the basis for economic comparison of the methods. This is the essence of scientific management—to devise the best method based on rigorous time and motion studies.
6. *Facilitate operations scheduling.* One of the data inputs to all scheduling systems is time estimates for work activities. These estimates are derived from work measurement.
7. *Establish wage incentives.* Under wage incentives, workers receive more pay for more output. Underlying these incentive plans is a time standard which defines 100 percent output.

Since there are so many different uses for work measurement, management must decide which of them will be selected. If work measurement is used for wage incentives, for example, one of the more accurate methods, such as the stopwatch, should be used and standards should be updated frequently. If work measurement is used for estimating capacity or planning work-force needs, not as much accuracy is required in each individual time estimate and other work-measurement methods can therefore be used.

In practice, some uses of work measurement occur more frequently than others. A 1977 survey of 1500 firms by Robert S. Rice evaluated uses of work measurement, as shown in Table 17.1. This study indicated that estimating and costing represented

TABLE 17.1 **USES OF WORK MEASUREMENT**

	Percentage of cases*
Wage incentives	59
Estimating and costing	89
Performance measurement only	41
Production scheduling	55
Manning and capacity planning	2
Other	4

Source: Robert S. Rice, "Survey of Work Measurement and Wage Incentives," *Industrial Engineering,* vol. 9, no. 7, July 1977, p. 20.

* Respondents could indicate more than one use in each case.

the greatest use of work measurement, followed by wage incentives, production scheduling, and performance measurement.

The principal result of some types of work-measurement activity is a production standard, also called a time standard or simply a standard. A standard can be formally defined as the amount of time it should take to execute a task or activity when a trained operator working at a normal pace uses a prescribed method. This definition includes several key features that require further clarification.

First, a standard is normative. It defines the amount of time which *should* be required for work under certain conditions. A standard is not merely the average of past times, because past averages reflect how much time a job has taken, not necessarily how much time it *should* have taken. Later, it will be shown, however, how actual time observations can be adjusted to arrive at a standard.

A standard also requires that a method be prescribed for the work or activity. Usually the "best" method is developed to eliminate wasted motions and to streamline the work whenever possible. The prescribed method is ordinarily put in written form.

Finally, a standard requires that a trained operator be doing the work at a normal pace. An operator who is suited for the type of work involved should be selected and this operator should be carefully trained to follow the method. A "normal pace" means that the operator is working neither too fast nor too slow but at a pace which could be sustained by most workers over an entire day.

A standard thus implies a number of conditions which must be met. If a worker cannot achieve the standard, any of the following causes might be identified. Perhaps the material has changed, the product has been redesigned, the worker has not been properly trained, or the individual's abilities do not match the job. When the cause of the deviation from standard has been found, action can be taken to correct the situation.

A standard can be expressed in two ways: either as the time required per unit of output or the reciprocal, output per unit of time. Examples are minutes per piece or pieces per minute. In complex cases where the job is a task or activity for which there is no convenient unit of output, a standard must be defined as the time required to complete the task or activity. In cases where a specific unit of output can be defined, either measure can be used.

17.2 METHODS STUDY

Most of the improvements resulting from work measurement stem from the underlying methods studies, which precede the time studies themselves. Although time standards are needed for management control purposes, the standards alone do not improve efficiency. A great source of productivity improvement during the twentieth century has been the application of methods studies.

A typical methods study proceeds along the following lines:

1. Define the objectives and constraints of the study.
2. Decide on the study approach to be used.

3. Announce the study to the workers.
4. Break the job into elements.
5. Study the method through the use of charts.
6. Decide on a method for each work element.

The objectives of the study might be to improve productivity by 50 percent or, alternatively, to increase efficiency using the present machines. Management must clearly define the objectives of the study, since so many possibilities exist.

The approach selected, in the second step, might consist of a very elaborate motion study, with filming or extensive visual observation, or a "quick and dirty" study which takes only a short time. The approach might include worker responsibility for the study, with industrial engineers as the advisers, or the reverse situation. The approach might use any number of different work-measurement techniques.

In the third step, the study is announced to the workers. A methods study should never be sprung on the work force as a surprise. Normally, workers should be informed of the study in writing or at a meeting where they have a chance to ask questions. When informing the workers, management should address the objectives and planned approach for the study along with issues of job security, work pace, and worker benefits.

The fourth step in a methods study is to break the job into elements.[2] This is done to facilitate analysis, because each element will require a specific method. If the job being analyzed is typing a specified business letter, for example, the following elements might be defined:

Read rough draft
Correct errors
Set up typewriter
Type letter
Proofread letter
Correct errors
Type envelope
Get signature
Mail letter

Each job element is then studied through observation and the use of charts. The purpose of the methods analysis is to devise a method which is efficient and economical while also considering the workers' social and psychological needs. Some of the method analysis charts which can be used are described below.

Finally, the job is designed by selecting a method for each work element. The decision may be made by the industrial engineer, the worker, or a manager. Which of these individuals holds final authority depends on the behavioral theory used by the firm. More on this issue will be presented later in the chapter.

Several different charts are used in studying work methods. The first type of

---

[2] An element is a part of a job which contains a closely related set of motions, activities, or tasks.

Operator	Time*	Machine	Time*
Take customer order	.3	Idle	
Load blender	.5	Load blender	.5
Idle	.6	Run blender	.6
Empty blender	.2	Empty blender	.2
Serve drink	.5	Idle	.5

**Figure 17.1
Activity chart for
mixing a drink in a
blender.**

*Time in minutes

chart is the process flowchart discussed in Chapter 7. The process flowchart describes the entire process and the interrelationships between jobs and activities. After the process flowchart has been constructed, attention shifts to the micro level of motion study for a particular job or work element. Three principal types of charts are used at the micro level of analysis: activity chart, operations chart, and Simo (simultaneous motion) chart.

**Figure 17.2
Operation chart
(signing a letter).**

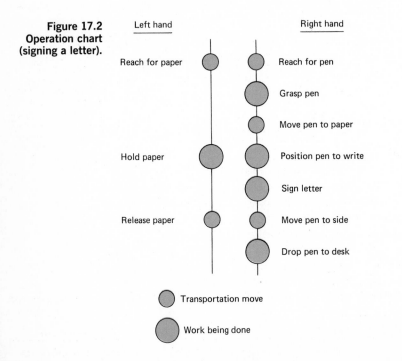

Left hand | Right hand

Reach for paper — Reach for pen
Grasp pen
Move pen to paper
Hold paper — Position pen to write
Sign letter
Release paper — Move pen to side
Drop pen to desk

Transportation move

Work being done

The activity chart (also called a "man-machine" chart) shows the relationship between the operator and machine. As an example, Figure 17.1 is an activity chart for the job of making drinks in an automatic blender at a bar. The chart shows what the machine is doing and what the operator is doing at each point in time. From this chart it is possible to determine idle time of the operator and the machine and to identify the operator- and machine-paced elements. With this information, one can determine whether the operator can operate another machine, or whether some changes in method are possible to utilize the machine or worker more efficiently.

The operation chart shows the detailed motions of a worker's hands during each step of a job. The operation chart in Figure 17.2 is intended to show the motions of the left hand and the right hand during the job of signing a letter. The small circles in the figure represent transportation move, while the large circles represent work being done on the job.

TABLE 17.2	PRINCIPLES OF MOTION ECONOMY

A check sheet for motion economy and fatigue reduction

These twenty-two rules or principles of motion economy may be profitably applied to shop and office work alike. Although not all are applicable to every operation, they do form a basis or a code for improving the efficiency and reducing fatigue in manual work.

Use of the human body

1. The two hands should begin as well as complete their motions at the same time.

2. The two hands should not be idle at the same time except during rest periods.

3. Motions of the arms should be made in opposite and symmetrical directions, and should be made simultaneously.

4. Hand and body motions should be confined to the lowest classification with which it is possible to perform the work satisfactorily.

5. Momentum should be employed to assist the worker wherever possible, and it should be reduced to a minimum if it must be overcome by muscular effort.

6. Smooth, continuous, curved motions of the hands are preferable to straight-line motions involving sudden and sharp changes in direction.

7. Ballistic movements are faster, easier, and more accurate than restricted (fixation) or "controlled" movements.

8. Work should be arranged to permit easy and natural rhythm wherever possible.

9. Eye fixations should be as few and as close together as possible.

Arrangement of the work place

10. There should be a definite and fixed place for all tools and materials.

11. Tools, materials, and controls should be located close to the point of use.

12. Gravity-feed bins and containers should be used to deliver material close to the point of use.

13. Drop deliveries should be used wherever possible.

14. Materials and tools should be located to permit the best sequence of motions.

15. Provisions should be made for adequate conditions for seeing. Good illumination is the first requirement for satisfactory visual perception.

16. The height of the work place and the chair should preferably be arranged so that alternate sitting and standing at work are easily possible.

17. A chair of the type and height to permit good posture should be provided for every worker.

Design of tools and equipment

18. The hands should be relieved of all work that can be done more advantageously by a jig, a fixture, or a foot-operated device.

19. Two or more tools should be combined wherever possible.

20. Tools and materials should be pre-positioned whenever possible.

21. Where each finger performs some specific movement, such as in typewriting, the load should be distributed in accordance with the inherent capacities of the fingers.

22. Levers, crossbars, and hand wheels should be located in such positions that the operator can manipulate them with the least change in body position and with the greatest mechanical advantage.

Source: Ralph M. Barnes, *Motion and Time Study: Design and Measurement of Work,* 6th ed., New York: Wiley, 1968, p. 220.

By first describing the current method in detail through use of an operation chart, one should be able to develop an improved method. This is done by analyzing the operations chart with regard to three aspects of the job: use of the human body, arrangement of the work place, and design of tools and equipment. These three aspects of method design are embodied in the principles of motion economy shown in Table 17.2. Through application of these principles, first developed by Frank and Lillian Gilbreth, it is possible to greatly simplify many jobs.

Another type of motion study chart, which is similar to the operation chart, is the Simo chart. The Simo chart also shows the motions of the left hand and right hand, but it includes the time for each movement using the standard Therblig symbols. In studying work, the Gilbreths determined that all hand motions could be divided into 17 distinct types. Each of these motions was called a Therblig (Gilbreth spelled backward with the t and h interchanged). The Gilbreths also stressed analysis of the time for each motion, usually determined by counting frames on a motion picture of the job. With this technique it was possible to combine, eliminate, or change the basic motions to develop an improved method. See Figure 17.3 for an example of a Simo chart for signing a letter.

The results of methods study can be dramatic. For example, on the basis of Gilbreth's 3-year study of bricklaying methods, the number of bricks laid per hour was increased from 120 to 350. This result was achieved by a new bricklaying method which reduced the number of motions per brick from 18 to 5. Through the use of special scaffolds, more consistent mortar, and prearranged bricks, this new method eliminated much of the stooping, bending, and lifting that had formerly been associated with bricklaying. Thus the workers were able to lay more bricks in a day while using about the same number of total motions, so that the new method actually represented a better use of human effort—not a speedup. As a catch phrase goes, "The bricklayers worked smarter, not harder."

Figure 17.3 Simo chart (signing a letter).

Description: Left hand	Therblig symbol	Time	Time in 2000 ths of a min	Therblig symbol	Time	Description: Right hand
Reach for paper	TE	6		TE	5	Reach for pen
				G	3	Grasp pen
				TL	7	Move pen to paper
				P	4	Position pen to write
Hold paper	H	32				
				U	19	Sign letter
Release paper	RL	4		TL	7	Move pen to side
				RL	3	Drop pen to desk

TE = Transport empty; H = Hold; G = Grasp; TL = Transport loaded; P = Position; U = Use; RL = Release

17.3 TYPES OF WORK MEASUREMENT

After the methods study is completed, work measurement can begin. There are several types of work-measurement techniques, each suited to different uses and each with different accuracies and costs. The work-measurement methods which have been most widely used and will receive primary attention in the rest of this chapter are the following:

1. Time study
2. Predetermined time data
3. Standard data
4. Historical data
5. Work sampling

The study by Rice, referred to previously, provides some interesting data on how these methods are used in industry. According to Rice, different methods are used to study direct and indirect labor. While direct labor is studied primarily by the first three methods, indirect labor is studied by the last two. This is because of the repetitive nature of direct labor and the greater accuracy required in direct-labor standards.

17.4 TIME STUDY

The time-study approach to work measurement uses a stopwatch or other timing device to determine the time required to complete given tasks. Assuming a standard is being set, the worker must be trained and must use the prescribed method while the study is being conducted.

To make a time study, one must:

1. Break the job into elements.
2. Develop a method for each element.
3. Select and train a worker or worker(s).
4. Time study each element.
5. Set the standard.

To illustrate these steps, let us use the typing job previously described and assume that the first three steps have already been completed according to the discussion of Section 17.2. The remaining tasks are to record time and set a standard. Figure 17.4 is a typical time-study chart used to record the data taken during a time study. Along the left side of the sheet is each element in the job. Along the top is each cycle or observation which is made. The time-study person would observe several cycles of work being performed and record the time for each element from a stopwatch. As a result, the times shown in Figure 17.4 are recorded.

The next step in the time study is to determine the rating for each job element. A rating is an estimate of work speed. A rating of 100 percent represents a normal work pace. A high percentage of trained workers should be able to work at 100 per-

Sheet: 1 of 1 sheets										Date: 10/9/80	
Operation: Prepare letter										Part no.:	
Operator's name: J. Lumkin										Part name:	
Observer: N.A. Jones										Shift: 1	
Begin: 9:30	Finish: 3:30		Units Finished: 10					Time in min.:			

Elements	1	2	3	4	5	6	7	8	9	10	Rating	Normal time
1. Read rough draft	.73	.85	.97	.65	.78	.84	.69	.74	.95	.88	95	.77
2. Correct errors	.30	.40	.21	.35	.25	.37	.41	.43	.48	.31	100	.35
3. Set up typewriter	.51	.63	.42	.30	.67	.51	.56	.40	.38	.41	105	.50
4. Type letter	1.65	2.03	2.15	1.50	2.20	1.80	1.93	1.75	1.76	1.85	110	2.05
5. Proofread letter	.60	.65	.50	.55	.67	.73	.69	.59	.68	.71	100	.64
6. Correct errors	.85	.90	.93	.70	.97	.71	.83	.76	.87	.91	105	.88
7. Type envelope	.60	.51	.54	.56	.63	.65	.68	.48	.46	.61	110	.63
8. Get signature	—	—	—	—	—	—	—	—	—	—		
9. Mail letter	.21	.20	.19	.18	.23	.21	.22	.23	.21	.19	100	.21
Allowances:								Total normal				6.03
Personal and fatigue 10% Delays 5%			15% Allowance					X1.15 Standard				6.93

Figure 17.4 Time-study observation sheet.

cent during the entire day or to exceed 100 percent without abnormal exertion or effort. If a worker is rated at 125 percent, more work is done in a given amount of time (i.e., the worker is working faster than normal).

On the basis of the rating factor (RF) for each element, observed times (OT) are converted to normal times (NT) by the following conversion formula:

$$NT = OT \ (RF/100)$$

For example, if the observed time is 1 minute and the rating factor is 120, then the normal time is 1.2 minutes.

The definition of the rating factor does not include allowances for unavoidable delays, rest for fatigue, personal time (e.g., washroom, coffee breaks), and so on. In other words, the normal time assumes that the person stays on the job the entire day, does not talk to the supervisor or take coffee breaks, and does not need to rest at intervals. To compensate for these additional factors, an allowance is provided. The allowance (A) is added to normal time (NT) to arrive at standard time (ST) as follows:

$$ST = NT \ (1 + A/100)$$

For example, if the allowance is 15 percent and the normal time is 20 minutes, then the standard time is 23 minutes.

Allowances vary depending on the type of working conditions. If the work is heavy or hot and requires frequent rest, allowances may be as much as 50 percent. An example of this is shoveling dirt on a construction site. For work under ideal conditions, allowances may be as low as 10 or 15 percent. Sometimes allowances are determined by separate work-sampling studies, and some allowances are even subject to union negotiations. Allowances are usually applied to the entire job and do not differ from one work element to the next. [See Niebel (1976), p. 365, for typical allowances.]

After applying allowances, the final standard is finished. A trained worker using the prescribed method should be able to meet or exceed this standard on a daily basis without overexertion.

One question which arises in time study is how many observations will be needed. Generally speaking, the more variability in the time of an element, the more observations will be required to achieve a desired accuracy level. This idea can be reduced to a formula for computing the number of observations for any particular case. [See Barnes (1968), pp. 359–360.]

Another question which arises in time study concerns the matter of rating. Rating is a controversial issue which raises questions about the validity of time study itself. The untrained person is very poor at rating work pace. For example, if a number of untrained people observe the same person working at a normal pace, their rating estimates will usually vary from about 70 to 130 percent of normal. This is significant because many managers form instinctive judgments about work pace around the office and in other work settings. With this much variation between individuals, judgments are often wrong.

Industrial engineers who have been trained in the rating of work pace will achieve more uniform ratings. In this case, the variation may be about ± 10 percent. One method used to achieve accuracy in ratings is to have time-study people watch movies of work which has previously been rated. These movies show people doing various types of jobs at various rates. Another method used to achieve accuracy in ratings is to establish benchmarks. For example, walking at a rate of 3 miles per hour is considered a 100 percent work pace by the industrial engineers. This is not an exceptionally fast rate of walking. Most people can walk at a speed of 4 miles per hour (133 percent) without undue exertion. An absolute maximum of about 5.4 miles per hour (180 percent) can be achieved without running. To the surprise of some people, it also takes a great deal of effort to walk at too slow a pace. At 2 miles per hour (66 percent), each foot must be carefully placed, since the muscles are being held back. Walking is typical of industrial work paces which range from 70 percent to about 140 percent in practice. For short periods of time, paces of 180 percent may be observed.

Another benchmark established by industrial engineers is dealing cards to represent hand-motion activity. A deck of 52 cards can be dealt into four piles on a table in 30 seconds at a 100 percent pace. You can test your own concept of normal pace by trying this experiment.

Despite its limitations, time study is a reasonably accurate method of work measurement. Because of its accuracy, it is widely used as a basis for incentive plans and in cases where disputes arise over standards. The principal disadvantage of time study is its psychological effect on workers. Some workers object to having a watch used on them while they are working. As a result, they may slow down, change methods, or use other means to manipulate the standards.

Fortunately, methods which can eliminate the need for the stopwatch have been developed. These methods are described in the remainder of this chapter.

17.5 PREDETERMINED DATA

Predetermined data are based on the clever idea that all work can be reduced to a basic set of motions. Times can then be determined for each of the basic motions—by means of a stopwatch or motion pictures—to create a bank of time data. Using the data bank, a time standard can be built up for any job that involves the basic motions.

Several predetermined time systems have been developed, the most common ones being work factor, basic motion time study (BMT), and methods time measurement (MTM). As an example, the "reach" motion from MTM is shown in Table 17.3. The other motions used in the MTM system are "grasp," "move," "turn," "apply pressure," "position," and "disengage." A very large percentage of industrial and clerical work can be described in terms of these seven basic motions.

The procedure used to set a standard from predetermined time data is as follows. First, each job element is broken down into its basic motions. Next, each basic motion is rated as to degree of difficulty. A reach to an object in a variable location, for example, is more difficult and takes more time than a reach for an object in a fixed location. Once the time required for each basic motion has been determined from the predetermined-time tables, the basic motion times are added to yield total normal time. An allowance factor is then applied to obtain standard time.

Some industrial engineers who have used predetermined times find that they are more accurate than stopwatch times. The improved accuracy is attributed to the large number of cycles used in building the initial predetermined-time tables.

However, some difficulties are involved in using predetermined-time methods. To set a standard, the analyst must break a job into basic motions and assign a degree of difficulty to each motion. Different analysts will develop different basic motions and assign different degrees of difficulty to each one. This results in some variation in standards for the same job.

The greatest advantages of predetermined-time systems is that they do not require rating or the use of stopwatches; they are also frequently less expensive. The ratings, based on a large number of observations of different people, are already built into the tables. There are, however, some jobs which do not fit into the framework of predetermined-time systems. Examples are jobs which are not highly routine in nature. Standards for these jobs must still be set by stopwatch. It is also common practice in companies that use predetermined-time systems to occasionally check some predetermined standards with a stopwatch.

TABLE 17.3   MTM PREDETERMINED TIME DATA FOR "REACH"

Distance moved, inches	Time TMU				Hand in motion		Case and description
	A	B	C or D	E	A	B	
¾ or less	2.0	2.0	2.0	2.0	1.6	1.6	**A** Reach to object in fixed location, or to object in other hand or on which other hand rests.
1	2.5	2.5	3.6	2.4	2.3	2.3	
2	4.0	4.0	5.9	3.8	3.5	2.7	
3	5.3	5.3	7.3	5.3	4.5	3.6	**B** Reach to single object in location which may vary slightly from cycle to cycle.
4	6.1	6.4	8.4	6.8	4.9	4.3	
5	6.5	7.8	9.4	7.4	5.3	5.0	
6	7.0	8.6	10.1	8.0	5.7	5.7	
7	7.4	9.3	10.8	8.7	6.1	6.5	**C** Reach to object jumbled with other objects in a group so that search and select occur.
8	7.9	10.1	11.5	9.3	6.5	7.2	
9	8.3	10.8	12.2	9.9	6.9	7.9	
10	8.7	11.5	12.9	10.5	7.3	8.6	
12	9.6	12.9	14.2	11.8	8.1	10.1	
14	10.5	14.4	15.6	13.0	8.9	11.5	**D** Reach to a very small object or where accurate grasp is required.
16	11.4	15.8	17.0	14.2	9.7	12.9	
18	12.3	17.2	18.4	15.5	10.5	14.4	
20	13.1	18.6	19.8	16.7	11.3	15.8	
22	14.0	20.1	21.2	18.0	12.1	17.3	**E** Reach to indefinite location to get hand in position for body balance or next motion or out of way.
24	14.9	21.5	22.5	19.2	12.9	18.8	
26	15.8	22.9	23.9	20.4	13.7	20.2	
28	16.7	24.4	25.3	21.7	14.5	21.7	
30	17.5	25.8	26.7	22.9	15.3	23.2	
Additional	0.4	0.7	0.7	0.6			TMU per inch over 30 inches.

17.6 STANDARD DATA

The use of standard data also involves the concept of a data bank, but the data comprise larger classes of motion than predetermined data. For example, a standard-data system may contain data on the time required to drill various-size holes through certain materials. When a standard is needed for a drilling operation, the standard data are used to estimate the required time. With standard data, it is not necessary to measure every different type of drilling operation; only a standard set of drilling operations are included in the data bank and formulas or graphs are provided to approximate other conditions.

Standard data are derived from either stopwatch data or predetermined-time data. According to Rice (1977), standard data are quite popular for measuring direct labor. This is because a large number of standards can be derived from a small standard-data set. Typically, each company will develop its own standard-data system.

Standard-data systems are useful when there are a large number of repetitive operations which are quite similar. For example, in a furniture factory, the time required to varnish a piece of furniture could probably be based on the number of square feet of surface area. In a typing pool, the time required for typing a letter could be related to the number of words in the letter plus a fixed time for the heading and signature blocks. By using relationships of this type in setting standards, a great deal of effort can be saved.

Standard-data systems have some of the same advantages as predetermined-time data. No stopwatch is needed; the data can be used to study new operations; and accuracy can be assured through continued use and refinement of the data.

17.7 HISTORICAL DATA

The use of historical data is perhaps one of the most overlooked approaches to work measurement. This is so because methods are not controlled with historical data and it would therefore be impossible to set a standard in the usual sense of the word. But with historical data a different approach to work measurement can be taken.

To measure work on the basis of historical data, each employee or the supervisor records the time required to complete each job. For example, if the job is to drill a certain type of hole in 100 pieces, the time per piece would be recorded. Later, if the job were done again, the time per piece would also be recorded and compared to the earlier data. In this way it is possible to keep continuous track of the time required per unit of work and to control departures from the historical average.

For some jobs the approach of using historical data may be preferable because the work itself is used to develop a "standard." No stopwatch is required, and flexibility in the method is permitted, encouraging innovation without the need to set a new standard. This approach can be especially effective when it is coupled with a wage incentive plan, where the objective is to make continual improvements over the historical levels. [See Sirota (1966) for more details.]

Historical data can also be used to develop time estimates for complicated jobs. Suppose, for example, that the time it takes for a worker in a laundry to iron a basket of clothes has been recorded in the past. The basket, however, never contains the

$$n = \log \phi / \log 2$$
$$\phi = \text{learning rate}$$
$$1 - \phi = \text{progress ratio}$$

Learning curves for different learning rates have been plotted in Figure 17.5. As may be noted, the lower the learning rate, the steeper the curve. Each of these curves, however, approaches a constant number of hours per unit as the value of x increases.

When the learning curve is plotted on log-log graph paper, a straight line is obtained. Use of log-log paper is thus helpful for plotting values of the learning curve and for fitting learning curves to actual production data.

Learning curves are essential for cost estimating, since the cost of the units will rapidly decline as volume is increased. Learning curves are also used to measure productivity and to set labor standards. [For a complete review of the uses of learning curves, see Yelle (1979) or Harvard Business School (1975).]

17.11 PROBLEMS ENCOUNTERED IN WORK MEASUREMENT

In practice, several problems are encountered in using work measurement properly. The first is the selection of an appropriate work-measurement technique (e.g., time study, work sampling, etc.). This problem can be solved by selecting a technique based on the following considerations:

1. Use
2. Cost
3. Accuracy
4. Type of work (e.g., repetitive)
5. Worker reaction

How the results of work measurement are to be used is a fundamental consideration. If the purpose is to establish wage incentive plans, a highly accurate technique such as time study, predetermined times, or standard data should be used. If a standard is to be set, an accurate technique will also be needed. If the aim is for planning and forecasting or job analysis, one of the less accurate methods can be used (e.g., work sampling or historical data).

Type of work is also an important consideration. For example, it does not usually pay to set a standard unless the work is repetitive. For nonrepetitive work, a historical data or work-sampling approach tends to be more appropriate.

In addition to these considerations of use, accuracy, and type of work, the cost of work measurement should be considered. The method employing historical data is the least costly to use provided that the data are readily available. When there are many time standards to set, the use of predetermined times and standard data is less expensive than time study. In every case cost must be balanced against the use and accuracy considerations.

Finally, worker reaction to the work-measurement technique must be considered. Ordinarily, workers do not like to be timed with a stopwatch. This makes the techniques other than time study more attractive from a psychological point of view. In many cases, management is becoming more and more sensitive to worker reactions and would prefer to avoid stopwatches. However, 89 percent of the companies surveyed by Rice still use the stopwatch for direct labor measurement. [See Rice (1977), p. 21.]

Another important issue in using work measurement is who is to set the standards. In some organizations, standards are set by industrial engineers; in others they are set by line management. Sirota and Wolfson (1972) give an interesting example of this dilemma in a large electronics manufacturing company. Faced with increasing cost competition, the company installed formal work measurement and hired a staff of industrial engineers to implement the program. Through work measurement and methods study, the industrial engineers improved efficiency by over 50 percent in a 2-year period. However, management also learned, through formal surveys before and after, that worker morale had decreased dramatically during this time.

Apparently, morale decreased because the workers considered some standards unfair and the industrial engineers were reluctant to change them. As a result, management decided to place the final decision for standards in the hands of first-level supervisors. If the supervisor felt the standard was unfair, the job could be placed "off standards" until it was studied once again by industrial engineers. After restudying the job, the first-line supervisor decided whether to put the job back on work measurement again. This approach resulted in no loss in productivity and a sharp improvement in worker morale. It also resulted, of course, in a loss of power for the industrial engineers.

The final problem encountered in using work measurement is the maintenance of the standards. Each time a work method changes, the standard should be updated through another study. The updates, however, are not always done with a resulting deterioration of standards. In some organizations, workers typically exceed the standards by 30 to 50 percent, and all standards must be adjusted before they are used for planning. A company faced with this situation should reevaluate its whole work-measurement approach and develop a program to revise the standards systematically.

17.12 KEY POINTS

The chapter's key points include the following:

- Work measurement can be used for various purposes including evaluating a worker's performance, planning work-force needs, planning capacity, setting prices, controlling costs, selecting a work method, scheduling operations, and establishing wage incentives. In industry, the greatest use of work measurement is for estimating and costing, followed by wage incentives, production scheduling, and performance measurement.
- In time studies, a trained worker who follows the prescribed method is timed by

a stopwatch or other timing device for a number of work cycles. The worker is then rated for work pace and allowances are added to arrive at a standard.

- Predetermined times and standard data are used to set standards without the use of a stopwatch. These approaches have important psychological and cost advantages.
- Work sampling and historical data can be used to study work but not to set time standards. With work sampling, random observations of an individual or group of workers lead to the development of a distribution of activity percentages. This approach often calls for a large number of observations.
- Learning curves are used to set labor-hour standards or to estimate costs of production when human learning is a significant factor in production. With an 85 percent learning curve, for example, each doubling of production volume reduces the labor required per unit by 85 percent.
- Several issues are encountered in using work measurement in practice; these involve selecting the proper method, maintaining worker morale, deciding who is to set the standards, and maintaining the standards.

QUESTIONS

1. It has been suggested that individual standards be set for each worker. Discuss the pros and cons of this idea.
2. Why is it essential to determine the uses for work measurement prior to selecting a method?
3. The ABC typing pool is considering an incentive pay system. What type of work-measurement methods might be appropriate?
4. At the Union Oil Company, a large number of complaints about standards that are "too tight" have been received. These standards have been set by industrial engineers on the basis of predetermined time systems. How would you solve this problem?
5. Why cannot work sampling and historical data be used to set standards?
6. Develop an activity chart to describe the procedure you use to start your car and drive it out of the driveway.
7. Develop an operation chart to describe the procedure used by a man to get his trousers out of the closet and to put them on.
8. What are the advantages and disadvantages of using stopwatch observations rather than predetermined times?
9. During a time study, the following times were observed: 40, 50, 45, 46, and 48 seconds. Using a rating factor of 90 percent and an allowance of 20 percent, determine a time standard for this job.
10. Consider the following problems:
    a. If NT = 100 and OT = 90, what is RF?
    b. If ST = 150, A = 20%, and RF = 90, what is OT?
11. A worker was heard to complain that he cannot work for 8 hours, all day, at the 100 percent pace set by the industrial engineers. What is your reaction to this complaint?
12. Describe the differences between predetermined data and standard data.
13. We think that the workers in the shipping department spend 15 percent of their time in nonproductive activities (delays, rest, etc.). We want to use work sampling to determine the true percentage of nonproductive time to within ± 1 percent with 95 percent confidence. How many observations are needed?

14. Suppose you are producing hand-held calculators to a 90 percent learning curve. The eighth unit takes 2 hours to assemble.
    a. How many labor hours did the first unit require?
    b. How many labor hours will the 100th unit require?
15. Suppose that an 80 percent learning curve can be used for the production of aircraft. The first unit takes 5000 labor hours.
    a. How many hours will the first 10 units take in total?
    b. What is the average amount of labor required per unit for the first 100 units?

SELECTED BIBLIOGRAPHY

BARNES, RALPH M.: *Motion and Time Study: Design and Measurement of Work,* 6th ed., New York: Wiley, 1968.

CARLSON, SUNE: *Executive Behavior, A Study of the Workload and the Working Methods of Managing Directors,* Stockholm: Strombergs, 1951.

HARVARD BUSINESS SCHOOL: *Experience and Cost: Some Implications for Manufacturing Policy,* Cambridge, Mass.: Harvard Business School, ICCH 9-675-228, 1975.

HEGSTAD, MICHAEL: "Executive Productivity and Time Management," graduate student paper, Minneapolis: University of Minnesota, 1979.

HEILAND, ROBERT, and WALLACE RICHARDSON: *Work Sampling,* New York: McGraw-Hill, 1957.

MAYNARD, HAROLD, G. J. STEGEMERTEN, and JOHN L. SCHWAB: *Methods-Time Measurement,* New York: McGraw-Hill, 1948.

MUNDEL, MARVIN E.: *Motivation and Time Study,* 5th ed., Englewood Cliffs, N.J.: Prentice Hall, 1978.

NADLER, GERALD: "Is More Measurement Better?" *Industrial Engineering,* March 1978, pp. 20–25.

————: *Work Design,* Homewood, Ill.: Irwin, 1963.

NIEBEL, BENJAMIN W.: *Motion and Time Study,* 6th ed., Homewood, Ill: Irwin, 1976.

RICE, ROBERT S.: "Survey of Work Measurement and Wage Incentives," *Industrial Engineering,* vol. 9, no. 7, July 1977, pp. 18–31.

SIROTA, DAVID: "Productivity Management," *Harvard Business Review,* vol. 44, no. 5, September–October 1966, pp. 111–116.

————and ALAN D. WOLFSON: "Work Measurement and Worker Morale," *Business Horizons,* August 1972, pp. 43–48.

YELLE, LOUIS E.: "The Learning Curve: Historical Review and Comprehensive Survey," *Decision Sciences,* vol. 10, no. 2, April 1979.

CHAPTER 18
PRODUCTIVITY

The media have made us aware of the serious productivity problem in business today. After several decades of rising productivity, productivity growth was arrested in the 1970s. Sagging productivity is a root cause of high inflation, unemployment, and adverse United States trade balances. Although most managers want to do something about the productivity problem, many are unsure about what actions should be taken.

Productivity is defined as the relationship between inputs and outputs of a productive system. It is often convenient to measure this relationship as a ratio of output divided by input. If more output is produced with the same inputs, productivity is improved. Likewise, if fewer inputs are used for the same output, productivity is also improved. A full discussion of how productivity can be measured will be given later in the chapter.

Operations managers are the spearhead for improving productivity in the firm. Over the years, operations managers have improved productivity in the factory. A similar challenge is now being accepted by operations managers in service industries. But it is not enough simply to improve productivity in the operations function; some of the largest areas for productivity improvement are in sales, finance, personnel, data processing, and other staff areas. In many organizations, the direct labor costs are already under good control, but high indirect costs are leading to low productivity. Productivity should, therefore, be thought of as an organizationwide issue.

BOX 18.1   **TYPICAL DECISION PROBLEM**

Ted Hickford at Pizza U.S.A. was looking over the latest profit figures, which were down for the third quarter in a row. Ted mused, "I've got to do something about productivity in operations. We've simply got to cut our costs without sacrificing quality or the level of customer service that we offer. Since our operation is highly labor-intensive, we must get greater productivity from our people. I wonder what we should do."

Ted called in Sherry Stahl, manager of operations analysis, to help with this problem. After reviewing the situation with Sherry, Ted observed, "Sherry, we need to be imaginative in our approach to improving productivity. First, we need to look at the staffing of our pizza stores. Can we devise ways to help our store managers do a better job of controlling personnel levels? If we can help them to forecast demand levels and if we can use alternate sources of part-time labor, perhaps we can cut staffing costs.

"We also need to improve the efficiency of the labor that we use. One thing I'm considering is a bonus or profit-sharing plan, so that the harder the employees work, the more they get paid. In our business, a group incentive plan makes the most sense, since we need teamwork from all individuals.

"I also think we need to examine whether some additional labor might be saved through automation. We haven't looked at this issue since the initial design of our stores several years ago.

"Finally, we need to decide how to measure productivity. I would like to use a ratio which measures output over input. The ratio should include as many inputs and outputs as possible. There is no point in instituting a comprehensive productivity improvement program if we cannot measure our progress.

"In studying productivity, Sherry, I want you to examine not only the issues I have mentioned but everything in operations from A to Z. I also want you to take a trip to several of our store sites and talk with the store managers about productivity. Maybe you could look at some of the best stores and some of the worst ones to get ideas about what they do differently. I want a full report on this problem in two months, with a progress report in one month."

In operations, productivity is affected by all decisions, including process design, capacity, inventory, and work-force decisions. This chapter on productivity improvement will, therefore, draw on all the previous chapters in the text and will serve as an integrative chapter around the productivity theme. This chapter is included with the work-force section of the text because managing the work force is frequently a pivotal element in productivity improvement efforts.

Different individuals often address the productivity problem from different angles. The economists concentrate on the effect of investment and government regulation. The industrial engineers stress the effects of methods and work flow on productivity. The psychologists and management people concentrate on job design or other human relations approaches. This chapter will summarize within a broad integrative framework, all the different approaches which have been suggested for productivity improvement. A typical productivity decision problem is given in Box 18.1.

18.1   NATIONAL PRODUCTIVITY

Although national productivity is often measured as a ratio of output divided by input, different ratios are possible, depending on the assumptions made. The total factor productivity ratio is obtained by dividing total output, measured by GNP, by the total of labor and capital inputs. Thus we have:

$$\text{Total factor productivity} = \frac{\text{GNP}}{\text{labor} + \text{capital}}$$

There are also two partial productivity ratios; one for labor and the other for capital:

$$\text{Labor productivity} = \frac{\text{GNP}}{\text{labor hours}}$$

$$\text{Capital productivity} = \frac{\text{GNP}}{\text{capital}}$$

The total factor productivity ratio is the best one to use when describing national productivity, because it includes all the inputs used. The partial ratios consider only one input or the other. For example, the labor productivity ratio gives labor credit for the whole GNP output, even though changes in output may be due to increased utilization of capital. Labor productivity ratios are often used, however, because the data are readily available.

National productivity ratios are typically expressed as indexes over time. The ratio from one time period is compared to the base period to derive a percentage of increase or decrease in the productivity ratio. These indexes are typically calculated for annual and quarterly time periods.

Table 18.1 shows the United States total factor and partial productivity ratios from the late 1800s, when productivity ratios were first calculated, until the present time. From 1889 to 1919, the total factor productivity in the United States increased at an annual rate of 1.3 percent. After World War I, from 1919 to 1948, the annual increase in total factor productivity grew to 1.8 percent, despite the general depression of the 1930s. This growth in productivity is generally attributed to the adoption of scientific management methods, increased R&D expenditures, increasing automation, and a rapid increase in the average education of the work force. After World War II, from 1948 to 1969, the postwar economic expansion boosted increases in total factor productivity to an annual average of 2.3 percent. Since 1969, however, the growth of total factor productivity has slowed considerably. This slowdown has led to great national interest in the productivity problem.

TABLE 18.1 **PRODUCTIVITY RATIOS**

Real GNP per unit of:	Average percentage increase per year			
	1889–1919	1919–1948	1948–1969	1969–1973
Labor (hours)	2.0	2.2	3.2	2.9
Capital	0.5	1.6	0.3	0.2
Total factor productivity	1.3	1.8	2.3	2.1

Source: John W. Kendrick, *Understanding Productivity*, Baltimore: Johns Hopkins, 1977.

In comparing productivity ratios over time, one must be very cautious about year-to-year fluctuations. Figure 18.1, for example, shows the annual labor productivity ratios for the period 1969–1979. Productivity is highly variable from year to year and no conclusions can be drawn on the basis of one or two years of figures. For example, in 1974, productivity decreased by 3.4 percent, only to be followed by increases in 1975 of 2.1 percent and in 1976 of 4.5 percent. The media sometimes portray the latest productivity figures as significant, when in fact only 5- to 10-year trends are stable enough to support conclusions about real changes in productivity.

Recent labor productivity is dropping, as shown by the long-run trend line in Figure 18.2. The productivity figures since 1973 are substantially below the 1947–1967 trend line of 3.2 percent per year. What the future holds is, however, very uncertain. Kendrick predicts that the total factor productivity in the 1976–1986 period will average about 2.0 percent increase per year.[1] This rate would be somewhat above the 1.7 percent rate of the 1966–1973 period but modestly below the 2.4 percent rate of the 1948–1966 period. If Kendrick's projections are correct, the productivity growth rate will be slower, but not as slow as some economists project.

Productivity should not be viewed merely at the national level but also by industries. Projections for a representative sample of industries in Table 18.2 show some interesting differences. The extractive industries of iron and coal mining have shown a drop in productivity over the 1967–1977 period. This has been attributed to governmental regulation, environmental concerns, and safety regulations. Some

[1] Kendrick's projection in output per hour for the same period is 3.0 percent per year.

**Figure 18.1
Real output per
hour worked (annual percentage
change).**
(Source: U.S. Department of Labor, Bureau of Labor Statistics.)

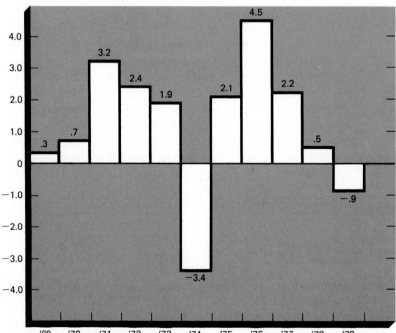

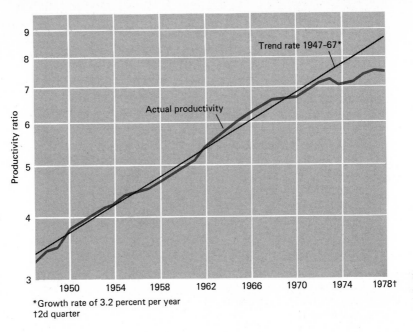

**Figure 18.2
Productivity in the
private business
sector, 1947–
1979 (1972 out-
put dollars per
hour).**
*(Source: U.S. Depart-
ment of Labor, Bureau of
Labor Statistics, in John
W. Kendrick, Under-
standing Productivity,
Johns Hopkins, 1977.)*

other industries with slow productivity growth are footwear, steel, railroads, restaurants, hotels, education, and retail food stores. As a general rule, productivity growth in the service industries has lagged behind that in manufacturing industries.

Some might wonder why productivity should be improved. How serious is the recent drop in United States productivity?

There are many benefits from improved productivity. First, increasing productivity creates more real per capita income. Since World War I, the availability of all inputs—land, labor, and capital—has risen about as rapidly as population. Thus all growth in real income over this period can be attributed to productivity improvements. The average growth in total factor productivity has been about 2 percent a year since 1920, resulting in a doubling in the standard of living (real per capita income) every 30 years. Since World War I, the United States standard of living has quadrupled.

Another benefit from improved productivity is the favorable effect on the United States's world trade balance. Since our industries compete in world markets, trade balances are directly affected by productivity in other countries. The labor productivity increases for the United States, Japan, and western European countries are shown in Figure 18.3. The low rate of improvement in United States productivity is one of the reasons for our increasingly adverse trade position.

Increased productivity will also tend to mitigate the effects of inflation. If productivity growth is 2 percent and wages are increased 8 percent, then 6 percent of the wage increase is inflationary and only 2 percent is real. Growth in productivity helps to maintain wage stability. Without offsetting increases in productivity, wage increases are purely inflationary.

TABLE 18.2 **INDUSTRY PRODUCTIVITY RATIOS**
Output per employee hour in selected industries, 1947–1967 and 1967–1977

Industry (in SIC order)	Average annual change, percent	
	1947–1967	1967–1977
Iron mining (usable ore)	3.9	−0.2
Coal mining	6.5	−3.8
Bakery products	2.1	1.5
Tobacco products	3.6	1.7
Hosiery	5.0	9.1
Sawmills	3.5*	1.7
Paper, paperboard, and pulp mills	5.8	3.3
Synthetic fibers	4.1†	8.2
Petroleum refining	6.0	3.0
Tires and tubes	4.2	2.3
Footwear	1.8	0.3
Glass containers	1.4	1.8
Steel	1.7	1.8
Metal cars	2.5	2.2
Major household appliances	6.4*	4.5
Radio and television receiving sets	5.8*	3.4
Motor vehicles and parts	4.5†	3.8
Railroads	4.8	2.8
Intercity trucking	2.7‡	3.1
Air transportation	7.9	4.4
Telephone communications	7.1§	5.8
Gas and electric utilities	7.2	3.0
Retail food stores	3.1*	0.0
Gasoline service stations	2.8*	4.5
Eating and drinking establishments	1.1*	0.5
Hotels and motels	3.0*	0.9
Laundry and cleaning services	1.5	0.8

Source: U.S. Department of Labor, Bureau of Labor Statistics.
* 1958–1967.
† 1957–1967.
‡ 1954–1967.
§ 1951–1967.

From the standpoint of management, productivity growth is a way to increase profits. As a matter of fact, in some cases increased productivity may be a better way to improve profits than increased sales. For example, suppose a company has sales of $100, $70 in variable costs, $20 in fixed costs, and a resulting profit of $10. If sales are now increased by 10 percent, profits will increase by 30 percent. See Table 18.3 for detailed calculations. On the other hand, if variable costs are decreased by 10 percent due to improvements in productivity, profits will improve by 70 percent. In this particular case, a 10 percent improvement in productivity has a much greater effect on profits than a 10 percent increase in sales. The relative strengths of these effects

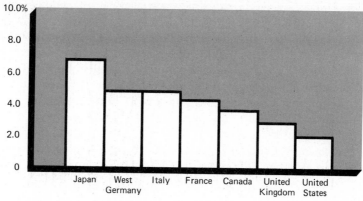

**Figure 18.3
International pro-
ductivity ratios
(output per hour
in manufacturing
—annual percent-
age change,
1960–1977).**
*(Source: National Center
for Productivity, Produc-
tivity in the Changing
World of the 1980's,
Washington, 1978,
p. 10).*

will, of course, depend on the numbers chosen. But, under certain conditions, productivity can have a greater effect on profits than sales.

Finally, from the worker's viewpoint, improvement in productivity can lead to increased wages. Nevertheless, the connection between wages and productivity may seem very tenuous to workers, who may therefore restrict output. After all, why should workers be willing to use better methods, suggest improved procedures, or put forward extra effort when the result is layoffs, more profits for the owners, and nothing for themselves? When a direct connection between productivity improvement and wages is evident, however, the result may be much different. How such a connection can be established will be discussed later in the chapter.

No one is sure why United States productivity growth has been arrested, although a number of theories have been advanced. For example, the National Center for Productivity and the Quality of Working Life has identified three reasons for the productivity slowdown of the 1970s [National Center Final Report (1978)].

1. The lower rate of growth in capital stocks per worker
2. The increasing proportion of inexperienced employees in the work force
3. Adverse changes in the industrial composition of employment

With respect to the lower growth of capital stocks, the National Center observed three trends. First, as people have emphasized consumption rather than sav-

TABLE 18.3   IMPROVEMENT IN PROFIT

	Before	After a 10% sales increase	After a 10% improvement in productivity
Sales	$100	$110	$100
Variable costs	70	77	63
Fixed costs	20	20	20
Profit	$10	$13 (+30%)	$17 (+70%)

ings, capital formation has slowed in this country. This has resulted in a reduction in the investment capital available per worker. At the same time, the productivity of capital appears to have decreased since 1967. These two capital effects are believed to account for most of the slowdown in productivity observed during the 1970s. Burton Malkiel (1979), a noted economist, has called for a reversal in this trend and an increase in investment to improve productivity. Malkiel notes that the slowdown in productivity has also been aggravated by social forces, including a reduction in the shift from farm to nonfarm work and a change in the mix of the labor force from older, experienced workers to many more young and untried workers with less experience. Although we cannot control these latter factors, Malkiel emphasizes that we *can* do something about the recent low level of business investment, the apparent reduction in R&D expenditures, and the effects of escalating government regulation.

18.2 MEASUREMENT OF PRODUCTIVITY

It has been said, "If you can't measure it, you can't manage it." This is particularly true of productivity. In the last section, we concentrated on national productivity measurements and problems. In this section, we will concentrate on productivity measurements for the firm starting at the firmwide level and proceeding to various subunit measures.

Some examples of firmwide productivity measures are:

$$\frac{\text{Sales}}{\text{Labor hours}}$$

$$\frac{\text{Sales}}{\text{Pay}}$$

$$\frac{\text{Shipments}}{\text{Direct labor} + \text{indirect labor} + \text{materials}}$$

$$\frac{\text{Shipments at standard price}}{\text{Labor} + \text{materials} + \text{overhead} + k(\text{capital invested})}$$

As at the national level, there are partial and total factor ratios at the level of the firm. The ratios of sales/labor hours and sales/pay are partial labor productivity ratios which ignore inputs of capital and material to the firm. These labor ratios should not be used unless they are the only measurements available. Furthermore, sales should not be used as a measure of output because sales figures are affected by inventory changes. Shipments is a far better measure of output than sales.

The best productivity ratio is the last one shown above, where shipments have been valued at standard price in the numerator and all inputs have been included in the denominator. In this case the capital input is represented by the unit cost of capital (k) times the amount of capital invested. The shipments should be valued at standard or constant prices (or costs) to weight the volumes of the various products. Since productivity is a measure of volume of output over input, changes in prices of outputs or inputs should not be allowed to affect the productivity ratio.

A variety of formulas used by industry are shown in Box 18.2. These formulas were chosen by each company to represent the availability of data and their particular needs for productivity measurement.

It is not enough simply to measure productivity at the firmwide level. Productivity ratios must also be developed at each level of the firm and for most if not all organizational units. Some examples of productivity measures for units or individual activities are:

$$\frac{\text{Sales}}{\text{Salespeople}} \qquad\qquad \frac{\text{Accounts receivable}}{\text{Credit employees}}$$

$$\frac{\text{Engineering drawings}}{\text{Designer}} \qquad\qquad \frac{\text{Square feet of floor cleaned}}{\text{Janitor}}$$

$$\frac{\text{Total pay}}{\text{Personal department pay}} \qquad\qquad \frac{\text{Yards of carpet laid}}{\text{Number of carpet layers}}$$

There are three principles which should be followed in measuring productivity at lower levels in the firm. First, department managers should be asked to develop their own measures, perhaps with the assistance of staff. Line department managers should set the measures, because managerial commitment is needed and the responsible line managers often know best how to measure outputs and inputs for their units. By having line managers determine the ratios, the firm will be able to develop a set of measurements unique to itself.

The second principle is that all productivity measurements should be linked in a hierarchical fashion, as shown in Figure 18.4. To ensure consistency of lower- and

BOX 18.2 **PRODUCTIVITY RATIOS WITHIN FIRMS**

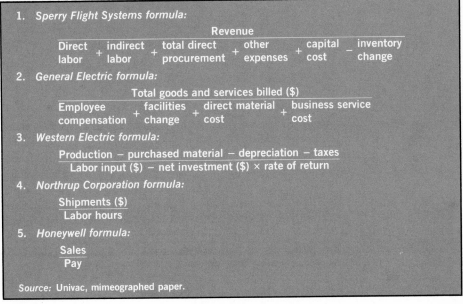

1. *Sperry Flight Systems formula:*

$$\frac{\text{Revenue}}{\substack{\text{Direct} \\ \text{labor}} + \substack{\text{indirect} \\ \text{labor}} + \substack{\text{total direct} \\ \text{procurement}} + \substack{\text{other} \\ \text{expenses}} + \substack{\text{capital} \\ \text{cost}} - \substack{\text{inventory} \\ \text{change}}}$$

2. *General Electric formula:*

$$\frac{\text{Total goods and services billed (\$)}}{\substack{\text{Employee} \\ \text{compensation}} + \substack{\text{facilities} \\ \text{change}} + \substack{\text{direct material} \\ \text{cost}} + \substack{\text{business service} \\ \text{cost}}}$$

3. *Western Electric formula:*

$$\frac{\text{Production} - \text{purchased material} - \text{depreciation} - \text{taxes}}{\text{Labor input (\$)} - \text{net investment (\$)} \times \text{rate of return}}$$

4. *Northrup Corporation formula:*

$$\frac{\text{Shipments (\$)}}{\text{Labor hours}}$$

5. *Honeywell formula:*

$$\frac{\text{Sales}}{\text{Pay}}$$

Source: Univac, mimeographed paper.

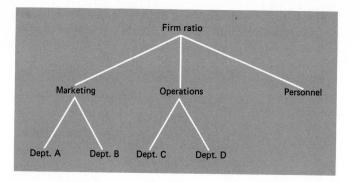

**Figure 18.4
Hierarchy of productivity ratios.**

higher-level ratios, departmental managers should not establish their own ratios until the higher-level ratios have been determined. For example, it does little good to tell the janitor that his goal is to maximize profits. The janitor's goal should be stated in terms of floors cleaned, walls cleaned, and whatever else is related to the janitor's responsibility. Ultimately, all responsibilities should be linked to the firm's goals.

The third principle is that productivity ratios should incorporate all job responsibilities to the extent possible. In some cases, this may require construction of several productivity ratios or a weighted overall ratio. Whatever ratios are defined, they should represent a reasonable measure of the total job.

At this point, a few examples from industry may be useful to illustrate the principles involved. In the first case, a group of University of Minnesota M.B.A. students developed a productivity ratio for a factory in the Minneapolis area. [See Johnson et al. (1977).] After considering a variety of ratios, the M.B.A. group suggested the following ratio:

$$\frac{\text{Production at fixed standard price}}{\text{Overhead + materials + labor + G/A}^2 + k(\text{controllable assets})}$$

In this case, the output of various products was weighted by standard prices previously developed by the company. The inputs consisted of all resources under the control of the plant manager.

Using actual company data, the M.B.A. students developed the graph shown in Figure 18.5. At first, the extreme fluctuation in the productivity ratio over time was disconcerting. How could standards or goals be established with such variability in performance? Upon closer examination, however, it was determined that 79 percent of the variability in the productivity ratio could be explained by volume of output; see Figure 18.6. Since volume was outside the control of the plant manager, the productivity goals for the plant manager could be set as a function of planned volume. As actual volume changed, the productivity goal would then be changed by use of the relationship in Figure 18.6. This case illustrates not only an actual measurement problem but also the important effect of volume on productivity.

The second case is the measurement of productivity for a data processing facil-

---

^{2} G/A = general and administrative expenses.

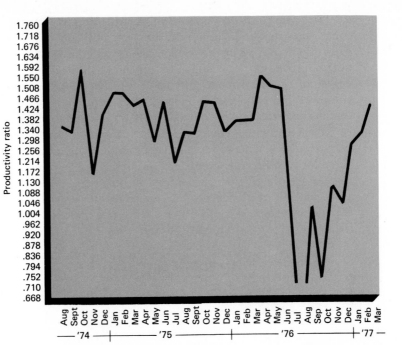

**Figure 18.5
Example of factory
productivity mea-
surement: produc-
tivity ratio over
time.**
*(Source: Todd Johnson
et al., "A Study of Plant
Productivity Measure-
ment," Plan B paper,
Minneapolis: University
of Minnesota, May
1977.)*

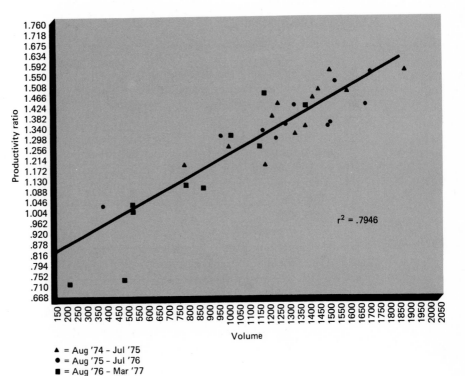

**Figure 18.6
Productivity ratio
versus volume
(productivity ratio
plotted to produc-
tion with re-
gression line).**
*(Source: Todd Johnson
et al., "A Study of Plant
Productivity Measure-
ment," Plan B paper,
Minneapolis: University
of Minnesota, May
1977.)*

$r^2 = .7946$

▲ = Aug '74 – Jul '75
● = Aug '75 – Jul '76
■ = Aug '76 – Mar '77

ity. [See Peeples (1978) for details.] Here the output is pure service, which further complicates the productivity measurement problem. To solve this problem, measures of effectiveness were developed along with measures of efficiency. Effectiveness of data processing was defined by timeliness in meeting output schedules and the degree of systems support provided. Efficiency was defined by the utilization of computer and peripheral support devices. Efficiency was measured by traditional output-input ratios, while effectiveness was related to the quality of output.

To combine the different effectiveness and efficiency measures, a point system was used. Each measure was allocated a number of points and a total score was computed for each time period under measurement. The result was a total effectiveness score and a total efficiency score for each time period. Productivity was then defined as the product of effectiveness multiplied by efficiency. Since there was no constant measure of output, the effectiveness score was multiplied by the more familiar efficiency (output-input) ratio as follows:

$$\text{Productivity} = \text{effectiveness} \times \frac{\text{output}}{\text{input}}$$

This case illustrates an important assumption regarding simple productivity ratios: that quality or effectiveness of output is held constant. For a factory under constant quality control standards, this may be a realistic assumption. However, for many operations, both quality and productivity vary over time. In this case, the more complicated productivity measure should be used.

18.3 FACTORS AFFECTING PRODUCTIVITY

Measurement is only the first step in improving productivity. The second step is understanding the factors which affect productivity and selecting the appropriate improvement factors in any given situation.

In the literature on productivity, a partial list of factors is often given. This results from a behavioral, economic, or technical point of view which emphasizes one particular approach to productivity improvement. In this section, a comprehensive view of productivity will be given, including all the factors which might affect the productivity of operations: external, product, process, capacity, inventory, and work-force factors. These various factors are summarized by the productivity wheel in Figure 18.7.

External factors—including government regulation, government investment policy, competition from other firms, and customer demand—are outside the control of the firm. The external factors may affect both volume of output and the availability of scarce inputs. In some cases, external factors *may* be so strong as to offset steps which the firm may take to improve productivity. Generally speaking, this is not true; firms can do much to improve productivity within the external constraints.

The product is a factor which can greatly affect productivity. It is generally recognized that R&D leads to new product technologies which improve productivity. On the other hand, too much product innovation may slow down process innovation and lead to productivity decline. Product diversity may lead to greater produc-

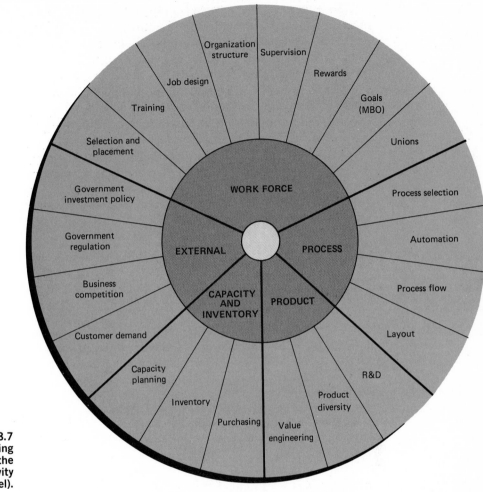

**Figure 18.7
Factors affecting
productivity (the
productivity
wheel).**

tivity through increased sales and economies of scale. But product diversity may reduce productivity too, by unfocusing the process and spreading operations too thin.

Value engineering is a product improvement approach used to produce the product more cheaply. The idea is to simplify the product or substitute materials so the product performs the same function at lower cost. An example is a metal part which is redesigned and made from plastic instead to reduce the cost of its production.

In Part II of this book, we covered many ideas in process design which can be used to improve productivity. These improvement factors include process flow, automation, layout, and selection of process types. If the process type is not properly matched to the product and market, inefficiencies can result. Within a given process, there are many ways to organize the flow of information, material, and customers. These flows can be improved by better layouts or by process flow analysis, with resulting increases in productivity.

One of the key methods used to improve productivity in the past has been automation, and it appears that the substitution of capital for labor can still be a powerful key to the improvement of productivity in the future. Many economists have identified investment slowdown as the primary reason for the United State's decline in productivity during the last decade.

Management of capacity and inventory is the fourth factor which can affect productivity. In the short run, excess capacity is often a factor which contributes to adverse productivity ratios. We have already seen, in the case of the M.B.A. study, how volume affected a factory's productivity because of fixed capacity costs. Capacity can almost never be matched exactly to demand, but careful capacity planning can reduce both excess capacity and bottlenecks due to insufficient capacity.

Along the same lines, inventory can be either a hindrance or a help to a firm's productivity. Too little inventory will lead to lost sales, reduced volume, and eventually lower productivity. Too much inventory will lead to higher cost of capital and lower productivity.

The fifth and last factor, work force, is perhaps the most important of all, and it is receiving a great deal of attention today. The work force, in turn, is associated with a great number of subfactors: selection and placement, training, job design, supervision, organizational structure, rewards, goals, and unions.

The management of human resources in operations should be viewed as an integrated task beginning with the recruitment and selection of workers and proceeding through the motivation of workers, the measurement of results, and the giving of rewards for performance. The recruitment, selection, and placement of workers determines the "raw material" of human resources available to the firm. These resources can be made productive through training within a given organizational context. The organization context itself can be altered through job design, supervision, or authority relationships. Finally, rewards and goals can be used to motivate the work force within the given organizational context and the available level of training.

While the work-force factors interact with each other, they also interact with all the variables in the productivity wheel. Thus management must carefully select a comprehensive approach to productivity improvement which may cut across many departmental lines and the entire range of variables. By using the productivity wheel in Figure 18.7, managers can view all the factors available and select those which promise the greatest improvement in productivity.

18.4 PRODUCTIVITY IMPROVEMENT PROGRAMS

While many companies believe productivity should be improved, they often have trouble getting started. One company, Honeywell, Inc., started by asking the following questions as part of a companywide productivity improvement program:

What is our competitor's productivity?
How do our competitors achieve productivity?
Is there a universal productivity measure?
How labor-intensive should we be?

Can the productivity of creative work be quantified?

Who is in charge of productivity improvement?

Where can a manager get help when he or she has a productivity improvement problem?

What is the minimally acceptable productivity rate for a division? Department? Employee?

How should productivity improvement be woven into annual planning?

[Honeywell (n.d.)]

Every company will have its own particular set of questions, depending on its circumstances and situation. Answers to the questions in particular cases will lead to a wide variety of different productivity programs. But there are some things which all these programs have in common: measurement of productivity, organizational commitment, and feedback on results achieved. No productivity improvement program can succeed without these important features.

Some of the steps which should be followed to achieve measurement, commitment, and feedback in a productivity improvement program are as follows:

1. Develop productivity measures at all levels of the organization. These measures should be developed by the responsible line managers with staff assistance as needed. Some organizational units may have more than one measure or an aggregated overall measure.
2. Set goals for productivity improvement in terms of the measures stated. These productivity goals should be realistic and time dependent. For example, a carpet-laying firm may set a productivity goal to improve yards of carpet laid per labor hour by 10 percent in the next year.
3. Develop plans to meet the goals. At this point the line management must decide exactly *how* the goals will be met. In the carpet-laying firm, for example, management might decide to purchase some new radio-dispatched trucks and to spend more money on training to reach the productivity improvement goals.
4. Implement the plan. This would normally be done through the line organization. Implementation is, of course, much easier if the line managers and work force have formulated the plan themselves, in the beginning.
5. Measure results. This step will require data collection and periodic assessment of progress in meeting goals set by step 2. If results are on track, no further action is required. If productivity improvement has fallen behind, corrective action will be needed or the goals should be revised in light of changing conditions.

The approach outlined above is nothing more than the standard method of management planning and control covered in most introductory business courses. The approach applies not only to productivity but also to quality, money, and other controllable factors. Furthermore, the planning and control process cannot be short-circuited, eliminated for the sake of convenience, or circumvented. Each step of the process is essential, even though the concept itself is quite simple.

A productivity improvement program which emphasizes measurement, feedback, and control requires the support and participation of top management. The improvement program must be given a high company priority and should be implemented from the top down. Since productivity improvement cuts across all organizational units, it should start with top management and focus on business goals and business strategy at the highest level.

For example, Honeywell's program started with the president and chairman of the board. Top management set productivity goals for the company, established staff support to plan and monitor the program, and insisted that line managers at every level measure and improve their productivity.

To improve productivity it will also be necessary to establish a formal program, perhaps giving it a catchy title such as Beech Aircraft's Employee Bonanza Plan. A person or committee should be appointed to establish the plan and monitor results. Incentives and prizes may be given to entice all employees to participate. The best productivity programs have found ways to stress productivity and to sell the plan to all managers and employees.

18.5 EXAMPLES OF PRODUCTIVITY IMPROVEMENT PROGRAMS

Two programs from industry illustrate the concepts described above. The first was initiated by Detroit Edison, a large utility supplying electricity to Detroit and Southeastern Michigan. This program emphasized productivity measurement and involvement by all company employees. Detroit Edison has about 10,000 employees and annual revenues of $1 billion. Since the mid 1950s, the company has measured its productivity by megawatts of electric output per employee. Due to rising costs and rate regulation, management decided to increase emphasis on productivity improvement by establishing a program called ACTION (All Committed to Improving Operations Now). This program was launched by the company president at a staff meeting attended by all members of management. He described ACTION as consisting of three phases:

Phase I: Meetings with all employees and supervisors to clarify roles and responsibilities

Phase II: Strengthening the companies' MBO system to make the objectives more measurable and concrete

Phase III: Establishing a productivity measurement and improvement program

As part of the ACTION program, a high-level productivity committee was established which interviewed managers in all 65 of the company's departments to determine what was currently being done to measure and improve productivity. One of the committee's principal findings was that only 50 percent of Detroit Edison's employees were currently under productivity measurement. A goal was then set to raise the figure to 75 percent of the employees within a year. The only employees exempted from measurement were those in functions that were extremely difficult to measure, such as the planning department and the public affairs office.

As a result of the measurement program, which led to the clarification of responsibilities and goals within the departments, productivity was improved. To keep the momentum going, an annual seminar on productivity was instituted; at that meeting, managers shared with each other the progress that had been achieved in their departments and discussed the methods they had used.

The Detroit Edison program shows how productivity can be improved through a formal, companywide measurement program initiated from the top down. The program involved all employees, and management insisted that a large portion of the departments in the company develop productivity measures.

The second productivity program, at Beech Aircraft, illustrates a different approach to productivity improvement. In this case, the company established specific programs aimed at product design, process design, and worker motivation, while measurement took a secondary role. This project was actually a series of programs initiated over a period of years.

Beech Aircraft is a manufacturer of small private and military aircraft; it has six plants in Kansas and Colorado. The first productivity improvement program to be established used work simplification. This program was based on the idea that each employee is the best judge of the work methods used on his or her job. Therefore each employee was asked to accept responsibility for improving productivity through self-initiated job changes. The industrial engineering staff was available to help and each employee received some training in industrial engineering methods and work measurement. As a result of the program, many employees simplified their jobs and productivity was improved throughout the Beech Aircraft factories.

The second Beech aircraft program was called the Employees' Bonanza Plan, which provided group wage incentives for increased productivity. The plan was based on equivalent airframe pounds manufactured per payroll dollar, using the year before the plan was put into effect as the base year. Any improvement in productivity over the base year was shared 50 percent by management and 50 percent by the workers. During the first year, Bonanza Plan payments totaled $1.6 million; in the second year, the payments were $2.2 million. For an employee who made the average wage, the bonus payments totaled $575.

The third Beech Aircraft productivity improvement program was based on value engineering (VE). In brief, the idea of VE is to redesign existing products so they perform the equivalent function at less cost. This might be done by using different materials, taking off frills, or simplifying the product. The program was initiated by establishing a VE group with full-time engineers assigned within the engineering function. Their responsibility was to review all designs for VE changes, initiate changes, and monitor these changes into production. The criterion used to initiate a change was that the development and investment cost had to be paid back in 1 year.

Finally, Beech Aircraft initiated a commonality program to promote the use of common parts and assemblies throughout all products. By reducing the number of different parts used to make a given product line, economies of scale and simplification of field service was achieved. The program was initiated by forming a commonality group in the engineering department, which studied each assembly and subassembly for possible changes to increase commonality and reduce the variety of parts. The same cost criterion was used to select commonality changes as in the VE program.

The Beech Aircraft programs emphasized productivity improvement in both production and engineering. In production, productivity was improved through work simplification and wage incentives. In engineering, productivity was improved through value engineering and increased commonality of parts. Beech Aircraft utilized a variety of different approaches to improve productivity over a period of several years.

These examples illustrate that there is no one sure-fire approach to productivity improvement. The best approach in any particular company will be tailored to the company's problems and situation. In all cases, however, management must stress productivity and develop programs to constantly improve it.

18.6 WAGE INCENTIVE PLANS

There has been a great deal of debate in the literature on the effect of pay on productivity. This debate was fueled by the human relations studies of the 1940s and later the work of Frederick Herzberg (1968). Herzberg's two-factor theory holds that factors intrinsic to the job itself (achievement, recognition, work, responsibility, and growth advancement) tend to satisfy workers, while extrinsic factors (pay, supervision, company policies, work conditions, etc.) are dissatisfiers. Some people have erroneously concluded from this research that pay is not a motivating factor. Herzberg's research, however, had nothing to do with performance or productivity; it simply addressed worker satisfaction.

There has been, however, a great deal of other research on the direct relationship between pay and productivity. This research generally supports the proposition that higher pay does lead to higher productivity. A careful study by Davison et al. (1958) examined the results of wage incentive plans on 15 operations in five different factories. Davison and his colleagues selected cases where all conditions were held constant except that a wage incentive plan was introduced; this plan paid higher wages for higher productivity. In all 15 cases, productivity improved from 7.5 to 291 percent, with half the cases falling between 43 and 76 percent improvement. These productivity increases were not temporary but were sustained over a period of time.

Another study of over 400 plants in the United States showed that work-measurement programs alone increased productivity by an average of 14.6 percent. When wage incentives were added to work measurement, productivity rose another 42.9 percent. The average increase from baseline to work measurement and incentives was 63.8 percent. [Fein (1973).]

The evidence indicates that wage incentives should be considered seriously as one way to improve productivity. Yet only 26 percent of United States workers are on some type of wage incentive program. In some industries such as steel and sewn products, up to 80 percent of employees are on incentive plans. But other industries have not even considered the use of incentives.

Mitchell Fein (1977) gives three reasons why management is reluctant to install wage incentive plans.

1. Some managers are concerned that incentives will diminish their ability to control the operations and over a period of time the incentives will deteriorate, causing labor problems.
2. Some managers believe that productivity improvement is largely created by management efforts; there is no need to share productivity gains.
3. Management's rights advocates believe that improvement is best shared periodically as increases in wages and benefits.

Although all these arguments have merit, they must be balanced against the potential motivating effect of pay.

Productivity is a goal of management, not of the work force. The workers want tangible economic rewards (pay and benefits), job security, and a suitable working environment. There is a fundamental conflict between management's desire for productivity on the one hand and the workers' interests on the other. Wage incentive plans are one way to reconcile this conflict by automatically sharing the results of productivity increases between management and workers. Another way to reconcile this conflict is through collective bargaining. In this case the sharing of productivity improvements is considered part of the bargaining process. Whatever method is used to resolve the conflict, productivity is something a worker will not automatically seek.

In many companies, there are disincentives to increase productivity and the workers actively (but not openly) seek to restrict output. Disincentives occur when workers believe that increased productivity may lead to layoffs, job reassignment, and work speedups. Under these circumstances, management knowingly or unknowingly seeks to coerce the worker into higher productivity. Wage incentive plans are one way to make it clear that both parties will benefit from improved productivity.

There are two general types of incentive plans: individual and group. The individual plans include a variety of types: straight piece rate, piece rate with minimum, gain-sharing, and measured day work.

The straight-piece-rate plan is based on the concept that workers are paid directly for production, X dollars per unit. The piece rate (X) is usually set by the work-measurement techniques covered in the last chapter and represents the base rate at 100 percent effort. The worker is rewarded directly for any additional production and penalized for any lower production. Piece rates are widely used in industries where jobs are of a repetitive nature and the output is under the worker's direct control (e.g., sewing clothes). Piece rates do not work well where group interaction is important, where jobs are machine-paced, or where the work is not highly repetitive.

Another problem with piece rates is that earnings may vary widely from week to week, sometimes because of circumstances outside the control of the worker. To alleviate this problem, some piece-rate plans have a minimum or floor wage rate per hour (e.g., the Manchester plan). In this case, the worker is guaranteed at least the minimum wage regardless of the output level.

A gain-sharing or bonus plan (Rowan or Halsey) guarantees a base rate and divides any excess production between management and the worker. It is common to divide the extra production on a fifty-fifty basis, although other percentage splits are also used. Suppose, for example, that the base production rate is 10 units per hour, the base wage is $5 per hour, and 2500 units are produced in the course of a week (160 hours). In this case, the worker gets credit for 250 hours of work (2500/10). The first 160 hours are paid at $5 per hour and the additional 90 hours at $2.50 per hour (fifty-fifty sharing). The total wages are:

$$160(5) + 90(2.50) = \$1025$$

Finally, the measured-day-work plan is similar to the others except that wages are adjusted every few weeks or months to provide more stability in take-home pay. Suppose, for example, wages are adjusted monthly. Each month, the hourly wage is computed on the basis of the number of units produced during the past month, the sharing percentage with management, and the minimum if applicable. This wage rate would then be paid for hours worked during the next month, after which the wage rate would again be recomputed.

The group plans are another form of wage incentive used to pay an entire department or entire plant at the same incentive bonus. These plans are used where jobs are highly interactive and one individual paces the work of another. Group plans are also used to bring indirect labor into the incentive plan, on the premise that they too should contribute to output. Two types of group incentive plans are in wide use: Scanlon and IMPROSHARE (Improving Productivity through Sharing).[3]

The Scanlon plan uses the idea of work groups and a plantwide incentive bonus. [See Geare (1976) for a review of Scanlon plans.] The work groups discuss work methods and procedures which may restrict output or decrease productivity. It has been found that many productivity bottlenecks can be eliminated through the sharing of common problems and concerns. The bonus in the Scanlon plan is usually based on past output divided by pay. If this ratio is improved, management and labor share the improvement on a fifty-fifty basis. The Scanlon plan or its variants is being used in about 500 plants in the United States [Kendrick (1977)].

There are three differences between the Scanlon plan and IMPROSHARE. First, with IMPROSHARE, the bonus is calculated on the basis of work standards adjusted for past actual output. Thus changes in product mix can be accurately reflected in the bonus paid. Second, changes in technology are reflected in IMPROSHARE. When productivity is improved by the addition of new machines, the workers get 10 percent of the improvement and management gets 90 percent. This gives management an incentive to continue to automate where it is economically justified. If machine productivity increases were shared with workers on a fifty-fifty basis, there would be a tendency to reduce automation and to create a competitive disadvantage for the company. Third, there is a ceiling on the incentive wages that can be paid and a buy-back provision to adjust the standards when the ceiling is reached. This limits management's risk to extraordinary productivity increases beyond the ceiling. Under the IMPROSHARE plan, group bonus payments are made weekly. Over 300 plants in the United States are using this plan.

There are many types of incentive plans; only a few of these have been discussed

---

[3] IMPROSHARE is a registered service mark of Mitchell Fein.

here merely to indicate how wage incentives can affect productivity. Management should carefully consider such plans as one component of a total productivity improvement program. Of course, these plans are effective only when a reasonable measure of output can be devised and quality standards are held constant over time. If the plan is to be effective, the productivity measure must be considered to be fair by both management and the workers.

18.7 KEY POINTS

A variety of different measures and methods to improve productivity are available. It is management's responsibility to measure productivity constantly and to act in conjunction with the workers to improve it. Unfortunately, productivity is not adequately measured in many firms and management is sometimes reluctant to act.

The chapter's key points include the following:

- National productivity can be measured by either total factor productivity or partial ratios. The total factor productivity ratio is the best one because it considers all inputs used to produce output.
- United States productivity has decreased in the 1970s. The decrease is thought to be caused by lower investment in R&D, plant, and equipment; by increased government regulation; and by the changing mix of the work force.
- Total firm productivity should be measured by the ratio of output at standard prices (or costs) to the sum of labor, material, overhead, and capital costs. When the productivity of a particular manager is being measured, only controllable inputs should be included in the denominator. These measures should be set by line management, and all measures should be linked in a hierarchical fashion. Measurements for individual managers should incorporate all job responsibilities, even if multiple ratios must be established. It is necessary to incorporate effectiveness in productivity measures when both effectiveness and efficiency vary over time.
- Many factors affect productivity in the firm, including external, product, process, capacity, inventory, and work-force factors. The proper mix of these factors must be selected for any particular productivity improvement program.
- Productivity improvement programs follow the standard planning and control process used in business. The steps required in these programs are: develop productivity measures, set productivity goals, develop plans to improve productivity, implement the plans, measure the results, and take corrective action. Regardless of the specific factors or approach selected to improve productivity, this planning and control process is essential.
- Productivity improvement is a goal of management. Workers cannot be expected to improve productivity unless there is a clear connection between productivity improvement and their welfare. One way to establish this connection is through wage incentive plans. Another way is through collective bargaining or through a consistent management track record of higher wages for improved productivity.
- Wage incentives have been shown to improve productivity in cases where an adequate productivity measure can be established and where management and workers support the wage incentive plan. Many types of individual and group

incentive plans have been used, including straight-piece-rate, bonus, measured-day-work, Scanlon, and IMPROSHARE plans.

QUESTIONS

1. The real GNP of a hypothetical country is shown below, along with the value of labor and capital inputs. Calculate the improvement in (a) total factor productivity and (b) partial productivity of labor and capital for years 2 and 3.

Years (billions of dollars)			
	1	2	3
Real GNP	800	850	920
Labor	500	560	600
Capital	200	210	220

2. Why is it desirable to improve productivity? Discuss from a national, management, and labor perspective.

3. For the following data, calculate the effect on profit margins of improving labor productivity by 10 percent.
   Labor cost $80
   Other costs $10
   Profit $10

4. A firm has the following data:

	Year 1	Year 2
Sales	$100	$120
Direct labor	40	45
Materials	20	25
G & A expense	10	15
Depreciation	10	10
Other expenses	5	5
Total expenses	85	100
Profit	15	20
Inventory	80	70
Plant and equipment	40	50

   a. Using a cost of capital of 15 percent, calculate the change in total factor productivity using shipments/all inputs. Assume that prices were increased an average of 5 percent between year one and year two.
   b. Using a ratio of sales/pay, calculate the change in productivity.
   c. Why do the measures calculated in a and b differ?

5. Devise a productivity measure for each of the following jobs:
   a. Plumber   d. Doctor
   b. Civil engineer   e. Professor
   c. Nurse

6. a. Evaluate the following hospital productivity measure:

$$\frac{\text{Beds filled}}{\text{Salaries of hospital personnel}}$$

   b. Devise a better productivity measure.

7. Classify the productivity changes made by Beech Aircraft according to the productivity factor wheel of Figure 18.7.
8. Amy Smith, who manages a bakery, says that productivity for her business cannot be measured. Suggest an approach that Amy could use. Amy also says that she has automated things to the maximum extent possible and that therefore no further improvements in productivity are possible. Discuss.
9. Discuss the pros and cons of using wage incentives to improve productivity.
10. When is it appropriate to use group incentives versus individual incentive plans?
11. There is a natural conflict between management and labor regarding productivity. Why does this conflict occur? What can be done about it?
12. A worker has produced 160 pieces of output in 6 hours. The hourly rate is $6 per hour and the standard production rate is 20 pieces per hour. Calculate the wages for the following incentive plans:
    a. Straight piece rate
    b. Fifty-fifty bonus-sharing plan

SELECTED BIBLIOGRAPHY

DAVISON, J. P., et al.: *Productivity and Economic Incentives,* London: G. ALLEN, 1958.
FEIN, MITCHELL: "An Alternative to Traditional Managing," working paper, Hillsdale, N.J., 1977.
————: "Designing and Operating an IMPROSHARE Plan," working paper, Hillsdale, N.J., 1976.
————: "Work Measurement and Wage Incentives," *Industrial Engineering,* September 1973.
GEARE, A. J.: "Productivity from Scanlon-Type Plans," *Academy of Management Review,* vol. 1, no. 3, July 1976, pp. 99–108.
GELLERMAN, SAUL W.: *Motivation and Productivity,* New York: American Management Association, 1963.
HEATON, HERBERT: *Productivity in Service Organizations,* New York: McGraw-Hill, 1977.
HERZBERG, FREDERICK: "One More Time: How Do You Motivate Employees?" *Harvard Business Review,* January–February 1968.
HONEYWELL, INC.: *People, Productivity, Honeywell,* Minneapolis, n.d.
HORNBRUCH, FREDERICK, Jr.: *Raising Productivity: Ten Case Histories and Their Lessons,* New York: McGraw-Hill, 1977.
JOHNSON, TODD, et al.: "A Study of Plant Productivity Measurement," Plan B paper, Minneapolis: University of Minnesota, May 1977.
KATZELL, RAYMOND A., PENNY BIENSTOCK, and PAUL FAERSTEIN: *A Guide to Worker Productivity Experiments in the United States, 1971–75,* New York: New York University Press, 1977.
KENDRICK, JOHN W.: *Understanding Productivity,* Baltimore: Johns Hopkins, 1977.
LEWIS, MARK R.: "Productivity as It Relates to Computer and Information Systems," Graduate School paper, Minneapolis: University of Minnesota, 1978.
MALI, PAUL: *Improving Total Productivity,* New York: Wiley, 1978.
MALKIEL, BURTON G.: "Productivity—The Problem behind the Headlines," *Harvard Business Review,* May–June 1979.
NATIONAL CENTER FOR PRODUCTIVITY AND QUALITY OF WORKING LIFE: *Improving Productivity: A Description of Selected Company Programs,* series 1, Washington: U.S. Government Printing Office, December 1975.
————: *Productivity in the Changing World of the 1980's,* final report, Washington: U.S. Government Printing Office, 1978.
PEEPLES, DONALD E.: "Measure for Productivity," *Datamation,* May 1978.
THATCHER, RALPH H.: "Designing a Productivity Control Process," *Business Horizons,* December 1975.

PART VI
QUALITY PLANNING AND CONTROL

CAPACITY

INVENTORY

PROCESS

WORK FORCE

- PLANNING QUALITY
- QUALITY CONTROL

QUALITY

Quality is one of the objectives of operations and one of the five decision-making responsibilities. In order to meet the quality objective, it is important to plan and control all aspects of quality. Chapter 19 begins this part with a discussion of planning quality, and Chapter 20, on quality control, completes it.

The planning of quality should encompass all aspects of quality, from design of the product or service through production and use. All quality efforts should be guided by a corporate policy on quality and a planning and control system which ensures a quality product. This system should involve all individuals in the firm and achieve the proper balance between the prevention of defects and detection of those defects that occur. This balance can be achieved by carefully managing the quality function.

Quality control, described in Chapter 20, is aimed at producing a product in conformance with product specifications. A proper quality control system can be defined by identifying key inspection control points in the delivery system for the product or service. At each of these control points, the product should be inspected in accordance with stated criteria and standards. In some cases, statistical sampling procedures can be used to reduce the amount of inspection required. Many of these statistical procedures are described in Chapter 20.

The main contribution of Part VI is a broad treatment of quality, which includes management, planning, and policy concerns in addition to the more traditional statistical topics. In practice, quality is primarily a management problem, and statistical methods are used within the context of planning and controlling quality to acceptable levels.

CHAPTER 19
PLANNING QUALITY

Quality is one of the four key objectives of most operations. While it is something the whole organization must be concerned with, the operations function is charged with the responsibility of producing quality for the customer. This responsibility can be carried out only by the proper planning and control of quality in all phases of operations.

This chapter is primarily concerned with the planning of quality, while control of quality is discussed in Chapter 20. Since operations is so vitally involved in quality, it is somewhat surprising that the subject of quality planning is given only cursory treatment in the literature of operations management. Perhaps the explanation is the preoccupation with formulas, statistics, and quantitative methods which has characterized the quality control field. As more attention shifts to management concerns, planning for quality will receive increased emphasis.

The term "quality" is used in a variety of different ways; there is no clear definition of it. From the customer's viewpoint, quality is often associated with value, usefulness, or even price. From the producer's viewpoint, quality is associated with conformance to specifications: with producing the product according to its design.

BOX 19.1 **TYPICAL DECISION PROBLEM**

Sherry Stahl presented her analysis of how productivity could be improved at Pizza U.S.A. Ted Hickford praised Sherry for the thorough and penetrating analysis she had made. He observed, "I'm proceeding to implement your recommendations beginning with the next meeting of our store managers. As a follow-up on this study, I'd like you to begin a new study of quality at Pizza U.S.A. All our present procedures and approaches to quality need a thorough review, similar to the productivity review that you have just completed."

Ted continued, "I'd like you to start by reviewing our current store operating manual which specifies our quality standards. I believe that a more comprehensive set of standards is needed, and we need to question seriously whether the quality standards reflect the type and level of service we want to offer.

"Next, I'd like you to review our training programs. Do these programs emphasize quality to a sufficient degree, and do they help the trainees to understand our quality procedures? If these programs aren't working, what can be done to improve them?

"I'd also like you to visit several stores and discuss the quality problems with the store managers. Find out whether the managers are able to follow the procedures in the store operating manual, what additional quality procedures they would suggest, and what training problems they are encountering in training their people. Perhaps you could visit some of the stores together with our inspection teams to gain further insights into the quality program.

"I'm particularly interested in whether we can improve quality by stressing 'zero defects' and 'doing it right the first time' with our work force. Will this approach work in reducing wasted effort and scrap while also making our workers more quality conscious, or should we emphasize some other approach?

"Finally, I'd like to have you make a thorough review of the inspection procedures we use. Are the stores inspected frequently enough? Are the inspectors properly qualified? Is the inspection helpful in actually improving quality?"

Ted finished by saying, "I'm particularly concerned that we review quality programs now. As we move to improve productivity, I want to be sure that quality is not sacrificed."

The conformance to design specifications is commonly referred to as quality control.

"Quality" has taken on different meanings through the years. In the early 1900s, it meant inspection. All finished products were inspected and any defects were corrected. In the 1940s, the word "quality" took on a statistical connotation. Pioneers in statistical quality control—like Shewhart, Dodge, Romig, and Nelson—developed the idea that any production process was subject to a certain level of natural variation. It was the job of quality control managers to discover this level through statistical methods and to assure control of the production process. In the 1960s, "quality" was extended outside of production to include all other functions using a concept of total quality control. With total quality control, the entire organization is mobilized to help produce a quality product. The meaning of the term "quality" is now being expanded to include product liability and a concern for the consumer movement. A typical quality decision problem is described in Box 19.1.

19.1 FITNESS FOR USE

"Quality" has been generally defined as "fitness for use." This means that the product or service meets the customer's needs, i.e., the product is fit for the customer's use. Fitness for use is related to value received by the customer and to customer satisfaction. Only the customer—not the producer—can determine it.

Fitness for use is a relative concept which varies from one customer to another. For example, while one customer may consider a Ford automobile perfectly fit for use, another may not. Each person defines quality in relation to his or her own needs.

From the producer's viewpoint, variation in quality cannot be tolerated. The producer must specify quality as concretely as possible and then strive to meet those specifications. Whether the resulting product is fit for use or not will then be judged by the customer.

According to Juran et al. (1974), fitness for use is based on the following five quality characteristics:

Technological (e.g., strength and hardness)
Psychological (e.g., taste, beauty, status)
Time-oriented (e.g., reliability and maintainability)
Contractual (e.g., guarantee provisions)
Ethical (e.g., courtesy of sales personnel, honesty)

Quality for a manufactured product may be defined primarily by technological and time-oriented characteristics, while a service product may involve all the characteristics listed above.

Quality is generally more difficult to define for services than for manufactured products. Whether the product is a service or a good, however, the following dimensions of quality may be defined:

Quality of design
Quality of conformance
The "abilities"
Field service

Quality of design is determined before the product is produced. In a manufacturing company, this determination is usually the primary responsibility of the engineering department, along with marketing and operations. In service organizations, quality of design is handled by whoever is responsible for designing services.

Quality of design is determined by market research, design concept, and specifications. Market research is ordinarily aimed at determining the customer's needs. Since there are different ways to meet these needs, a particular design concept must be developed. For example, the customer may need inexpensive and energy-efficient transportation—a need that can be met by a large number of different automobiles, each representing a different design concept. The design concept then results in a set of specifications for the product, e.g., a blueprint, bill of materials, or service specification.

Quality of conformance means producing a product to meet the specifications. When the product conforms to specifications, it is considered by operations as a quality product even though the quality of design may be low. For example, an inexpensive pair of shoes will have high "quality" if they are made according to specifications, and they will have low "quality" if they do not meet specifications. Quality of design and quality of conformance thus represent two different uses of the term "quality."

Another aspect of quality involves the so-called abilities: availability, reliability, and maintainability. Each of these terms has a time dimension and thus extends the meaning of "quality" beyond the beginning or starting quality level. The addition of time to the definition of quality is, of course, necessary to reflect the fitness for continued use by the customer.

"Availability" defines the continuity of service to the customer. A product is available if it is in an operational state and not down for repairs or maintenance. In the military, availability is equated with operational readiness. Availability can be measured quantitatively as follows:

$$\text{Availability} = \frac{\text{uptime}}{\text{uptime} + \text{downtime}}$$

"Reliability" refers to the length of time that a product can be used before it fails. Formally speaking, reliability is the probability that a product will function for a specified period of time without failure. The reliability of a light bulb for 1000 hours might, for example, be 80 percent. In this case, if many light bulbs are tested for 1000 hours, 80 percent of them will burn the entire time and 20 percent will fail. The reliability of a product is also related to mean time between failure (MTBF), which is just the average time that the product functions from one failure to the next. The longer the MTBF, the more reliable the product.

"Maintainability" refers to the restoration of a product to service once it has failed. All customers consider maintenance or repairs a nuisance. Thus a high degree of maintainability is desired so that a product can be restored to use quickly. Maintainability can be measured by the mean time to repair (MTTR) the product.

Returning to availability, we see that availability is a combination of reliability and maintainability. If a product is high in both reliability and maintainability, it will also be high in availability. This relationship can be expressed formally as:

$$\text{Availability} = \frac{\text{MTBF}}{\text{MTBF} + \text{MTTR}}$$

If a product has an MTBF of 8 hours and an MTTR of 2 hours each time it fails, then its availability will be 80 percent.

The last dimension of quality is field service, which represents warranty and repair or replacement of the product after it has been sold. Field service is also called customer service, sales service, or just service. Field service is intangible, since it is related to such variables as promptness, competence, and integrity. The customer expects that any problems will be corrected quickly, in a satisfactory manner, and with a high degree of honesty and courtesy. Unfortunately, field service is often one of the least well defined and most poorly controlled dimensions of quality.

The four different dimensions of quality are summarized in Figure 19.1. As can

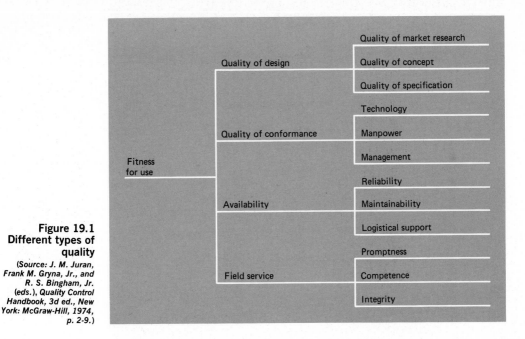

**Figure 19.1
Different types of
quality**
(Source: J. M. Juran,
Frank M. Gryna, Jr., and
R. S. Bingham, Jr.
(eds.), Quality Control
Handbook, 3d ed., New
York: McGraw-Hill, 1974,
p. 2-9.)

be seen, quality is more than just good product design; it extends to quality control of production, quality over the service life of the product, and quality of field service after the sale. In Section 19.2, we will show how these dimensions of quality can be specified by the process of quality planning and control.

19.2 PROCESS OF QUALITY PLANNING AND CONTROL

The process of quality planning and control requires a continuous interaction between the customer, operations, and other parts of the organization. Figure 19.2 illustrates how these interactions occur through a quality cycle. The customer specifies needs, usually through the marketing function. These needs are either expressed directly by the customer or discovered through a process of market research. Engineering, in turn, designs a product to meet those needs or works with the customer on design modifications which fit within production capabilities.

Once the design concept and specifications have been completed, the quality of design has been established. Engineering must then work with operations to produce the product specified or, if difficulties are encountered, to modify the specifications. Operations must continually ensure that the product is produced as specified by insisting on quality of conformance. This is ordinarily done through proper training, supervision, machine maintenance, and inspection.

Finally, the product is delivered to the customer, who uses it and determines whether it meets his or her needs. The quality cycle then repeats.

Figure 19.2 is primarily a manufacturing specification of the quality cycle, and Figure 19.3 is a similar description of the quality cycle for a mass transit system.

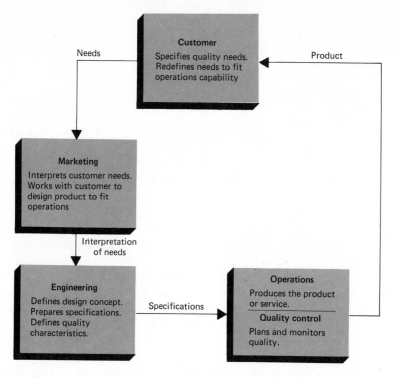

**Figure 19.2
The quality cycle.**

In this case, a planning agency, in place of marketing, interprets the customer's needs. Another planner, working in greater detail, then determines the design concept and the specifications for service. The operations function delivers the service, and the public then restates its needs or confirms that the present service is satisfactory. The quality cycle should, therefore, exist in every organization to ensure that all aspects of quality are planned and continually controlled.

**Figure 19.3
The quality cycle
in a mass transit
system.**
(*Source: John P. Van
Gigch, "Quality—Producer
and Consumer Views,"
Quality Progress, April
1977, p. 31.*)

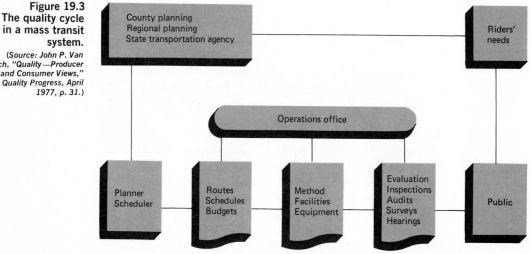

To implement planning and control of quality through the quality cycle requires the following sequence of steps:

1. Define quality attributes.
2. Decide how to measure each attribute.
3. Set quality standards.
4. Establish an inspection program.
5. Find and correct causes of poor quality.

Planning for quality control must always start with the product attributes. The quality planner determines which attributes are important to fitness for use and which are not. For example, the manufacturers of L'eggs panty hose have determined three important quality attributes for their product: (1) a comfortable fit, (2) an attractive appearance, and (3) a wear life that is considered reasonable by the customer [Mabe (1978)]. They have also decided that the correct amount of material in various parts of the panty hose will provide a comfortable fit; that fabric dyed in popular colors and free from defects will provide an attractive appearance; and that choice yarns and selected stitch formations will provide acceptable wear life.

A method must then be devised to test and measure quality for each of the product attributes. For example, the manufacturers of L'eggs have developed a special cross-stretcher which can be used to test the strength of their product, and this is used on a certain percentage of all their panty hose. L'eggs are also inspected visually for fabric defects, seaming defects, and shade variations.

After deciding on the measurement techniques to use, the quality planner should set standards that describe the amount of quality required on each attribute. Usually these standards are stated as tolerances (± quantities) or minimum and maximum acceptable limits. For example, a standard on L'eggs panty hose is the amount of pressure which the garment must withstand on the cross-stretcher.

After standards have been set, an inspection program should be established. In the case of L'eggs, this program is based on sampling procedures, since it would be far too costly to inspect each of the 120 million pairs of panty hose that is produced each year. How such inspection plans can be set up will be treated in the next chapter.

It is not enough simply to inspect the products for defects. As the saying goes, "You cannot inspect quality into a product." Upon discovering defects, quality personnel should find the underlying cause and correct it. Causes for poor quality could include improper raw material, lack of training, unclear procedures, a faulty machine, and so on. When the causes of poor quality are regularly found and corrected, the production system will be under constant control and the quality of conformance will be high.

In order to plan and control quality, inspections and tests should be made on the inputs, the process, and the outputs. As shown in Figure 19.4, product (or service) design should guide the testing of materials (or inputs) prior to the production process, during the process, and after production. When all stages of production are monitored, a high level of quality can be achieved.

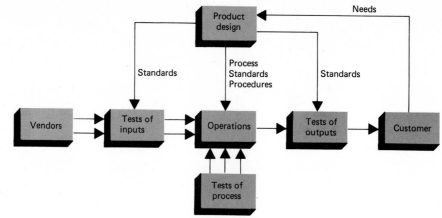

**Figure 19.4
Quality control
points.**

19.3 QUALITY POLICY

To initiate the process of quality planning, a quality policy should be set by top management. The quality policy, in turn, should be derived from a corporate strategy. As an aid to setting these policies and strategies, the Strategic Planning Institute has done a study called PIMS (Project Impact of Market Strategy) [Mertz (1977)]. The basic purpose of this study was to determine what factors affected return on investment and by how much. One of its findings was that high-quality products and services are the most profitable as shown in Figure 19.5. In this case, the quality of the firm was defined as the percentage of the products superior to competition minus the percentage of products inferior to competition.

With respect to market position, the PIMS study demonstrated that quality and market share usually go together. Firms with high-quality products also have the largest share of the market and benefit most from market growth. From the standpoint of policy, companies in a weak market position should emphasize quality as a way to build market share. They should use quality in preference to price or high marketing expenditures, since improvement in quality provides the greatest poten-

**Figure 19.5
PIMS data. High-
quality products
and services are
most profitable.**
*(Source: PIMS, Strategic
Planning Institute, n.d.)*

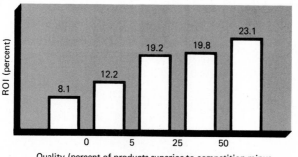

tial for ROI. The PIMS study illustrates the role of quality in strategy, which has sometimes been overlooked in the past.

After considering the strategic factors, top management should set a quality policy. Juran et al. (1974) give one example of such a policy:

> It is the policy of the company to provide products and services of a quality that meets the initial and continuing needs and expectations of customers in relation to the price paid and to the nature of competitive offerings, and in doing so, to be the leader in product quality reputation.
>
> It is the policy of the corporation that its products shall meet all specified and implied standards of performance, reliability and quality.

Juran goes on to point out that this policy statement is rather vague and thus provides little guidance for quality actions. However, it might be corrected by making it more specific and by incorporating guidance on the following questions:

1. What type of market segment is being targeted with respect to quality and price?
2. What emphasis is placed on beginning quality versus availability, reliability, and maintainability?
3. What is the role of the line and staff in meeting quality requirements?

Notice, some of the questions that should be answered in a quality policy involve marketing considerations. Since quality is fitness for use, this should be no surprise. Therefore, marketing has an important stake in helping to define a clear quality policy along with operations. When the policy statement is finished, it should be put in written form and distributed throughout the firm. In most companies policy statements on quality can be found in the quality control manual, along with procedures and standards which ensure quality control.

Policy statements should be followed up with detailed quality objectives set on a periodic basis, usually annually. If the company has a management by objectives (MBO) system, the quality objectives should be incorporated into it.[1] Quality objectives should appear not only in the quality manager's MBO statement but in the statements of each manager involved in quality; e.g., marketing, engineering, and field service.

Some examples of quality objectives are as follows:

Raise the outgoing quality level to 99.9 percent (1 defect out of 1000 units) as measured by sampling procedures.

Make sure that all employees receive a one-day training course on quality procedures.

Form quality control circles of workers and staff to meet weekly, to identify causes of poor quality, and to take appropriate corrective action.

---

[1] "MBO" refers to a system where each manager agrees to written objectives with his or her supervisor, usually on an annual basis. Managerial performance is then defined in relation to the objectives which have been set.

Once the objectives are formulated and have been assigned to specific managers, they will provide the short-range vehicle to improve quality and to carry out the company's quality policy.

19.4 QUALITY AND THE CONSUMER

In recent years the consumer has become a more important factor in quality planning and control. This development is due to increasing consumer awareness of quality and greater attention to consumer rights as well as to product liability legislation. All these factors are having a great effect on quality professionals as they are thrust into a role of consumer protection within the firm.

More and more consumers are becoming concerned about the quality of the products and services that they use. For example, a 1976 Roper survey that tested consumer confidence in well-known products found that consumer confidence was highest in canned goods and prescription drugs, with two-thirds of the people saying they got good quality in most or almost all instances [Brokaw (1977), p. 26]. On automobiles and small appliances, opinion was equally split—only half of the people surveyed said they received good-quality products in most or almost all cases. In another survey of services, the top ratings were received by medical services, telephone service, and life insurance. All these services were rated by about half the panel as excellent or good values. At the bottom of the service ratings were TV repair, home repair, government services, and auto repair. Only about 25 percent of those surveyed rated these as excellent or good values.

These surveys point to the lack of consumer confidence in quality. The problem is also illustrated by the large increase in product liability suits in recent years. In the United States in 1965, insurance claims for product liability were $500 million. This figure increased to about $50 billion by 1975, a hundredfold increase in 10 years. As a result of these increases, the time-honored phrase *caveat emptor* (let the buyer beware) is being replaced by *caveat vendor* (let the seller beware).

Nelson (1976) observes that most product liability suits fall into one of five categories:

Poor or improper design of the product
Manufacturing defects
Assembly defect
Improper repair or service
Failure to warn the customer

The most difficult category is the "failure to warn," which does not even require proof of a defective product. For example, in Illinois a product liability judgment for $5,225,500 was awarded after a man sustained leg injuries from a rented trailer [Nelson (1976), p. 23]. The suit alleged that the trailer rental company had failed to warn the man that a proper weight-equalizing hitch should be used.

In other suits, the product itself is found to be defective. One of the most famous cases was the $128 million award made to Richard Grimshaw as a result of the Ford

Pinto gas tank suit. The prosecution argued that even though Ford's own testing had found weaknesses in Pinto gas tanks, the company chose not to spend the $10 per car it would have taken to correct those weaknesses [*Time* (1978), p. 65].

Quality is therefore becoming increasingly important as businesses become more concerned about product liability and consumer protection. Some firms have gone so far as to take special organizational measures to ensure that only quality products reach the market. For example, Gillette has appointed a vice president of product integrity, Robert Giovacchini. His responsibility is to oversee corporate quality control and the Gillette Medical Evaluation Laboratory. If an existing or new product is found to represent unacceptable risks, he can pull the product off the market, often to the dismay of marketing and operations executives. For example, he held up the introduction of a new shaving cream because the aerosol pumps would push out only 3 of the can's 4-ounce contents. Mr. Giovacchini said, "You couldn't hear the stuff left inside and the cans felt pretty light, so marketing executives wanted to launch the product and replace the bad pumps in later production runs." Giovacchini said no. "The fact that the consumer doesn't know the difference doesn't make it right" [Martin (1975)].

In another action, Giovacchini instituted the $1.5 million recall of two new Gillette antiperspirants because of questions about the long-term effects of inhaling the zirconium propellant. This was done after Gillette's tests on animals indicated the possibility of lung irritations due to the chemicals. Eighteen months later, an advisory panel of the FDA recommended, on the basis of its own laboratory tests, that zirconium propellant be removed from the market.

What can be done, then, to respond to the consumer's concern for better quality and to protect the company from product liability? One thing companies can do is to be more careful during product design. Better quality control can also be instituted to improve the quality of conformance. Organizational changes such as the one made by Gillette can be made. When quality is made a part of the corporate strategy and of every manager's objectives, quality will receive the emphasis it deserves and the consumer will be better served.

19.5 ORGANIZATION FOR QUALITY AND THE TOTAL QUALITY CONCEPT

In addition to policy and objectives, organizational structure is one of the issues that should be decided as part of quality planning. In manufacturing companies, two basic types of organizational structures are used. First, the quality department may be independent of manufacturing and report directly to the general manager, as shown in Figure 19.6*a*. Second, the quality department may be a part of manufacturing and report to the manufacturing manager, as shown in Figure 19.6*b*.

Whether quality should be under manufacturing or not has raised a great deal of controversy. Those who argue for a separate quality function reporting to the general manager claim that quality should be independent to avoid compromising quality in the effort to meet schedules or to reduce costs. This view has been especially strong in companies that do government contracting. In some cases, the government

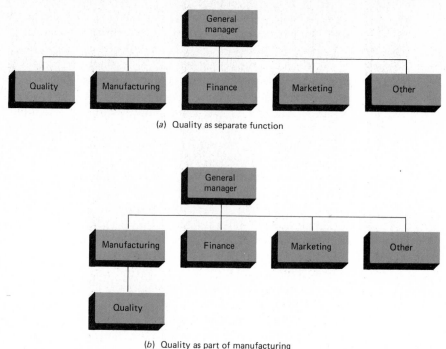

(a) Quality as separate function

(b) Quality as part of manufacturing

**Figure 19.6
Organization of
quality.**

insists that quality be organized separately to protect the government's interests as a customer.

Those who argue that quality should be under manufacturing point out that you cannot inspect quality into a product and that quality requires close coordination with the work force, purchasing, and all phases of operations. They argue that the manager of manufacturing is the best person to coordinate the quality department and all other departments in manufacturing which affect quality.

In recent years, as the concept of total quality has been developed, the precise organizational arrangement which is used has become less important. Using the total quality concept, the quality department is seen as the organizational coordinator for all other departments which affect quality: manufacturing, purchasing, marketing, and engineering. Under a total quality program, each department must identify its precise role in quality and must set objectives to maintain acceptable quality of design and conformance.

The total quality concept requires the quality department to spend more time on planning and less on inspection and control. A total quality approach stresses prevention of defects and recognizes the role of all organizational units in achieving quality goals. Prevention is not something which can be done by any one department because it requires attention to vendor relations (purchasing), training (personnel), design (engineering), customer needs (marketing), and production of the product (operations). A total systems approach is required which cuts across the entire organization. In this case, the quality department is not responsible for quality; rather, quality is everybody's responsibility. The quality department serves a coordinating role to ensure that everyone contributes to quality objectives.

Lack of a total quality concept is seen every day in industry. When a quality problem is discovered, the general manager often turns to quality control to fix the problem. In reality, quality control can do little, since the problem was caused by engineering, manufacturing, or marketing in the first place. It is a mistake to call most problems quality problems; they should be called by the names of the departments which caused them.

It is not enough simply to recognize the importance of total quality control; rather, a positive program must be implemented throughout the organization. The program should specify how the total quality effort will be organized, how all individuals can be made aware of their role in quality, and how the results of the total quality approach will be measured. [Whirlpool (1977) offers an example of how a total quality program can be implemented.]

19.6 COSTS OF QUALITY

A new idea in the quality area is to calculate and control the cost of quality. For cost-of-quality calculations, we assume that product specifications are given. The cost of quality is therefore the cost of nonconformance. By assigning a cost to quality, it can be managed and controlled like any other cost. Since managers speak the language of money, putting quality in cost terms offers a powerful means of communication and control.

Most companies have no idea how much they spend to plan and control quality. Those who have measured them find that the costs are about 10 percent of sales, with ranges from 5 to 15 percent [Crosby (1979)]. Since these figures are equal to profit margins in many companies, a reduction in the cost of quality can lead to a significant improvement in profit. The best-managed companies have been able to reduce their costs of quality from 10 or 15 percent of sales to as little as 3 to 5 percent over a period of several years [Crosby (1979)]. This has been done while improving the quality of the product. The potential for doing this in most companies is untapped.

The cost of quality may be divided into two components: control costs and failure costs. The control costs are related to activities which remove defects from the production stream. This can be done in two ways: by prevention and by appraisal. The prevention costs include activities such as quality planning, new-product reviews, training, and engineering analysis. These activities occur prior to production and are aimed at preventing defects before they occur. The other category of control costs comprises appraisal or inspection aimed at eliminating defects after they occur but before the products reach the customer.

The failure costs are incurred either during the production process (internal) or after the product is shipped (external). The internal failure costs include such items as

TABLE 19.1	COSTS OF QUALITY

Prevention costs

Quality planning: Costs of preparing an overall plan, numerous specialized plans, quality manuals, procedures.

New-product review: Review or prepare quality specifications for new products, evaluation of new designs, preparation of tests and experimental programs, evaluation of vendors, marketing studies to determine customers' quality requirements.

Training: Developing and conducting training programs.

Process planning: Design and develop process control devices.

Quality data: Collecting data, data analysis, reporting.

Improvement projects: Planned failure investigations aimed at chronic quality problems.

Appraisal costs

Incoming materials inspection: The cost of determining quality of incoming raw materials.

Process inspection: All tests, sampling procedures, and inspections done while the product is being made.

Final goods inspection: All inspections or tests conducted on the finished product in the plant or the field.

Quality laboratories: The cost of operating laboratories to inspect materials at all stages of production.

Internal failure

Scrap: The cost of labor and material for product which cannot be used or sold.

Rework: The cost of redoing product which can be made to conform.

Downgrading: Product which must be sold at less than full value due to quality problems.

Retest: Cost of inspection and tests after rework.

Downtime: Idle facilities and people due to quality failures.

External failure

Warranty: The cost of refunds, repairing, or replacing products on warranty.

Returned merchandise: Merchandise which is returned to the seller.

Complaints: The cost of settling customer complaints due to poor quality.

Allowances: Cost of concessions made to customers due to substandard quality.

Source: Adapted from J. M. Juran, Frank M. Gryna, Jr., and R. S. Bingham, Jr. (eds.), *Quality Control Handbook*, 3d ed., New York: McGraw-Hill, 1974, pp. 5–4 to 5–5, and Whirlpool, *Total Quality Assurance: Total Cost of Quality*, May 1978, pp. 5–6.

scrap, rework, quality downgrading, and machine downtime. The external failure costs include warranty charges, returned goods, allowances, and the like. A more complete listing of all of these costs is given in Table 19.1.

The total cost of quality can thus be expressed as a sum of the following costs.

$$\text{Total cost of quality} = (\text{control costs}) + (\text{failure costs})$$

$$= \begin{pmatrix} \text{prevention} \\ \text{costs} \end{pmatrix} + \begin{pmatrix} \text{appraisal} \\ \text{costs} \end{pmatrix} + \begin{pmatrix} \text{internal} & \text{external} \\ \text{failure} & + & \text{failure} \\ \text{costs} & & \text{costs} \end{pmatrix}$$

Prevention costs	Control costs	Total cost of quality
Appraisal costs		
Internal failure costs	Failure costs	
External failure costs		

The total cost of quality can be minimized by observing the relationship between cost of quality and degree of conformance, as in Figure 19.7. When the degree of conformance is very high (low defects), the costs of failures are low but the costs of control are quite high. When the degree of conformance is low (high defects), the opposite situation exists. Thus there is, between the two extremes, an optimal level of conformance where total quality costs are minimized.

Good quality management also requires the proper balance between appraisal and prevention costs, so that total control costs are at the minimum. Table 19.2 is a cost table from the Whirlpool Corporation showing the tradeoff between these costs. The numbers in the table are millions of dollars of total quality cost for particular expenditures on prevention and appraisal in the margins. For example, suppose

Figure 19.7 Cost of quality.

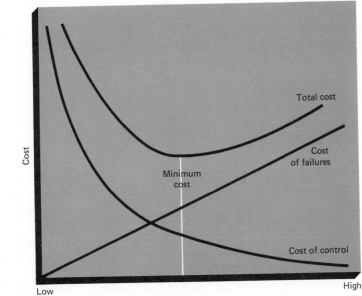

TABLE 19.2   **TRADEOFFS IN QUALITY COSTS**

		Range of prevention costs (dollars per unit)								
		0.60	0.80	1.00	1.20	1.40	1.60	1.80	2.00	2.20
Range of appraisal costs (dollars per unit)	0.60	20.05	20.29	20.18	19.40	15.90	12.22	10.09	9.82	10.22
	0.80	20.40	20.64	20.54	19.78	16.34	11.72	10.62	10.36	10.77
	1.00	20.52	20.77	20.69	19.96	16.63	12.16	11.11	10.87	11.28
	1.20	20.20	20.46	20.42	19.77	16.66	12.47	11.51	11.31	11.73
	1.40	18.08	18.40	18.47	18.03	15.58	12.25	11.56	11.50	11.95
	1.60	15.17	15.56	15.77	15.62	14.02	11.79	11.46	11.53	12.06
	1.80	14.62	15.03	15.29	15.23	13.91	12.03	11.81	11.99	12.48
	2.00	14.63	15.06	15.34	15.32	14.14	12.44	12.28	12.48	12.98
	2.20	15.09	15.52	15.80	15.80	14.64	12.98	12.83	13.04	13.54

Source: Whirlpool, *Total Quality Assurance: Total Cost of Quality*, May 1978, p. 2.

$1.4 million is spent on appraisal and $1 million on prevention. Then the total cost of quality will be $18.47 million.

Most companies have a tendency to operate in the lower left-hand corner of this table by spending a great deal on appraisal and little on prevention. But the total cost is minimized in the upper right-hand corner, where more is spent on prevention and less on appraisal. The typical company would therefore benefit by reducing its appraisal costs and simultaneously increasing its prevention costs.

The costs of quality should be reported to all levels of management. There are several ways in which these costs can be tabulated:

By organizational unit
By time
By cost-of-quality categories
By product

Quality costs should also be normalized for volume using one or more of the following measures.

Per direct labor hours. This is one of the best-known measures of volume and is readily available for calculation in most operations.

Per direct labor cost. This measure has the advantage of dividing dollars by dollars and thus reducing the effects of inflation.

Per dollar of standard manufacturing cost. This extends the direct labor index by adding material and overhead. The resulting index has greater stability because it is not affected as much by automation.

Per dollar of sale. This measure has the advantage of being readily understood by top managers. It has the disadvantage of being affected by pricing and costs outside operations.

Per equivalent unit of product. When products are fairly homogenous, this measure is useful because it is unaffected by extraneous costs and prices.

The measures that are selected will be a function of the particular company and its reporting practices. Whatever measures are used, however, should be calculated by the accountants, just like other financial information. The accounting reports should then be interpreted by quality managers, who should also recommend appropriate actions to reduce the costs of quality.

The cost of quality can be a powerful tool for quality control when it is properly used. It focuses management attention on waste due to excess failures or high control costs. It also provides a quantitative basis for monitoring progress in reducing quality costs to the desired level. The cost of quality is easily understood; it brings quality out of a "goodness" or "value" area which cannot be measured to a dollars-and-cents basis.

19.7 MAKE IT RIGHT THE FIRST TIME

Suppose we find that the cost of quality is too high. How can it be reduced? What can management do? One approach is to adopt the total quality view described above. Another approach is to stress prevention: to produce "zero defects" or to "make it right the first time."

It is generally accepted that there has been a reduction in craftsmanship and pride in work over the past decade. This problem is believed to stem from worker attitudes, but workers often reflect the attitudes of their managers. To reverse the decline in quality, management must be the first to change.

The advocates of the zero defects philosophy argue that we are conditioned to believe it is all right to make errors. They point to such common sayings as "To err is human," "Everybody makes mistakes," and "Nobody's perfect," all of which serve to justify the lack of conformance in the work place. The problem is further compounded by inspectors whose job it is to catch the errors made by workers.

Why should we settle for poor quality in the work place? The usual reply is that high quality costs too much. But in fact high quality may cost less. Perhaps it is cheaper to make the product right the first time than to correct errors or to pay for scrap, rework, or failures in the field.

Of course, it is unrealistic to expect that the delivered product will literally have zero defects, but—according to the zero defects approach—the workers should strive toward this as the goal. Even when they do, however, a few defective items may be produced and be shipped to the customer. When the zero defects approach is being used, the work force should strive to make the product exactly to specifications or get the specifications changed. No worker should knowingly produce defects on the grounds that it is too expensive to do it right the first time.

Zero defects programs have usually been introduced into industry as motivational efforts. Awards and prizes are given to those workers who produce zero defects over a period of time. But prizes are not enough; the worker should be made responsible for quality. This requires the worker to do most of his or her own inspection, to receive feedback information on quality, and to accept personal responsibility for making a quality product. This can be done if management is willing to delegate authority to the line and to the work force and to expect a quality product in return.

Zero defects programs can have a dramatic effect on quality and the cost of quality. In the Martin Company, an audited savings of $1,650,000 was recorded over the first 2 years, with a 54 percent drop in defects produced. General Electric had a $2 million drop in rework and scrap during the first 2 years of their program. With respect to individual efforts, one forklift driver moved over 15 million pounds of delicate electronic hardware without a single incident of damage. A solderer made almost ½ million connections without error [Halpin (1966), pp. 16–17]. Since these studies were not controlled research efforts, it is difficult to determine the cause of the low number of defects. Nevertheless, it appears that workers are capable of delivering high quality and high productivity at the same time if the job is properly designed and management sets the climate for producing a quality product.

19.8 QUALITY CIRCLES

Recently, there has been a great deal of interest in the idea of quality circles. A quality circle is simply a group of employees that meets periodically to solve problems on the job. A quality circle involves more than just employee participation in decision making. Employees are trained in problem-solving techniques, and they actively gather data and solve problems together.

A quality circle consists of all employees who work closely together on the job. The leader of the quality circle may be an employee or one of the supervisors. The group meets periodically, often one hour a week, to discuss problems and seek solutions. Problems may be identified by individual employees or given to the group by management. Some groups even keep a logbook of problems which have been identified and solved.

Quality circles are based on the idea that employees can best identify and solve many of their own problems—assuming, of course, that they have the problem-solving skills, the data required, the time, and financial support. The employees acquire problem-solving skills through training sessions which include technical information and data-analysis techniques. The employees are given time off from their jobs and management support in their efforts. When the suggestions from a quality circle require financial resources, their request must be justified the same as any other capital request in the company.

Quality circles reduce some of the resistance to change encountered in organizations, because the employees themselves develop the solutions. They can also lead to better solutions, since several minds are working on the same problem. Although the solution to a problem may be improved, quality circles may require more time to reach a solution and they may result in compromises and poorer solutions. Therefore, it is important that members of quality circles be trained in problem-solving techniques and that they use an objective approach to problem solving.

Quality circles were first formed in Japan in 1962, when the country was plagued with low-quality goods. Now one out of every eight Japanese workers belongs to a quality circle. The Lockheed Missile and Space Company is credited with introducing the quality-circle idea to the United States beginning in the early 1970s. Several hundred U.S. companies now employ quality circles. [See Willis (1980) for more details.]

Quality circles not only improve quality, they often improve productivity too. Since many problems involve both low quality and low productivity, quality circles develop solutions which improve both of these simultaneously. Therefore, a better name for quality circles might be "performance circles," in recognition of their contribution to both quality and productivity.

19.9 AMERICAN AND JAPANESE QUALITY

It is appropriate to end this chapter on quality planning with a comparison of American and Japanese quality practices. Since the Japanese seem to be doing a better job of producing quality than the United States, perhaps something can be learned from them.

Juran conducted an in-depth analysis of Japanese and American quality with particular attention to the color TV set. He observed the following differences in quality practices between the two countries [Juran (1978)]:

1. SCRUBDOWN OF NEW PRODUCTS. In Japan, a very careful procedure is followed prior to the introduction of a new product to ensure the quality of design and conformance. This process of pilot production is called "scrubdown" and is aimed at getting the bugs out of the product before regular production begins. In the United States, scrubdown procedures are also used, but inevitably the conflict between the schedule and quality emerges. In most cases, the United States companies decide to go to market and meet the schedule while correcting the quality defects on the fly. In the end, the correction programs rarely materialize because of other, more pressing priorities and other new products. The Japanese scrubdown procedure is more careful and deliberate.

2. EMPHASIS ON QUALITY CHARACTERISTICS. A TV set has three principal quality characteristics: picture quality, cabinet appeal, and reliability. It appears that Japan has emphasized reliability to a much greater extent than the United States while competing favorably on picture quality and cabinet appeal. Juran estimates, for example, that United States color TV sets were failing in service about five times as often as Japanese sets in the middle '70s. Although the Americans have been attempting to close the gap, the Japanese still have the lead in quality and particularly in reliability.

3. **MARKETING STRUCTURE.** In Japan, the major TV producers have their own retail outlets and service shops. In Japan, their sets are not sold through huge retail chains and repaired by independent dealers, as TV sets are in the United States. The manufacturer in Japan does it all. As a result, the manufacturers pay more of the real cost of failure; logically, therefore, they stress reliability.

4. **COMPONENTS.** As any TV manufacturer knows, a key to quality is the use of quality components. The Japanese carefully test all components prior to putting them in a set. They also select vendors carefully to get the best possible supplier from a quality-price standpoint. The Americans do less screening and end up with a much higher rate of in-plant failures. For example, the typical American TV manufacturer has about 150 defects per 100 sets during production, while the Japanese have about 5 defects per 100 sets.

5. **TRAINING.** The Japanese emphasize quality training at all levels. Top management attends classes on quality principles. Before receiving assignments as design engineers, engineers must all spend some time in operations to learn about the problems of production. Workers must attend training sessions (in QC circles) as a regular part of their jobs.

6. **EMPLOYEE RELATIONS.** The Japanese stress teamwork and worker responsibility for quality. There is a pride in workmanship which starts with top management and permeates the entire organization. The line managers and workers are put in a decision-making role and the staff is advisory. As a result, the work force knows it is responsible for producing a quality product and accepts that responsibility. There is a great emphasis in Japan on the total quality concept described above and on doing things right the first time.

Many people feel that the Japanese methods may be all right for Japan but that they will not work in America. This view has already been shown to be wrong in three cases. One involved the Motorola (Quasar Electronics) factory which was taken over by Matsushita in 1974. Prior to the takeover, Motorola was experiencing 150 defects per 100 sets. In a relatively short period of time, the defect rate was reduced to 3 or 4 defects per 100 sets in the same factory, with the same workers, and the same quality control people. The only difference was a few Japanese managers who instituted the Japanese approach to quality management [Juran (1978), p. 14].

Americans have a tendency to reject ideas which are not invented here. In the case of quality, we should not only study the Japanese approach but be willing to accept Japanese ideas and improve on them where we can. As quality becomes more and more of a determinant of market share, a major change in American quality practices will be needed. Much can be learned from the Japanese, who have already succeeded in transforming their World War II image of cheap Japanese goods to the current image of cheap but *high-quality* Japanese goods.

19.10 THE INTEGRATION OF DECISION MAKING AND QUALITY

Decisions made during product and process design as well as in managing the work force directly affect quality. Product design decisions should specify quality objectives and give specifications for the product or service being designed. These product decisions can effectively reduce product liability and quality costs which might otherwise be incurred. In a similar way, the process can be designed from a quality perspective to ensure the meeting of quality objectives. A high-volume line-flow process will ensure consistent quality, while quality is more difficult to control for intermittent and project processes. The next chapter will include detailed examples of how process design can incorporate quality considerations directly in the design of the process.

We have indicated in this chapter how work-force decisions can affect product quality through training, job design, and motivation of the work force. In the case of a zero defects approach, the workers' attitude toward quality is important in reaching the quality objectives of operations. In a similar way, many work-force decisions affect quality in operations.

The total approach to quality stresses the interrelationship between quality, decisions in operations, and other parts of the business. Since product design, process design and work-force management decisions affect quality, these decisions must be properly integrated with quality decisions.

19.11 KEY POINTS

The chapter's key points include the following:

- Quality can be defined as fitness for use by the customer. There are four dimensions of quality which contribute to fitness for use: quality of design, quality of conformance, the "abilities," and field service.
- There is a cycle of product quality—from customer needs through quality of design, production, quality of conformance, and use by the customer. This cycle is controlled by specifying quality attributes, determining how to measure each attribute, setting quality standards, establishing an inspection program, and finding and correcting causes of poor quality. Quality controls should be specified for inputs, process, and outputs of operations.
- Management should set an overall quality policy, and this should be implemented through specific objectives set by managers at all levels.
- The consumer movement is exerting an influence on quality planning through consumer protection legislation and product liability. Management can restore consumer confidence by stressing quality and by placing primary responsibility for quality on the line management and the work force.
- The total quality concept utilizes a systems approach to quality by integrating quality programs and objectives across organizational lines. In most organizations a positive program is needed to implement the concept of total quality.
- The cost of quality measures the lack of conformance to quality standards. Qual-

ity costs can conveniently be divided into control costs and failure costs. Control costs are due to prevention or appraisal. Failure costs may be due to internal or external failures. Every company should measure and control these costs of quality.

- The philosophy that says "Make it right the first time" serves to prevent defects from occurring. The work force can be trained to reduce defects drastically if it is given the responsibility.
- The Japanese have succeeded in using the concepts of total quality and making the product right the first time. As a result, Japanese quality sometimes exceeds that of American products selling at the same price.

QUESTIONS

1. How can quality be measured for the following products?
   a. Telephone service
   b. Automobile repair
   c. Manufacture of ballpoint pens
2. Describe the differences between the quality of design and the quality of conformance.
3. Product A has an MTBF of 30 hours and an MTTR of 5 hours. Product B has an MTBF of 40 hours, and an MTTR of 2 hours.
   a. Which product has the higher reliability?
   b. Which product has greater maintainability?
   c. Which product has greater availability?
4. Suppose you manufacture 10,000 wooden pencils per day. Describe a quality planning and control system for this product including possible attributes, measures of quality, tests, etc.
5. Suppose you own and operate a small appliance repair service. Give an example of a quality policy which addresses all the important issues.
6. Give some examples of quality objectives for Question 5.
7. Name some products or services which in your opinion have relatively poor quality.
8. Name some products which have a high degree of product liability. Can this product liability be attributed to quality?
9. What are the pros and cons of placing the quality department under the operations manager?
10. The following costs have been recorded:

Incoming materials inspection	$10,000
Training of personnel	30,000
Warranty	45,000
Process planning	15,000
Scrap	9,000
Quality laboratory	30,000
Rework	25,000
Allowances	10,000
Complaints	12,000

What are the costs of prevention, appraisal, external failure, and internal failure?

11. Suppose the following cost functions are available:

    Cost of failure $F = 1500 + 40X$

    Cost of control $C = \dfrac{2000}{X}$

    where X = percent defective

    What is the minimum cost of quality and the optimal percent defective?
12. How does the minimum percent-defective philosophy agree with the idea of zero defects?
13. The cost of quality and volume figures for a hotel are as follows:

	1979	1980
Cost of quality	$100,000	$150,000
Sales	$1,000,000	$2,000,000
Number of customers	50,000	80,000
Direct labor cost	800,000	1,200,000

    Has the unit cost of quality increased or decreased?
14. How could a zero defects policy be applied to student term papers?

SELECTED BIBLIOGRAPHY

Booth, William E.: "Financial Reporting of Quality Performance," *Quality Progress*, February 1976, pp. 14–15.

Brokaw, Charles: "Quality Control for Consumer Confidence," *Quality Progress*, July 1977, pp. 26–28.

Crosby, Philip B.: *Quality Is Free*, New York: McGraw-Hill, 1979.

Enrick, Norbert L.: *Quality Control and Reliability*, 7th ed., New York: Industrial Press, 1977.

Feigenbaum, A. V.: "Total Quality Control," *Harvard Business Review*, November–December 1956, pp. 93–101.

———: *Total Quality Control: Engineering and Management*, New York: McGraw-Hill, 1961.

Gryna, Frank M., Jr.: "Quality Costs: User vs. Manufacturer," *Quality Progress*, June 1977, pp. 10–13.

Halpin, James F.: *Zero Defects*, New York: McGraw-Hill, 1966.

Harris, Douglas, and Frederick Chaney: *Human Factors in Quality Assurance*, New York: Wiley, 1969.

Juran, J. M.: "Japanese and Western Quality—A Contrast," *Quality Progress*, December 1978.

———, Frank M. Gryna, Jr., and R. S. Bingham, Jr. (eds.): *Quality Control Handbook*, 3d ed., New York: McGraw-Hill, 1974.

Kirkpatrick, Elwood G.: *Quality Control for Managers and Engineers*, New York: Wiley, 1970.

Lester, Ronald H., Norbert Enrick, and Harry Mottley: *Quality Control for Profit*, New York: Industrial Press, 1977.

Mabe, G. Mike: "Quality Control and L'Eggs Panty Hose," *Quality Progress*, February 1978, pp. 12–14.

Martin, Richard: "Gilette's Giovacchini Rules on the Quality Safety of 850 Products," *The Wall Street Journal*, Dec. 12, 1975.

Mellin, Barbara: "Shearton's Quality Improvement Program," *Quality Progress*, December 1977, pp. 12–14.

Mertz, Orville: "Quality's Role in ROI," *Quality Progress*, October 1977, pp. 14–17.

Miller, Ross F.: "America's Awakening Consumerism: The Long-Term Effect on Quality Control," *Quality Progress*, July 1978, pp. 26–28.

Nelson, Paul C.: "Current Impact of Product Liability," *Quality Progress*, August 1976, pp. 22–27.

PETERS, GEORGE A.: "New Product Safety Legal Requirements," *Quality Progress,* August 1978, pp. 34–36.

SCHROCK, EDWARD: "How to Manufacture a Quality Product," *Quality Progress,* August 1977, pp. 25–27.

SEGRAVES, DONALD: "Product Liability Problems—Growing Toward Crisis," *Quality Progress,* January 1977, pp. 16–18.

STRATEGIC PLANNING INSTITUTE: "PIMS-Profit Impact of Market Strategy," n.d.

VAN GIGCH, JOHN P.: "Quality—Producer and Consumer Views," *Quality Progress,* April 1977.

VAUGHN, RICHARD C.: *Quality Control,* Ames, Iowa: Iowa State Press, 1974.

WHIRLPOOL: *Total Quality Assurance: Systems Requirements,* 2d ed., August 1977.

————: *Total Quality Assurance: Total Cost of Quality,* May 1978.

WILLIS, JUDITH: "Quality Circles Breed Enthusiasm," *Minneapolis Star,* April 2, 1980.

CHAPTER 20
QUALITY CONTROL

As indicated in the last chapter, the field of quality control has a rich and long history. In the early 1900s, quality control was associated with inspection, which evolved from a responsibility of individual workers to that of an organized quality control department. While this evolution facilitated independent quality control, it sometimes created tension between the workers and quality control inspectors. In some organizations such tension is still evident today.

In 1924, Walter A. Shewhart of the Bell Telephone Laboratories published a paper which outlined the principles of statistical quality control charts. Two other Bell System men, H. F. Dodge and H. G. Romig, further developed the theory of statistical sampling for quality control in the 1930s. However, little of this theory found its way into industry until the 1940s, when the advent of World War II created a huge demand for mass-produced goods which could only be inspected by means of statistical methods. Imagine the problems faced by the U.S. government when it ordered millions of combat boots, millions of rifles, and huge quantities of other military equipment. As a result of these difficulties, the military and the government required suppliers to use statistical sampling methods to ensure compliance with government quality standards. These government-required sampling methods then spread throughout industry to all forms of manufacturing.

The spread of quality control methods has been much slower in service industries. While some service organizations have adopted comprehensive quality control programs, others are still neglecting quality or searching for the appropriate tools and principles.

BOX 20.1   **TYPICAL DECISION PROBLEM**

> Mary Lipton, vice president of operations at Radarwave, Inc., was reviewing the planned change to the assembly line with her boss, Tom Renford (see Boxes 16.1 and 17.1). Mary observed, "Tom, we've designed a novel assembly line which should reduce the levels of job boredom while still providing a great deal of efficiency. Roger Kirk and Ron Belfy are now designing detailed time standards and job descriptions for the line. When they finish, we'll be ready to go!"
>
> Tom replied, "One thing we need to ensure is quality control. I know we have good quality standards for our product, but how do we make sure that these standards are met? To enforce them, we need a well-designed statistical sampling program."
>
> "For example, in the receiving department, we now inspect a portion of all incoming materials. Are these samples being selected properly? Is the size of the sample proper to control our risks of accepting a bad lot or rejecting a good lot? We'll need to redesign all these sampling procedures as we change over to higher-volume production on the new line."
>
> Mary replied, "Tom, you're right, we need to look carefully at our acceptance sampling procedures in receiving. You'll be glad to know that quality control is already being designed into the line. We plan to have inspection stations at each critical point in the assembly of the ovens. For example, the chassis will be inspected after the magnetron tube has been installed. If the electrical tests are OK, then the outside case will be added to the oven and it will be inspected again. Since we are engaged in high-volume production, not every unit will be inspected at each inspection point on the line. Instead, we'll maintain statistical control charts based on samples to monitor the assembly process. If the process drifts out of control, we'll catch it and find the causes of the problem. We feel that this procedure will ensure quality products while keeping inspection costs under control."
>
> Tom replied, "I approve of your approach to quality control. Let's get on with the design of our new quality control system."

After the war, in 1946, the American Society of Quality Control (ASQC) was formed. While the initial emphasis of the society was on statistical quality control methods, the ASQC has recently addressed problems of reliability, product liability, zero defects, and total quality control. The ASQC has also made an effort to spread the use of quality control ideas throughout the service industries.

As we address the problems of quality control in this chapter, our emphasis will be on the traditional topics of inspection and statistical quality control. The modern focus in the quality area has shifted to the planning of quality, which was covered in the last chapter.

Quality control is defined as conformance to specifications. As a result, we assume that product or service specifications have been defined by the product design. The problem of quality control then is to ensure that the specifications are met by operations during production. This can be done by proper design of a quality control system. A typical decision problem encountered in the design of such a system is described in Box 20.1.

20.1 DESIGN OF QUALITY CONTROL SYSTEMS

All quality control must start with the process itself. Critical control points in the process, where inspection of the product should take place, should be identified. The types of measurements or tests required and the amount of inspection required at each of these points should be determined. Finally, management should decide who will do the inspection, the work force itself or separate inspectors. Once these decisions are made, it is possible to design a complete system of quality control which ensures conformance to the product or service specifications.

The first step in designing a quality control system is to identify the critical points in the process where inspection is needed. The guidelines for doing this are as follows:

1. Inspect incoming raw materials to ensure vendor compliance with raw-materials specifications. This inspection constitutes a screening process whereby defective material may be returned to the vendor and acceptable material passed on to production. The vendor should be kept informed of the results of this inspection process and especially of any quality problems. A method for doing this is described by Falvo (1977).

2. Inspect work in process or the service while it is being delivered. As a general rule, the product or service should be inspected before irreversible operations take place or before a great deal of value is added to the product. In these cases the cost of inspection is less than the cost of adding more value to the product.

    A precise determination of where the product should be inspected should be made from the process flowchart. One example of this procedure is shown in Figure 20.1, which makes use of symbols originally defined in Chapter 7. The flowchart defines points for lot approval, 100 percent inspection, process inspection, roving inspection, and sample inspection. It also indicates, through a combination operation and inspection symbol, where the operator uses self-inspection.

    An example of process flowcharting for the drug industry is shown in Figure 20.2. In this case a very extensive quality control system is used, consisting of more than 950 analytical control tests, 130,000 visual inspections, and physical control tests to ensure the quality of drugs for human consumption. In addition, the U.S. Food and Drug Administration tests the products independently at various points in the production process.

3. The third critical inspection point is the finished product or service. In manufacturing, final products are frequently inspected prior to shipment or prior to placing the product in inventory. At one automobile assembly plant, for example, a sample of cars is taken directly off the assembly line and thoroughly inspected for appearance and function. The defects are noted and fed back to assembly-line personnel so that they can correct the underlying causes. The defects are also used to compute a quality score for comparison among assembly plants. Another form of final-product inspection at this plant involves having each supervisor in the plant drive a new car home each evening. The supervisor writes up the defects the next morning and corrective action is taken in the daily plant meeting. These final-product checks are in addition to numerous in-process and raw-materials inspections.

    For services, the final product is more difficult and sometimes impossible to

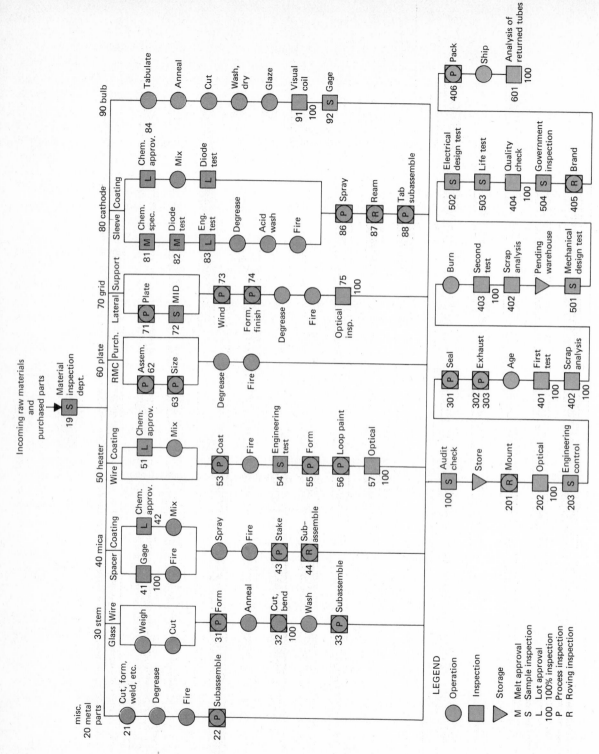

Incoming raw materials and purchased parts

misc. 20 metal parts

21 Cut, form, weld, etc.   Degrease   Fire   22 P Subassemble

30 stem | Glass | Wire

Weigh   Cut   31 P Form   Anneal   32 Cut, bend 100   Wash   33 P Subassemble

40 mica | Spacer | Coating

41 Gage 100   Fire   42 L Chem. approv.   Mix   Spray   Fire   43 P Stake   44 R Sub-assemble

50 heater | Wire | Coating

51 L Chem. approv.   Mix   53 P Coat   Fire   54 S Engineering test   55 P Form   56 P Loop paint   57 Optical 100

60 plate | RMC | Purch.

62 P Assem.   63 P Size   Degrease   Fire

70 grid | Lateral | Support

71 P Plate   72 S MID   73 P Wind   74 P Form, finish   Degrease   Fire   75 Optical insp. 100

80 cathode | Sleeve | Coating

81 M Chem. spec.   82 M Diode test   83 L Eng. test   Degrease   Acid wash   Fire
84 L Chem. approv.   Mix   Diode test
86 P Spray   87 R Ream   88 P Tab subassemble

90 bulb

Tabulate   Anneal   Cut   Wash, dry   Glaze   91 Visual coil 100   92 S Gage

19 S Material inspection dept.

100 S Audit check   Store   201 R Mount   202 Optical 100   203 S Engineering control

301 P Seal   302 P Exhaust 303   Age   401 First test 100   402 Scrap analysis 100

Burn   403 Second test 100   402 Scrap analysis   501 Pending warehouse   Mechanical design test

502 S Electrical design test   503 S Life test   404 S Quality check 100   504 S Government inspection   405 R Brand

406 P Pack   Ship   601 Analysis of returned tubes 100

LEGEND

Operation   Inspection   Storage

M Melt approval
S Sample inspection
L Lot approval
100 100% inspection
P Process inspection
R Roving inspection

542

inspect. Since the service delivered is intangible, the customer must be asked to rate the quality of the service delivered. Hotels and restaurants typically have cards which they ask customers to complete. Many universities ask students and alumni to rate the quality of education they received. All these "inspections" are aimed at assessing the quality of the finished product or service.

The second step in designing a quality control system is to decide on the type of measurement to be used at each inspection point. There are generally two options: measurement based either on variables or on attributes. Variable measurement utilizes a continuous scale for such factors as length, height, and weight. Attribute measurement uses a discrete scale by counting the number of defective items or the number of defects per unit.

When the quality specifications are complex, it will usually be necessary to use attribute measurements. In this case a complicated set of criteria can be used to define a defective unit or a defect. For example, a color TV set may be classified as defective if any of a number of functional tests fail or if the appearance of the cabinet is not satisfactory. In inspecting cloth, a defect can be defined as a flaw in the material and the number of defects per 100 yards can be counted during inspection. Determining the type of measurement to use also involves the specification of measuring equipment. A wide variety of devices are available for measurement. However the selection of these devices is beyond the scope of this text.

The third step in defining the quality control system is to decide on the amount of inspection to use. The choices are generally 100 percent inspection or a sample of a portion of the output. The guiding principle for this decision is to compare the cost of passing defects to the cost of inspection. For example, suppose that a defective unit sent to the customer costs $100 in terms of repair work, warranty, and future lost profits. Futhermore, suppose that a lot of 500 units contains an average of 2 percent defectives (10 defective units in the lot). Then the expected cost of not inspecting the lot is $1000 ($100 × 10). If it costs less than $1000 to inspect the entire lot ($2 per unit), the lot should be 100 percent inspected and the defective units screened out.[1]

There are other considerations besides cost which determine the amount of inspection. When human lives are at stake, 100 percent inspection at multiple points is often used (e.g., the drug example, Figure 20.2). When the product must be destroyed during testing, a sample must, of course, be used. Cost combined with these other considerations is used to set the proper level of inspection.

The final step in designing a quality control system is deciding who should do the inspection. Usually a combination of inspections by the workers themselves and by outside inspectors is used. If a philosophy of "zero defects" or "make it right the first time" is used, the workers will be given much of the responsibility for inspection and only a minimum of outside inspection will be used. There is some evidence to suggest that a prevention program along with a zero defects approach will be less expensive than an extensive outside inspection program.

Figure 20.1 (Opposite) Quality flow diagram for electronic tubes.
[Source: J. M. Juran, Frank Gryna, Jr., and R. S. Bingham (eds.), Quality Control Handbook, 3d ed., New York: McGraw-Hill, 1974,, pp. 6–13.]

[1] This assumes that all defective units are detected by the inspection procedure.

Drug and allied industries

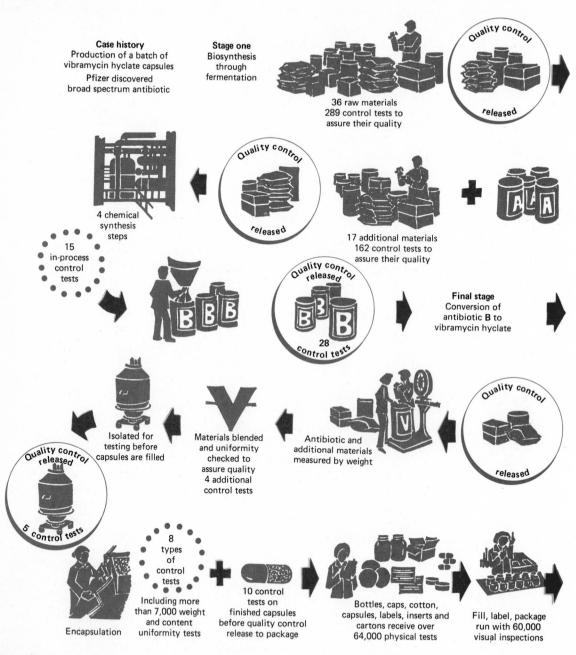

Case history
Production of a batch of
vibramycin hyclate capsules
Pfizer discovered
broad spectrum antibiotic

Stage one
Biosynthesis
through
fermentation

Quality control
released

36 raw materials
289 control tests to
assure their quality

4 chemical
synthesis
steps

Quality control
released

15
in-process
control
tests

17 additional materials
162 control tests to
assure their quality

Quality control
released

B B B

Quality control
released
B 3 B
28
control tests

Final stage
Conversion of
antibiotic B to
vibramycin hyclate

Isolated for
testing before
capsules are filled

Materials blended
and uniformity
checked to
assure quality
4 additional
control tests

Antibiotic and
additional materials
measured by weight

Quality control
released

Quality control
released
5 control tests

8
types
of
control
tests
Including more
than 7,000 weight
and content
uniformity tests

Encapsulation

10 control
tests on
finished capsules
before quality control
release to package

Bottles, caps, cotton,
capsules, labels, inserts and
cartons receive over
64,000 physical tests

Fill, label, package
run with 60,000
visual inspections

Figure 20.2
Controls on a drug (antibiotic) production process.
[*Source: J. M. Juran, Frank Gryna, Jr., and R. S. Bingham (eds.), Quality Control Handbook, 3d ed., New York: Mc-Graw-Hill, 1974, pp. 6–13.*]

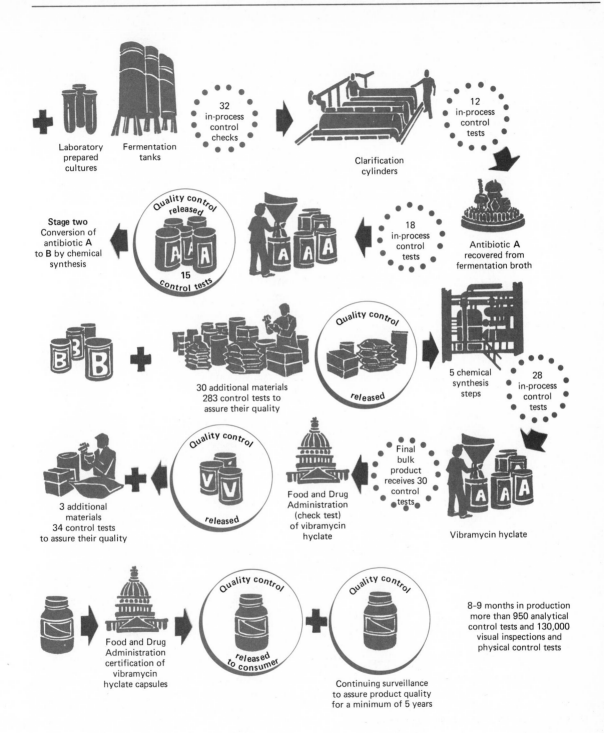

Laboratory prepared cultures

Fermentation tanks

32 in-process control checks

Clarification cylinders

12 in-process control tests

18 in-process control tests

Antibiotic **A** recovered from fermentation broth

Quality control released — 15 control tests

Stage two Conversion of antibiotic **A** to **B** by chemical synthesis

30 additional materials 283 control tests to assure their quality

Quality control released

5 chemical synthesis steps

28 in-process control tests

3 additional materials 34 control tests to assure their quality

Quality control released

Food and Drug Administration (check test) of vibramycin hyclate

Final bulk product receives 30 control tests

Vibramycin hyclate

Food and Drug Administration certification of vibramycin hyclate capsules

Quality control released to consumer

Quality control

Continuing surveillance to assure product quality for a minimum of 5 years

8-9 months in production more than 950 analytical control tests and 130,000 visual inspections and physical control tests

In some cases, the customer will be involved in inspecting the product. Service customers always take this role as they receive the service. Some customers station inspectors at the vendor plants to examine and accept or reject shipments before they are sent on to the customer. The government has inspectors in a variety of industries to ensure quality in the interest of public health and safety. Thus, a variety of people may be involved in the inspection process.

A well-designed quality control system requires a series of management judgments. The control principles themselves are elementary, requiring performance standards, measurement, and feedback of results to correct the process. The application of these principles in any given situation is complex. One of the aids which helps define the proper degree of control, however, is to utilize the cost-of-quality concept (see Chapter 19).

20.2 STATISTICAL QUALITY CONTROL

One of the cornerstones of quality control is the use of statistical methods to determine how much inspection to use. In many cases, a great deal can be saved by taking a sample rather than making a 100 percent inspection. In other cases, there is no alternative but to take a sample (e.g., destructive testing).

In using statistical methods, it is inferred from the sample whether or not the product conforms to specifications. This inference is made by inspecting the sample and deciding on that basis whether the entire output meets the quality standards. This process always involves the possibility of error, since sample information is being used to reach a decision.

Two types of errors can be made in statistical sampling, one being to accept the lot when it does not in fact meet the quality standards. This error occurs when the random sample happens to contain a low number of defective units even though there are many in the lot. The second type of error is to reject a lot which meets the quality standards. This error occurs when the random sample happens to contain a large number of defects even though the lot itself has only a few. Although these errors cannot be eliminated, they can be controlled at any desired level of accuracy by proper selection of a sampling plan.

Two distinct types of statistical methods are available: acceptance sampling and process control. Acceptance sampling applies to lot inspection where a decision to accept or reject a lot of material is made on the basis of a random sample drawn from the lot. This type of inspection is frequently used for incoming raw materials or for finished goods prior to shipment.

Process-control sampling is used during production while the product is being made. The decision in this case is whether to continue the process or to stop production and look for an assignable cause of defects, which may stem from the materials, the operator, or the machine. This decision is based on periodic random samples taken from the process. Once a process is brought under statistical control, it should remain there unless an assignable cause is present. By monitoring the process through sampling, a constant state of control can be maintained.

These two types of statistical quality control are conceptually different. While

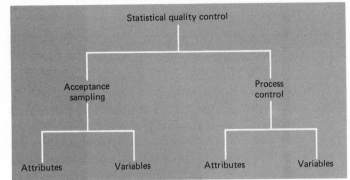

**Figure 20.3
Statistical quality
control methods.**

acceptance sampling is done either before or after production, process control is done during production. These methods are not mutually exclusive; they may both be used as part of a system of quality control at different points in the process.

Each of the two quality control methods can be used with either measurement of attributes or variables. This gives rise to four distinct cases, as shown in Figure 20.3. These four cases are important, since each one requires different statistical methods and formulas. The four cases also give rise to different sample sizes and different philosophies of control, as will be discussed in the remainder of the chapter.

20.3 ACCEPTANCE SAMPLING

Acceptance sampling is defined as taking one or more samples at random from a lot of items, inspecting each of the items in the sample(s), and deciding—on the basis of the inspection results—whether to accept or reject the entire lot. This type of inspection can be used by a customer to ensure that the supplier is meeting quality specifications or by the producer to ensure that quality standards are met prior to shipment. Acceptance sampling is used in preference to 100 percent inspection wherever the cost of inspection is high in relation to the cost of passing defective items to the customer—that is, in instances where it might be too costly to inspect the entire lot.

In the following discussion, we will restrict our attention to acceptance sampling by attributes. Thus, we assume that each item inspected is classified as good or defective on the basis of quality specifications or standards.

In single acceptance sampling, one sample is taken from a lot and the decision whether to accept or reject the lot is made after the sample is inspected. Formally, we let:

n = sample size
c = acceptance number
x = number of defective units found in the sample

For single sampling, the decision rule whether to accept or reject the lot after inspecting the sample is as follows:

If $x \leq c$, accept the lot

If $x > c$, reject the lot

As an example, suppose we have a lot of 10,000 items and we decide to take a random sample of 100 items ($n = 100$). We inspect the 100 items and find 3 defectives ($x = 3$). Assume the acceptance number in this case is two ($c = 2$). Therefore the lot of 10,000 items will be rejected, since the number of defective units in the sample exceeds the acceptance number ($x > c$).

Single sampling can be extended to double or multiple sampling by taking two or more separate samples. In this case, after the first sample, a decision is made whether to (a) accept the lot, (b) reject the lot, or (c) take a second sample. If the number of defectives in the sample is very low, the decision will be to accept the lot; if the number of defectives is very high, the decision will be to reject the lot; and if the number of defective units in the sample is in between, the decision will be to take another sample. Thus, very good lots or very bad lots will usually require only one sample, while lots of medium quality may require two or more samples to reach a decision.

Multiple sampling will usually result in a smaller total sample size than single sampling, sometimes only half as large. However, it might be difficult to take more than one sample, and multiple plans are slightly more complicated to understand. Despite these drawbacks, multiple sampling should be used whenever it is justified to obtain a reduction in sample size.

The performance of any sampling plan will depend on the quality of the items in the incoming lot or lots. If the incoming lots contain a low number of defectives, a high percentage of the lots will be accepted, which is the desired result. This occurs because the number of defectives in most samples is below the acceptance number. On the other hand, if the incoming lots contain a high number of defectives, a low percentage of lots will be accepted, which is also desirable. This occurs because most samples will have a high number of defectives and the lots will be rejected.

The precise relationship between the quality of the incoming lot or lots and the probability of accepting (P_a) any given lot is shown by the operating characteristic (OC) curve in Figure 20.4. The y axis of the OC curve represents the probability of accepting a lot (or the percentage of lots accepted for multiple lots), while the x axis shows the percentage of defective units in the incoming lot or lots. The OC curve thus shows the performance of a given sampling plan for any hypothetical incoming lot quality.

While the OC curve can be used to describe the performance of a given sampling plan (specified n and c), it can also be used to help evaluate alternative sampling plans and to select the preferred plan. To do this, management must first specify acceptable error levels. As described above, there are two types of errors: rejecting a lot which is considered to be of good quality (type I) and accepting a lot which is considered to be bad quality (type II). These errors can be specified quantitatively by selecting an acceptable quality level (AQL) and a lot tolerance percent defective (LTPD).

When incoming lots have a fraction defective less than or equal to AQL, they

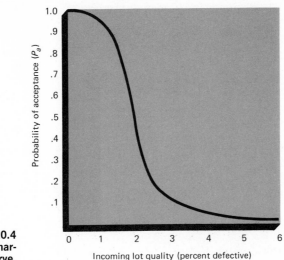

**Figure 20.4
Operating characteristic curve.**

should be accepted. Any lot with incoming quality less than or equal to AQL which is rejected by the sampling procedure is considered a type I error. This error is specified by the symbol α and is considered the producer's risk, since a good lot is rejected. Thus, we have:

α = probability (reject a lot when fraction defective = AQL)

When lots have a fraction defective equal to or greater than LTPD, they should be rejected. Accepting a lot with quality $\geq$ LTPD constitutes a type II error, which is considered the consumer's risk, since a lot of bad quality is accepted. The probability of a type II error is specified by the symbol β and defined as follows:

β = probability (accept a lot when fraction defective = LTPD)

The two pairs α, AQL and β, LTPD specify two points on the OC curve, as shown in Figure 20.5. When these two points are specified, they completely determine the entire OC curve as well as the required values of n and c. The two points on the OC curve thus specify a particular sampling plan. By controlling the specification of these two error points, management will control the plan selected and the associated sampling costs.

Management should select the values of α, AQL and β, LTPD on the basis of the economics of the situation. If the cost of rejecting a good lot (with quality $\leq$ AQL) is high, then a low value of α should be selected to control the type I error. Similarly, if the cost of accepting a bad lot is high, then a low value of β should be selected to control the type II error. Whether these costs incurred by sampling are considered subjectively or mathematically, management should take them into account in selecting the α, AQL and β, LTPD parameters for a sampling plan.

A nomograph for calculating the values of n and c from the error probability pairs α, AQL and β, LTPD is given in Figure 20.6. This nomograph is based on the

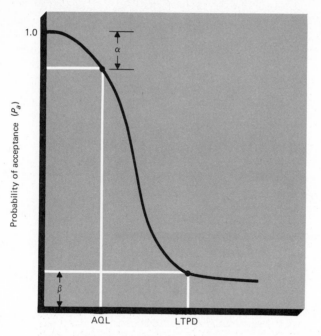

Figure 20.5 Error specifications.

binomial probability distribution and provides a convenient method of computation. An example of these computations is given in Box 20.2.

The nomograph in Figure 20.6 can also be used in reverse to calculate the OC curve or type I and II errors for any given sampling plan values of n and c. This particular computation is shown in Box 20.3. (See also Figure 20.7.)

OC curves also help the manager visualize how the performance of a sampling plan changes as the values of n and c are changed. In Figure 20.8a, OC curves are shown for various values of n, holding c constant. As n increases, the OC curve moves to the left and becomes more rectangular. When n equals the lot size (100 percent inspection), the OC curve is a vertical line through AQL; all lots with qual-

BOX 20.2   **COMPUTATION OF A SAMPLING PLAN FROM SPECIFIED ERROR PROBABILITIES**

The ABC hardware store has just received a shipment of 1000 wrenches. If the AQL is 20 defective items in the shipment (2 percent) and the LTPD is 8 percent, find a sampling plan (n and c) which will provide a type I error of .05 and a type II error of .10.

Using the nomograph in Figure 20.6, find the lot proportion defective for AQL = .02 on the left-hand scale and the probability of acceptance $1 - \alpha = .95$ on the right-hand scale. Connect these two points with a straight line, as illustrated in the inset in Figure 20.6. Next, locate the value of LTPD = .08 on the left-hand scale and $\beta = .10$ on the right-hand scale, also illustrated in the inset. Connect these two points with a second straight line. Where the two lines intersect on the nomograph, read off the values of n and c. In this case, $n = 96$ and $c = 4$. The hardware store should inspect 96 wrenches and accept the entire lot if the number of defective units in the sample is less than or equal to 4.

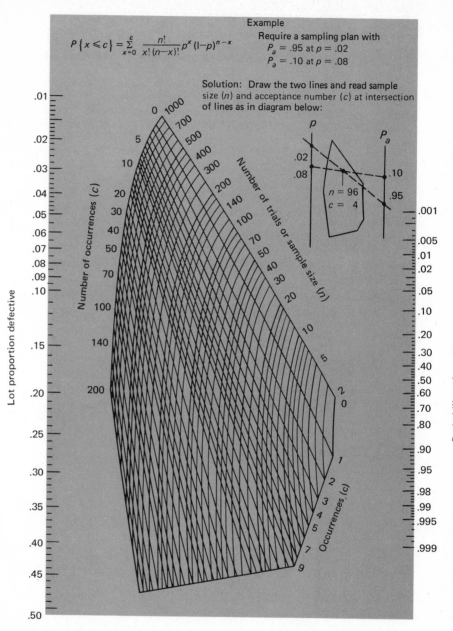

**Figure 20.6
Nomograph of the
cumulative bi-
nomial distribu-
tion.**

*(Source: Adapted from
Harry R. Larson,
"A Nomograph of the
Cumulative Binomial
Distribution," Western
Electric Engineer, April
1965.)*

BOX 20.3 **COMPUTATION OF AN OC CURVE FOR A GIVEN PLAN**

Suppose the ABC hardware store decides to tighten up the inspection plan computed in Box 20.2 by making $c = 2$ while holding $n = 96$. What are the associated values of the OC curve for this revised plan? To compute the OC curve, locate the point $n = 96$, $c = 2$ on the nomograph. Pivot a ruler around this point and read off successive pairs of values from the left-hand and right-hand scales. For example, when the lot proportion defective $p = .01$ on the left-hand scale, we have probability of acceptance $P_a = .93$ on the right-hand scale. A table of pairs of values is then as follows:

p	.01	.02	.03	.04	.05	.06	.07	.08	.09	.10
Pa	.93	.72	.48	.28	.16	.08	.04	.02	.01	.004

This OC curve is plotted in Figure 20.7. By comparison with Box 20.2, notice at $p = AQL = .02$ the type I error has been increased by tightening the plan to $1 - P_a = .28$. At the same time, the type II error at $p = .08$ has been reduced to $P_a = .02$.

ity less than or equal to AQL are accepted with probability = 1, and all lots with quality greater than AQL are rejected with probability = 1. Inspection of the entire lot is the case of perfect information where no statistical errors are made and the costs of errors are assumed to be infinite.

Similarly in Figure 20.8*b* a series of OC curves is shown for constant n and various values of c. As c is reduced, the OC curve moves to the left and the sampling plan becomes "tighter." Reducing c or increasing n has a similar effect; both tend to tighten the inspection plan, thereby decreasing both type I and type II errors.

In industry a widely accepted basis for selecting an acceptance sampling plan for

Figure 20.7
OC curve for
Box 20.3.

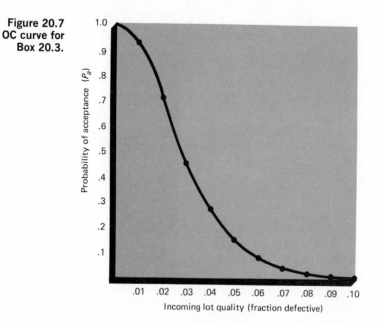

Incoming lot quality (fraction defective)

TABLE 20.2   USE OF QC TECHNIQUES BY INDUSTRY

Technique	S_1	S_2	S_3	S_4	S_5	All
			Firm size			
Percentage of firms using the listed acceptance sampling technique						
Single sample fraction defective with specified AQL and LTPD	43	76	77	70	89	72
Double sample fraction defective with specified AQL and LTPD	26	29	23	37	22	28
Multiple sample fraction defective with specified AQL and LTPD	22	16	7	25	19	18
Dodge/Romig AOQL	4	10	10	20	22	16
Dodge/Romig LTPD	9	8	7	14	15	10
Item-by-item sequential sampling	9	16	20	10	15	13
Group sequential sampling	0	11	13	10	11	9
Defects-per-unit sampling	30	24	17	23	15	19
Continuous sampling plans	30	53	47	47	55	48
Military standards						
MIL-STD-105D	65	87	73	71	82	76
MIL-STD-414	4	13	3	22	26	15
MIL-STD-1235 (Ord)	0	8	7	8	15	8
Percentage of firms using the listed control chart technique						
x chart (mean/average)	69	66	77	78	70	71
R chart (range)	56	61	67	71	67	64
chart (standard deviation)	35	40	67	53	70	51
p chart (proportion)	13	47	43	61	67	48
c chart (number of defects)	35	53	39	43	59	45
chart (defects per unit)	17	24	20	18	44	22
CUSUM chart (cumulative sum)	4	13	17	10	11	11
T^2 chart (multivariate average)	0	3	0	2	4	2
Moving average chart	13	31	27	35	44	32
Moving range chart	4	11	13	18	22	15
Test for runs	13	21	7	18	19	16
Median chart	9	13	10	6	26	12
Midrange chart	4	13	0	2	4	5
Geometric moving average	13	3	0	6	4	4
Lot plot method	0	16	2	12	11	9

Source: Erwin M. Saniga and Larry E. Shirland, "Quality Control in Practice—A Survey," *Quality Progress,* May 1977, p. 31.

Note: S_i in the table heading refers to firm size from small (S_1) to large (S_5).

The survey further discovered that the most widely reported problem was the lack of familiarity of quality control methods by people not directly involved in the quality function. Apparently, this problem is more difficult to solve than the technical problems associated with quality control methods. On the basis of this study, it would seem that the most important issue facing industry today is to teach people outside the quality control function about quality control procedures.

The survey indicates that quality control methods are widely used in manufacturing companies. While a few service companies also responded to the survey, the sample was not large enough to be conclusive for services. It is well known, however, that service organizations do not use quality control principles and methods to the same degree as manufacturing companies.

Industry has responded to quality control needs by computerizing the calculation of control charts, acceptance plans, and inspection itself. Evinrude, for example, has a computerized method for producing the control charts used in its manufacture of outboard motors. Figure 20.11 shows an $\bar{x}$ and R control chart produced by Evinrude's Wang computer. In addition to calculating the control limits for the charts, the computer performs statistical tests to determine the validity of the control chart assumptions. The computer also provides advantages in ensuring uniformity of data and correct calculations provided that the data input is correct.

Industry is beginning to use computers for voice input of inspection data; that is, the inspector reads the measurements being taken directly into the computer. The

Figure 20.11 Computer generated control charts.

(Source: Ronald J. Jensen, "Evinrude's Computerized Quality Control Productivity," Quality Progress, September 1977, p. 13.)

EVINRUDE MOTORS
PROCESS RELIABILITY CHART

PART NO. 606461
CHART NO. 1
DATE: 10/29/75

PART NAME: LAWNBOY CRANKSHAFT   MACHINE: 2919   ANALYST: JOEL D. TAFF   SPEC LIMITS: .8737/.8742 IN.

OPERATION: FINISH JOURNAL GRIND   MATERIAL: 86B17   INSPECTOR: J. CAMERON   UNIT OF MEASURE: .00001 IN.

OPERATOR: AUTOMATIC   CYCLE TIME: AUTOMATIC   GAGE: FEDERAL DIGITAL   ZERO EQUALS: .87 IN.

STD CONTROL CHART: SLOPE NOT SIGNIFICANT   FOR SLOPE, t(cr) = 1.96   t = 1.6427   STD DEV, R/d2 = 5.99
AVERAGE RANGE = 13.93   GRAND AVERAGE = 387.54   PROCESS CAPABILITY = 35.94
UCLR = 29.47   UCLX = 395.58
LCLX = 379.5

1	2	3	4	5	6	7	8	9	10	11	12	13	14	15	16	17	18	19	20	21	22	23	24	25
383	383	390	381	382	384	385	382	383	382	388	379	389	388	382	380	385	384	383	385	394	395	385	386	383
387	394	382	387	380	391	388	389	387	377	388	386	384	383	385	381	388	388	393	393	380	387	409	393	391
389	382	378	381	405	388	382	375	389	397	388	396	385	389	390	383	387	404	393	396	396	385	400	393	385
395	380	383	380	385	395	380	386	394	380	387	386	387	386	386	382	390	388	386	404	377	399	384	391	388
397	381	382	383	396	386	396	387	383	393	394	389	388	381	383	387	397	385	384	388	384	385	384	380	387
390.2	384.0	383.0	382.4	389.6	388.8	386.2	383.8	387.2	385.8	389.0	387.2	386.6	385.4	385.2	382.6	389.4	389.8	387.8	393.2	386.2	390.2	392.4	389.6	386.8
14	14	12	7	25	11	16	14	11	20	7	17	5	8	8	7	12	20	10	19	19	14	25	18	8
1	2	3	4	5	6	7	8	9	10	11	12	13	14	15	16	17	18	19	20	21	22	23	24	25

AVERAGES

RANGES

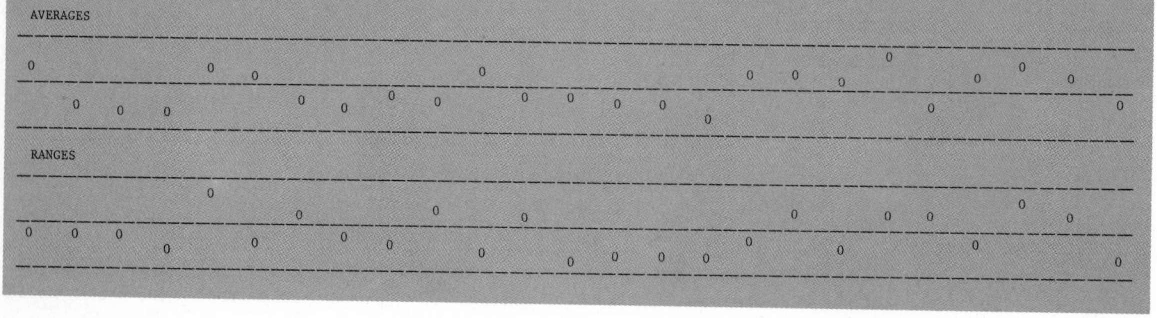

computer then compares the measurements to standards and may even prompt the operator on what to do next. An example of the use of "no-hands inspection" through voice input is the television faceplate inspection at Owens-Illinois Corp. [Belle (1977), pp. 34–35]:

> This application requires a complex series of 53 inspection steps, taking dimensional measurements. The inspections are a complex sequence of measurements requiring the inspector to use both hands to move the faceplate and use the gages. As the inspector collects the different faceplate samples to be inspected, his supervisor enters, via a central teleprinter, the type of faceplate to be inspected, the inspector's employee number, shift, date and time. This information is used for the heading on a final summary inspection report printed at the conclusion of the inspection operation.
>
> The system prompts the inspector through the sequence and indicates the measurement to be taken and the nominal value in the sample currently being inspected. As each dimensional entry is entered by voice and verified visually, it is compared by the computer to the predetermined standards. If a particular measurement is outside acceptable limits, an audio/visual indication of the unacceptable condition is provided so the inspector can alert the proper people of that situation.

The inspector working with a color-TV faceplate must use both hands to manipulate, orient, and measure the item being inspected. In such cases, computer-assisted inspection can improve productivity by a factor of 2 while also improving the accuracy of inspection results and the quality of inspection records.

Quality control in the service industries has lagged behind that in manufacturing for several reasons. First, services are more difficult to measure because they are intangible, while the characteristics of a manufactured product can be measured and specified. For example, steel can be measured by its strength, hardness, ductility, and other properties. The quality of a service is related to intangibles such as atmosphere in a restaurant, the waiter's smile, and the customer's sense of well-being. Nevertheless, quality cannot be controlled unless it is measured. Therefore it is imperative that the service industries measure what they can and develop new, innovative measurement techniques for the "intangible" services.

Juran (1974) has identified three aspects of service quality which should be measured: timeliness, consumer well-being, and continuity of service. "Timeliness" refers to the time from the customer's initiation of an order to its satisfactory delivery. The total time may be broken into components, each of which can be measured and managed independently. Consumer well-being refers to atmosphere, feeling of importance, safety, courtesy, and so on. These dimensions of service can generally be measured only by customer perceptions. To assess them, it is necessary to contact a sample of customers and ask for their evaluation of quality. Continuity of service is especially important for suppliers of services such as electricity, water, and transportation. Continuity can be measured in a similar way as reliability.

Another problem in managing quality of services is the perishability of the product, which requires that quality be controlled while the service is being delivered. As a result, a greater burden for service quality is placed on the work force, and the customer is immediately aware of it when bad quality is being delivered. Thus, service organizations should emphasize selection of the proper employees, specification of procedures whenever possible, and work-force training.

20.6 KEY POINTS

This chapter's key points include the following:

- Quality control is defined as the conformance to given product or service specifications. Quality of conformance is achieved through the design of a quality control system. This system design should specify *where* inspection takes place, *what* type of measurements are used, *how much* inspection is done, and *who* does the inspecting.
- Inspection should be considered for the inputs, as part of the process, and for the outputs. The critical control points for inspection are best described by a flowchart of the process. As a general rule, inspection is done when the expected cost of processing defective units further through the production process exceeds the cost of inspection.
- Statistical quality control can be based on acceptance sampling or process control. With either of these approaches, measurement may be by attributes or by variables.
- In acceptance sampling, one or more samples is taken from a lot of items. If the quality measurement in the sample is found acceptable, the entire lot is accepted; otherwise the lot is rejected or another sample is selected before a decision is made.
- In acceptance sampling, there are two types of errors: rejecting a good lot and accepting a bad lot. These errors can be controlled to any desired level by selecting a proper sample size and acceptance number.
- In process quality control, periodic samples are taken from a continuous production process. As long as the sample measurements fall within the control limits, production is continued. When the sample measurements fall outside the control limits, the process is stopped and a search is made for an assignable cause—operator, machine, or material. With this procedure, a production process is maintained in a continual state of statistical control.
- In industry a high percentage of manufacturing companies use both acceptance sampling and process quality control. The use of these statistical methods has much less acceptance in the service industries.

QUESTIONS

1. Why did statistical quality control ideas catch on in the 1940s?
2. Suppose you make electronic calculators which contain a chip purchased from a local vendor. How would you decide how much inspection to perform on the chips supplied to you?

3. Draw a process flowchart for the student registration system at your college. Identify all the current inspection points on the chart. Does the registration system use proper quality control checkpoints?

4. For the following situations, comment on whether inspection by variables or by attributes might be more appropriate.
   a. Filling feed bags to the proper weight
   b. Inspection for defects in yard goods
   c. Inspection of appliances for surface imperfections
   d. Determining the sugar content of candy bars

5. It has been said that workers should be given more control over the inspection of their own work. Discuss the pros and cons of this proposition.

6. Is it possible to eliminate both type I and type II errors? How?

7. Contrast and compare acceptance sampling and process quality control.

8. Describe the main use of an OC chart.

9. Define type I and type II errors.

10. Your boss has suggested that the sample size on an acceptance sampling plan be increased. What will this do to the OC curve?

11. Why is it that most processes are not in statistical control when they are first sampled for control chart purposes?

12. It has been suggested that a sample of six items be taken four times a day to control a particular process. How would you go about evaluating this suggestion?

PROBLEMS

1. In manufacturing a small part, your customer has decided to institute an acceptance sampling plan. She will take a sample of size 100 and accept the lot if 3 or less defective units are found. Calculate the OC curve for this plan. What is your risk as consumer when the lot quality is 8 percent defective?

2. What happens in Problem 1 when n and c are changed as follows:
   a. $n = 300, c = 3$
   b. $n = 100, c = 1$

3. Suppose you are the auditor for a bank operation. You have decided to consider error rates acceptable when there is one error or less in 100 days. You want to clear the bank (accept their procedures) with 95 percent confidence when the error rate is this low. On the other hand, if the error rate climbs to five per 100 days or more, you want to reject the bank's procedure with 90 percent probability. How many days of the bank's books should be audited? How many days can you find the bank in error and still pass it on the audit?

4. Given AQL = .01, $\alpha = .08$, LTPD = .06, and $\beta = .10$, find n and c.

5. An acceptance sampling plan has $n = 200$ and $c = 3$. What is the type I error at AQL = .01?

6. We have taken 12 samples of 100 letters each from a typing pool and have found the following percentages of defective letters: .01, .02, .02, .00, .01, .03, .02, .01, .00, .04, .03, and .02. A letter is considered defective when one or more errors is detected.
   a. Calculate the control limits for a p control chart.
   b. A sample of 100 letters has just been taken and 6 letters were found to be defective. Is the process still in control?

7. In a control chart application, we have found that the grand average over all past samples of size 5 is $\bar{\bar{x}} = 30$ and $\bar{R} = 5$.
   a. Set up a control chart for this application.
   b. The following measurements are taken: 38, 35, 27, 30, and 32. Is the process still in control?

SELECTED BIBLIOGRAPHY

BELLE, PEINOLD T.: "Quality Control through Voice Data Entry," *Quality Process,* June 1977, pp. 34–36.

DUNCAN, ACHESON J.: *Quality Control and Industrial Statistics,* 4th ed., Homewood, Ill.: Irwin, 1974.

FALVO, VINCENT A.: "A Computerized Vendor Rating System," *Quality Progress,* June 1977, pp. 20–23.

JENSEN, RONALD J.: "Evinrude's Computerized Quality Control Productivity," *Quality Progress,* September 1977, pp. 12–16.

JURAN, J. M., FRANK GRYNA, JR., and R. S. BINGHAM, JR. (eds.): *Quality Control Handbook,* 3d ed., New York: McGraw-Hill, 1974.

LARSON, HARRY R.: "A Nomograph of the Cumulative Binomial Distribution," *Western Electric Engineer,* April 1965.

SANIGA, ERWIN M., and LARRY E. SHIRLAND: "Quality Control in Practice—A Survey," *Quality Progress,* May 1977, pp. 30–33.

remainder of this chapter will describe how operations can be focused and thus become a vital basis for competing. See Box 21.1 for a typical strategic decision problem in operations.

21.1 OPERATIONS OBJECTIVES

Management's first step in focusing and integrating operations must be to recognize the different objectives and performance criteria applied to operations. Wheelwright (1978) has identified four different operations objectives: cost, quality, dependability, and flexibility.[2]

COST. The cost of operations includes both capital costs and annual operating costs. If the objective of operations is to minimize cost, a highly capital-intensive operation will be developed, with a resulting loss in flexibility to rapidly introduce new products. Equipment will be used as long as possible, and it will be inexpensively maintained. Minimum inventories will be held to facilitate efficient production but not to enhance customer service. Quality control will stress reduction of rework and scrap costs. Examples of operations which stress the cost objective are discount department stores, fast-food outlets, and commodity producers (e.g., milk, copper, steel).

QUALITY. "High quality" should be defined as quality which is significantly higher than that of the competition and high enough to command sales even in the face of higher prices. When quality is stressed in operations, emphasis is placed on both the quality of design and the quality of conformance. High-quality objectives may be reflected in operations, for example, by much attention to product design, a large number of inspectors, and intensive training of the work force. Examples of operations which pursue high quality as an objective are Hewlett-Packard calculators and Rolls Royce automobiles.

DEPENDABILITY. This objective refers to the ability of operations to meet customer delivery requirements consistently. In make-to-stock operations, dependability might be measured by a low level of stockouts. In make-to-order operations, dependability might be measured by meeting a high percentage of promised delivery dates. Dependability is ensured not only by a high stock of parts but also by an ability to manufacture additional products quickly.

FLEXIBILITY. In operations, flexibility means fast reaction to volume changes and new-product introduction. Flexibility can be assured by utilizing equipment and people which can rapidly adapt to new requirements. A flexible operation will probably operate at less than full capacity so that increased demand can be met rapidly. It will also have equipment and a work force which can be easily changed to introduce new products.

[2] These objectives, originally defined in Chapter 2, are described in more detail here.

TABLE 21.1   CURRENT AND REQUIRED PRIORITIES
As assessed by vice-presidents (VP)* and manufacturing managers (MM)*

	Cost		Quality		Dependability		Flexibility	
	VP	MM	VP	MM	VP	MM	VP	MM
Product 1								
As is	42	44	17	15	25	26	16	15
Should be	28	46	24	16	31	26	17	12
Needs more (less)	(14)	2	7	1	6	0	1	(3)
Product 2								
As is	26	20	37	43	24	22	13	15
Should be	26	30	36	38	26	20	12	12
Needs more (less)	0	10	(1)	(5)	2	(2)	(1)	(3)
Product 3								
As is	34	36	27	28	23	19	16	17
Should be	34	38	29	24	24	20	13	18
Needs more (less)	0	2	2	(4)	1	1	(3)	1
Product 4								
As is	24	34	30	22	19	17	27	27
Should be	39	44	20	25	23	15	18	16
Needs more (less)	15	10	(10)	3	4	(2)	(9)	(11)
Product 5 (Parts)								
As is	45	37	21	14	18	31	16	18
Should be	22	31	24	13	35	35	19	21
Needs more (less)	(23)	(6)	3	(1)	17	4	3	3

Source: Steven C. Wheelwright, "Reflecting Corporate Strategy in Manufacturing Decisions," *Business Horizons,* February 1978, p. 65.

* Criteria totals for VP and MM for each priority = 100.

It is often assumed that the primary objective of operations is to minimize costs. When the cost objective is pursued exclusively, however, there are corresponding losses in quality, dependability, and flexibility. An operation cannot simultaneously optimize all four dimensions of operations performance. Because of this, the role of corporate strategy is to guide the relative priority of the four objectives.

Wheelwright (1978) reports on an interesting experiment carried out in one company after a vice president returned from a seminar on operations strategy. When the vice president was, half jokingly, asked what he had learned, he decided to ask each of the other vice presidents in the company to rank the four objectives of operations for each of the five product lines in the company.

For each product line, a total of 100 points was allocated among the four objectives of operations, both for "as is" currently and for "should be." As might be expected, there was considerable diversity among the vice presidents. After a few meetings to resolve the differences, however, the priorities in Table 21.1 were agreed to.

As a result of this exercise, it was decided that:

Product 1 should have modest increases in quality and dependability at the expense of cost efficiencies.

Products 2 and 3 should have no significant changes.

Product 4 should have a significant improvement in cost at the expense of quality and flexibility.

Product 5 should have a significant increase in dependability at the expense of cost efficiencies.

In following up on these actions, the vice president of operations decided to survey his own middle managers in operations. As a result, he found that they stressed cost considerably more than the other objectives (see Table 21.1). Since the "should be" objectives were derived by the vice presidents of the corporation at the policy level, the vice president of operations proceeded to reorient operations for those products which were out of line with corporate objectives. The executives were pleased with this approach as a way to deal with conflicting objectives and to communicate to all concerned the proper focus for operations.

21.2 DECISION TRADEOFFS IN OPERATIONS

The view prevails that a good operation is one that achieves low cost along with high quality, high dependability, and high flexibility. According to popular folklore, this can be done by maintaining modern equipment, a good information system, satisfied workers, and professional operations managers. There is, however, no such thing as a universally good operation; in every operation, tradeoff decisions must be made in the face of the conflicting objectives described above.

Wickham Skinner (1969) has identified some of the key tradeoff decisions required in manufacturing in his classic article "Manufacturing—Missing Link in Corporate Strategy." These tradeoff decisions can easily be generalized to service operations, and they can conveniently be described by the five decision categories used in this textbook.

PROCESS. Some of the important tradeoffs faced in process design are whether to select a line, intermittent, or project process; whether to make or buy; whether to use general-purpose or special-purpose equipment; how much automation to provide; and what layout to use. All these decisions affect the four objectives in operations.

CAPACITY. Tradeoff decisions in this area include whether to have one large facility or several smaller facilities, whether to have a level work force or to chase demand, whether to have more capacity and less inventory, and whether to emphasize performance or time in managing project schedules.

INVENTORY. The classic tradeoff in inventory decisions is whether to have high ordering cost or high inventory holding cost. Other tradeoffs include whether to carry a large safety stock or accept lower customer service; whether to stress extensive MRP systems or simpler systems; and whether to provide many different inventory buffers or only a few. In the inventory area, the tradeoffs have been well defined and quantified by mathematical models.

WORK FORCE. Tradeoff decisions in this area include whether to design jobs for specialized or generalized skills, whether to use more supervision or less supervision, whether to use wage incentives or hourly pay, and whether to stress work measurement or not. Work-force decisions are highly interactive with all other decisions in operations and therefore require numerous tradeoffs.

QUALITY. In this decision area, examples of tradeoffs are whether to stress defect prevention or detection, whether to screen defects before shipment or to correct them in the field, whether to use a great deal of inspection or only a little, and whether to use process control or acceptance sampling.

As indicated by the above examples, there are a great many decisions in operations requiring tradeoffs. If low cost is the primary rationale for operations, one set of decisions will be made; if dependability is the primary objective, a different set will be selected. Thus, operations must be guided by a corporate strategy which specifies the priority among objectives and helps operations management develop a consistent set of tradeoff decisions.

21.3 THE POLICY DETERMINATION PROCESS IN OPERATIONS

The method of policy determination for operations which we have been discussing is summarized in Figure 21.1. The figure indicates that operations policy and strategy should be formulated from the top down, beginning with a corporate strategy. This strategy should help define the appropriate degree of emphasis among the four operations objectives: cost, quality, dependability, and flexibility. And these objectives, in turn, should guide all the tradeoff decisions made in operations. Through this approach, a focused operation will be developed which is well coordinated within operations and also integrated with the other business functions.

This approach should be contrasted with the more traditional one followed in operations. Using the traditional approach, operations seems to evolve over time as various decisions are made which are not always coordinated with one another. Often the implicit objective underlying these decisions is cost. As new products are added and new process technologies are developed, the operations function becomes unfocused. A consistent rationale to guide all activities and decisions does not exist.

This problem is compounded by the variety of staff specialties in operations. The quality control people tend to develop the "best" quality control system. The production and inventory control people try to develop the "best" system in their area. The engineers try to develop the "best" technology, and so on. As a result, a great deal of suboptimization occurs, where each function is defined by the various specialists but there is no coordinated whole. It is the responsibility of the operations manager to set overall policy for operations to ensure coordination of the various specialties.

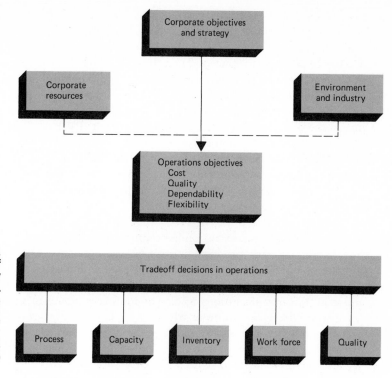

**Figure 21.1
The process of
operations policy
determination.**

*(Source: Adapted from
Steven C. Wheelwright,
"Reflecting Corporate
Strategy in Manufactur-
ing Decisions," Business
Horizons, February
1978.)*

This top-down approach to operations policy stands in contrast to Frederick Taylor's scientific management approach and to traditional industrial engineering. The primary objective in Taylor's approach was cost-efficiency. This objective was achieved through increasing automation and job specialization, which often limited flexibility, quality, or dependability objectives. In other words, operations were designed from the bottom up without attention to corporate objectives or consideration of the inherent tradeoffs in operations objectives. As a result, operations were ultimately less efficient than they were thought to be. The bottom-up approach will inevitably result in suboptimization and will not provide a competitive, well-focused operation. When operations is viewed from the top down, it will no longer be merely the producer of the companies' products or services at the lowest cost but a means of competing in the marketplace.

21.4 FOCUSED OPERATIONS

The primary advantage of a top-down approach to operations policy making is that it helps focus operations to achieve a coordinated set of policies. Wickham Skinner, who developed this approach for manufacturing companies, has called this a focused factory. He tells the story of an electronic instrument company that made fuel gauges and automatic-pilot instruments in the same plant. [Skinner (1978), p. 60.]

After years of failure to make a profit on fuel gauges, the company was ready to sell off that portion of the business. As a last resort, the plant manager decided instead to build a wall around the fuel-gauge production facilities and manage them separately. As a result, the equipment and process technology was segregated, production and inventory control was handled separately, the fuel gauge operation had its own quality control function, and work-force policies were separated to some extent. After 4 months, the fuel-gauge business had become profitable, apparently due to the development of a plant within a plant (PWP).

The explanation for this result is that the autopilot production requirements had been imposing more stringent quality control policies, a different type of production and inventory control system, and work-force policies which were not appropriate to both types of production. As a result the production of the fuel gauges was excessively costly. This story indicates how incompatible product lines within the same plant can reduce effectiveness.

The rationale for production has traditionally been economies of scale. Through the addition of more products, it is supposedly possible to spread fixed costs over more units and to achieve production efficiencies. While this strategy works in some cases, it does not work in others, because additional products increase complexity and may unfocus operations to the point where economies are lost. Traditional economies of scale do not occur when management adds staff to coordinate the additional complexity imposed by more products in the same facility. The economies in direct labor are then more than offset by the diseconomies in indirect labor. Skinner argues that some plants have been made too large and complex under the banner of economies of scale. In these cases, the plant should be divided and focused on a specific product or product group which demands a consistent set of manufacturing tasks. Each smaller plant or PWP could then concentrate on the particular set of cost, quality, dependability, and flexibility objectives which are most appropriate to it. Thus the plants would once again become weapons of corporate strategy rather than attempting to be "all things to all people."

Marketing managers clearly understand the problem of focus. Market segmentation is aimed at finding that part of the market in which the corporation can compete. In a similar way, operations should find that set of policies which implement the corporate strategy and focus the efforts of operations on a particular set of tasks which can be well done. This set of tasks has been called the "distinctive competence" of operations. It defines those operations activities which give the business a unique competitive advantage.

For years the distinctive competence of the Harvard Business School has been the case study method. This distinctive competence influenced all parts of operations: staffing, facilities, student admissions, etc. Faculty who were good at teaching and developing cases were selected and promoted. Special classrooms were developed to teach cases, and the curriculum was developed to help students analyze them. The Harvard Business School is a good example of the "focused factory" concept.

In general, there is an astounding lack of focused operations in practice. The principal reasons for this lack of focus appear to be:

1. The rise in professional staff within each profession (quality, accounting, engineering, production, inventory control, etc.) pursuing its own set of internal standards. Professionals need to be guided by general management toward a consistent set of operations objectives.
2. The addition of more and more products to existing facilities in the name of economies of scale. This futile attempt to reduce costs has unfocused operations and made the operation less competitive.
3. Failure to define the distinctive competence of the operation. As a result, various elements of operations develop in an uncoordinated way over time and the inconsistencies are often never recognized.
4. A change of focus in operations while most staff and service departments continue to serve prior goals.

In an attempt to avoid these problems, Skinner (1974) has identified how focused operations can be designed and managed from the top down. The four steps required are:

1. *Develop an explicit, brief statement of corporate objectives and strategy.* This statement should cover the next 3 to 5 years and it should be developed in cooperation with all functional managers, including operations, marketing, finance, and personnel. One such statement from a manufacturer of mechanical equipment says:

    "Our corporate objective is directed toward increasing market share during the next five years via a strategy of (1) tailoring our product to individual customer needs, (2) offering advanced and special product features at a modest price increment, and (3) gaining competitive advantage via rapid product development and service orientation to customers of all sizes."

2. *Translate the objectives-and-strategy statement into what this means to operations.* What must operations be able to do particularly well? What is its principal task and objective? Operations must, in short, determine its required focus. In the case of the equipment manufacturer, the primary task of operations was stated as follows:

    "Our manufacturing task for the next three years will be to introduce specialized, custom-tailored new products into production, with lead times that are substantially less than those of our competitors. Since the technology in our industry is changing rapidly, and since product reliability can be extremely serious for our customers, our most difficult problems will be to control the new product introduction process, so as to solve technical problems promptly and to maintain reliability amid rapid changes in the product itself."

3. *Carefully examine each element of the operations system for consistency with the stated policy.* What is the distinctive competence of operations at the present time? How is operations organized, staffed, equipped, and controlled in relation to the operations policy? How must operations be changed to meet the primary task and the policy?

TABLE 21.2   FOCUS FOR AN EQUIPMENT MANUFACTURER

Production system elements	Present approach (conventional factory)	Implicit manufacturing tasks of present approach	Changed approach (focused factory)
Equipment and process policies	One large plant, special-purpose equipment, high-volume tooling, balanced capacity with functional layout.	Low manufacturing costs on steady runs of a few large products with minimal investment	Separate old, standardized products and new customized products into two plants within a plant (PWP). For each new PWP, provide general-purpose equipment, temporary tooling, and modest excess capacity with product-oriented layout.
Work-force management policies	Specialized jobs with narrow job content, incentive wages, few supervisors, focus on volume of production per hour.	Low costs and efficiency	Create fewer jobs with more versatility. Pay for breadth of skills and ability to perform a variety of jobs. Provide more supervisors for solving technical problems at work place.
Production scheduling and control	Detailed, frequent sales forecasts; produce for inventory economic lot sizes of finished goods; small, decentralized production scheduling group.	Short delivery lead times.	Produce to order special parts and stock of common parts based on semiannual forecast. Staff production control to closely schedule and centralize parts movements.
Quality control	Control engineers and large inspection groups in each department.	Extremely reliable quality.	No change.
Organizational structure	Functional; production control under superintendents of each area; inspection reports to top.	Top performance of the objectives of each functional department (i.e., many tasks).	Organize each PWP by program and project in order to focus organizational effort on bringing new products into production smoothly and on time.

Source: Wickham Skinner, "The Focused Factory," *Harvard Business Review,* May–June 1974.

4. *Reorganize the structure of operations to provide a congruent focus.* The reorganization should coordinate all elements of operations to focus them on the primary task as defined.

The example of the equipment manufacturer is completed in Table 21.2. Notice how each element of operations was analyzed and changed as necessary to support the new focus. It is surprising how many elements had to be changed in this case in order to achieve consistency and focus.

At this point, some readers may be concerned that the focused operation will require a large investment in new facilities. In some cases, this may be true. In most cases, however, focus can be achieved by using the plant-within-a-plant concept. A large factory can be reorganized into a cluster of smaller PWPs. Each small plant has its own focus and is ideally suited to compete for its product or groups of products.

21.5   EXAMPLE

The following example illustrates the two main ideas presented in this chapter: a top-down approach to operations policy and a focused operation. The company, which manufactures specialized products in the Midwest, spent several months formulating a corporate strategy for 5 years into the future. The strategy called for dramatic changes in both marketing and manufacturing in order to move the division from a custom job shop toward a more standard product line with multiple customers for each product. As a result, marketing would have to turn toward developing markets instead of simply selling to each customer individually. In manufacturing, the corporate strategy required the following changes:

1.   Manufacturing was required to become more cost-conscious. Instead of simply passing all costs through to the customer, manufacturing had to begin to compete on a cost basis. This required more attention to manufacturing methods, process flows, standards, and cost-control programs. The industrial engineering function had to be expanded to help achieve these cost goals.
2.   The corporate strategy also implied that a first-rate materials-management system was needed in manufacturing. In making products to stock, finished-goods inventories would be accumulated for the first time. Manufacturing would also be exposed to competition on delivery lead time. As a result, production and inventory control had to be geared to replenishment of stock and strict control of delivery promises.
3.   Manufacturing eventually had to gain control of its own purchasing and quality functions. Initially, these functions were handled outside the division on a centralized corporate basis. As these functions became more critical to manufacturing objectives, the organizational structure itself had to be changed.
4.   It was determined that the corporate strategy required operations managers to become more professional in their approach to operations. As a result, all managers were encouraged to join local professional societies and to attend outside workshops. In some cases, outside personnel were hired where operations could not be strengthened from within.

In this case, the corporate strategy triggered a series of changes in operations objectives toward cost-consciousness and delivery performance. These changes, in turn, created a series of adjustments in systems, organization, personnel, and professionalism to focus operations on the required task.

21.6 KEY POINTS

This chapter discusses the integration of operations through policy and strategy. Its key points include the following:

- Operations is under conflicting pressures from marketing, finance, personnel, and top management. A corporate strategy is required to resolve these pressures and to direct operations toward corporate goals.
- Top management often takes a limited view of operations, expecting that operations policy and practices will follow automatically from marketing and financial strategy. Operations policy should be an integral part of the formulation of corporate strategy and not merely an afterthought.

- Operations objectives are cost, quality, dependability, and flexibility. The relative priority among these objectives should be derived from the corporate strategy.
- The implementation of a particular set of operations objectives requires a large number of tradeoff decisions. These tradeoff decisions should be made on a consistent basis to support the operations objectives.
- The process of determining an operations policy should work from the top down, beginning with corporate strategy, moving to operations objectives, and resulting in specific tradeoff decisions. If this process is properly used, the result will be a focused operation.
- The top-down approach to operations policy stands in contrast to traditional industrial engineering or the scientific method, which emphasizes cost efficiency. The top-down approach recognizes cost as only one objective among four and requires a corporate strategy to guide operations.
- In a focused operation, all aspects of operations—process, capacity inventory, work force, and quality—are focused on the primary task of operations. Focus is achieved by grouping product lines into separate facilities, trimming product lines, or organizing a "plant within a plant." In this way, each focused facility has a consistent set of cost, dependability, quality, and flexibility objectives.
- The causes of lack of focus in operations include a professional staff with their own internal standards and objectives, the addition of more products in the attempt to achieve economies of scale, a lack of operations leadership to define the primary task, and a gradual diffusion of focus in operations.

QUESTIONS

1. Describe the differences between a top-down and a bottom-up approach to operations policy and strategy.
2. Why is a top-down approach to operations strategy preferred?
3. Evaluate your local hospital in terms of its emphasis on the four operations objectives: cost, dependability, quality, and flexibility. Are all departments in the hospital focused on the same objectives?
4. What are the symptoms of an unfocused operation?
5. What kinds of tradeoff decisions are required in the operation of a grocery supermarket?
6. How would the decisions in Question 5 be made if the primary objective of operations were:
   a. Cost
   b. Quality
   c. Dependability
   d. Flexibility
7. What are the pros and cons of organizing a plant within a plant?
8. What prerequisites must be met prior to focusing operations?
9. Why are traditional scientific management and industrial engineering approaches inadequate as a basis for managing operations?
10. The president of a fast-food chain has asked you to look at his operation from the point of view of this chapter. How would you proceed to evaluate his operation?

SELECTED BIBLIOGRAPHY

ANSOFF, IGOR H., and JOHN M. STEWART: "Strategies for a Technology-Based Business," *Harvard Business Review,* November–December 1967, pp. 71–83.

BANKS, ROBERT L., and STEVEN WHEELWRIGHT: "Operations vs. Strategy: Trading Tomorrow for Today," *Harvard Business Review,* May–June 1979, pp. 112–120.

CHASE, RICHARD B.: "Where Does the Customer Fit in a Service Operation?" *Harvard Business Review,* November–December 1978, pp. 137–142.

HOBBS, JOHN M., and DONALD F. HEAVY: "Coupling Strategy to Operating Plans," *Harvard Business Review,* May–June 1971, pp. 119–126.

SHAPIRO, BENSON: "Can Marketing and Manufacturing Coexist?" *Harvard Business Review,* September–October 1977, pp. 104–114.

SKINNER, WICKHAM: "The Anachronistic Factory," *Harvard Business Review,* January–February 1971, pp. 61–70.

————: "The Focused Factory," *Harvard Business Review,* May–June 1974, pp. 113–121.

————: *Manufacturing in the Corporate Strategy,* New York: Wiley, 1978.

————: "Manufacturing—Missing Link in Corporate Strategy," *Harvard Business Review,* May–June 1969, pp. 136–145.

————: "Production under Pressure," *Harvard Business Review,* November–December 1966, pp. 139–146.

WHEELWRIGHT, STEVEN C.: "Manufacturing Strategy and Plant Focus: A Review of the Literature," working paper HBS 79-1, Cambridge, Mass.: Harvard Business School, 1979.

————: "Reflecting Corporate Strategy in Manufacturing Decisions, *Business Horizons,* February 1978, pp. 57–66.

PART VIII
CASE STUDIES

The case studies in Part VIII are designed to provide practice in both the formulation and solution of problems. Although the cases require an understanding of the techniques and concepts covered in the text, they also require the application of common sense and integration of the material from the various chapters. None of the cases is simply a straightforward application of the techniques from the text. Creativity and the extension of concepts are needed.

All the cases are based on real business problems. In some instances the problems have been simplified or "pared down" to make them more manageable. The names of the companies and individuals have also been disguised in some of the cases. Nevertheless, the problems and situations are real.

The cases are organized according to the major divisions of the text. The appropriate chapters and material in each part should be covered prior to studying each particular case.

INTRODUCTION
>   FHE, Inc.
>   Merriwell Bag Company

PROCESS DESIGN
>   Benihana of Tokyo
>   Eastern Gear, Inc.
>   First City National Bank

CAPACITY PLANNING AND SCHEDULING
>   Commonwealth Ice Cream Company
>   Lawn King, Inc.
>   World Industrial Abrasives

INVENTORY MANAGEMENT
>   Slayton's Furniture Store
>   Consolidated Electric
>   Hot Line, Incorporated

WORK-FORCE MANAGEMENT
>   Southwestern University
>   Donaldson Company
>   Minnesota Diversified Industries

QUALITY PLANNING AND CONTROL
>   General Appliance Company
>   Bayfield Mud Company

INTEGRATION OF OPERATIONS
>   Sheldhal

FHE, INC.

In April 1978, Lum Donaldson, product development engineering manager at FHE, Inc., was reviewing the process his company used to introduce new products.[1] Mr. Donaldson was responsible for the technical direction of all new-product development and revisions of existing products. He wondered whether the procedures, organization, and project-control systems used at FHE might be improved to make new-product introductions go more smoothly.

FHE is a manufacturer of pumps and related fluid-handling equipment. The company supplies products used to transfer liquids of all types including paint, adhesives, and food products. The pumps supplied by the company are used by the automobile and appliance industries, in vehicle servicing, in home construction, and in other ways. In 1978, sales were $105,200,000 and profit after tax was $5,470,000. Over the last 5 years the company has been improving both sales and profits through aggressive new-product introductions.

ORGANIZATION

The organization of the engineering and marketing departments at FHE is shown in Exhibit 1. Phil Thomas, the vice president of corporate development and marketing, has responsibility for both marketing and design engineering functions in the company. This arrangement is intended to facilitate cooperation between marketing and engineering, particularly on new-product introductions.

On the engineering side of the organization, three technical program managers (TPMs) report to Mr. Donaldson. These program managers are generally responsible for the technical direction of the projects assigned to them. Detailed responsibilities of the TPM are shown in Exhibit 2.

On the marketing side of the organization, three product managers report to Vince Kramer, the United States marketing manager. These product managers are generally responsible for developing new-product ideas and managing the business impact of new products. Detailed responsibilities of the product manager are shown in Exhibit 3.

A great deal of coordination is required between the product managers in marketing and the TPMs in engineering to successfully introduce a new product. When development problems arise, it is not always clear who has the primary responsibility for resolving them. As a result, product managers and TPMs must work closely together during the development process.

NEW-PRODUCT DEVELOPMENT PROCESS

The new-product development process begins with a formal marketing request which specifies in general terms the type of product needed and the market it will serve. As a result of the marketing request, a concept conference is conducted between marketing and engineering to determine whether to proceed, and if so, how. If the decision is made to proceed, a *Technical Specification Action Report* (TSAR) is prepared by engineering.

[1] This case was prepared as a basis for class discussion, not to illustrate either effective or ineffective handling of an administrative situation.

583

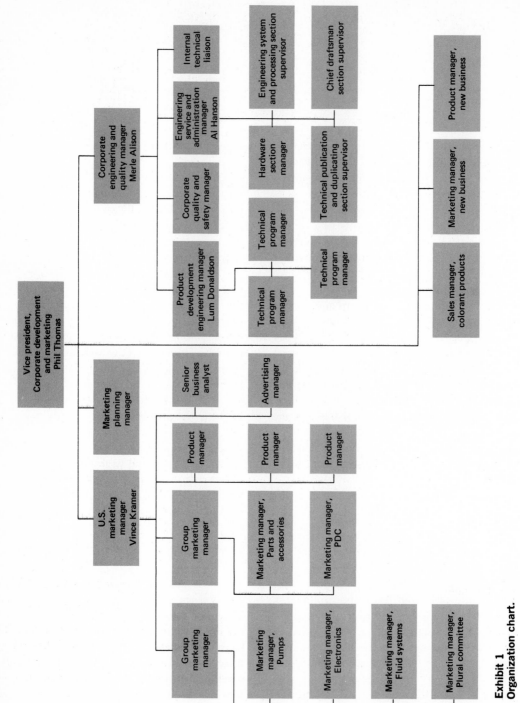

Exhibit 1
Organization chart.

TECHNICAL PROGRAM MANAGER—NEW PRODUCT DEVELOPMENT

General Summary Statement

The technical program manager—new product department reports to the manager
of product engineering and is responsible for planning, coordinating, and
directing the activities of projects in the program area(s) assigned to him or her.
(A "program area" is composed of one or more projects related to a particular
product application area, such as sanitary, plural components, and hydraulics.)
The technical program manager—new product department is responsible for personnel
assignments and the administration and control of all design personnel reporting to
him or her.

Typical Duties and Responsibilities

1. Assigns technical staff to maintain development schedules for all projects
    within his or her areas of program responsibility. Maintains the communication
    between development sections to ensure usage of critical skills and keep
    the state-of-the-art awareness with all personnel assigned.

2. Directs the design activities of a specific program area or areas to
    develop the design, select materials, prepare technical descriptions,
    conduct tests, meet performance, schedule, and cost objectives; is
    responsible for the program costs and status and presents timely reports
    and technical conclusions when directed; communicates with product managers,
    development engineers, and other design personnel, and maintains technical
    project files.

3. Coordinates with product management in defining technical customer
    specifications of currently planned product and product which is
    contemplated for future effort.

4. Reviews and directs the detail analysis prepared by development engineers,
    and is responsible for testing programs to ensure overall product design
    conformance to specifications. Reviews all cost inputs and directs
    completion of cost estimates.

5. Interfaces with all departments of company to coordinate product design
    completion; negotiates work schedules with hardware and software groups,
    purchasing, etc.

6. Identifies technical problem areas which will result in altered time, cost
    and/or performance schedules; defining alternative courses of action to
    meet same; and/or making visible to management these problems so that
    proper corrective management action can be taken.

7. Maintains continuing contact with product management, manufacturing, fluid
    systems, etc., where appropriate in obtaining the best technical solutions
    to the problems associated with his or her program area and in ensuring that
    product resulting from his team's efforts can be economically produced.

Exhibit 2
Position description

The TSAR contains a great deal of detail on development costs, product costs, schedules, and product technical specifications. If the TSAR is approved, the project is formally authorized and engineering development begins. The project then proceeds through a series of steps, as summarized in Exhibit 4 for a typical project. These steps include actual design of the physical product, major design reviews, testing, and finally release to production if the product is successfully developed.

Although the new-product development

<u>PRODUCT MANAGER RESPONSIBILITY PROFILE</u>

A product manager's basic responsibility is to the development of new products and to ensuring that the entire product line is properly servicing the needs of the marketplace. The product manager would generally have a strong technical background and a working knowledge of marketing concepts. He or she must possess leadership qualities in that the tasks to be accomplished are through others over whom the product manager has no direct control.

<u>MAJOR DUTIES</u>

I. New Product

    A. Develop product strategies that are in support of corporate objectives.

    B. Coordinate project definition.

        1. Evaluate the content of new product proposals (the product specification) and programs, responding to market opportunities identified by U.S., Eurafrica, and regional international marketing groups.

        2. Evaluate the content of the technical specification and the project schedule assuring conformity with the product specification and market timing requirements.

        3. Evaluate anticipated project costs.

        4. Analyze anticipated profitability of proposed programs (ROI).

        5. Generate the project authorization.

    C. Monitor project activity and take action where necessary to ensure integrity of project.

    D. Insure vendor quality.

    E. Ensure the coordination of all technical resources related to new product development and introduction; to include engineering, manufacturing, marketing and service.

Exhibit 3
Job description.

process is well defined at FHE, Mr. Donaldson has several reservations about its operation. First he continually encounters problems in coordinating the technical program managers and the product managers. Perhaps the division of responsibility is not as clear as it might be. He is also concerned about the fluctuating workload in the engineering services department.

ENGINEERING SERVICES

The engineering services department, managed by Al Hanson, includes drafting services, the model shop, testing facilities, and technical documentation services. Because all projects use these services, the workload for engineering services is unpredictable and bottlenecks frequently oc-

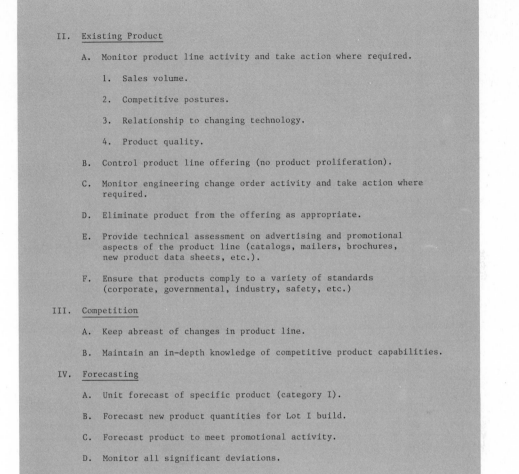

II. Existing Product

    A. Monitor product line activity and take action where required.

        1. Sales volume.

        2. Competitive postures.

        3. Relationship to changing technology.

        4. Product quality.

    B. Control product line offering (no product proliferation).

    C. Monitor engineering change order activity and take action where required.

    D. Eliminate product from the offering as appropriate.

    E. Provide technical assessment on advertising and promotional aspects of the product line (catalogs, mailers, brochures, new product data sheets, etc.).

    F. Ensure that products comply to a variety of standards (corporate, governmental, industry, safety, etc.)

III. Competition

    A. Keep abreast of changes in product line.

    B. Maintain an in-depth knowledge of competitive product capabilities.

IV. Forecasting

    A. Unit forecast of specific product (category I).

    B. Forecast new product quantities for Lot I build.

    C. Forecast product to meet promotional activity.

    D. Monitor all significant deviations.

Exhibit 3 (*Continued*)

cur in this department. At any one time, as many as 20 new-product development projects may be in progress, and they all seem to require the same engineering services at the same time. Al Hanson has continually asked the technical program managers to give him more advanced notice, but—due to uncertainties in project schedules—requirements are often unknown until the last minute.

DISCUSSION QUESTIONS

1. What steps should Mr. Donaldson take to improve the new-product development process at FHE?
2. What could be done to clarify the organizational relationship between product managers and technical program managers?

| | FHE NEW PRODUCT DEVELOPMENT PLANNING SCHEDULE | PROJECT ENGINEER _JIM POWERS_ | SHEET _1_ |

PROJECT NAME _FLUID REGULATOR_   PROJECT NUMBER _7720_   PROGRAM MANAGER _MIKE ABELE_   PRODUCT MANAGER _GARY SINCLAIR_   OF _1_   DATE INITIATED _10-6-77_

EVENT NO.	DEFINE ACTIVITIES
105	Project team established
120	Marketing need defined
160	Conceptual cost estimate
165	Technical specification completed
170	First model completed
180	First model testing
190	Design review meeting
203	Hazard analysis
205	Agency approval plan
210	Construct field test models
215	Conduct field test
240	Review laboratory & field test results
254	Preliminary MFG cost estimate
265	Design review meeting
270	Update ROI
282	Submit tooling decision package
291	Release design to MFG. ENG'R'G
305	Conduct MFG Commitment mtg
316	Order purchased parts
330	Production of lot I
348	Lab test of lot I units
360	Release lot I for sale

DEPT.	APPROVAL/DATE	ESTIMATED MAN-HRS.	TOTAL	Oct.	Nov.	Dec.	Jan.	Feb.	Mar.	Apr.	May	June	July	Aug.	Sept.	Oct.
		PROG. MGR.	150	20	20	10	10	10	10	10	10	10	10	10	10	10
	JBP	ENGR.	320	60	60	40	40	20	20	20	20	20	10	10		
		IND. DES.														
482	WEB 11/2/77	DRAFT.	100		40	40				20						
		TECH PUBS.	40										30	10		
483	JCW 11-2-77	MOD. SHOP	120			120										
		TEST LAB.	200				100	80							20	
CASH EXPENDITURES	EXPENSE — Mat'l, Outside Labor, Travel, Etc.		$ 500							250	250					
	CAPITAL EQUIPMENT		$ —													
SCHEDULE REVISIONS	REVISED BY															
	DATE															

Exhibit 4
Gantt chart.

3. Evaluate the new-product development process and the level of detail used in planning new-product introductions.

4. What can be done to better manage the workload of the engineering services department?

MERRIWELL BAG COMPANY

Merriwell Bag Company is a small, family-owned corporation located in Seattle, Washington.[1] The stock of the company is equally divided among five members of the Merriwell family (husband, wife, and three sons), but the acknowledged leader is the founder and patriarch, Ed Merriwell. Ed Merriwell formed the company 20 years ago when he resigned as a mill supervisor for a large paper manufacturer. Ironically, the same manufacturer formed a container division five years ago and is presently one of Merriwell's competitors.

COMPANY STRATEGY

The family attributes the success of Merriwell Bag Company to the fact that it has found a market niche and has no "serious" competition. Merriwell supplies stock bags to many small chain stores scattered over a wide geographical area. It ships the bags directly to small regional warehouses or drop ships directly to the individual stores. The family reasons that the large bag manufacturers cannot profitably provide service to accounts on that small of a scale. In fact, Ed Merriwell formed the business with one second-hand bagging machine to provide bags for a

[1] Reprinted with permission of Charles E. Merrill Publishing Company.

small discount store chain and a regional chain of drug stores. These two organizations have grown tremendously over the years, and Ed Merriwell proudly points out that the bag company has grown with them. Today, these two original clients are Merriwell's largest customers.

The Merriwell family does not want its business to be too heavily reliant on any one customer. Hence, they have a policy that no single customer can account for over 15 percent of sales. In fact, Merriwell Bag Company encourages its major customers to establish alternative sources of bag supply for insurance against stock outs because of paper shortages, freight line difficulties, local trucking/warehousing strikes, and production problems that may locally affect Merriwell's ability to supply bags.

Merriwell does not aggressively pursue new bag customers, yet it has over 500 customers. The smallest customers order five bales per year (smallest order processed and shipped), and the largest order 15,000 bales per year. The number of bags per bale varies according to the weight of paper used and the size of the bag. Merriwell manufactures only pinch-bottom general merchandise bags, ranging in size from small $2\frac{1}{2}'' \times 10''$ pencil bags to large $20'' \times 2'' \times 30''$ bags used for larger items sold in discount stores. They make no flat bottom (grocery) bags or bags that require sophisticated printing (specialty bags). Bag labels are restricted to 20 percent face coverage and one-ink color placed on one side only. Hence, Merriwell's central strategy is built around low unit cost production due to standardization which allows a selling price that is competitive with the large bag manufacturers. At the same time, Merriwell provides the shipping and inventory services that are on too small of a scale for most of the large manufacturers. The Merriwell family takes great pride in "taking care of" a customer who has an emergency need for additional bags or who would like Merriwell to warehouse a bag order for a given time because of storage problems at the customer's warehouse.

FORECASTING DEMAND

Providing this personal service requires tight inventory control and production scheduling at Merriwell's bag plant. A highly accurate demand forecast allows Merriwell to service the special customer requests by use of Merriwell's own warehouse facilities and routing schedules of the company's truck line. Heretofore, Ed Merriwell could manage the demand forecasting and pro-

duction scheduling by "feel." Because of the ever-growing number of accounts and changes in personnel in customer purchasing departments, the accuracy of Merriwell's forecasting has been rapidly declining. The percentage of short-shipped accounts for particular types of bags is increasing alarmingly. Conversely, the warehouse is becoming overstocked with other types of bags. As a result, a severe demurrage penalty on three boxcars of incoming rolls of paper was recently paid because the paper warehouse was partially used to store finished bags that spilled over from the finished-bag warehouse. This caused a delay in unloading the boxcars until space could be created in the raw-material warehouse.

Demand forecasting has historically been difficult due to the seasonal nature of the product. There is always a surge in demand for bags prior to a holiday season. The exact timing of the surge in demand for particular types of bags depends upon customer stocking policies and the dates that holiday promotional activities begin.

The Merriwell family needs a forecasting method that would take this seasonal factor into consideration. Moreover, they want a method

	Sales (in no. of bales)				
Month	1972	1973	1974	1975	1976
January	2,000	3,000	2,000	5,000	5,000
February	3,000	4,000	5,000	4,000	2,000
March	3,000	3,000	5,000	4,000	3,000
April	3,000	5,000	3,000	2,000	2,000
May	4,000	5,000	4,000	5,000	6,000
June	6,000	8,000	7,000	6,000	6,000
July	6,000	4,000	7,000	10,000	8,000
August	6,000	8,000	10,000	14,000	10,000
September	10,000	12,000	15,000	16,000	20,000
October	12,000	12,000	15,000	16,000	20,000
November	14,000	16,000	18,000	20,000	22,000
December	8,000	10,000	8,000	12,000	8,000
	77,000	90,000	99,000	114,000	112,000

that exhibits stability, because their market is relatively stable with a large number of repeat customers. Finally, they want a forecasting method that anticipates the growth patterns of their respective customers. A forecasting method with these specifications would greatly enhance the company's ability to service its market profitably. It is believed that if such a method could be applied to forecasting aggregate demand, the same method could be used to gain additional accuracy by forecasting demand of its larger customers. By having an accurate forecast of aggregate demand and demand of larger customers, the requirements of the smaller customers could be processed within the existing warehousing and shipping flexibility.

To develop such a method, the Merriwell family compiled the aggregate demand data shown on the previous page. Actual demand through the first quarter of 1977 was 14,000 bales.

DISCUSSION QUESTIONS

1. Develop and justify a forecasting method that fulfills the company's specifications.
2. Forecast aggregate demand for the balance of 1977 and the first quarter of 1978.
3. In addition to forecasting demand of larger customers and aggregate demand, how might the accuracy of the forecast be improved?
4. What role should Ed Merriwell's "feel" of the market play in establishing new sales forecasts?

BENIHANA OF TOKYO

"Some restaurateurs like myself have more fun than others," says Hiroaki (Rocky) Aoki, youthful president of Benihana of Tokyo.[1] Since 1964 he has gone from a deficit net worth to becoming president of a chain of 15 restaurants which grosses over $12 million per year. He sports a $4,000 sapphire ring, maintains a $250,000 home, keeps five cars including three Rolls-Royces. One wall of his office is completely covered with photographs of Rocky with famous personalities who have eaten at a Benihana. Rocky firmly believes: "In America money is always available if you work hard."

BACKGROUND

Benihana is basically a steakhouse with a difference—the food is cooked in front of the customer by native chefs and the decor is that of an authentically detailed Japanese country inn. From a humble 40-seat unit opened in midtown Manhattan in 1964, Benihana has grown to a chain of 15 units across the country. Nine are company-owned locations: New York (3), San Francisco, Chicago, Encino and Marina del Rey, Cal., Portland, Ore., and Honolulu. Five are franchised: Boston, Fort Lauderdale, Beverly Hills, Seattle,

and Harrisburg, Pa. The last unit, Las Vegas, is operated as a joint venture with Hilton Hotels Corporation. Rocky, who is a former Olympic wrestler, describes his success as follows:

> In 1959, I came to the United States on a tour with my university wrestling team. I was twenty at the time. When I reached New York, it was love at first sight! I was convinced that there were more opportunities for me in America than Japan. In fact, the minute I was able to forget that I was Japanese, my success began. I decided to enroll in the School of Restaurant Management at City College basically because I knew that in the restaurant business I'd never go hungry. I earned money those early years by washing dishes, driving an ice cream truck and acting as a tour guide. Most importantly, I spent three years making a systematic analysis of the U.S. restaurant market. What I discovered is that Americans enjoy eating in exotic surroundings, but are deeply mistrustful of exotic foods. Also I learned that people very much enjoy watching their food being prepared. So I took $10,000 I had saved by 1963 and borrowed $20,000 more to open my first unit on the West side and tried to apply all that I had learned.

The origins of the Benihana of Tokyo actually date back to 1935. That was when Yunosuke Aoki (Rocky's father) opened the first of his chain of restaurants in Japan. He called it Benihana, after the small red flower that grew wild near the front door of the restaurant.

The elder Aoki ("Papasan"), like his son who was to follow in the family tradition, was a practical and resourceful restaurateur. In 1958, concerned about rising costs and increased competition, he first incorporated the hibachi table

[1] This case was made possible by the cooperation of the Benihana Corporation and Mr. Russ Carpenter, Executive Editor of the magazine *Institutions/Volume Feeding*. It was prepared by Mr. John Klug, Research Assistant, under the direction of Assistant Professor W. Earl Sasser as the basis for class discussion rather than to illustrate either effective or ineffective handling of an administrative situation.

592

concept into his operations. Rocky borrowed this method of cooking from his father and commented as follows:

> One of the things I learned in my analysis, for example, was that the number-one problem of the restaurant industry in the U.S. is the shortage of skilled labor. By eliminating the need for a conventional kitchen with the hibachi table arrangement, the only "skilled" person I need is the chef. I can give an unusual amount of attentive service and still keep labor cost to 10%–12% of gross sales (food and beverage) depending whether a unit is at full volume. In addition, I was able to turn practically the entire restaurant into productive dining space. Only about 22% of the total space of a unit is back-of-the-house including preparation areas, dry and refrigerated storage, employee dressing rooms and office space. Normally a restaurant requires 30% of its total space as back-of-the-house. (Operating statistics for a typical service restaurant are included in Exhibit 1.)
>
> The other thing I discovered is that food storage and wastage contribute greatly to the overhead of the typical restaurant. By reducing my menu to only three simple "Middle American" entrees—steak, chicken, and shrimp, I have virtually no waste and can cut food costs to between 30% and 35% of food sales depending on the price of meat.
>
> Finally, I insist on historical authenticity. The walls, ceilings, beams, artifacts, decorative lights of a Benihana are all from Japan. The building materials are gathered from old houses there, carefully disassembled, shipped in pieces to the U.S., where they are reassembled by one of my father's two crews of Japanese carpenters.

Rocky's first unit on the West side was such a success that it paid for itself in six months. He then built in 1966 a second unit 3 blocks away on the East side simply to cater to the overflow of the Benihana West. The Benihana East quickly developed a separate clientele and prospered. In 1967, Barron Hilton, who had eaten at a Benihana, approached Rocky concerning the possibility of locating a unit in the Marina Towers in Chicago. Rocky flew to Chicago, rented a car

and while driving to meet Mr. Hilton saw a vacant site. He immediately stopped, called the owner, and signed a lease the next day. Needless to say, a Benihana didn't go into the Marina Towers.

The #3 unit in Chicago has proved to be the company's largest money maker. It was an instant success and grosses approximately $1.3 million per year. The food and beverage split is 70/30 and management is able to keep food (30%), labor (10%), advertising (10%), and rent (5%) expense percentages at relatively low levels.

The fourth unit was San Francisco and the fifth was a joint venture with International Hotel in Las Vegas in 1969. By this time literally hundreds of people were clamoring for franchises. Rocky sold a total of six until he decided in 1970 that it would be much more to his advantage to own rather than franchise. Following are the franchises that were granted:

Puerto Rico (Not successful due to economic turndown)
Harrisburg, Penn.
Ft. Lauderdale
Portland (Company bought unit back)
Seattle
Beverly Hills
Boston

The decision to stop franchising was because of a number of problems. First, all the franchises were bought by investors, none of whom had any restaurant experience. Second, it was difficult for the American investor to relate to a predominantly native Japanese staff. Finally, control was considerably more difficult to maintain with a franchisee than a company employee manager. During the period to 1970 several groups attempted to imitate the Benihana success. One even included a group with intimate knowledge of the Benihana operation who set up in very close proximity to one Benihana unit. They, however, folded within the year. Bolstered by the confidence that the Benihana success could

EXHIBIT 1

OPERATING STATISTICS FOR A TYPICAL AMERICAN SERVICE RESTAURANT

	Ranges
Sales	
Food	70.0 –80.0
Beverage	20.0 –30.0
Other income	
Total sales	100.0%
Cost of sales	
Food cost (raw food from suppliers)	38.0 –48.0
Beverage cost	25.0 –30.0
Other cost	
Total cost of sales	35.0 –45.0
Gross profit	55.0 –65.0
Operating expenses	
Controllable expense	
Payroll	30.0 –35.0
Employee benefits	3.0 – 5.0
Employee meals	1.0 – 2.0
Laundry, linen, uniforms	1.5 – 2.0
Replacements	0.5 – 1.0
Supplies (guest)	1.0 – 1.5
Menus & printing	0.25– 0.5
Misc. contract expense (cleaning, garbage, extermination, equipment rental)	1.0 – 2.0
Music & entertainment (where applicable)	0.5 – 1.0
Advertising & promotion	0.75– 2.0
Utilities	1.0 – 2.0
Management salary	2.0 – 6.0
Administration expense (including legal and accounting)	0.75– 2.0
Repairs & maintenance	1.0 – 2.0
Occupation expense	
Rent	4.5 – 9.0
Taxes (real estate & personal property)	0.5 – 1.5
Insurance	0.75– 1.0
Interest	0.3 – 1.0
Depreciation	2.0 – 4.0
Franchise royalties (where applicable)	3.0 – 6.0
Total operating expenses	55.0 –65.0
Net profit before income tax	0.5 – 9.0%

Source: Bank of America *Small Business Reporter,* vol. 8, no. 2, 1968.

not be easily replicated, management felt that one of the classic pressures to franchise was eliminated—i.e., to expand extremely rapidly to preempt competitors.

The amount of space devoted to the bar/lounge/holding area accurately indicates when the unit was built. When Rocky opened his first unit, he saw the business as primarily food-service sales. The Benihana West has a tiny bar which seats about eight and has no lounge area. Rocky quickly learned that amount of bar space was insufficient and at the second unit, Benihana East, he doubled the size of the bar/lounge area. But since the whole unit is larger, the ratio of space is not too different. A typical floor plan is included as Exhibit 2.

His third Manhattan operation, called Benihana Palace, opened about two years ago. Here, the bar/lounge area is enormous, even in ratio to size. Current figures bear out the wisdom of the growth. At West, beverage sales represent about 18% of total sales. At East, they run 20%–22%. And at the Palace, they run a handsome 30%–33% of total sales. The beverage cost averages 20% of beverage sales.

The heart of the "show biz" lies in the dining

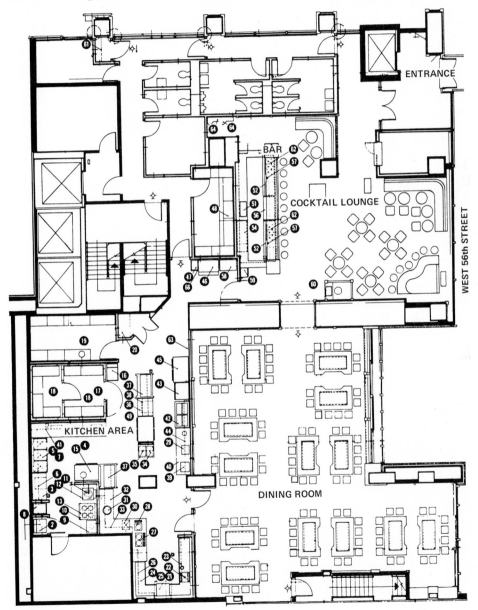

Exhibit 2
A typical Benihana floor plan.

area. The "teppanyaki" table is comprised of a steel griddle plate, with a 9½" wooden ledge bordering it to hold the ware. It is gas-fired. Above every table is an exhaust hood to remove cooking steam and odors and much of the heat from the griddle. Service is by a chef and waitress; each such team handles two regular tables.

The four food items—steak, filet mignon, chicken and shrimp—can either be had as single entree items or in combinations. A full dinner has three, with the shrimp as appetizer. The accompaniments are unvaried: beansprouts, zucchini, fresh mushrooms, onions and rice.

Normally, a customer can come in, be seated, have dinner and be on his way out in 45 minutes, if need be. The average turnover is an hour, up to an hour-and-a-half in slow periods.

The average check, including food and beverage, runs about $6 at lunch, about $10 at dinner. These figures include a drink (average price $1.50) at lunch, an average of one-plus at dinner.

The big purchase is meat. Only U.S.D.A. Prime Grade, tightly specified tenderloin and boneless strip loins are used. The steaks are further trimmed in-house. Only a bit of fat at the tail is left, and this is for effect. When the chef begins cooking the meat, he dramatically trims this part off and pushes it aside before cubing the remaining meat.

The hours of operation for the 15 units vary according to local requirements. All are open for lunch and dinner, though not necessarily every day for each. Lunch business is important; overall it accounts for about 30% to 40% of the total dollar volume despite a significantly lower check average. Essentially the same menu items are served for meals; the lower menu price average at lunch reflects smaller portions and fewer combinations.

SITE SELECTION

Because of the importance of lunch time business, Benihana has one basic criterion for site selection—high traffic. Management wants to be sure that a lot of people are nearby or going by both at lunch and at dinner. Rent normally runs 5–7% of sales for 5000–6000 square feet of floor space. Most units are located in a predominantly business district, though some have easy access to residential areas. Shopping center locations have been considered, but none accepted as yet.

TRAINING

Because the chef is considered by Benihana to be a key to its success, they are very highly trained. All are young and single native Japanese and all are "certified" which means that they have completed a three-year formal apprenticeship. They are then given a three- to six-month course in Japan in the English language and American manner as well as the Benihana form of cooking, which is mostly showmanship. The chefs are brought to the U.S. under a "trade treaty" agreement.

Training of the chefs within the U.S. is a continuous process also. In addition to the competition among the chefs to perfect their art in hopes of becoming the chief chef, there is also a traveling chef who inspects each unit periodically as well as being involved in the grand opening of new units.

While Benihana finds it relatively difficult to attract chefs and other personnel from Japan due to the general level of prosperity there as well as competition from other restaurants bidding for their talents, once in the U.S. they are generally not anxious to leave. This is due to several factors. One is the rapidity with which they can rise in the U.S. Benihana operation versus the rather rigid hierarchy based on class, age, and education they would face in Japan. A second and major factor is the paternal attitude that Benihana takes toward all its employees. While personnel are well paid in a tangible sense, a large part of the compensation is intangible based on job security and a total commitment of Benihana to the well-being of its employees. As a result, turnover of personnel within the U.S. is very low, although most do eventually return to Japan. To fully appreciate the Benihana success, one must appreciate the unique combination of Japanese paternalism in an American setting. Or, as Rocky puts it: "At Benihana we combine Japanese workers with American management techniques."

ORGANIZATION AND CONTROL

Each restaurant carries a simple management structure. It has a manager ($15,000/year), an assistant manager ($12,000/year) and 2–3 "front men" ($9000/year), who might be likened to maitre d's. These latter are really potential managers in training. All managers report to manager of operations Allen Saito who, in turn, reports to Bill Susha, vice president in charge of operations and business development. (See Exhibit 3.)

Susha came with Benihana in 1971, follow-

ing food and beverage experience with Hilton, Loew's and the Flagship Hotel division of American Airlines. He described his job as follows:

I see management growth as a priority objective. My first step was to establish some sort of control system by introducing sales goals and budgets. At the most recent manager workshop meeting in New York, with managers attending from all over the country, I asked each to project his sales goal on an annual basis, then break it out by month, then by week, then by day. After I reached agreement with a manager on the individual quota figures, I instituted a bonus plan. Any unit that exceeds its quota on any basis— daily, weekly, monthly, yearly—will get a proportionate bonus, which will be prorated across the entire staff of the unit. I've also built up an accounting staff and controller to monitor our costs. It's been a slow but steady process. We have to be very careful to balance our needs for control with the amount of overhead we can stand. We can justify extra "front men" standing around in the

Exhibit 3
Organization chart.

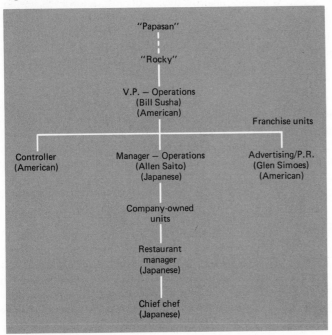

"Papasan"

"Rocky"

V.P. — Operations
(Bill Susha)
(American)

Franchise units

Controller
(American)

Manager — Operations
(Allen Saito)
(Japanese)

Advertising/P.R.
(Glen Simoes)
(American)

Company-owned
units

Restaurant
manager
(Japanese)

Chief chef
(Japanese)

units. At the corporate level, however, we have to be very careful. In fact, at the present the company is essentially being run by three people—Rocky, myself and Allen Saito.

ADVERTISING POLICY

Rocky considers that a vitally important factor in Benihana's success is a substantial investment in creative advertising and public relations. The company invests 8–10 percent of its gross sales on reaching the public.

Glen Simoes, the director of advertising and public relations summed it up:

> We deliberately try to be different and original in our advertising approach. We never place advertisements on the entertainment pages of newspapers on the theory that they would be lost among the countless other restaurant advertisements.
>
> We have a visual product to sell. Therefore, Benihana utilizes outstanding visuals in its ads. The accompanying copy is contemporary, sometimes offbeat. A recent full-page advertisement which appeared in the *New York Times, Women's Wear Daily* and *New York Magazine* did not contain the word "restaurant." We also conduct a considerable amount of market research to be sure we know who our customers really are.

Exhibit 4 shows the results of our market research survey. Exhibit 5 is a further discussion of Benihana advertising policy. Exhibits 6, 7, and 8 are examples of Benihana advertising copy.

FUTURE EXPANSION

Bill Susha summed up the problems of the future as he saw them:

> I think the biggest problems facing us now are how to expand. We tried franchising and decided to discontinue the program for several reasons. Most of our franchisees were business men looking for investment opportunities and did not really know and understand the restaurant business—this was a problem. The Japanese staff we provided were our people and we have obligations to them that the franchisee could not or would not cope with which at the time made us unhappy. The uniqueness of our operation in the hands of novices to the business made control more difficult and finally, we found it more profitable to own and operate the restaurants ourselves.
>
> Presently, we are limited to opening only 5 units a year because that is as fast as the two crews of Japanese carpenters we have can work. We are facing a decision and weighing the advantages and disadvantages of going into hotels with our type of restaurant. We are presently in two Hilton Hotels (Las Vegas and Honolulu) and have recently signed an agreement with Canadian Pacific Hotels. What we have done in these deals is to put "teeth" in the agreements so that we are not at the mercy of the hotel company's management.
>
> Further, one of our biggest constraints is staff. Each unit requires approximately 30 people who are all Oriental. Six to eight of these are highly trained chefs.
>
> Finally, there is the cost factor. Each new unit costs us a minimum of $300,000. My feeling is that we should confine ourselves to the major cities like Atlanta, Dallas, St. Louis, etc., in the near future. Then we can use all these units to expand into the suburbs.
>
> We've been highly tempted to try to grow too fast without really considering the full implications of the move. One example was the franchise thing, but we found it unsatisfactory. Another example is that a large international banking organization offered to make a major investment in us which would have allowed us to grow at a terrific rate. But when we looked at the amount of control and autonomy we'd have to give up, it just wasn't worth it, at least in my mind.
>
> Another thing I'm considering is whether it's worth it to import every item used in construction from Japan to make a Benihana 100% "authentic." Does an American really appreciate it and is it worth the cost? We could use material available here and achieve substantially the same effect. Also is it worth it to use Japanese carpen-

ters and pay union carpenters to sit and watch? All these things could reduce our costs tremendously and allow us to expand much faster.

Rocky described his perception of where the firm should go:

I see three principal areas for growth, the U.S., overseas, and Japan. In the U.S. we need to expand into the primary marketing areas Bill talked about that do not have a Benihana. But I think through our franchises we also learned that secondary markets such as Harrisburg, Pa. and Portland, Ore. also have potential. While their volume potential obviously will not match that of a primary market, these smaller units offer fewer headaches and generate nice profits. Secondary markets being considered include Cincinnati and Indianapolis.

The third principal area I see for growth is in

Exhibit 4
Market survey.

What the Customers Think

Every foodservice operator thinks he knows why customers come to his operation. Benihana, which has served two-and-a-quarter million customers in eight years, a high percentage of which were repeat business, thought it knew.

But when he joined as v-p of operations a year-and-a-half ago, Bill Susha wanted to be sure the hallowed presumptions were true. He devised a questionnaire, and arranged that it be handed to departing customers. A remarkable number took the time to fill out and return the form.

The percentage figures shown here are averages of six stores. While there were many variations from unit to unit, the general thrust was constant, so the six-store figures have been averaged to save space.

The six units included the three in New York City, plus Chicago, Encino, Cal., and Portland, Ore. The questions and averages are as follows:

Are you from out-of-town?
Yes	38.6%
No	61.4

Here on:
Business	38.7%
Pleasure	61.3

Do you live in the area?
Live	16.0%
Work	35.9
Both	45.1

Have you been to a Benihana in another city?
Yes	22.9%
No	77.3

How did you learn of us?
Newspaper	4.0%
Magazine	6.9
Radio	4.6
Recommended	67.0
TV show	1.0
Walk by	5.0
Other	11.5

Is this your first visit?
Yes	34.3%
No	65.7

What persuaded you to come?
Good food	46.7%
Service	8.2
Preparation	13.1
Atmosphere	13.3
Recommendation	5.7
Other	13.1

Food was:
Good	2.0%
Satisfactory	20.1
Excellent	77.9

Portions were:
Satisfactory	21.8%
Good	33.0
Excellent	45.4

Service was:
Satisfactory	9.8%
Good	21.6
Excellent	71.3

Atmosphere is:
Satisfactory	6.3%
Good	29.9
Excellent	63.2

Would you consider yourself a lunch or dinner customer?
Lunch	17.3%
Dinner	59.0
Both	23.7

Which aspect of our restaurant would you highlight?
Food	38.2%
Atmosphere	13.0
Preparation	24.6
Service	16.3
Different	2.2
Friendly	2.4
Other	3.3

How frequently do you come to Benihana?
Once a week or more	12.1%
Once a month or more	32.5
Once a year or more	55.6

Age:
10–20	4.2%
21–30	28.3
31–40	32.0
41–50	21.4
51–60	10.1
60 and over	4.0

Sex:
Male	71.4%
Female	28.6

Income:
$ 7,500–$10,000	16.8%
$10,000–$15,000	14.2
$15,000–$20,000	17.3
$20,000–$25,000	15.0
$25,000–$40,000	17.9
$40,000 and over	18.7

Occupation:
Managerial	23.0%
Professional	26.6
White Collar	36.9
Student	6.9
Housewife	5.0
Unskilled	1.1

No icky, sticky, slimy stuff

"Part of what makes Benihana successful," Rocky Aoki believes, "is our advertising and promotion. It's different, and it makes us seem different to people."

Indeed it is, and does. Much of the credit belongs to Glen Simoes, the hip director of advertising and public relations for Benihana of Tokyo. With a background mostly in financial public relations, Simoes joined the chain a little over two years ago to help open the flagship Benihana Palace. Since then, he's created a somewhat novel, all-embracing public relations program that succeeds on many levels.

"My basic job," he explains, "is guardian of the image. The image is that of a dynamic chain of Japanese restaurants with phenomenal growth." Keeping the image bright means exposure. Part of the exposure is a brilliant advertising campaign; part is publicity.

Each has its own function. Advertising is handled by Kracauer and Marvin, an outside agency, under Simoes' supervision and guidance. Its function is to bring in new customers.

"Our ads," Simoes points out, "are characterized by a bold headline statement and an illustration that make you want to read on. The copy itself is fairly clever and cute. If it works properly, it will keep you reading until you get the message—which is to persuade a stranger to come into Benihana.

"The ads are designed to still fears about icky, sticky, slimy stuff," he adds. "We reassure folks that they will get wholesome, familiar food, with unusual, unique and delicious preparation, served in a fun atmosphere. We want to intrigue the people celebrating an anniversary or taking Aunt Sally out to dinner. A Japanese restaurant would normally never cross their minds. We're saying we're a fun place to try, and there's no slithery, fishy stuff.

"We have an impact philosophy. We go for full pages in national publications on a now-and-then basis, rather than a regular schedule of small ads. We want that impact to bring the stranger into Benihana for the first time. After that, the restaurant will bring him back again and again, and he will bring his friends.

"We do a good media mix," Simoes concludes. "We advertise in each of the cities in which we operate. Within each market we aim for two people: the resident, of course, but even more, the tourist-visitor. With them you know you're always talking to new people. We appear in city entertainment guides and work with convention and visitor bureaus to go after groups and conventions."

The second factor is publicity. Here, the intent is not the quantity of mentions or exposure, but the type. As Simoes sees it, "We are building. Each mention is a building block. Some are designed to bring customers into the store. Some are designed to bring us prospective financing, or suppliers, or friends, or whatever. We work many ways against the middle. And the middle is the company, the people, Rocky, the growth and all of it put together that makes the image."

Publicity takes many forms, it's media stories, and TV demonstrations. Simoes cites clipping and viewing services to prove that every day of the year, something about Benihana appears either in print or on radio or TV, a record he believes is unique. Publicity is department store demonstrations, catering to celebrities, hosting youth groups, sending matchboxes to conventions and chopsticks to ladies clubs, scheduling Rocky for interviews and paying publicists to provide oneliners to columnists.

But no engine runs without fuel. And Rocky believes that advertising and promotion are a good investment. Believes so strongly, in fact, that he puts an almost unprecedented $1 million a year into advertising, and probably half that again into promotion, for a total expenditure of nearly 8% of gross sales in this area.

A few months back, Simoes, wholeheartedly pitching his company to a skeptical magazine writer, said heatedly there are "at least 25 reasons people come to Benihana." Challenged on the spot, he came back a few days later with a list of 31. They are:

1) the quality of the food; 2) the presentation of the food; 3) the preparation of the food; 4) the showmanship of the chef; 5) the taste of the food; 6) authenticity of construction; 7) authenticity of decor; 8) continuity of Japanese flavor throughout; 9) communal dining; 10) service—constant attention.

11) Youthfulness of staff; 12) frequent presence of celebrities; 13) excitement created by frequent promotions; 14) type of cuisine; 15) moderate price; 16) the uniqueness of appeal to the five senses; 17) the recent growth in popularity of things Japanese; 18) quick service; 19) unusual advertising concept; 20) publicity.

21) No stringent dress requirements; 22) recommendations from friends; 23) the basic meal is low-calorie; 24) banquet and party facilities; 25) the presence of Rocky Aoki, himself; 26) chance to meet people of the opposite sex; 27) the presence of many Japanese customers (about 20%); 28) locations in major cities giving a radiation effect; 29) acceptance of all major credit cards; 30) the informality of the dining experience; and 31) the use of the restaurant as a business tool.

Exhibit 5
Summary of Benihana marketing philosophy.

suburbia. No sites have yet been set, but I think it holds a great potential. A fourth growth area, not given the importance of the others, is further penetration into existing markets. Saturation is not a problem as illustrated by the fact that New York and greater Los Angeles have three units each, all doing well.

We are also considering someday going pub-

Exhibit 6
Advertisement.

lic. In the meantime, we are moving into joint ventures in Mexico and overseas. Each joint venture is unique in itself. We negotiate each on the basis that will be most advantageous to the parties concerned taking into account the contributions of each party in the form of services and cash. Once this is established, we agree on a formula for profits and away we go.

Four deals have now been consummated. Three are joint ventures out of the country. An agreement has already been reached to open a Benihana in the Royal York Hotel, Toronto, Canada. This will provide the vanguard for a march across Canada with units in or outside Canadian Pacific Hotels.

Second is a signed agreement for a new unit

Two philosophies of the steak.

The basic philosophy of the American restaurant.

The chef throws a slab of raw steak into the kitchen broiler. It sits there until it's rare, medium or well-done.

The waiter brings it to your table.

You eat it.

The Benihana philosophy.

The chef comes right up to your hibachi table. (Why shouldn't you see the man who's actually creating your meal?)

He bows. (There's no reason why a chef can't be a gentleman.)

He sets the raw steak in front of you. (Isn't it nice to see for yourself that you're getting the very freshest, prime cuts?)

He asks you how you want it. (There's no luxury like the luxury of dealing directly with your chef.)

He cuts your steak into bite-size morsels. (Why should you have to perform any labor?)

His knife begins a snappy, rhythmic attack on the onions. (We believe there's as much drama in a dancing onion as in a dancing chorus girl.)

He slams the pepper shaker against the grill. (It's not good for a chef to suppress his excitement.)

As he cooks he adds all kinds of Japanese sauces and seasonings. (No, Worcester sauce is not part of our theory.)

At last he puts the sizzling steak directly on your plate. (The world's fastest waiter couldn't serve you better.)

You eat it. (Tell us. Has there ever been a more palatable philosophy?)

BENIHANA of TOKYO

New York — Benihana Palace 15 W. 44 St., 682-7120 • Benihana East 120 E. 56 St., 593-1627 • Benihana West 61 W. 56 St., 581-0930
Boston, Harrisburg, Fort Lauderdale, Chicago, Seattle, Portland Ore., San Francisco, Las Vegas, Encino, Marina Del Rey, Beverly Hills, Honolulu, Tokyo.

Exhibit 7
Advertisement.

in Mexico City. From here, negotiations are under way on a new hotel to be built in Acapulco. Benihana stands ready to build and operate a unit in the hotel or, if possible, to take over management of the entire hotel. These units would form a base for expansion throughout Mexico.

The third extra-territorial arrangement was recently signed with David Paradine, Ltd., a British firm of investors headed by TV personality David Frost. Again, this is a joint venture, with the Paradine group to supply technical assistance, public relations, advertising and financing, Benihana the management and know-how. This venture hopes ultimately to have Benihana restaurants not only throughout Great Britain but across the Continent.

Rocky also has a number of diversification plans:

We have entered into an agreement with a firm that is researching and contacting large food processors in an effort to interest them into producing a line of Japanese food products under the Benihana label for retail sale. There has been a great deal of interest and we are close to concluding a deal.

I worry a lot. Right now we cater to a middle-income audience, not the younger generation. That makes a difference. We charge more, serve better quality, have a better atmosphere and more service. But we are in the planning stages for operations with appeal to the younger generation.

For instance, there is no Japanese quick service operation in this country. I think we should go into a combination Chinese-Japanese operation like this. The unit would also feature a dynamic cooking show exposed to the customers. Our initial projections show margins comparable to our present margins with Benihana of Tokyo. I see a check of about 99 cents. We are negotiating with

Exhibit 8
Advertisement.

The Mission of Rocky Aoki

When Rocky Aoki, owner of Benihana, came to America six years ago, this was how a great many Americans felt about Japanese food:

(1) It wasn't as good as Chinese food.
(2) It was mostly sukiyaki and soup that tasted like hot brown water.
(3) If you ordered anything besides sukiyaki, you'd wind up with raw, slithery fishy things.
(4) OK, the food was very prettily arranged. But you walked out twice as hungry as when you walked in.
(5) It wasn't as good as Chinese food.

"My task is clear," said Rocky. "I'm going to change the way Americans think about Japanese food. I'm going to introduce America to Hibachi cooking."

(Hibachi cooking or cooking on a grill, is nothing at all like the highly stylized classical Japanese cuisine.)

And so, in 1964, Rocky opened the first Benihana. It broke all the rules. You couldn't get sukiyaki there. Or raw fish. There wasn't even a conventional kitchen. You just sat around this big Hibachi table—a combination grill and dining table—and waited for your chef to appear.

When he did, he came bearing a feast. Basket upon basket of beautiful fresh meat, poultry and vegetables. Then, right in front of you, he sprang into action. Slicing, seasoning and cooking, he prepared your meal with a speed and skill bordering on wizardry.

It was hard to believe. No exquisitely carved carrot slices. No wispy vegetables arranged in perfect flower patterns. Instead, solid food in abundance. Jumbo shrimps sauteed with lemon. Succulent chunks of steak. Young chicken dusted with sesame seeds. Mushrooms, scallions, beansprouts—served not together in some kind of mish-mash, but individually. It was enough to bring joy to the most jaded gourmet, bliss to the most ravenous appetite.

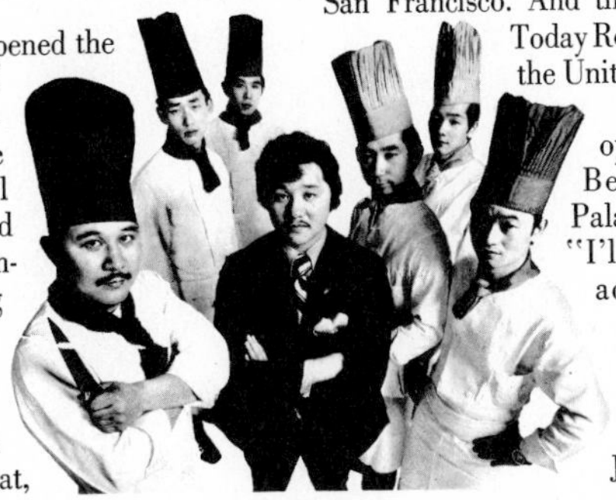

Well, the first New York Benihana was an enormous success. Within a year, Rocky had to open another one. That too became a smash. Soon Rocky was opening a Benihana in Chicago. And then one in San Francisco. And then another in Las Vegas. Today Rocky has Benihanas all over the United States.

Earlier this year, after opening his third New York Benihana—the Benihana Palace—Rocky Aoki declared: "I'll consider my mission accomplished when everyone in America has tried Hibachi cooking at least once."

Come in and give a nice Japanese boy a break.

BENIHANA of TOKYO
No slithery, fishy things.

New York—Benihana Palace 15 W. 44 St., 682-7120 Benihana East 120 E. 56 St., 593-1627 Benihana West 61 W. 56 St., 581-0930
Chicago, Los Angeles, Las Vegas, San Francisco, Harrisburg, Fort Lauderdale, Portland, Ore., Puerto Rico, Honolulu, Tokyo.

an oil company to put small units in gas stations. They could be located anywhere—on turnpikes or in the Bronx. I think we should do this very soon. I think I will get a small store in Manhattan and try it out. This is the best kind of market research in the U.S. Market research works in other countries, but I don't believe in it here. We are also negotiating for a site on Guam and to take over a chain of beer halls in Japan.

The restaurant business is not my only business. I went into producing; I had two unsuccessful Broadway shows. The experience was very expensive, but I learned a great deal and learned it very fast. It's all up to the critics there. In the restaurant business, the critics don't write much about you if you're bad; but even if they do they can't kill you. On Broadway they can. They did.

I promoted a heavyweight boxing match in Japan. It was successful. I am going into promoting in the entertainment field in Japan. I am doing a Renoir exhibition in Japan with an auction over television. I am thinking about buying a Japanese movie series and bringing it here. I am also thinking of opening a model agency, probably specializing in Oriental models.

But everything always works back to Benihana. For instance, if I open a model agency, I will let the girls come to Benihana to eat. Twenty beautiful girls at the restaurant would mean 400 guys, which would mean 600 girls, and so.

My philosophy of the restaurant business is simply to make people happy. We do it many ways in Benihana. As we start different types of operations, we will try to do it in other ways. I have no real worries about the future. The U.S. is the greatest country in the world to make money. Anybody can do it who wants to work hard and make people happy.

Russ Carpenter, a consultant and editor for *Institutions/Volume Feeding* magazine summed up his perceptions as follows:

I basically see two main problems.

What is Benihana really selling? Is it food, atmosphere, hospitality, a "watering hole" or what? Is having entertainment in the lounge, for example, consistent with the over-all image? All the advertising emphasizes the chef and the food, but is that really what the public comes for? I don't know. I'm only raising the questions.

The other thing is how do you hedge your bets? Is Benihana really on the forefront of a trend of the future with their limited menu, cooking in front of you and Oriental atmosphere or is it just a fad? This relates to whether it should emphasize restaurant operations only.

EASTERN GEAR, INC.

Eastern Gear, Inc., in Philadelphia, Pa., is a manufacturer of custom-made gears ranging in weight from a few ounces to over 50 pounds.[1] The gears are made of different metals depending on the customer's requirements. Over the past year, 40 different types of steel and brass alloys have been used as raw materials. See Exhibit 1 for details.

Eastern Gear sells its products primarily to engineering research and development laboratories or very small manufacturers. As a result, the number of gears in most orders is small; rarely is exactly the same gear ordered more than once. The distribution of order sizes for March 1980 is shown in Exhibit 2.

[1] This case was prepared as a basis for class discussion, not to illustrate either effective or ineffective handling of an administrative situation.

EXHIBIT 1
RAW MATERIALS

Type of material	1979 usage $(000)
A	$ 36
B	10
C	15
D	43
E	110
F	18
G	32
H	75
I	40
J	60
K	30
All others	53
Total	$522

EXHIBIT 2
SALES, MARCH 1980

Order size	Number of orders	Total $ value of orders
1	80	$ 3,200
2	53	4,250
3	69	8,163
4	32	4,800
5	82	16,392
8	47	15,987
10	64	26,871
15	22	13,172
20	42	31,555
25	27	23,682
30	18	21,600
40	22	32,000
50	10	18,693
100	4	12,500
200	2	14,068
400	1	9,652
700	2	35,600
1000	1	20,000
	578	$312,185

ORDER ENTRY

When a customer wishes to order a gear, the order is taken by James Lord, sales manager and marketing vice president. The customer specifies the type of gear desired by submitting a blueprint or sketch. The quantity of gears required and the type of material are also specified by the customer. On occasion, the customer's engineer will call up after the order has been placed and request a change in the design. In these cases, it may be necessary to stop production and wait for new raw materials or for the design to be clarified. The customer's prints submitted with the order do not always contain the tolerances or finishes required during machining. As a result, the customer is contacted directly when the information is needed.

After the order is received, one copy is sent to the production supervisor, Joe Irvine, and the second copy is sent to Sam Smith, the controller. Upon receipt of the customer's order, Mr. Smith places a purchase order for the raw materials required. These materials often take from 1 to 2 weeks to arrive, depending on the supplier and the type of material ordered.

After receiving the customer order, the supervisor reviews the order and places it on file until the raw material arrives. The customer order is then routed through the shop along with the materials. In the past, the production process for most gears has taken about 2 weeks after receipt raw materials. Recently this production time has increased to 4 weeks.

Joe Irvine expressed concern about the bot-

tlenecks which appear in the production process. One week the bottleneck may be in one machine center, and the next week it is in another. These bottlenecks make it difficult to get the orders out on time.

PHYSICAL LAYOUT AND MATERIALS FLOW

Eastern Gear utilizes a standard job-shop layout, as shown in Exhibit 3. Each work center has a common set of machines or processes. The materials flow from one work center to another, depending on the operations needed for a particular order.

A typical order will take the following path. First, the raw material, a gear blank, is sent to the milling work center. Here the teeth are cut into the edge of the gear according to the customer's specifications. Next, the gear blanks are sent to the drilling work center, where one or more holes may be drilled in the gear. The gear is

**Exhibit 3
Layout.**

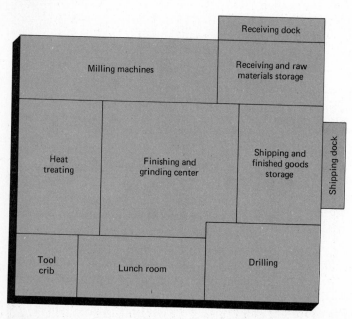

then sent to a grinding center, where a finish is put on the gear teeth and the surface of the gear. Next, the gear may be sent to heat-treating if this operation is required by the customer. After the batch of gears is completed, they are inspected by the next available worker and shipped to the customer.

COMPANY BACKGROUND

Business has been booming at Eastern Gear. For the first 2 years the company lost money, but over the last several months a small profit has been made. Sales are up by 100 percent in the last quarter. See Exhibit 4 for more details.

Although sales are rapidly increasing, a recent market survey has indicated that sales can be expanded even more in the next few years. According to the market survey, sales will be $5 million in calendar 1980 if the current delivery lead time of 5 to 6 weeks is maintained. If total delivery lead time can be reduced to the former 3 to 4 weeks, sales could be expanded to $6 million instead of $5 million.

Because of increased delivery lead times, the company has recently added an expediter, Matt Williams. Each morning Matt reviews the work in progress in the shop and selects those orders which appear to be behind schedule. Each order which is behind receives a red tag, indicating that it should be treated on a rush basis. At the present time about 20 percent of the orders have rush tags on them. Mr. Williams also spends his time looking for past-due raw materials and lost orders as well as explaining late orders to customers.

The organization chart for the company is shown in Exhibit 5. Roger Rhodes is the president and founder of Eastern Gear. Mr. Rhodes handles contacts with some of the large customers, arranges the financing needed by the company, and sits in on the weekly production meeting. During these meetings, scheduling problems, employee problems, and other production problems are discussed.

The company engineer is Sam Bartholomew. His responsibilities include design of the company's products, procurement and maintenance of equipment, and overseeing of the supervisor, Joe Irvine. Mr. Bartholomew also attends the weekly production meetings, and he spends about 10 hours a week on the factory floor talking with individual workers.

The company is currently experiencing about a 7 percent return rate on completed orders due to poor quality. In 75 percent of the cases, the

EXHIBIT 4
FINANCIAL DATA

	1977	1978	1979	First quarter, 1980
Sales	560*	1500	3100	1063
Manufacturing costs				
Materials	63	273	522	214
Labor	136	587	1063	327
Overhead	70	216	412	140
Depreciation	172	398	422	150
Total manufacturing costs	441	1474	2419	831
Sales expenses	70	130	263	80
G & A expense	75	110	297	93
Total costs	586	1714	2979	1004
Profit before tax	(26)	(214)	121	59

* All figures in thousands of dollars.

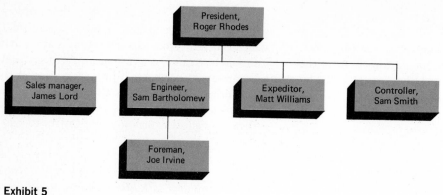

Exhibit 5
Organization chart.

returned orders have failed to undergo one or more operations or the operations have been improperly done. For example, in one returned order, all the gears were missing a hole.

Occasionally, the company will receive rush orders from its customers. In this case the order is referred directly to Roger Rhodes for approval. If the order is accepted, the raw materials are rush-ordered and received the next day. After receipt of the raw materials, the order is rushed through production in 4 days. This is accomplished by Fred Dirkson, a trusted employee, who hand-carries the rush orders through all operations. About 10 percent of the orders are handled on a rush basis.

The work force consists of 50 employees who are highly skilled or semiskilled. The mill-ing machine operators, for example, are highly skilled and require at least 2 years of vocational-technical training plus several months of on-the-job training. Within the last quarter, 10 new employees have been added to the work force. The employees are not unionized and good labor relations exist. The work force is managed using a family-type approach.

DISCUSSION QUESTIONS

1. What are the major problems being faced by Eastern Gear?
2. What action should Mr. Rhodes take to solve his problems?

FIRST CITY NATIONAL BANK

In March 1979, David Craig, vice president of operations for First City National Bank of Philadelphia, was considering a change in teller operations.[1] Currently, the bank's tellers were arranged in pods to handle customer transactions. There were four pods containing three teller stations each. One pod was used primarily for savings accounts, since some savings transactions took longer than other types of deposits or withdrawals. The major problem with the pod system was that one pod might be crowded while another was vacant. The distance between pods was such that customers were unwilling to move from one to another.

Mr. Craig was considering two alternatives to the pod system. The first was a single-line teller arrangement as shown in Exhibit 1. Using this plan, all customers would wait in a single line until a teller became available. The person at the head of the line would then move to the open

[1] This case was prepared as a basis for class discussion, not to illustrate either effective or ineffective handling of an administrative situation.

Exhibit 1
Teller arrangements.

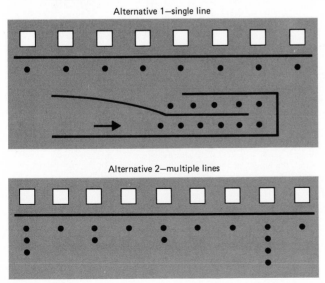

Alternative 1—single line

Alternative 2—multiple lines

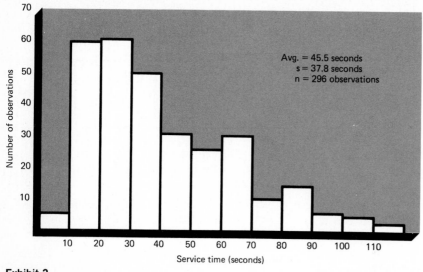

Exhibit 2
Histogram— Service-time distribution.

teller. Mr. Craig thought that about 10 tellers would be required to handle the bank's usual business. However, he could not be sure of the exact number without further study.

Exhibit 1 also shows the second alternative teller arrangement. Using this more conventional plan, the customers would form separate lines in front of each of the teller windows. Thus for 10 tellers, a total of 10 different lines could be formed.

Exhibit 3

Histogram—Arrival-time distribution.

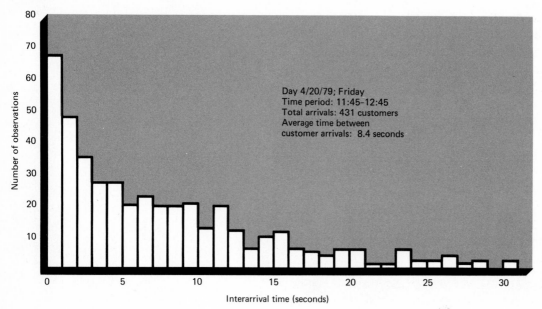

In evaluating these alternatives, several issues were of utmost importance. First, Mr. Craig was concerned with both customer waiting time and teller efficiency. On the basis of past experience, Mr. Craig felt that more than 3 minutes of waiting time would be unacceptable to most customers. He also felt that teller utilization should be as high as possible, perhaps in the 80 to 90 percent range. Since demand varied during the day, the number of tellers provided would have to vary to meet the customer-service and teller-utilization goals.

The statistical distribution of service time and arrival time is shown in Exhibits 2 and 3.

The service time averages 45 seconds per customer and does not vary by time of day. On the other hand, the average time between arrivals does vary with the time of day. For example, between 11:45 and 12:45 on one particular day sampled, 431 customers arrived at the bank, with an average of 8.4 seconds between customers.

To estimate the average arrival rate during different times of the day, the data in Exhibit 4 was collected. Over the period between November 1 and February 28, 1979, arrivals were counted for each half-hour period. The days were then divided into normal days, peak days, and super-peak days, depending on the intensity

EXHIBIT 4
CHART OF AVERAGE CUSTOMER ARRIVAL RATES

Time of day	Normal days		Peak days		Super-peak days	
	Total number of arrivals	Average arrival rate*	Total number of arrivals	Average arrival rate*	Total number of arrivals	Average arrival rate*
8–8:30	803	19	625	22	331	25
8:30–9	919	22	758	27	418	32
9–9:30	1207	29	863	31	571	44
9:30–10	2580	63	2033	72	1228	94
10–10:30	2599	63	2237	80	1382	106
10:30–11	2870	70	2283	82	1337	103
11–11:30	3384	83	2625	94	1577	121
11:30–12	4548	111	4060	145	2325	179
12–12:30	5804	142	5329	190	2908	224
12:30–1	5351	131	4923	176	2724	210
1–1:30	4355	106	3983	142	2271	175
1:30–2	3632	89	3150	113	1991	153
2–2:30	2321	57	2012	72	1282	99
2:30–3	1935	47	1960	70	1206	93
3–3:30	2151	52	2064	74	1250	96
3:30–4	2115	52	2238	80	1328	102
4–4:30	2291	55	2340	84	1346	104
4:30–5	2054	50	2191	78	1216	93
5–5:30	1598	39	1763	63	924	71

Total normal days = 41, total peak days = 28, total super peak days = 13.

* The total number of arrivals is divided by the number of days to arrive at the average arrival rate.

of the flow. Although the average number of arrivals varied during each hour of the day, the statistical pattern of arrivals was stable during each particular hour.

In order to arrive at a decision, Mr. Craig requested an analysis of the single- and multiple-line teller arrangements. For a given number of tellers, Mr. Craig wanted to know which arrangement provided the best customer service. He also specified that the analysis should include a calculation of the number of tellers required at various times of the day, so that a teller staffing plan could be devised.

In addition to the statistical analysis, Mr. Craig wondered what the customer reaction to the single- or multiple-line arrangement might be. Would the appearance of a long single line drive customers away, or would the customers perceive fast service from the rapidly moving line? Mr. Craig also wondered what the other advantages and disadvantages of a single line relative to the multiple lines might be.

DISCUSSION QUESTIONS

1. Which alternative arrangement of teller lines should Mr. Craig select? Support your recommendation with appropriate analysis and consideration of customer reaction.
2. For the alternative you recommend, develop appropriate staffing levels for each hour of the day.
3. Should other alternatives, not described in the case, be considered?

COMMONWEALTH ICE CREAM COMPANY

The Commonwealth Ice Cream Company manufactures and distributes ice cream in the state of Virginia.[1] At the present time the company owns four ice cream plants located at Alexandria, Norfolk, Roanoke, and Richmond. These plants are used to manufacture and distribute ice cream throughout the state on a daily basis.

Due to the high rate of population growth in the Washington, D.C., area, the company is considering building a new plant at Arlington, Virginia. If the new plant were built, one or more of the existing plants might be phased out, depending on the economics of the situation and future demand levels.

[1] This case was prepared as a basis for class discussion, not to illustrate either effective or ineffective handling of an administrative situation.

The four plants distribute ice cream to six marketing areas, as shown in Exhibit 1. While each plant currently distributes to its own marketing area, this practice is not required. Any plant can distribute ice cream to any marketing area in the state.

The capacity of each plant and the costs of production are shown in Exhibit 2. As indicated, the costs of production vary from one location to another due to different labor costs, different costs of materials, and different plant efficiencies. If the new plant is built in Arlington, it will have a capacity of 1200 cwt (hundredweight, or 100 pounds) per day and a cost of production of $21 per cwt.

The current distribution plan is shown in Exhibit 3, along with the projected market demands for 5 years into the future. Demand in each market area with the exception of Danville and Alexandria is expected to increase by about

Exhibit 1
Marketing areas and plant locations.

EXHIBIT 2
PLANT DATA

Plant	Plant capacity cwt per day	Production cost per cwt
Alexandria	1000	$25
Richmond	800	23
Norfolk	800	21
Roanoke	500	22
Total	3100	

EXHIBIT 3
MARKET DATA

Market	Current demand cwt/day	5-year demand cwt/day	Currently served by plant at
Alexandria	500	750	Alexandria
Charlottesville	200	240	Alexandria
Roanoke	300	360	Roanoke
Danville	150	150	Roanoke
Richmond	600	720	Richmond
Norfolk	500	600	Norfolk
Total	2250	2820	

EXHIBIT 4
TRANSPORTATION COSTS ($ per cwt)

Market	Alexandria	Richmond	Norfolk	Roanoke	Arlington
Alexandria	$2.50	$3.80	$5.20	$4.60	$2.60
Charlottesville	3.40	3.20	4.10	3.10	3.50
Roanoke	4.60	3.10	3.80	2.90	4.70
Danville	5.20	2.90	3.10	3.30	5.10
Richmond	3.80	2.80	2.90	3.10	3.70
Norfolk	4.60	2.90	2.60	4.40	4.50

20 percent. Demand in the Danville area is expected to remain constant, while demand in the Alexandria area is expected to increase by 50 percent.

The shipping costs between each plant and each marketing area are shown in Exhibit 4. These costs vary because of the distances involved and the mode of transportation used. Projected shipping costs for the new plant at Arlington are also shown in Exhibit 4.

If the new plant is built at Arlington, it will cost $2 million to construct, and the plant will have approximately a 20-year lifetime. The company would utilize the new Arlington plant and existing plants, which would be kept open, for approximately 300 days each year.

DISCUSSION QUESTIONS

1. Should the new ice cream plant be built at Arlington, Virginia?
2. What other actions should the company take?
3. What assumptions are required in your answer to Question 1?
4. What risks are there in building the new plant now?

LAWN KING, INC.

John Conner, marketing manager for Lawn King, looked over the beautiful countryside as he drove to the corporate headquarters in Moline, Ill.[1] John had asked his boss, Kathy Wayne, the general manager of Lawn King, to call a meeting in order to review the latest forecast figures for fiscal year 1981.[2] When he arrived at the plant, the meeting was ready to begin. Others in attendance at the meeting were James Fairday, plant manager; Joan Peterson, controller; and Harold Pinter, personnel officer.

John started the meeting by reviewing the latest situation. "I've just returned from our annual sales meeting and I think we lost more sales last year than we thought, due to back-order conditions at the factory. We have also reviewed the forecast for next year and feel that sales will be 110,000 units in fiscal year 1981. The marketing department feels this forecast is realistic and could be exceeded if all goes well."

At this point, James Fairday interrupted by saying, "John, you've got to be kidding. Just three months ago we all sat in this same room and you predicted sales of 98,000 units for fiscal '81. Now you've raised the forecast by 12 percent. How can we do a reasonable job of production planning when we have a moving target to shoot at?"

Kathy interjected, "Jim, I appreciate your concern, but we have to be responsive to changing market conditions. Here we are in September

and we still haven't got a firm plan for fiscal '81, which has just started. I want to use the new forecast and develop an aggregate plan for next year as soon as possible."

John added, "We've been talking to our best customers and they're complaining about back orders during the peak selling season. A few have threatened to drop our product line if they don't get better service next year. We have to produce not only enough product but also the right models to service the customer."

MANUFACTURING PROCESS

Lawn King is a medium-sized producer of lawn-mower equipment. Last year, sales were $14.5 million and pretax profits were $2 million, as shown in Exhibit 1. The company makes four lines of lawn mowers: an 18-inch push mower, a 20-inch push mower, a 20-inch self-propelled mower, and a 22-inch deluxe self-propelled mower. All these mowers are made on the same assembly line. During the year, the line is changed over from one mower to the next to meet the actual and projected demand.

The changeover cost of the production line depends on which type of mower is being produced and the next production model planned. For example, it is relatively easy to change over from the 22-inch push mower to the 22-inch self-propelled mower, since the mower frame is the same. The self-propelled mower has a propulsion unit added and a slightly larger engine. The company estimated the changeover costs as shown in Exhibit 2.

Lawn King fabricates the metal frames and

[1] This case was prepared as a basis for class discussion, not to illustrate either effective or ineffective handling of an administrative situation.

[2] The Lawn King 1981 fiscal year runs from September 1, 1980, to August 31, 1981.

615

EXHIBIT 1
PROFIT AND LOSS STATEMENT ($000)

	FY79	FY80
Sales	$11,611	$14,462
Cost of goods sold		
Materials	6,340	8,005
Direct labor	2,100	2,595
Depreciation	743	962
Overhead	256	431
Total CGS	9,439	11,993
G & A expense	270	314
Selling expense	140	197
Total expenses	9,849	12,504
Pretax profit	1,762	1,958

metal parts for their lawn mowers in their own machine shop. These fabricated parts are sent to the assembly line along with parts purchased directly from vendors. In the past year, approximately $8 million in parts and supplies were purchased, including engines, bolts, paint, wheels, and sheet steel. An inventory of $1 million in purchased parts is held to supply the machine shop and the assembly line. When a particular mower is running on the assembly line, only a few days of parts are kept at the plant, since supplies are constantly coming into the factory.

A total of 100 employees work at the main plant in Moline, Ill. These employees include 60 workers on the assembly line, 25 workers in the machine shop, 10 maintenance workers, and 5 office staff. A beginning assembly-line worker is paid $7.15 per hour plus $2.90 an hour in benefits. Senior maintenance and machine-shop employees earn as much as $14 per hour.

It generally takes about 2 weeks for a new employee to reach full productivity on the assembly line. After 3 months, an employee can request rotation to other jobs on the line if job variety is desired. At least some of the workers find the work quite repetitive and boring.

The plant is unionized, but relations between the union and the company have always been good. Nevertheless, employee turnover has been high. In the past year, approximately 50 percent of the employees left the company, representing a total training cost of $42,000 for the year. There is also a considerable absenteeism, especially on Mondays and Fridays, causing production disruptions. To handle this situation, six "fillers" are kept on the work force to fill in for people who are absent on a given day. These fillers also help train the new employees when they are not needed for direct production work.

EXHIBIT 2
LINE CHANGEOVER COST MATRIX

		Changed to			
		18″	20″	20″ SP*	22″ SP*
Changed from	18″	—	$2000	$2000	$2500
	20″	$2000	—	$500	$1500
	20″ SP	$2000	$500	—	—
	22″ SP	$2500	$1500	$1500	—

* SP denotes "self-propelled." Changeover cost includes the wages of the work force used to adjust the assembly line from one model configuration to another.

PRODUCTION PLANNING

The actual sales and forecasts are shown in Exhibit 3. Not only are the sales highly seasonal but total sales are dependent on the weather. If the weather is good in early spring, customers will be more inclined to buy a new mower. A good grass-growing season also encourages sales during the summer.

It appears that customers are more likely to buy the high-priced self-propelled mowers in good economic times. In recessionary periods, the bottom-of-the-line 18-inch mower does better.

The production strategy in current use might be described as a one-shift level workforce strategy with overtime used as needed. The work force is not always exactly level due to turnover and short-run production requirements. Nevertheless, the policy is to keep the work force as level as possible. Overtime is used when the regular work force cannot meet production requirements.[3]

The actual monthly production output and sales for fiscal year 1980 are shown in Exhibit 4. Differences between sales and production were absorbed by the inventory. If stockouts occurred, the order was backlogged and filled from the next available production run. Lawn King utilized a 30 percent carrying cost per year for inventory.[4]

Each June, an aggregate production plan is prepared for the upcoming fiscal year. The plan shows the level of production for each model type and month of the year. The aggregate plan is used for personnel planning, inventory planning, and budget preparation. Each month during the year, the plan is revised on the basis of the latest conditions and data.

BACK TO THE MEETING

The meeting continued with Joan Peterson saying, "We must find a way to reduce our costs. Last year we carried too much inventory, which required a great deal of capital. At 30 percent carrying cost, we cannot afford to build up as much inventory again next year."

Harold Pinter added, "If we reduce our inventories by more nearly chasing demand, the labor force will fluctuate from month to month and our hiring and firing costs will increase. It currently costs $800 to hire an employee, including the lower productivity on the line during the training period and the effort required to find new employees. I also believe it costs $1500 to fire an employee, including the severance costs

[3] Overtime work is paid at 150 percent of regular time.

[4] This cost includes capital costs (20 percent), obsolescence (5 percent), and warehouse costs (5 percent).

EXHIBIT 3
SALES DATA IN UNITS

	FY79 forecast	FY79 actual	FY80 forecast	FY80 actual	Latest FY81 forecast
18″	30,000	25,300	23,000	22,300	24,000
20″	11,900	15,680	20,300	23,500	35,500
20″ SP	15,600	14,200	20,400	21,200	31,500
22″ SP	10,500	14,320	21,300	17,600	19,000
Total	68,000	69,500	85,000	84,600	110,000

	18"	20"	20" SP	22" SP	Overtime hours
Beginning inventory	4,120	3,140	6,250	3,100	
Sept. 79 Production	3,000	3,100	—	—	—
Sales	210	400	180	110	
Oct. 79 Production	—	—	3,400	3,500	—
Sales	600	510	500	300	
Nov. 79 Production	3,000	3,800	—	—	—
Sales	1,010	970	860	785	
Dec. 79 Production	—	—	4,400	3,750	1000
Sales	1,200	1,420	1,030	930	
Jan. 80 Production	4,000	4,100			1500
Sales	1,430	1,680	1,120	1,120	
Feb. 80 Production	—	—	4,400	3,500	1620
Sales	2,140	2,210	2,180	1,850	
Mar. 80 Production	3,000	3,000	2,000	—	1240
Sales	4,870	5,100	4,560	3,210	
Apr. 80 Production	—	—	2,000	4,500	—
Sales	5,120	4,850	5,130	3,875	
May 80 Production	3,000	2,000	2,000	—	—
Sales	3,210	3,310	2,980	2,650	
June 80 Production	1,000		2,000	3,000	—
Sales	1,400	1,500	1,320	800	
July 80 Production	2,000	3,000	2,000		—
Sales	710	950	680	1,010	
Aug. 80 Production	2,000	2,000		2,000	—
Sales	400	600	660	960	
Total FY80 Production	21,000	21,000	22,200	20,250	
Sales	22,300	23,500	21,200	17,600	
End inventory (8/31/80)	2,820	640	7,250	5,750	
Nominal production rate/day*	300	350	400	420	

Exhibit 4
Units of production and sales, fiscal year 1980.

and supplemental unemployment benefits that we pay."

James Fairday expressed concern that a new shift might have to be added to accommodate the higher forecast. "We are already at plant capacity, and the additional units in the new forecast can't be made with one shift. I want to be sure these sales forecasts are realistic before we go through the trouble of hiring an entire second shift."

Lunchtime had arrived and the meeting was drawing to a close. Kathy Wayne emphasized that she wanted a new production plan developed soon. "Jim, I want you to develop an aggregate production plan that considers the costs of inventory, overtime, hiring, and firing. If your plan results in back orders we will have to incur greater costs later in the year to meet demand. I will not allow the same stockout situation that we experienced last year." The meeting adjourned for lunch.

DISCUSSION QUESTIONS

1. Develop a forecast to use as a basis for aggregate production planning.

2. Develop an aggregate production plan by model type and month for fiscal '81. Consider the use of several different production strategies. Which strategy do you recommend?

3. What are the proper batch sizes for Lawn King to use in production scheduling?

WORLD INDUSTRIAL ABRASIVES

The World Industrial Abrasives Company produces grit used in the manufacture of sandpaper and other products.[1] The production process starts with either aluminum oxide or silicon carbide as primary raw material, which is shipped to the company's crushing plant in railroad cars. The raw material passes through a series of crusher rollers, a furnace treatment, and screening operations to produce the finished grit in the desired sizes and shapes. The resulting grit can be glued to backing materials to form sandpaper and other abrasive products.

THE PRODUCTION PROCESS

A schematic representation of the grit production process is shown in Exhibit 1. Crude mineral is fed into a primary crush operation which produces a pea-sized grit referred to as "5 and Finer." Three pairs of secondary crushing rolls are available for processing the 5-and-Finer grit size; one pair is dedicated to aluminum oxide, another to silicon carbide, and the third pair may be used for crushing either mineral. Several different operations or machine settings can be utilized for crushing the 5-and-Finer grit size. Each second-

ary crushing operation normally produces three ranges of grit sizes, called splits, and a miscellaneous grit output. Because crushing operations cannot produce single grits, overproduction of some grits is often unavoidable.

Output from secondary crushing operations is normally heat-treated, giving the mineral the proper characteristics required for adherence to the backing. The capacity of this furnace treatment operation is the primary constraint on system throughput time.

Eight screening machines, each having several setups, are available for separating the furnace-treated splits into individual grits. It is the combination of secondary crushing and screening operations which determines the relative yield for each grit. A final sifting step, known as "dropping," purifies the individual grits. Approximately 10 percent of the input into the dropping operation is rejected because it is outside the quality tolerance range.

The buildup of both in-process and finished-grit inventories is an unavoidable consequence of the manufacturing process. The in-process inventory is necessary to decouple the various stages of production. The excessive finished-grit inventories are the result of the characteristics of the crushing operations, wherein single grits cannot be selectively produced. Storage of these excessive inventories represents another constraint on production. The limitations of on-site

[1] This case was prepared as a basis for class discussion, not to illustrate either effective or ineffective handling of an administrative situation.

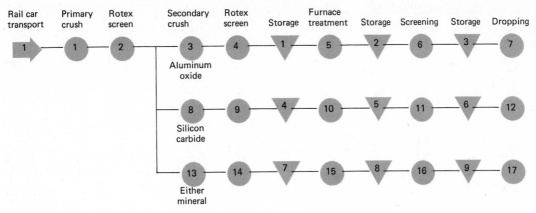

Exhibit 1
Grit-crushing system-flow-process diagram.

storage capacity require transportation of some mineral to a remote storage location at considerably greater cost.

A second unavoidable result of the production process is the recrushing of approximately 20 percent of the previously crushed mineral. Specific secondary crushing operations are dedicated to this function. The additional expense of these operations requires that original crushing and screening operations be chosen to minimize the need for recrushing.

Additionally, the difficulty of meeting the requirements exactly often results in the need to purchase finished, graded grit from outside suppliers at a premium price. This, combined with the problems of excess inventory and recrushing, requires the scheduler to make tradeoff decisions. Recognition of the costs associated with each tradeoff decision facilitates development of a production plan to minimize total costs.

PRODUCTION SCHEDULING

Each week a printout specifying the amounts of each grit size required is given to the production scheduler. These requirements are generated by an MRP program considering final demand, inventory available, and production lead time. The

scheduler's job is to determine the amount of input (silicon dioxide and aluminum oxide) and the best crushing and screening operations to be used to produce the required amounts of each grit size. In most cases, all requirements cannot be satisfied, but the scheduler attempts to come as close as possible to the required amounts of each grit size.

The development of a schedule for crushing and screening operations begins with the determination of net requirements by grit type. The scheduler analyzes the MRP requirements for an 8-week period, with primary emphasis placed on the next 4 weeks.

After reviewing the requirements, the scheduler selects a particular combination of crushes and screens and an input weight of silicon dioxide or aluminum oxide material. For these conditions the output of the production process is calculated. Performing the large number of calculations is a long and tedious process. The historical percentage outputs from each crushing and screening operation are obtained from a series of tables and used to predict the yields of the individual grits. Next, these yields must be compared to the requirements. If the yields do not compare favorably, the entire calculating process must be repeated using an alternative combination of crushes and screens. Because of the time involved in performing the calculations, only a limited number of alternatives can be considered. Therefore, experienced personnel are required to select the preferred combinations in a few trials. All together, there are 19 different crushing settings, 19 different primary screening operations, and 4 secondary screening operations which might be selected by the scheduler.

THE PROBLEM

In assessing the situation, Judy Samson, a systems analyst in the manufacturing department, felt that the situation could be improved by use of an interactive computer program. The proposed system would assist the scheduler in evaluating crushing and screening options. If an optimal solution could be identified, that would be desirable, but optimality was not required by the scheduling department. The objective of the scheduling department was to meet the requirements for crushed mineral at a reasonably low cost.

DISCUSSION QUESTIONS

1. Develop a detailed flowchart which replicates the manual method currently used by the scheduler.
2. Evaluate the advisability of using linear programming, simulation, heuristic rules, or the present scheduling method to solve this problem.
3. Develop a conceptual model to solve this problem. Specify the inputs, outputs, and computational algorithm you would use.

SLAYTON'S FURNITURE STORE

Joan Jeffery, furniture buyer for Slayton's Furniture Store, received a call from Eric Townsend, the Wexel Furniture sales representative.[1] Eric began, "Joan, I can give you a better deal on our standard Dovetail bedroom furniture set if you buy a larger quantity. We have just received a new rate from our trucking firm which reduces the shipping cost from $10 per cwt (hundredweight, or 100 pounds) to $9 per cwt provided we ship a minimum of 100 cwt. This would require you to order at least 10 bedroom sets at a time instead of your current order size of 6 sets. If you order 10 at a time, we will pass along the freight savings to you: a saving of $10 a set just on freight alone. What do you think of the deal?"

Upon hearing the offer, Joan replied, "Eric, it sounds good, but I will have to do some checking and a little pencil pushing before I can decide what to do." Joan added, "Would there be further economy if we ordered 15 sets at a time?" Excited by the prospects of more business, Eric responded, "The freight company would not reduce its price further, but we could give you a 2 percent price discount ($12 a set) if you order 15 sets or more. Why don't you think it over and I'll call you back next week to get your decision."

As Joan hung up the phone, she wondered what to do. There was room in the warehouse to store up to 15 bedroom sets, but there would be an opportunity cost, since the space would not be available for other merchandise. Also, interest rates had been soaring in recent months, and the additional capital would be costly to obtain. Joan decided to work through the problem using available economic data for the product (see Exhibit 1).

EXHIBIT 1
DOVETAIL BEDROOM SET

Selling price (each)	$1000.00
Unit cost (each)*	$600.00
Average annual sales	60 sets
Ordering cost†	$40 per order
Annual carrying cost‡	30%
Safety stock	2 sets
Weight per set	1000 lb
Lead time (average)	4 weeks

* Excludes freight cost.

† This cost includes receiving ($20 per order) and paperwork ($20 per order).

‡ This cost includes the cost of capital (20%), insurance (3%), warehouse space (5%), and obsolescence (2%).

DISCUSSION QUESTIONS

1. What should Joan do?
2. What assumptions are implicit in your analysis of the situation?

---

[1] This case was prepared as a basis for class discussion, not to illustrate either effective or ineffective handling of an administrative situation.

CONSOLIDATED ELECTRIC

Joe Henry, the sole owner and president of the Consolidated Electric Company, reflected on his inventory management problems.[1] He was a major wholesale supplier of equipment and supplies to electrical contractors, and his business hinged on the efficient management of inventories to meet his customers' needs. While Mr. Henry had built a very successful business, he was nearing retirement age and wanted to pass along a good inventory management system.

Mr. Henry's two sons-in-law were employed in the company. Carl Byerly, the older of the two, had a college degree in mathematics and was very interested in inventory formulas and computers. The other son-in-law, Edward Wright, had a degree in biology and was manager of one of the company's wholesale warehouses.

Joe Henry started the Consolidated Electric Company in the 1940s and built it into a highly profitable business. In 1979, the company had achieved $10 million dollars in sales and earned $1 million dollars in pretax profits. Consolidated Electric was currently the twelfth largest electrical wholesaler in the country.

Consolidated Electric operates through four warehouses in Iowa (Des Moines, Cedar Rapids, Sioux City, and Davenport). From these sites contractors in Iowa, Minnesota, Nebraska, Wisconsin, Illinois, and Missouri are supplied with a wide range of electrical equipment including wire, electrical boxes, connectors, lighting fixtures, and electrical controllers. The company stocks 20,000 separate line items in its inventory purchased from 200 different manufacturers. (A

line item is defined as a particular item carried at a particular location.) These items range from less than 1 cent each to several hundred dollars for the largest electrical controllers.

Of the 20,000 line items, a great many are carried to provide a full line of service. For example, the top 2000 items account for 50 percent of the sales and the bottom 10,000 items for only 20 percent. The remaining 8000 items account for 30 percent of the sales.

The company has continually purged its 20,000 inventory items to carry only those which are demanded at least once a year. As Mr. Henry says, "We live and die by good customer service at a reasonable selling price. If we do not meet this objective, the customer will go to another wholesaler or buy directly from the manufacturer."

Mr. Henry explained that he currently managed inventory by using an "earn and turn" concept. According to this concept, the earnings margin multiplied by the inventory turn ratio must equal a constant value of 2.0. For example, if a particular electrical item costs $6 to purchase wholesale and is sold for $10, then the earnings margin is $4 and the earn ratio for this item is $4/$10 = .40. If this item has a turn ratio of 5 times a year (sales is 5 times the average inventory carried), then the product of earn and turn is .4(5) = 2.0. If another item earns more, it can turn slower; if it earns less, it must turn faster.

Each year Mr. Henry sets a target earn-turn ratio for the entire business and a value for each product line. These targets are based on the estimated costs of operations and the return-on-investment goal for the company. As stated above, the current target ratio for the business is 2.0. The purchasing agents and inventory managers

[1] This case was prepared as a basis for class discussion, not to illustrate either effective or ineffective handling of an administrative situation.

at each location are measured by their ability to meet the target earn-turn ratios on their product lines. The actual ratios are reported monthly.

Although earn-turn ratios work quite well in controlling profitability of the business and entire product lines, they do not work very well for individual inventory items. Some line items tend to be in excess supply, while others are often out of stock.

The inventory is currently managed by use of a Cardex system. A card for each item is kept in a large file and a clerk posts transactions on the card as units are received or issued, thus keeping a running on-hand inventory balance. Periodically, a purchasing agent reviews the cards for a particular supplier. Then, using the order point and the quantity printed on the card, the purchasing agent places an order for all items which are below their reorder point.

If the total quantities of all items required from a supplier do not meet the purchase discount minimums or a truckload lot, additional items near their reorder points are added to the order. This is not done when the total order size is too far from the minimums, since excessive inventories would build up.

The order quantity and reorder point printed on each card are based on judgment and past experience. Generally speaking, a 3-month supply is ordered for low-cost items and as little as a 1-month supply for expensive items. Most lines are reviewed on a weekly basis.

Over the past 2 years, Consolidated Electric had been converting its inventory records to the computer. At the present time, an on-hand balance is maintained on the computer and an accurate history of all orders placed, receipts, and issues is kept. A demand history for a typical item is shown in Appendix 1 on the next page.

Mr. Henry was anxious to automate the calculation of reorder points and order quantities, but he was unsure of the exact formulas to use. Using standard textbooks in the inventory field, Mr. Henry and Carl Byerly developed the formulas given in Exhibit 1. The EOQ formula uti-

lizes a carrying cost of 28 percent and an ordering cost of $4.36 per order placed. These figures were based on past cost history at the company.

The formulas were programmed into the computer and tested on a pilot basis. For some items, the formulas seemed to work quite well, but for others they resulted in drastic departures from current practice and from common sense. For example, on one electrical box, the formulas would have ordered a 2-year supply. Mr. Henry wanted to get the new computerized system up as soon as possible, but he was not sure that the formulas would work properly. He wondered whether the formulas would meet the customer-service objectives of the business. Would they take advantage of truckload lots or purchase discounts whenever appropriate, and would the formulas result in reasonable inventory levels?

DISCUSSION QUESTIONS

1. Design an inventory control system for this business.
2. Describe how the system you have designed will help the company meet customer-service and cost objectives.

EXHIBIT 1

Delivery delay
$$= \frac{\text{maximum lead time} - \text{average lead time}}{\text{average lead time}}$$

Safety allowance
$$= \text{usage} \times \text{average lead time} \times 0.8 \times \text{delivery delay}$$

Order point
$$= \text{usage} \times \text{average lead time} + \text{safety allowance}$$

$$\text{EOQ} = \sqrt{\frac{2 \times 4.36 \times \text{daily usage} \times 365}{0.28 \times \text{unit cost}}}$$

$$\text{Line point} = \text{daily usage} \times 7 + \text{order point}$$

Quantity to order = (order point) − (quantity on order) − (quantity on hand) + quantity allocated + EOQ

Note: The line point is used to generate orders for all items in a line which are within 1 week of their order points. These orders may be used to meet truckload minimums or purchase discount minimums.

Appendix 1
Demand history for a typical item.

```
PRINT1
      VENDOR- ABMO    CATALOG NO.- 700N200A1           AUDIT TRAIL
RECORD    CUSTOMER TICKET                              BRANCH- ST. PAUL
                                                         U
  TYPE     NUMBER  NUMBER    QUANTITY    DATE            N       COST        SELL
SALES     12000-00 730606-0        1   8/10/79           E      16.32       21.60
SALES     19461-00 729425-0       60   8/02/79           E      16.32       18.72
SALES     22315-00 695421-0       65   7/31/79           E      16.32       18.72
SALES     34515-00 728883-0        2   7/30/79           E      16.32       21.60
SALES     02691-00 723670-0        1   7/24/79           E      16.32       21.60
SALES     02145-00 723482-0        1   7/23/79           E      16.32       21.60
SALES     81666-00 720920-0        8   7/23/79           E      16.32       18.72
SALES     02535-00 722026-0        4   7/20/79           E      16.32       21.60
SALES     81666-00 722637-0        6   7/16/79           E      16.32       18.72
SALES     01209-00 722413-0        7   7/13/79           E      16.32       18.72
SALES     81666-00 722409-0        8   7/13/79           E      16.32       18.72
SALES     23556-00 722001-0        1   7/13/79           E      16.32       18.72
SALES     51616-00 722418-0        3   7/11/79           E      16.32       21.60
SALES     81666-00 722408-0        6   7/11/79           E      16.32       18.72
SALES     26535-00 721861-0       20   7/11/79           E      16.32       18.72
PRINT1 S0015643
      VENDOR- ABMO    CATALOG NO.- 700N200A1           AUDIT TRAIL
RECORD    CUSTOMER TICKET                              BRANCH- ST. PAUL
                                                         U
  TYPE     NUMBER  NUMBER    QUANTITY    DATE            N       COST        SELL
SALES     86190-00 721088-0        1   7/11/79           E      16.32       21.60
SALES     18954-00 722080-0        4   7/10/79           E      16.32       18.72
SALES     32550-00 698856-0        1   7/06/79           E      16.32       21.60
SALES     53726-00 722205-0        4   7/05/79           E      16.32       21.60
SALES     80925-02 721015-0        4   7/03/79           E      16.32       24.00
SALES     39132-00 721235-0        6   7/02/79           E      16.32       21.60
SALES     22315-00 695420-0       65   6/27/79           E      16.32       18.72
SALES     15951-00 713019-0        5   6/26/79           E      16.32       18.72
SALES     77137-00 712992-0        6   6/26/79           E      16.32       21.60
SALES     14468-00 713269-0        2   6/25/79           E      16.32       21.60
SALES     63180-00 701603-0       15   6/22/79           E      16.32       18.72
SALES     12000-00 709765-0        2   6/15/79           E      16.32       18.72
SALES     32550-00 709795-0        2   6/14/79           E      16.32       21.60
SALES     29058-00 710405-0        1   6/13/79           E      16.32       21.60
SALES     17862-00 710524-0·       1   6/12/79           E      16.32       18.72
PRINT1 S0015626
      VENDOR- ABMO    CATALOG NO.- 700N200A1           AUDIT TRAIL
RECORD    CUSTOMER TICKET                              BRANCH- ST. PAUL
                                                         U
  TYPE     NUMBER  NUMBER    QUANTITY    DATE            N       COST        SELL
SALES     81666-00 699732-0        6   6/12/79           E      16.32       18.72
SALES     26535-00 710223-0       40   6/11/79           E      16.32       18.72
SALES     34515-00 710679-0        1   6/04/79           E      16.32       21.60
SALES     99940-00 710659-0        1   5/30/79           E      16.32       16.32
SALES     15951-00 699254-0        5   5/29/79           E      16.32       18.72
SALES     69576-00 710367-0        1   5/25/79           E      16.32       24.00
SALES     15951-00 695114-0        1   5/25/79           E      16.32       18.72
SALES     22315-00 695419-0       65   5/21/79           E      16.32       18.72
SALES     12051-00 701595-0        2   5/18/79           E      16.32       21.60
SALES     20631-00 701454-0        1   5/16/79           E      16.32       18.72
SALES     40315-00 701018-0       20   5/14/79           E      16.32       18.72
SALES     12051-00 700314-0       34   5/07/79           E      16.32       18.72
SALES     39132-00 700208-0        2   5/04/79           E      16.32       21.60
SALES     40315-00 691238-0       10   5/04/79           E      16.32       18.72
SALES     74607-02 699132-0        2   4/30/79           E      16.32       18.72
PRINT1 S0015607
      VENDOR- ABMO    CATALOG NO.- 700N200A1           AUDIT TRAIL
RECORD    CUSTOMER TICKET                              BRANCH- ST. PAUL
                                                         U
  TYPE     NUMBER  NUMBER    QUANTITY    DATE            N       COST        SELL
SALES     22315-00 689584-0       65   4/26/79           E      16.32       18.72
SALES     99999-00 698384-0        1   4/20/79           E      16.32       21.60
SALES     39132-00 695746-0        2   4/19/79           E      16.32       21.60
SALES     34515-00 695597-0        1   4/17/79           E      16.32       21.60
SALES     99999-00 695286-0        1   4/13/79           E      16.32       24.00
SALES     39132-00 695198-0        3   4/13/79           E      16.32       21.60
SALES     12000-00 694933-0        2   4/13/79           E      16.32       21.60
SALES     36348-00 694138-0        2   4/11/79           E      16.32       18.72
SALES     99940-00 694352-0       12   4/10/79           E      16.32       16.32
SALES     40315-00 694047-0       25   4/06/79           E      15.36       17.52
SALES     19760-00 691495-0        5   4/04/79           E      15.36       20.16
SALES     17862-00 691365-0        5   4/04/79           E      15.36       17.52
SALES     17862-00 691364-0       20   4/04/79           E      15.36       17.52
SALES     34515-00 691409-0        1   4/03/79           E      15.36       20.16
SALES     83226-00 691303-0        5   4/03/79           E      15.36       20.16
PRINT1 S0015588
      VENDOR- ABMO    CATALOG NO.- 700N200A1           AUDIT TRAIL
RECORD    CUSTOMER TICKET                              BRANCH- ST. PAUL
                                                         U
  TYPE     NUMBER  NUMBER    QUANTITY    DATE            N       COST        SELL
SALES     14966-00 691504-0        2   4/02/79           E      15.36       20.16
SALES     74607-02 689937-0        5   3/29/79           E      15.36       17.52
SALES     34515-00 690284-0        4   3/28/79           E      15.36       20.16
SALES     21333-00 690394-0        1   3/27/79           E      15.36       20.16
SALES     01209-00 689985-0        1   3/23/79           E      15.36       17.52
SALES     86190-00 690018-0        2   3/21/79           E      15.36       20.16
SALES     02535-00 689959-0        2   3/20/79           E      15.36       20.16
SALES     32550-00 670521-0        3   3/16/79           E      15.36       20.16
SALES     17862-00 683189-0        1   3/14/79           E      15.36       17.52
SALES     21333-00 681910-0        2   2/27/79           E      15.36       20.16
SALES     48477-00 682354-0       10   2/26/79           E      15.36       17.52
SALES     18954-00 682573-0        4   2/23/79           E      15.36       17.52
SALES     19461-00 682104-0       50   2/22/79           E      15.36       17.52
SALES     61842-00 681738-0        1   2/20/79           E      15.36       23.28
SALES     74607-02 678243-0       12   2/20/79           E      15.36       17.52
PRINT1 S0015573
      VENDOR- ABMO    CATALOG NO.- 700N200A1           AUDIT TRAIL
RECORD    CUSTOMER TICKET                              BRANCH- ST. PAUL
                                                         U
  TYPE     NUMBER  NUMBER    QUANTITY    DATE            N       COST        SELL
SALES     74607-02 678239-0        7   2/20/79           E      15.36       17.52
SALES     74607-02 681673-0        5   2/19/79           E      15.36       17.52
SALES     02535-00 681458-0        2   2/13/79           E      15.36       20.16
SALES     63180-00 678329-0       12   2/12/79           E      15.36       17.52
SALES     99899-00 678188-0        1   2/07/79           E      15.36       23.28
SALES     99940-00 677897-0        1   2/02/79           E      15.36       15.36
SALES     40315-00 677869-0        8   2/02/79           E      15.36       15.36
SALES     79638-00 675976-0        4   2/01/79           E      15.36       17.52
SALES     19461-00 668836-0       10   1/30/79           E      15.36       17.52
SALES     39132-00 675497-0        1   1/26/79           E      15.36       20.16
SALES     72650-00 670481-0       25   1/24/79           E      15.36       17.52
SALES     39132-00 675474-0       10   1/23/79           E      15.36       20.16
SALES     15951-00 656858-0        2   1/15/79           E      15.36       17.52
SALES     22315-00 646309-0      100   1/15/79           E      15.36       17.52
SALES     64974-00 669143-0        2   1/12/79           E      15.36       17.52
PRINT1 S
                         ITEM INVENTORY FILE    ST. PAUL
  VEND CATALOG NO.       DESCRIPTION                   INV/CLS   CARRIED IN
ABMO 700N200A1           700N200A1 CONTROL RELAY          A      S
  QTY. ON      QTY. ON     QTY         ORDER                     LEAD
   HAND        ORDER     ALLOCATED     POINT     E.O.Q.          TIME
   371          200          0          38        453          1  11
                                                               2  10
                                                               3  15
                                                             MAX 20
  QTY. SOLD        JUNE        MAY       APRIL      MARCH
  BY MONTH         121         154        76         203
  QTY. SOLD     JAN-MAR     OCT-DEC    JUL-SEP     APR-JUN
  BY QUARTER      356         292        505         201
```

HOT LINE, INCORPORATED

Early in the morning of August 28, 1972, Mr. Ted Capitani, Vice President of Manufacturing for Hot Line was discussing a proposal to adopt a new system for planning and controlling production with Hal Jaskiewicz.[1] Jaskiewicz, Manager of Production Planning and a recent MBA had proposed the new system in a memo (Exhibit 1), several weeks earlier. As Capitani rose from his desk to end the meeting, he said:

> Hal, I don't know. What you have described makes sense so far. But so did the system that those consultants designed for us three years ago. We paid them $65,000 to design and install our present system and put a lot of our own time and effort into it. But the end result was the same as it always seems to be when we open up this can of worms. Some people are enthusiastic, others get very upset, and in the end it turns out that inventories, stockouts and costs are as high as ever. Our foremen, and other people on the shop floor, have devised their own way of doing things to make up for the deficiencies in our present system, and Jack Wyzicki (VP Marketing) still hasn't forgiven us for all the lost sales which resulted when we went through the startup phase, and for all the extra work that his people have to do to make it work. I'm going to have to give some more thought to this issue, and its implications for the whole company, before I can commit.

---

[1] This case was prepared as a basis for class discussion rather than to illustrate either effective or ineffective handling of an administrative situation. Copyright © 1975 by the President and Fellows of Harvard College. Reproduced by permission. This case was prepared by Jeffrey G. Miller.

COMPANY BACKGROUND

Hot Line began operations in 1956 when they introduced their Hot Line series of monofilament fishing lines. The rapid growth of this product line led to the development and manufacture of a companion line of spin casting reels. More recently, the company had started to manufacture and market a pilot line of spinning rods. These products were marketed through distributors to small sporting goods and hardware stores, and on a direct basis to large retailers. As might be expected, sales were seasonal, with peaks in the spring, and in December. Hot Line had adopted an aggressive marketing strategy to complement their high-quality products. Sales and profits (Exhibit 2) had been increasing at a rapid rate.

Manufacturing operations for the three product lines were all carried out in Hot Line's new facility in South Bend, Indiana. Monofilament line and plastic rod blanks were molded in the plastics department of the plant where plastic reel covers and handles were also fabricated. Completed plastic component parts were stored in the manufactured component parts storeroom. These parts were periodically withdrawn from stock, along with parts from the purchased component parts stockroom, and used in one of the three assembly areas of the plant. The first assembly line was devoted to line winding and packaging, the second line to the assembly of spinning reels, and the third line was for spinning rod assembly. Exhibit 3 shows the manufacturing organization and a partial organization chart

TO: T. Capitani   August 11, 1972

FROM: H. Jaskiewicz

RE: Production Planning and Control Systems

    Our recent problems with finished goods stockouts and high inventories
have been somewhat ameliorated since we began to hold our monthly scheduling
meetings. I believe that the improved communications which have resulted are
largely responsible for the decline in backorders as a percent of sales from 9%
to 8%, and the improvement in inventory turnover from 4 times per year to 4.5
times per year. However, I do not believe that we have yet uncovered the root
of our problems. Clearly, we still have a long way to go before our operating
statistics are as good as those of our competitors.

    Since I took over as Manager of Production Planning and Control last
spring, I have been uneasy about our present system for planning and controlling
production. I began to study it closely a few months ago, and I believe that more
than anything else, it is the reason for our remaining inventory and stockout
problems. It is now easy for me to explain why this is true. Look at the reason
for most of our stockouts. It's because we simply don't have all of the <u>component
parts</u> required to assemble our products at the time that we have scheduled assembly
runs to take place. When this happens, we can't produce on time to replenish
finished goods inventory, and backorders result. Similarly, if we look at where
most of the inventory is in our system, we find that a substantial portion of it
is in <u>component parts</u>, either those purchased outside or produced from within.
Clearly, our problem is that we have <u>too many</u> of the <u>wrong</u> component parts in
inventory.

    This occurs because in our present planning and control system, we treat
assembly and parts production and ordering as two separate, unrelated entities. For
example, last month we had 2,000 Model 1198 spinning reels scheduled for assembly
on line number two. But, when we went to get the parts which were to be assembled,
we found we only had 1,200 drag gears in stock. Why did we only have 1,200 instead
of 2,000? Because under our system we schedule assembly as if we had all the parts
we needed, and we schedule parts production and purchases using an EOQ, reorder
point rule which acts as if component parts were finished goods items. On drag
gears, our rule is to order 4,000 parts (the EOQ) every time our stock levels are
drawn down to 1,000 parts (the reorder point). The reorder point is set by
determining the average demand for drag gears over the lead time it takes to
purchase them. The problem is, we never assemble an "average" amount since demand
just doesn't behave that way.

    I am recommending that we adopt a requirements planning system to
replace our present system. Requirements planning ties together assembly and
parts production and will certainly allow us to reduce both inventories and
stockouts significantly. Essentially it works like this. First, we make out our
master assembly schedule much as we do now. Then, instead of hoping that the
component parts are there when we expect to need them for assembly, we "explode"
parts requirements using a <u>bill of materials</u>. Bills of materials are lists of all
the parts required to assemble one unit of a finished product. Explosion means
that we multiply the quantity of items we have scheduled for assembly in a month
by the number of units of each component part which is required to assemble it.
For instance, if we had 2,000 Model 1198's scheduled for production in two months,
by exploding we could see that we need to have 2,000 drag gears on hand at the
time of assembly, no more, no less. Since we know the purchasing lead time on
drag gears is about one month, then we can plan to order 2,000 one month from
now. This way, we'll keep inventories down since we won't be ordering and
holding parts before we need them. Stockouts will be reduced because we'll have
the right parts on hand when we need them.

    I am sure that you can appreciate the beauty of the requirements
planning system that I am proposing. It is elegant in its simplicity. Moreover,
I am sure that it will be easy to adapt to. We will need to purchase a larger
computer to handle the explosions for our 123 finished goods items and 3,700
parts, and we will need to construct bills of materials. But after these tasks
are completed, and we have a few training sessions with the people involved, I
am sure that we will have it up and running in no time.

    I shall schedule a meeting with you in the next few weeks to define and
discuss this proposal with you further.

**Exhibit 1
Memorandum.**

EXHIBIT 2
FINANCIAL DATA

Income statements (in $000's)
Years ending December 31, 1970 and
December 31, 1971

	1971	1970
Net sales	$36,300	$28,670
Cost of goods sold		
Direct labor	4,060	2,960
Materials	14,750	10,510
Manufacturing overhead	4,290	3,500
	$23,100	$16,970
Gross profit	$13,200	$11,700
General and administrative	1,930	1,520
Marketing	10,470	8,610
	$12,400	$10,130
Profit before taxes	$ 800	$ 1,570
Provision for income taxes	330	720
Net profit	$ 470	$ 850

Balance sheets as of December 31, 1970 and December 31, 1971
(in $000's)

	December 31, 1971	December 31, 1970
ASSETS		
Current assets		
Cash	60	530
Accounts receivable	6,460	4,990
Inventory	8,066	7,180
Other	190	240
Total current assets	$14,776	$12,940
Fixed assets		
Net fixed assets	2,340	2,260
Total assets	$17,116	$15,200
LIABILITIES		
Current liabilities		
Notes payable	2,866	3,520
Accounts payable	4,720	2,980
Accruals	1,760	1,400
Total current liabilities	$ 9,346	$ 7,900
Long-term debt	$ 2,030	$ 2,030
Capital stock and surplus	1,500	1,500
Earned surplus	4,240	3,770
Net worth	$ 5,740	$ 5,270
Total liabilities	$17,116	$15,200

for Hot Line. Exhibit 4 shows the layout of Hot Line's manufacturing facility.

HOT LINE'S CURRENT PRODUCTION PLANNING AND CONTROL SYSTEM

Each month, production planning at Hot Line began with a six-month sales forecast that was prepared by marketing for each final product. The production planning and control department then compared the forecasted demand for each final product with the inventory balance to determine when an assembly lot should be scheduled. Sometimes, when Hal Jaskiewicz thought that marketing was too optimistic or pessimistic in their forecast, he revised them.

The size of an assembly lot was determined by an economic lot size analysis prepared by inventory controllers in the production planning and control department for each product. This analysis considered a product's annual requirements, the cost of holding inventory (estimated at 24% of item cost per year) and the assembly line changeover cost (estimated at $200 every time a line was prepared for the assembly of a different model).

The next step in the production planning process involved the preparation of a master assembly schedule. The master schedule was composed of three separate schedules, one for each assembly line. It indicated the planned starting and completion dates for each assembly lot for each item, for the next six months. Assembly

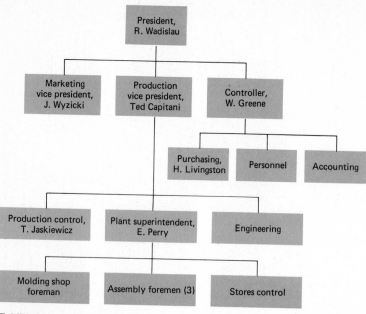

Exhibit 3
Simplified organization chart.

master scheduling was done to ensure that those products in the most danger of stocking out were assembled first, and to check to see if sufficient assembly capacity existed to produce the lots which were scheduled. If the number of lots scheduled for a particular assembly line was greater than the capacity of an assembly line during a month, the start dates for lots were shifted around or overtime was scheduled. If too few lots were scheduled to keep the assembly line

Exhibit 4
Plant layout.

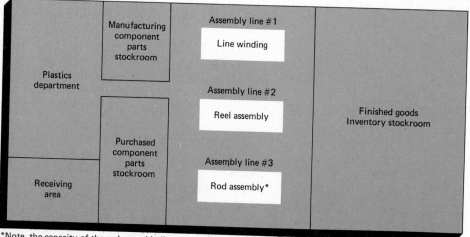

*Note, the capacity of the rod assembly line was 120 rods per day (2400 rods per month). Two days were required to change over the line for producing a new product.

EXHIBIT 5
MASTER SCHEDULE
Assembly line #2—six-month reel production master schedule (in units)

Model number	September	October	November	December	January	February
1198	1400		1640	1600		1400
1167		1100		1110		1120
1120		1240		1500		1600
1080	2750		2210		3270	
1010					4000	
1012	2000	1000		1200	1100	

workers busy, the start dates for some assembly lots were shifted forward to balance the workload. Exhibit 5 illustrates a portion of the master schedule for August.

The master schedule at this stage was discussed in the monthly scheduling meeting attended by Jaskiewicz, Capitani, Wyzicki, Perry, and Greene. These meetings served to notify those concerned of the current status of production, and plans for the immediate future. Frequently, the meetings resulted in changes in the master schedule, reflecting the desire of the plant superintendent to maintain a balanced workload, or of desires to keep inventories low. Last-minute changes in forecasts were also a reason for changes in the master schedule. Jack Wyzicki, was the first to admit that marketing's forecasts were not very good. The three most recent forecasts for one rod model shown below (Table 1) illustrates his point. He felt that he could forecast distributor demand fairly well, but had difficulty forecasting the timing of large orders from major retailers.

The completed master assembly schedule was distributed to the foremen at the start of each month. The foremen were responsible for obtaining the component parts needed to assemble scheduled final products, and for seeing that the assembly lines were set up according to schedule. They were also responsible for assigning their people to the various assembly stations, and for supervising the actual assembly operation.

The component parts for most of the company's products were inventoried in the appropriate stock rooms in the plant (see Exhibit 4). Many of these components were manufactured by Hot Line. Other parts were purchased from outside vendors. Both the manufactured and purchased parts were ordered in economic lot sizes. These lot sizes reflected an average ordering cost of $25, as well as the cost of carrying inventory. The reorder points for these component parts, i.e., the stock levels at which replenishment orders were triggered, were determined using historical demand data.

In spite of the careful attention that Jaskiewicz's inventory controllers paid to determining these reorder points and order quantities, one

TABLE 1
FORECAST

Date of forecast	July	August	September	October	November	December	January	February
June 15	1000	1000	900	900	1300	1500		
July 20		800	700	700	1000	1200	500	
August 20			600	600	800	900	300	300

EXHIBIT 6
SPINNING ROD SALES UNIT FORECAST

	Inventory balance (units)	September	October	November	December	January	February
Model 1107 5 foot rod	1,540	600	600	800	900	300	400
Model 1269 6 foot rod	320	200	200	400	500	500	500
Model 1301 7 foot rod	500	600	700	900	1000	800	800

or more component parts were frequently unavailable on the designated date at which the assembly of an item was scheduled. This resulted in delays in production, idle workers, or partially assembled products that sat in in-process inventory until the required component part could be obtained. The assembly foremen tried to avoid this problem by checking inventory levels themselves in advance of assembly, and, if need be, requesting that the molding shop foremen hurry up the production of required items, or that purchasing expedite the delivery of purchased components.

THE WALK TO BARNEY'S DINER

As Hal Jaskiewicz walked to Barney's Diner for lunch with Hank Livingston, a grizzled veteran from the purchasing department, he described his meeting with Capitani that morning, and the plan he had subsequently come up with:

I don't know if I've got Capitani's support for this system or not. But I really believe that we need it if we're going to set things straight. I think I could start using it for rod manufacturing and assembly right now. I've got the latest rod forecast from

EXHIBIT 7
MODEL 1107 BILL OF MATERIALS

Part number	Description	Number required per finished unit	Cost/unit*	Lead time†	Current inventory	On order‡
1107	Assembled rod	1	$3.00	—	1,540	—
610	Rod blank	1	1.00	1 month	300	—
107	Plastic beads§	.3 lb	.33/lb	1 month	3,000 lbs	—
720	Cork handle and reel holder	1	.75	2 months	2,890	845
647	Line guides	2	.05	1 month	6,720	—
648	Line guides	2	.05	1 month	5,400	—
649	Tip guide	1	.07	1 month	3,210	

* The unit costs represent the cost per unit for a component item, not the cost per unit of finished product. The costs are cumulative, e.g., the cost of part 610 includes the cost of the plastic beads, and the cost of the assembled rod includes all direct labor and material costs to that point.

† Note, all component parts for spinning rod assemblies are purchased from outside vendors except for the rod blanks, which are molded by Hot Line.

‡ The order of cork handles is scheduled to arrive on October 1.

§ Plastic beads provide the raw material from which the rod blanks are made.

EXHIBIT 8
MODEL 1269 BILL OF MATERIALS

Part number	Description	Number required per finished unit	Cost/unit	Lead time	Current inventory	On order
1269	Assembled rod	1	$4.00	—	320	—
611	Rod blank	1	1.50	1 month	2,210	—
107	Plastic beads	.3 lb	.33/lb	1 month	3,000 lbs	—
720	Cork handle and reel holder	1	.75	2 months	2,890	845
647	Line guides	3	.05	1 month	6,720	—
648	Line guides	2	.05	1 month	5,400	—
649	Tip guide	1	.07	1 month	3,210	—

marketing (Exhibit 6) and I've prepared bills of materials for each rod which contain cost and lead time data for all the component parts (Exhibits 7, 8, and 9).

Livingston:

Come on, you'll never make any kind of system work here. Look at what happens now. Those dingbats in marketing lie to you each month when they give you their inflated forecasts so they won't miss any sales. You adjust their forecasts and turn them into a master schedule. That's your lie. It's designed to keep the heat off you by making sure that we don't run out of finished goods. You give your lie to the assembly foremen who lie to the molding shop foreman so they can get their parts on time. You all come to me with your lies and get me to expedite purchased parts. So then I lie to a field rep by telling him I need a part in one week when I know I need it in two. He knows I'm lying but compounds it by reporting to his company that I need it in two days. Then their marketing dingbats lie to their production control people and so on and I eventually get the part in two weeks just like I knew I would. That is, unless you then tell me to cancel the order, in which case our vendors don't know whether to believe my lies or not. How the hell do you ever expect to come up with a production control system that will work in a business filled with liars and dingbats?

EXHIBIT 9
MODEL 1301 BILL OF MATERIALS

Part number	Description	Number required per finished unit	Cost/unit	Lead time	Current inventory	on order
1301	Assembled rod	1	$5.00	—	500	—
617	Rod blank	1	2.00	1 month	1,030	—
107	Plastic beads	.3 lb	.33/lb	1 month	3,000 lbs	—
720	Cork handle and reel holder	1	.75	2 months	2,890	845
647	Line guides	3	.05	1 month	6,720	—
648	Line guides	3	.05	1 month	5,400	—
649	Tip guide	1	.07	1 month	3,210	—

SOUTHWESTERN UNIVERSITY

The mathematics department at Southwestern University employs 6 secretaries, 20 professors, and 40 graduate-student teaching assistants.[1] Since Robert Kirk took over the duties of department chairman a year ago, he has been wrestling with administrative problems. In particular, Professor Kirk has been trying to streamline the secretarial jobs, improve productivity, and raise morale among the secretaries.

Secretarial turnover in the department has been high. Of the six secretaries on the staff, one has worked in the office for 4 years, one for 2 years, and the other four have been in the office for less than a year (see Exhibit 1). Of the four secretaries who left the office in the past year, one moved to another city when her husband graduated from college, another took a job in the physics department, one returned to college to get a degree, and one went to work in a downtown office building. As a result of this turnover, a great deal of additional training has been required.

Absenteeism has also been a problem in the office. Over the past year, a total of 50 days of work have been missed by the six secretaries. A detailed list of days missed and longevity on the job is given in Exhibit 1. In most cases, the reason given for missing work was personal illness. Other reasons include car problems, dentist appointments, and illness in the family.[2]

Several secretaries have expressed dissatisfaction with the working conditions. One said, "All we get around here is a lot of work and not much thanks from the professors." Another said, "I see no future in this job. The work itself is mechanical and does not provide a challenge."

[1] This case was prepared as a basis for class discussion, not to illustrate either effective or ineffective handling of an administrative situation.

[2] The universitywide absenteeism rate averaged 5 days a year with a standard deviation of 2 days.

EXHIBIT 1
JOB DATA

	Title	Days absent last year	Months since hired
Betty Brier	Administrative assistant	3	48
Joan Erickson	Supervisor	2	24
Cheryl Peterson	Typist II	15	12
Cindy North	Typist I	6	8
Mary Short	Typist I	7	2
Sharon Homer	Typist I	17	6

There is a general feeling in the office among the secretaries that they are "used" and not really treated like professional clerical employees. While all the secretaries like some typing, the four new secretaries feel they do too much typing and not enough creative work.

Pay in the department is relatively low. A starting secretary makes $610 a month, as a typist I. A typist II makes $720 a month, a supervisor makes $815 a month, and an administrative assistant makes $960 a month. If a secretary is not promoted, a salary increase of about 8 percent a year can be expected provided performance is good. There is a merit pay system in effect at the university, but most employees receive the same increase. The civil service union has made it clear that longevity will receive more emphasis in pay increases than merit.

Recently women's liberation has been a factor in the office. One secretary complained to Professor Kirk about the sexist remarks made by a professor. Another secretary has refused to get coffee for professors, claiming this is not in her job description as a typist I.

Over the past year, the office has been experimenting with word processing equipment. The department purchased CPT equipment which can be used to store typewritten material on magnetic tape.[3] The tape can be saved for later use and corrected when errors or changes occur. The CPT typewriter can be used to insert paragraphs or words into the text, and it prints out the finished material at the rate of 175 words per minute. The machine has been used primarily for form letters and for papers written by the professors. Some papers go through as many as four or five revisions before they are published. Occasionally the CPT is used to type 10 to 20 copies of a form letter that is mailed to different addresses.

The department uses a secretarial pool concept. Secretaries do not work for individual professors; instead, they are given individual clerical

---

[3] CPT refers to the Cassette Power Typewriter Corporation.

EXHIBIT 2
INTERVIEW WITH SHARON HOMER

Case writer: How do you like your job here?

Ms. Homer: There are certain parts of my job that I like very much and other parts that I do not like. I like a variety of activities. When I have to type for several hours straight, which happens occasionally, I go home very tired and depressed at night.

Case writer: Do you get a sense of accomplishment from your work?

Ms. Homer: I do take pride in a job well done. When the pressure is on to meet deadlines, however, I find it hard to maintain quality standards. All I ever hear from the professors is complaints about problems—never a word of thanks for good work.

Case writer: I notice you have been absent a number of times in the last six months. Is there some reason for this?

Ms. Homer: I have been ill twice since I came to work here. I also get migraine headaches from time to time and cannot come to work.

Case writer: How do you get along with the other secretaries?

Ms. Homer: That depends. Another girl and I are very good friends. I can work well with all of the others in the office, but I do not consider them personal friends. Occasionally, Joan gets on my nerves when she puts pressure on me.

Case writer: What do you like the least about your job?

Ms. Homer: The worst thing is the uneven workload. Some days, I sit around for several hours with nothing to do. The next day I will be swamped with work. Some of the deadlines seem arbitrary. Just last week one of the girls started crying because she could not get all of her work out on time.

Case writer: What do you like best about your job?

Ms. Homer: I really like to work with other people, provided I am not under too much pressure to get the work out. I get a sense of pride from a neatly typed letter and a job well done. I do like some challenge in my work. I hope I will not be stuck in the same job forever.

---

jobs from the incoming work basket. All work is given to the office supervisor by the professors and teaching assistants. The supervisor then gives the work to the secretaries as they become available.

In addition to these typing assignments, the following duties are assigned to the secretarial staff:

Betty Brier (administrative assistant). Betty is the administrative assistant to the department chairman. Her duties include assisting with budget preparation, faculty staffing, teaching-assistant appointments, new-student applications, course scheduling, and liaison with the university's central administration.

Joan Erickson (supervisor). Joan is responsible for supervising the four typists in the office. She assigns the typing work to the other secretaries as it comes in. She is responsible for hiring new secretaries and evaluating their performance on the job. Joan also does typing when she is not busy running the office.

Cheryl Peterson (typist II). Cheryl is responsible for typing papers and long reports. She is trained to operate the CPT typewriter and is a very productive worker. Cheryl also handles all student grade reports for the department.

Cindy North (typist I). Cindy does general typing work on class syllabi, letters, and reports. Cindy is not an extremely fast typist, but she is dependable and does high-quality work.

Mary Short (typist I). As the newest member of the department, Mary is in charge of all copy work on the duplicating machine. It is the tradition in the department that the newest member does the copying. Mary spends an average of 4 hours a day on the duplicating machine. Some days she does copying work for the entire 8 hours. When she is not copying, Mary does general typing.

Sharon Homer (typist I). Sharon acts as the receptionist and telephone operator for the department. When professors are not in, Sharon takes phone messages. She also answers student questions and provides information to outside callers. Sharon does typing when she is not busy on the phone.

In reviewing the general situation, Professor Kirk was concerned about the recent friction between the secretaries and the professors, the uneven workload in the department, the high rate of secretarial turnover and absenteeism, and the need for improved productivity. Professor Kirk knew that something had to be done, but he was unsure of what to do next.

DISCUSSION QUESTIONS

1. What problems is Professor Kirk facing in dealing with the work force and how should he handle these problems?
2. Design a method for measuring productivity in this office.
3. How can productivity be improved?
4. Describe a way to use job enrichment in this situation.

DONALDSON COMPANY

COMPANY BACKGROUND

The Donaldson Company is a Minneapolis-based firm engaged in the production and sale of air cleaners and filters, hydraulic filters, mufflers, and various dust collectors and control devices.[1] Donaldson products are distributed worldwide, principally to original equipment manufacturers in the truck and bus, construction and mining, farm equipment, railroad, and manufacturing industries.

The Donaldson Company has several operating divisions: the Fluid Power Products Division produces hydraulic filters, Torit Division produces air pollution control equipment for industrial applications, and the Liquid Systems Division manufactures equipment designed to remove particles from liquids. The Donaldson Division, the largest of the divisions and the subject of this case, manufactures heavy-duty air cleaners, replacement filter elements, mufflers, silencers, dust-control devices for mining operations, and various other specialized filters. The Donaldson Division produces approximately 70 percent of the Donaldson Company's total sales.

ORGANIZATION OF THE DONALDSON DIVISION

The Donaldson Division's manufacturing operations are conducted at eight plants located primarily in the Midwest. Production is geared to orders received, and plants typically carry only a small finished-goods inventory. Individual products are set up and run approximately five to eight times per year.

Each plant produces a portion of the approximately 25,000 different line items that the division markets. Plant outputs vary considerably in terms of volume, product mix, market application, and manufacturing requirements. In addition, while some plants produce end-use products, others manufacture components that require further assembly at another plant.

Individual plants collect and maintain data on inventory levels and labor efficiency. However, most of the accounting for the individual plants is done at division headquarters in Bloomington, Minn. Individual plants are connected through a batch processing system with a computer in Bloomington for purposes of information processing.

Plant managers have substantial control over many aspects of a plant's operations and minimal control over a few areas. Certain functions—including marketing, purchasing, and accounting—are performed at the division level. Generally, a plant manager does not have significant control over production levels, sales prices, or raw-materials prices.

The division staff in Bloomington performs the marketing function. Individual plant production forecasts are developed from the marketing forecasts, assigning production to a plant in line with the anticipated demand for the products made at that plant. Since the plant manager does not have effective control over the marketing ef-

[1] The case was prepared as a basis for class discussion, not to illustrate either effective or ineffective handling of an administrative situation.

fort and subsequent production requirements, the manager cannot control the plant utilization level as it relates to coverage of fixed expenses.

A second aspect of the centralized marketing function is that the plant managers have little impact on the prices at which the plant's production is sold. Pricing policies are determined at the division level, with prices based on market conditions as well as cost considerations. As will be explained later, these pricing policies have a significant impact on the measurement of current plant performance.

Finally, purchasing of significant materials is performed at the division level. Thus, the prices of raw materials at the plant level are largely beyond the control of the plant manager.

Apart from production volume, sales prices, and raw-materials prices, the plant manager has substantial control over all other aspects of plant operations. Because of the impact on profits of the variables that the plant manager does not control, management feels it is more appropriate to view the individual plants as cost centers rather than profit centers.

EVALUATION OF A PLANT MANAGER'S PERFORMANCE

The Donaldson Division is oriented toward acceptable rates of profitability and return on assets. While profitability is easily measured at the division level, it is more difficult to measure the plant manager's contributions to profits. Since a plant manager controls only some of the variables that affect plant profits, plant net profit does not adequately reflect the plant manager's contribution.

The Donaldson Division currently utilizes a management by objectives (MBO) system. The MBO system defines nine measures for which the plant manager is held responsible. Three of these areas relate to division or corporate profitability; five are concerned with customer service,

quality control, labor efficiency, inventory turnover, and return on assets employed. The other measure, called the profit improvement goal, attempts to measure the plant manager's contribution to profit by measuring the direct costs incurred at the plant level.

The nine measures have varying weights in the computation of the overall MBO performance appraisal. The weight of the profit improvement goal measure varies between 10 and 15 percent of a manager's total appraisal, depending on the plant involved. The vehicle for measuring a manager's accomplishment of the profit improvement goal is a montly report titled the *Plant Goal Analysis* (PGA).

Recently, the Donaldson Division has questioned the use of the PGA report as an effective means of measuring a plant manager's achievement of the profit improvement goal. The stated objective of the profit improvement goal is to increase profit through reduction of direct plant costs. These costs are defined as material, direct labor, overhead, and direct plant general and administrative (G&A) expense. Performance is measured by a ratio of actual direct plant costs to target direct plant costs.

The PGA shows the actual and target direct plant costs on a monthly and year-to-date basis. Before looking at the PGA report itself, the budgeting process should be reviewed. An understanding of the flow of the budgeting process is essential to understanding the problems inherent in the PGA method.

BUDGETING PROCESS

The first step in the budgeting process is the division sales plan. Based on the division sales plan, production is assigned to the individual plants. Plant costs are then budgeted based on assigned production. Budgeted plant standard costs are computed as percentages of sales at the current selling price. If no price increases were planned, standard costs would be a constant percentage of sales throughout the year. However, because price increases are planned, standard costs decrease as a percentage of budgeted sales. No allowance is made in budgeted standard costs for cost increases because standards are fixed throughout the year. Expected cost increases are reflected in budgeted variances. An example of the profit and loss (P&L) budget for one plant is shown in Exhibit 1. The corresponding PGA for the plant is shown in Exhibit 2.

DESCRIPTION OF THE PLANT GOAL ANALYSIS

The plant manager is not responsible for purchasing or sales, therefore some of the budget variances on the PGA are beyond the manager's control. The PGA analyst identifies the variances which the plant manager controls in order to measure the manager's contribution to division profits. That is accomplished by converting the P&L budget, which is a fixed budget, into a variable budget. To do that, the items in the PGA are divided into three categories:

1. Uncontrollable
2. Fixed
3. Variable

The uncontrollable items are sales, purchase variances, absorbed overhead, and new model tooling. For these items the plan is set equal to the actual, so that the variance is always zero. The fixed items are the reserves for shrink and direct G&A. For these items the plan is taken directly from the P&L budget.

The variable items are standard materials, standard labor, standard overhead, and the methods variances. The planned amounts for these items are computed as percentages of actual sales based on the corresponding percentages on the P&L budget. For example, if budgeted sales

are $1 million and budgeted standard materials are $400,000 (on the P&L budget), and if actual sales are $1.1 million, then planned standard materials on the PGA would be $440,000. The result is that the manager is not penalized for costs over budget which are the result of sales over budget, nor is the manager rewarded for cost reductions which are the result of sales reductions.

Manufacturing expense is semivariable. The fixed and variable components are identified and the plan amounts are computed separately. In addition, the variable component is broken down into two parts. Planned costs for direct departments are computed on the basis of direct hours, and planned costs for nondirect departments are based on product dollars produced. Exhibit 3 summarizes the calculation of the plan amounts for the various items.

The manager's performance on the profit improvement goal is computed by comparing total actual to total plan costs, as follows:

Actual 98.5 percent of plan is 100 percent accomplishment.
Actual 100 percent of plan is 50 percent accomplishment.
Actual 101.5 percent of plan is 0 percent accomplishment.

Interpolation is used between the stated benchmarks. No allowance is made for accomplishment above 100 percent or below 0 percent. The percent accomplishment is included in each manager's MBO evaluation.

Donaldson management has identified three weaknesses in the formulation of the PGA which result in inadequacies in the measurement process:

1. The use of sales and cost of sales instead of production and cost of production
2. The inclusion of uncontrollable items in the totals
3. The use of sales as a basis for computing variable costs

EXHIBIT 1
PROFIT & LOSS STATEMENT, Dinkytown Plant
Period of 6 months ended January 31, 1980
(000's omitted)

	Current month					Current year-to date					Prior year-to-date			
	Actual	% of sales	Plan	% of sales	Over/(under) plan	Actual	% of sales	Plan	% of sales	Over/(under) plan	Actual	% of sales	Incr./(decr.) Amount	%
Sales														
Customer	$1,176	86.7	$1,355	88.6	$(179)	$7,293	88.4	$6,955	88.4	$338	$4,637	86.1	$2,656	57.3
Interplant	180	13.3	175	11.4	5	960	11.6	910	11.6	50	748	13.9	212	28.3
Total	1,356	100.0	1,530	100.0	(174)	8,253	100.0	7,865	100.0	388	5,385	100.0	2,868	53.3
Cost of sales														
Material	584	43.1	699	45.7	(115)	3,760	45.5	3,584	45.6	176	2,381	44.2	1,379	57.9
Labor	99	7.3	119	7.8	(20)	641	7.8	609	7.7	32	422	7.8	219	51.9
Burden	354	26.1	314	20.5	40	1,895	23.0	1,742	22.2	153	1,436	26.7	459	32.0
Tooling	21	1.5	21	1.4	—	125	1.5	125	1.6	—	109	2.0	16	14.7
Total	1,058	78.0	1,153	75.4	(95)	6,421	77.8	6,060	77.1	361	4,348	80.7	2,073	47.7
Gross margin	298	22.0	377	24.6	(79)	1,832	22.2	1,805	22.9	27	1,037	19.3	795	76.7
Operating expenses														
Marketing	22	1.6	26	1.7	(4)	142	1.7	154	2.0	(12)	113	2.1	29	25.7
Physical distribution	20	1.5	16	1.0	4	110	1.3	94	1.2	16	70	1.3	40	57.1
Product engineering	57	4.2	57	3.7	—	323	3.9	348	4.4	(25)	305	5.7	18	5.9
Production development	—		—		—	—		—		—	—		—	
Plant G&A	22	1.6	21	1.4	1	130	1.6	125	1.6	5	100	1.9	30	20.0
Division G&A	32	2.4	35	2.3	(3)	190	2.3	212	2.7	(22)	151	2.8	39	25.8
Corporate services	5	.3	5	.3	—	31	.4	29	.3	2	44	.8	(13)	(29.5)
Sub-total	158	11.6	160	10.4	(2)	926	11.2	962	12.2	(36)	783	14.6	143	18.3
Other														
Other income	—		—		—	—		—		—	—		—	
Other expense	1	.1	—		1	1		—		1	—		1	
Total	1	.1	—		1	1		—		1	—		1	
Total	159	11.7	160	10.4	(1)	927	11.2	962	12.2	(35)	783	14.6	144	18.4
Direct operating profit	$ 139	10.3	$ 217	14.2	$ (78)	$ 905	11.0	$ 843	10.7	$ 62	$ 254	4.7	$ 651	256.3

Manufacturing expense through 6 months has been increased by $51 due to adjustments of accruals. $39 of this total was adjusted in January.

EXHIBIT 2
DONALDSON COMPANY, INC.—PLANT GOAL ANALYSIS
Plant: Dinkytown
Month: January 1981
(000's omitted)

Description	Actual	%	Plan	%	Cum. actual	%	Cum. plan	%
Sales—customer	1,176	86.7	1,176	86.7	7,303	88.5	7,303	88.5
interplant	180	13.3	180	13.3	960	11.6	960	11.6
returns	—	—	—	—	(10)	(.1)	(10)	(.1)
Total net sales	1,356	100.0	1,356	100.0	8,253	100.0	8,253	100.0
COST OF SALES								
Direct material								
Std. mat'l.—reg.	387	32.9	425	36.1	2,522	34.6	2,627	36.0
Std. mat'l.—I.P.	80	44.4	76	42.2	411	42.8	405	42.2
Pur. var.—reg.	9	.7	9	.7	30	.4	30	.4
Pur. var.—I.P.	105	7.7	105	7.7	779	9.4	779	9.4
Res. for shrink	—	—	—	—	—	—	—	—
Methods variance	3	.2	3	.2	18	.2	18	.2
Total act. material	584	43.1	618	45.6	3,760	45.5	3,859	46.7
Direct labor								
Std. labor—regular	79	6.7	85	7.2	527	7.2	527	7.2
Std. labor—I.P.	10	5.6	11	6.1	61	6.4	60	6.3
Res. for shrink	1	.1	—	—	5	.1	4	—
Methods variance	9	.7	9	.7	48	.6	48	.6
Total act. labor	99	7.3	105	7.8	641	7.8	639	7.7
Manufacturing overhead								
Std. O.H.—reg.	195	16.6	200	17.0	1,300	17.8	1,255	17.2
Std. O.H.—I.P.	26	14.4	26	14.4	149	15.5	143	14.9
Mfg. expense*	339	25.0	291	21.4	1,825	22.1	1,745	21.1
Less: abs. overhead*	(228)	(16.8)	(228)	(16.8)	(1,505)	(18.2)	(1,505)	(18.2)
Unabsorbed overhead	111	8.2	63	4.6	320	3.9	240	2.9
Reserve for shrink	2	.1	2	.1	12	.1	12	.1
Methods variance	20	1.5	20	1.5	114	1.4	114	1.4
Total actual overhead	354	26.1	311	22.9	1,895	23.0	1,764	21.4
New model tooling	21	1.5	21	1.5	125	1.5	125	1.5
Total cost of sales	1,058	78.0	1,055	77.8	6,421	77.8	6,387	77.3
Less new model tooling	(21)	(1.5)	(21)	(1.5)	(125)	(1.5)	(125)	(1.5)
Plus direct G&A	22	1.6	21	1.5	130	1.6	125	1.5
Total direct plant costs	1,059	78.1	1,055	77.8	6,426	77.9	6,387	77.3

* Not included in totals
Manufacturing expense through 6 months has been increased by $51 due to adjustments of accruals. $39 of this total was adjusted in January.
Donaldson Division Accounting

Date _____ February 10, 1981

Goal measurement
  98.5% of plan = 100% accomplishment
  100.0% of plan = 50% accomplishment
  101.5% of plan = 0% accomplishment

Cumulative plant goal achievement: 30%

EXHIBIT 3
DONALDSON COMPANY, INC.—PLANT GOAL ANALYSIS
Plant _____
Month _____
(000's omitted)

Description	Actual	%	Plan	%	Cum. actual	%	Cum. plan	%
Sales—customer	*							
interplant	*							
returns	*							
Total net sales								
COST OF SALES								
Direct material	*							
Std. mat'l.—reg.	***							
Std. mat'l.—I.P.	***							
Pur. var.—reg.	*							
Pur. var.—I.P.	*							
Res. for shrink	**							
Methods variance	***							
Total act. material								
Direct labor								
Std. labor—regular	***							
Std. labor—I.P.	***							
Res. for shrink	**							
Methods variance	***							
Total act. labor								
Manufacturing overhead								
Std. O.H.—reg.	***							
Std. O.H.—I.P.	***							
Mfg. expense*	****							
Less: abs. overhead*	*							
Unabsorbed overhead								
Reserve for shrink	**							
Methods variance	***							
Total actual overhead								
New model tooling	*							
Total cost of sales								
Less new model tooling	*							
Plus direct G&A	**							
Total direct plant costs								

KEY—
   * Uncontrollable—Plan is set equal to actual.
  ** Fixed—Plan is taken directly from the P&L budget.
 *** Variable—Plan is computed as a percentage of sales.
**** Semi-variable—Fixed and variable components of the plan are computed separately.

Goal measurement
  98.5% of plan = 100% accomplishment
 100.0% of plan = 50% accomplishment
 101.5% of plan = 0% accomplishment

Cumulative plant goal achievement: _____

Inventory at month end = _____

Donaldson Division Accounting

Date _____

DONALDSON'S DILEMMA

Faced with these problems in measurement of plant performance, the management of the Donaldson Division recognized two alternatives. The first was to improve the PGA measurement system to more accurately reflect actual plant performance. The second alternative, representing an entirely different approach, was to abandon the PGA form and develop a productivity measure for plant performance. The productivity measure could represent actual output divided by input and it could be compared from one period to the next independent of the plan. While a productivity measure might eliminate some of the problems with the PGA, it might create still other problems in the measurement of plant performance.

QUESTIONS

1. How should the current PGA measurement system be improved to more accurately reflect plant performance?
2. Devise a productivity measure for the Donaldson Company plants.
3. Discuss the pros and cons of using the PGA approach as opposed to the productivity measurement approach to evaluating plant performance.

MINNESOTA DIVERSIFIED INDUSTRIES

Minnesota Diversified Industries (MDI) is a national model of an affirmative industry firm.[1] (An affirmative industry is a nonprofit organization whose primary goal is to provide employment to people who are handicapped.) Over 80 percent of the employees at MDI have social, physical, or mental handicaps. Although MDI is very similar to a business run for profit, there is one major distinction: whereas the for-profit business is primarily concerned with earning profit for investors, the affirmative industry is concerned with providing meaningful employment opportunities to handicapped people who have traditionally been unable to work.

MDI engages in packaging operations, the recycling of returnable containers, the repair of wooden pallets, and other operations which can be performed by handicapped employees. Because MDI is a nonprofit organization, it must raise capital from donations by government and nongovernment sources. Aside from the source of capital, the company is competitive in every respect with other business firms. On price, for example, MDI competes in the marketplace with other firms that do not employ handicapped workers. As a result, the employees of MDI must perform productive work in relation to the amount they are paid.

[1] This case was prepared as a basis for class discussion, not to illustrate either effective or ineffective handling of an administrative situation.

With respect to wages, MDI pays an hourly rate based on the level of production achieved. As a result, some of the severely handicapped employees earn as little as 10 or 25 percent of the minimum wage rate when they are first employed. As the employees are trained and become more productive, their wage rate is increased to reflect improved output. Many employees have equaled or exceeded the minimum wage rate after a period of time with the company. Some employees were originally so severely handicapped they were released from sheltered workshop programs as "untrainable."

MDI also employs a number of "competitive" workers who do not have handicaps. These competitive workers serve as role models: they help train the handicapped workers and are used to define the 100 percent work pace. All together, 320 handicapped workers and 80 competitive workers are employees at MDI.

The MDI wage rate system is essential to the survival of the company. It allows MDI to control its costs on a competitive basis and, more importantly, it provides the handicapped worker with a sense of progress and pride as the worker's productivity improves. One of the goals of the company is to monitor each employee carefully and help him or her to achieve wage improvement during each quarter of the year.

To implement the MDI wage policy, each employee who earns less than the minimum wage is subjected to time study five times per

EXHIBIT 1
TIME STUDY SUMMARY
12/26/77 to 3/25/79

Period covered	Status of those studied	# studied	# of individuals studied—times per quarter													Under five studies per individual		Of those studied less than 5 times—not studied in previous quarter	
			1	2	3	4	5	6	7	8	9	10	11	12	13	#	%	#	%
12/26/77 to 3/25/78	Main plant employees	87	9	12	14	13	9	9	8	2	3	6	1	1		48	55		
3/26/78 to 6/25/78	Main plant employees	92	23	9	11	12	9	12	5	6		5				55	60		
	Main plant trainees	30	5	5	5	1	4	1	6	1	2					16	53		
	Plant 1 employees	41	6	5	8	2	2	5	5	2	2	1	2		1	21	51		
6/26/78 to 9/25/78	Main plant employees	104	23	24	17	19	13		5	3						83	80	32	39
	Main plant trainees	37	7	10	3	4	6	4	1	2						24	65	12	50
	Plant 1 employees	45	19	13	11		2									43	96	12	28
9/26/78 to 12/25/78	Main plant employees	117	29	19	35	13	11	8	2							96	82	26	27
	Main plant trainees	46	9	8	13	5	8	2	1	1						35	76	19	54
	Plant 1 employees	51	9	7	15	7	9	2	1	1						38	75	9	24
12/26/78 to 3/25/79	Main plant employees	93	28	20	17	12	7	4	5							77	83	9	12
	Main plant trainees	37	9	8	5	1	4	3	3	2	2					23	62	9	39
	Plant 1 employees	28	16	9	3											28	100	0	0

quarter. Each time study lasts 10 minutes, during which the actual production rate is compared to the employee's current base rate for pay purposes. On the basis of the five quarterly time studies, the pay rate for the next quarter is set.

The pay rate for every employee is determined in relation to the pay for a competitive worker. Suppose, for example, that on a particular job the competitive worker earns $4 per hour and produces a standard output of 10 pieces per hour. The piece rate for this job is therefore 40¢ per piece produced. If a particular handicapped employee produces 5 pieces per hour, that employee's pay rate will then be 5 × 40¢ = $2 per hour.

For each employee, an efficiency is also defined relative to the minimum wage. Suppose, for example, the minimum wage is $2.90 per hour. Then a worker earning the minimum wage should produce 2.90/.40 = 7.25 pieces per hour. The efficiency of the worker who produces 5 pieces per hour is therefore 5/7.25 = 69 percent. It is the goal of the company to improve the efficiency and therefore the pay rate of each worker.

Recently MDI has begun to review the method of time study used to set wage rates and efficiencies. Data in Exhibit 1, for example, indicate that substantial numbers of employees were not time studied five times during each quarter due to overloading of the single time-study employee available. It also was not possible to standardize the method and to rate each employee's pace in accordance with normal industrial engineering practice. As a result, the management of MDI felt that a better work measurement system could be devised. Perhaps the improved system could use actual production records to determine the pay rate and efficiency figures. For certain purposes, properly conducted time studies might also be used. The company was eager to explore these options and to implement an improved work measurement system.

DISCUSSION QUESTIONS

1. What are the alternative approaches to work measurement that the company might use?
2. Describe a work measurement approach that you would recommend to the management of MDI.
3. How would you go about implementing the system that you recommend?

GENERAL APPLIANCE COMPANY

The Milwaukee Division of General Appliance Company manufactures freezers, vacuum cleaners, ice makers, and other consumer appliances.[1] For the General Appliance Company, quality has always been a source of pride and a competitive advantage. In view of the company's quality image, George Rodgers, director of quality assurance for the Milwaukee Division, was concerned about the quality of parts which were used on the freezer assembly line. While the quality of the finished product had, apparently, not suffered, "irregularities" had occurred in the quality control system, and Mr. Rodgers wanted to correct these. He therefore decided to conduct a complete review of the parts quality control system at the Milwaukee Division freezer plant.

Mr. Rodgers and Dick West, his quality control engineer, requested that a team of four MBA students from Marquette University be assigned to conduct a quality audit. In briefing the MBA team, Mr. West stated that he wanted the team to cover all aspects of parts quality from receiving of incoming parts through sample parts inspection and management policies. In Mr. West's words, "No stones should be left unturned in reviewing the present quality control system and in recommending improvements."

The MBA team set out to define the problems in more detail and to develop a methodology for the quality audit. As part of the problem definition, the team interviewed all managers and supervisors at the freezer plant about how the quality system functioned and about the problems they saw in its operation. In all, about 20 managers were interviewed. The team also collected information on the flow of parts from the time they were received until they reached the freezer line, and they collected copies of all written quality policies and procedures in effect. As a result of these initial efforts, several issues were identified for in-depth study.

A formal questionnaire was then designed to aid in detailed study of the issues and formulation of recommendations. The questionnaire was administered to 10 directors, 21 managers, 32 supervisors, and 32 engineers. A sample of some of the results of the questionnaire is shown in Exhibit 1.

The questionnaire seemed to indicate a certain lack of understanding of the "total" quality concept, where all departments are collectively responsible for producing a quality product. This problem was compounded by conflicting departmental goals, a lack of teamwork, and poor communications between the various departments. However, as may be noted in Exhibit 1, the agreement on these issues by the people interviewed was by no means unanimous.

---

[1] This case was prepared as a basis for class discussion, not to illustrate either effective or ineffective handling of an administrative situation.

EXHIBIT 1
QUALITY SURVEY

ITEM 3

What percentage of your time is devoted to quality assurance–related activities?

	Row pct.	Total count
1. None	7.4	7
2. 1–20% of the time	38.9	37
3. 21–30% of the time	11.6	11
4. 31–40% of the time	10.5	10
5. 41–50% of the time	7.4	7
6. 51–60% of the time	7.4	6
7. More than 61% of the time	17.9	17

Marginally significant (.0929) differences in time spent on quality-related activities occurred depending upon job title. Overall, foremen and the supervisor/engineer group spent more time with quality tasks than other groups. Sixty percent of the managers spent less than 20 percent of their time on quality-related activities.

ITEM 7

How often do you accept responsibility (blame) for a quality-related problem? Answer in terms of times you have accepted responsibility within the *last 6 months*.

	Row pct.	Total count
1. Never	31.2	29
2. Once	12.9	12
3. Twice	6.5	6
4. Three times	4.3	4
5. Four times	9.7	9
6. More than four times (specify)	35.5	33
(2 missing observations)		

This question revealed response differences depending on job title (.0018) as well as product line (.0613). Overall foremen represent the group which said they accepted blame most often, engineers were second. Responses for directors were at opposite ends of the response scale— 60 percent indicated they accepted blame more than five times in the last 6 months while 40 percent responded "never."

ITEM 9

How would you rate the quality of the product(s) you are associated with?

	Row pct.	Total count
1. Excellent	15.4	14
2. Very good	49.5	45
3. Good	29.7	27
4. Fair	3.3	3
5. Poor	2.2	2
(4 missing observations)		

EXHIBIT 1 (*Continued*)

ITEM 10
How would you rate the job that the quality control department does?

	Row pct.	Total count
1. Outstanding	0	0
2. Very good	28.0	26
3. Good	51.6	48
4. Fair	18.3	17
5. Poor	2.2	2

(2 missing observations)

ITEM 11
If your answer for question 10 was below "outstanding," what is the major factor preventing quality control from performing in an outstanding way?

	Row pct.	Total count
1. Lack of technical expertise in Q. C. department	7.9	7
2. Poor financial support	10.9	9
3. No commitment from other departments	14.6	13
4. Lack of direction	15.7	14
5. Low status of Q. C. department compared to other departments	7.9	7
6. None of the above (specify)	31.5	28
7. I rated the Q. C. department as outstanding	0.0	0
8. More than one reason	12.4	11

ITEM 21
Do you have quantifiable measures of performance in your management objectives which relate to quality?

	Row pct.	Total count
1. Yes	47.4	45
2. No	16.8	16
3. I have quality related objectives, but they are not easily measured; in other words, they are qualitative measures.	35.8	34

ITEM 24
Do you feel that quality goals from department to department are in conflict?

	Row pct.	Total count
1. Yes	62.2	56
2. No	37.8	34

(5 missing observations)

Respondent comment: "Yes, budget control versus quality program implementation."

EXHIBIT 1 (*Continued*)

ITEM 26

Should the line be shut down more often for problems relating to quality?

	Row pct.	Total count
1. Yes	48.4	45
2. No	51.6	48
(2 missing observations)		

The majority within the managers, directors, and supervisor/engineers groups favored shutting down the line more often for quality-related problems. Foremen did not agree. This difference was significant at .0645.

ITEM 27

It has been said that too many decisions are attempted through *committees*. Do you feel that *individuals* should assume more responsibility for quality decisions?

	Row pct.	Total count
1. Yes	71.3	67
2. No	28.7	27
(1 missing observation)		

Respondent comments: "Let's get managers acting like managers." "When QC foremen make a decision too many times it is overridden by somebody higher up in quality control." "On some items it would be much better if individuals made the decisions."

ITEM 28

Would you be willing to accept such responsibility for quality decisions relating to your area of responsibility?

	Row pct.	Total count
1. Yes	89.4	84
2. No	10.6	10
(1 missing observation)		

ITEM 29

Do you feel that people will try to short-cut quality procedures because they take too much time?

	Row pct.	Total count
1. Yes	72.6	69
2. No	27.4	26

In reviewing the results of the questionnaire, Mr. Rodgers felt that something should be done, but the proper action was not clear. He recognized that it was always easy to blame the quality control department when things went wrong. He wondered how this situation could be improved.

DISCUSSION QUESTIONS

1. What precisely are the problems in managing quality at General Appliance?
2. How should the management problems be resolved?
3. What steps should be taken in the short run and the long run?

BAYFIELD MUD COMPANY

In November, 1976, John Wells, a customer service representative of Bayfield Mud Company, was summoned to the Houston, Texas, warehouse of Wet-Land Drilling, Inc. to inspect three boxcars of mud treating agents which Bayfield Mud Company had shipped to the Houston firm.[1] (Bayfield's corporate offices and its largest plant are located in Orange, Texas, which is just west of the Louisiana-Texas border.) Wet-Land Drilling had filed a complaint that the 50-pound bags of treating agents that it had just received from Bayfield were short-weight by approximately 5 percent.

The light-weight bags were initially detected by one of Wet-Land's receiving clerks who noticed that the railroad scale tickets indicated that the net weights were significantly less on all three of the boxcars than those of identical shipments received on October 25, 1976. Bayfield's traffic department was called to determine if lighter weight dunnage or pallets were used on the shipments. (This might explain the lighter net weights.) Bayfield indicated, however, that no changes had been made in the loading or palletizing procedures. Hence, Wet-Land randomly checked 50 of the bags and discovered that the average net weight was 47.51 pounds. They noted from past shipments that the bag net weights averaged exactly 50.0 pounds, with an acceptable standard deviation of 1.2 pounds. Consequently, they concluded that the sample indicated a significant short-weight. (The reader may wish to verify the above conclusion.) Bayfield was then contacted, and Wells was sent to

investigate the complaint. Upon arrival, Wells verified the complaint and issued a 5 percent credit to Wet-Land.

Wet-Land's management, however, was not completely satisfied with only the issuance of credit for the short shipment. The charts followed by their mud engineers on the drilling platforms were based on 50-pound bags of treating agents. Lighter weight bags might result in poor chemical control during the drilling operation and might adversely affect drilling efficiency. (Mud-treating agents are used to control the pH and other chemical properties of the cone during drilling operation.) This could cause severe economic consequences because of the extremely high cost of oil and natural gas well-drilling operations. Consequently, special use instructions had to accompany the delivery of these shipments to the drilling platforms. Moreover, the light-weight shipments had to be isolated in Wet-Land's warehouse, causing extra handling and poor space utilization. Hence, Wells was informed that Wet-Land's Drilling might seek a new supplier of mud treating agents if, in the future, it received bags that deviated significantly from 50 pounds.

The quality control department at Bayfield suspected that the light-weight bags may have resulted from "growing pains" at the Orange plant. Because of the 1973 energy crisis, oil and natural gas exploration activity had greatly increased. This increased activity, in turn, created increased demand for products produced by related industries, including drilling muds. Consequently, Bayfield had to expand from a one-shift (6:00 A.M. to 2:00 P.M.) to a two-shift (6:00 A.M. to 10:00 P.M.) operation in mid-1974 and finally to a three-shift operation (24 hours per day) in the fall of 1976.

The additional night-shift bagging crew was staffed entirely by new employees. The most experienced foremen were temporarily assigned to supervise the night-shift employees. Most emphasis was placed on increasing the output of bags to meet the ever-increasing demand. It was suspected that only occasional reminders were made to double-check the bag weight-feeder. (A double-check is performed by systematically weighing a bag on a scale to determine if the proper weight is being loaded by the weight-feeder. If there is a significant deviation from 50 pounds, corrective adjustments are made to the weight-release mechanism.)

To verify this expectation, the quality control staff randomly sampled the bag output and prepared the following chart. Thirty-six bags were sampled and weighed each hour.

Time	Avg. weight (pounds)	Range	
		Smallest	Largest
6:00 A.M.	49.6	48.7	50.7
7:00	50.2	49.1	51.2
8:00	50.6	49.6	51.4
9:00	50.8	50.2	51.8
10:00	49.9	49.2	52.3
11:00	50.3	48.6	51.7
12:00 Noon	48.6	46.2	50.4
1:00 P.M.	49.0	46.4	50.0
2:00	49.0	46.0	50.6
3:00	49.8	48.2	50.8
4:00	50.3	49.2	52.7
5:00	51.4	50.0	55.3
6:00	51.6	49.2	54.7
7:00	51.8	50.0	55.6
8:00	51.0	48.6	53.2
9:00	50.5	49.4	52.4
10:00	49.2	46.1	50.7
11:00	49.0	46.3	50.8
12:00 Midnight	48.4	45.4	50.2

Time	Avg. weight (pounds)	Range	
		Smallest	Largest
1:00 A.M.	47.6	44.3	49.7
2:00	47.4	44.1	49.6
3:00	48.2	45.2	49.0
4:00	48.0	45.5	49.1
5:00	48.4	47.1	49.6
6:00	48.6	47.4	52.0
7:00	50.0	49.2	52.2
8:00	49.8	49.0	52.4
9:00	50.3	49.4	51.7
10:00	50.2	49.6	51.8
11:00	50.0	49.0	52.3
12:00 Noon	50.0	48.8	52.4
1:00 P.M.	50.1	49.4	53.6
2:00	49.7	48.6	51.0
3:00	48.4	47.2	51.7
4:00	47.2	45.3	50.9
5:00	46.8	44.1	49.0
6:00	46.8	41.0	51.2
7:00	50.0	46.2	51.7
8:00	47.4	44.0	48.7
9:00	47.0	44.2	48.9
10:00	47.2	46.6	50.2
11:00	48.6	47.0	50.0
12:00 Midnight	49.8	48.2	50.4
1:00 A.M.	49.6	48.4	51.7
2:00	50.0	49.0	52.2
3:00	50.0	49.2	50.0
4:00	47.2	46.3	50.5
5:00	47.0	44.1	49.7
6:00	48.4	45.0	49.0
7:00	48.8	44.8	49.7
8:00	49.6	48.0	51.8
9:00	50.0	48.1	52.7
10:00	51.0	48.1	55.2
11:00	50.4	49.5	54.1
12:00 Noon	50.0	48.7	50.9
1:00 P.M.	48.9	47.6	51.2
2:00	49.8	48.4	51.0
3:00	49.8	48.8	50.8

Time	Avg. weight (pounds)	Range	
		Smallest	Largest
4:00	50.0	49.1	50.6
5:00	47.8	45.2	51.2
6:00	46.4	44.0	49.7
7:00	46.4	44.4	50.0
8:00	47.2	46.6	48.9
9:00	48.4	47.2	49.5
10:00	49.2	48.1	50.7
11:00	48.4	47.0	50.8
12:00 Midnight	47.2	46.4	49.2
1:00 A.M.	47.4	46.8	49.0
2:00	48.8	47.2	51.4
3:00	49.6	49.0	50.6
4:00	51.0	50.5	51.5
5:00	50.5	50.0	51.9

DISCUSSION QUESTIONS

1. What is your analysis of the bag weight problem?
2. What procedures would you recommend to maintain proper quality control?

In April 1978, James Wallace, general manager of the Advanced Products Division at Sheldahl, was considering a change in manufacturing strategy.[1] Recently, Mr. Wallace and his staff had revised the business stategy of the division. As a result, it became apparent that the marketing, engineering, and manufacturing strategies should also be revised.

The Sheldahl Company started in the aerospace business in the 1960s. In the early years, the company developed and produced the Echo weather satellites which were launched into space. More recently, the Sheldahl Company had diversified into three divisions located in Northfield, Minn.: the Electrical Products Division (EPD), the Materials Division (MD), and the Advanced Products Division (APD). EPD produced a variety of circuit boards and other electrical products for mass markets. MD produced laminated plastic materials which were sold to EPD, APD, and outside customers. APD manu-

[1] This case was prepared as a basis for class discussion, not to illustrate either effective or ineffective handling of an administrative situation.

factured specialty products to customer order. The sales growth and profitability of the company have been good over the past 5 years, as shown in Exhibit 1. Sales and profits of the APD division, however, have been somewhat erratic, also as shown in Exhibit 1.

The main product of the APD division is the aerostat, which is a large lighter-than-air blimp resembling the famous Goodyear blimp. These aerostats are sold to communications companies, the United States government, and foreign countries for communications uses. At the present time the APD division produces about 12 aerostats per year, and the aerostat accounts for about 50 percent of the APD division's sales.

The APD division also produces a variety of other specialty products made to customer order. These products include mine stoppers used to seal mining passages for ventilation control (see Exhibit 2) and blade liners used as inserts in helicopter blades to detect cracks. One unifying feature of these specialty products is that they are made from the laminated plastic materials supplied by the MD division of Sheldahl.

EXHIBIT 1
FINANCIAL DATA

	$ Thousands				
	1974	1975	1976	1977	1978
			Sheldahl Corp.		
Sales	34,884	41,029	46,824	41,914	37,857
Profits (after tax)	1,256	1,324	363	(1,035)	379
			APD Division		
Sales	5,977	6,508	4,080	7,600	5,179
Profits (after tax)	703	597	223	1,139	150

Sheldahl

Advanced Products Division
Northfield, Minnesota 55057
(507) 645-5633

Reusable Ventilation Control Stopping for Underground Mines
Part No. 10687

DESCRIPTION

- A **DIFFERENT BRATTICE** FOR EMERGENCY AND PRODUCTION VENTILATION CONTROL

- INSTALL IN MINUTES

- SELF SEALING

- REUSABLE

- RESISTANT TO BLAST FORCES

- FLAME RESISTANT (To NFPA 701-75 Spec. and ASTM E162 with Flame Spread Index of less than 25.)

- AN ACCESSORY HARNESS IS AVAILABLE TO CONVERT THIS UNIT INTO A "PARACHUTE" SINGLE POINT ATTACHMENT STOPPING

SIZING

For Airways smaller than 7'x8' order the **10687-012** Stopping.
For Airways between 7'x8' and 11'x12' order the **10687-016** Stopping.

Exhibit 2
Product description.

In formulating his business strategy, Mr. Wallace envisioned a gradual shift toward products which are sold to multiple customers and manufactured on a volume basis. The business strategy developed by Wallace and his staff is summarized as follows:

APD will continue to do what it has historically done best—respond to *individual customer* design requirements tailoring new products to unique customer applications. This business is characterized by low volume but sole-source products, by customer funding for product development, and by large year-to-year variations in sales and profits.

Concurrently and increasingly, APD will become more *market*-focused in its business and will apply resources toward market and product development programs. Our objective shall be to reduce but not eliminate APD dependence on short-run *customer*-specified products or projects and to bring on stream new products with higher-volume continuous production. APD will restrict its market development resources to certain market segments or "niches" of growth and to mature industries where there is a realistic opportunity and expectation of occupying a dominant or strong competitive position.

This heavy emphasis on marketing strategies will require enlargement of market research, market development, and sales distribution systems. Technologically, materials and systems engineering capabilities will have to be strengthened, as will the production engineering and production control disciplines. We will need to concentrate heavily on planning, and we must have the patience to focus on and stick to our strategies to see them through to fruition.

The business unit is growth-oriented with substantial resources directed to new-product/new-market strategies, making it a medium- to high-risk operation. Although investment in product development and capital equipment will be required, the business should retain its low-capital, high-labor-intensive character. Over the 5-year planning period, sales, profits, and asset levels should produce a return on net assets

(RONA) in the 30 to 40 percent range. Additionally, the business will be a net cash user.

According to Mr. Wallace, the shift in business strategy will require a corresponding change in manufacturing strategy. Manufacturing will need to develop facilities, people, and production control systems to support the gradual change from low-volume one-of-a-kind production to higher-volume standardized product lines. Among the results of this change in strategy could be changes in organization. The present organizational structure of the APD division is shown in Exhibit 3.

Mr. Wallace also felt that the shift in business strategy might affect the production and inventory control area. At the present time, production and inventory control is handled by two individuals who were transferred from the storeroom and the production floor. They have been trained on the job, and they have evolved a manual system of record keeping and production planning. The system appears to work quite well for the present situation, but constant expediting and stock chasing are necessary to keep production moving.

Inventory stock status is computerized by means of punched cards. Receipts and disbursements are sent to data processing and keypunched for entry into the computer. Because of time lags and problems of record accuracy, the production and inventory control people also keep manual records on the most important parts.

The Sheldahl Company recently signed a contract with Hewlett-Packard for a new computer which will arrive in the fall of 1978 and replace the current Honeywell equipment. As part of the new computer conversion, the company has investigated software packages available from Hewlett-Packard. The production and inventory control (MRP) software package appears quite good, but conversion of existing computer software will have priority over new systems. The first priority, after the new computer is in-

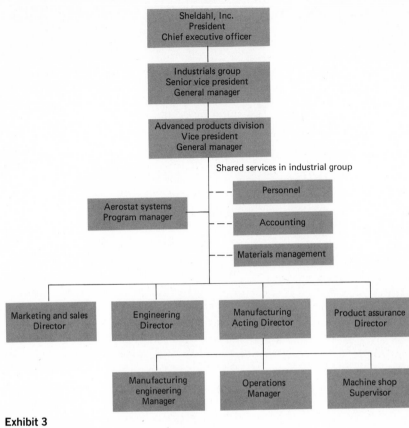

Exhibit 3
Organization chart.
(Detail only shown in manufacturing area.)

stalled, will be the conversion of existing accounting and financial systems.

In viewing the situation, Mr. Wallace wondered what the manufacturing strategy over the next 5 years should be and how the strategy should be implemented. He knew that manufacturing should support the new divisional business strategy but was unsure about exactly what direction manufacturing should take.

DISCUSSION QUESTIONS

1. What strategy should be adopted in manufacturing with respect to cost, delivery, quality, and flexibility objectives?
2. How should the strategy in manufacturing be implemented through process, organization, equipment, work force, and production and inventory control systems?

APPENDIXES

APPENDIX A
AREAS UNDER THE STANDARD NORMAL PROBABILITY DISTRIBUTION

Values in the table represent the proportion
of area under the normal curve between the
mean ($\mu = 0$) and a positive value of z.

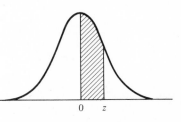

z	.00	.01	.02	.03	.04	.05	.06	.07	.08	.09
0.0	0.0000	0.0040	0.0080	0.0120	0.0160	0.0199	0.0239	0.0279	0.0319	0.0359
0.1	0.0398	0.0438	0.0478	0.0517	0.0557	0.0596	0.0636	0.0675	0.0714	0.0753
0.2	0.0793	0.0832	0.0871	0.0910	0.0948	0.0987	0.1026	0.1064	0.1103	0.1141
0.3	0.1179	0.1217	0.1255	0.1293	0.1331	0.1368	0.1406	0.1443	0.1480	0.1517
0.4	0.1554	0.1591	0.1628	0.1664	0.1700	0.1736	0.1772	0.1808	0.1844	0.1879
0.5	0.1915	0.1950	0.1985	0.2019	0.2054	0.2088	0.2123	0.2157	0.2190	0.2224
0.6	0.2257	0.2291	0.2324	0.2357	0.2389	0.2422	0.2454	0.2486	0.2517	0.2549
0.7	0.2580	0.2611	0.2642	0.2673	0.2703	0.2734	0.2764	0.2794	0.2823	0.2852
0.8	0.2881	0.2910	0.2939	0.2967	0.2995	0.3023	0.3051	0.3078	0.3106	0.3133
0.9	0.3159	0.3186	0.3212	0.3238	0.3264	0.3289	0.3315	0.3340	0.3365	0.3389
1.0	0.3413	0.3438	0.3461	0.3485	0.3508	0.3531	0.3554	0.3577	0.3599	0.3621
1.1	0.3643	0.3665	0.3686	0.3708	0.3729	0.3749	0.3770	0.3790	0.3810	0.3830
1.2	0.3849	0.3869	0.3888	0.3907	0.3925	0.3944	0.3962	0.3980	0.3997	0.4015
1.3	0.4032	0.4049	0.4066	0.4082	0.4099	0.4115	0.4131	0.4147	0.4162	0.4177
1.4	0.4192	0.4207	0.4222	0.4236	0.4251	0.4265	0.4279	0.4292	0.4306	0.4319
1.5	0.4332	0.4345	0.4357	0.4370	0.4382	0.4394	0.4406	0.4418	0.4429	0.4441
1.6	0.4452	0.4463	0.4474	0.4484	0.4495	0.4505	0.4515	0.4525	0.4535	0.4545
1.7	0.4554	0.4564	0.4573	0.4582	0.4591	0.4599	0.4608	0.4616	0.4625	0.4633
1.8	0.4641	0.4649	0.4656	0.4664	0.4671	0.4678	0.4686	0.4693	0.4699	0.4706
1.9	0.4713	0.4719	0.4726	0.4732	0.4738	0.4744	0.4750	0.4756	0.4761	0.4767
2.0	0.4772	0.4778	0.4783	0.4788	0.4793	0.4798	0.4803	0.4808	0.4812	0.4817
2.1	0.4821	0.4826	0.4830	0.4834	0.4838	0.4842	0.4846	0.4850	0.4854	0.4857
2.2	0.4861	0.4864	0.4868	0.4871	0.4875	0.4878	0.4881	0.4884	0.4887	0.4890
2.3	0.4893	0.4896	0.4898	0.4901	0.4904	0.4906	0.4909	0.4911	0.4913	0.4916
2.4	0.4918	0.4920	0.4922	0.4925	0.4927	0.4929	0.4931	0.4932	0.4934	0.4936
2.5	0.4938	0.4940	0.4941	0.4943	0.4945	0.4946	0.4948	0.4949	0.4951	0.4952
2.6	0.4953	0.4955	0.4956	0.4957	0.4959	0.4960	0.4961	0.4962	0.4963	0.4964
2.7	0.4965	0.4966	0.4967	0.4968	0.4969	0.4970	0.4971	0.4972	0.4973	0.4974
2.8	0.4974	0.4975	0.4976	0.4977	0.4977	0.4978	0.4979	0.4979	0.4980	0.4981
2.9	0.4981	0.4982	0.4982	0.4983	0.4984	0.4984	0.4985	0.4985	0.4986	0.4986
3.0	0.4987	0.4987	0.4987	0.4988	0.4988	0.4989	0.4989	0.4989	0.4990	0.4990

27767	43584	85301	88977	29490	69714	94015	64874	32444	48277
13025	14338	54066	15243	47724	66733	74108	88222	88570	74015
80217	36292	98525	24335	24432	24896	62880	87873	95160	59221
10875	62004	90391	61105	57411	06368	11748	12102	80580	41867
54127	57326	26629	19087	24472	88779	17944	05600	60478	03343
60311	42824	37301	42678	45990	43242	66067	42792	95043	52680
49739	71484	92003	98086	76668	73209	54244	91030	45547	70818
78626	51594	16453	94614	39014	97066	30945	57589	31732	57260
66692	13986	99837	00582	81232	44987	69170	37403	86995	90307
44071	28091	07362	97703	76447	42537	08345	88975	35841	85771
59820	96163	78851	16499	87064	13075	73035	41207	74699	09310
25704	91035	26313	77463	55387	72681	47431	43905	31048	56699
22304	90314	78438	66276	18396	73538	43277	58874	11466	16082
17710	59621	15292	76139	59526	52113	53856	30743	08670	84741
25852	58905	55018	56374	35824	71708	30540	27886	61732	75454
46780	56487	75211	10271	36633	68424	17374	52003	70707	70214
59849	96169	87195	46092	26787	60939	59202	11973	02902	33250
47670	07654	30342	40277	11049	72049	83012	09832	25571	77628
94304	71803	73465	09819	58869	35220	09504	96412	90193	79568
08105	59987	21437	36786	49226	77837	98524	97831	65704	09514
64281	61826	18555	64937	64654	25843	41145	42820	14924	39650
66847	70495	32350	02985	01755	14750	48968	38603	70312	05682
72461	33230	21529	53424	72877	17334	39283	04149	90850	64618
21032	91050	13058	16218	06554	07850	73950	79552	24781	89683
95362	67011	06651	16136	57216	39618	49856	99326	40902	05069
49712	97380	10404	55452	09971	59481	37006	22186	72682	07385
58275	61764	97586	54716	61459	21647	87417	17198	21443	41808
89514	11788	68224	23417	46376	25366	94746	49580	01176	28838
15472	50669	48139	36732	26825	05511	12459	91314	80582	71944
12120	86124	51247	44302	87112	21476	14713	71181	13177	55292
95294	00556	70481	06905	21785	41101	49386	54480	23604	23554
66986	34099	74474	20740	47458	64809	06312	88940	15995	69321
80620	51790	11436	38072	40405	68032	60942	00307	11897	92674
55411	85667	77535	99892	71209	92061	92329	98932	78284	46347
95083	06783	28102	57816	85561	29671	77936	63574	31384	51924
90726	57166	98884	08583	95889	57067	38101	77756	11657	13897
68984	83620	89747	98882	92613	89719	39641	69457	91339	22502
36421	16489	18059	51061	67667	60631	84054	40455	99396	63680
92638	40333	67054	16067	24700	71594	47468	03577	57649	63266
21036	82808	77501	97427	76479	68562	43321	31370	28977	23896
13173	33365	41468	85149	49554	17994	91178	10174	29420	90438
86716	38746	94559	37559	49678	53119	98189	81851	29651	84215
92581	02262	41615	70360	64114	58660	96717	54244	10701	41393
12470	56500	50273	93113	41794	86861	39448	93136	25722	08564
01016	00857	41396	80504	90670	08289	58137	17820	22751	36518
34030	60726	25807	24260	71529	78920	47648	13885	70669	93406
50259	46345	06170	97965	88302	98041	11947	56203	19324	20504
73959	76145	60808	54444	74412	81105	69181	96845	38525	11600
46874	37088	80940	44893	10408	36222	14004	23153	69249	05747
60883	52109	19516	90120	46759	71643	62342	07589	08899	05985

APPENDIX C
PRESENT-VALUE FACTORS FOR FUTURE SINGLE PAYMENTS

Single Payment Factor PV_i

$$\frac{1}{(1+i)^2}$$

Periods until payment	1%	2%	4%	6%	8%	10%	12%	14%	15%	16%	18%	20%	22%	24%	25%	26%	28%	30%
1	0.990	0.980	0.962	0.943	0.926	0.909	0.893	0.877	0.870	0.862	0.847	0.833	0.820	0.806	0.800	0.794	0.781	0.769
2	0.980	0.961	0.925	0.890	0.857	0.826	0.797	0.769	0.756	0.743	0.718	0.694	0.672	0.650	0.640	0.630	0.610	0.592
3	0.971	0.942	0.889	0.840	0.794	0.751	0.712	0.675	0.658	0.641	0.609	0.579	0.551	0.524	0.512	0.500	0.477	0.455
4	0.961	0.924	0.855	0.792	0.735	0.683	0.636	0.592	0.572	0.552	0.516	0.482	0.451	0.423	0.410	0.397	0.373	0.350
5	0.951	0.906	0.822	0.747	0.681	0.621	0.567	0.519	0.497	0.476	0.437	0.402	0.370	0.341	0.328	0.315	0.291	0.269
6	0.942	0.888	0.790	0.705	0.630	0.564	0.507	0.456	0.432	0.410	0.370	0.335	0.303	0.275	0.262	0.250	0.227	0.207
7	0.933	0.871	0.760	0.665	0.583	0.513	0.452	0.400	0.376	0.354	0.314	0.279	0.249	0.222	0.210	0.198	0.178	0.159
8	0.923	0.853	0.731	0.627	0.540	0.467	0.404	0.351	0.327	0.305	0.266	0.233	0.204	0.179	0.168	0.157	0.139	0.123
9	0.914	0.837	0.703	0.592	0.500	0.424	0.361	0.308	0.284	0.263	0.225	0.194	0.167	0.144	0.134	0.125	0.108	0.094
10	0.905	0.820	0.676	0.558	0.463	0.386	0.322	0.270	0.247	0.227	0.191	0.162	0.137	0.116	0.107	0.099	0.085	0.073
11	0.896	0.804	0.650	0.527	0.429	0.350	0.287	0.237	0.215	0.195	0.162	0.135	0.112	0.094	0.086	0.079	0.066	0.056
12	0.887	0.788	0.625	0.497	0.397	0.319	0.257	0.208	0.187	0.168	0.137	0.112	0.092	0.076	0.069	0.062	0.052	0.043
13	0.879	0.773	0.601	0.469	0.368	0.290	0.229	0.182	0.163	0.145	0.116	0.093	0.075	0.061	0.055	0.050	0.040	0.033
14	0.870	0.758	0.577	0.442	0.340	0.263	0.205	0.160	0.141	0.125	0.099	0.078	0.062	0.049	0.044	0.039	0.032	0.025
15	0.861	0.743	0.555	0.417	0.315	0.239	0.183	0.140	0.123	0.108	0.084	0.065	0.051	0.040	0.035	0.031	0.025	0.020
16	0.853	0.728	0.534	0.394	0.292	0.218	0.163	0.123	0.107	0.093	0.071	0.054	0.042	0.032	0.028	0.025	0.019	0.015
17	0.844	0.714	0.513	0.371	0.270	0.198	0.146	0.108	0.093	0.080	0.060	0.045	0.034	0.026	0.023	0.020	0.015	0.012
18	0.836	0.700	0.494	0.350	0.250	0.180	0.130	0.095	0.081	0.069	0.051	0.038	0.028	0.021	0.018	0.016	0.012	0.009
19	0.828	0.686	0.475	0.331	0.232	0.164	0.116	0.083	0.070	0.060	0.043	0.031	0.023	0.017	0.014	0.012	0.009	0.007
20	0.820	0.673	0.456	0.312	0.215	0.149	0.104	0.073	0.061	0.051	0.037	0.026	0.019	0.014	0.012	0.010	0.007	0.005
21	0.811	0.660	0.439	0.294	0.199	0.135	0.093	0.064	0.053	0.044	0.031	0.022	0.015	0.011	0.009	0.008	0.006	0.004
22	0.803	0.647	0.422	0.278	0.184	0.123	0.083	0.056	0.046	0.038	0.026	0.018	0.013	0.009	0.007	0.006	0.004	0.003
23	0.795	0.634	0.406	0.262	0.170	0.112	0.074	0.049	0.040	0.033	0.022	0.015	0.010	0.007	0.006	0.005	0.003	0.002
24	0.788	0.622	0.390	0.247	0.158	0.102	0.066	0.043	0.035	0.028	0.019	0.013	0.008	0.006	0.005	0.004	0.003	0.002
25	0.780	0.610	0.375	0.233	0.146	0.092	0.059	0.038	0.030	0.024	0.016	0.010	0.007	0.005	0.004	0.003	0.002	0.001
26	0.772	0.598	0.361	0.220	0.135	0.084	0.053	0.033	0.026	0.021	0.014	0.009	0.006	0.004	0.003	0.002	0.002	0.001
27	0.764	0.586	0.347	0.207	0.125	0.076	0.047	0.029	0.023	0.018	0.011	0.007	0.005	0.003	0.002	0.002	0.001	0.001
28	0.757	0.574	0.333	0.196	0.116	0.069	0.042	0.026	0.020	0.016	0.010	0.006	0.004	0.002	0.002	0.002	0.001	0.001
29	0.749	0.563	0.321	0.185	0.107	0.063	0.037	0.022	0.017	0.014	0.008	0.005	0.003	0.002	0.002	0.001	0.001	0.001
30	0.742	0.552	0.308	0.174	0.099	0.057	0.033	0.020	0.015	0.012	0.007	0.004	0.003	0.002	0.001	0.001	0.001	0.001

663

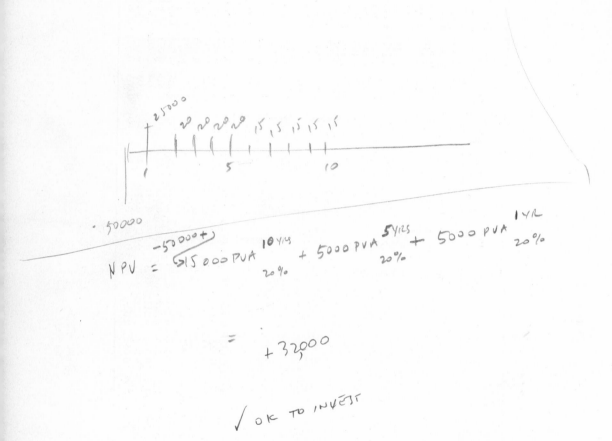

$$NPV = -50000 + 15000\ PVA^{10\ YRS}_{20\%} + 5000\ PVA^{5\ YRS}_{20\%} + 5000\ PVA^{1\ YR}_{20\%}$$

$$= +32000$$

✓ OK TO INVEST

Years (N)	1%	2%	4%	6%	8%	10%	12%	14%	15%	16%	18%	20%	22%	24%	25%	26%	28%	30%
1	0.990	0.980	0.962	0.943	0.926	0.909	0.893	0.877	0.870	0.862	0.847	0.833	0.820	0.806	0.800	0.794	0.781	0.769
2	1.970	1.942	1.886	1.833	1.783	1.736	1.690	1.647	1.626	1.605	1.566	1.528	1.492	1.457	1.440	1.424	1.392	1.361
3	2.941	2.884	2.775	2.673	2.577	2.487	2.402	2.322	2.283	2.246	2.174	2.106	2.042	1.981	1.952	1.923	1.868	1.816
4	3.902	3.808	3.630	3.465	3.312	3.170	3.037	2.914	2.855	2.798	2.690	2.589	2.494	2.404	2.362	2.320	2.241	2.166
5	4.853	4.713	4.452	4.212	3.993	3.791	3.605	3.433	3.352	3.274	3.127	2.991	2.864	2.745	2.689	2.635	2.532	2.436
6	5.795	5.601	5.242	4.917	4.623	4.355	4.111	3.889	3.784	3.685	3.498	3.326	3.167	3.020	2.951	2.885	2.759	2.643
7	6.728	6.472	6.002	5.582	5.206	4.868	4.564	4.288	4.160	4.039	3.812	3.605	3.416	3.242	3.161	3.083	2.937	2.802
8	7.652	7.325	6.733	6.210	5.747	5.335	4.968	4.639	4.487	4.344	4.078	3.837	3.619	3.421	3.329	3.241	3.076	2.925
9	8.566	8.162	7.435	6.802	6.247	5.759	5.328	4.946	4.772	4.607	4.303	4.031	3.786	3.566	3.463	3.366	3.184	3.019
10	9.471	8.983	8.111	7.360	6.710	6.145	5.650	5.216	5.019	4.833	4.494	4.192	3.923	3.682	3.571	3.465	3.269	3.092
11	10.368	9.787	8.760	7.887	7.139	6.495	5.937	5.453	5.234	5.029	4.656	4.327	4.035	3.776	3.656	3.544	3.335	3.147
12	11.255	10.575	9.385	8.384	7.536	6.814	6.194	5.660	5.421	5.197	4.793	4.439	4.127	3.851	3.725	3.606	3.387	3.190
13	12.134	11.343	9.986	8.853	7.904	7.103	6.424	5.842	5.583	5.342	4.910	4.533	4.203	3.912	3.780	3.656	3.427	3.223
14	13.004	12.106	10.563	9.295	8.244	7.367	6.628	6.002	5.724	5.468	5.008	4.611	4.265	3.962	3.824	3.695	3.459	3.249
15	13.865	12.849	11.118	9.712	8.559	7.606	6.811	6.142	5.847	5.575	5.092	4.675	4.315	4.001	3.859	3.726	3.483	3.268
16	14.718	13.578	11.652	10.106	8.851	7.824	6.974	6.265	5.954	5.669	5.162	4.730	4.357	4.033	3.887	3.751	3.503	3.283
17	15.562	14.292	12.166	10.477	9.122	8.022	7.120	6.373	6.047	5.749	5.222	4.775	4.391	4.059	3.910	3.771	3.518	3.295
18	16.398	14.992	12.659	10.828	9.372	8.201	7.250	6.467	6.128	5.818	5.273	4.812	4.419	4.080	3.928	3.786	3.529	3.304
19	17.226	15.678	13.134	11.158	9.604	8.365	7.366	6.550	6.198	5.877	5.316	4.844	4.442	4.097	3.942	3.799	3.539	3.311
20	18.046	16.351	13.590	11.470	9.818	8.514	7.469	6.623	6.259	5.929	5.353	4.870	4.460	4.110	3.954	3.808	3.546	3.316
21	18.857	17.011	14.029	11.764	10.017	8.649	7.562	6.687	6.312	5.973	5.384	4.891	4.476	4.121	3.963	3.816	3.551	3.320
22	19.660	17.658	14.451	12.042	10.201	8.772	7.645	6.743	6.359	6.011	5.410	4.909	4.488	4.130	3.970	3.822	3.556	3.323
23	20.456	18.292	14.857	12.303	10.371	8.883	7.718	6.792	6.399	6.044	5.432	4.925	4.499	4.137	3.976	3.827	3.559	3.325
24	21.243	18.914	15.247	12.550	10.529	8.985	7.784	6.835	6.434	6.073	5.451	4.937	4.507	4.143	3.981	3.831	3.562	3.327
25	22.023	19.523	15.622	12.783	10.675	9.077	7.843	6.873	6.464	6.097	5.467	4.948	4.514	4.147	3.985	3.834	3.564	3.329
26	22.795	20.121	15.983	13.003	10.810	9.161	7.896	6.906	6.491	6.118	5.480	4.956	4.520	4.151	3.988	3.837	3.566	3.330
27	23.560	20.707	16.330	13.211	10.935	9.237	7.943	6.935	6.514	6.136	5.492	4.964	4.524	4.154	3.990	3.839	3.567	3.331
28	24.316	21.281	16.663	13.406	11.051	9.307	7.984	6.961	6.534	6.152	5.502	4.970	4.528	4.159	3.992	3.840	3.568	3.331
29	25.066	21.844	16.984	13.591	11.158	9.370	8.022	6.983	6.551	6.166	5.510	4.975	4.531	4.159	3.994	3.841	3.569	3.332
30	25.808	22.396	17.292	13.765	11.258	9.427	8.055	7.003	6.566	6.177	5.517	4.979	4.534	4.160	3.995	3.842	3.569	3.332

INDEX